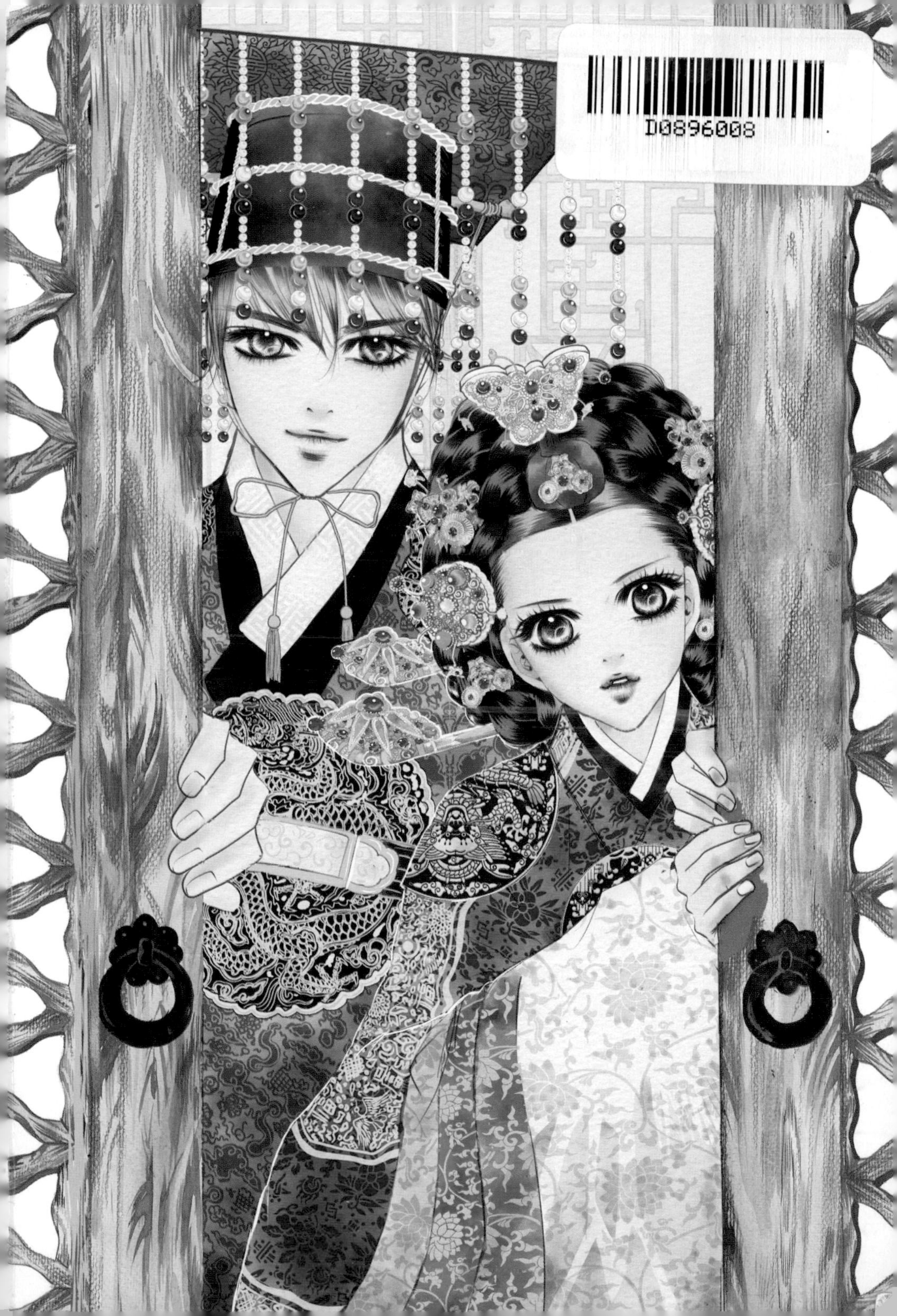

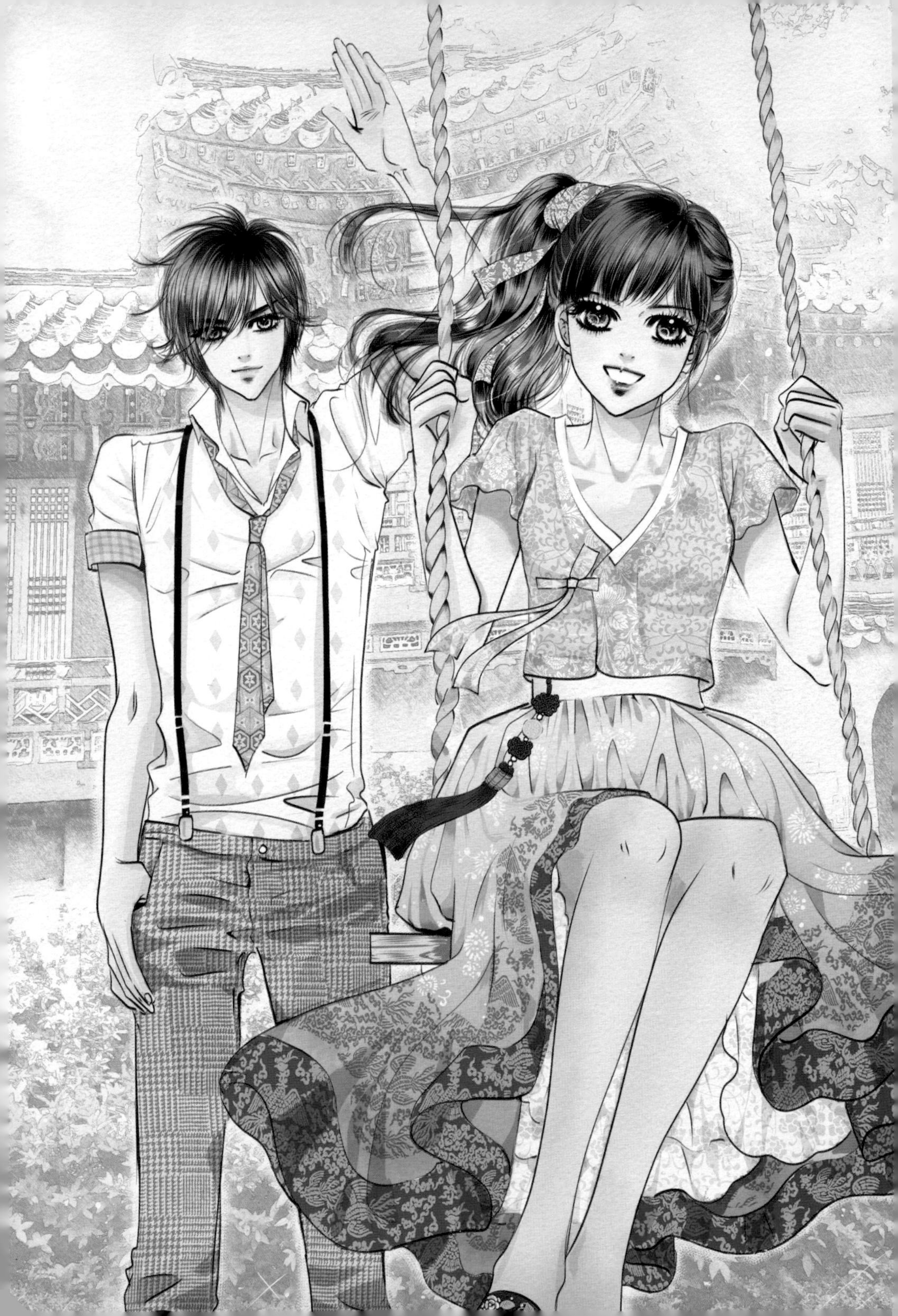

vol. 18

Park SoHee

Yen Press

Words from the Creator

Volume 27

Yes, it's finally ending. There's a saying that a story is a living thing. So even if *Goong* ends, the story doesn't stop. It carries on. Although I, the storyteller, am leaving, the story will live on in your heart. I believe...a different version of *Goong* continues in every reader. I would like to thank my editors, my assistants, and the readers who have cheered me on and given me constructive criticism. Thanks to everyone who has made my life memorable. Please take care until I come back with the next book. I hope you'll look forward to the *Goong* side stories in the next volume~!!!

SoHee Park

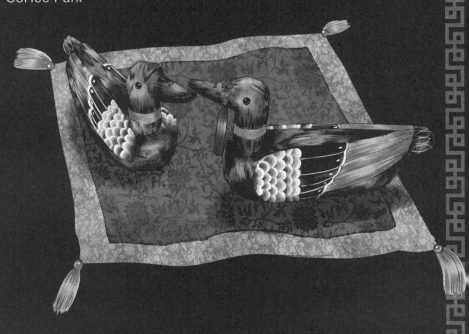

Words from the Creator

Volume 28

At first, it was hard to work on these side stories for *Goong*. I didn't know what to do because I didn't expect this difficult feeling at all. But I finally realized that the toughest part was already over the moment I crossed the finish line by completing the main story. After that, the extra stories were like a victory lap awaiting me. It was an arduous but gratifying time. Many thanks to my editors, who endured my complaining and whining. I'd like to blow a kiss to you, the readers of this side-story volume of *Goong*.

SoHee Park

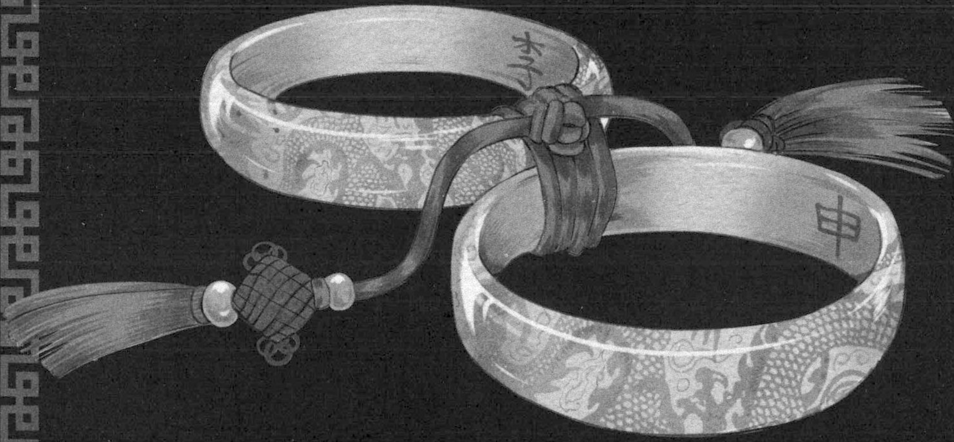
李
申

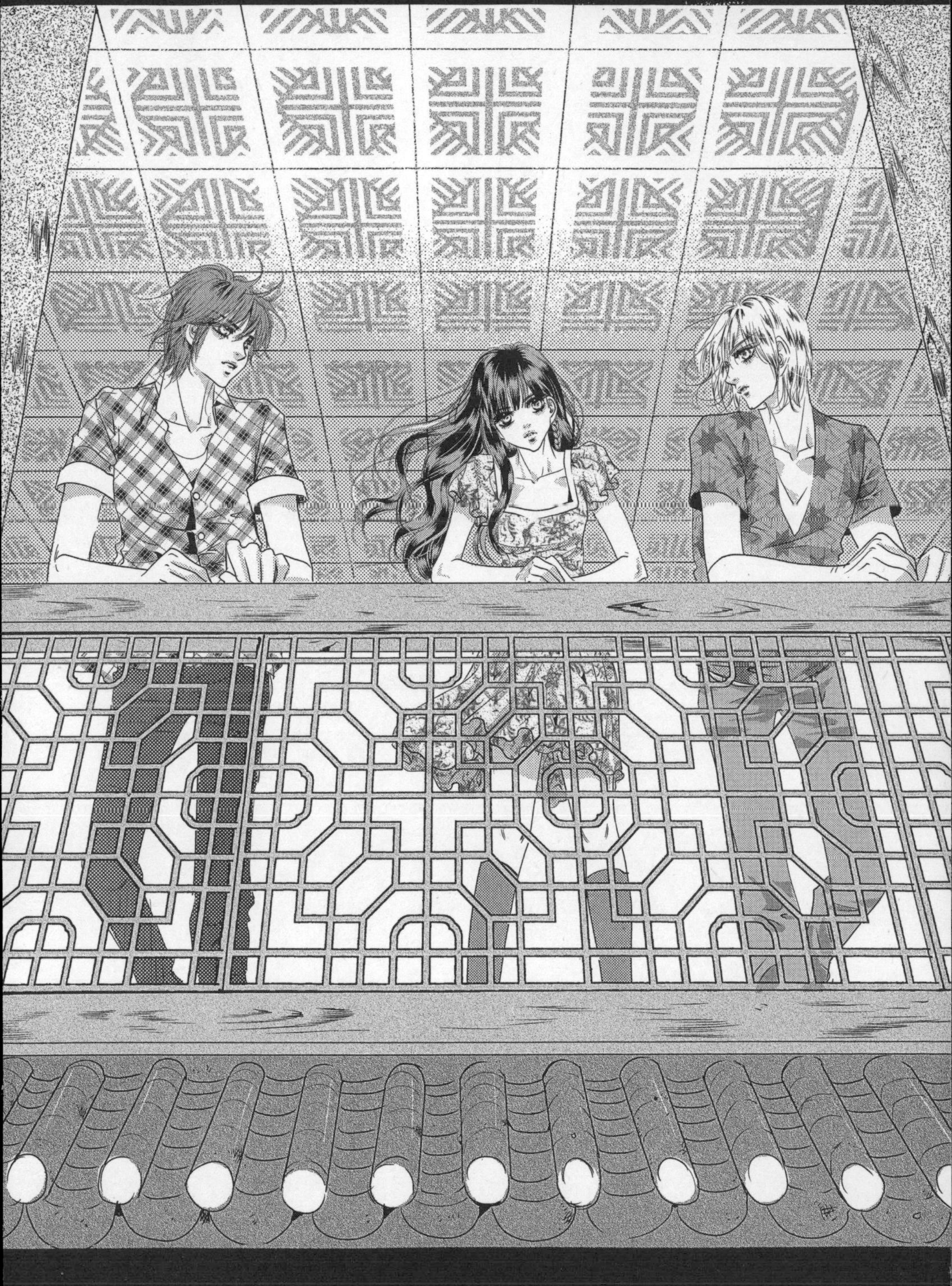

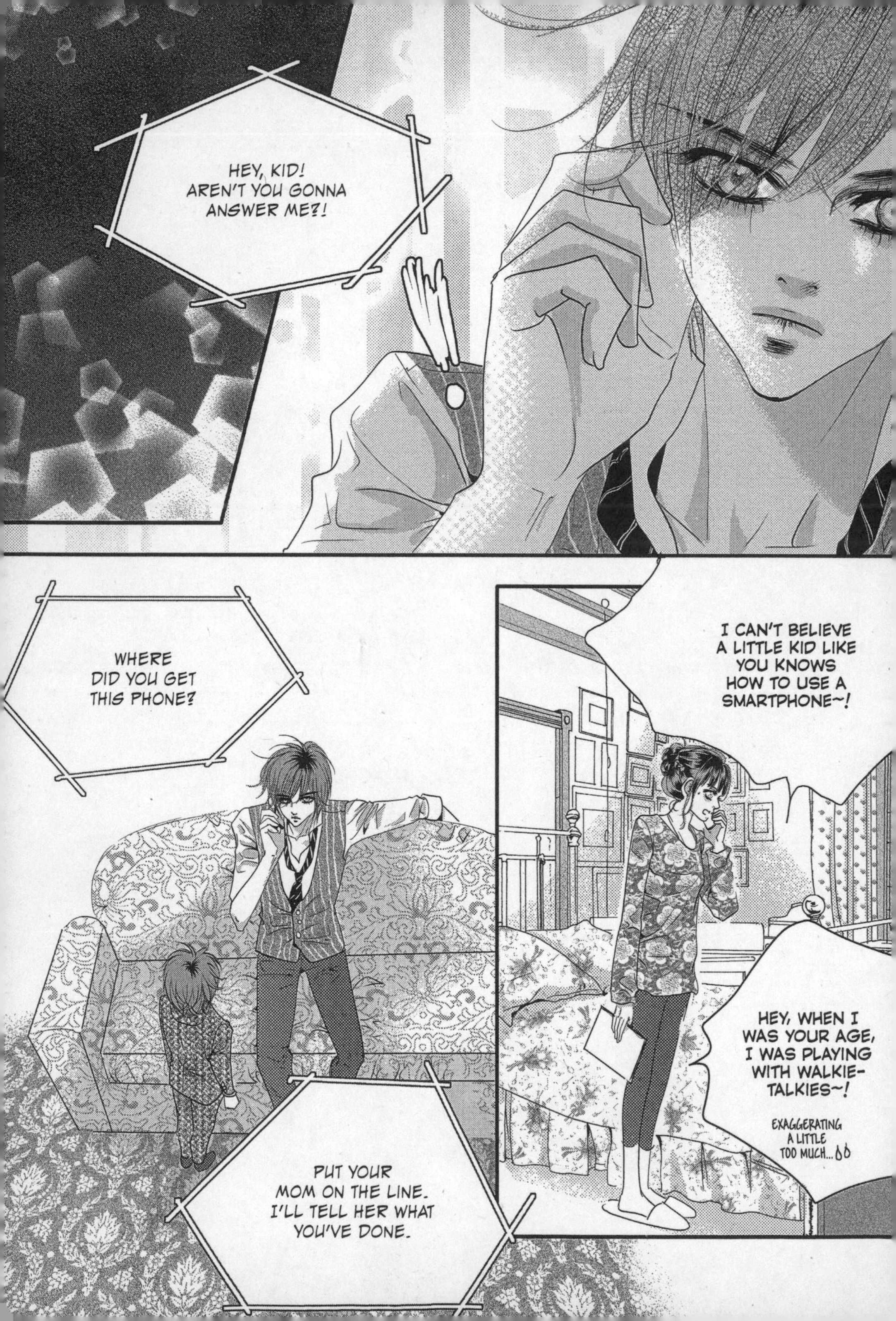
HEY, KID! AREN'T YOU GONNA ANSWER ME?!
WHERE DID YOU GET THIS PHONE?
PUT YOUR MOM ON THE LINE. I'LL TELL HER WHAT YOU'VE DONE.
I CAN'T BELIEVE A LITTLE KID LIKE YOU KNOWS HOW TO USE A SMARTPHONE~!
HEY, WHEN I WAS YOUR AGE, I WAS PLAYING WITH WALKIE-TALKIES~!
EXAGGERATING A LITTLE TOO MUCH...

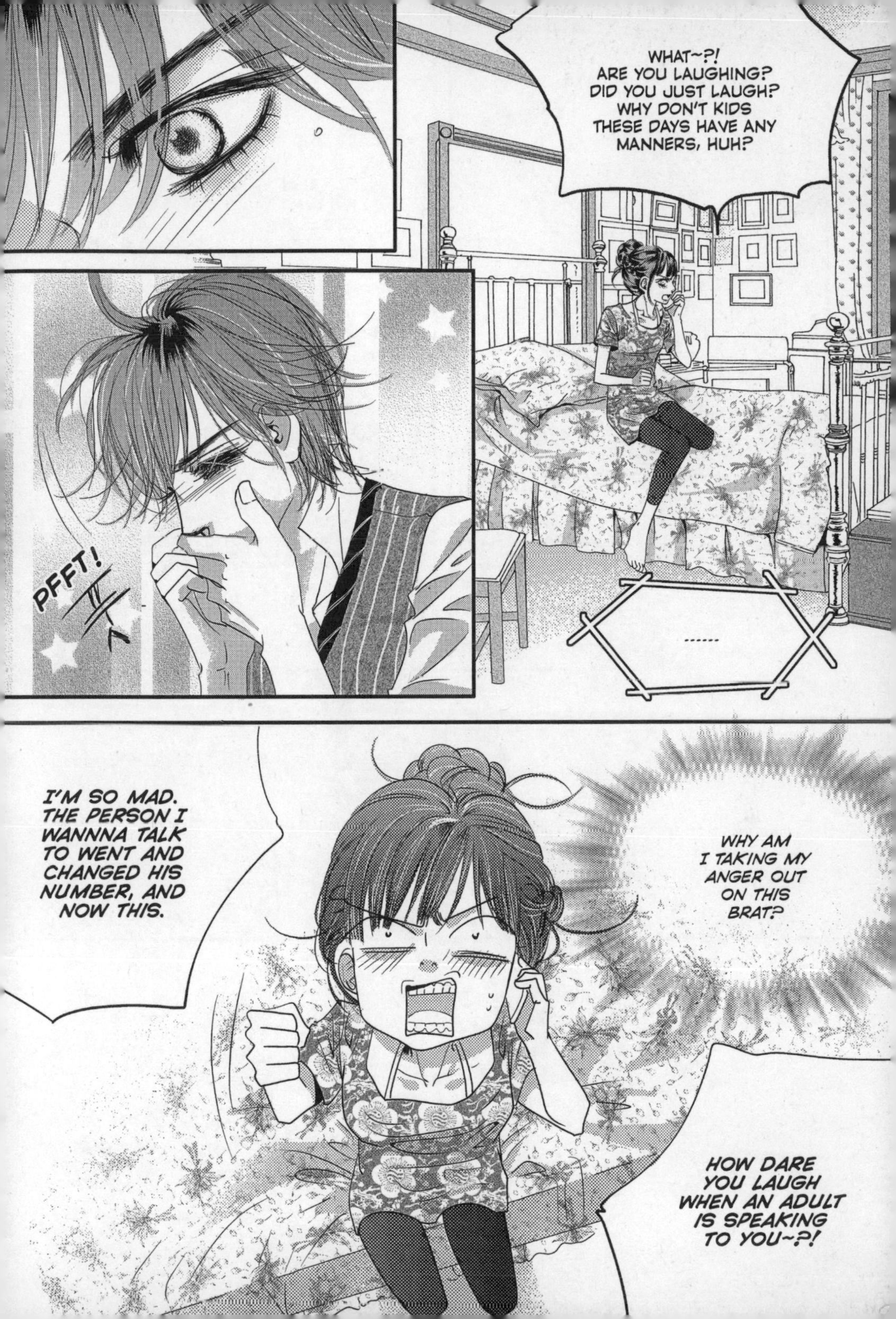
PFFT!
WHAT~?! ARE YOU LAUGHING? DID YOU JUST LAUGH? WHY DON'T KIDS THESE DAYS HAVE ANY MANNERS, HUH?
......
I'M SO MAD. THE PERSON I WANNA TALK TO WENT AND CHANGED HIS NUMBER, AND NOW THIS.
WHY AM I TAKING MY ANGER OUT ON THIS BRAT?
HOW DARE YOU LAUGH WHEN AN ADULT IS SPEAKING TO YOU~?!

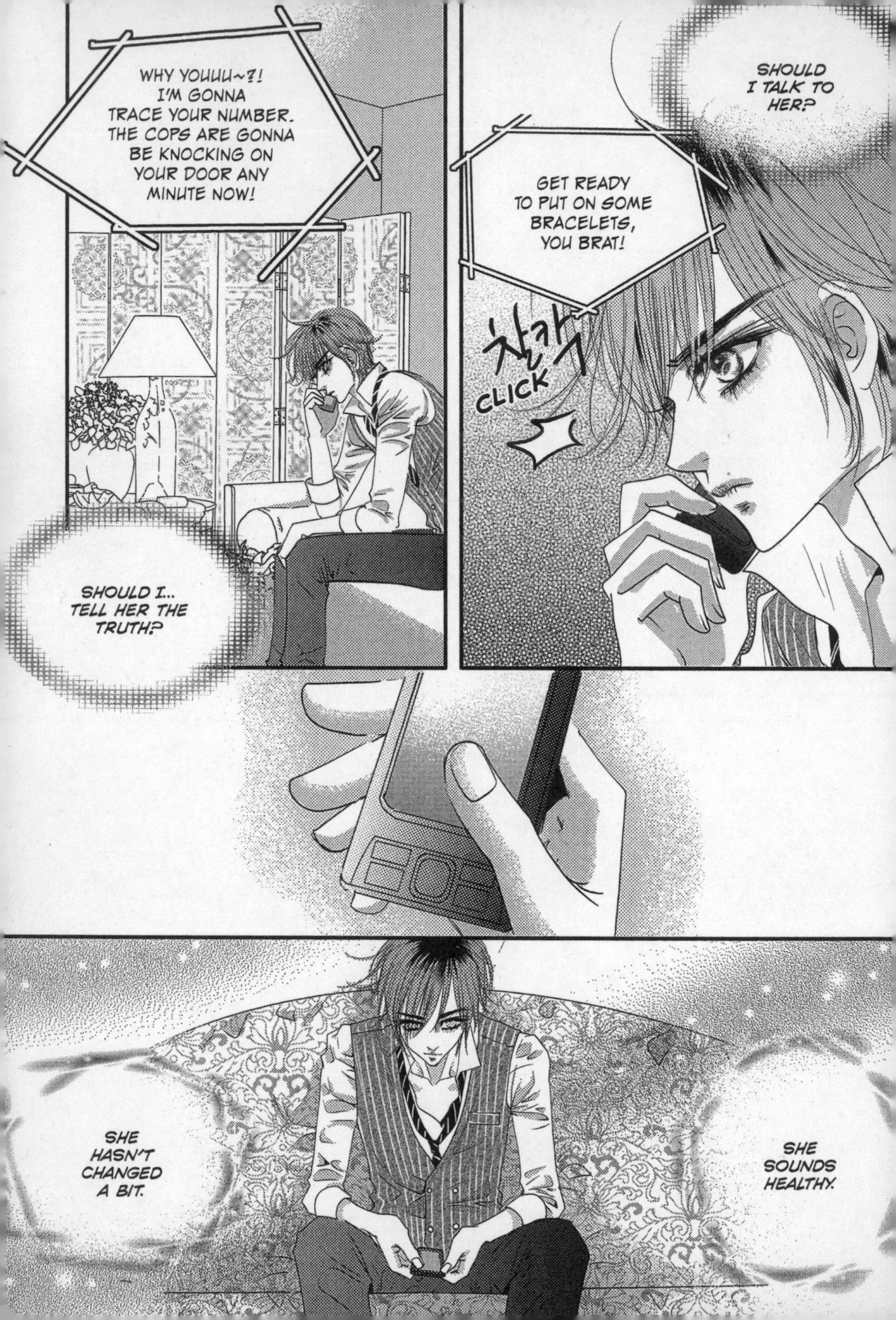
WHY YOUUU~?! I'M GONNA TRACE YOUR NUMBER. THE COPS ARE GONNA BE KNOCKING ON YOUR DOOR ANY MINUTE NOW!
SHOULD I... TELL HER THE TRUTH?
GET READY TO PUT ON SOME BRACELETS, YOU BRAT!
찰칵
CLICK
SHOULD I TALK TO HER?
SHE HASN'T CHANGED A BIT.
SHE SOUNDS HEALTHY.

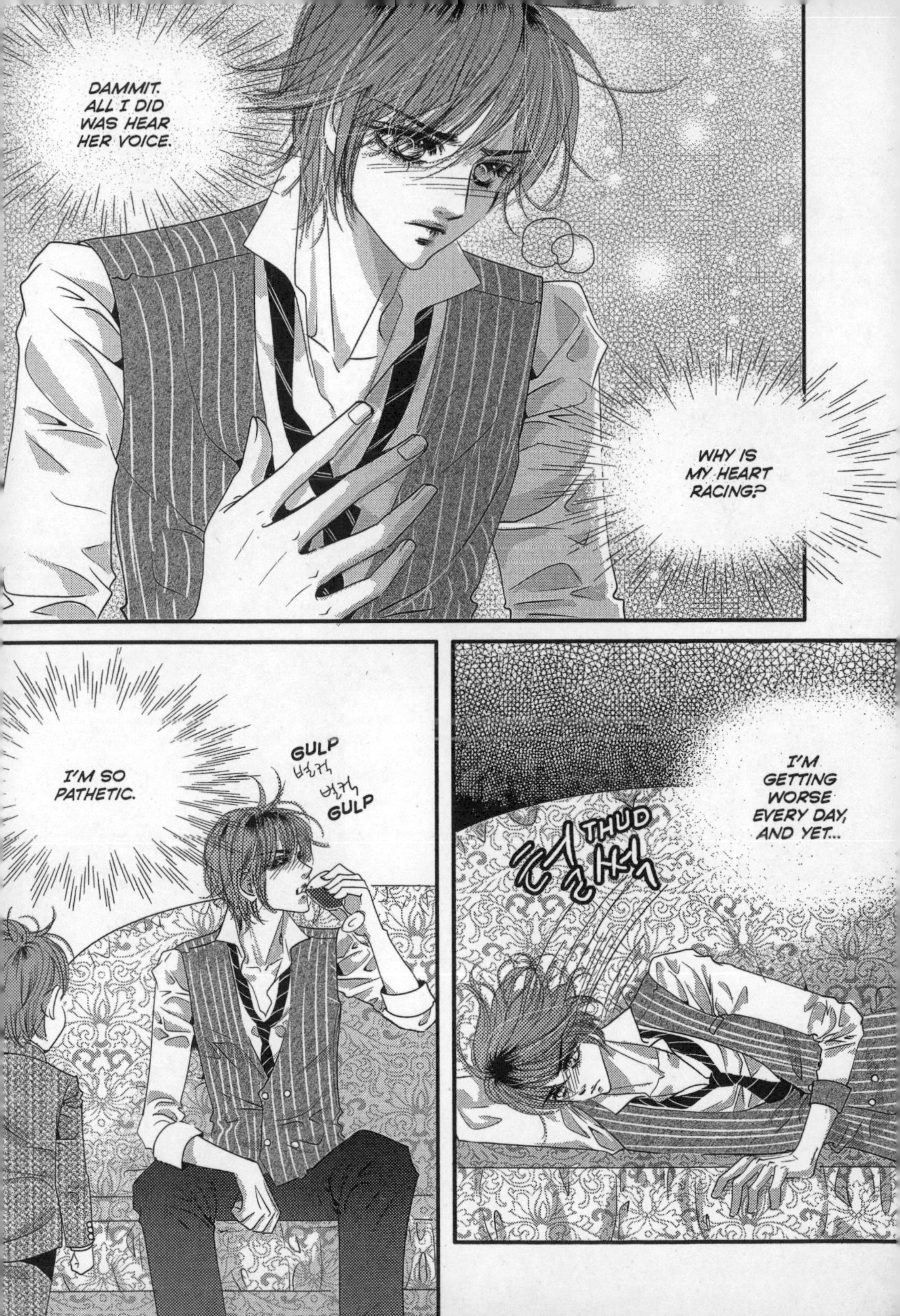
DAMMIT. ALL I DID WAS HEAR HER VOICE.
WHY IS MY HEART RACING?
I'M SO PATHETIC.
GULP 벌컥
벌컥 GULP
I'M GETTING WORSE EVERY DAY, AND YET...
THUD 털썩

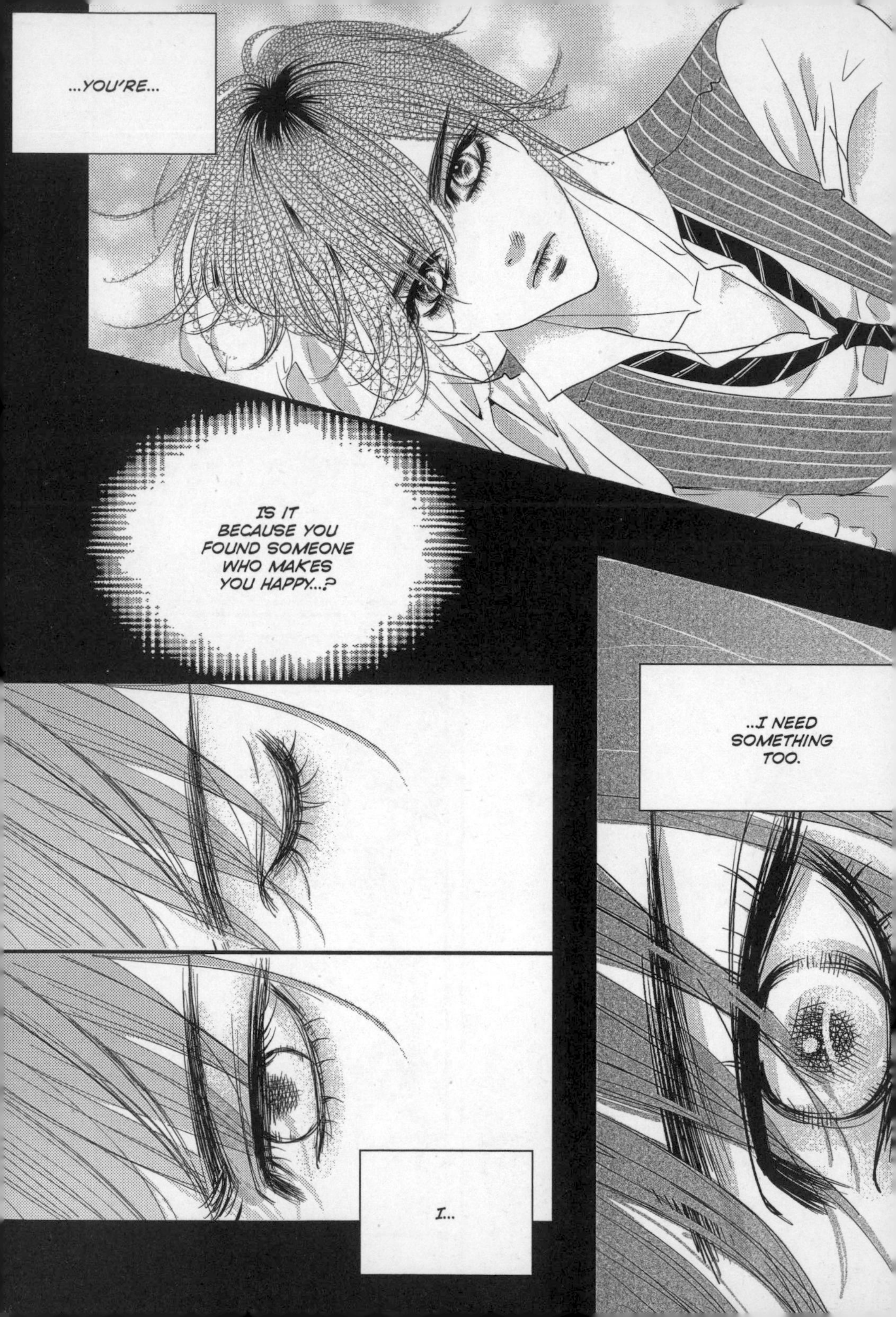
...YOU'RE...
IS IT BECAUSE YOU FOUND SOMEONE WHO MAKES YOU HAPPY...?
I...
..I NEED SOMETHING TOO.

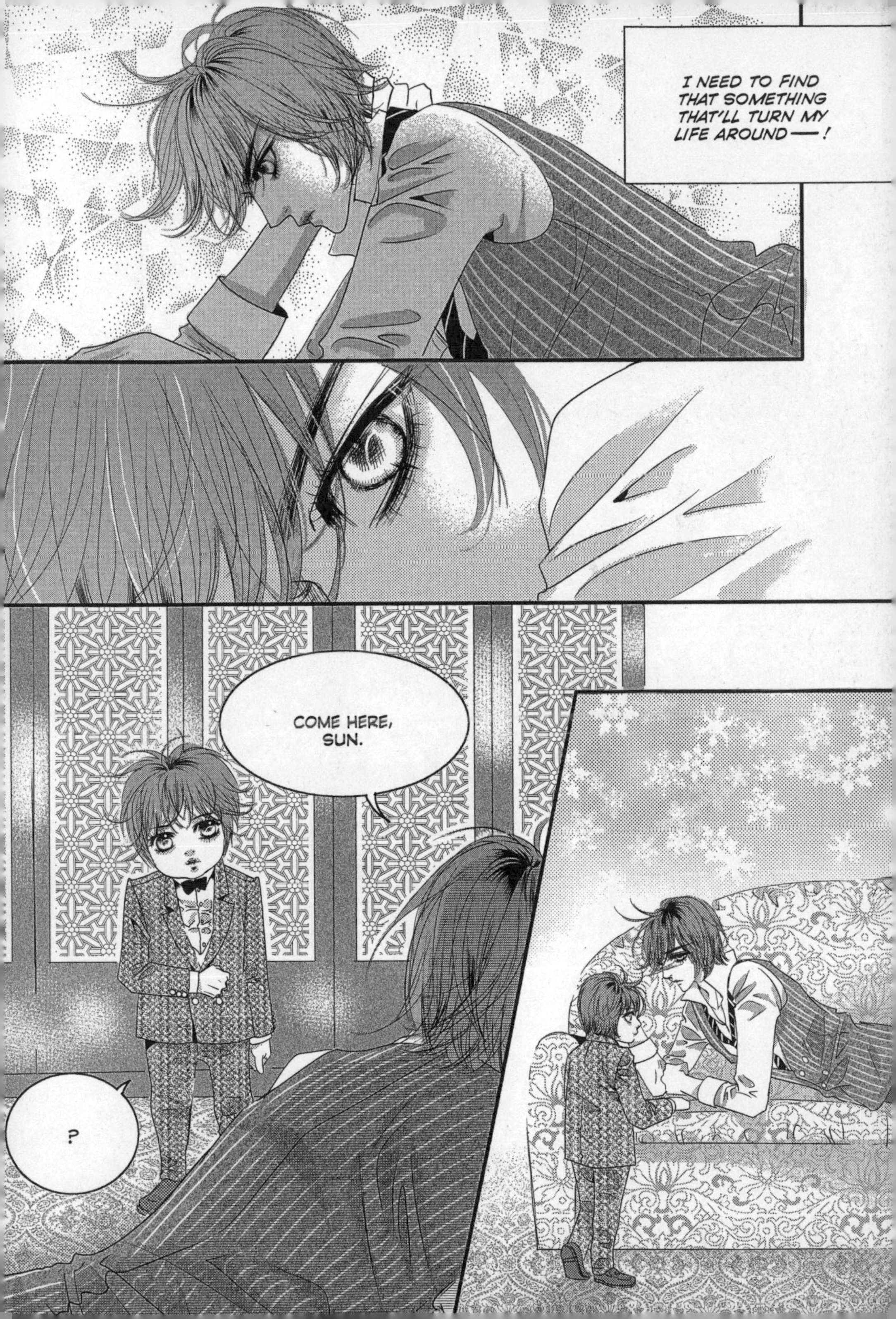
I NEED TO FIND THAT SOMETHING THAT'LL TURN MY LIFE AROUND—!
COME HERE, SUN.
?

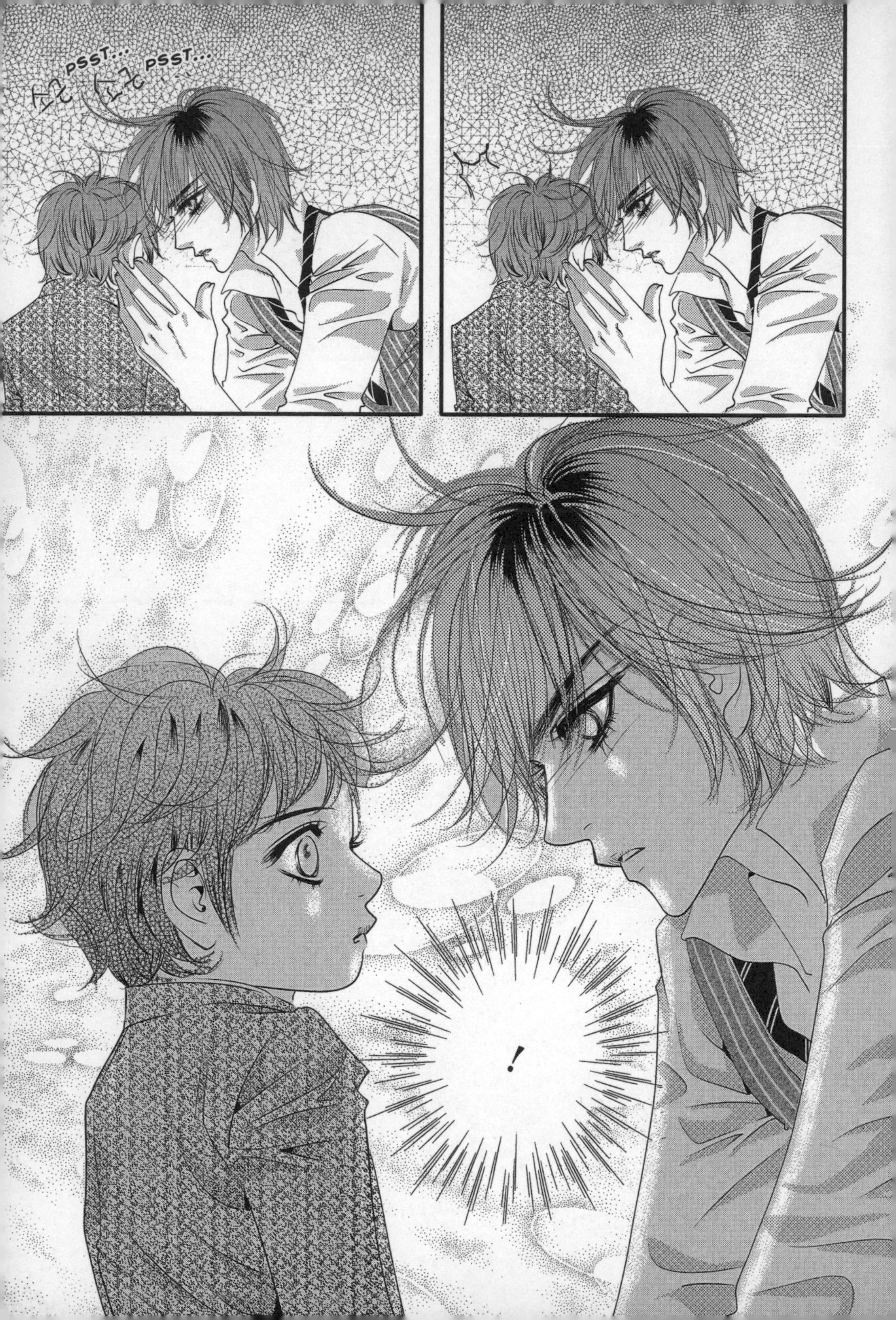
PSST... PSST...
!

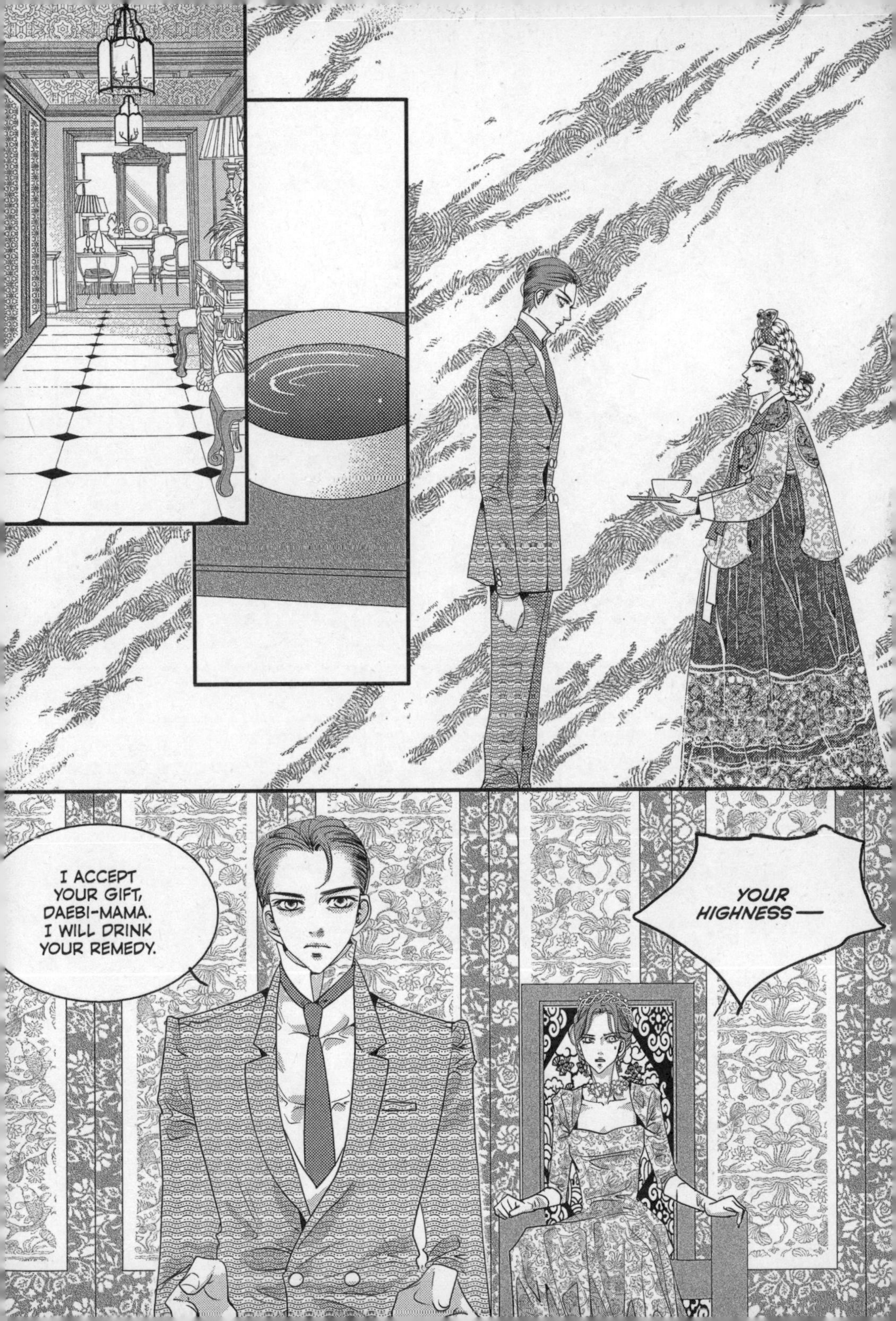
I ACCEPT YOUR GIFT, DAEBI-MAMA. I WILL DRINK YOUR REMEDY.
YOUR HIGHNESS—

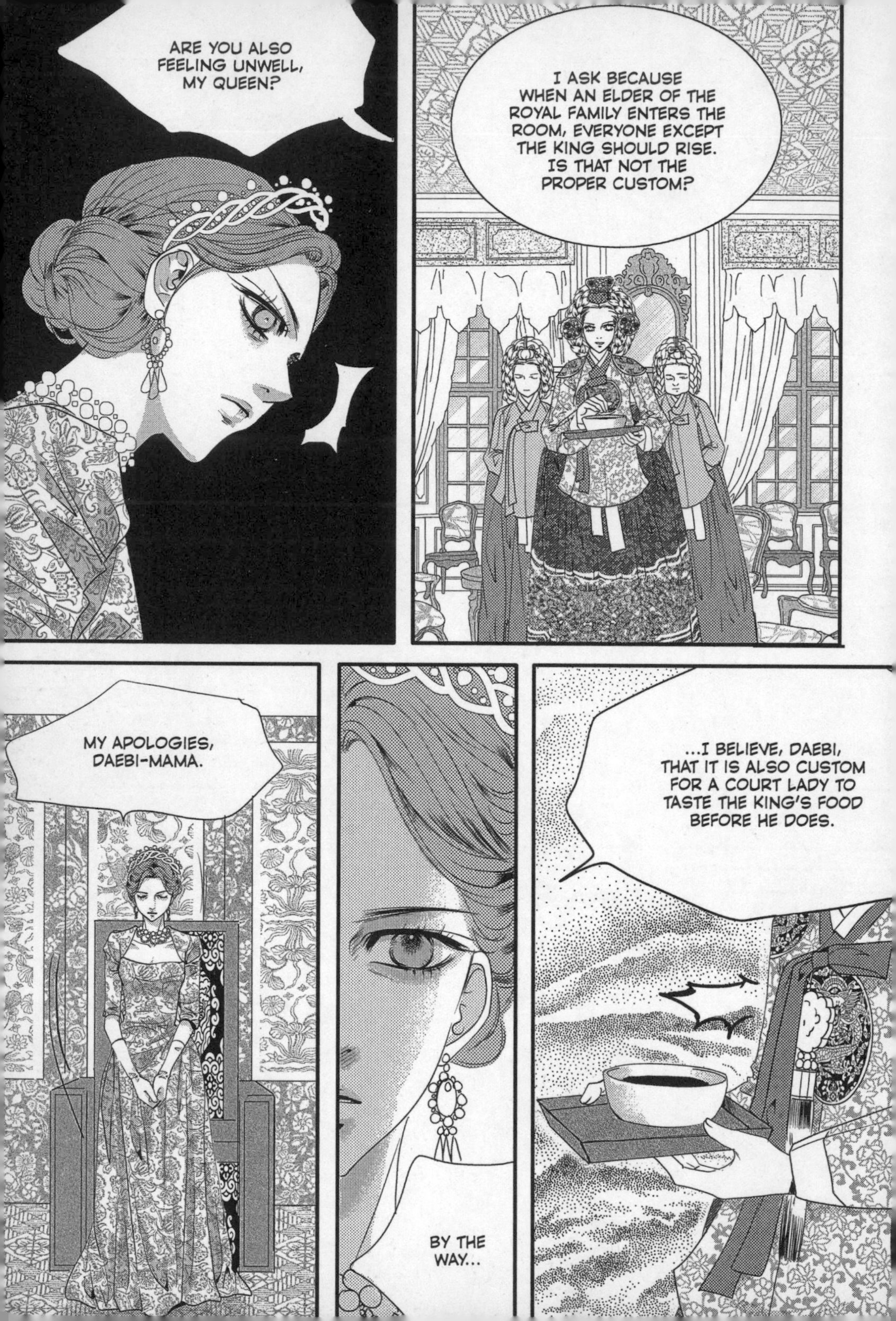
ARE YOU ALSO FEELING UNWELL, MY QUEEN?
I ASK BECAUSE WHEN AN ELDER OF THE ROYAL FAMILY ENTERS THE ROOM, EVERYONE EXCEPT THE KING SHOULD RISE. IS THAT NOT THE PROPER CUSTOM?
MY APOLOGIES, DAEBI-MAMA.
BY THE WAY...
...I BELIEVE, DAEBI, THAT IT IS ALSO CUSTOM FOR A COURT LADY TO TASTE THE KING'S FOOD BEFORE HE DOES.

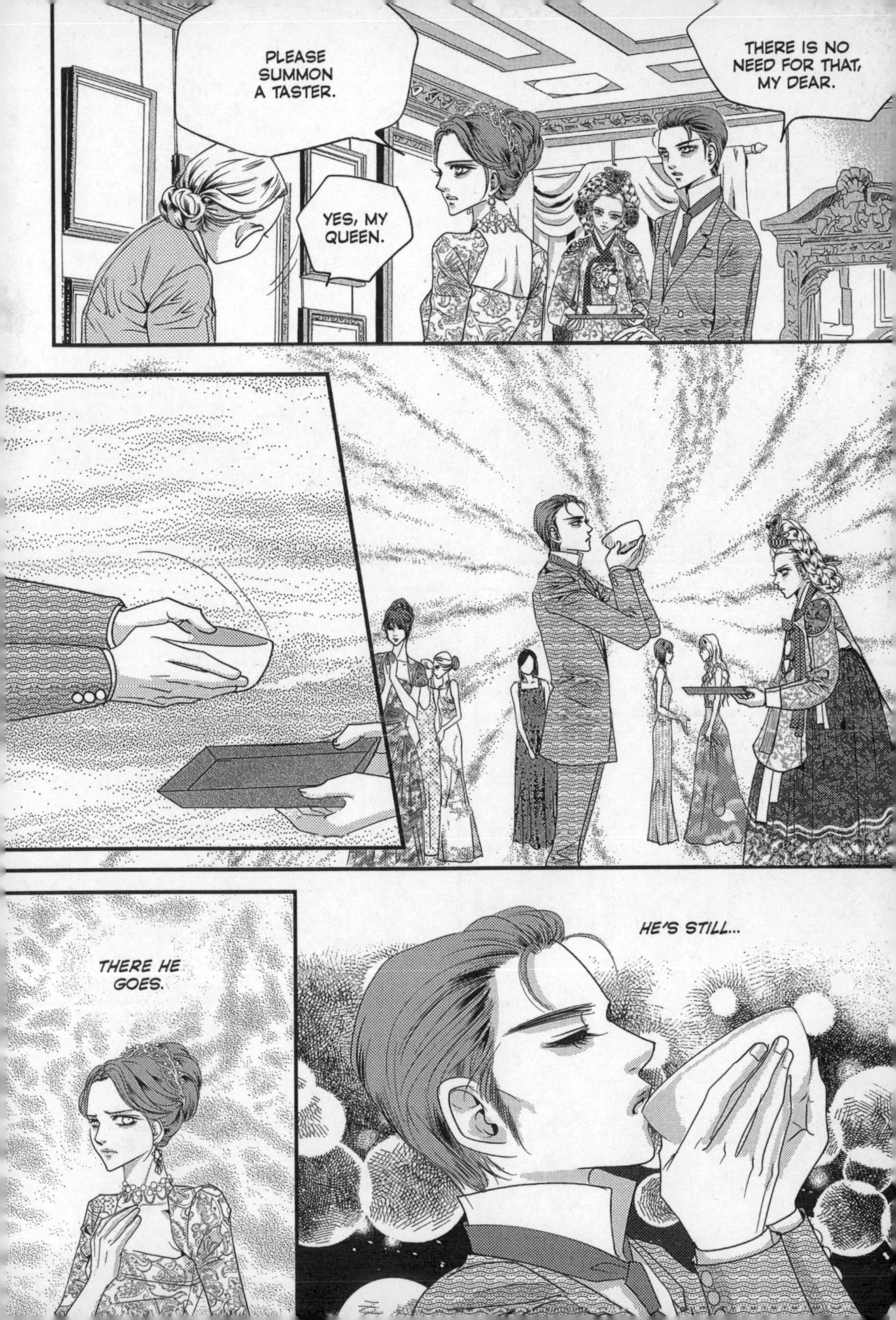
PLEASE SUMMON A TASTER.
YES, MY QUEEN.
THERE IS NO NEED FOR THAT, MY DEAR.
THERE HE GOES.
HE'S STILL...

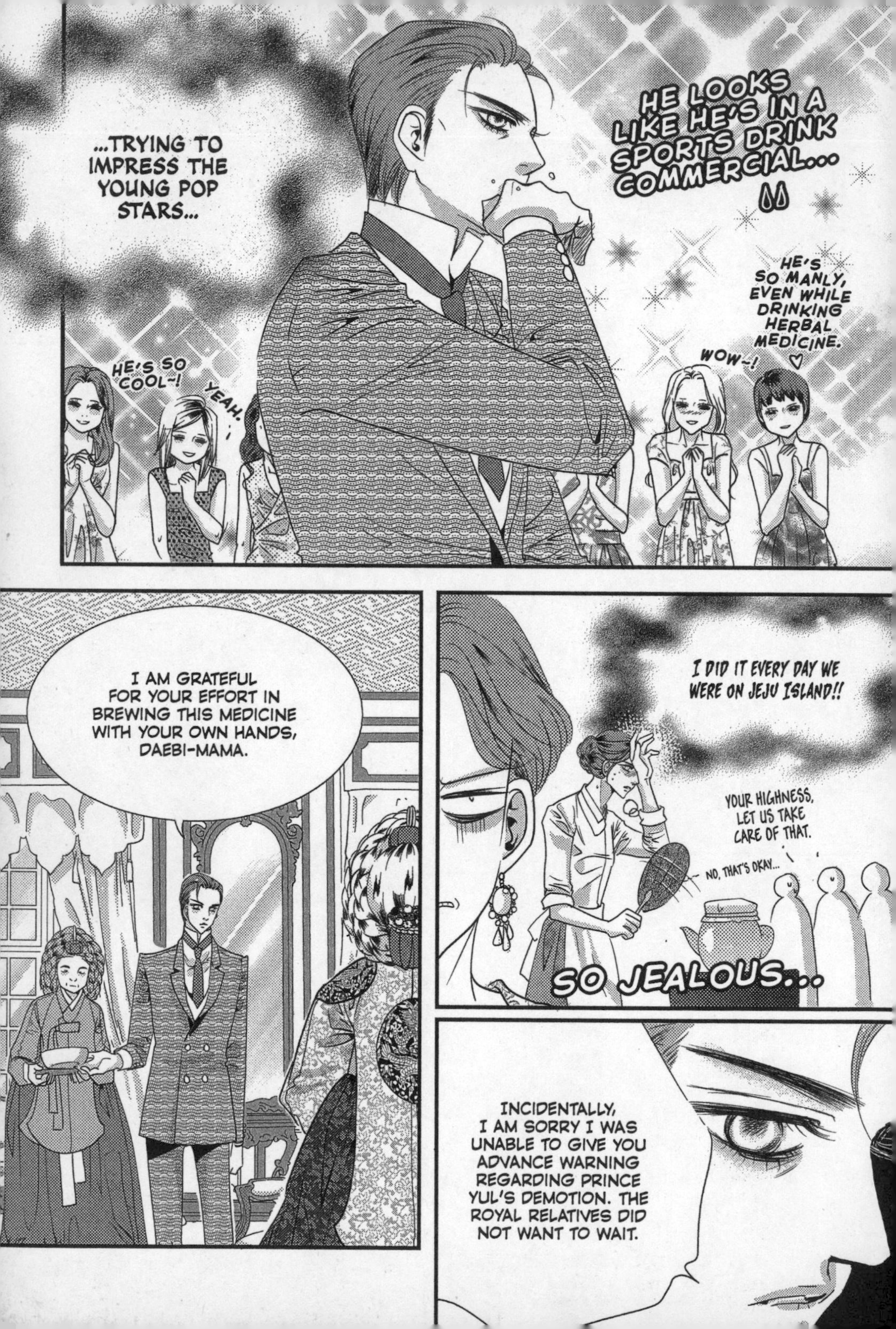
...TRYING TO IMPRESS THE YOUNG POP STARS...
HE LOOKS LIKE HE'S IN A SPORTS DRINK COMMERCIAL...
HE'S SO COOL~!
YEAH.
WOW~!
HE'S SO MANLY, EVEN WHILE DRINKING HERBAL MEDICINE. ♡
I AM GRATEFUL FOR YOUR EFFORT IN BREWING THIS MEDICINE WITH YOUR OWN HANDS, DAEBI-MAMA.
I DID IT EVERY DAY WE WERE ON JEJU ISLAND!!
YOUR HIGHNESS, LET US TAKE CARE OF THAT.
NO, THAT'S OKAY...
SO JEALOUS...
INCIDENTALLY, I AM SORRY I WAS UNABLE TO GIVE YOU ADVANCE WARNING REGARDING PRINCE YUL'S DEMOTION. THE ROYAL RELATIVES DID NOT WANT TO WAIT.

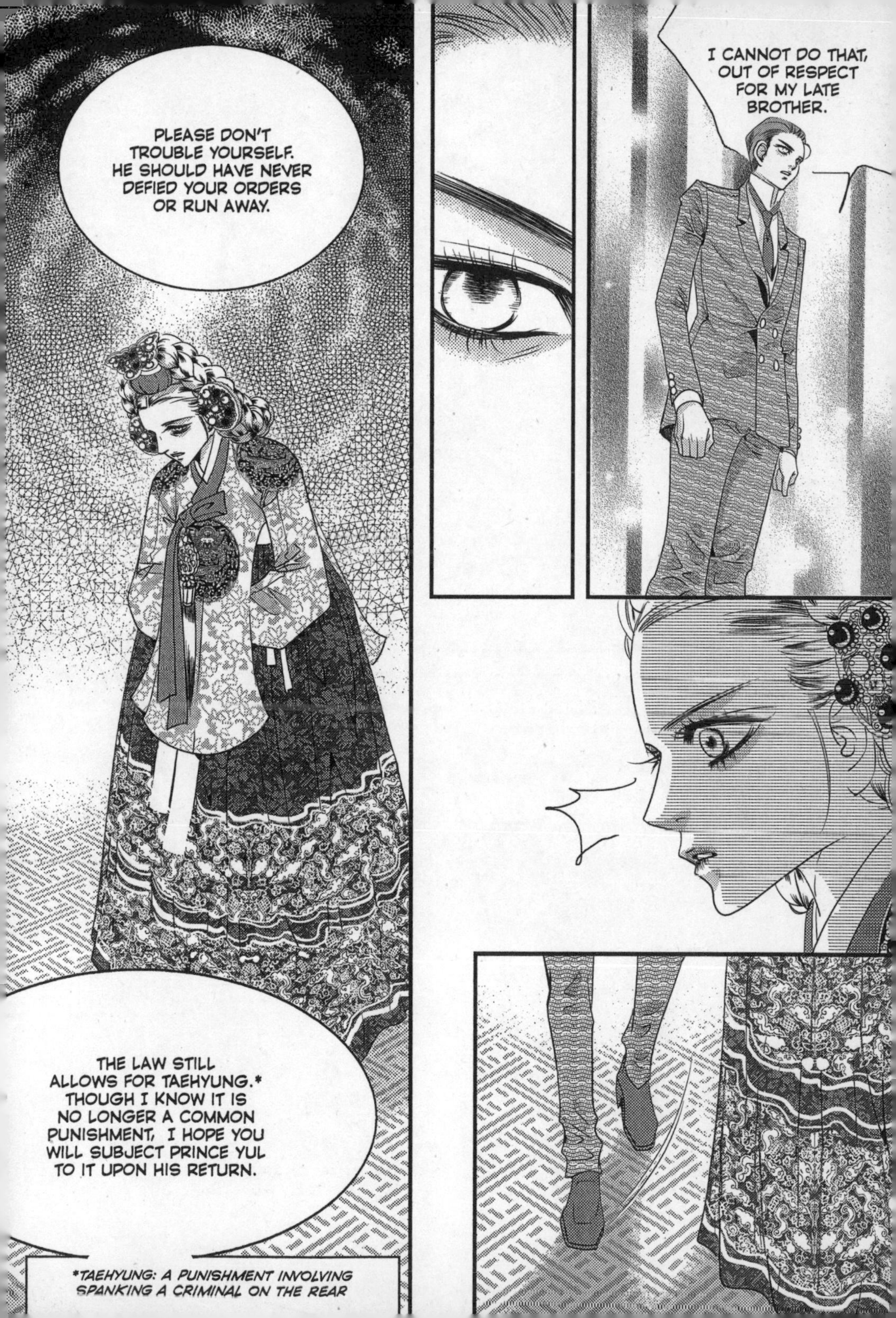
PLEASE DON'T TROUBLE YOURSELF. HE SHOULD HAVE NEVER DEFIED YOUR ORDERS OR RUN AWAY.
THE LAW STILL ALLOWS FOR TAEHYUNG.* THOUGH I KNOW IT IS NO LONGER A COMMON PUNISHMENT, I HOPE YOU WILL SUBJECT PRINCE YUL TO IT UPON HIS RETURN.
*TAEHYUNG: A PUNISHMENT INVOLVING SPANKING A CRIMINAL ON THE REAR
I CANNOT DO THAT, OUT OF RESPECT FOR MY LATE BROTHER.

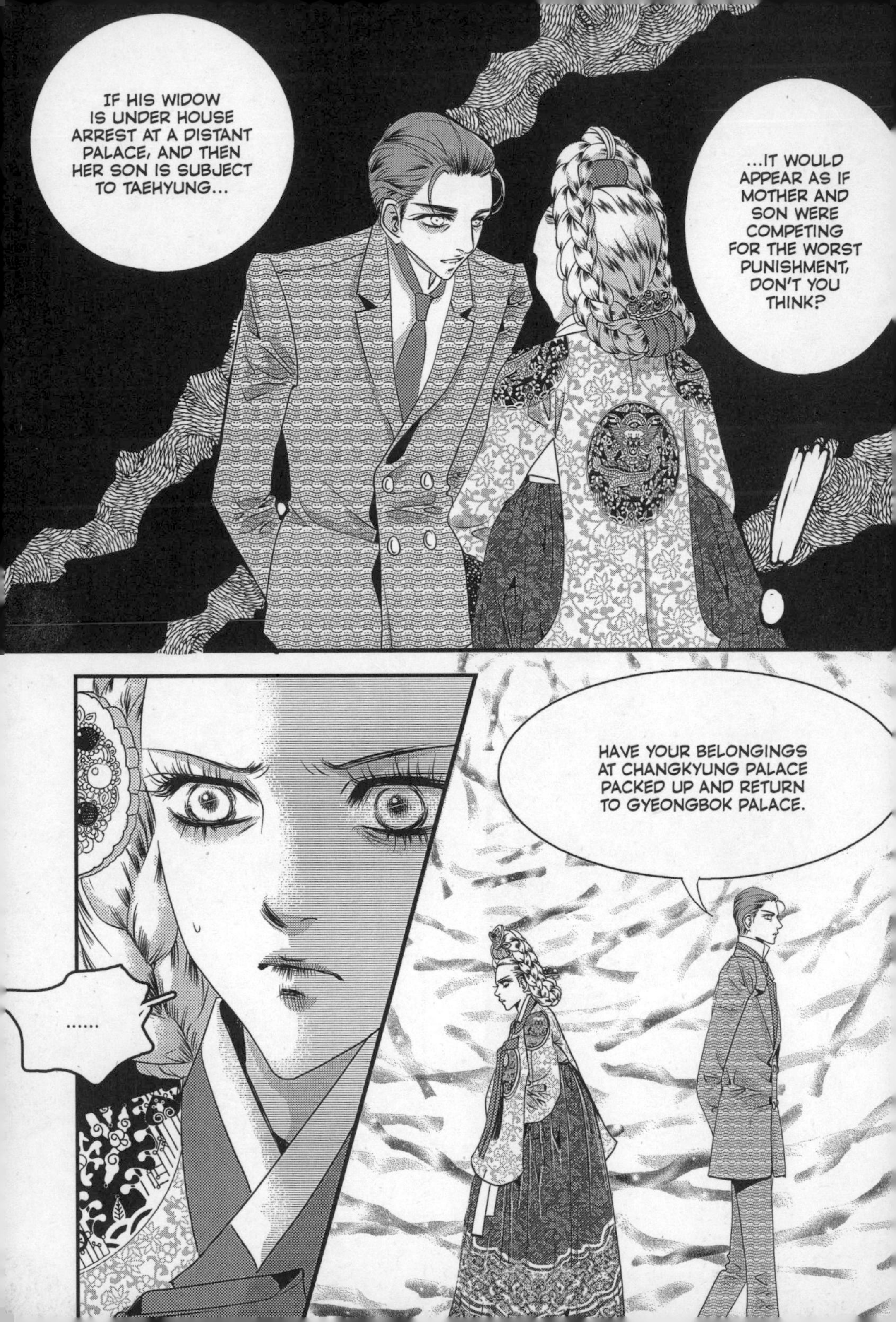
IF HIS WIDOW IS UNDER HOUSE ARREST AT A DISTANT PALACE, AND THEN HER SON IS SUBJECT TO TAEHYUNG...
...IT WOULD APPEAR AS IF MOTHER AND SON WERE COMPETING FOR THE WORST PUNISHMENT, DON'T YOU THINK?
......
HAVE YOUR BELONGINGS AT CHANGKYUNG PALACE PACKED UP AND RETURN TO GYEONGBOK PALACE.

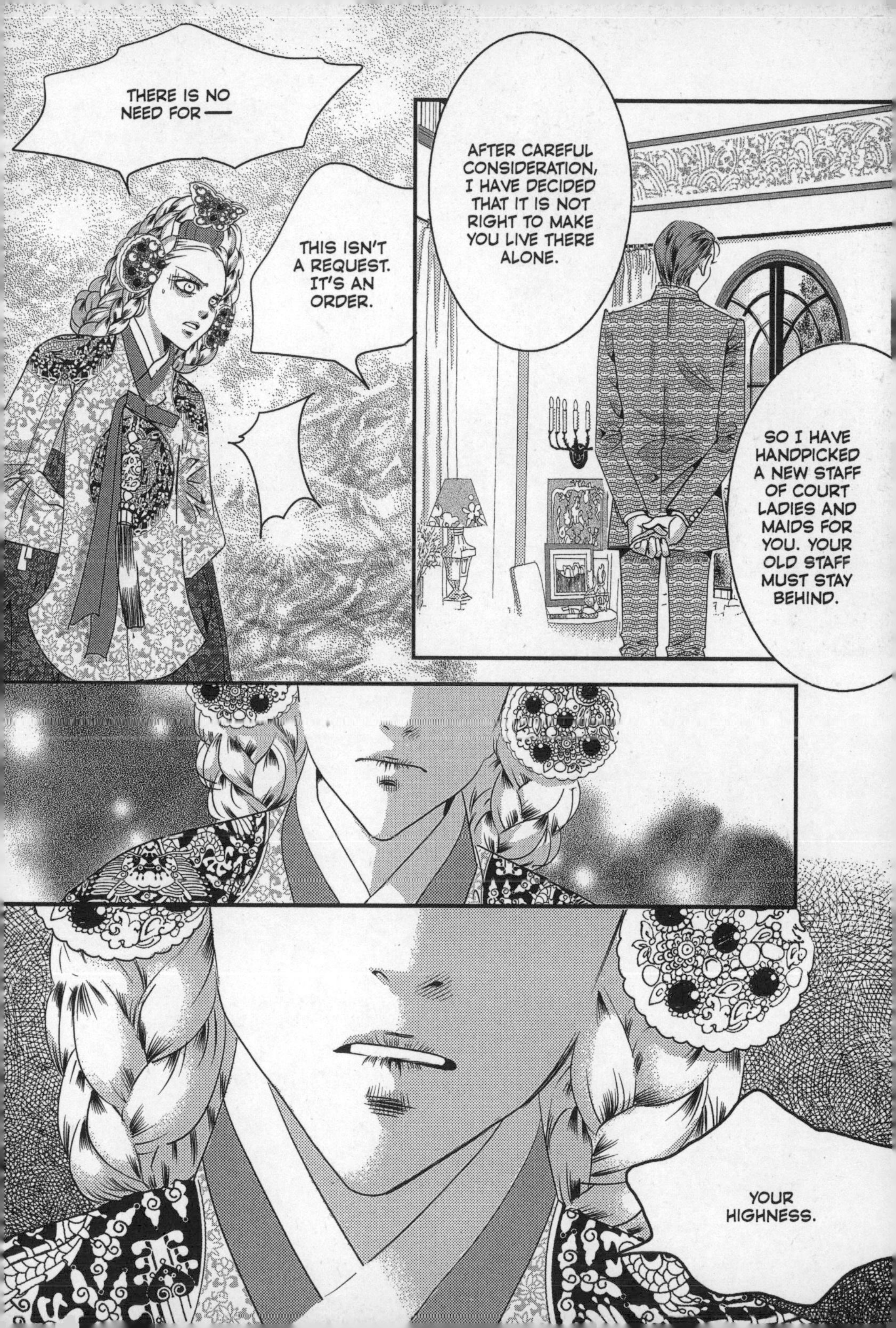
THERE IS NO NEED FOR—
THIS ISN'T A REQUEST. IT'S AN ORDER.
AFTER CAREFUL CONSIDERATION, I HAVE DECIDED THAT IT IS NOT RIGHT TO MAKE YOU LIVE THERE ALONE.
SO I HAVE HANDPICKED A NEW STAFF OF COURT LADIES AND MAIDS FOR YOU. YOUR OLD STAFF MUST STAY BEHIND.
YOUR HIGHNESS.

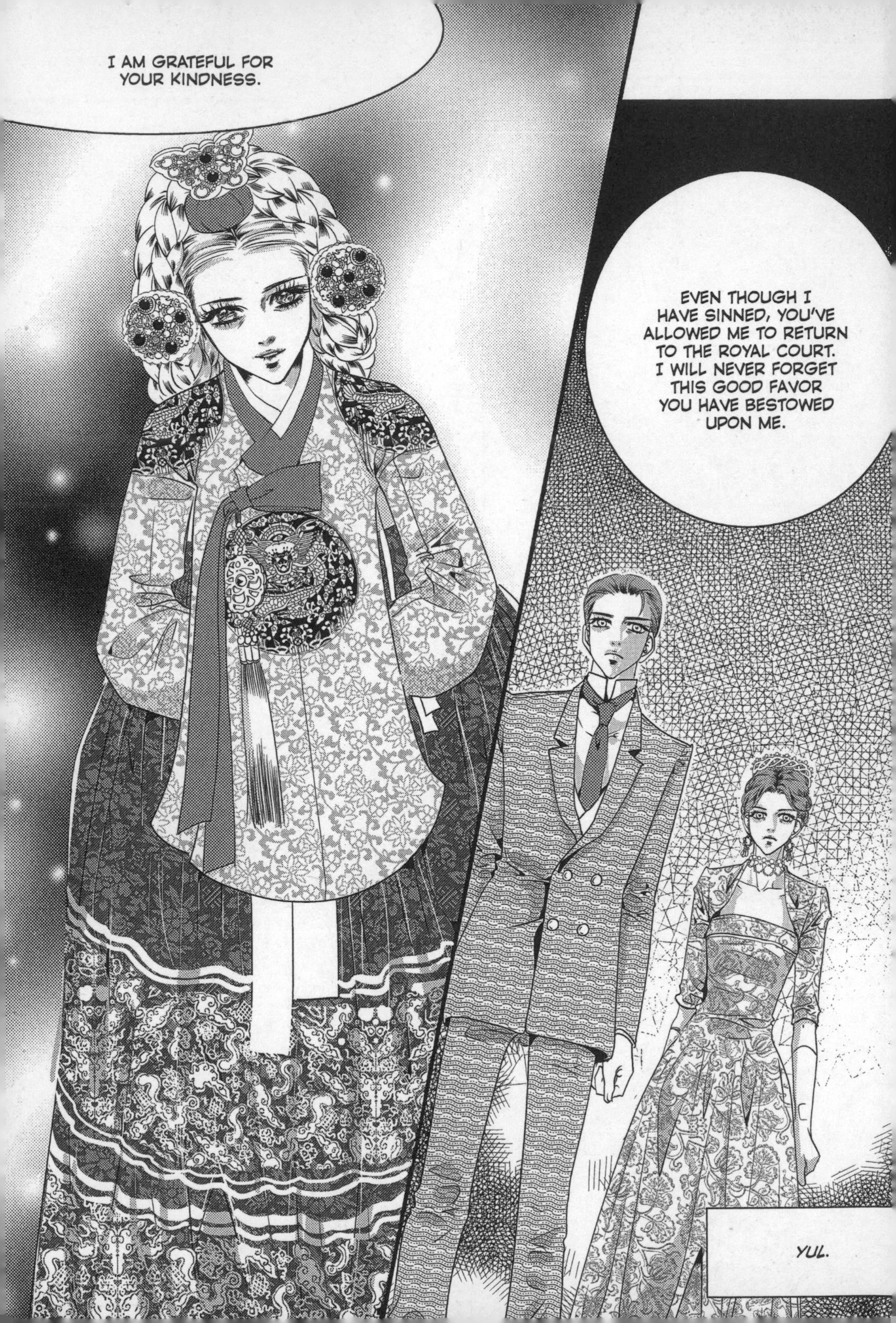
I AM GRATEFUL FOR YOUR KINDNESS.
EVEN THOUGH I HAVE SINNED, YOU'VE ALLOWED ME TO RETURN TO THE ROYAL COURT. I WILL NEVER FORGET THIS GOOD FAVOR YOU HAVE BESTOWED UPON ME.
YUL.

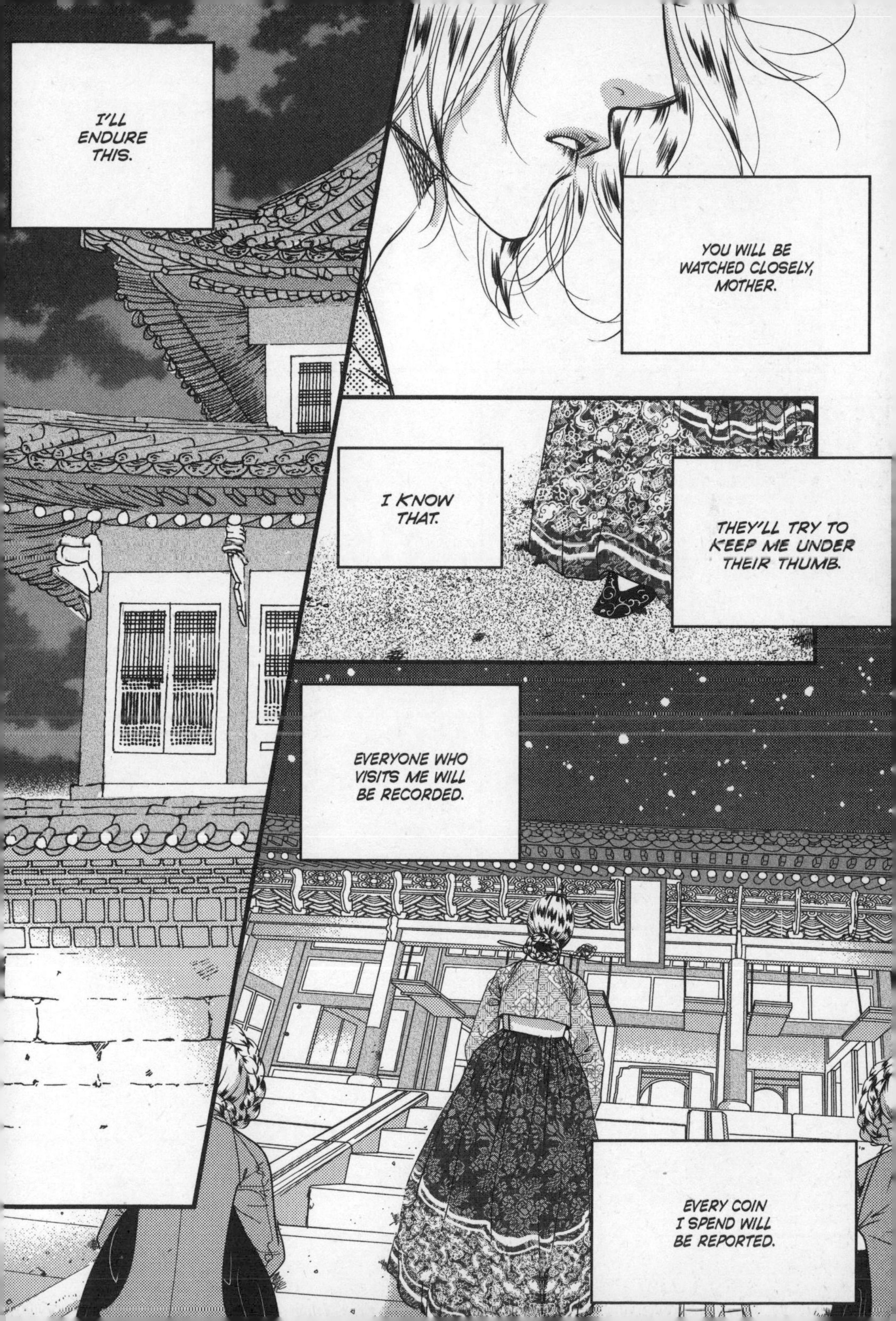
I'LL ENDURE THIS.
YOU WILL BE WATCHED CLOSELY, MOTHER.
I KNOW THAT.
THEY'LL TRY TO KEEP ME UNDER THEIR THUMB.
EVERYONE WHO VISITS ME WILL BE RECORDED.
EVERY COIN I SPEND WILL BE REPORTED.

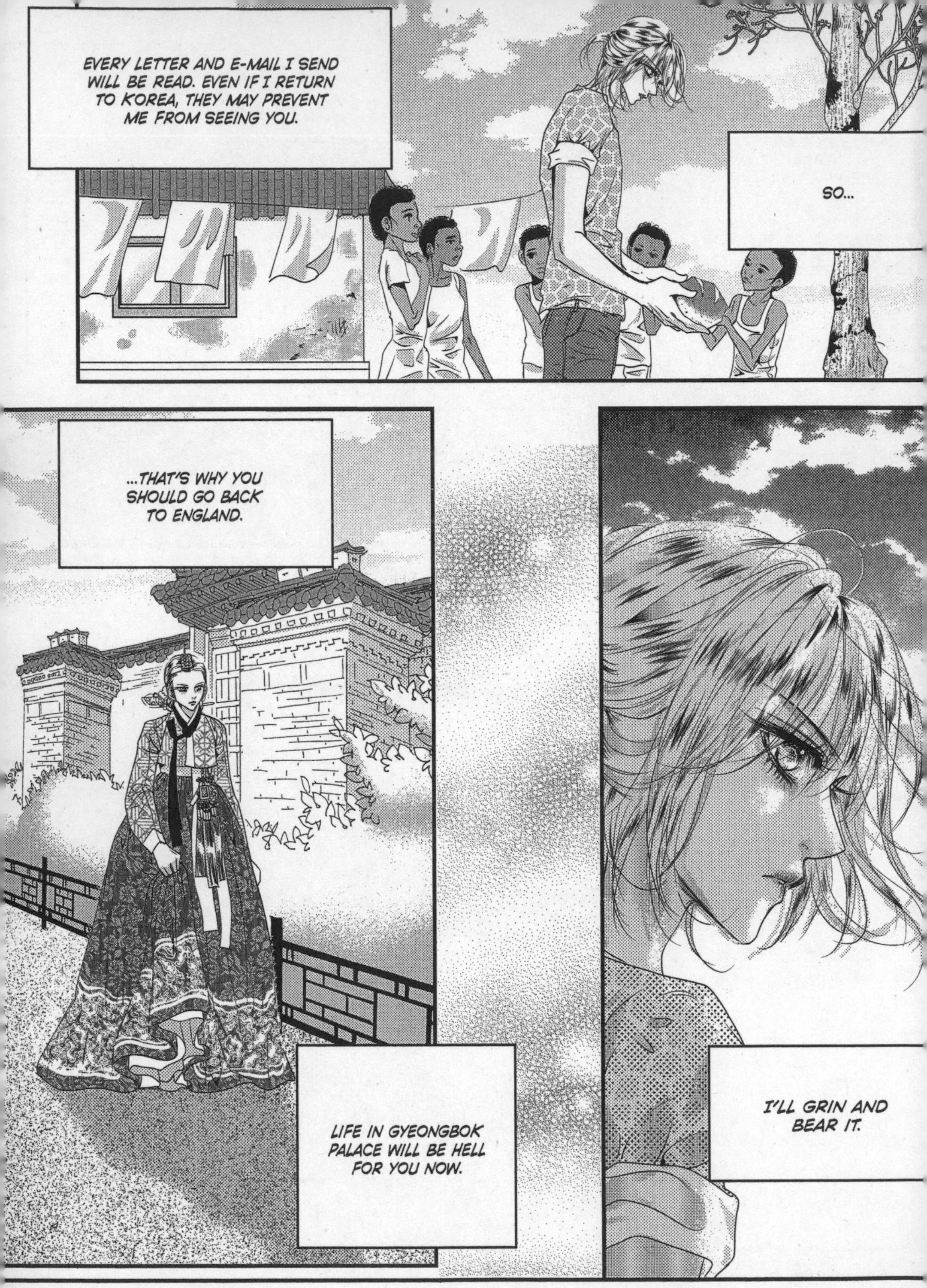
EVERY LETTER AND E-MAIL I SEND WILL BE READ. EVEN IF I RETURN TO KOREA, THEY MAY PREVENT ME FROM SEEING YOU.
SO...
...THAT'S WHY YOU SHOULD GO BACK TO ENGLAND.
LIFE IN GYEONGBOK PALACE WILL BE HELL FOR YOU NOW.
I'LL GRIN AND BEAR IT.

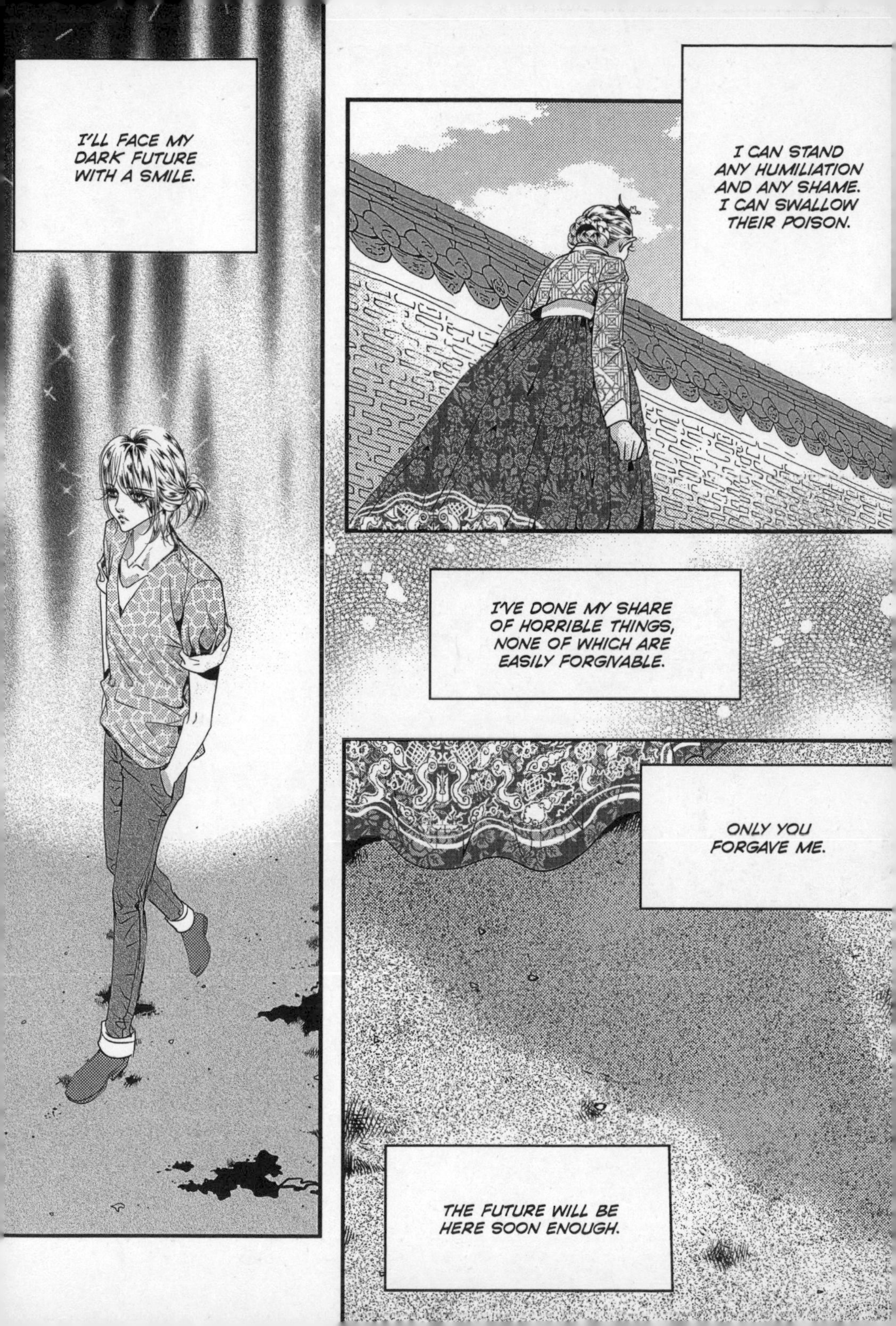
I'LL FACE MY DARK FUTURE WITH A SMILE.
I CAN STAND ANY HUMILIATION AND ANY SHAME. I CAN SWALLOW THEIR POISON.
I'VE DONE MY SHARE OF HORRIBLE THINGS, NONE OF WHICH ARE EASILY FORGIVABLE.
ONLY YOU FORGAVE ME.
THE FUTURE WILL BE HERE SOON ENOUGH.

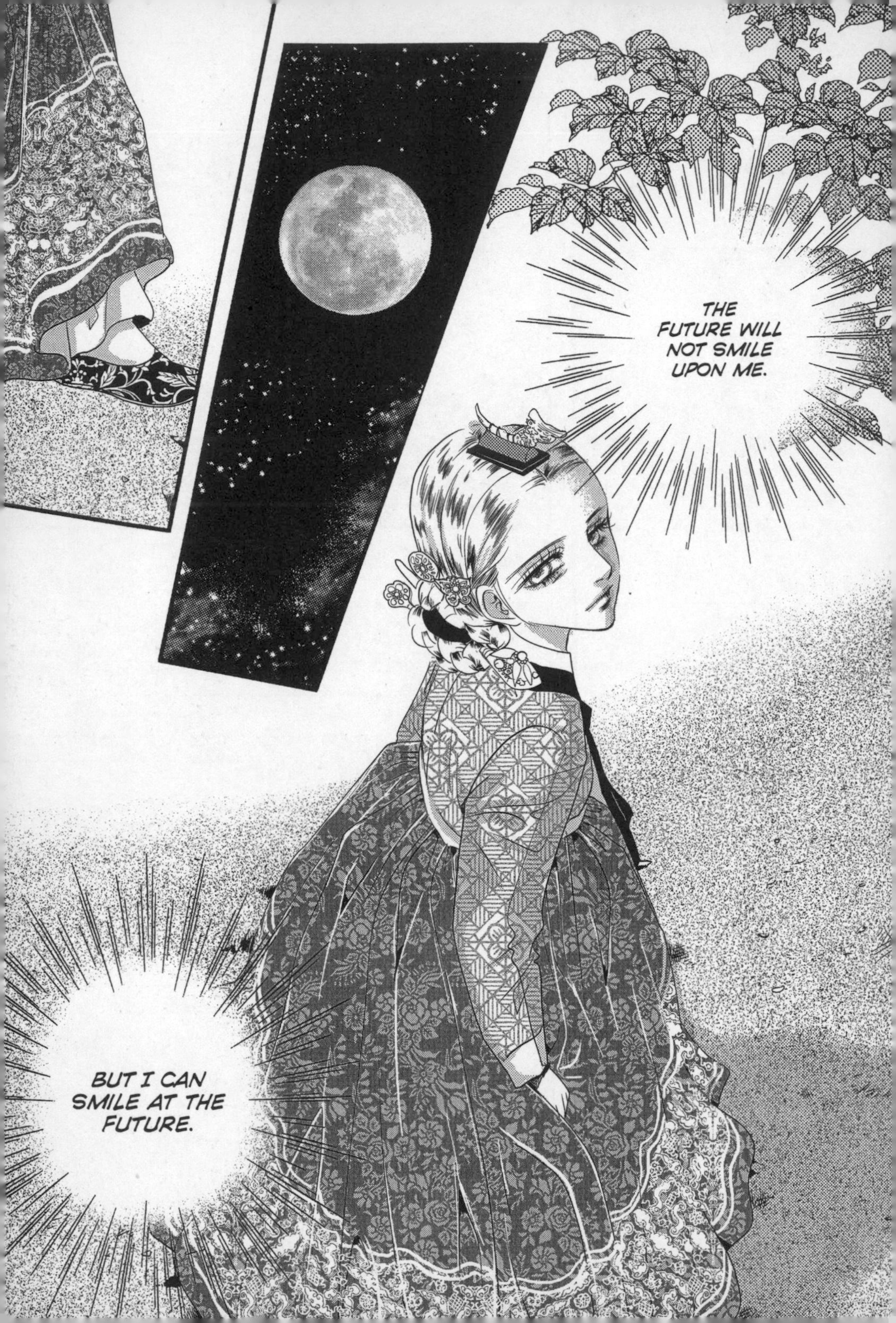
THE FUTURE WILL NOT SMILE UPON ME.
BUT I CAN SMILE AT THE FUTURE.

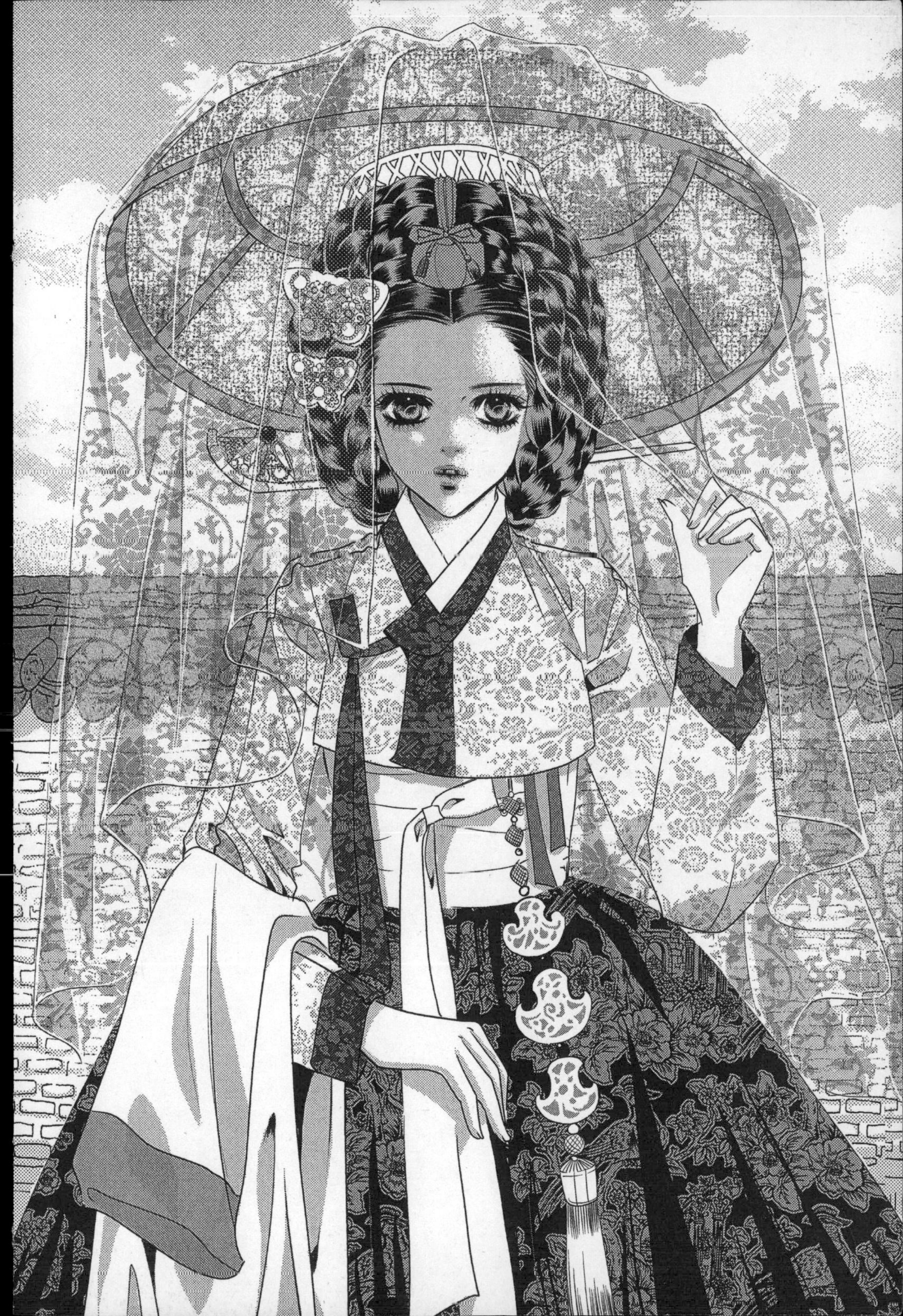

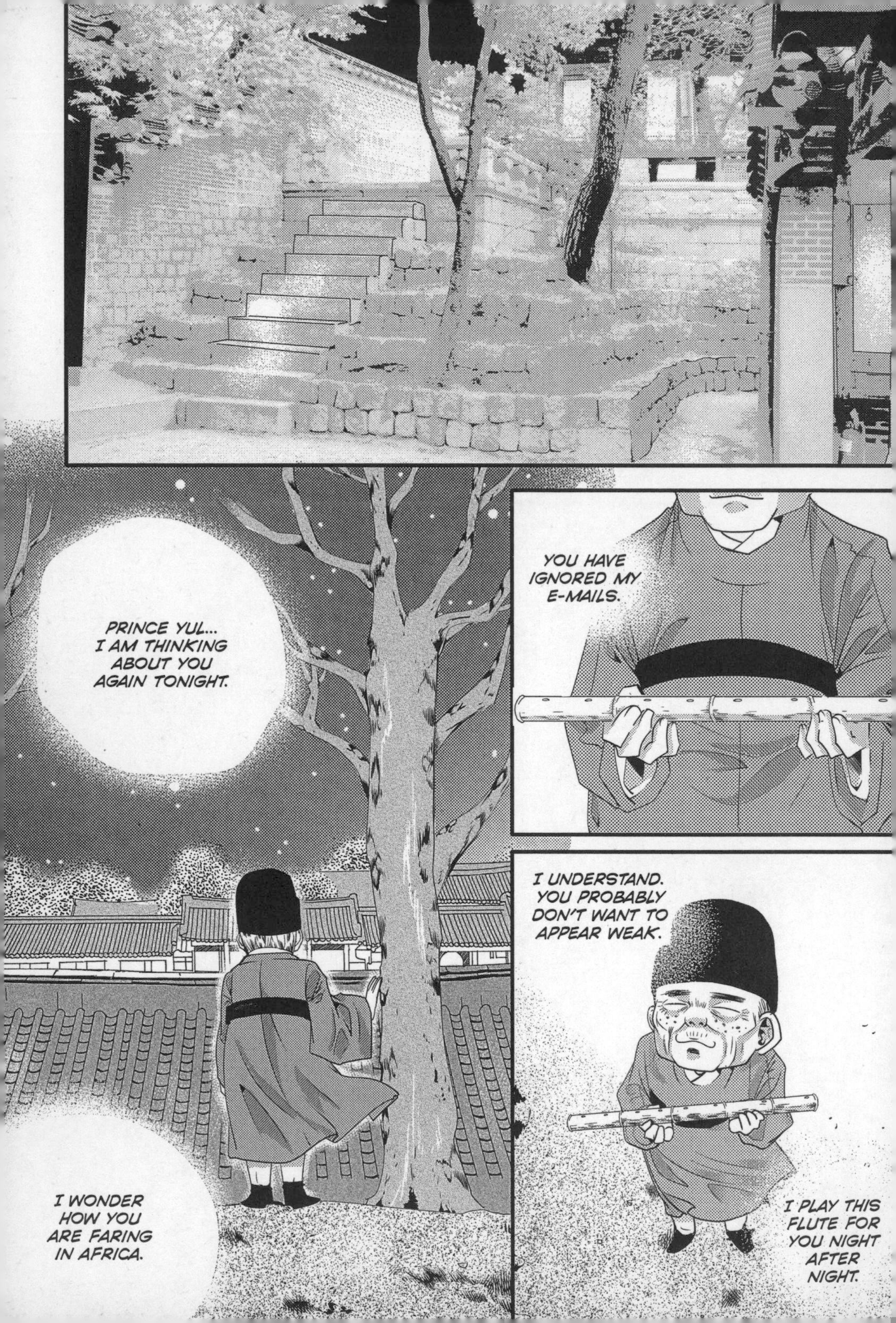
PRINCE YUL... I AM THINKING ABOUT YOU AGAIN TONIGHT.
I WONDER HOW YOU ARE FARING IN AFRICA.
YOU HAVE IGNORED MY E-MAILS.
I UNDERSTAND. YOU PROBABLY DON'T WANT TO APPEAR WEAK.
I PLAY THIS FLUTE FOR YOU NIGHT AFTER NIGHT.

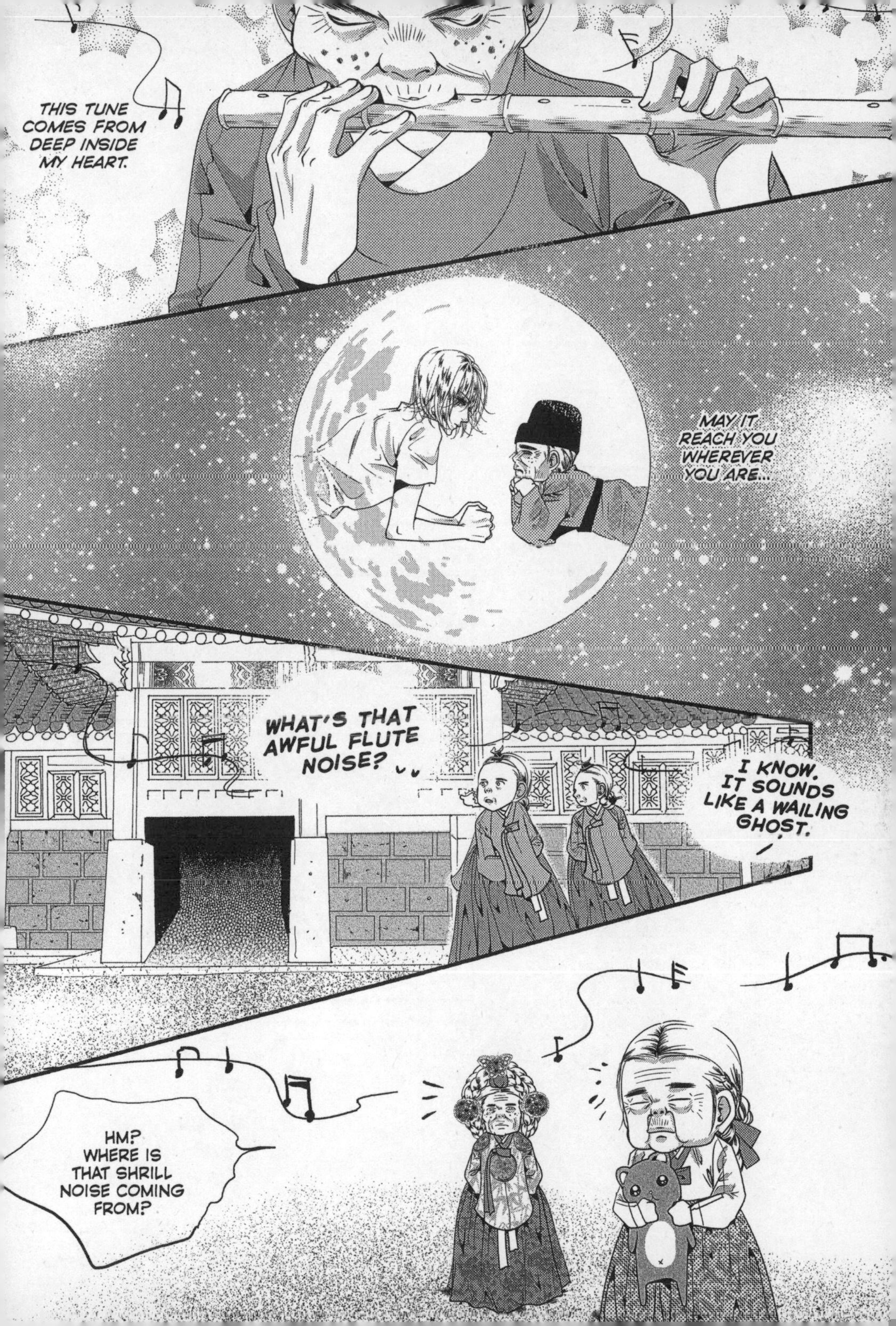
THIS TUNE COMES FROM DEEP INSIDE MY HEART.
MAY IT REACH YOU WHEREVER YOU ARE...
WHAT'S THAT AWFUL FLUTE NOISE?
I KNOW. IT SOUNDS LIKE A WAILING GHOST.
HM? WHERE IS THAT SHRILL NOISE COMING FROM?

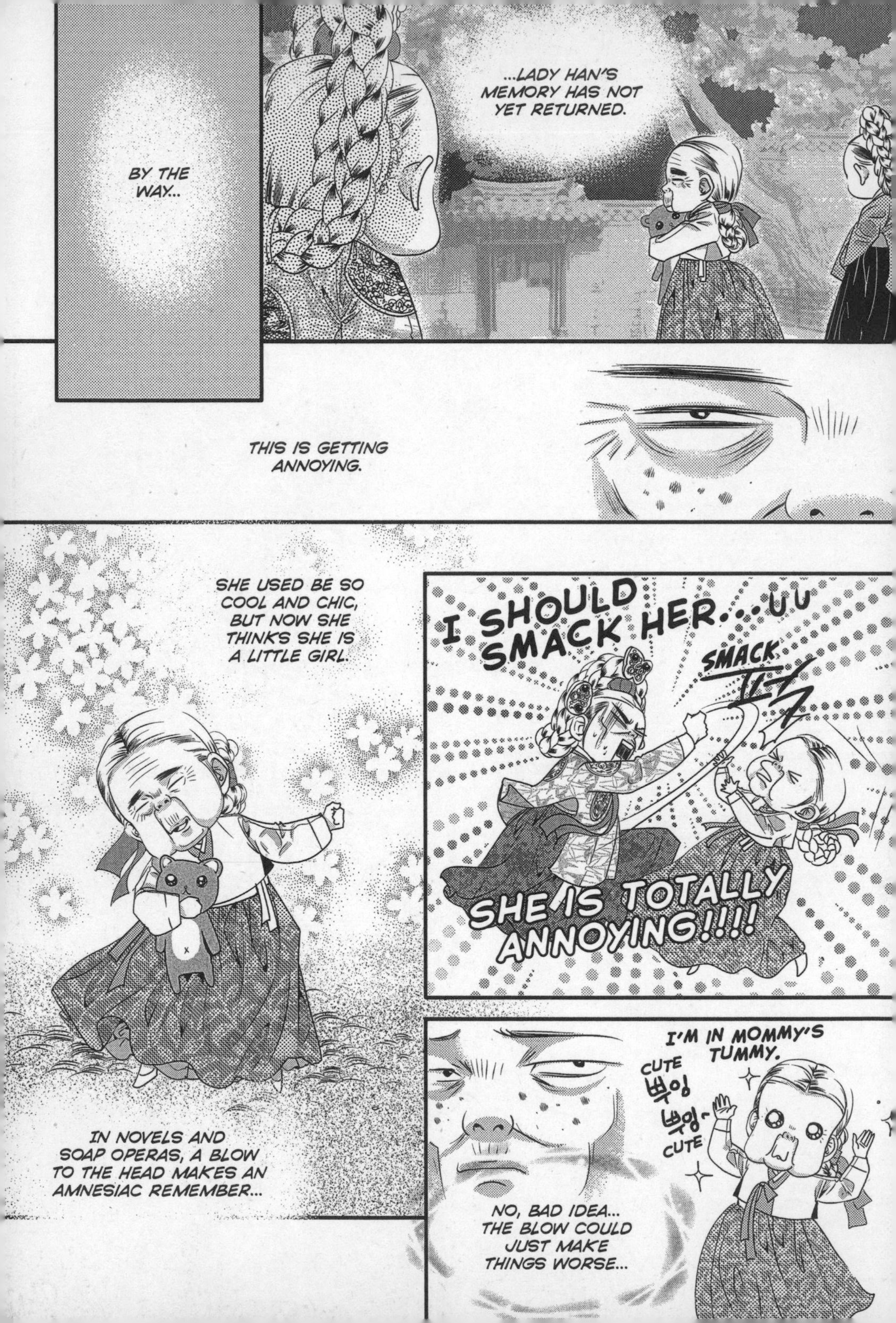
BY THE WAY...
...LADY HAN'S MEMORY HAS NOT YET RETURNED.
THIS IS GETTING ANNOYING.
SHE USED BE SO COOL AND CHIC, BUT NOW SHE THINKS SHE IS A LITTLE GIRL.
IN NOVELS AND SOAP OPERAS, A BLOW TO THE HEAD MAKES AN AMNESIAC REMEMBER...
I SHOULD SMACK HER...UU
SMACK
SHE IS TOTALLY ANNOYING!!!!
I'M IN MOMMY'S TUMMY.
CUTE
뿍잉
뿍잉-
CUTE
NO, BAD IDEA... THE BLOW COULD JUST MAKE THINGS WORSE...

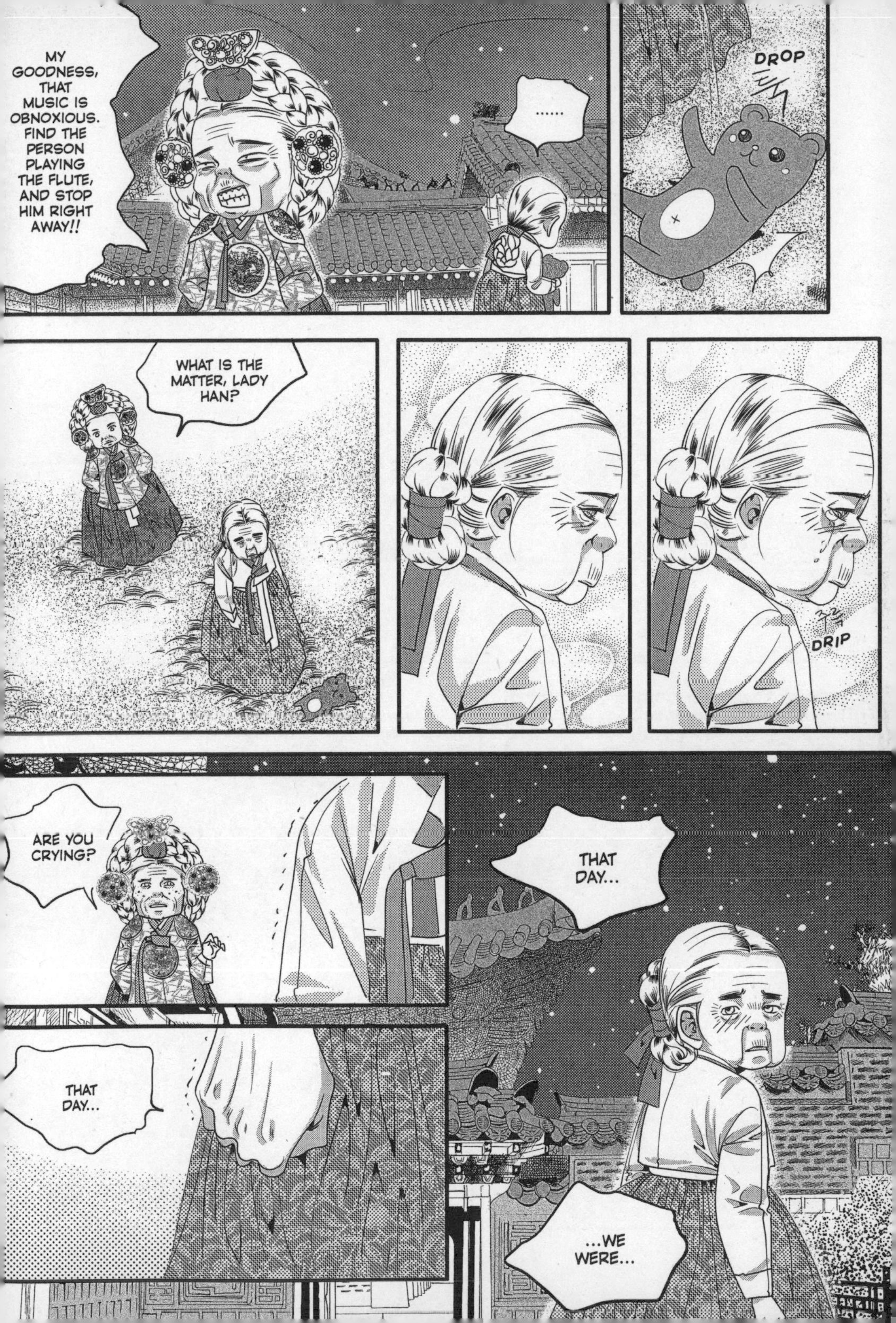
MY GOODNESS, THAT MUSIC IS OBNOXIOUS. FIND THE PERSON PLAYING THE FLUTE, AND STOP HIM RIGHT AWAY!!
......
DROP
WHAT IS THE MATTER, LADY HAN?
DRIP
ARE YOU CRYING?
THAT DAY...
THAT DAY...
...WE WERE...

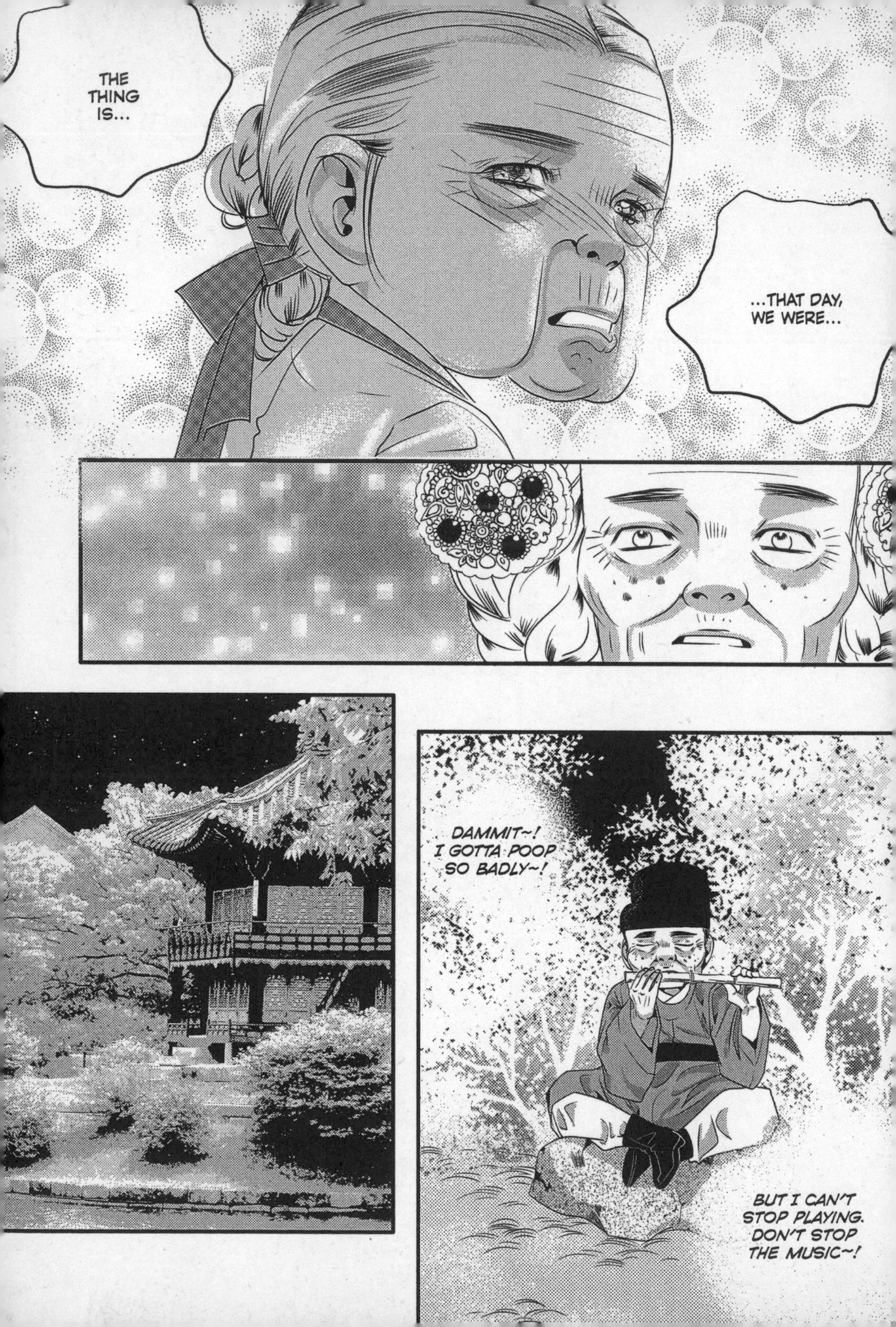
THE THING IS...
...THAT DAY, WE WERE...
DAMMIT~! I GOTTA POOP SO BADLY~!
BUT I CAN'T STOP PLAYING. DON'T STOP THE MUSIC~!

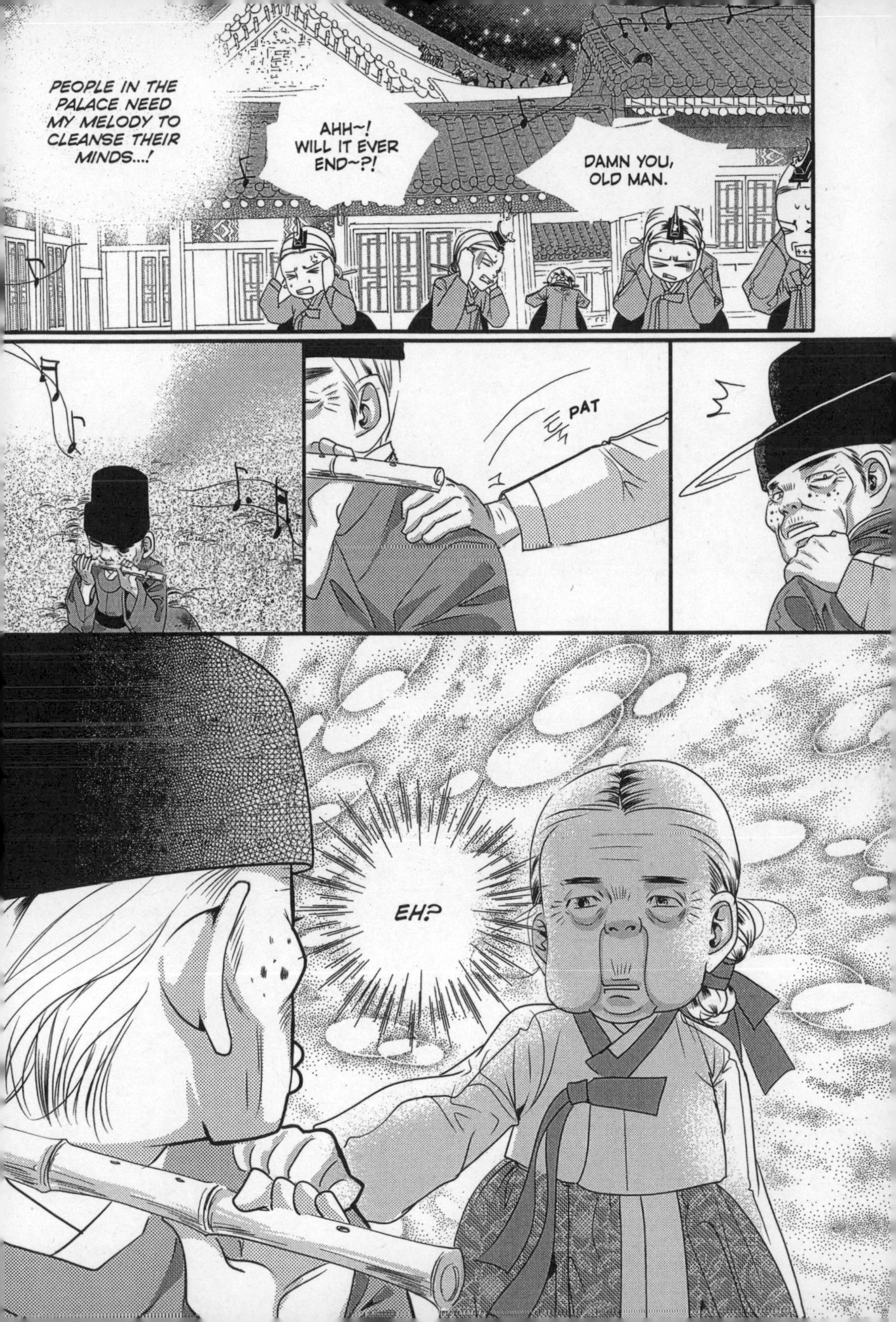
PEOPLE IN THE PALACE NEED MY MELODY TO CLEANSE THEIR MINDS...!
AHH~! WILL IT EVER END~?!
DAMN YOU, OLD MAN.
PAT
EH?

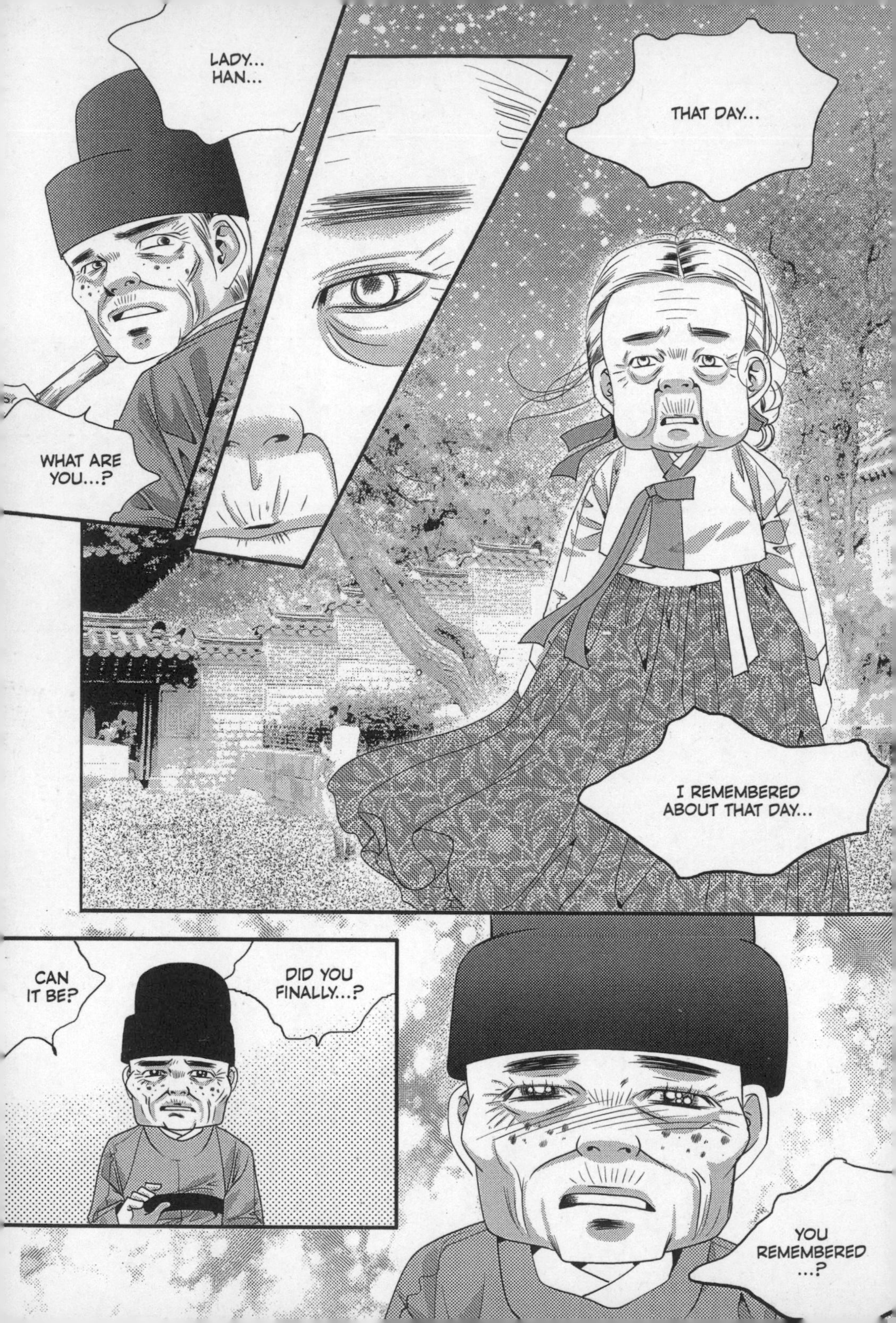
LADY... HAN...
WHAT ARE YOU...?
THAT DAY...
I REMEMBERED ABOUT THAT DAY...
CAN IT BE?
DID YOU FINALLY...?
YOU REMEMBERED ...?

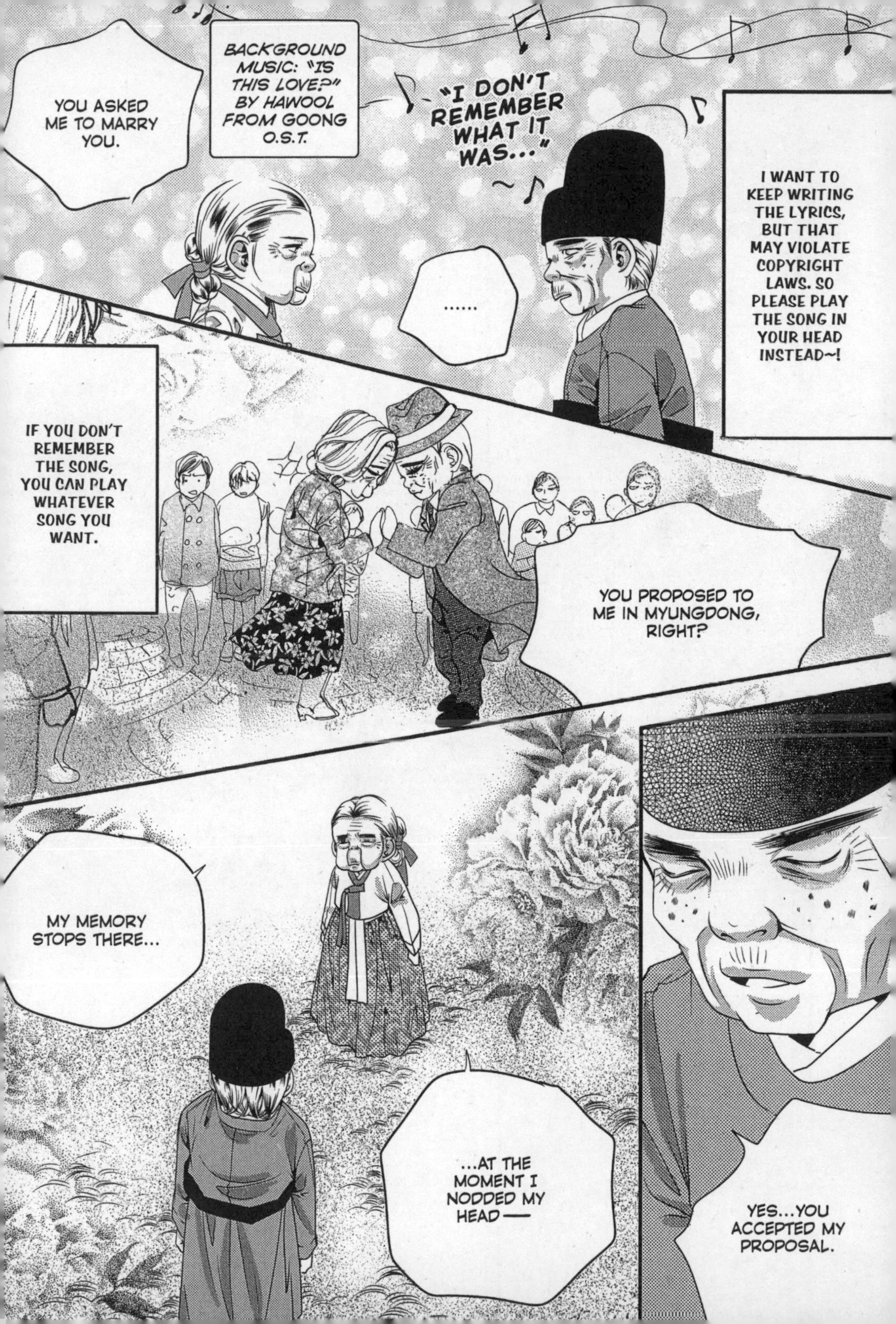
YOU ASKED ME TO MARRY YOU.
BACKGROUND MUSIC: "IS THIS LOVE?" BY HAWOOL FROM GOONG O.S.T.
"I DON'T REMEMBER WHAT IT WAS..."
......
I WANT TO KEEP WRITING THE LYRICS, BUT THAT MAY VIOLATE COPYRIGHT LAWS. SO PLEASE PLAY THE SONG IN YOUR HEAD INSTEAD~!
IF YOU DON'T REMEMBER THE SONG, YOU CAN PLAY WHATEVER SONG YOU WANT.
YOU PROPOSED TO ME IN MYUNGDONG, RIGHT?
MY MEMORY STOPS THERE...
...AT THE MOMENT I NODDED MY HEAD—
YES...YOU ACCEPTED MY PROPOSAL.

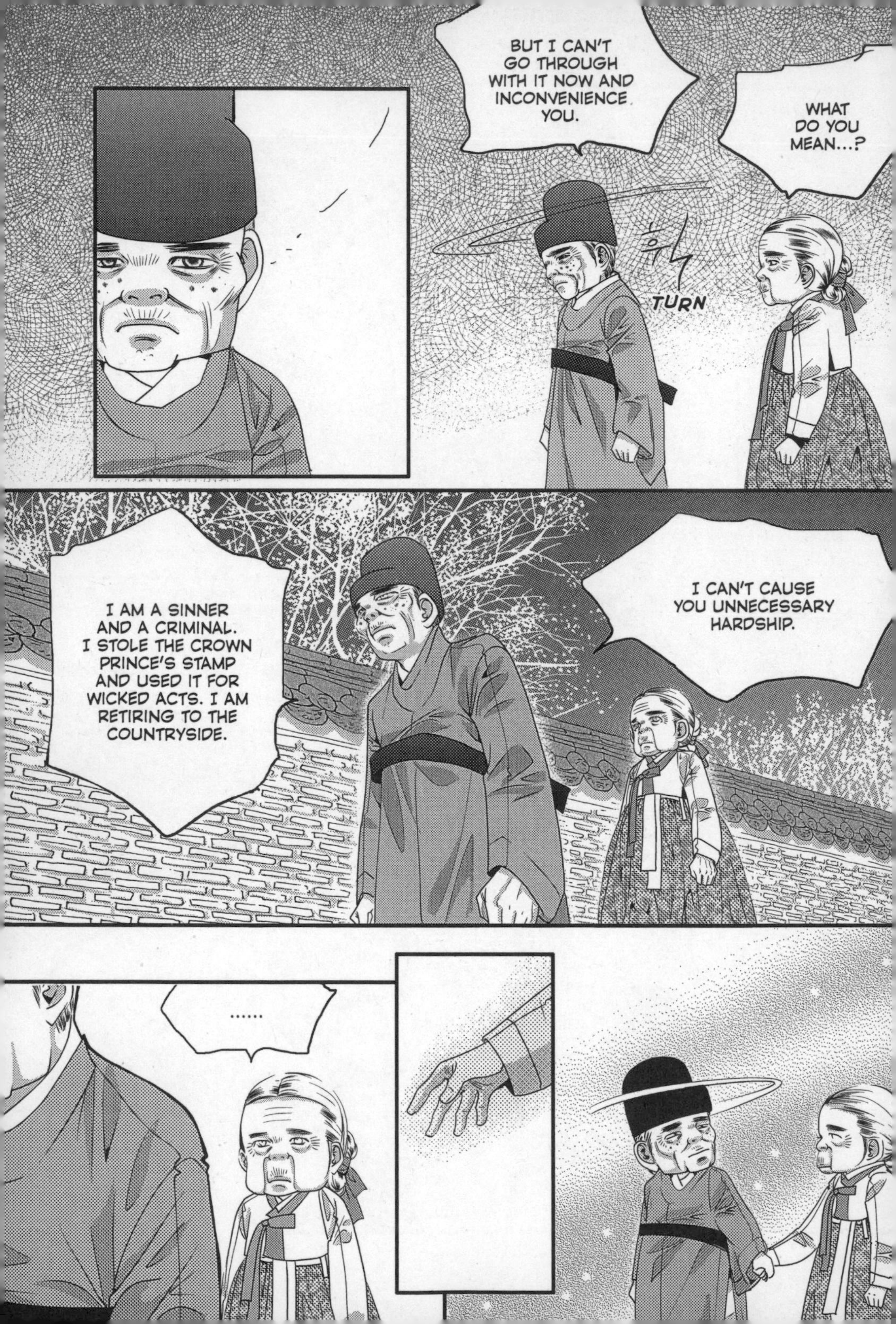
BUT I CAN'T GO THROUGH WITH IT NOW AND INCONVENIENCE YOU.
WHAT DO YOU MEAN...?
TURN
I AM A SINNER AND A CRIMINAL. I STOLE THE CROWN PRINCE'S STAMP AND USED IT FOR WICKED ACTS. I AM RETIRING TO THE COUNTRYSIDE.
I CAN'T CAUSE YOU UNNECESSARY HARDSHIP.
......

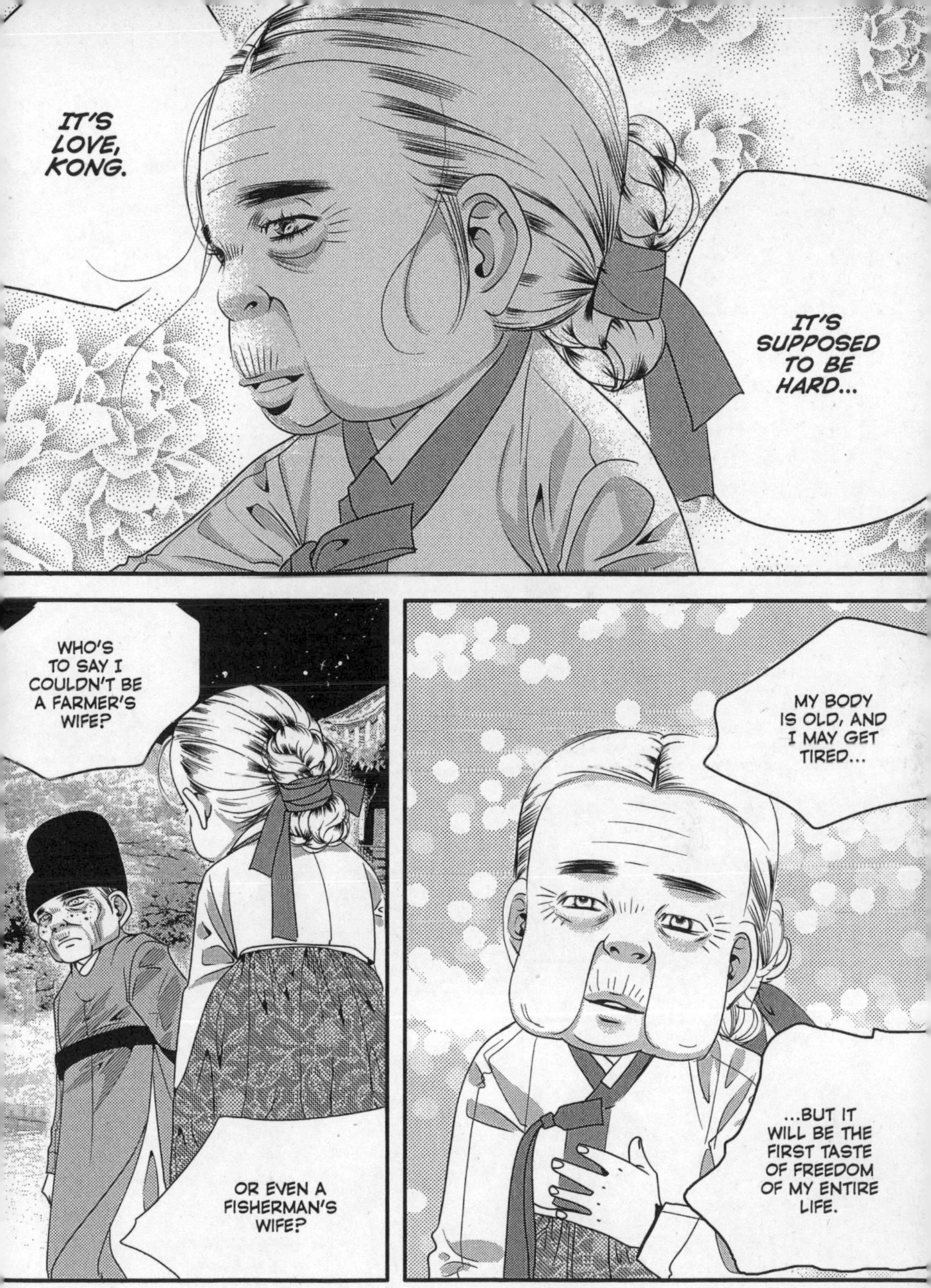
IT'S LOVE, KONG.
IT'S SUPPOSED TO BE HARD...
WHO'S TO SAY I COULDN'T BE A FARMER'S WIFE?
OR EVEN A FISHERMAN'S WIFE?
MY BODY IS OLD, AND I MAY GET TIRED...
...BUT IT WILL BE THE FIRST TASTE OF FREEDOM OF MY ENTIRE LIFE.

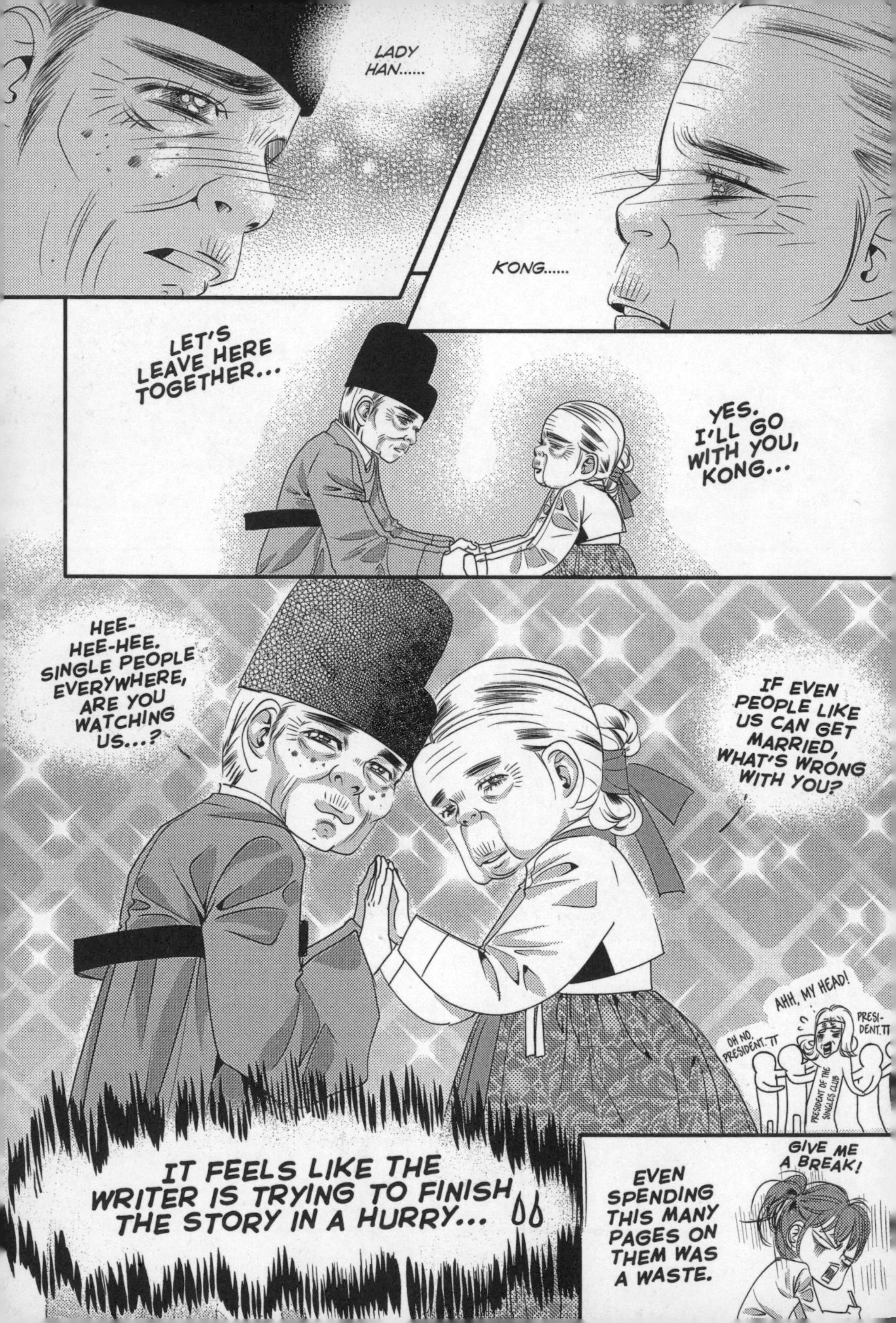
LADY HAN......
KONG......
LET'S LEAVE HERE TOGETHER...
YES. I'LL GO WITH YOU, KONG...
HEE-HEE-HEE. SINGLE PEOPLE EVERYWHERE, ARE YOU WATCHING US...?
IF EVEN PEOPLE LIKE US CAN GET MARRIED, WHAT'S WRONG WITH YOU?
OH NO, PRESIDENT. TT
AHH, MY HEAD!
PRESI-DENT. TT
PRESIDENT OF THE SINGLES CLUB
IT FEELS LIKE THE WRITER IS TRYING TO FINISH THE STORY IN A HURRY...
EVEN SPENDING THIS MANY PAGES ON THEM WAS A WASTE.
GIVE ME A BREAK!

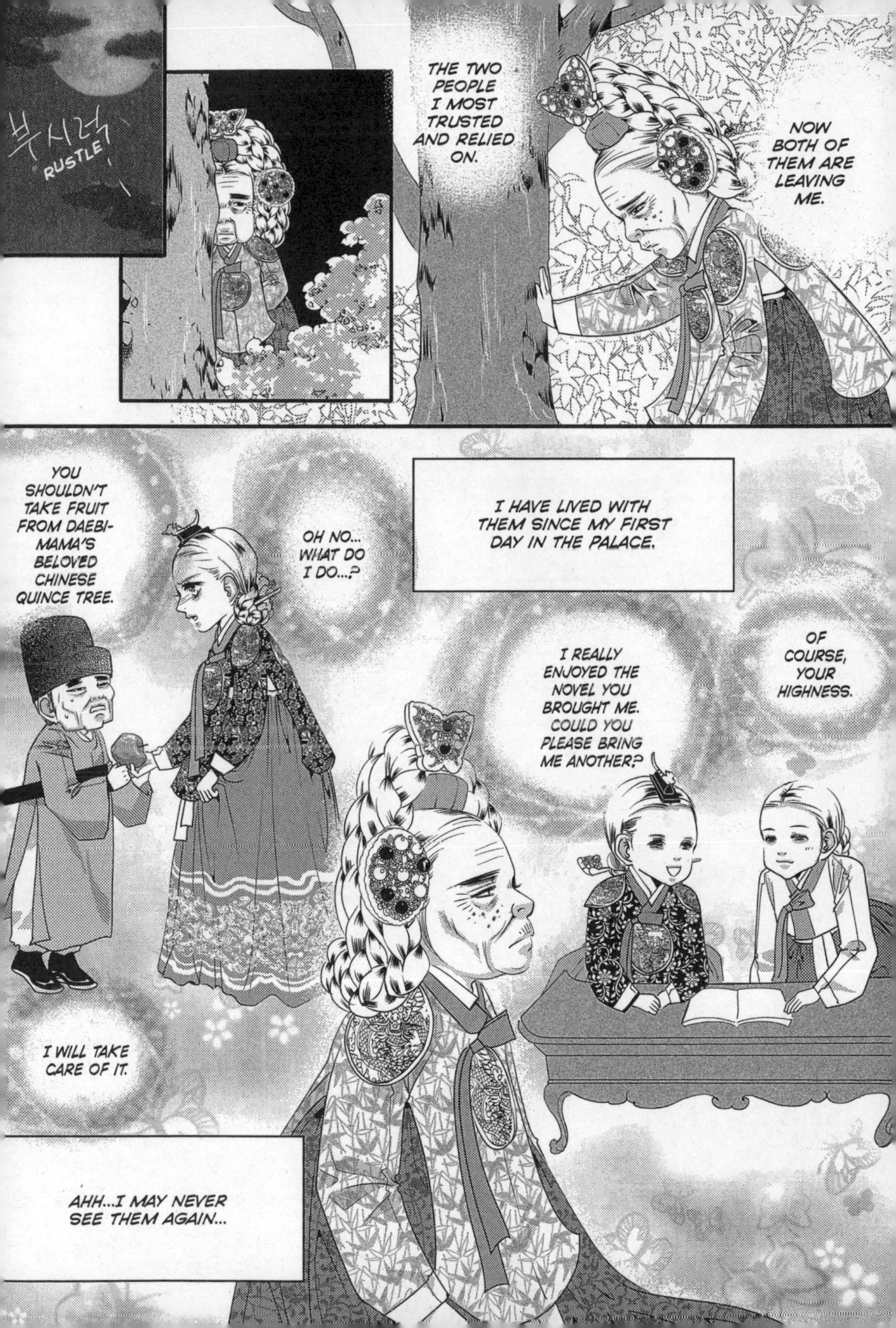
부시럭
RUSTLE
THE TWO PEOPLE I MOST TRUSTED AND RELIED ON.
NOW BOTH OF THEM ARE LEAVING ME.
YOU SHOULDN'T TAKE FRUIT FROM DAEBI-MAMA'S BELOVED CHINESE QUINCE TREE.
OH NO... WHAT DO I DO...?
I HAVE LIVED WITH THEM SINCE MY FIRST DAY IN THE PALACE.
I REALLY ENJOYED THE NOVEL YOU BROUGHT ME. COULD YOU PLEASE BRING ME ANOTHER?
OF COURSE, YOUR HIGHNESS.
I WILL TAKE CARE OF IT.
AHH...I MAY NEVER SEE THEM AGAIN...

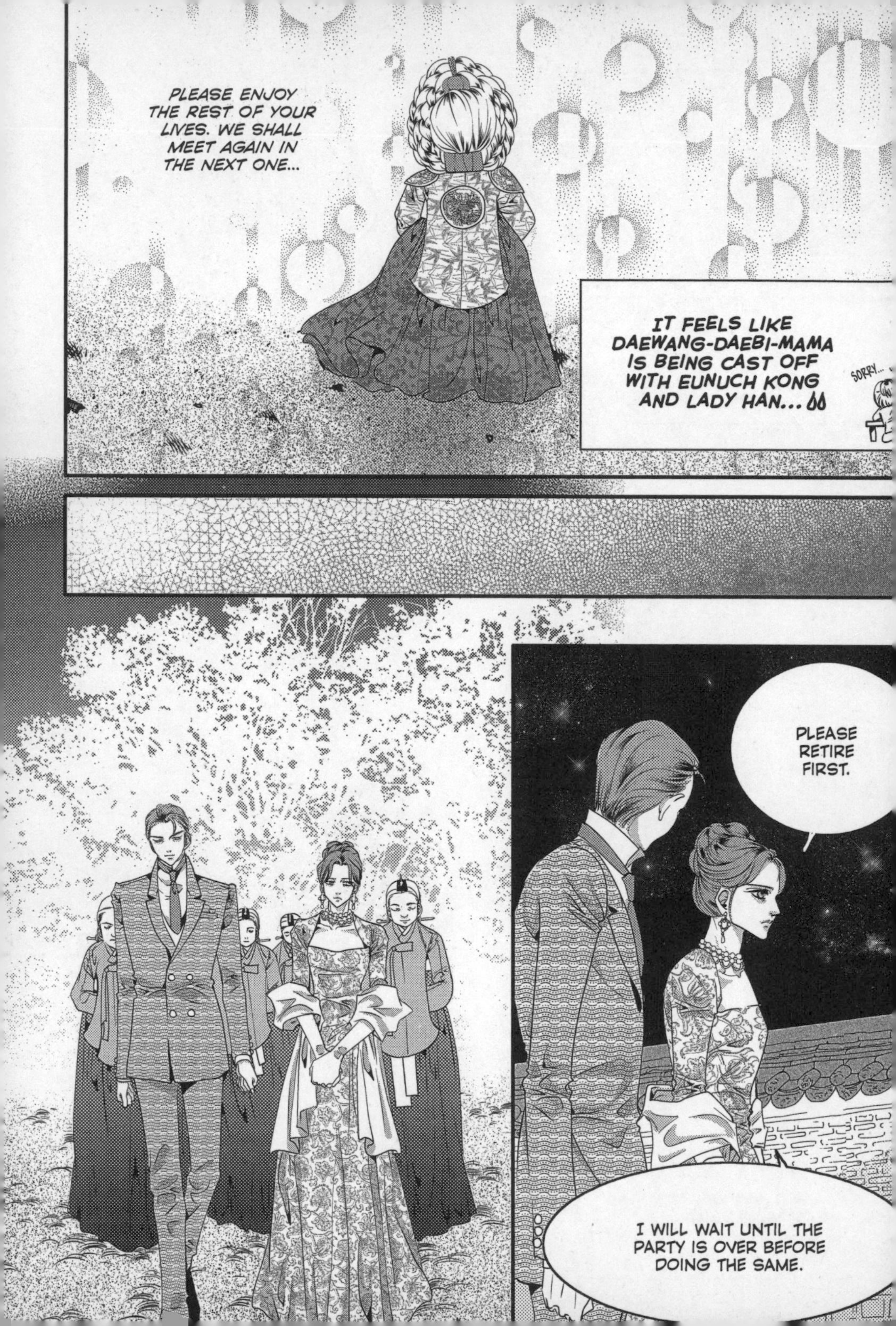
PLEASE ENJOY THE REST OF YOUR LIVES. WE SHALL MEET AGAIN IN THE NEXT ONE...
IT FEELS LIKE DAEWANG-DAEBI-MAMA IS BEING CAST OFF WITH EUNUCH KONG AND LADY HAN...
SORRY...
PLEASE RETIRE FIRST.
I WILL WAIT UNTIL THE PARTY IS OVER BEFORE DOING THE SAME.

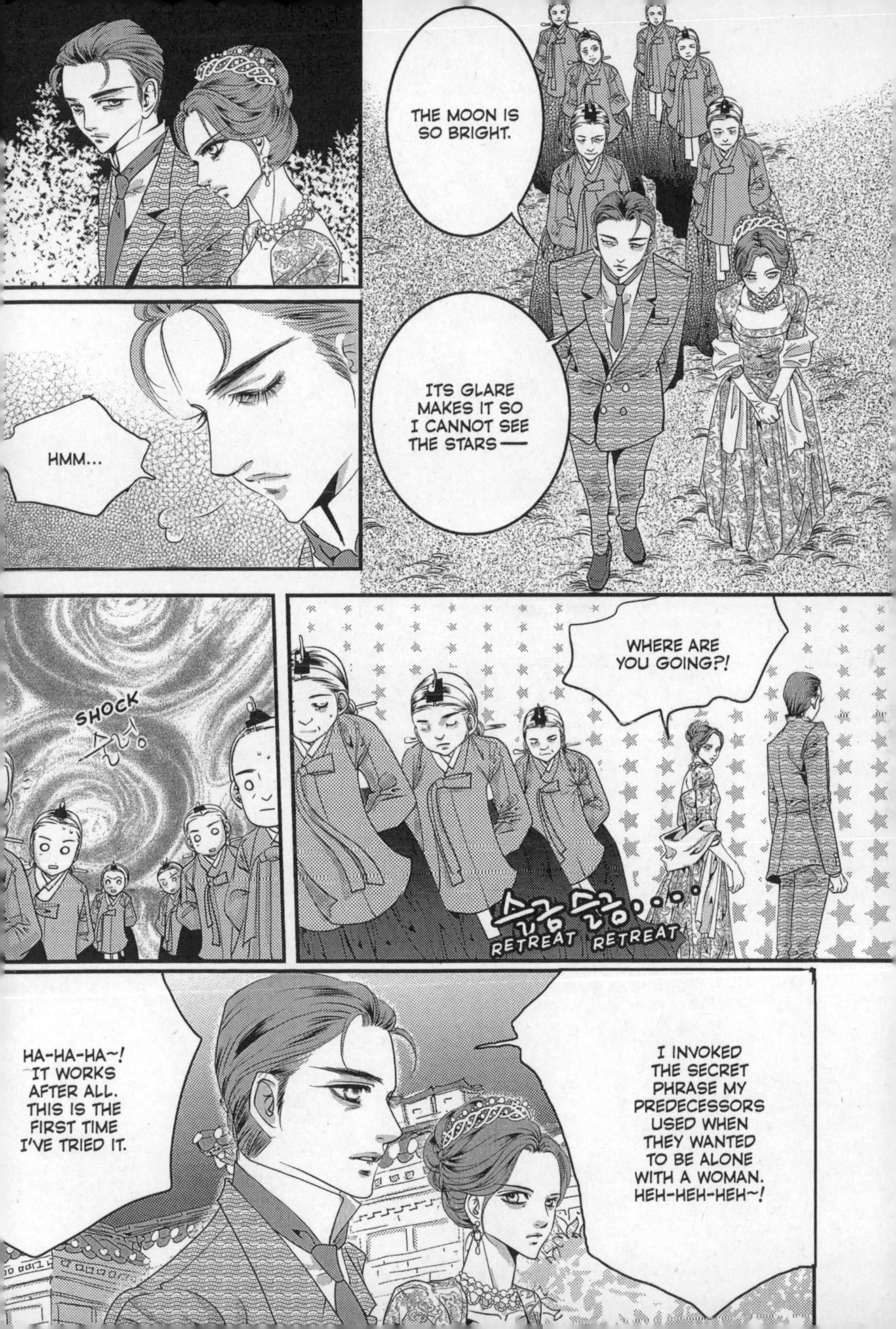
HMM...
THE MOON IS SO BRIGHT.
ITS GLARE MAKES IT SO I CANNOT SEE THE STARS—
SHOCK
WHERE ARE YOU GOING?!
RETREAT RETREAT
HA-HA-HA~! IT WORKS AFTER ALL. THIS IS THE FIRST TIME I'VE TRIED IT.
I INVOKED THE SECRET PHRASE MY PREDECESSORS USED WHEN THEY WANTED TO BE ALONE WITH A WOMAN. HEH-HEH-HEH~!

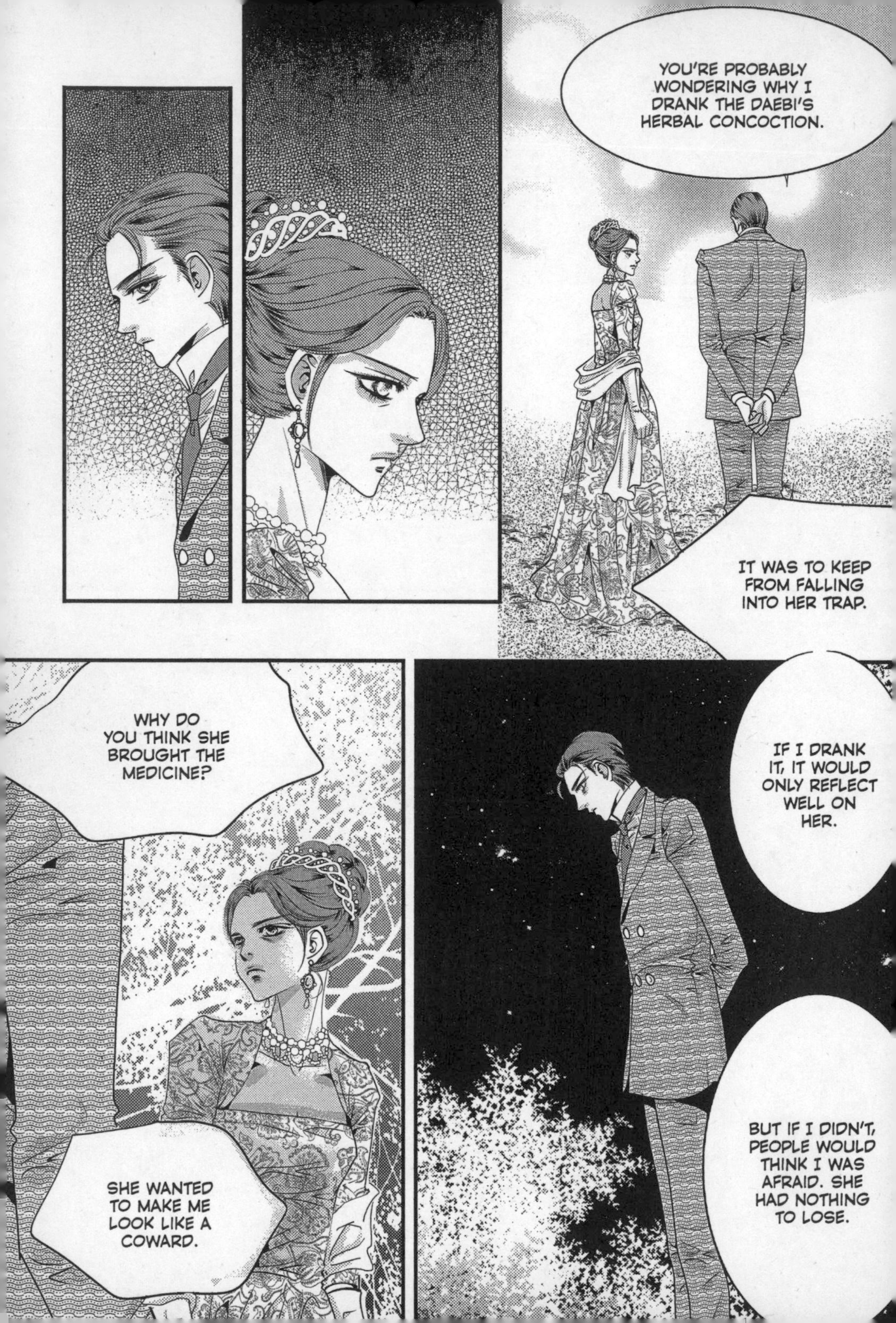
YOU'RE PROBABLY WONDERING WHY I DRANK THE DAEBI'S HERBAL CONCOCTION.
IT WAS TO KEEP FROM FALLING INTO HER TRAP.
WHY DO YOU THINK SHE BROUGHT THE MEDICINE?
SHE WANTED TO MAKE ME LOOK LIKE A COWARD.
IF I DRANK IT, IT WOULD ONLY REFLECT WELL ON HER.
BUT IF I DIDN'T, PEOPLE WOULD THINK I WAS AFRAID. SHE HAD NOTHING TO LOSE.

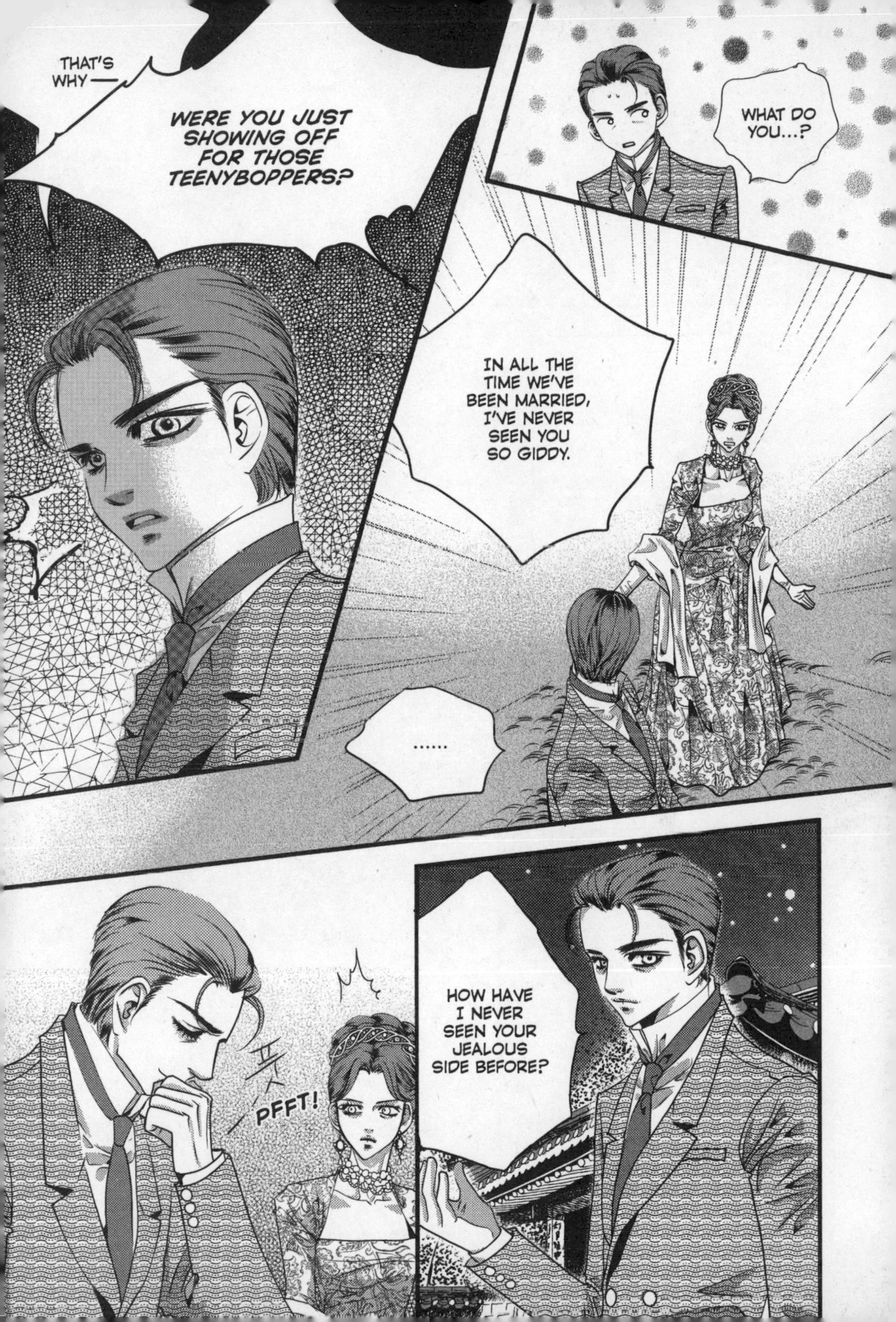
THAT'S WHY—
WERE YOU JUST SHOWING OFF FOR THOSE TEENYBOPPERS?
WHAT DO YOU...?
IN ALL THE TIME WE'VE BEEN MARRIED, I'VE NEVER SEEN YOU SO GIDDY.
......
PFFT!
HOW HAVE I NEVER SEEN YOUR JEALOUS SIDE BEFORE?

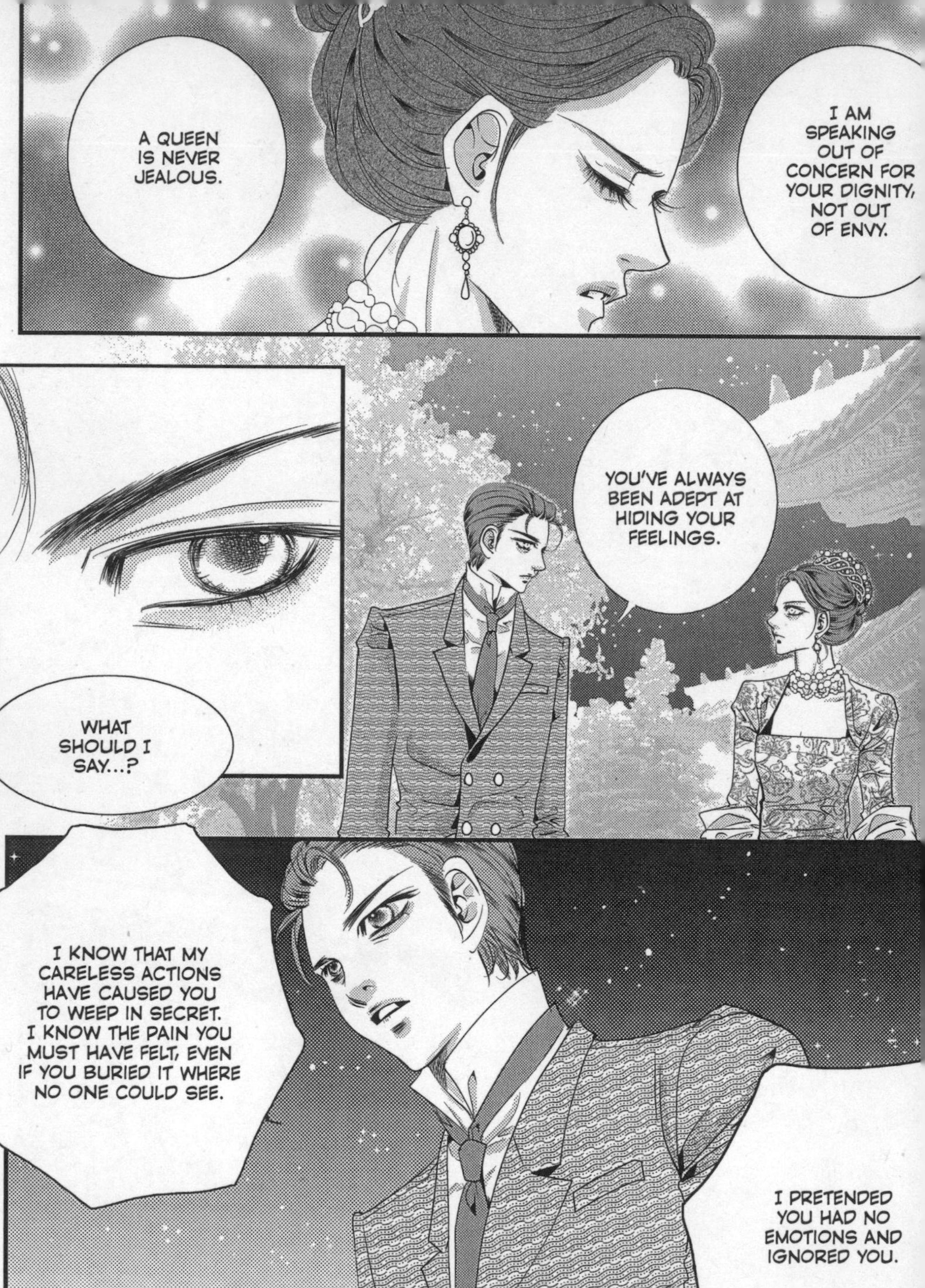
A QUEEN IS NEVER JEALOUS.
I AM SPEAKING OUT OF CONCERN FOR YOUR DIGNITY, NOT OUT OF ENVY.
YOU'VE ALWAYS BEEN ADEPT AT HIDING YOUR FEELINGS.
WHAT SHOULD I SAY...?
I KNOW THAT MY CARELESS ACTIONS HAVE CAUSED YOU TO WEEP IN SECRET. I KNOW THE PAIN YOU MUST HAVE FELT, EVEN IF YOU BURIED IT WHERE NO ONE COULD SEE.
I PRETENDED YOU HAD NO EMOTIONS AND IGNORED YOU.

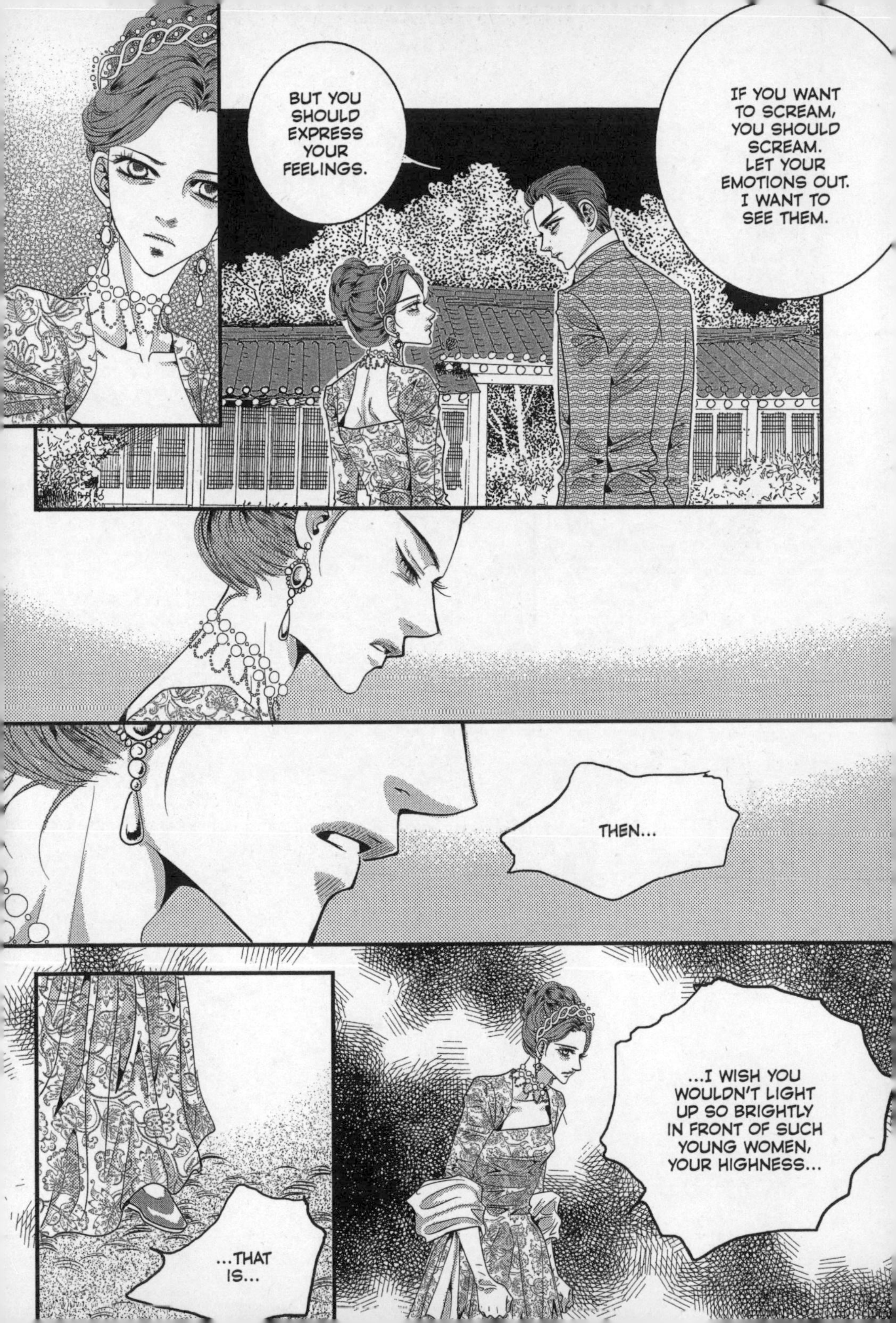
BUT YOU SHOULD EXPRESS YOUR FEELINGS.
IF YOU WANT TO SCREAM, YOU SHOULD SCREAM. LET YOUR EMOTIONS OUT. I WANT TO SEE THEM.
THEN...
...THAT IS...
...I WISH YOU WOULDN'T LIGHT UP SO BRIGHTLY IN FRONT OF SUCH YOUNG WOMEN, YOUR HIGHNESS...

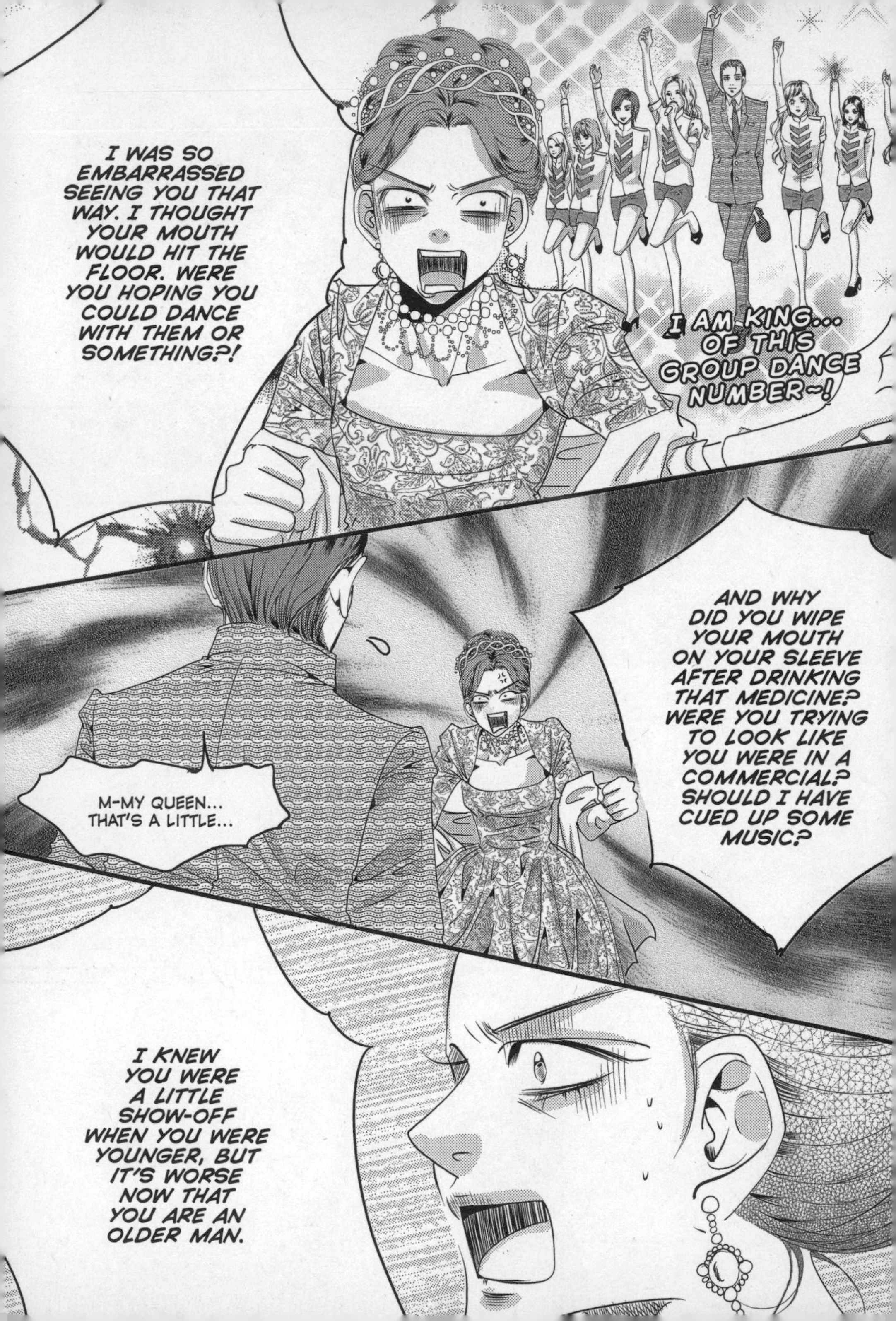
I WAS SO EMBARRASSED SEEING YOU THAT WAY. I THOUGHT YOUR MOUTH WOULD HIT THE FLOOR. WERE YOU HOPING YOU COULD DANCE WITH THEM OR SOMETHING?!
I AM KING... OF THIS GROUP DANCE NUMBER~!
M-MY QUEEN... THAT'S A LITTLE...
AND WHY DID YOU WIPE YOUR MOUTH ON YOUR SLEEVE AFTER DRINKING THAT MEDICINE? WERE YOU TRYING TO LOOK LIKE YOU WERE IN A COMMERCIAL? SHOULD I HAVE CUED UP SOME MUSIC?
I KNEW YOU WERE A LITTLE SHOW-OFF WHEN YOU WERE YOUNGER, BUT IT'S WORSE NOW THAT YOU ARE AN OLDER MAN.

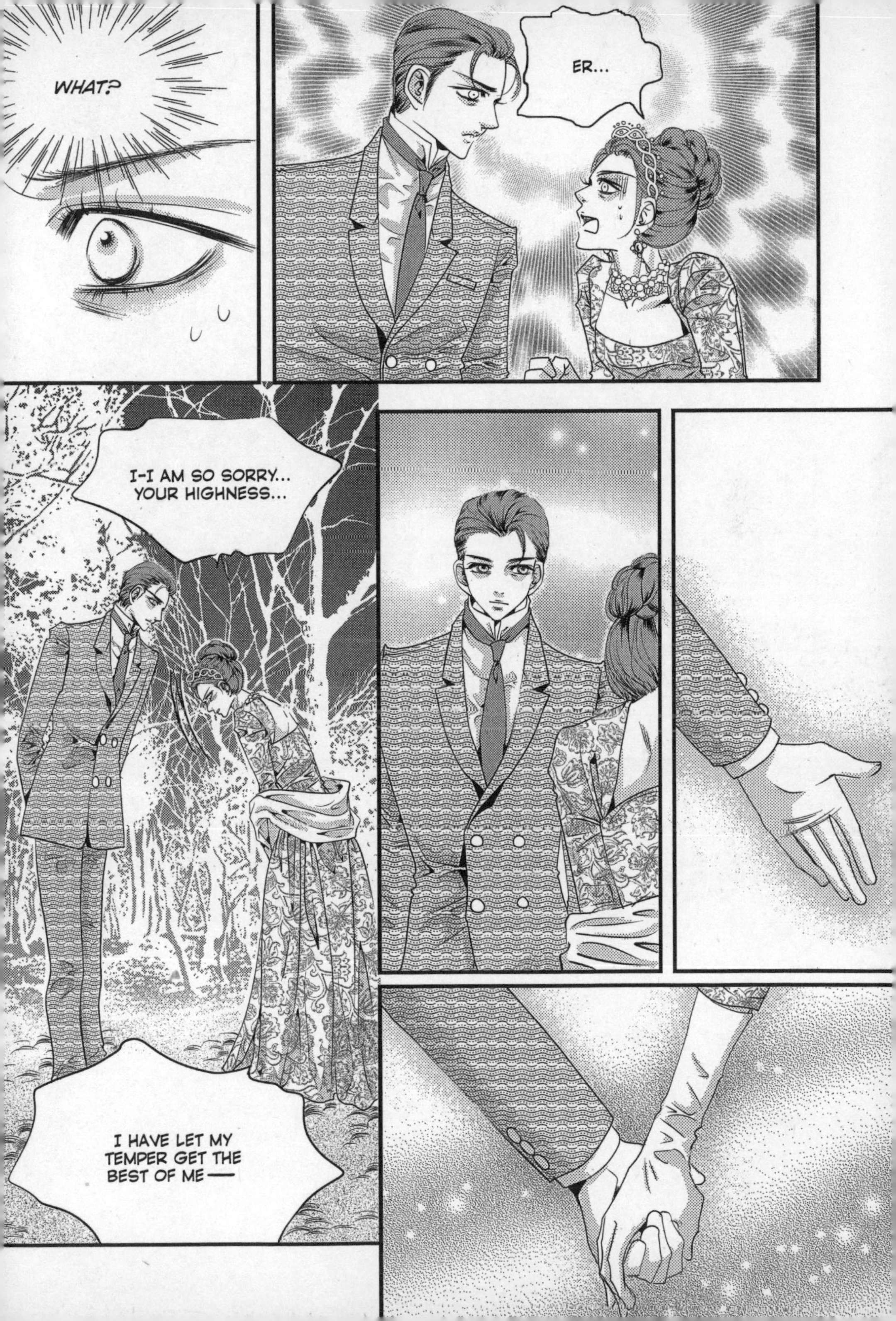
WHAT?
ER...
I-I AM SO SORRY... YOUR HIGHNESS...
I HAVE LET MY TEMPER GET THE BEST OF ME—

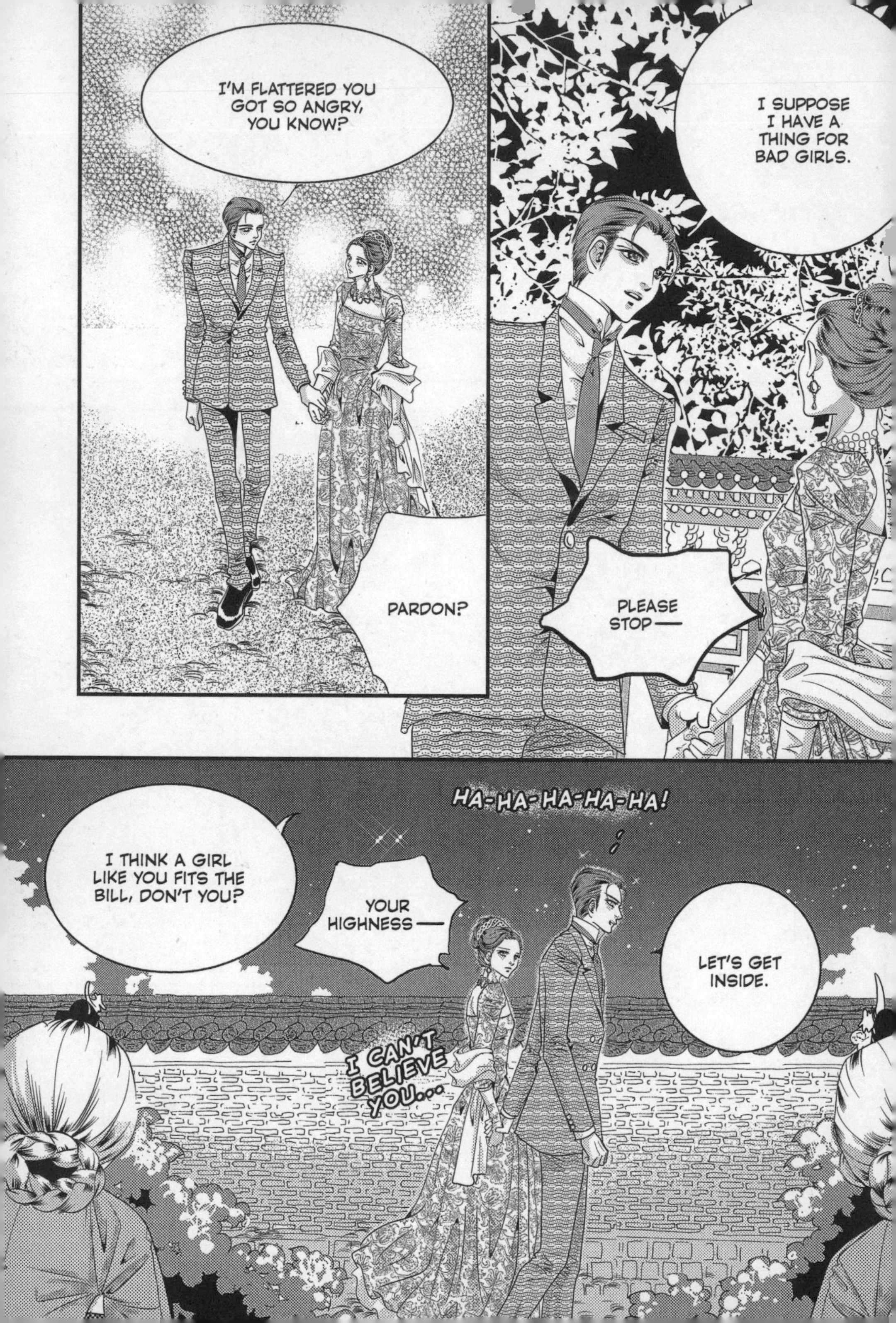
I'M FLATTERED YOU GOT SO ANGRY, YOU KNOW?
PARDON?
I SUPPOSE I HAVE A THING FOR BAD GIRLS.
PLEASE STOP—
HA-HA-HA-HA-HA!
I THINK A GIRL LIKE YOU FITS THE BILL, DON'T YOU?
YOUR HIGHNESS—
I CAN'T BELIEVE YOU...
LET'S GET INSIDE.

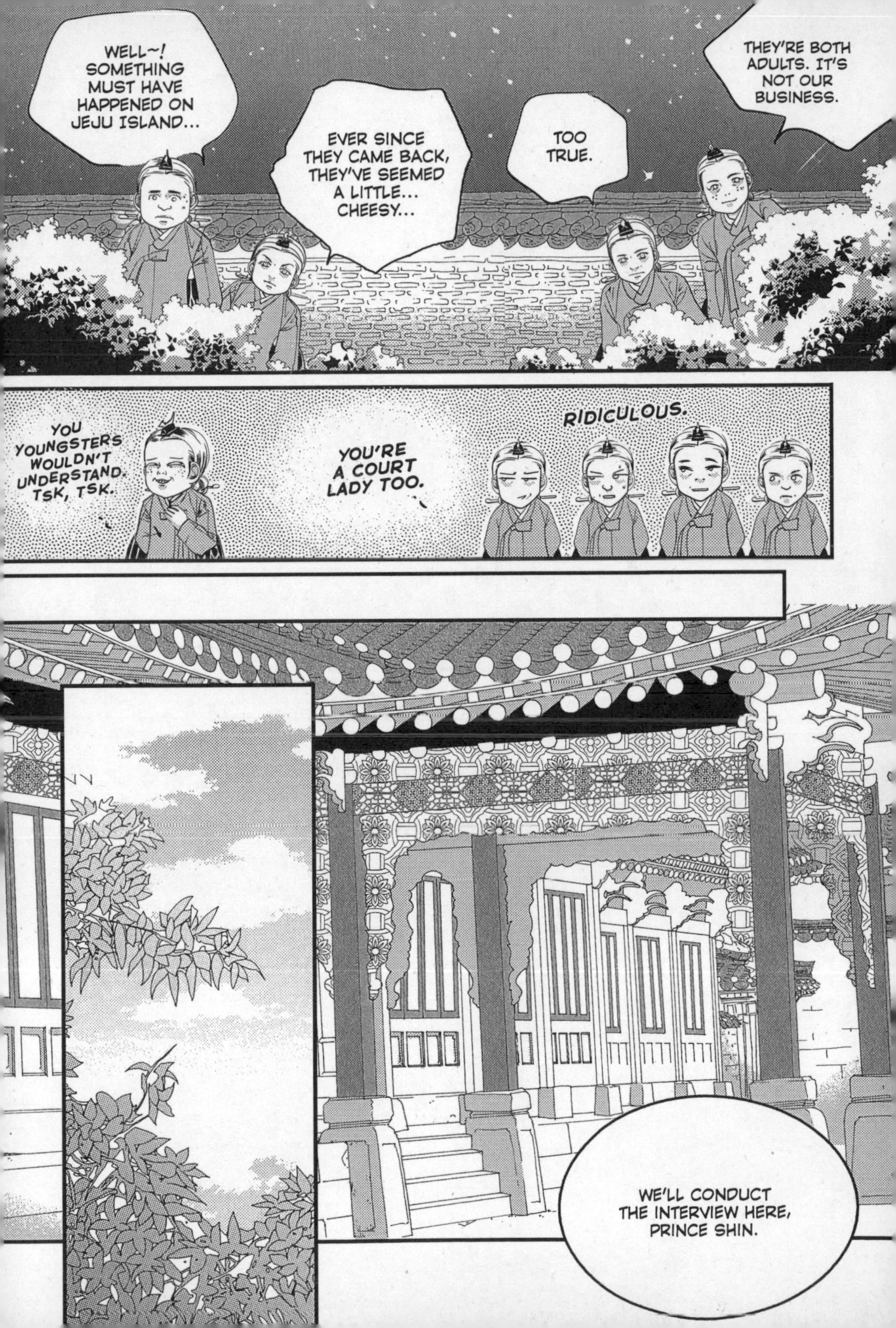
WELL~! SOMETHING MUST HAVE HAPPENED ON JEJU ISLAND...
EVER SINCE THEY CAME BACK, THEY'VE SEEMED A LITTLE... CHEESY...
TOO TRUE.
THEY'RE BOTH ADULTS. IT'S NOT OUR BUSINESS.
YOU YOUNGSTERS WOULDN'T UNDERSTAND. TSK, TSK.
YOU'RE A COURT LADY TOO.
RIDICULOUS.
WE'LL CONDUCT THE INTERVIEW HERE, PRINCE SHIN.

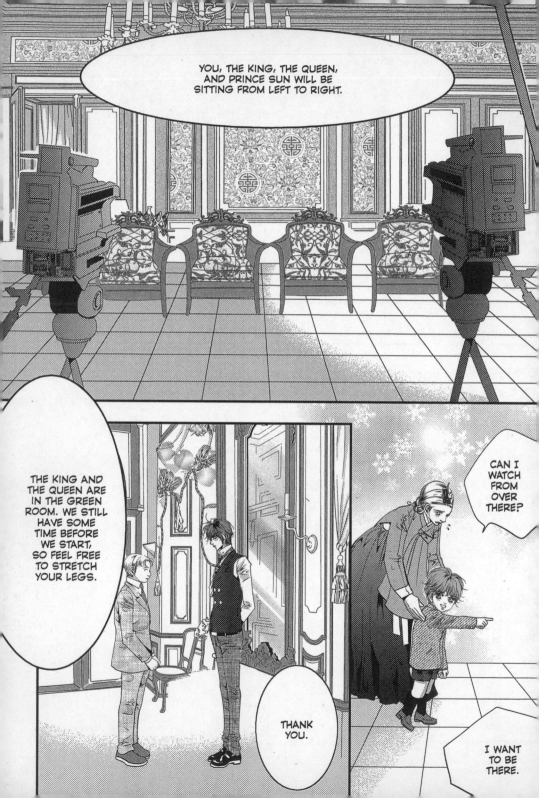

YOU, THE KING, THE QUEEN, AND PRINCE SUN WILL BE SITTING FROM LEFT TO RIGHT.

THE KING AND THE QUEEN ARE IN THE GREEN ROOM. WE STILL HAVE SOME TIME BEFORE WE START, SO FEEL FREE TO STRETCH YOUR LEGS.

CAN I WATCH FROM OVER THERE?

THANK YOU.

I WANT TO BE THERE.

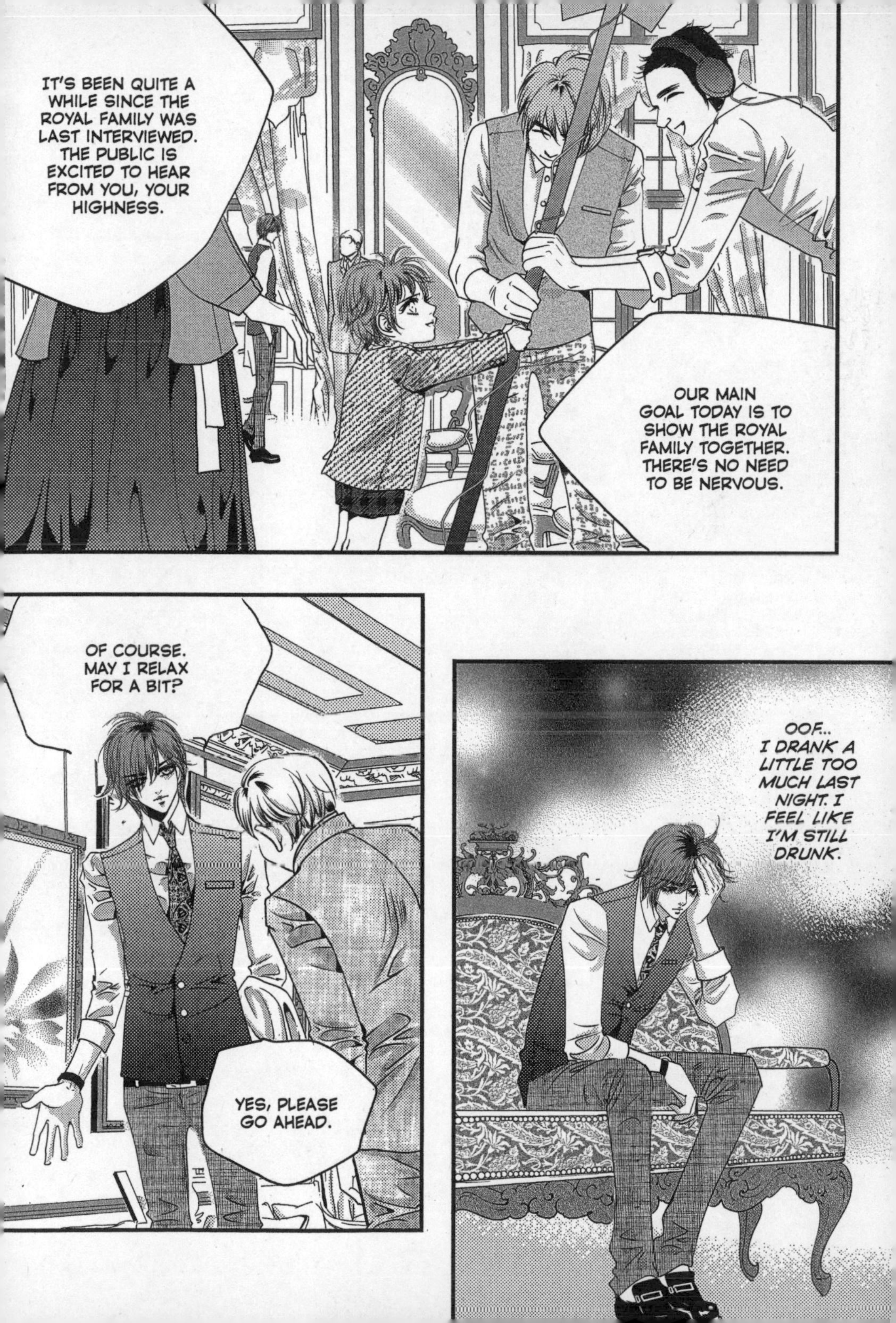
IT'S BEEN QUITE A WHILE SINCE THE ROYAL FAMILY WAS LAST INTERVIEWED. THE PUBLIC IS EXCITED TO HEAR FROM YOU, YOUR HIGHNESS.
OUR MAIN GOAL TODAY IS TO SHOW THE ROYAL FAMILY TOGETHER. THERE'S NO NEED TO BE NERVOUS.
OF COURSE. MAY I RELAX FOR A BIT?
YES, PLEASE GO AHEAD.
OOF... I DRANK A LITTLE TOO MUCH LAST NIGHT. I FEEL LIKE I'M STILL DRUNK.

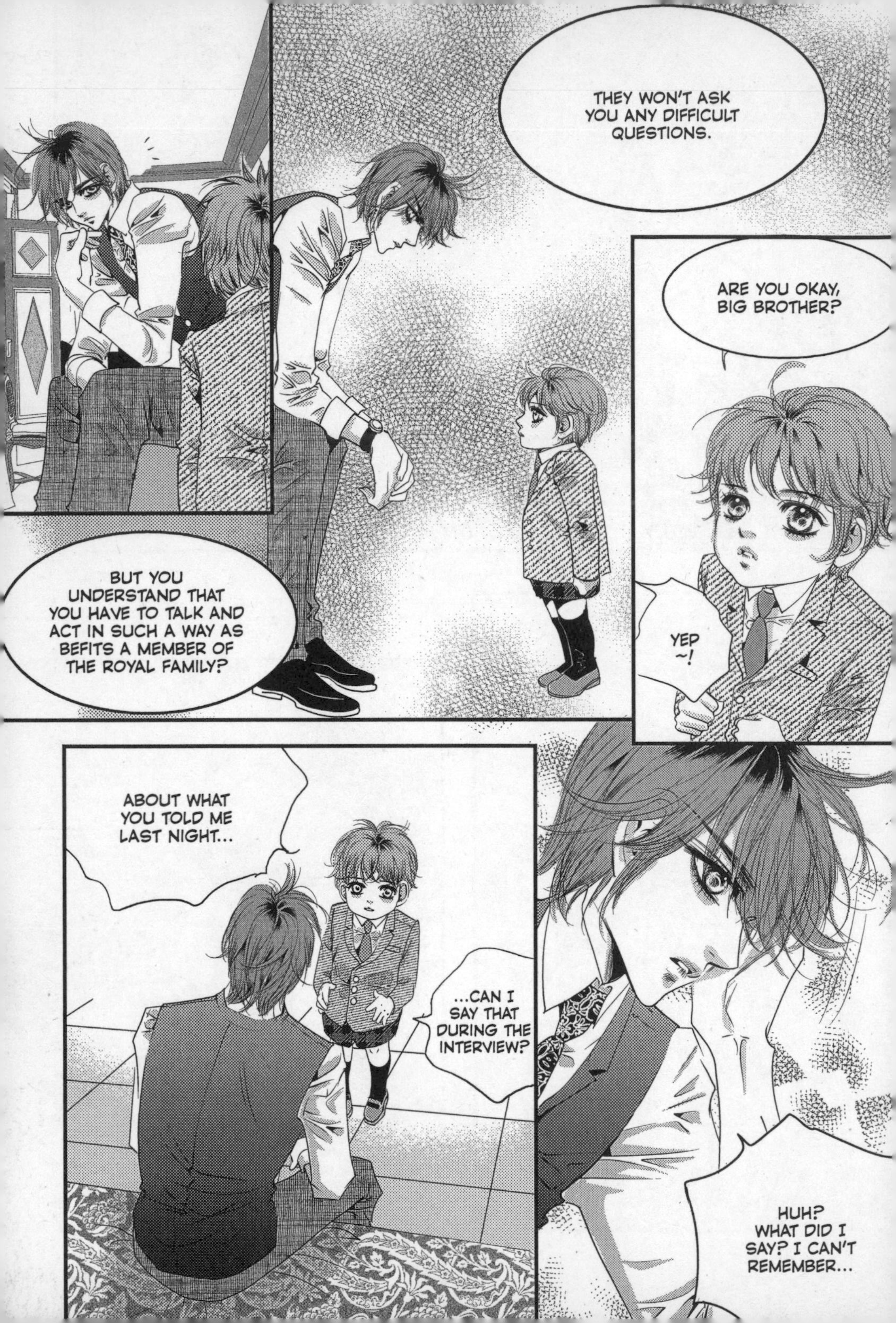
THEY WON'T ASK YOU ANY DIFFICULT QUESTIONS.
BUT YOU UNDERSTAND THAT YOU HAVE TO TALK AND ACT IN SUCH A WAY AS BEFITS A MEMBER OF THE ROYAL FAMILY?
ARE YOU OKAY, BIG BROTHER?
YEP ~!
ABOUT WHAT YOU TOLD ME LAST NIGHT...
...CAN I SAY THAT DURING THE INTERVIEW?
HUH? WHAT DID I SAY? I CAN'T REMEMBER...

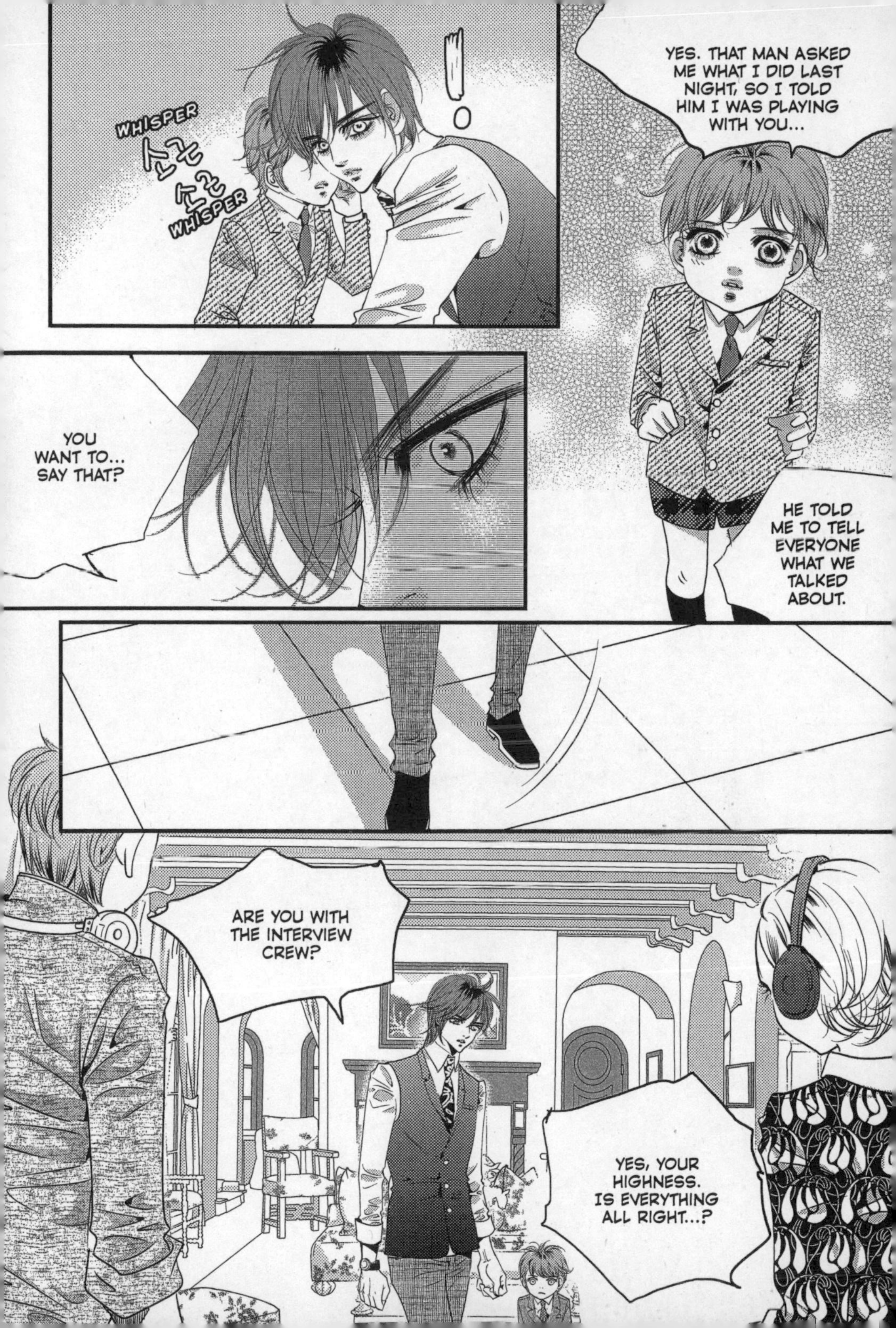
WHISPER
소곤
소곤
WHISPER
YOU WANT TO... SAY THAT?
YES. THAT MAN ASKED ME WHAT I DID LAST NIGHT, SO I TOLD HIM I WAS PLAYING WITH YOU...
HE TOLD ME TO TELL EVERYONE WHAT WE TALKED ABOUT.
ARE YOU WITH THE INTERVIEW CREW?
YES, YOUR HIGHNESS. IS EVERYTHING ALL RIGHT...?

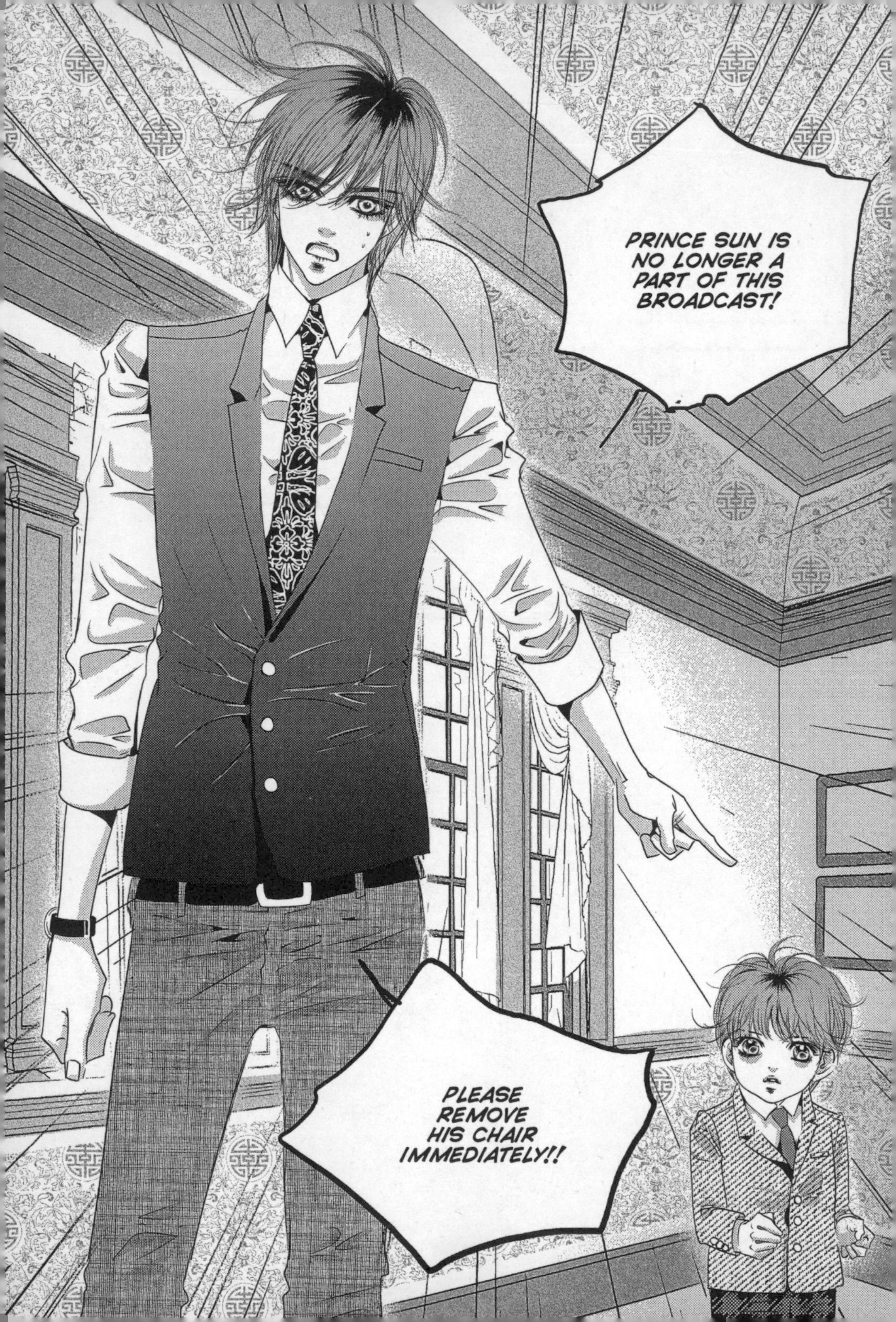
PRINCE SUN IS NO LONGER A PART OF THIS BROADCAST!
PLEASE REMOVE HIS CHAIR IMMEDIATELY!!

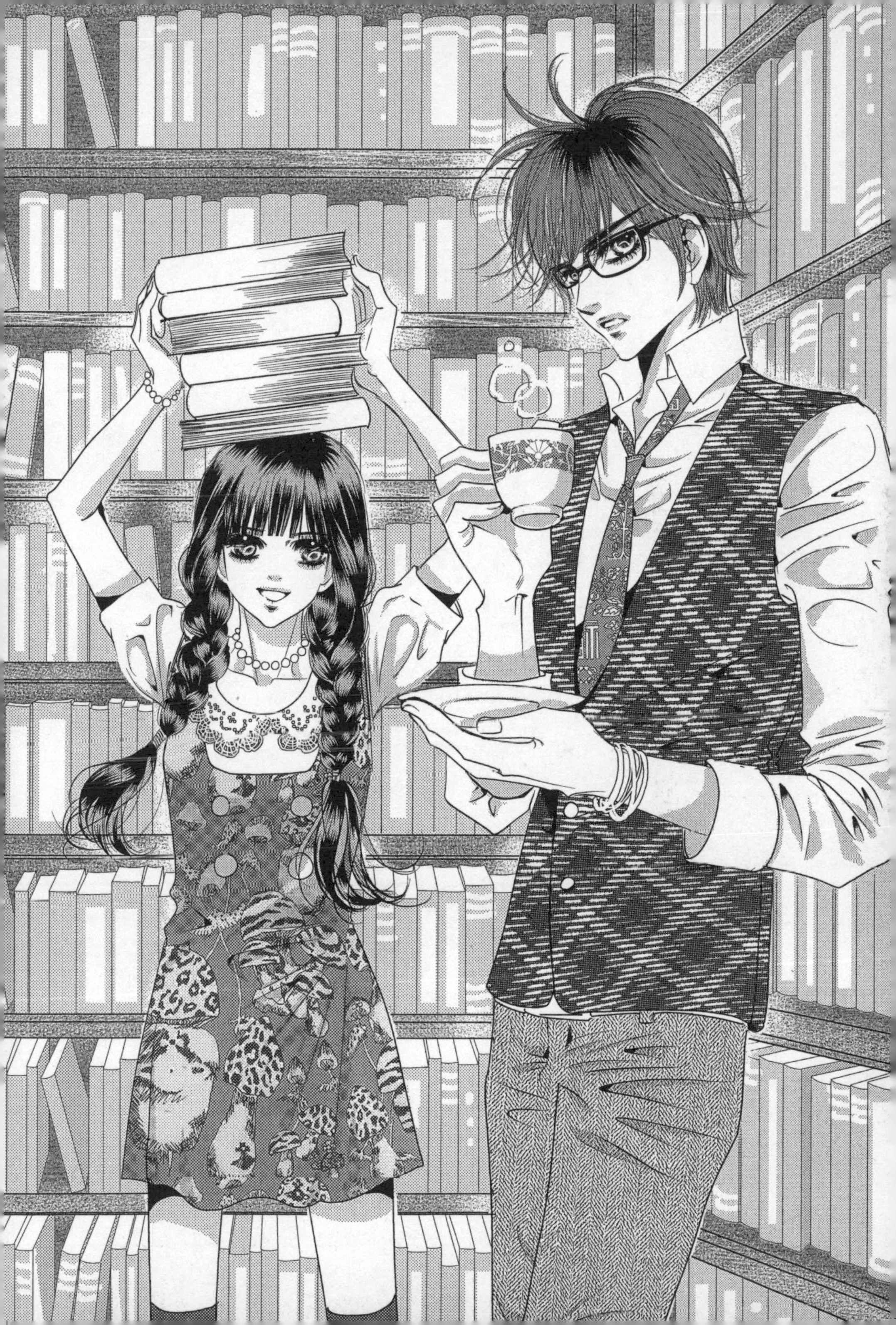

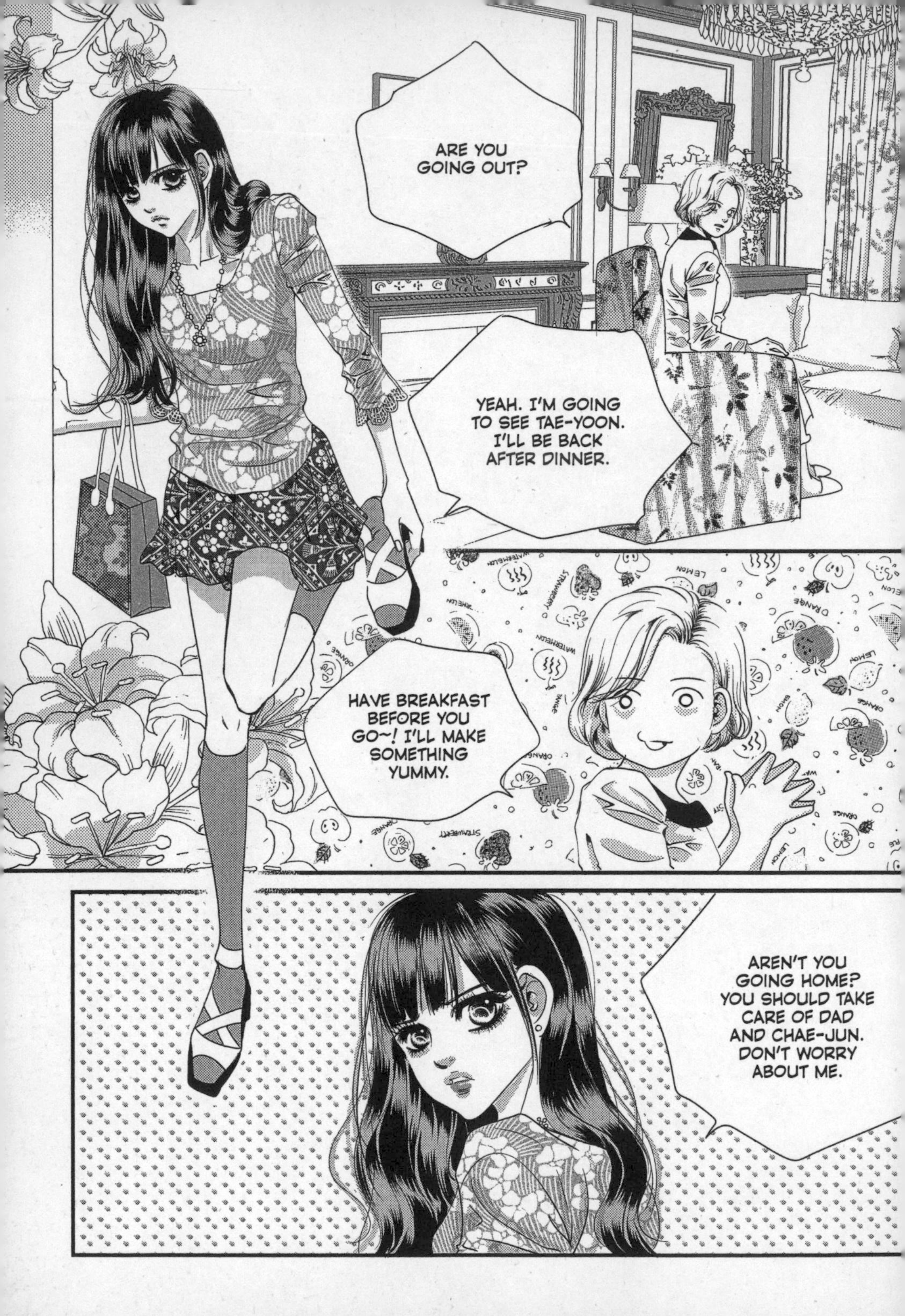
ARE YOU GOING OUT?
YEAH. I'M GOING TO SEE TAE-YOON. I'LL BE BACK AFTER DINNER.
HAVE BREAKFAST BEFORE YOU GO~! I'LL MAKE SOMETHING YUMMY.
AREN'T YOU GOING HOME? YOU SHOULD TAKE CARE OF DAD AND CHAE-JUN. DON'T WORRY ABOUT ME.

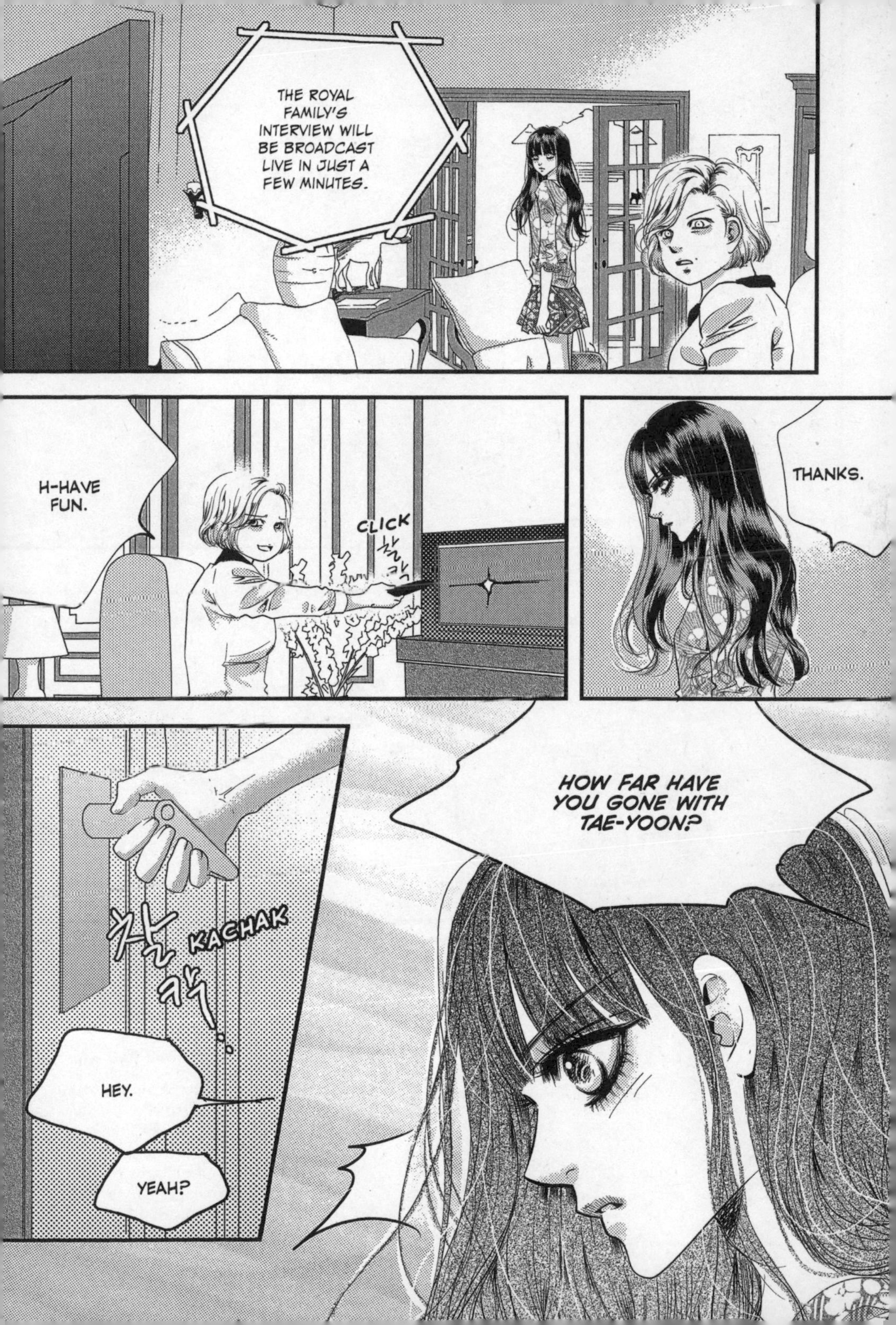
THE ROYAL FAMILY'S INTERVIEW WILL BE BROADCAST LIVE IN JUST A FEW MINUTES.
H-HAVE FUN.
CLICK
THANKS.
KACHAK
HEY.
YEAH?
HOW FAR HAVE YOU GONE WITH TAE-YOON?

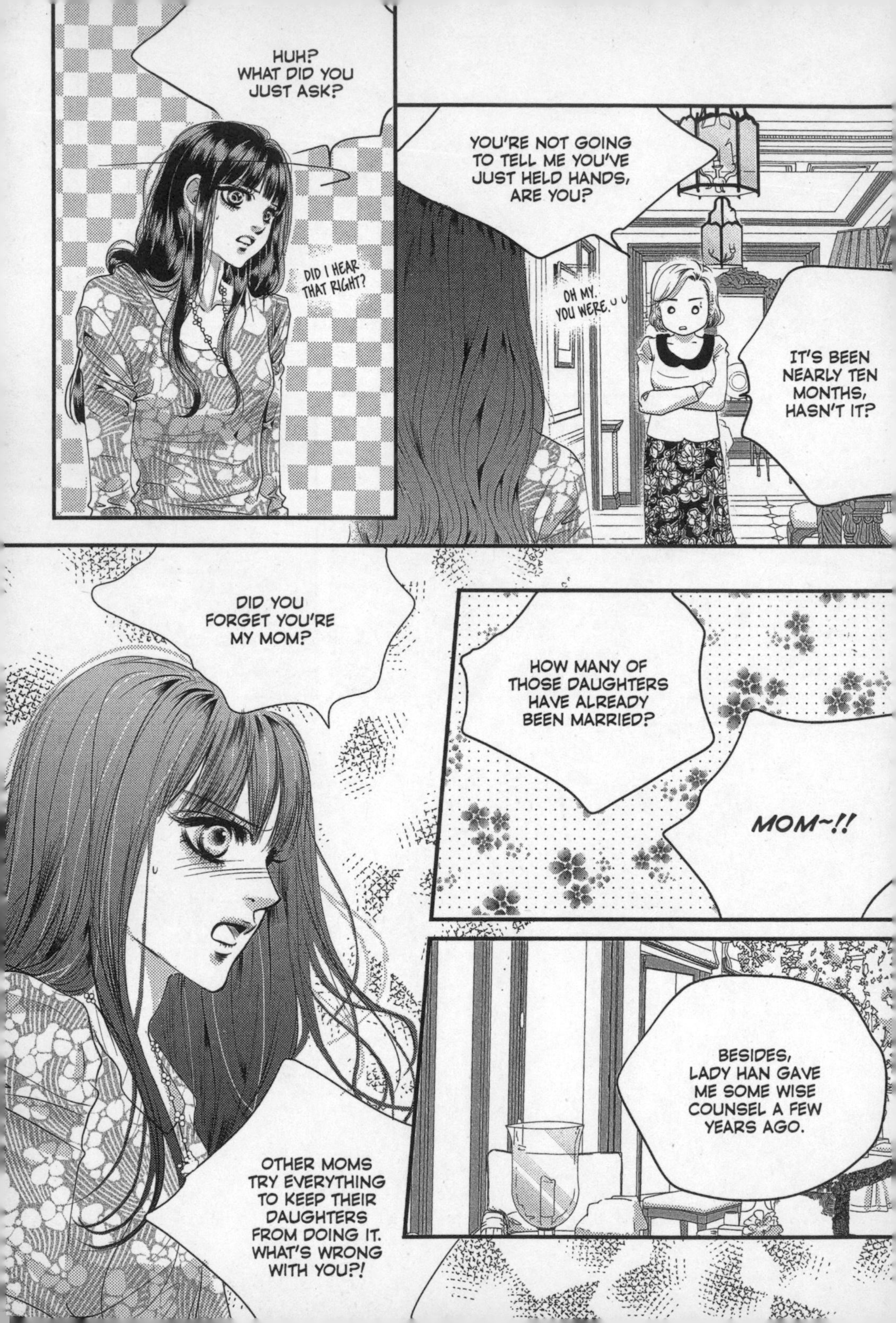
HUH? WHAT DID YOU JUST ASK?
DID I HEAR THAT RIGHT?
YOU'RE NOT GOING TO TELL ME YOU'VE JUST HELD HANDS, ARE YOU?
OH MY. YOU WERE.
IT'S BEEN NEARLY TEN MONTHS, HASN'T IT?
DID YOU FORGET YOU'RE MY MOM?
OTHER MOMS TRY EVERYTHING TO KEEP THEIR DAUGHTERS FROM DOING IT. WHAT'S WRONG WITH YOU?!
HOW MANY OF THOSE DAUGHTERS HAVE ALREADY BEEN MARRIED?
MOM~!!
BESIDES, LADY HAN GAVE ME SOME WISE COUNSEL A FEW YEARS AGO.

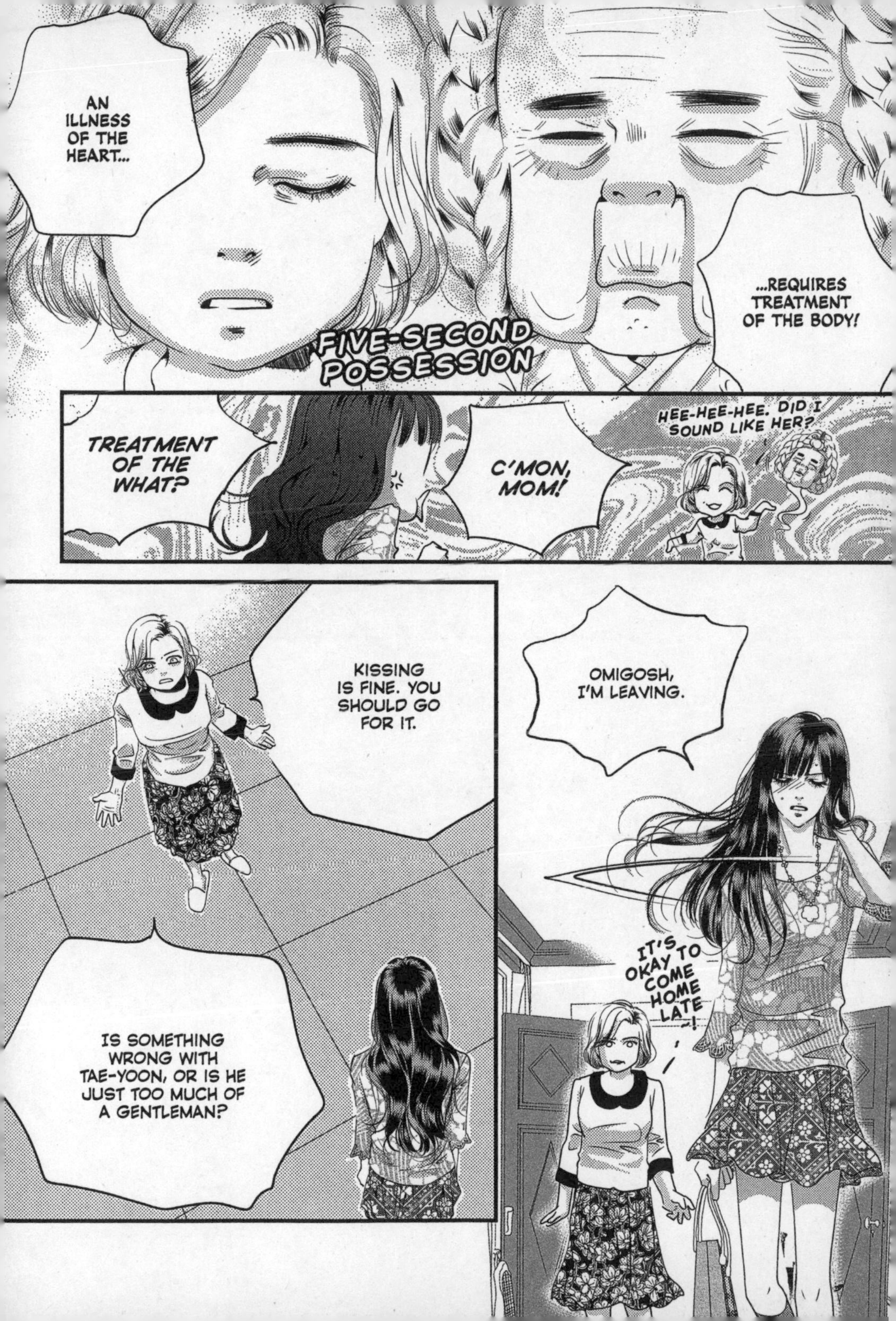
AN ILLNESS OF THE HEART...
FIVE-SECOND POSSESSION
...REQUIRES TREATMENT OF THE BODY!
TREATMENT OF THE WHAT?
C'MON, MOM!
HEE-HEE-HEE. DID I SOUND LIKE HER?
KISSING IS FINE. YOU SHOULD GO FOR IT.
IS SOMETHING WRONG WITH TAE-YOON, OR IS HE JUST TOO MUCH OF A GENTLEMAN?
OMIGOSH, I'M LEAVING.
IT'S OKAY TO COME HOME LATE--!

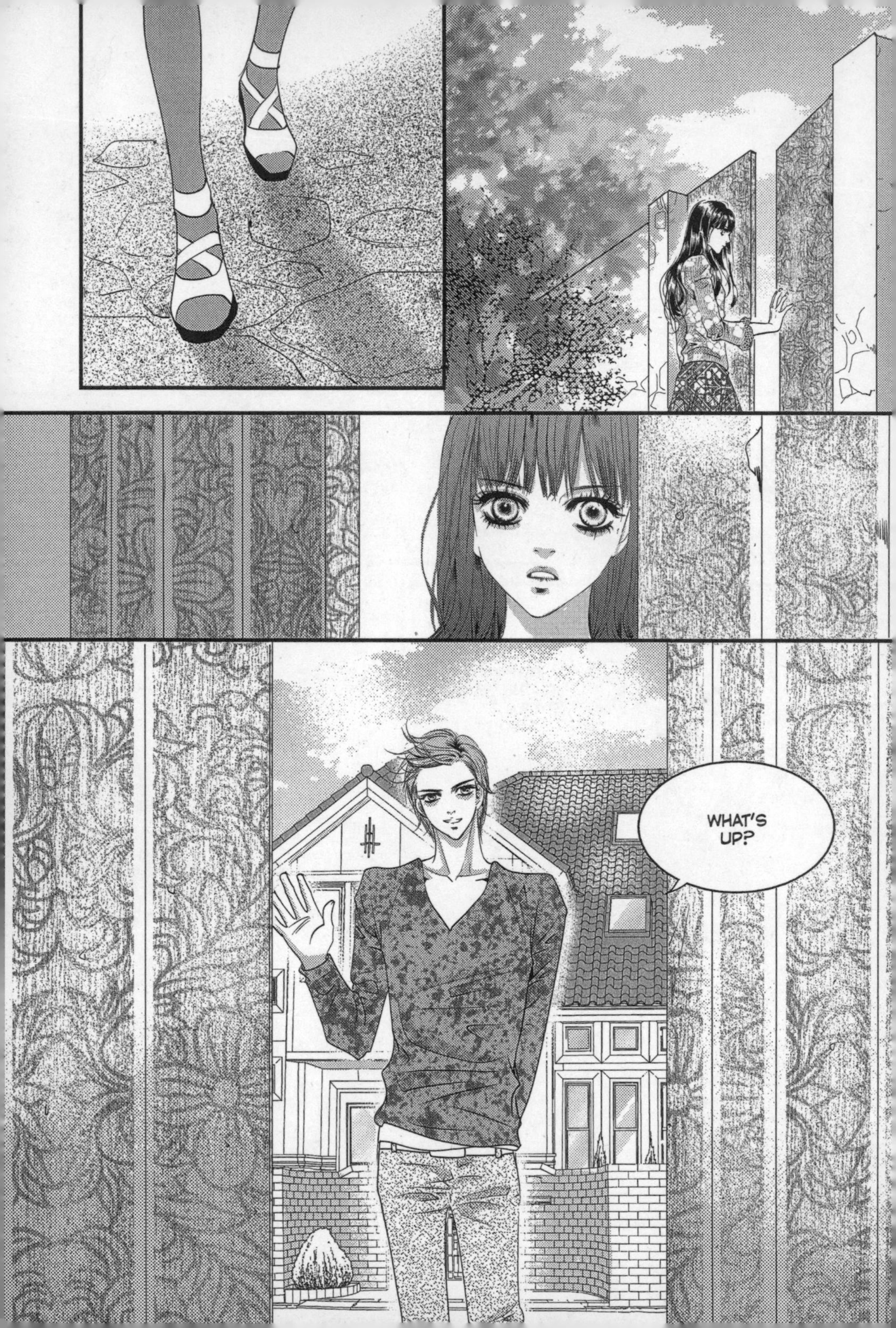
WHAT'S UP?

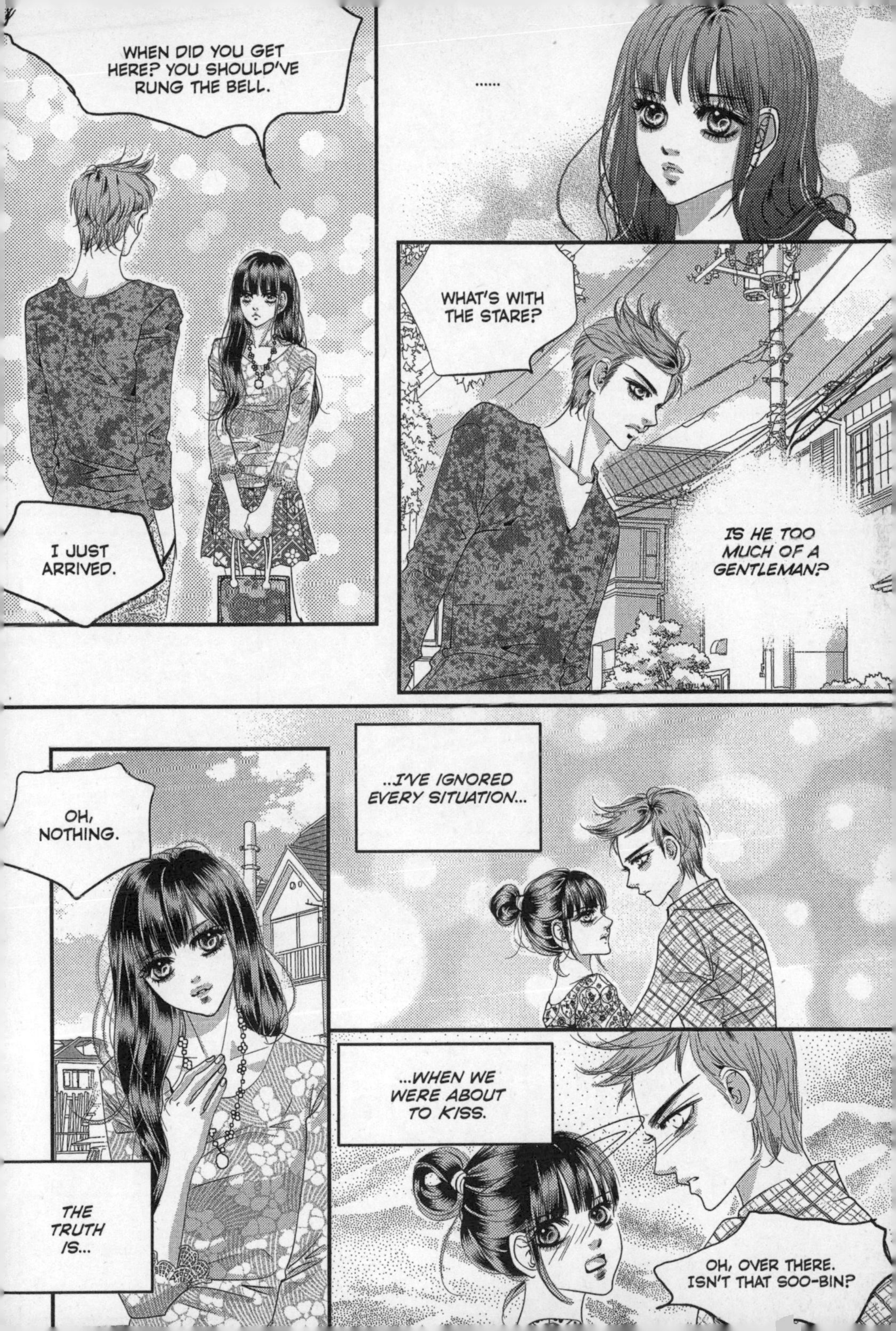
WHEN DID YOU GET HERE? YOU SHOULD'VE RUNG THE BELL.
I JUST ARRIVED.
......
WHAT'S WITH THE STARE?
IS HE TOO MUCH OF A GENTLEMAN?
OH, NOTHING.
THE TRUTH IS...
...I'VE IGNORED EVERY SITUATION...
...WHEN WE WERE ABOUT TO KISS.
OH, OVER THERE. ISN'T THAT SOO-BIN?

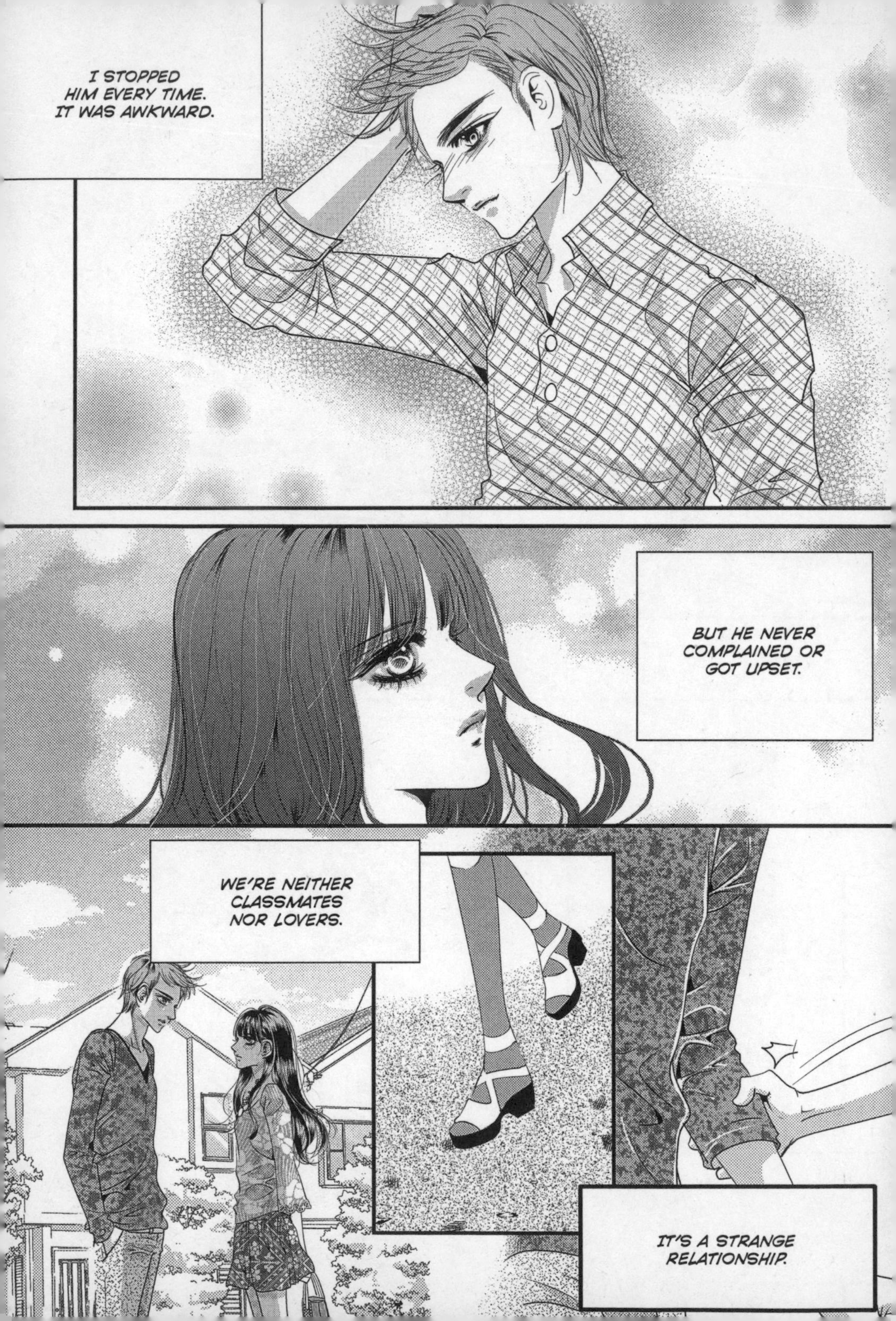
I STOPPED HIM EVERY TIME. IT WAS AWKWARD.
BUT HE NEVER COMPLAINED OR GOT UPSET.
WE'RE NEITHER CLASSMATES NOR LOVERS.
IT'S A STRANGE RELATIONSHIP.

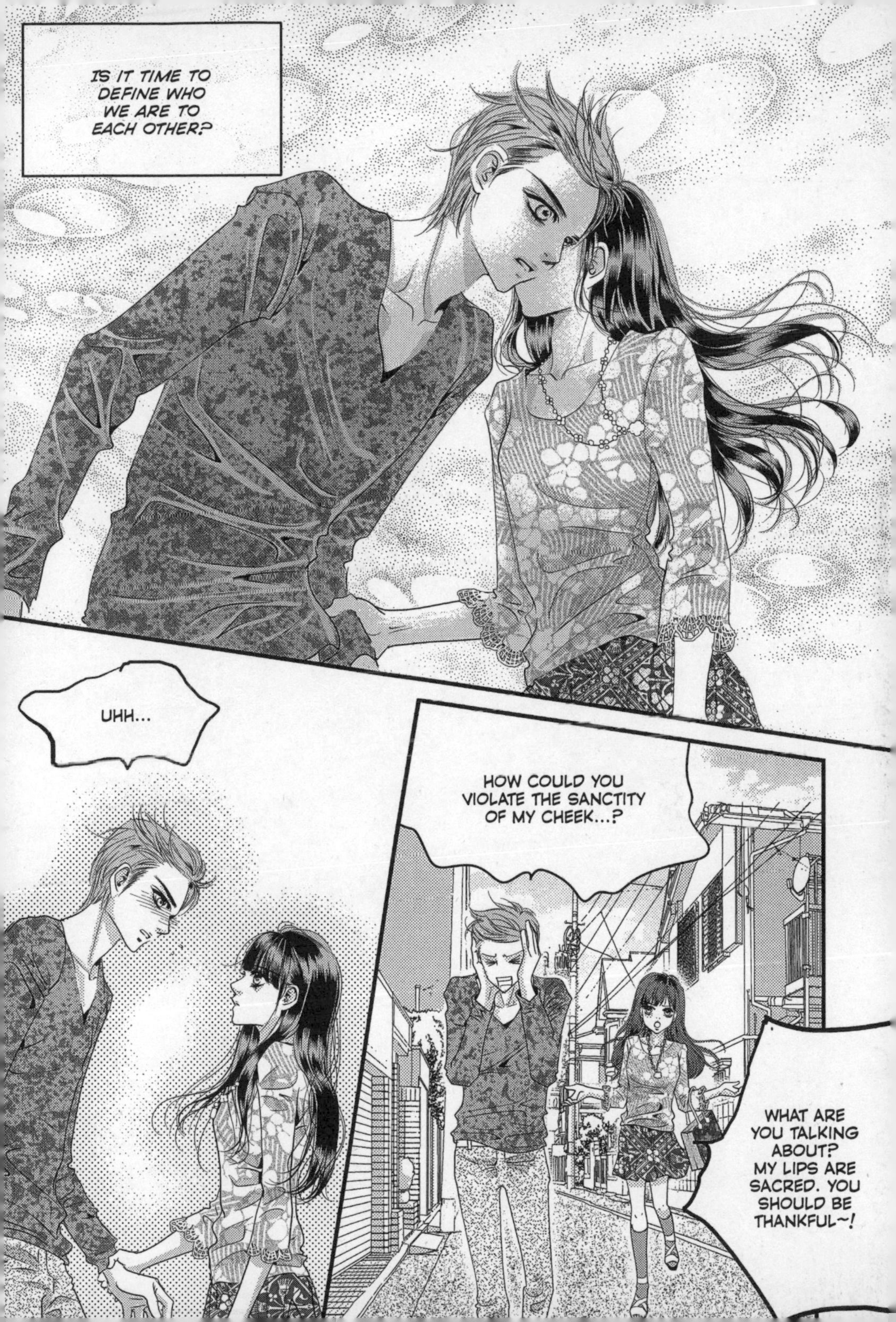
IS IT TIME TO DEFINE WHO WE ARE TO EACH OTHER?
UHH...
HOW COULD YOU VIOLATE THE SANCTITY OF MY CHEEK...?
WHAT ARE YOU TALKING ABOUT? MY LIPS ARE SACRED. YOU SHOULD BE THANKFUL~!

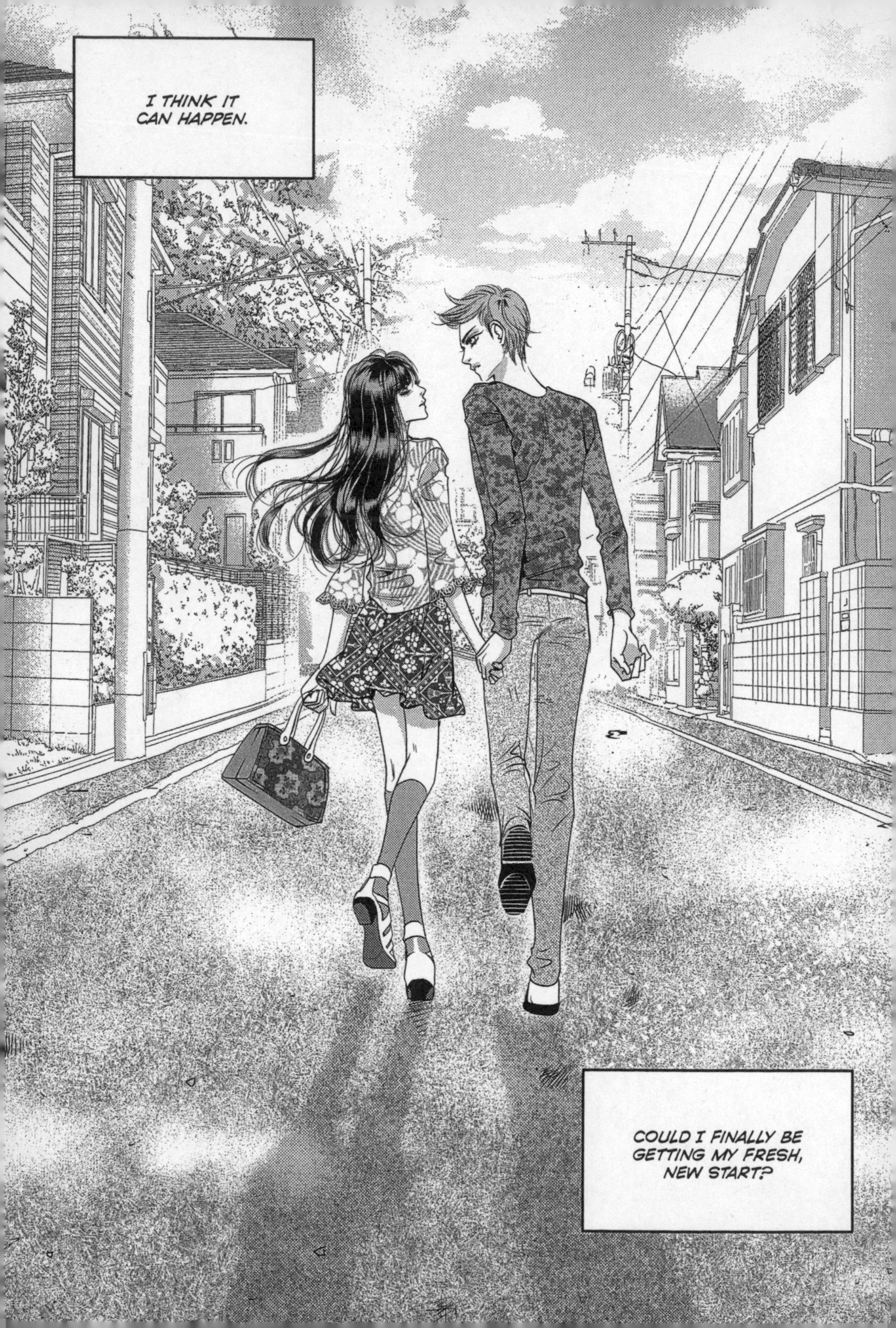
I THINK IT CAN HAPPEN.
COULD I FINALLY BE GETTING MY FRESH, NEW START?

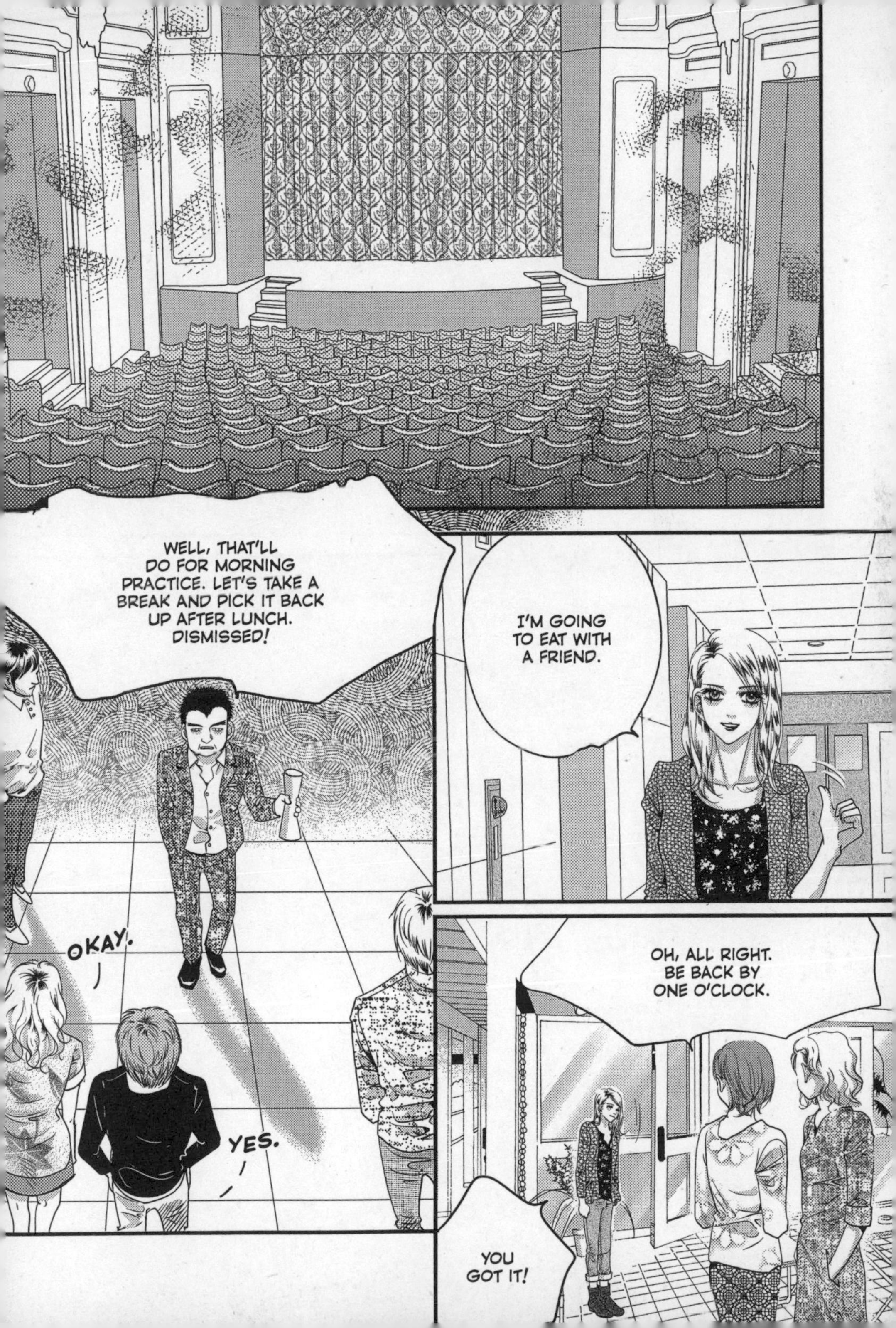
WELL, THAT'LL DO FOR MORNING PRACTICE. LET'S TAKE A BREAK AND PICK IT BACK UP AFTER LUNCH. DISMISSED!
OKAY.
YES.
I'M GOING TO EAT WITH A FRIEND.
OH, ALL RIGHT. BE BACK BY ONE O'CLOCK.
YOU GOT IT!

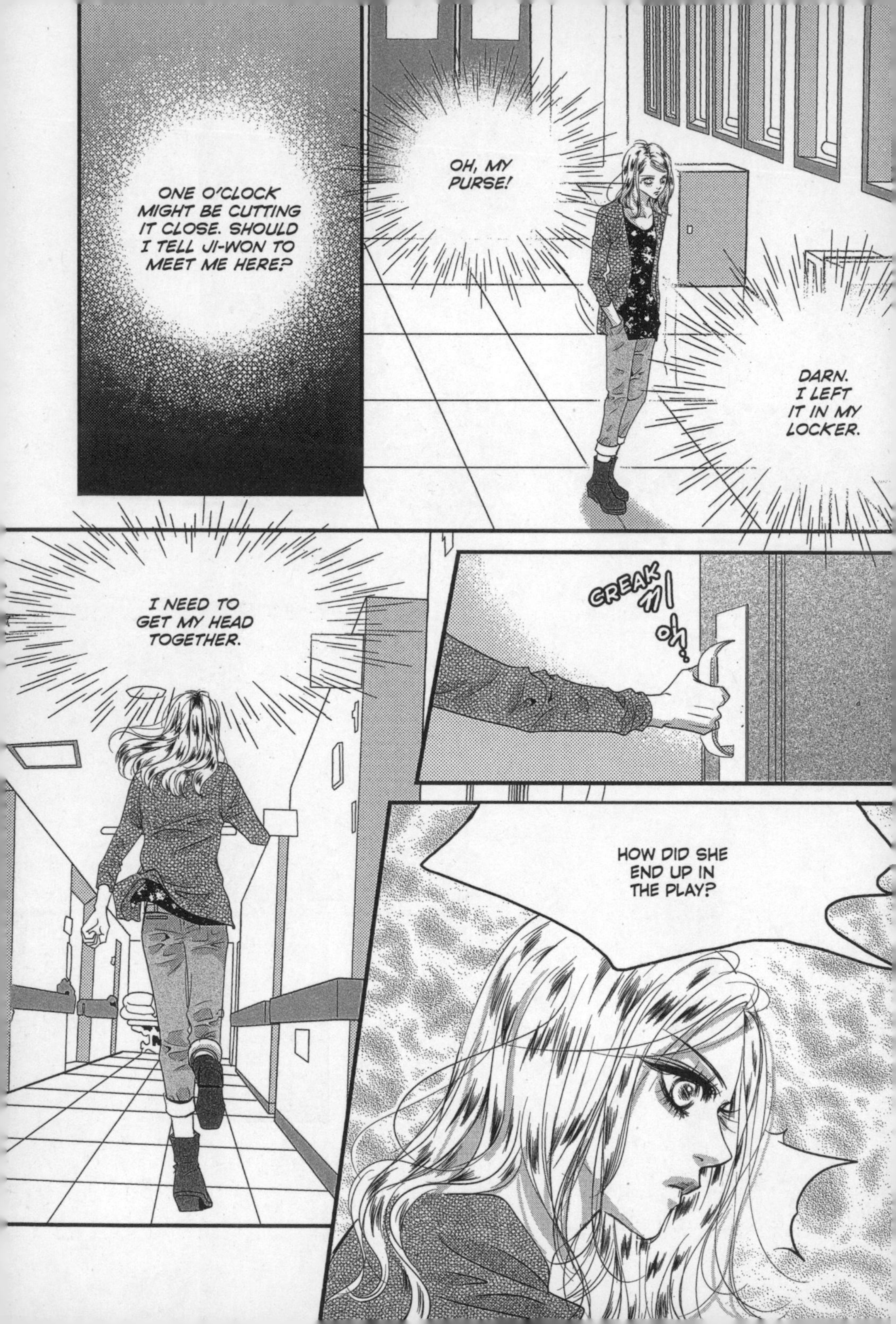
ONE O'CLOCK MIGHT BE CUTTING IT CLOSE. SHOULD I TELL JI-WON TO MEET ME HERE?
OH, MY PURSE!
DARN. I LEFT IT IN MY LOCKER.
I NEED TO GET MY HEAD TOGETHER.
CREAK
끼이
HOW DID SHE END UP IN THE PLAY?

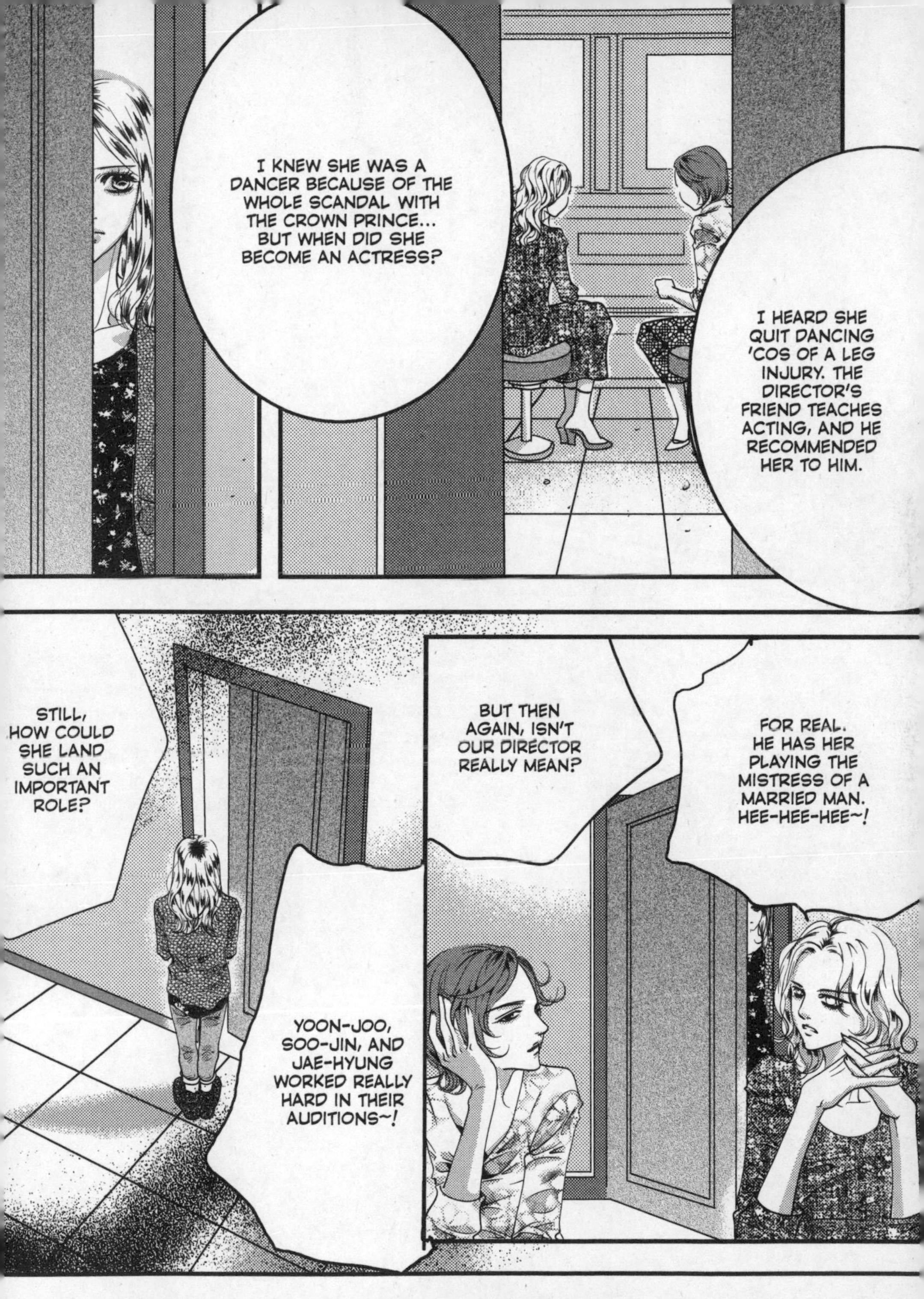
I KNEW SHE WAS A DANCER BECAUSE OF THE WHOLE SCANDAL WITH THE CROWN PRINCE... BUT WHEN DID SHE BECOME AN ACTRESS?
I HEARD SHE QUIT DANCING 'COS OF A LEG INJURY. THE DIRECTOR'S FRIEND TEACHES ACTING, AND HE RECOMMENDED HER TO HIM.
STILL, HOW COULD SHE LAND SUCH AN IMPORTANT ROLE?
YOON-JOO, SOO-JIN, AND JAE-HYUNG WORKED REALLY HARD IN THEIR AUDITIONS~!
BUT THEN AGAIN, ISN'T OUR DIRECTOR REALLY MEAN?
FOR REAL. HE HAS HER PLAYING THE MISTRESS OF A MARRIED MAN. HEE-HEE-HEE~!

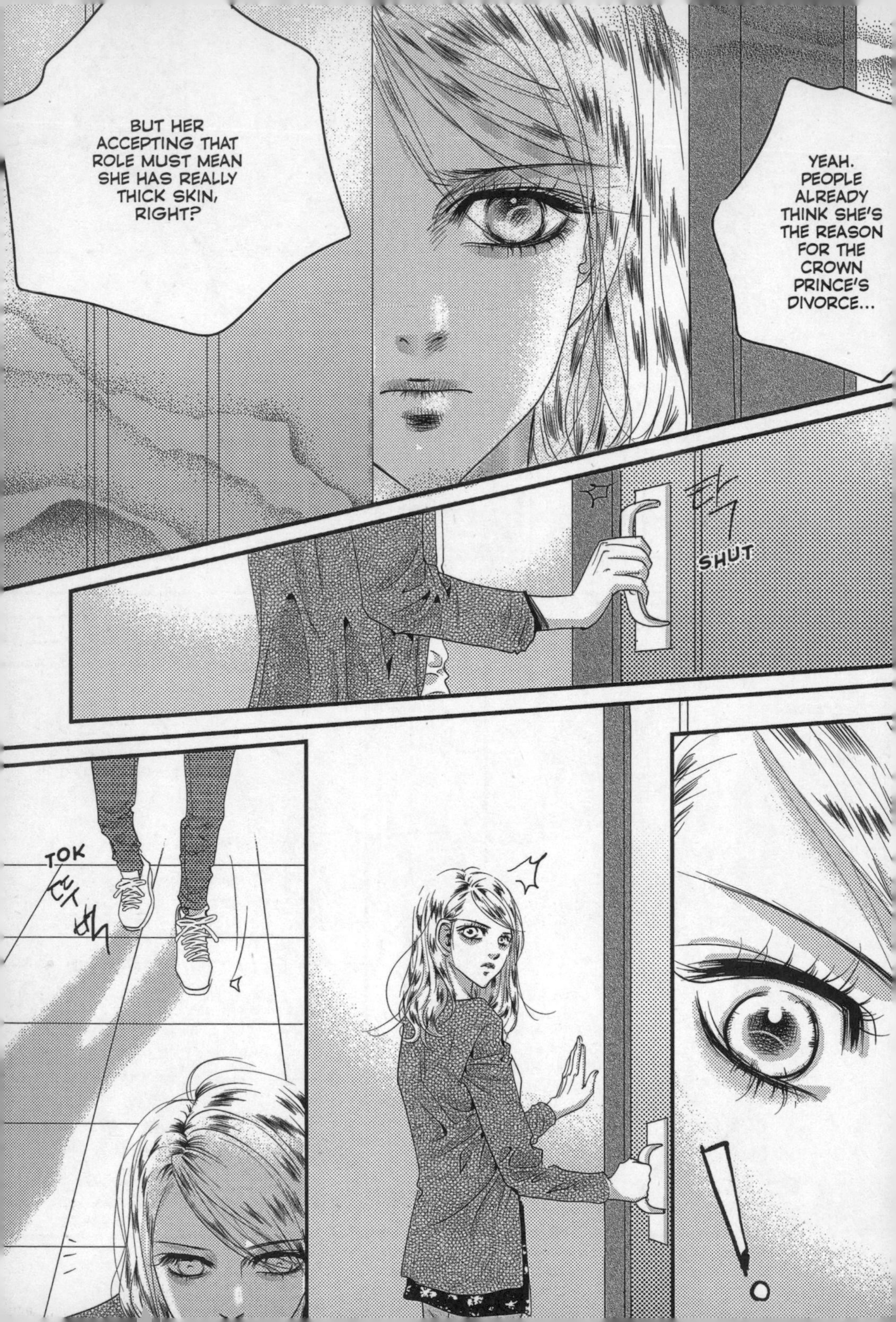
BUT HER ACCEPTING THAT ROLE MUST MEAN SHE HAS REALLY THICK SKIN, RIGHT?
YEAH. PEOPLE ALREADY THINK SHE'S THE REASON FOR THE CROWN PRINCE'S DIVORCE...
SHUT
TOK
!

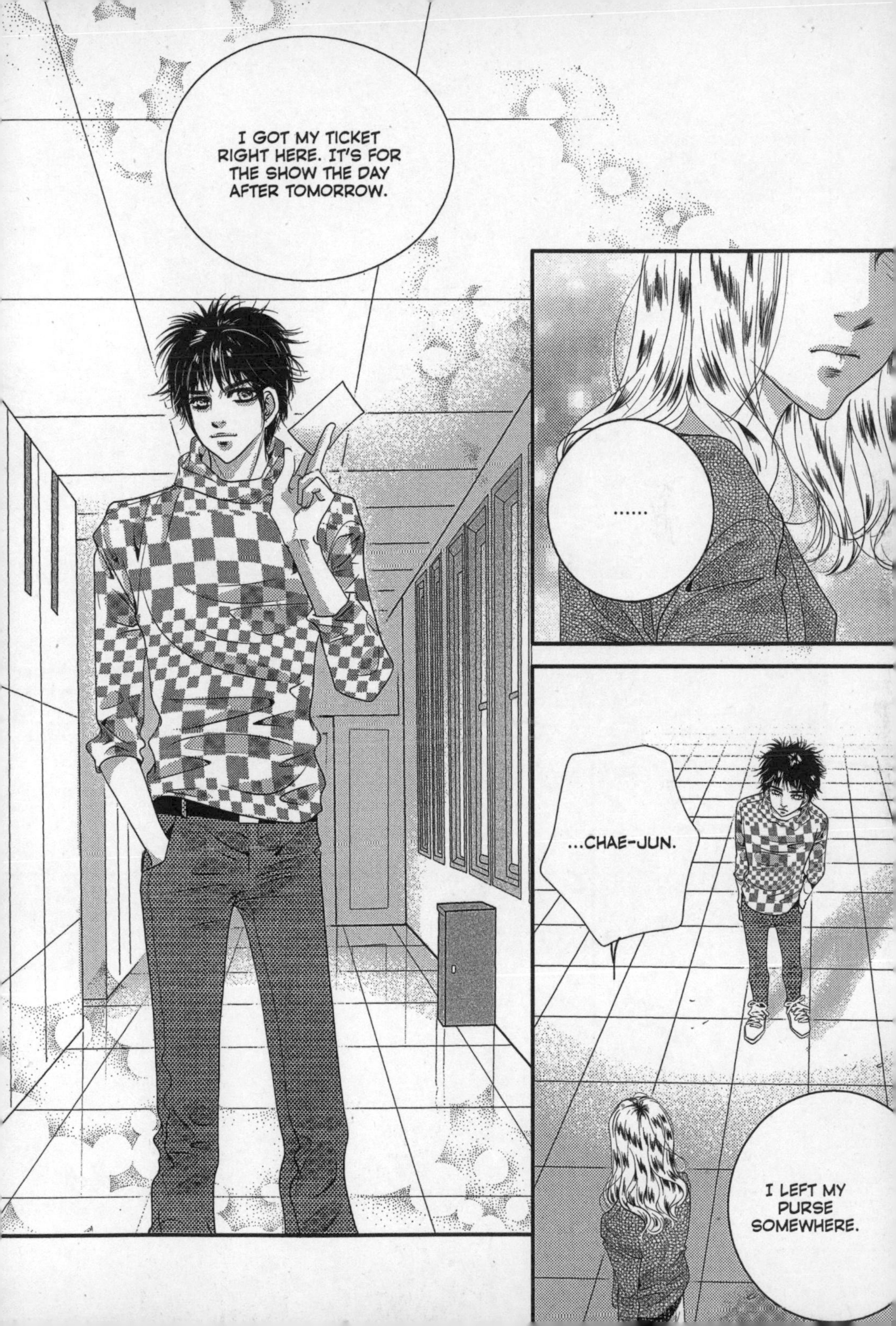
I GOT MY TICKET RIGHT HERE. IT'S FOR THE SHOW THE DAY AFTER TOMORROW.
......
...CHAE-JUN.
I LEFT MY PURSE SOMEWHERE.

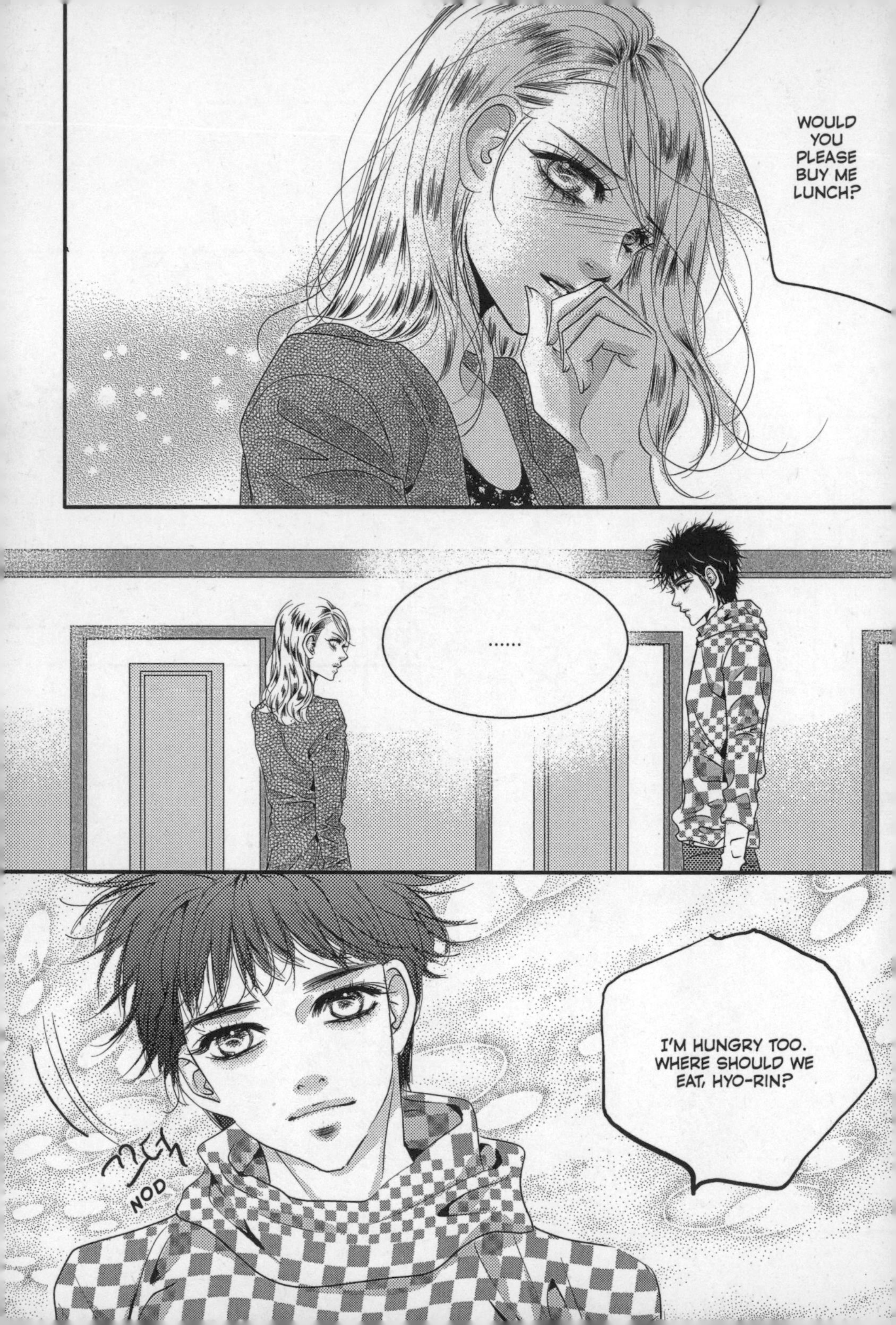
WOULD YOU PLEASE BUY ME LUNCH?
......
I'M HUNGRY TOO. WHERE SHOULD WE EAT, HYO-RIN?
NOD

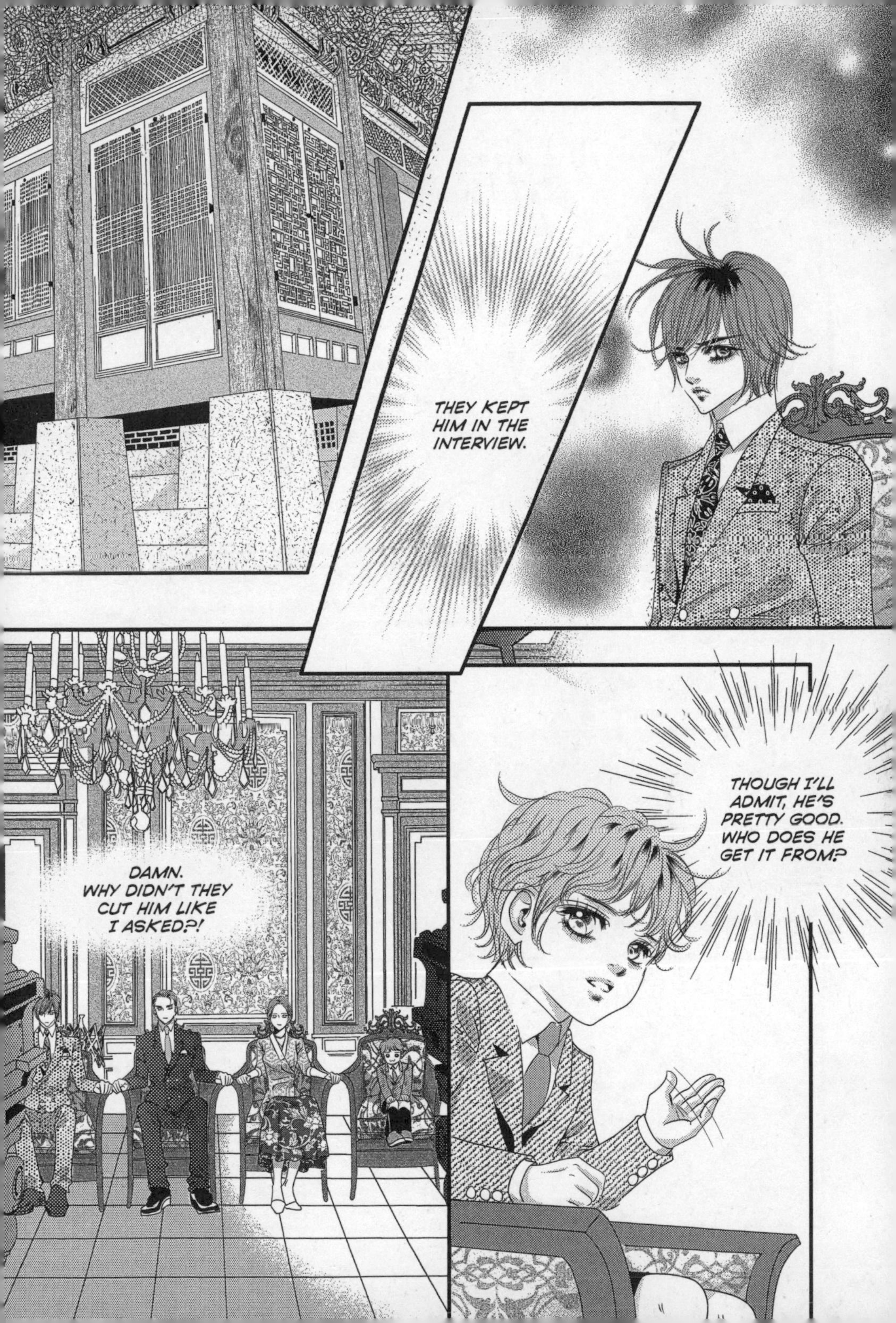
THEY KEPT HIM IN THE INTERVIEW.
DAMN. WHY DIDN'T THEY CUT HIM LIKE I ASKED?!
THOUGH I'LL ADMIT, HE'S PRETTY GOOD. WHO DOES HE GET IT FROM?

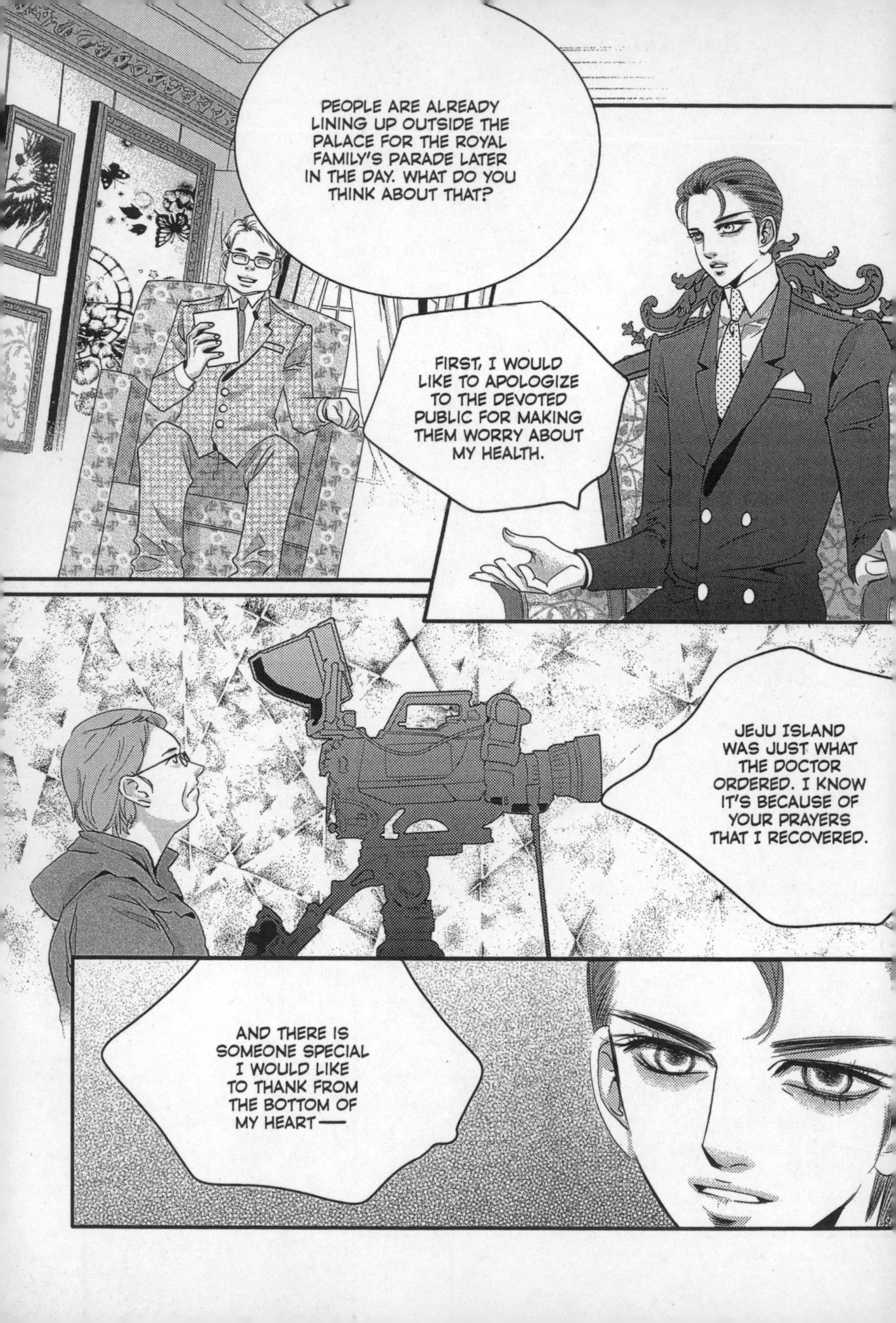
PEOPLE ARE ALREADY LINING UP OUTSIDE THE PALACE FOR THE ROYAL FAMILY'S PARADE LATER IN THE DAY. WHAT DO YOU THINK ABOUT THAT?
FIRST, I WOULD LIKE TO APOLOGIZE TO THE DEVOTED PUBLIC FOR MAKING THEM WORRY ABOUT MY HEALTH.
JEJU ISLAND WAS JUST WHAT THE DOCTOR ORDERED. I KNOW IT'S BECAUSE OF YOUR PRAYERS THAT I RECOVERED.
AND THERE IS SOMEONE SPECIAL I WOULD LIKE TO THANK FROM THE BOTTOM OF MY HEART—

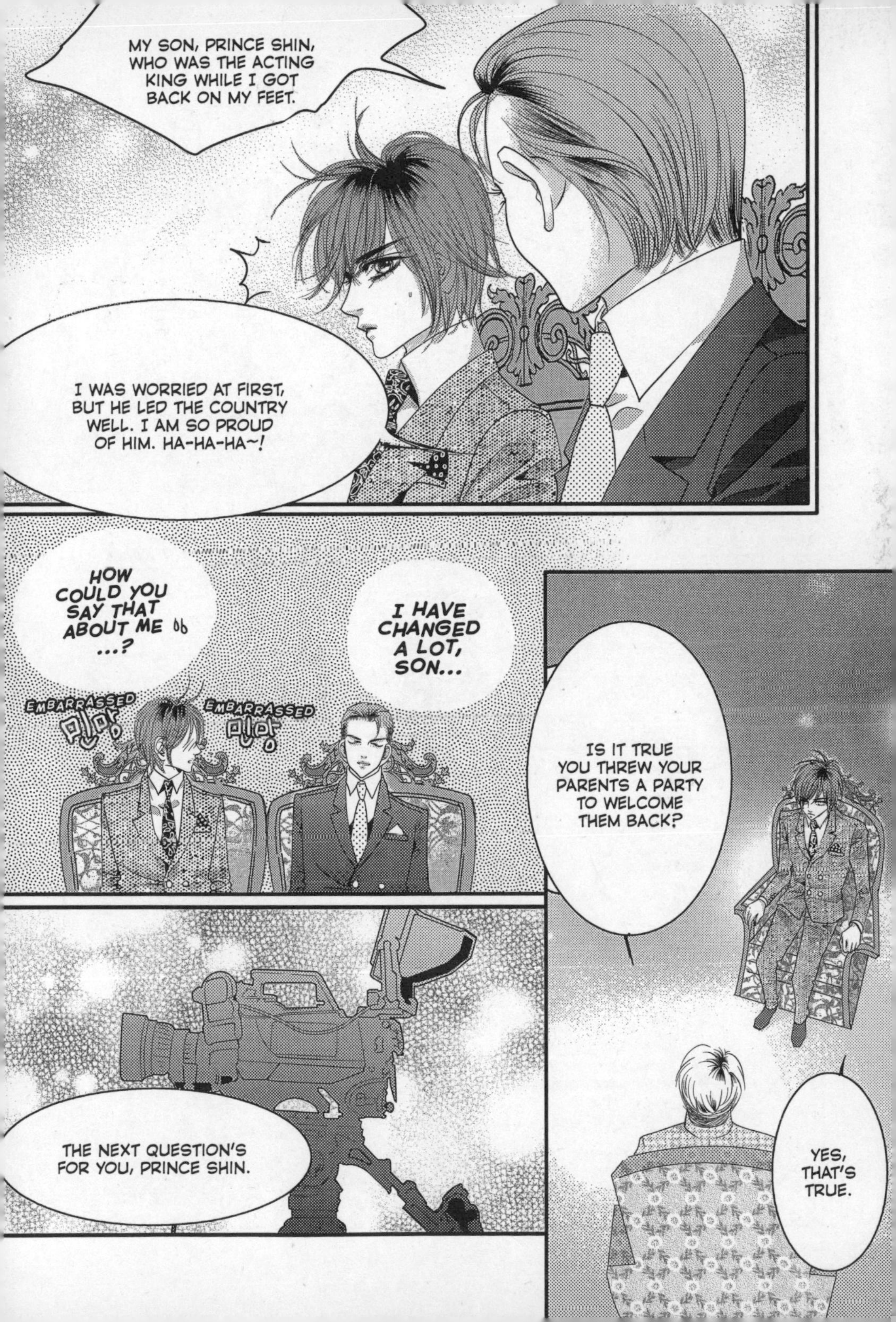
MY SON, PRINCE SHIN, WHO WAS THE ACTING KING WHILE I GOT BACK ON MY FEET.
I WAS WORRIED AT FIRST, BUT HE LED THE COUNTRY WELL. I AM SO PROUD OF HIM. HA-HA-HA~!
HOW COULD YOU SAY THAT ABOUT ME ㅂㅂ ...?
I HAVE CHANGED A LOT, SON...
EMBARRASSED
민망
EMBARRASSED
민망
THE NEXT QUESTION'S FOR YOU, PRINCE SHIN.
IS IT TRUE YOU THREW YOUR PARENTS A PARTY TO WELCOME THEM BACK?
YES, THAT'S TRUE.

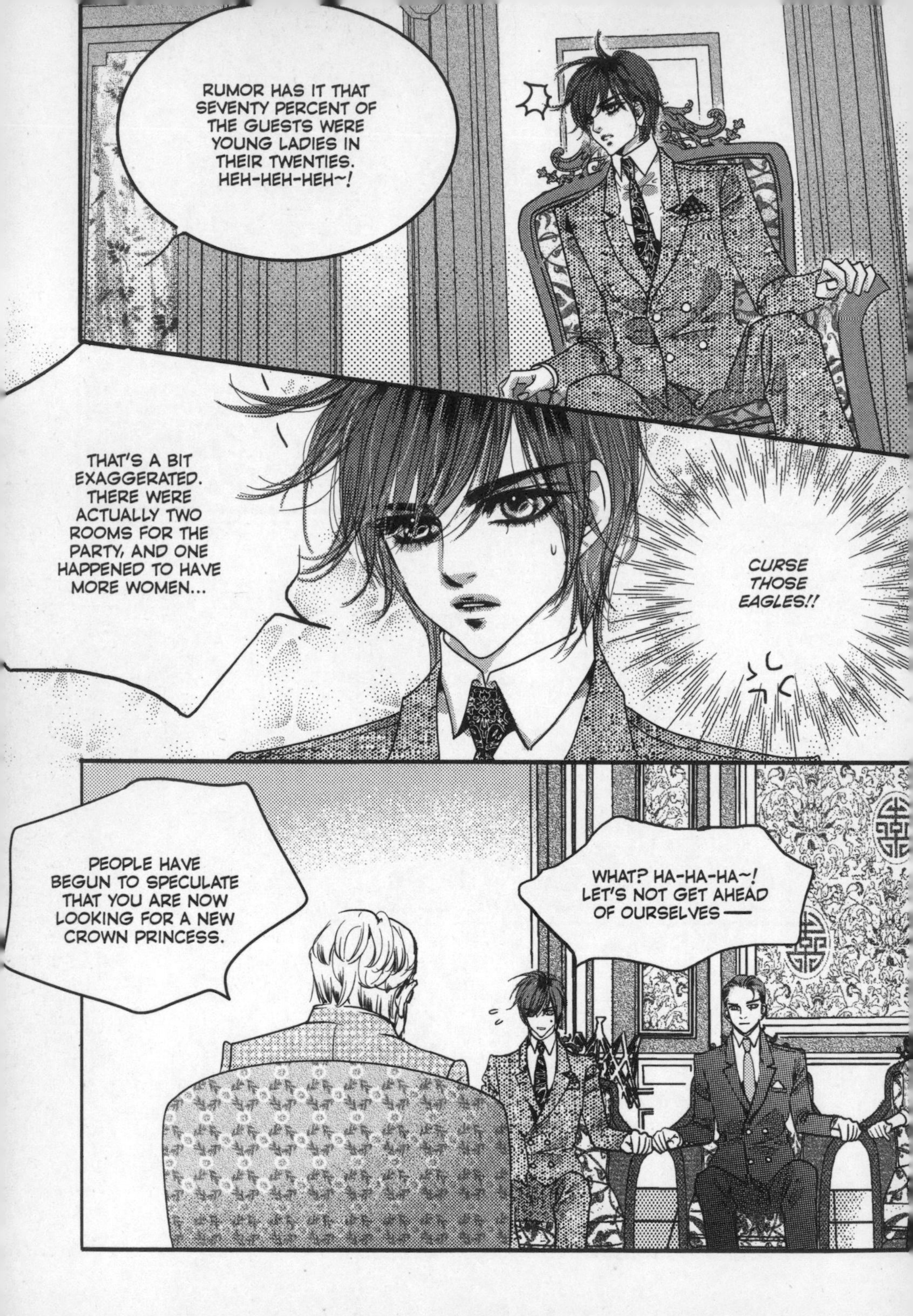
RUMOR HAS IT THAT SEVENTY PERCENT OF THE GUESTS WERE YOUNG LADIES IN THEIR TWENTIES. HEH-HEH-HEH~!
THAT'S A BIT EXAGGERATED. THERE WERE ACTUALLY TWO ROOMS FOR THE PARTY, AND ONE HAPPENED TO HAVE MORE WOMEN...
CURSE THOSE EAGLES!!
PEOPLE HAVE BEGUN TO SPECULATE THAT YOU ARE NOW LOOKING FOR A NEW CROWN PRINCESS.
WHAT? HA-HA-HA~! LET'S NOT GET AHEAD OF OURSELVES—

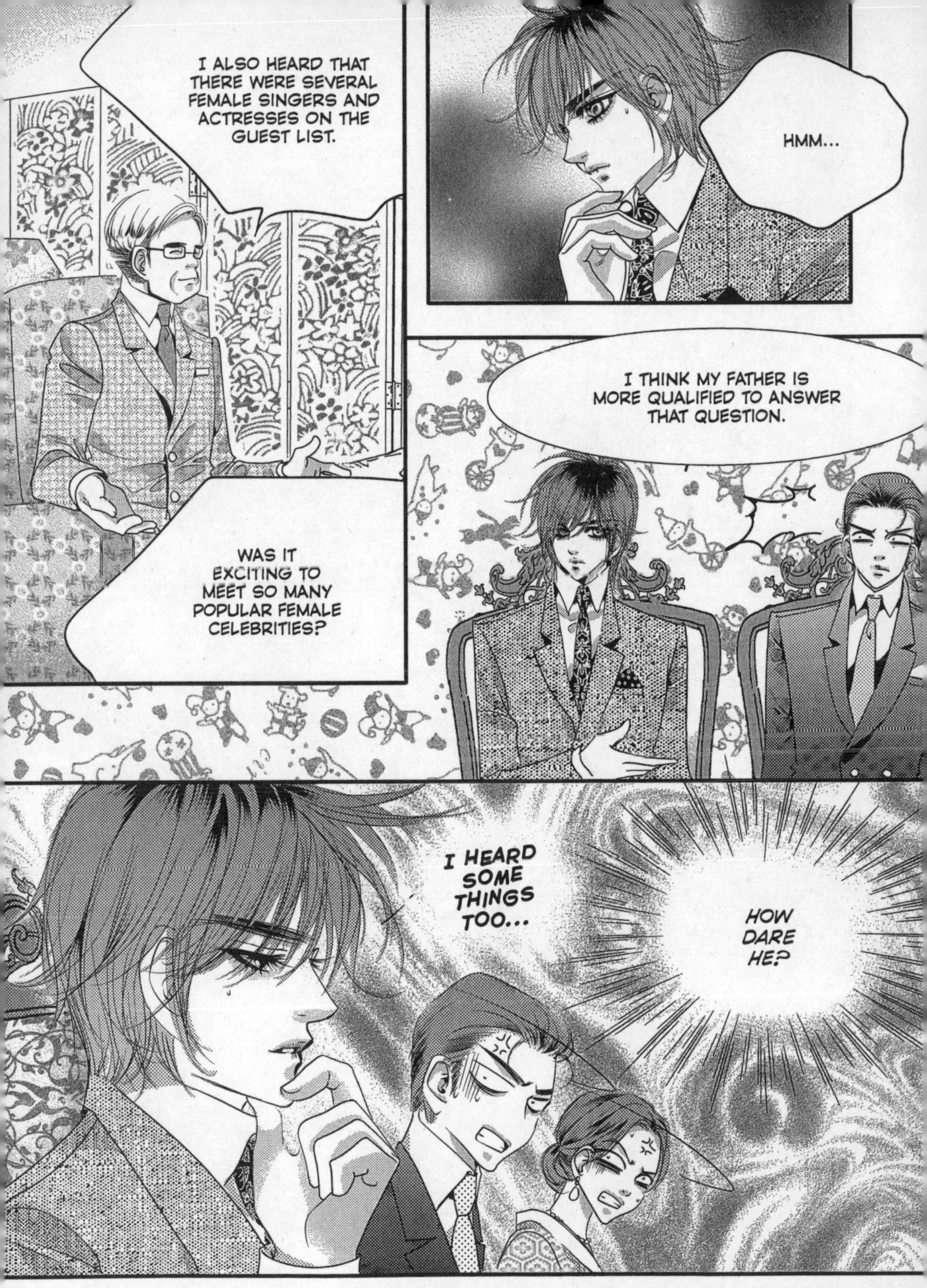
I ALSO HEARD THAT THERE WERE SEVERAL FEMALE SINGERS AND ACTRESSES ON THE GUEST LIST.
WAS IT EXCITING TO MEET SO MANY POPULAR FEMALE CELEBRITIES?
HMM...
I THINK MY FATHER IS MORE QUALIFIED TO ANSWER THAT QUESTION.
I HEARD SOME THINGS TOO...
HOW DARE HE?

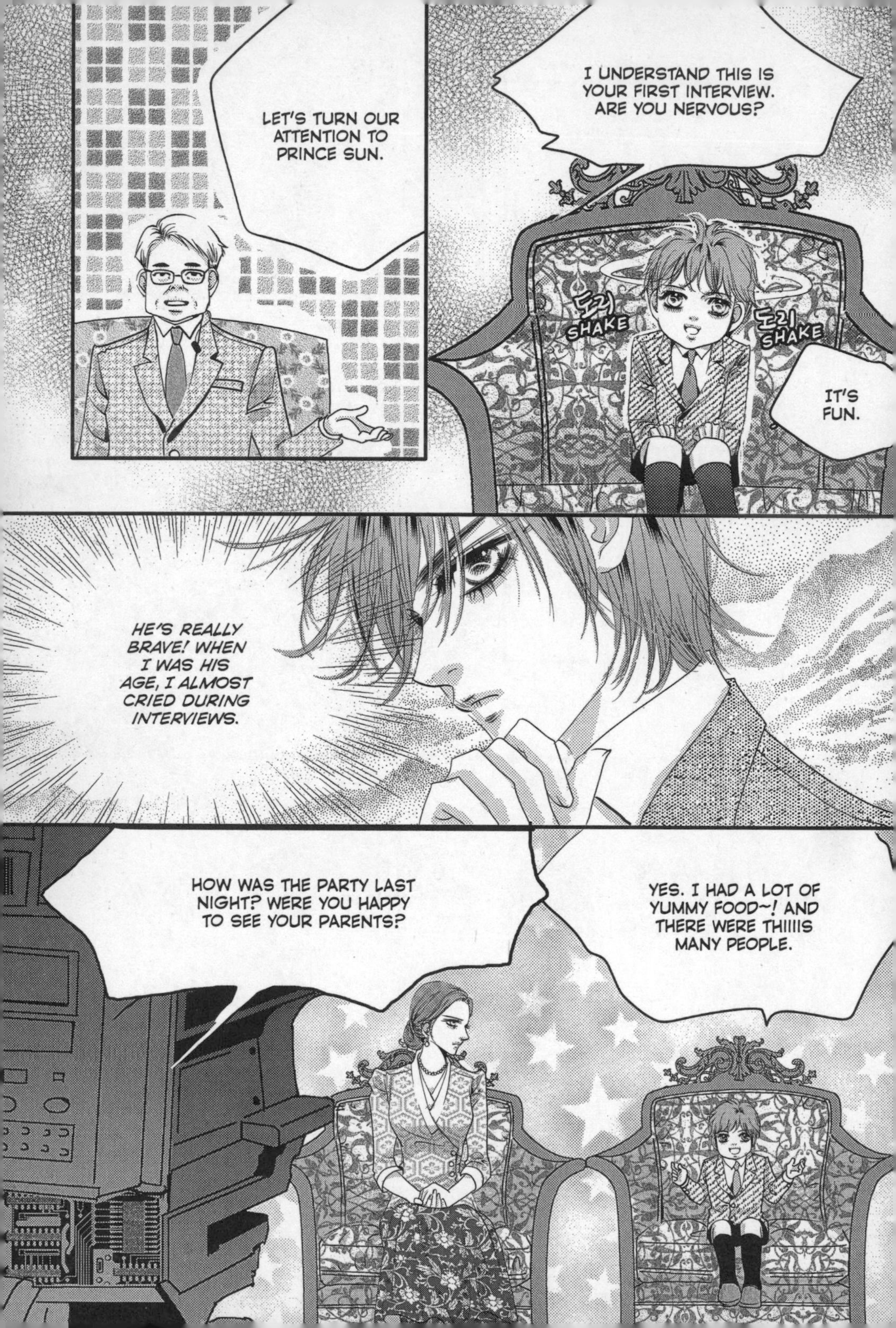
LET'S TURN OUR ATTENTION TO PRINCE SUN.
I UNDERSTAND THIS IS YOUR FIRST INTERVIEW. ARE YOU NERVOUS?
도리 SHAKE
도리 SHAKE
IT'S FUN.
HE'S REALLY BRAVE! WHEN I WAS HIS AGE, I ALMOST CRIED DURING INTERVIEWS.
HOW WAS THE PARTY LAST NIGHT? WERE YOU HAPPY TO SEE YOUR PARENTS?
YES. I HAD A LOT OF YUMMY FOOD~! AND THERE WERE THIIIIS MANY PEOPLE.

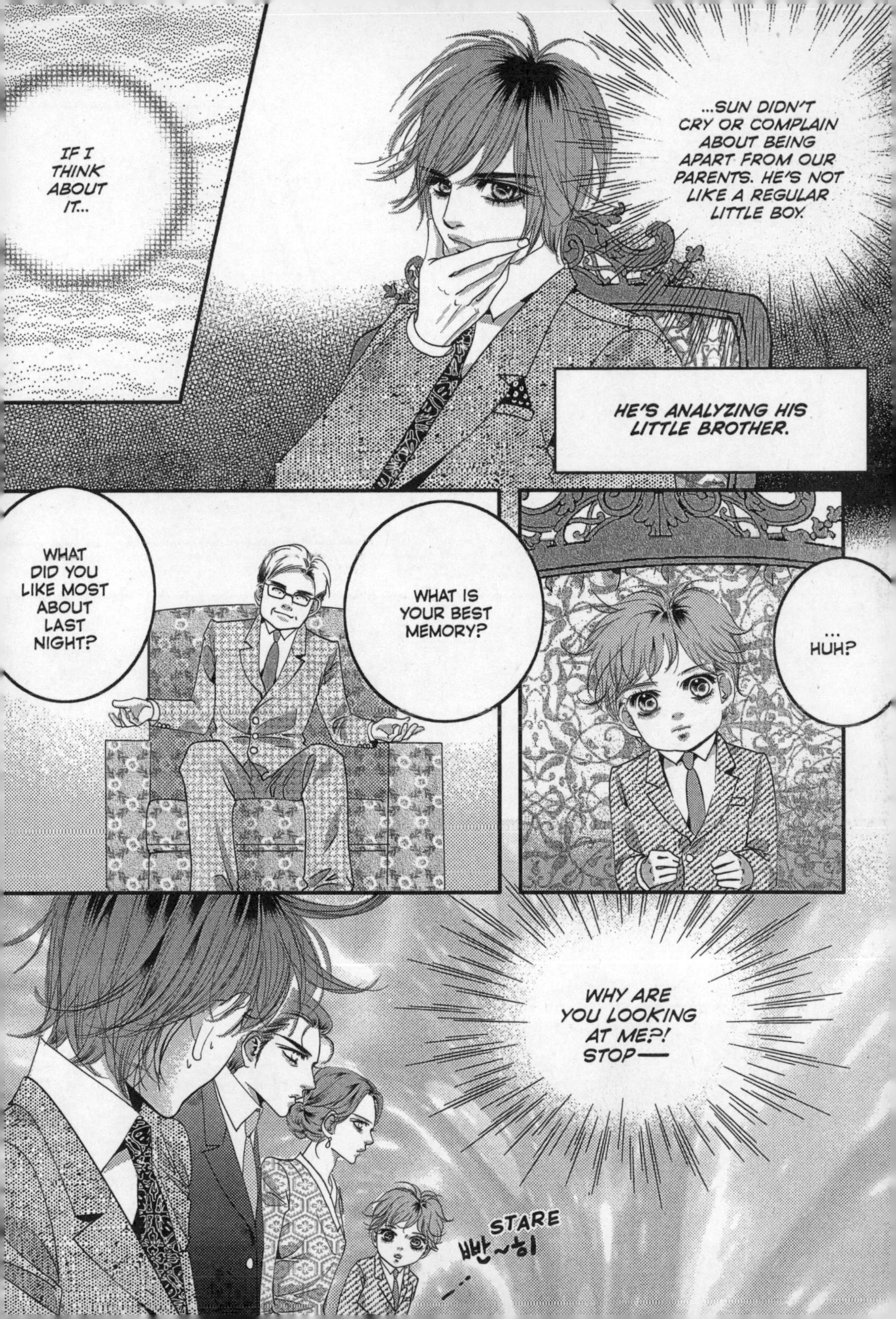
IF I THINK ABOUT IT...
...SUN DIDN'T CRY OR COMPLAIN ABOUT BEING APART FROM OUR PARENTS. HE'S NOT LIKE A REGULAR LITTLE BOY.
HE'S ANALYZING HIS LITTLE BROTHER.
WHAT DID YOU LIKE MOST ABOUT LAST NIGHT?
WHAT IS YOUR BEST MEMORY?
... HUH?
WHY ARE YOU LOOKING AT ME?! STOP—
STARE
빤~히

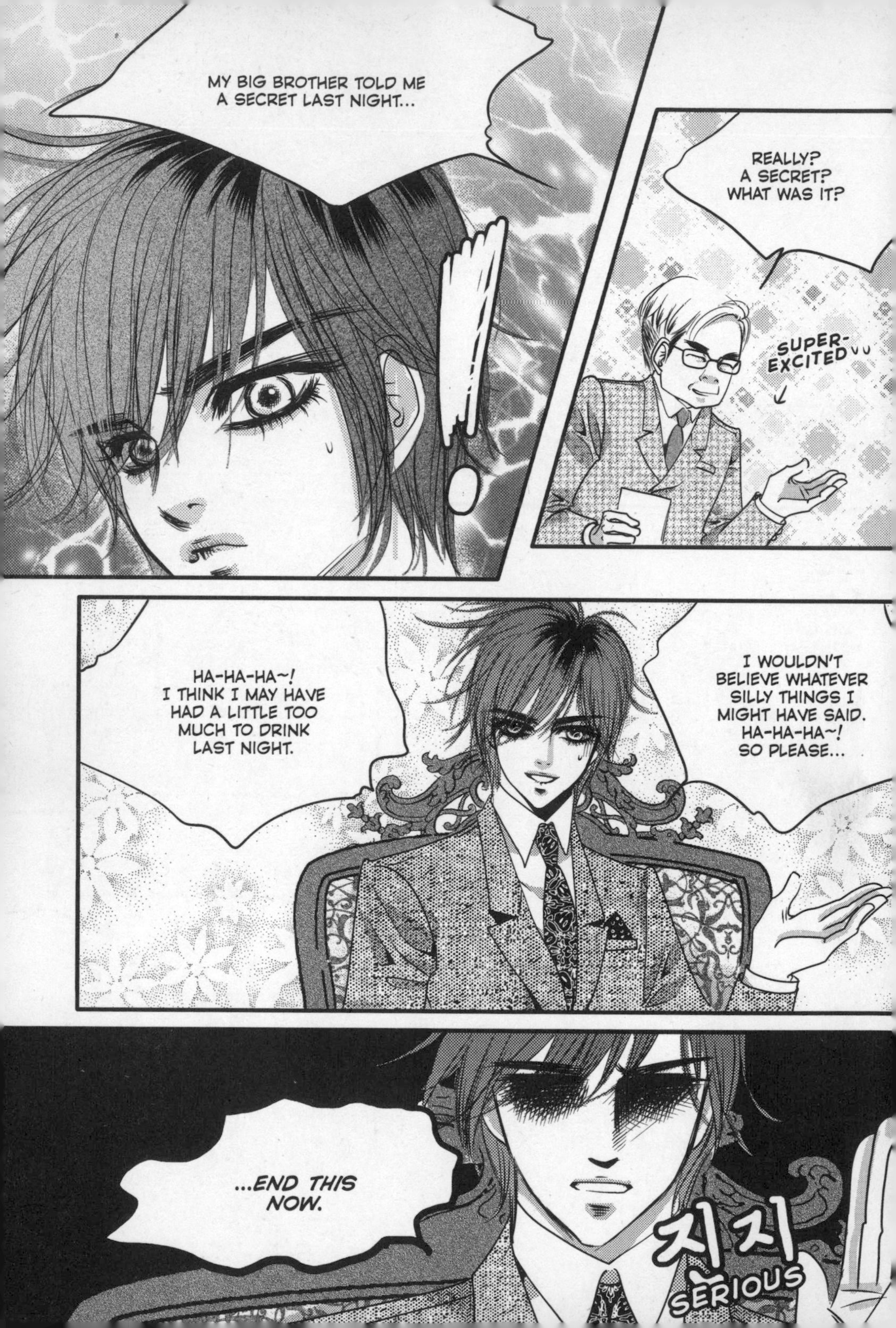
MY BIG BROTHER TOLD ME A SECRET LAST NIGHT...
REALLY? A SECRET? WHAT WAS IT?
SUPER-EXCITED
HA-HA-HA~! I THINK I MAY HAVE HAD A LITTLE TOO MUCH TO DRINK LAST NIGHT.
I WOULDN'T BELIEVE WHATEVER SILLY THINGS I MIGHT HAVE SAID. HA-HA-HA~! SO PLEASE...
...END THIS NOW.
지지
SERIOUS

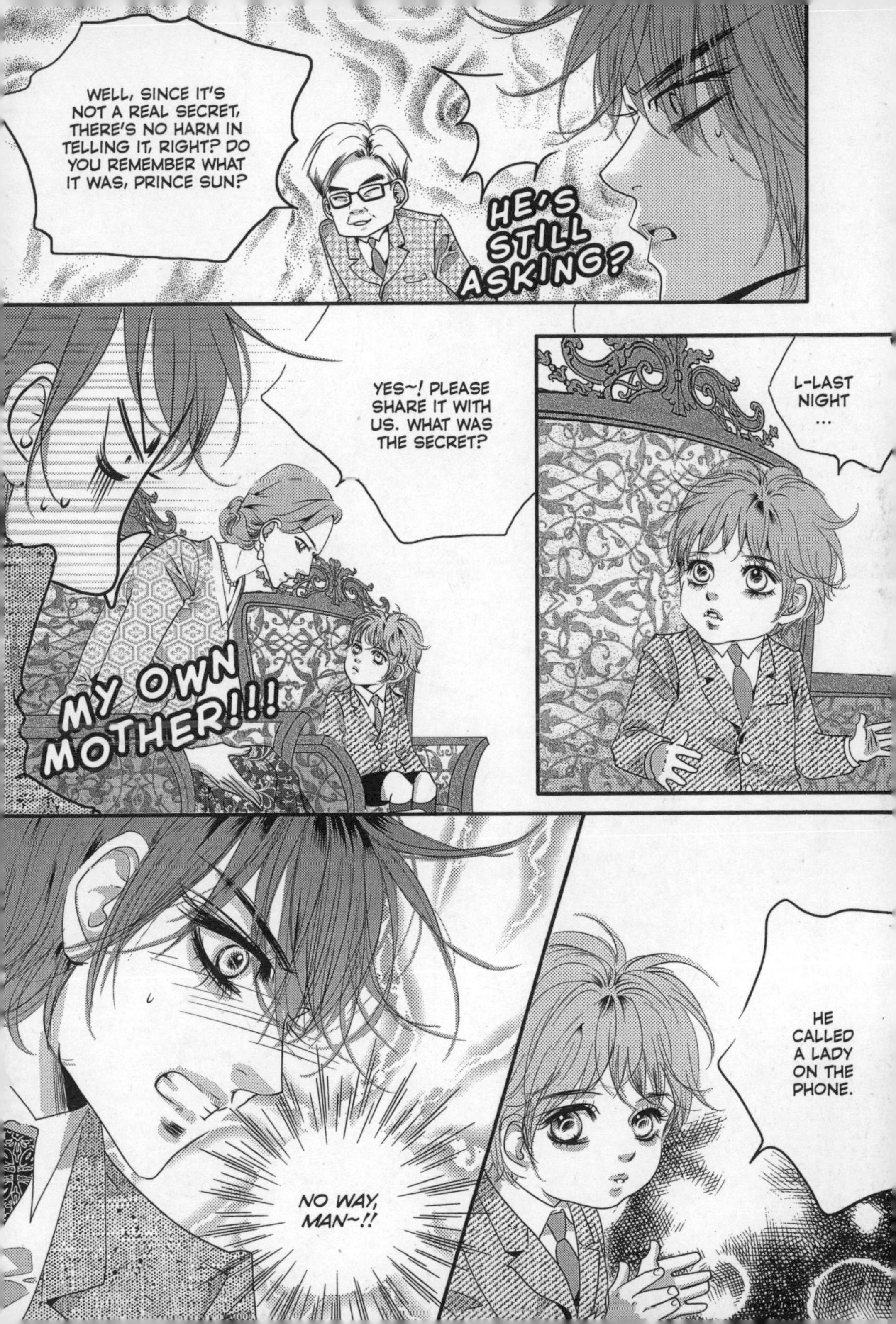
WELL, SINCE IT'S NOT A REAL SECRET, THERE'S NO HARM IN TELLING IT, RIGHT? DO YOU REMEMBER WHAT IT WAS, PRINCE SUN?
HE'S STILL ASKING?
YES~! PLEASE SHARE IT WITH US. WHAT WAS THE SECRET?
MY OWN MOTHER!!!
L-LAST NIGHT ...
NO WAY, MAN~!!
HE CALLED A LADY ON THE PHONE.

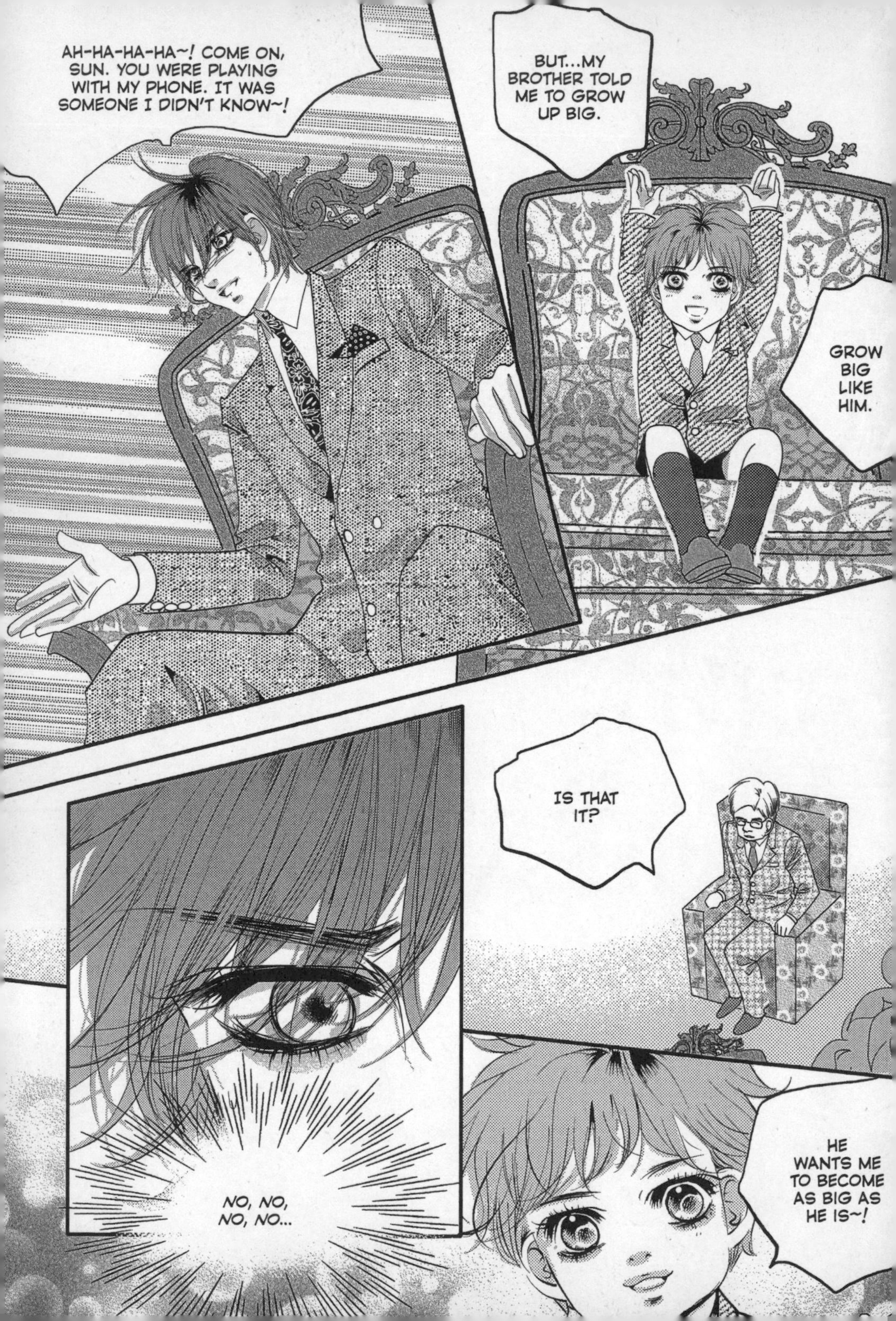
AH-HA-HA-HA~! COME ON, SUN. YOU WERE PLAYING WITH MY PHONE. IT WAS SOMEONE I DIDN'T KNOW~!
BUT...MY BROTHER TOLD ME TO GROW UP BIG.
GROW BIG LIKE HIM.
IS THAT IT?
NO, NO, NO, NO...
HE WANTS ME TO BECOME AS BIG AS HE IS~!

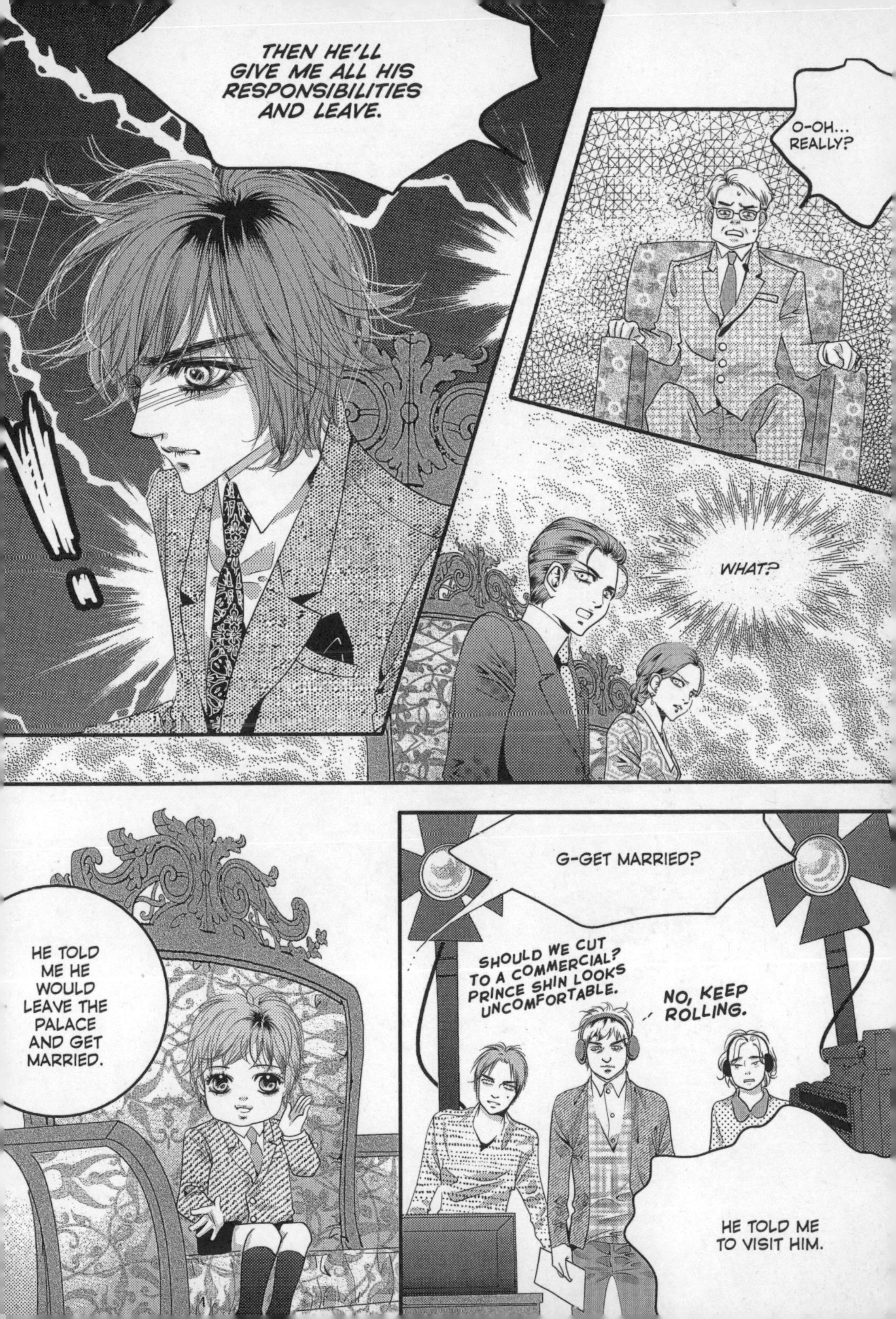
THEN HE'LL GIVE ME ALL HIS RESPONSIBILITIES AND LEAVE.
O-OH... REALLY?
WHAT?
HE TOLD ME HE WOULD LEAVE THE PALACE AND GET MARRIED.
G-GET MARRIED?
SHOULD WE CUT TO A COMMERCIAL? PRINCE SHIN LOOKS UNCOMFORTABLE.
NO, KEEP ROLLING.
HE TOLD ME TO VISIT HIM.

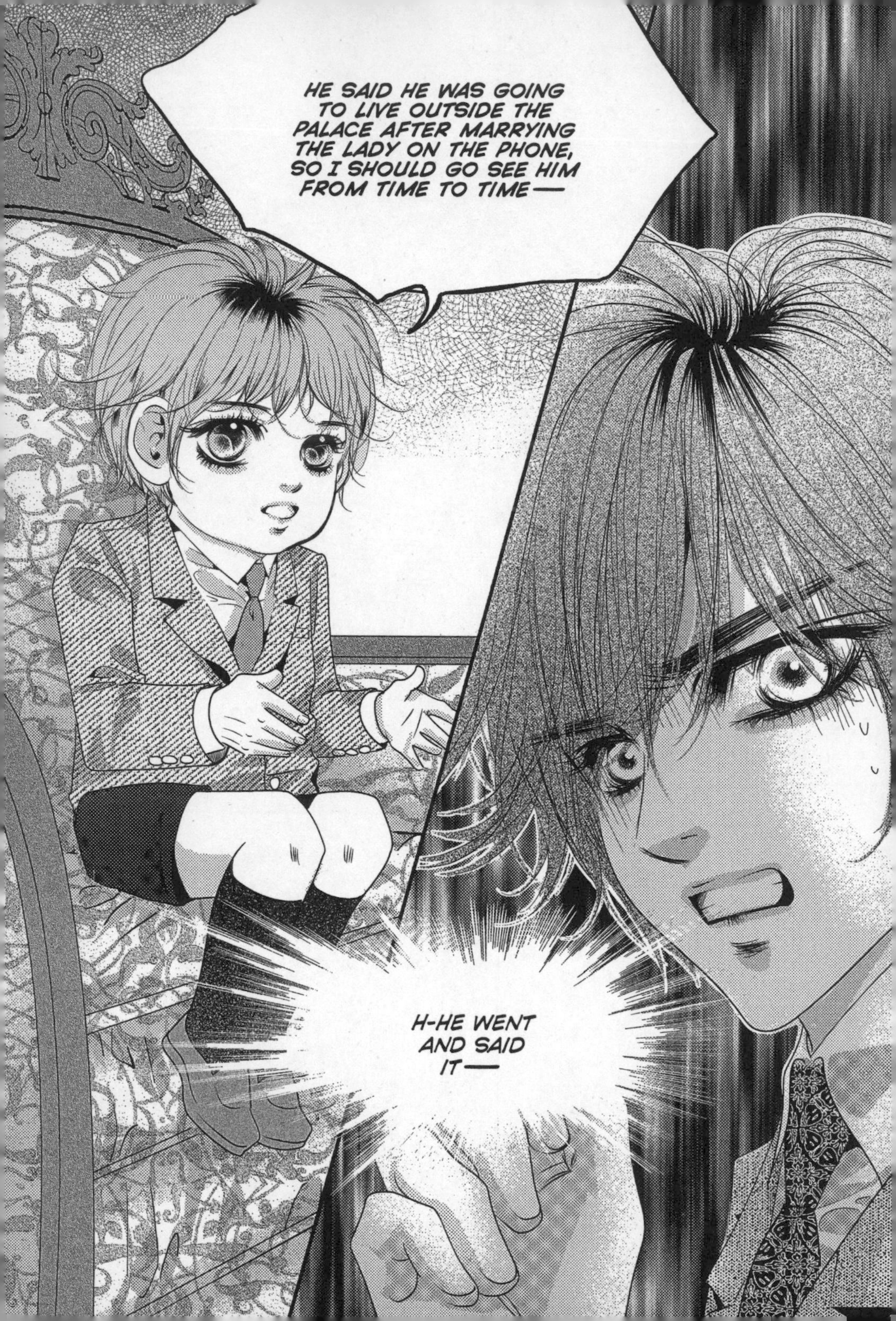
HE SAID HE WAS GOING TO LIVE OUTSIDE THE PALACE AFTER MARRYING THE LADY ON THE PHONE, SO I SHOULD GO SEE HIM FROM TIME TO TIME—
H-HE WENT AND SAID IT—

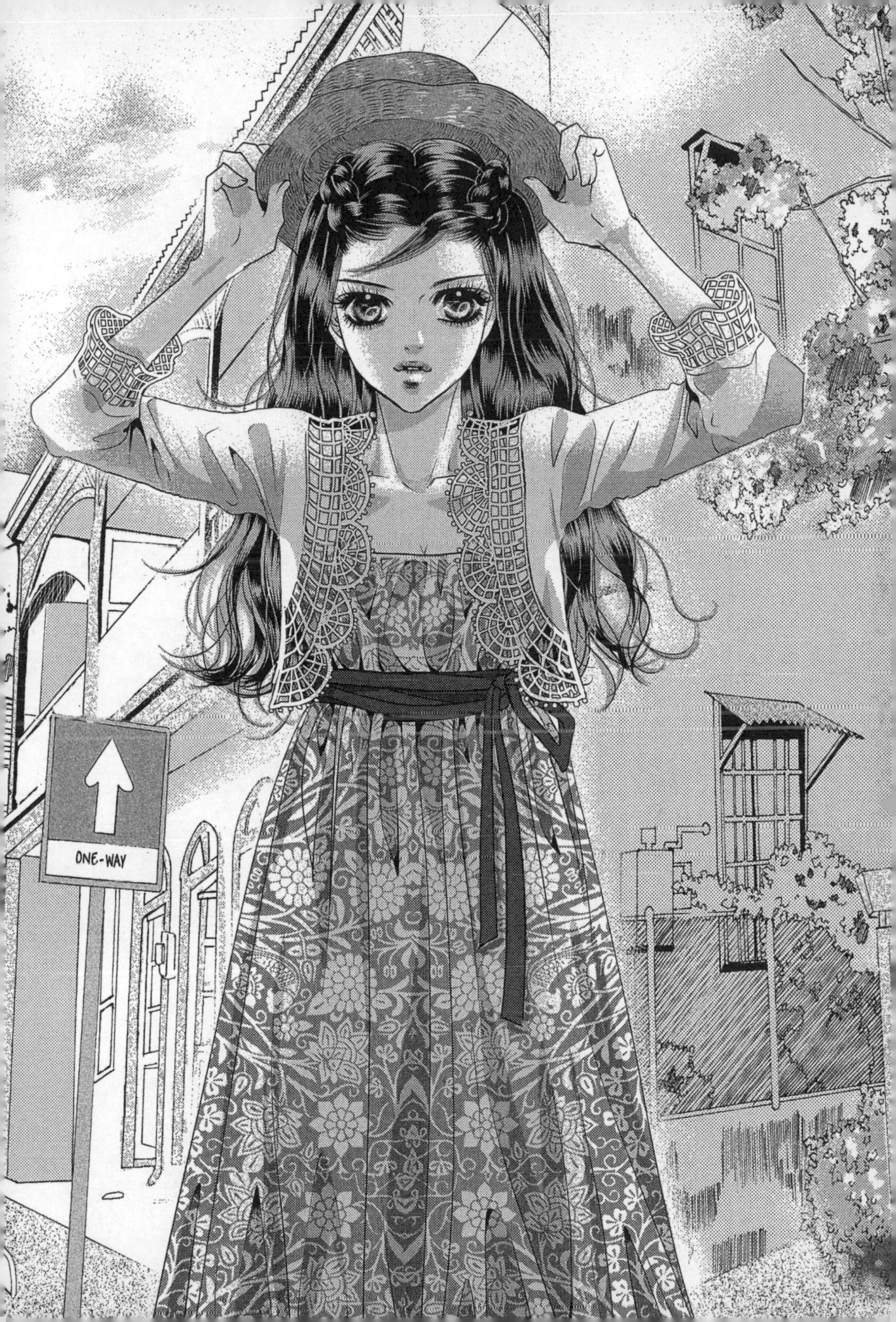
ONE-WAY

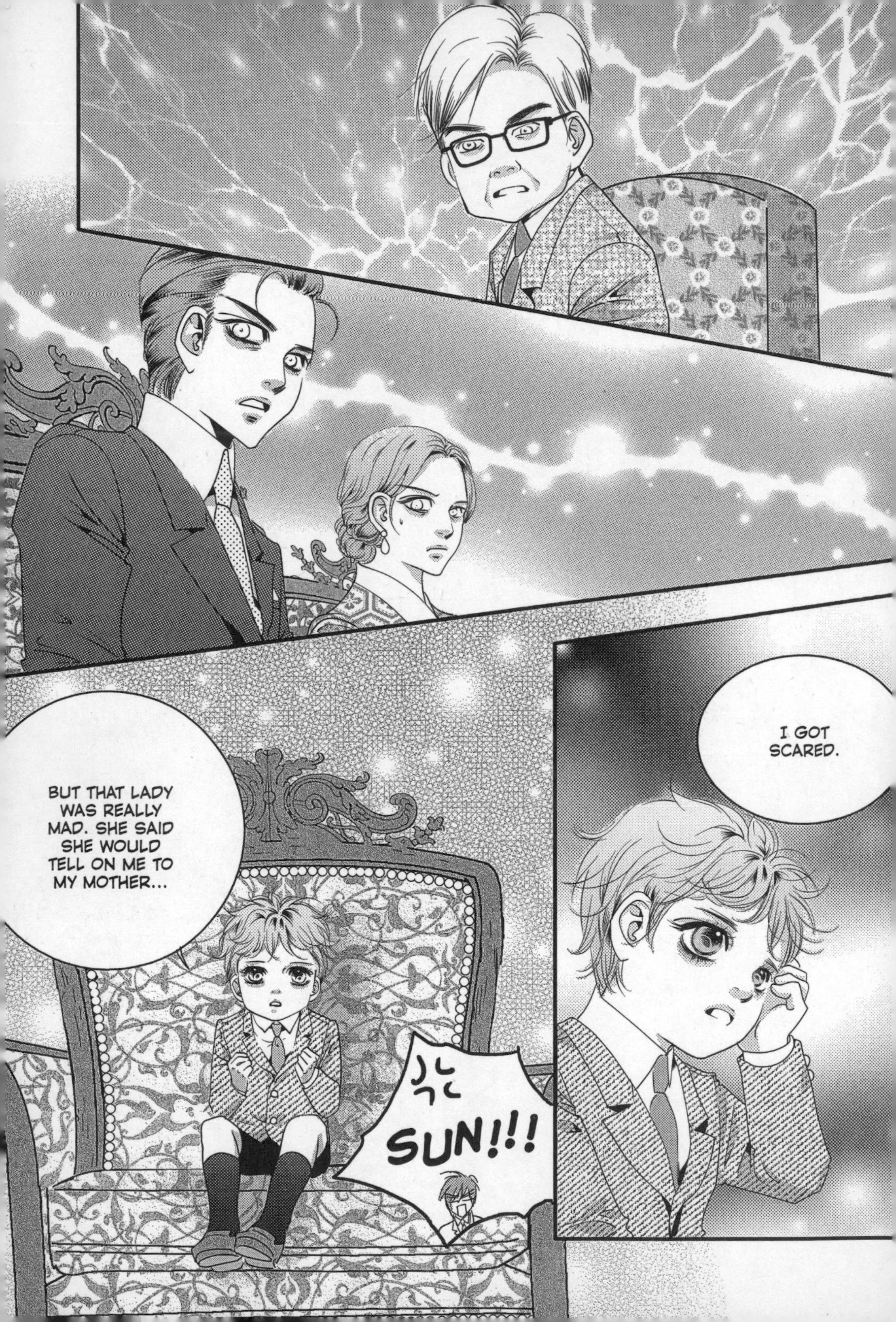
BUT THAT LADY WAS REALLY MAD. SHE SAID SHE WOULD TELL ON ME TO MY MOTHER...
SUN!!!
I GOT SCARED.

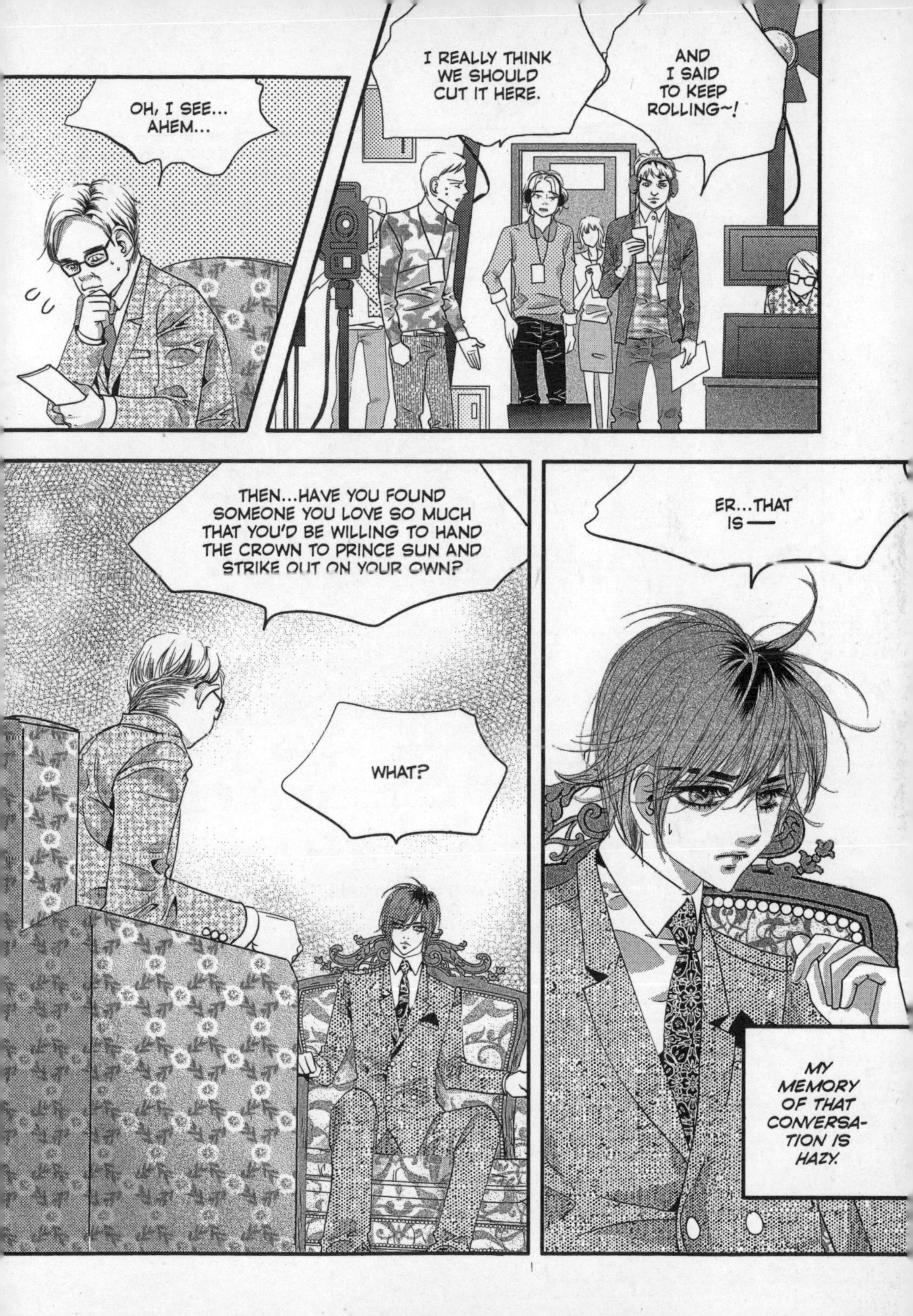
OH, I SEE... AHEM...
I REALLY THINK WE SHOULD CUT IT HERE.
AND I SAID TO KEEP ROLLING~!
THEN...HAVE YOU FOUND SOMEONE YOU LOVE SO MUCH THAT YOU'D BE WILLING TO HAND THE CROWN TO PRINCE SUN AND STRIKE OUT ON YOUR OWN?
WHAT?
ER...THAT IS—
MY MEMORY OF THAT CONVERSATION IS HAZY.

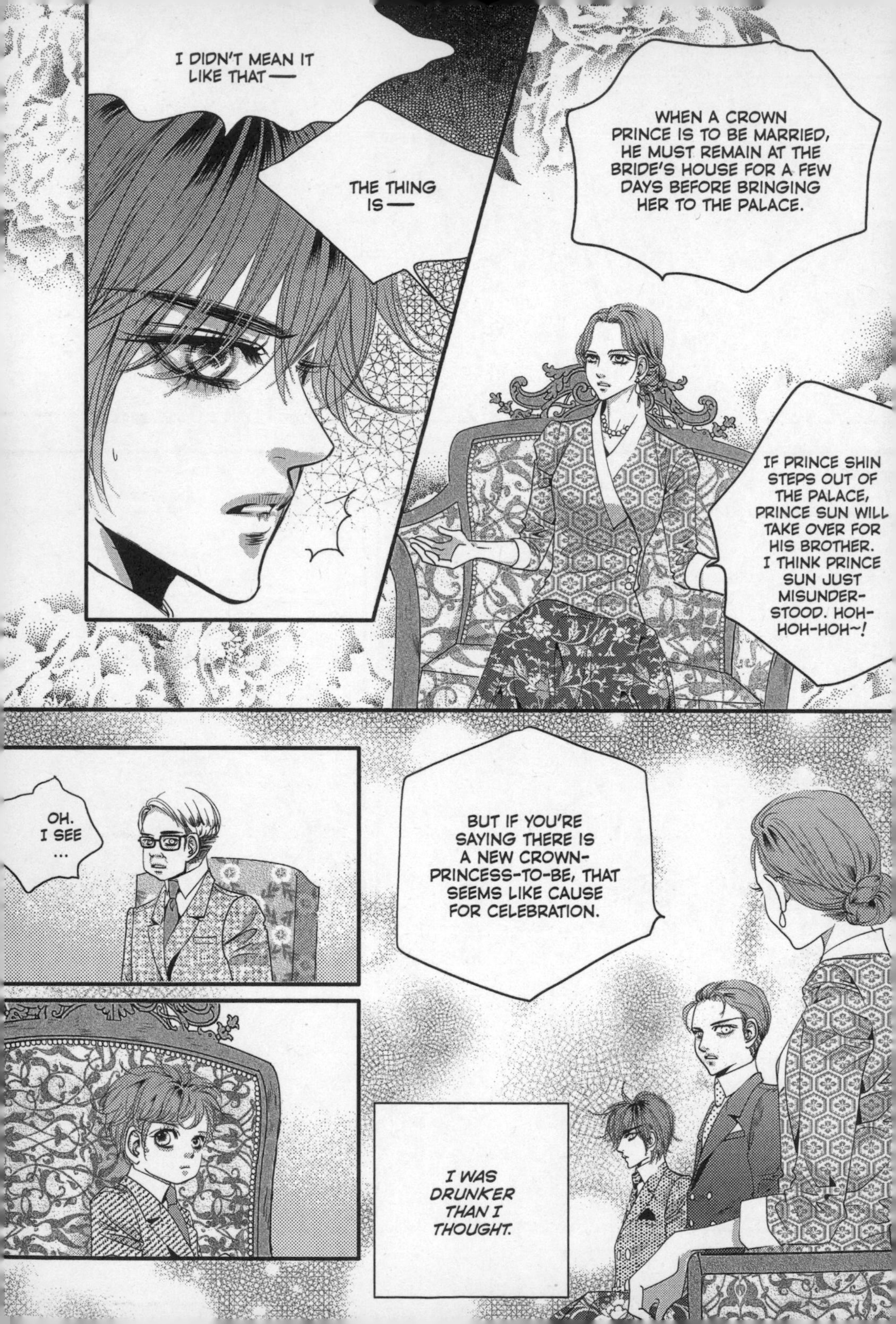
I DIDN'T MEAN IT LIKE THAT—
THE THING IS—
WHEN A CROWN PRINCE IS TO BE MARRIED, HE MUST REMAIN AT THE BRIDE'S HOUSE FOR A FEW DAYS BEFORE BRINGING HER TO THE PALACE.
IF PRINCE SHIN STEPS OUT OF THE PALACE, PRINCE SUN WILL TAKE OVER FOR HIS BROTHER. I THINK PRINCE SUN JUST MISUNDER-STOOD. HOH-HOH-HOH~!
OH. I SEE ...
BUT IF YOU'RE SAYING THERE IS A NEW CROWN-PRINCESS-TO-BE, THAT SEEMS LIKE CAUSE FOR CELEBRATION.
I WAS DRUNKER THAN I THOUGHT.

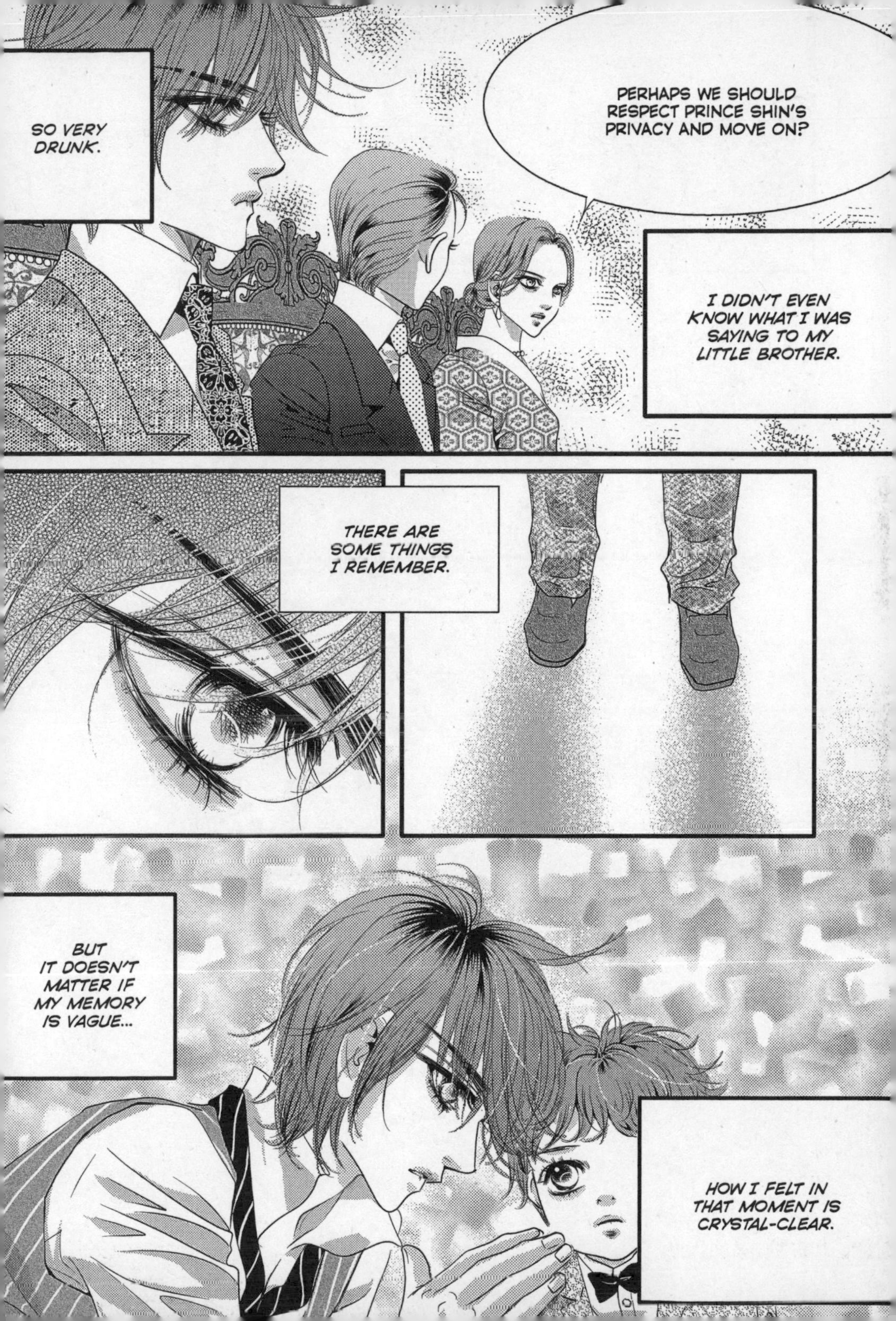
SO VERY DRUNK.
PERHAPS WE SHOULD RESPECT PRINCE SHIN'S PRIVACY AND MOVE ON?
I DIDN'T EVEN KNOW WHAT I WAS SAYING TO MY LITTLE BROTHER.
THERE ARE SOME THINGS I REMEMBER.
BUT IT DOESN'T MATTER IF MY MEMORY IS VAGUE...
HOW I FELT IN THAT MOMENT IS CRYSTAL-CLEAR.

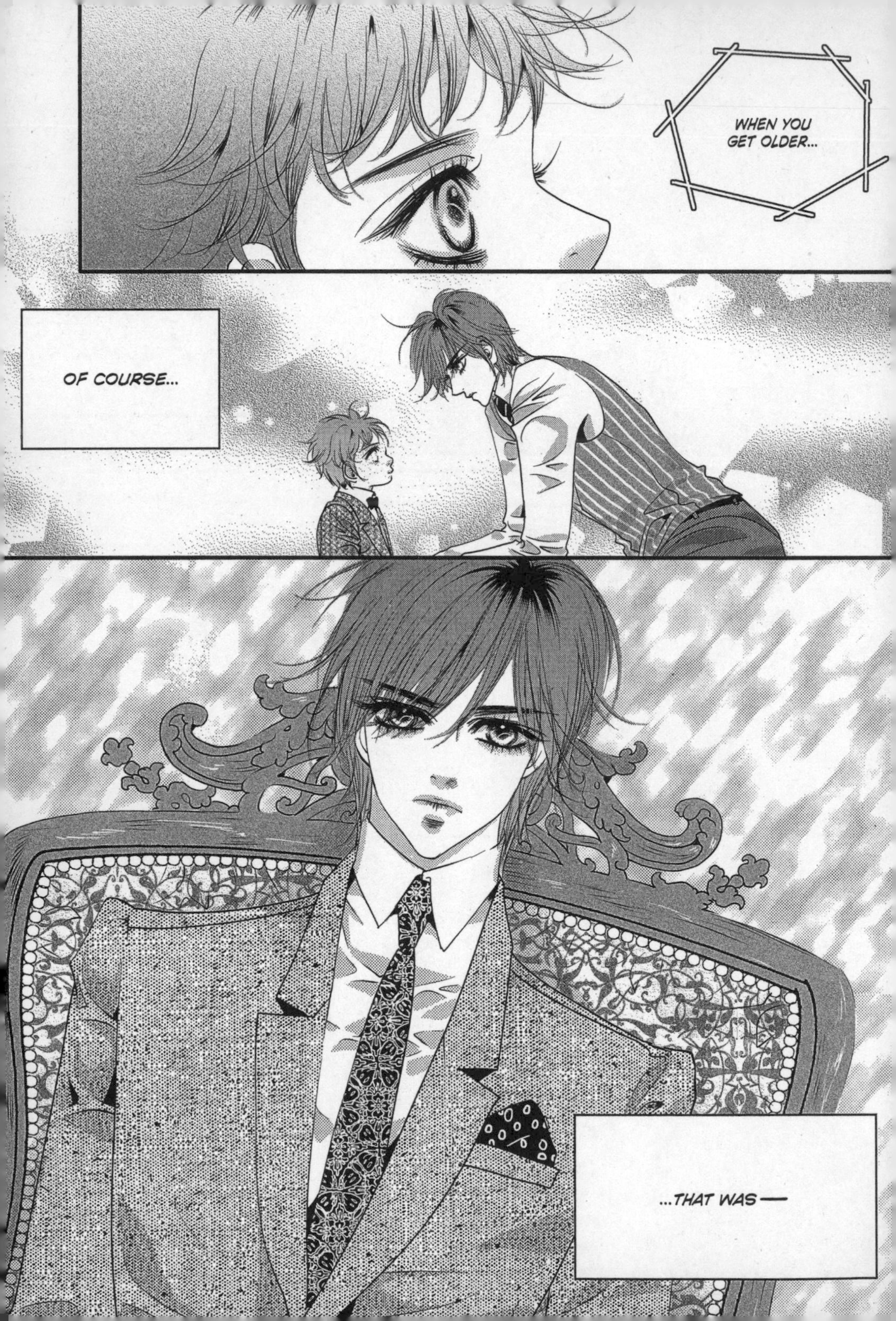
WHEN YOU GET OLDER...
OF COURSE...
...THAT WAS—

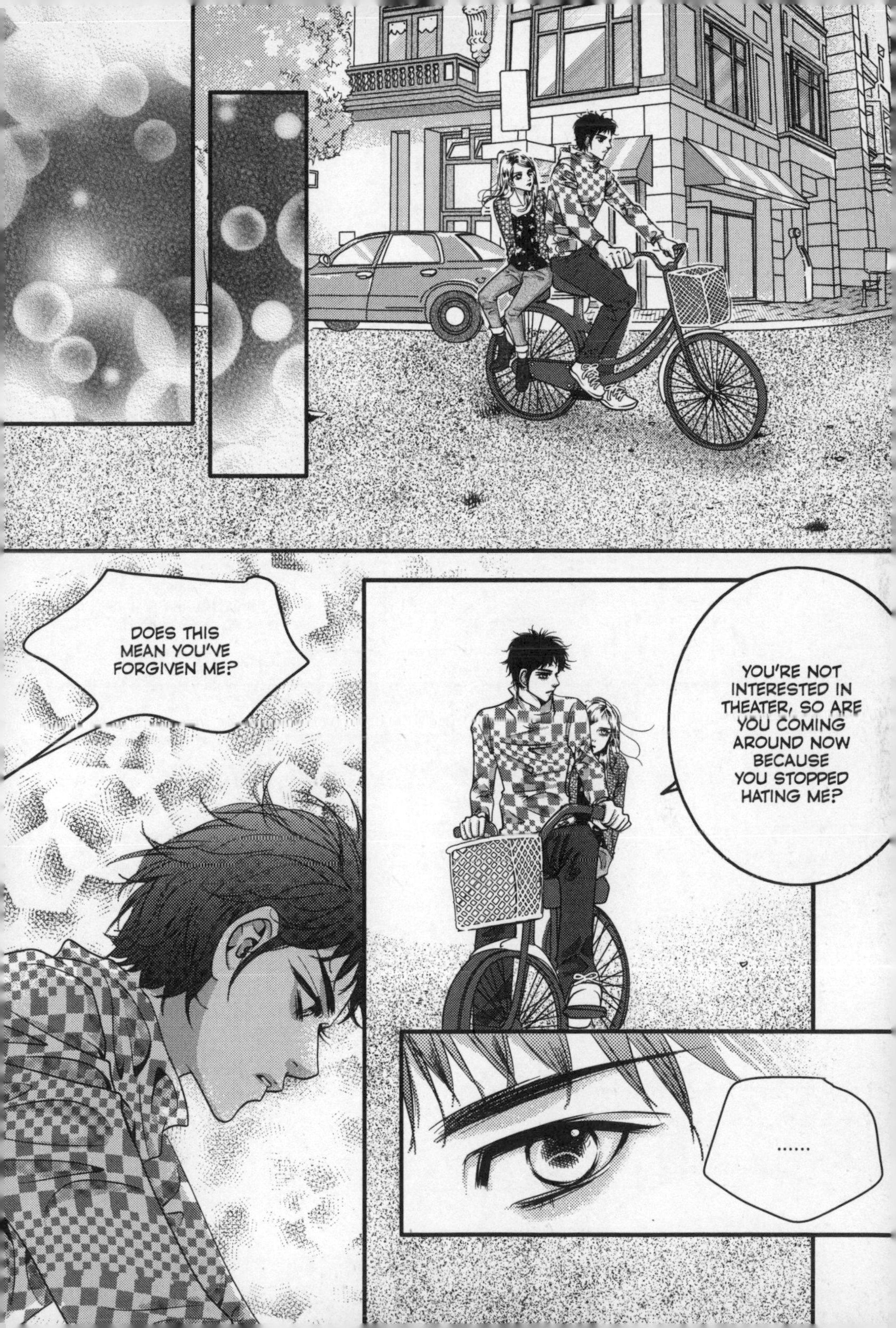
DOES THIS MEAN YOU'VE FORGIVEN ME?
YOU'RE NOT INTERESTED IN THEATER, SO ARE YOU COMING AROUND NOW BECAUSE YOU STOPPED HATING ME?
......

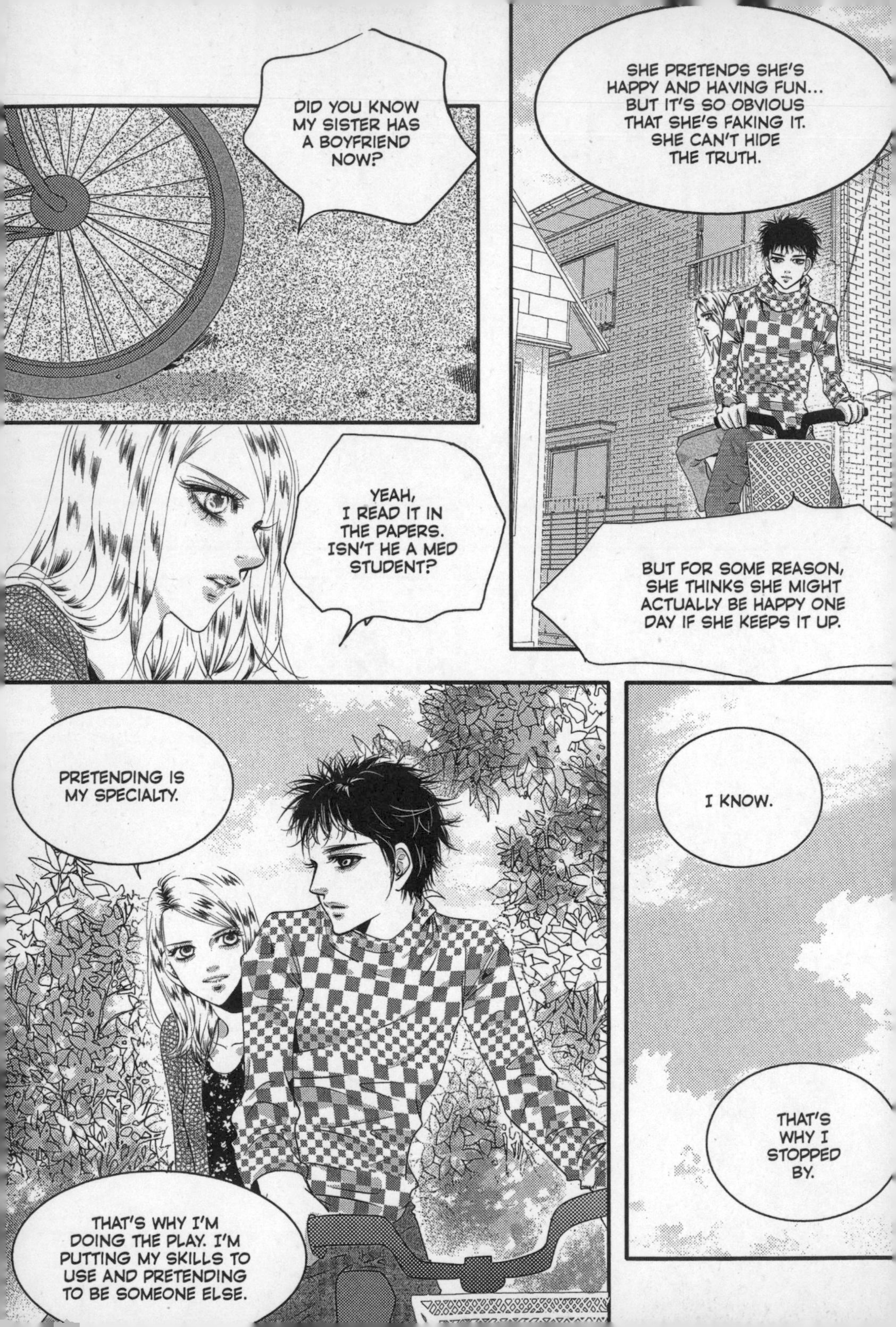
DID YOU KNOW MY SISTER HAS A BOYFRIEND NOW?
YEAH, I READ IT IN THE PAPERS. ISN'T HE A MED STUDENT?
SHE PRETENDS SHE'S HAPPY AND HAVING FUN... BUT IT'S SO OBVIOUS THAT SHE'S FAKING IT. SHE CAN'T HIDE THE TRUTH.
BUT FOR SOME REASON, SHE THINKS SHE MIGHT ACTUALLY BE HAPPY ONE DAY IF SHE KEEPS IT UP.
PRETENDING IS MY SPECIALTY.
THAT'S WHY I'M DOING THE PLAY. I'M PUTTING MY SKILLS TO USE AND PRETENDING TO BE SOMEONE ELSE.
I KNOW.
THAT'S WHY I STOPPED BY.

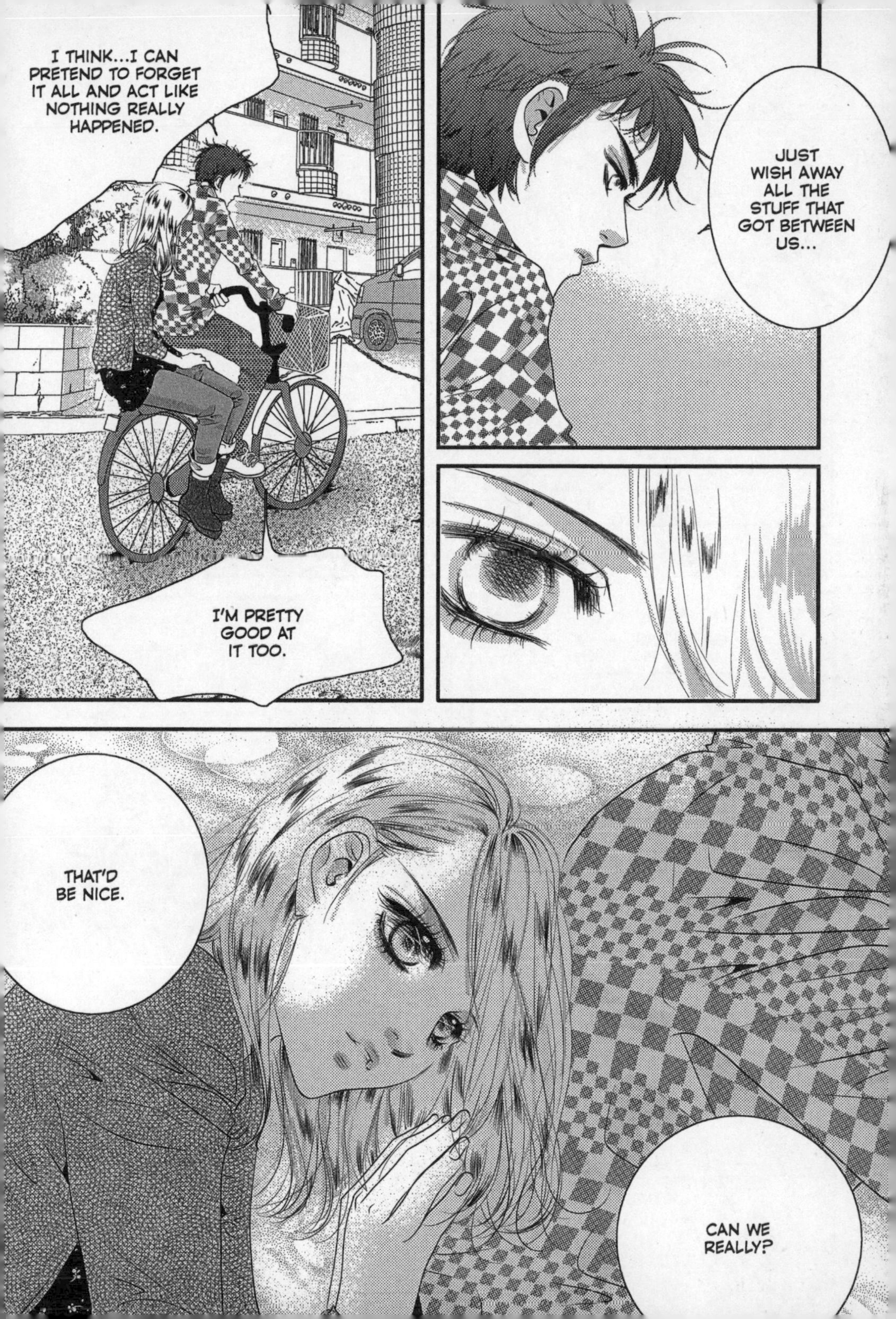
I THINK...I CAN PRETEND TO FORGET IT ALL AND ACT LIKE NOTHING REALLY HAPPENED.
I'M PRETTY GOOD AT IT TOO.
JUST WISH AWAY ALL THE STUFF THAT GOT BETWEEN US...
THAT'D BE NICE.
CAN WE REALLY?

WHY DID YOU LEAVE YOUR CAR AT SCHOOL?

MY FRIENDS ASKED ME TO PICK THEM UP 'COS THEY'D BEEN DRINKING.

BUT I ENDED UP DRINKING WITH THEM AND GOT DRUNK—— HA-HA-HA~!

THEN FIND YOUR CAR AND COME TO THE CLUBROOM. I'M GONNA GO SEE MYUNG-SOOK THERE.

OKAY~! SEE YOU SOON.

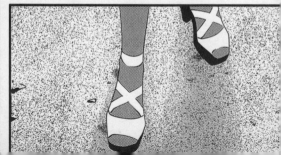

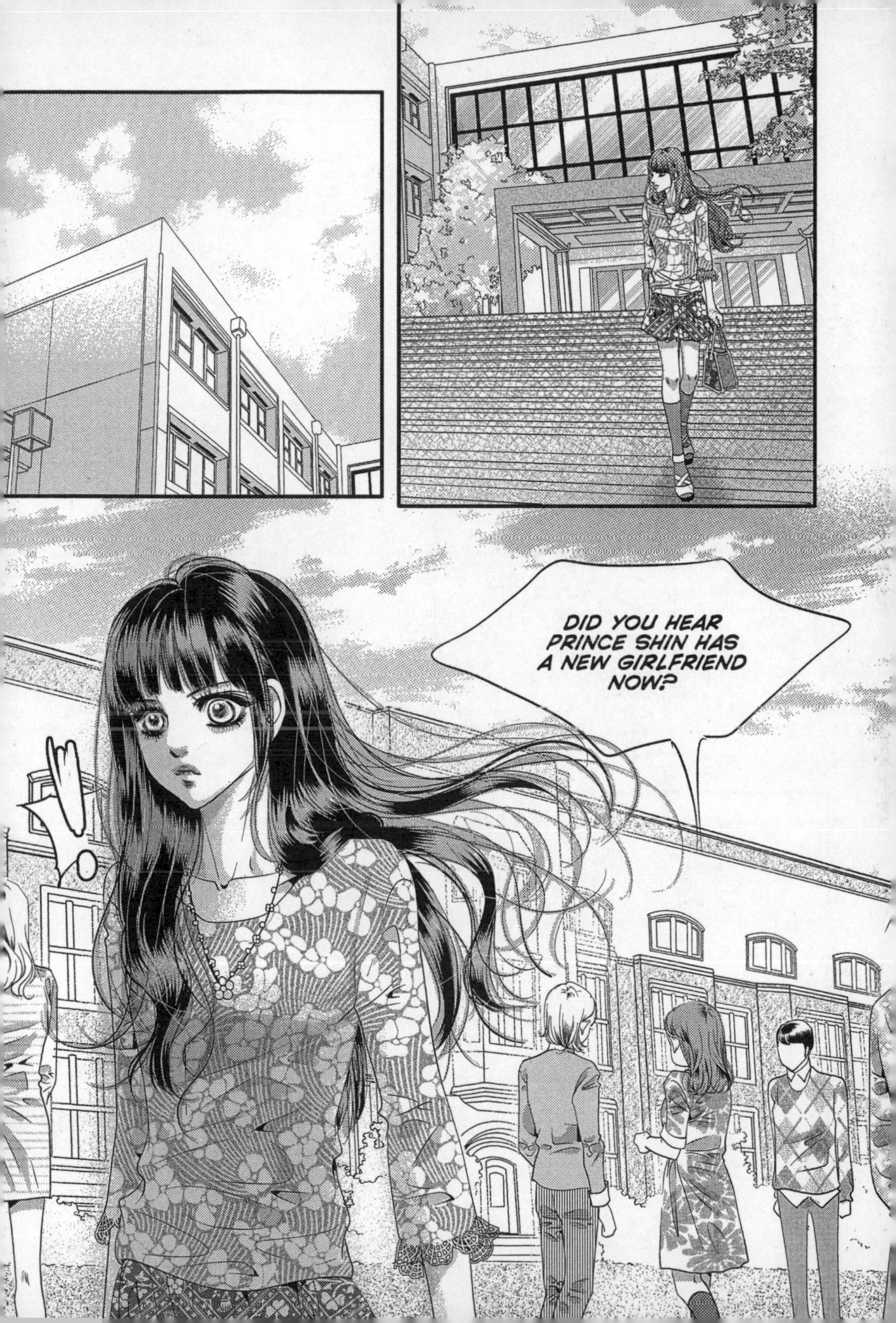
DID YOU HEAR PRINCE SHIN HAS A NEW GIRLFRIEND NOW?

APPARENTLY HE GOT DRUNK AND CALLED HER LAST NIGHT.

AWW, MAN~! I WAS HOPING HE'D DO A PUBLIC SEARCH SO I COULD APPLY~!

YOU'D BE DISQUALIFIED IN THE FIRST ROUND~!

HE TRIED TO HIDE IT, BUT PRINCE SUN SPILLED THE BEANS~! IT'S CRAZY~! TEE-HEE~!

THAT'S WHY...

...HE CHANGED HIS NUMBER.

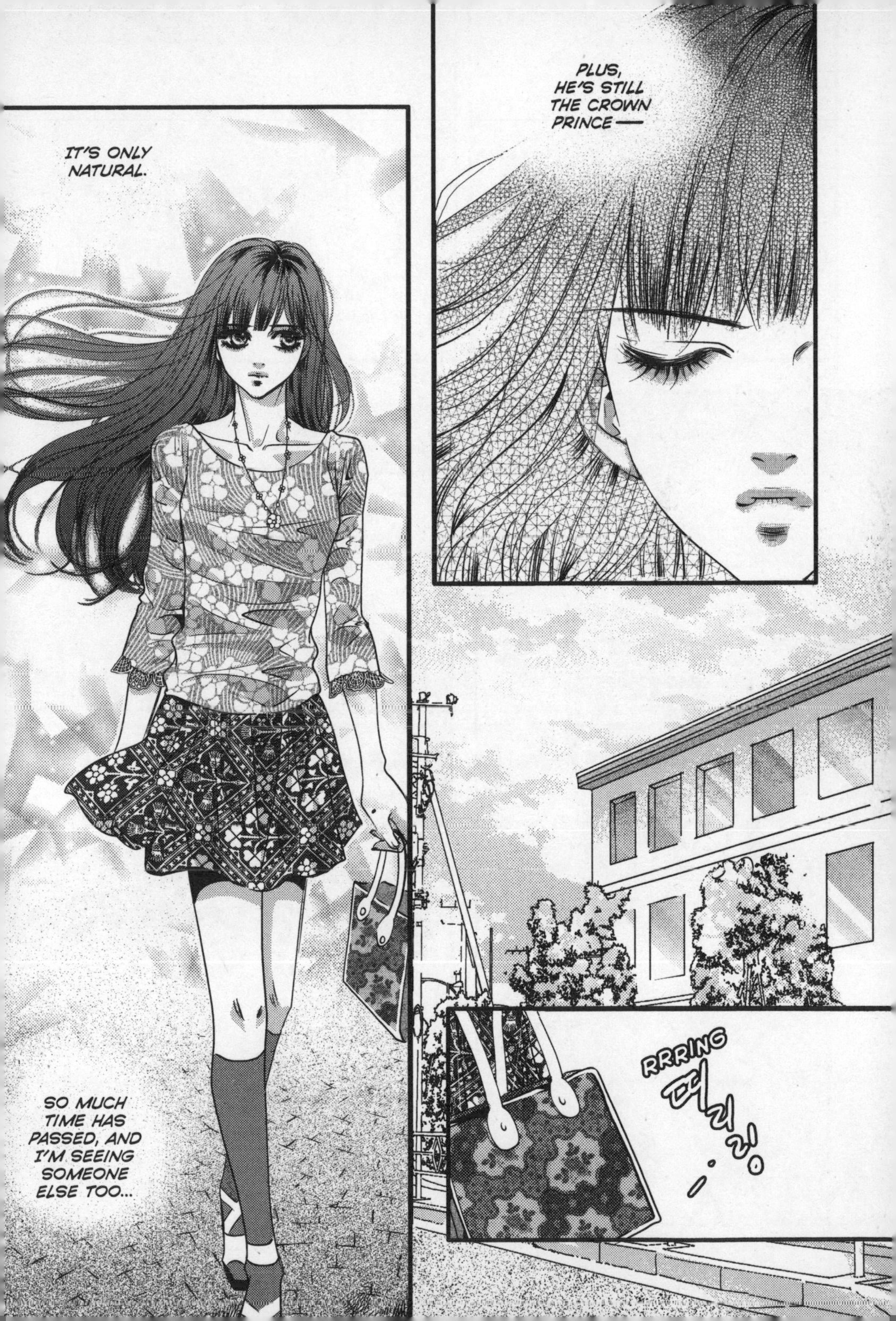
IT'S ONLY NATURAL.
SO MUCH TIME HAS PASSED, AND I'M SEEING SOMEONE ELSE TOO...
PLUS, HE'S STILL THE CROWN PRINCE—
RRRING

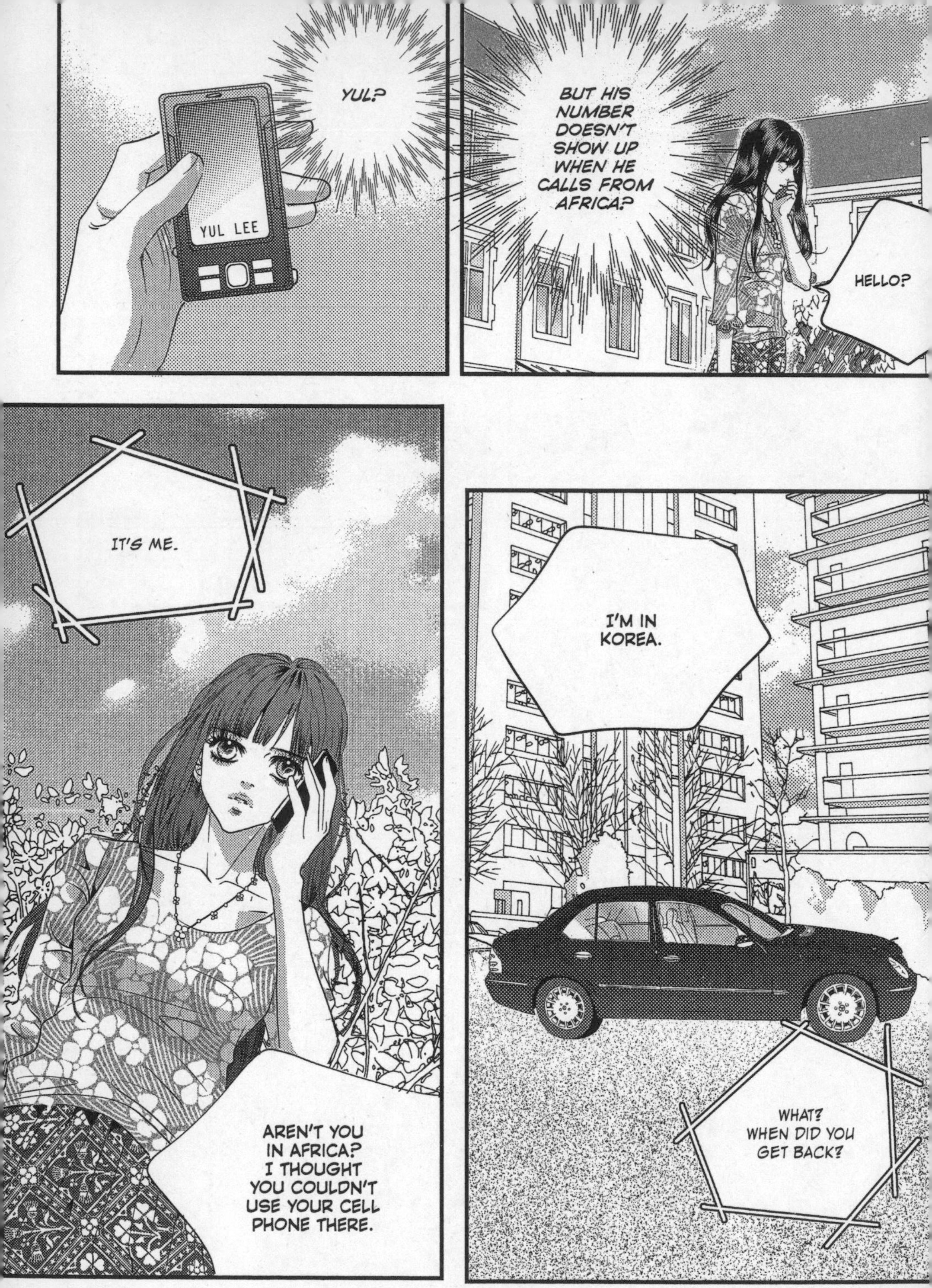
YUL LEE
YUL?
BUT HIS NUMBER DOESN'T SHOW UP WHEN HE CALLS FROM AFRICA?
HELLO?
IT'S ME.
AREN'T YOU IN AFRICA? I THOUGHT YOU COULDN'T USE YOUR CELL PHONE THERE.
I'M IN KOREA.
WHAT? WHEN DID YOU GET BACK?

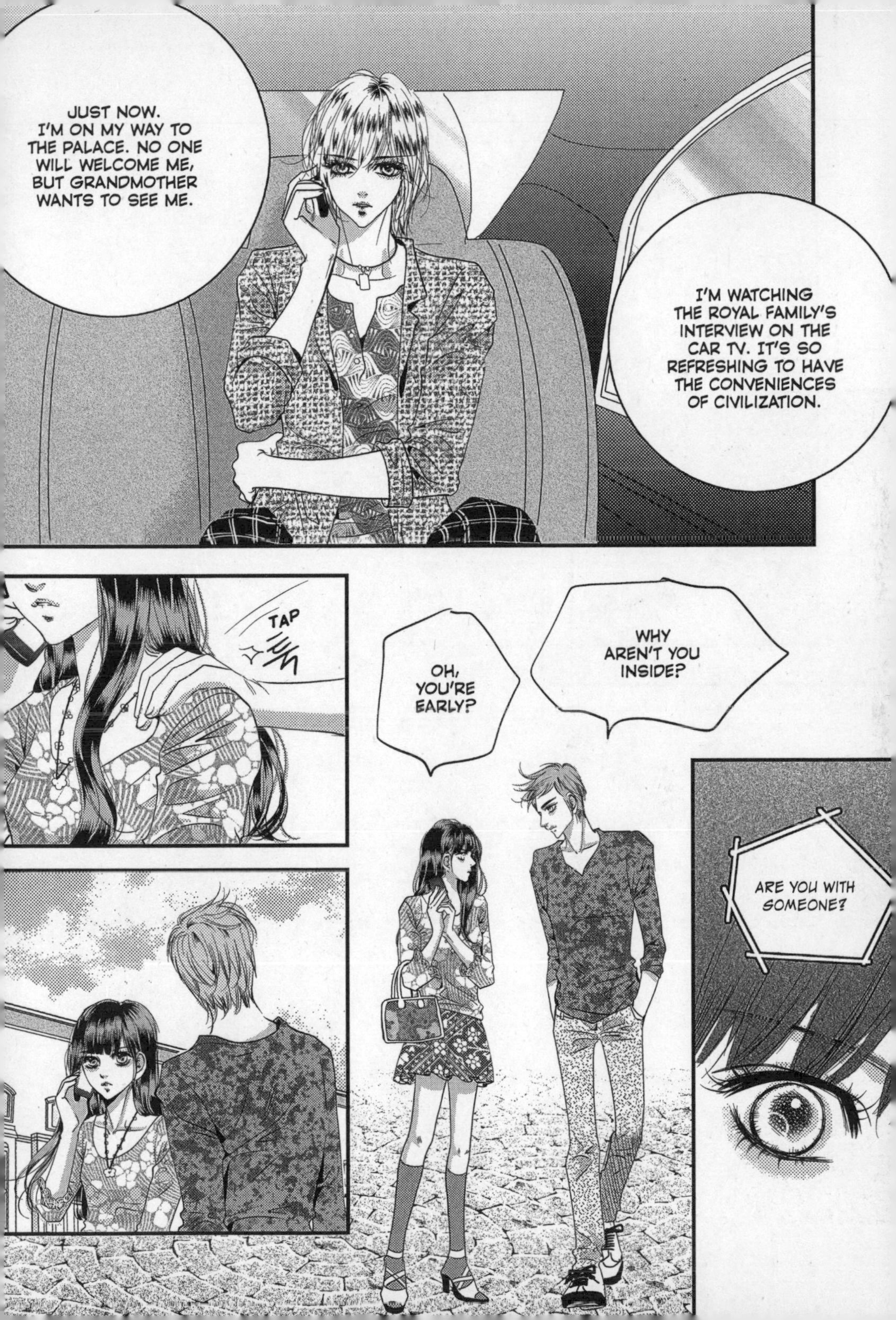
JUST NOW. I'M ON MY WAY TO THE PALACE. NO ONE WILL WELCOME ME, BUT GRANDMOTHER WANTS TO SEE ME.
I'M WATCHING THE ROYAL FAMILY'S INTERVIEW ON THE CAR TV. IT'S SO REFRESHING TO HAVE THE CONVENIENCES OF CIVILIZATION.
TAP
OH, YOU'RE EARLY?
WHY AREN'T YOU INSIDE?
ARE YOU WITH SOMEONE?

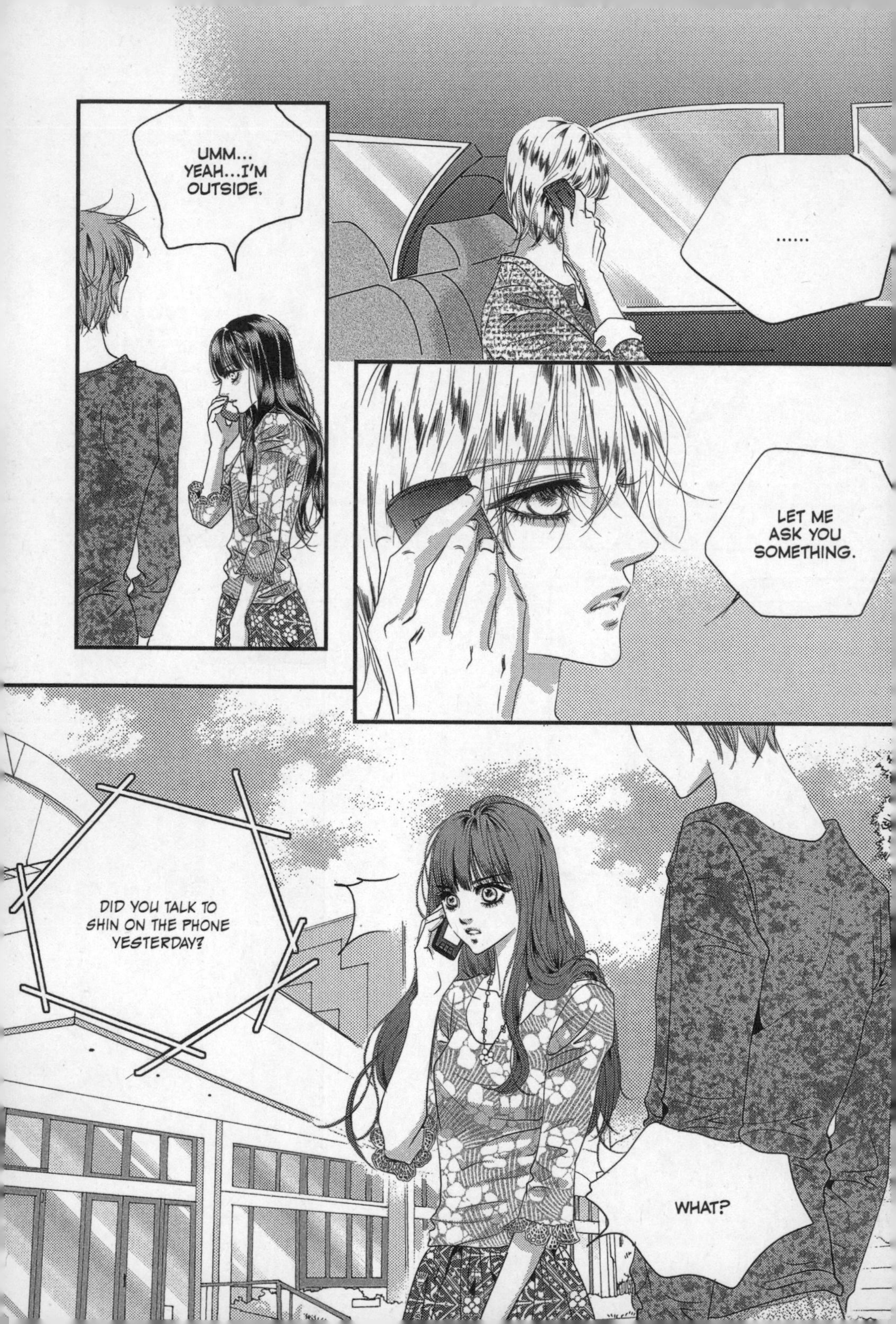
UMM... YEAH...I'M OUTSIDE.
......
LET ME ASK YOU SOMETHING.
DID YOU TALK TO SHIN ON THE PHONE YESTERDAY?
WHAT?

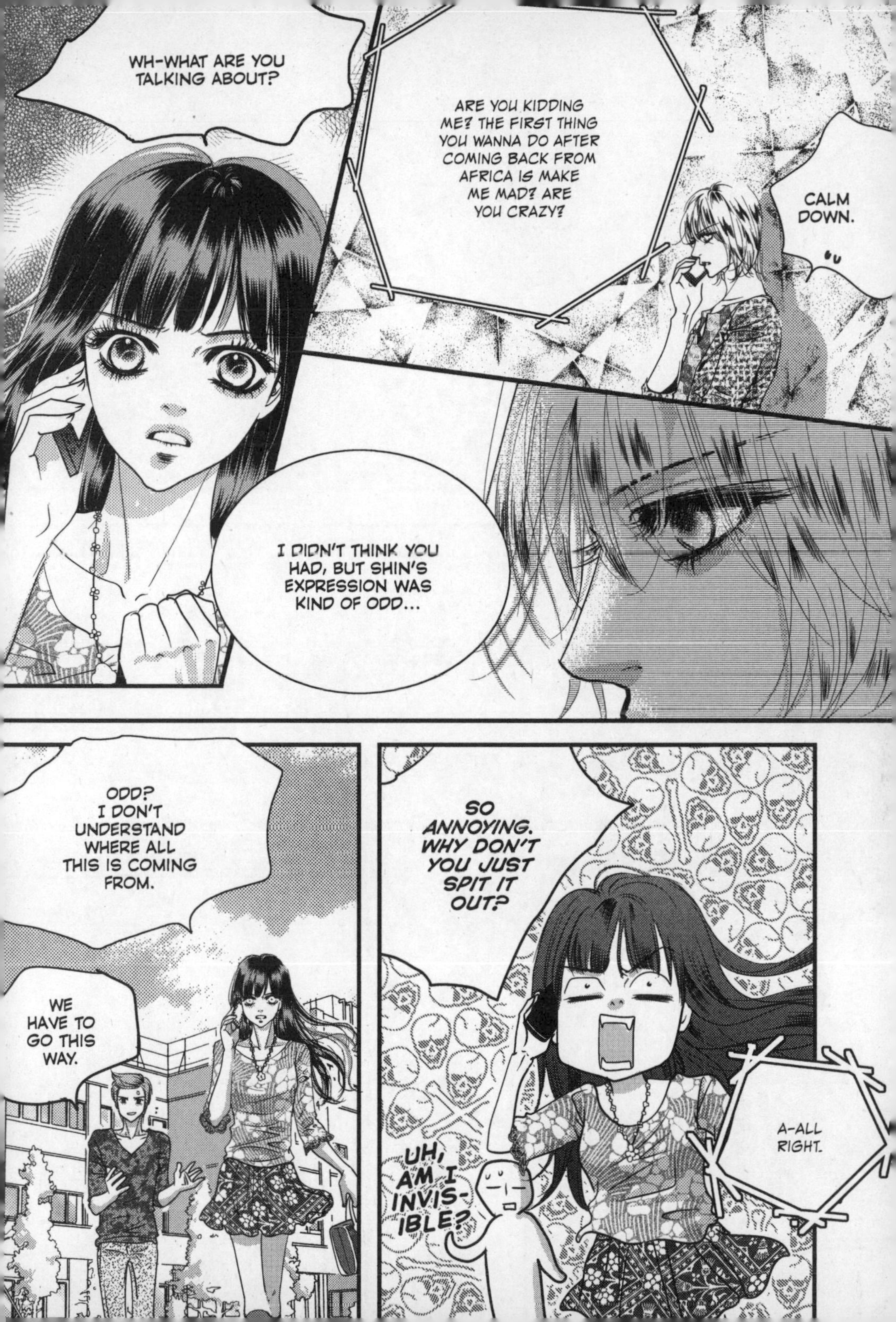
WH-WHAT ARE YOU TALKING ABOUT?
ARE YOU KIDDING ME? THE FIRST THING YOU WANNA DO AFTER COMING BACK FROM AFRICA IS MAKE ME MAD? ARE YOU CRAZY?
CALM DOWN.
I DIDN'T THINK YOU HAD, BUT SHIN'S EXPRESSION WAS KIND OF ODD...
ODD? I DON'T UNDERSTAND WHERE ALL THIS IS COMING FROM.
WE HAVE TO GO THIS WAY.
SO ANNOYING. WHY DON'T YOU JUST SPIT IT OUT?
UH, AM I INVIS-IBLE?
A-ALL RIGHT.

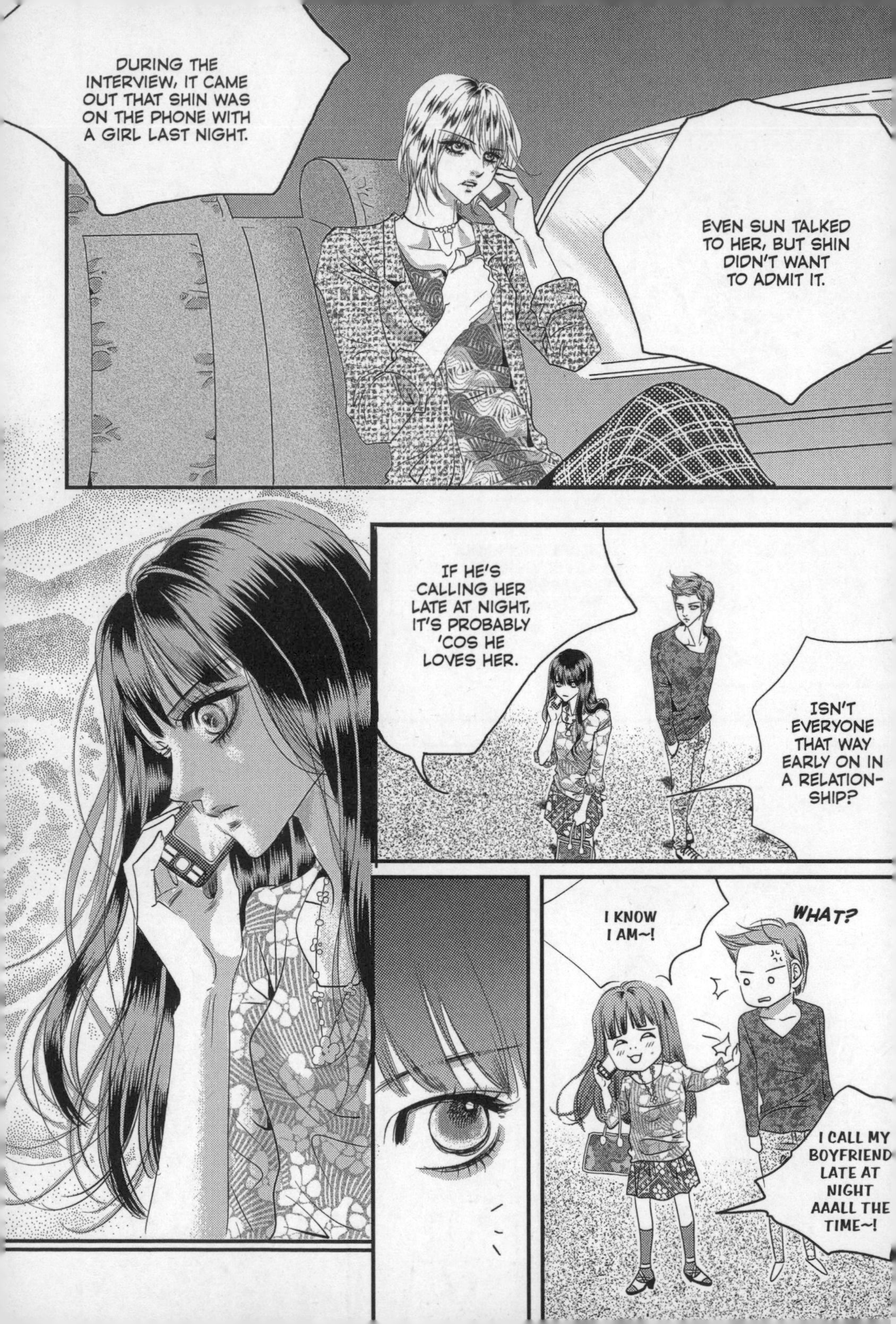
DURING THE INTERVIEW, IT CAME OUT THAT SHIN WAS ON THE PHONE WITH A GIRL LAST NIGHT.
EVEN SUN TALKED TO HER, BUT SHIN DIDN'T WANT TO ADMIT IT.
IF HE'S CALLING HER LATE AT NIGHT, IT'S PROBABLY 'COS HE LOVES HER.
ISN'T EVERYONE THAT WAY EARLY ON IN A RELATION-SHIP?
I KNOW I AM~!
WHAT?
I CALL MY BOYFRIEND LATE AT NIGHT AAALL THE TIME~!

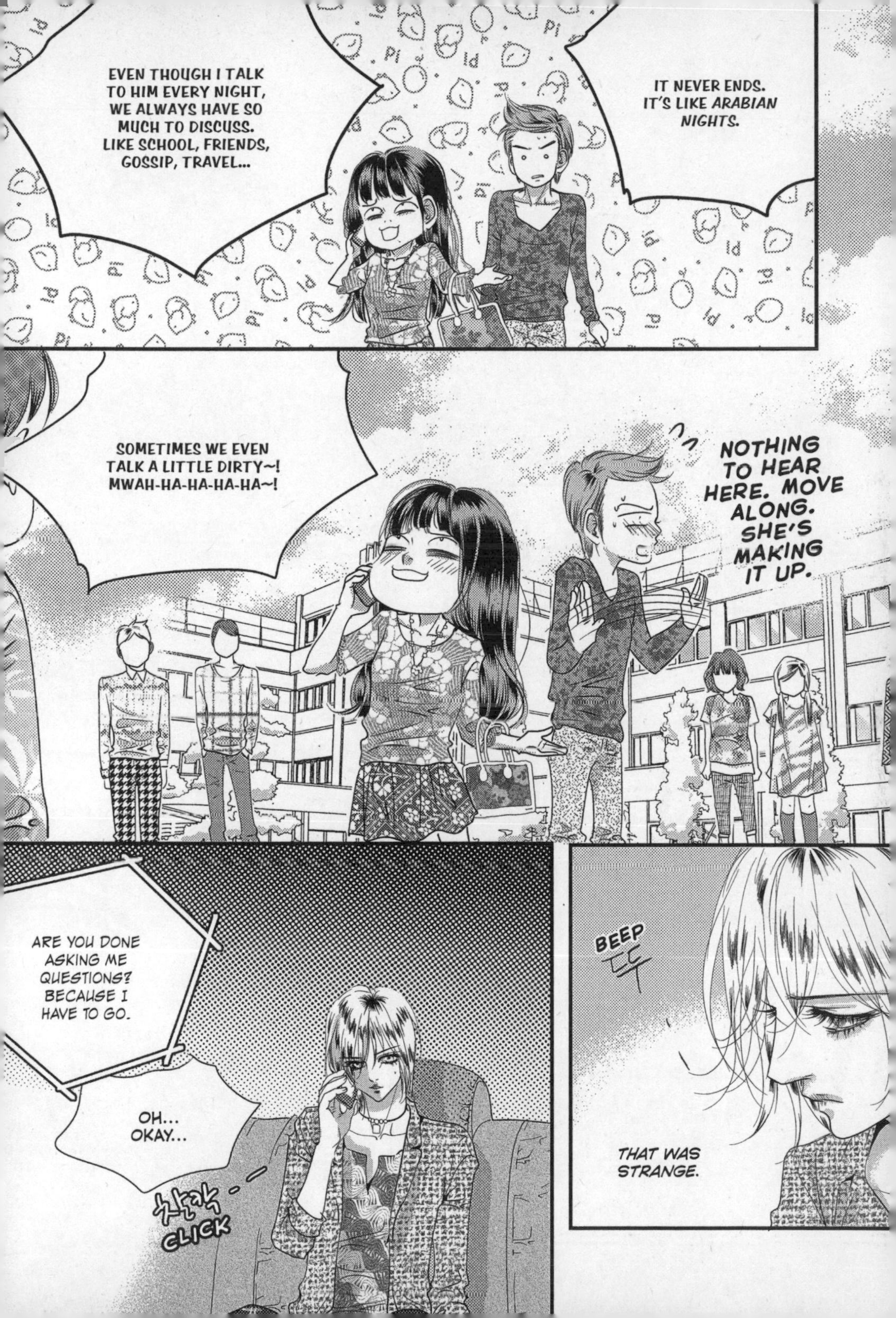
EVEN THOUGH I TALK TO HIM EVERY NIGHT, WE ALWAYS HAVE SO MUCH TO DISCUSS. LIKE SCHOOL, FRIENDS, GOSSIP, TRAVEL...
IT NEVER ENDS. IT'S LIKE *ARABIAN NIGHTS.*
SOMETIMES WE EVEN TALK A LITTLE DIRTY~! MWAH-HA-HA-HA-HA~!
NOTHING TO HEAR HERE. MOVE ALONG. SHE'S MAKING IT UP.
ARE YOU DONE ASKING ME QUESTIONS? BECAUSE I HAVE TO GO.
OH... OKAY...
찰칵
CLICK
BEEP
THAT WAS STRANGE.

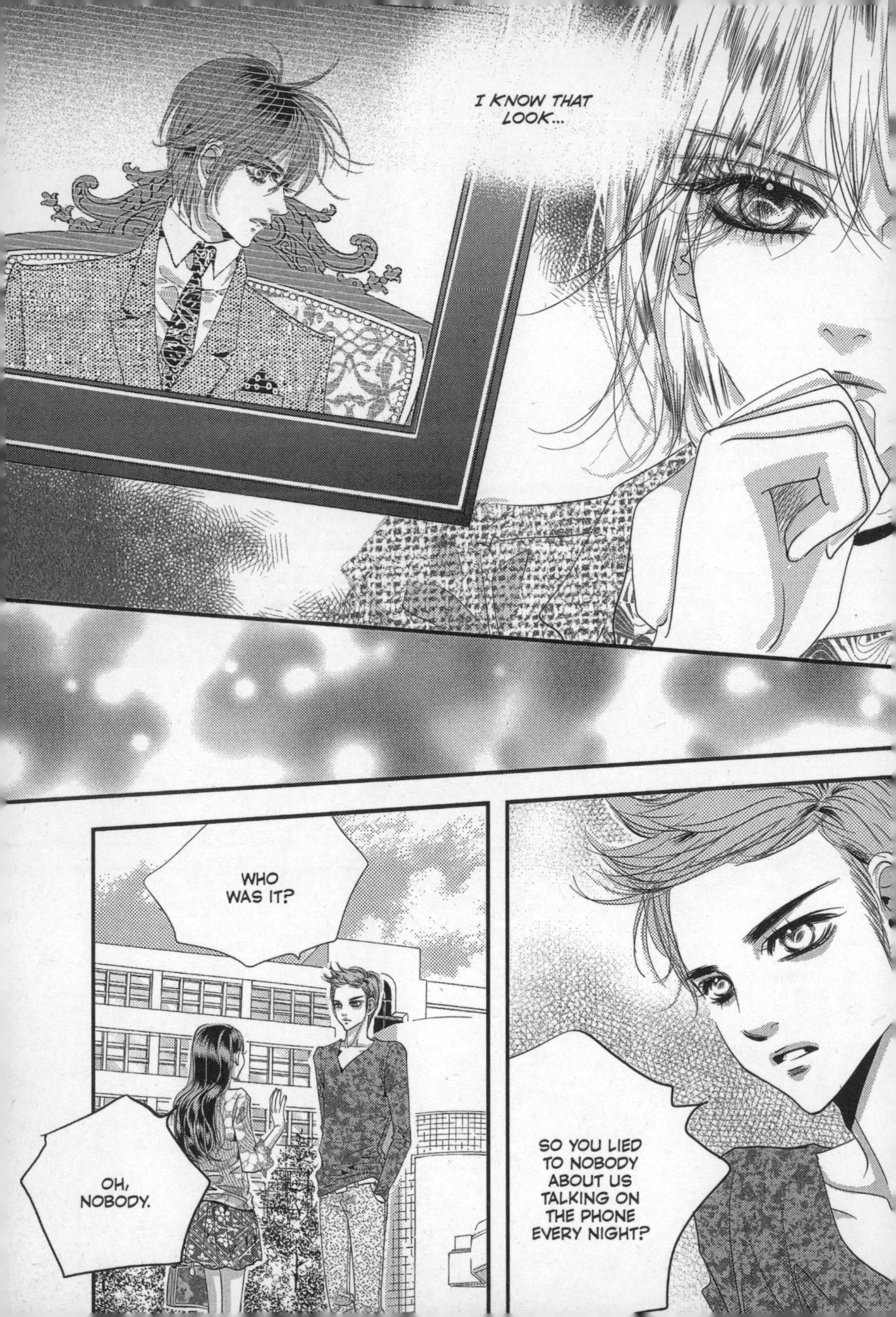
I KNOW THAT LOOK...
WHO WAS IT?
OH, NOBODY.
SO YOU LIED TO NOBODY ABOUT US TALKING ON THE PHONE EVERY NIGHT?

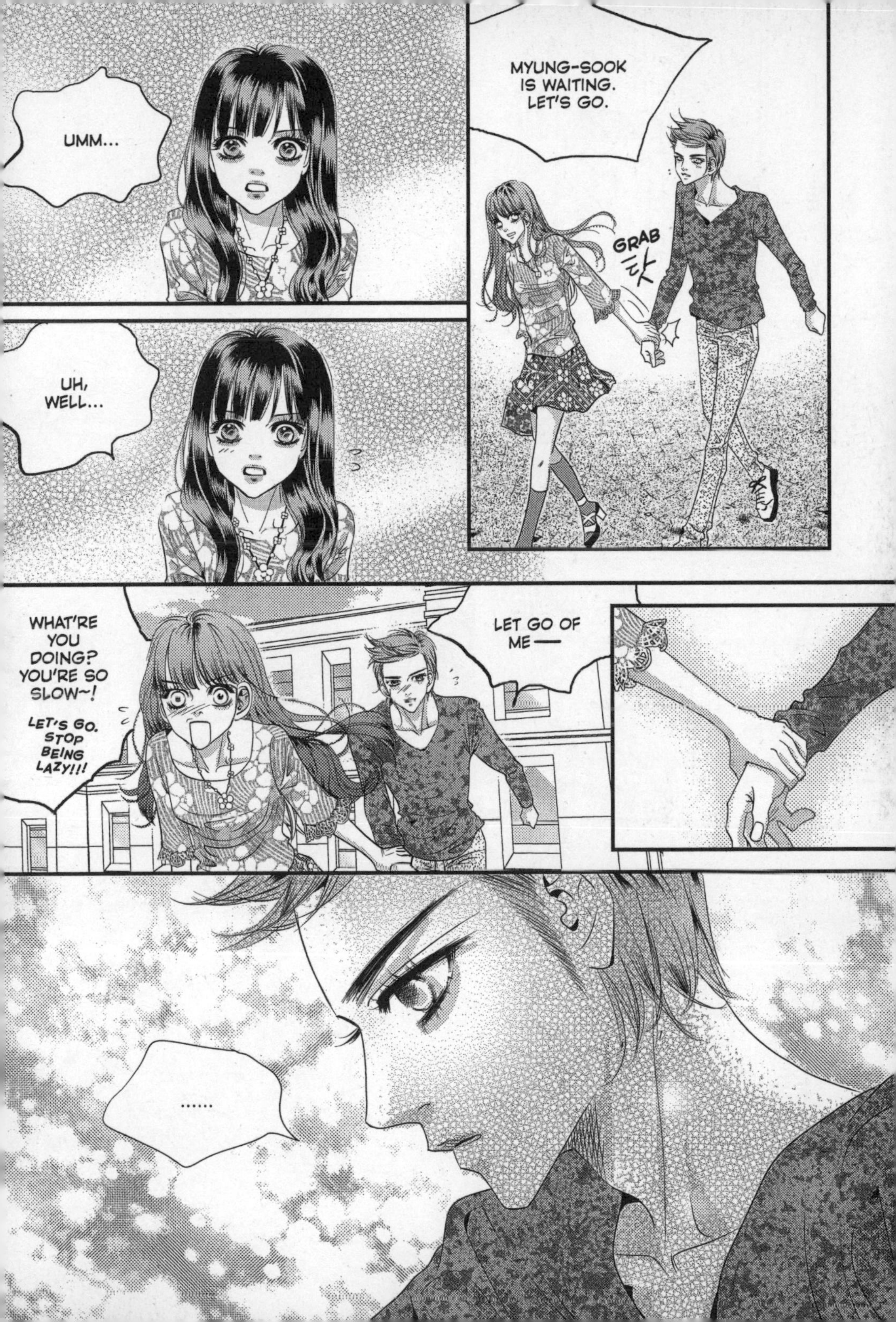
UMM...
UH, WELL...
MYUNG-SOOK IS WAITING. LET'S GO.
GRAB
WHAT'RE YOU DOING? YOU'RE SO SLOW~!
LET'S GO. STOP BEING LAZY!!!
LET GO OF ME—
......

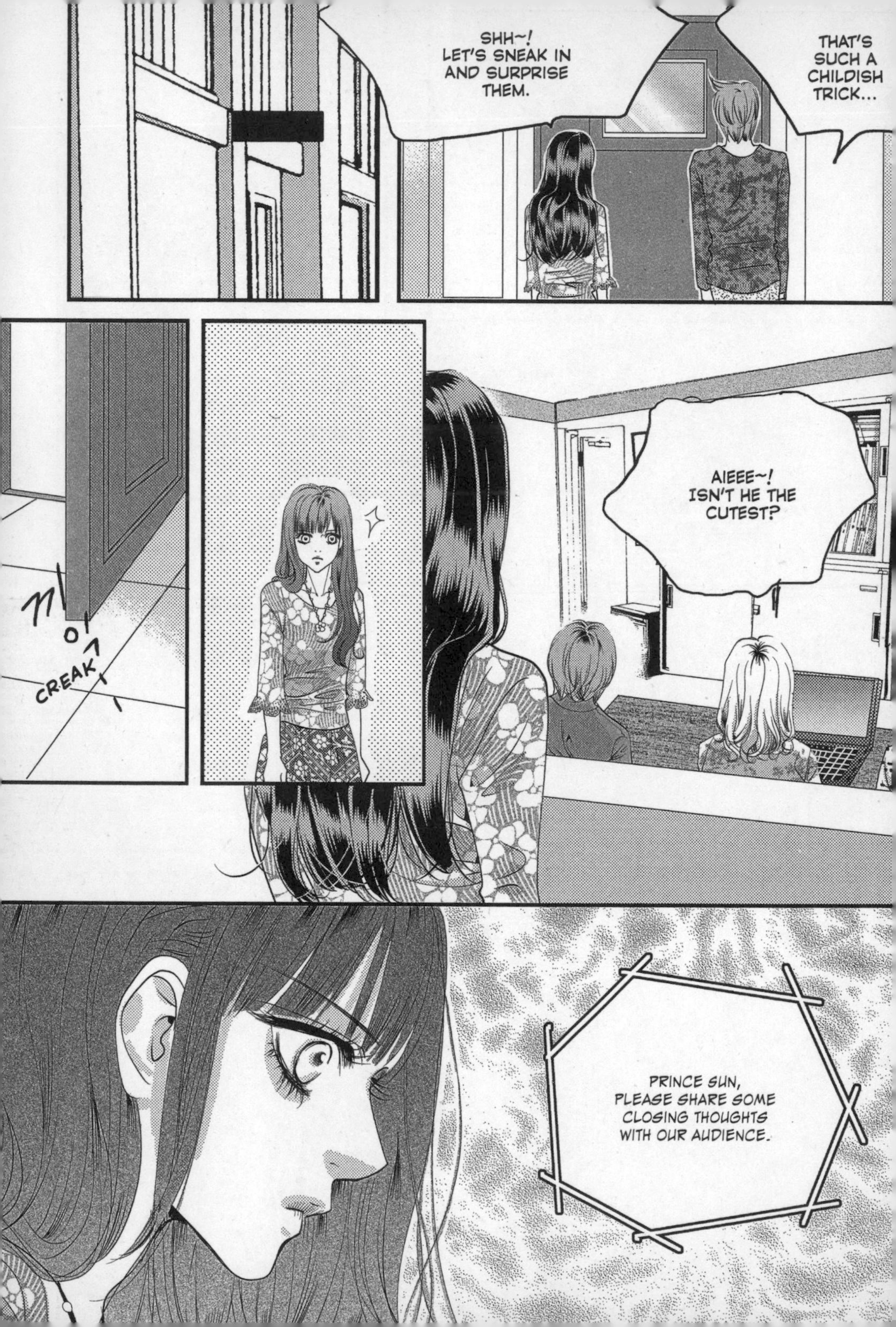
SHH~! LET'S SNEAK IN AND SURPRISE THEM.
THAT'S SUCH A CHILDISH TRICK...
CREAK
AIEEE~! ISN'T HE THE CUTEST?
PRINCE SUN, PLEASE SHARE SOME CLOSING THOUGHTS WITH OUR AUDIENCE.

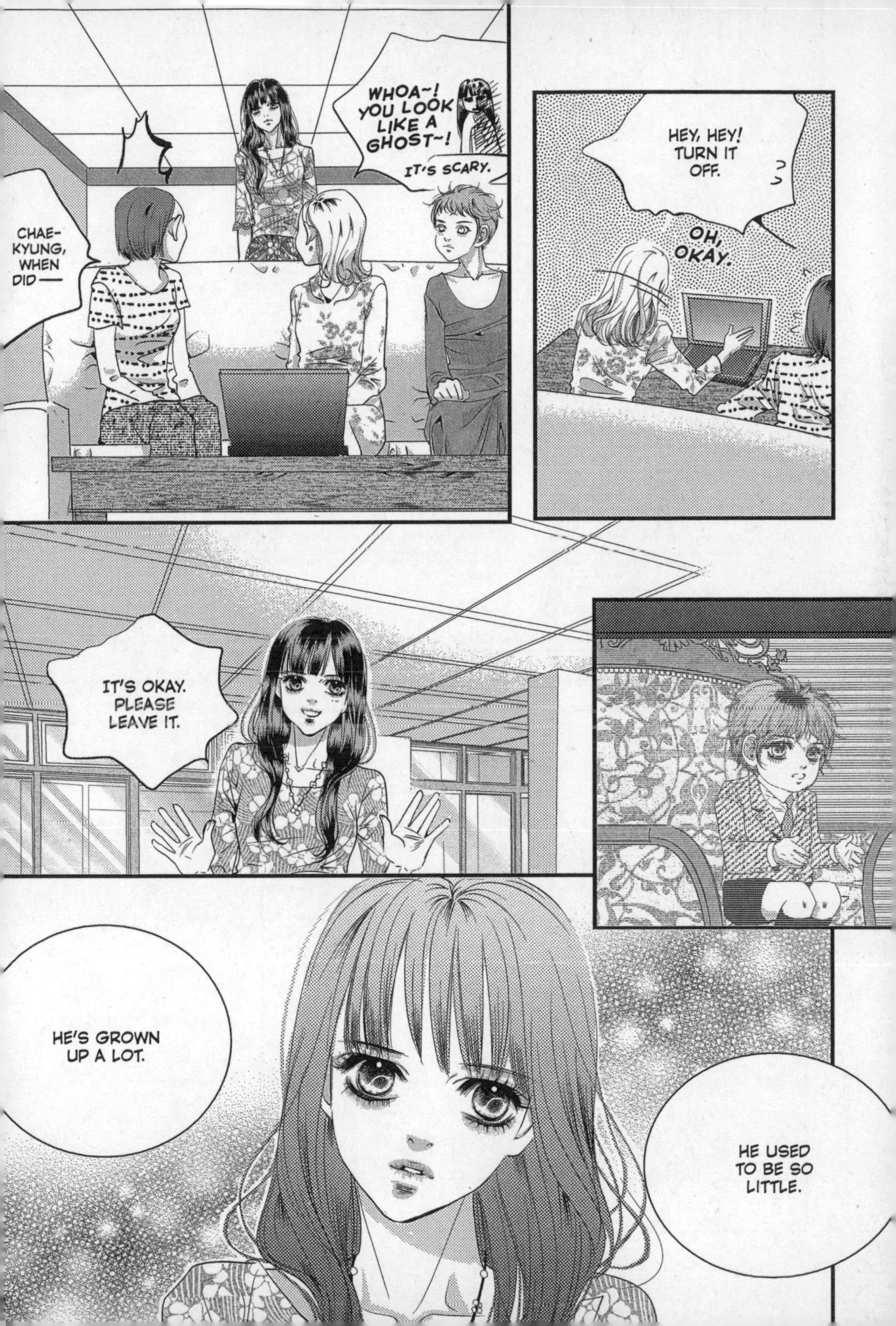
CHAE-KYUNG, WHEN DID—
WHOA~! YOU LOOK LIKE A GHOST~!
IT'S SCARY.
HEY, HEY! TURN IT OFF.
OH, OKAY.
IT'S OKAY. PLEASE LEAVE IT.
HE'S GROWN UP A LOT.
HE USED TO BE SO LITTLE.

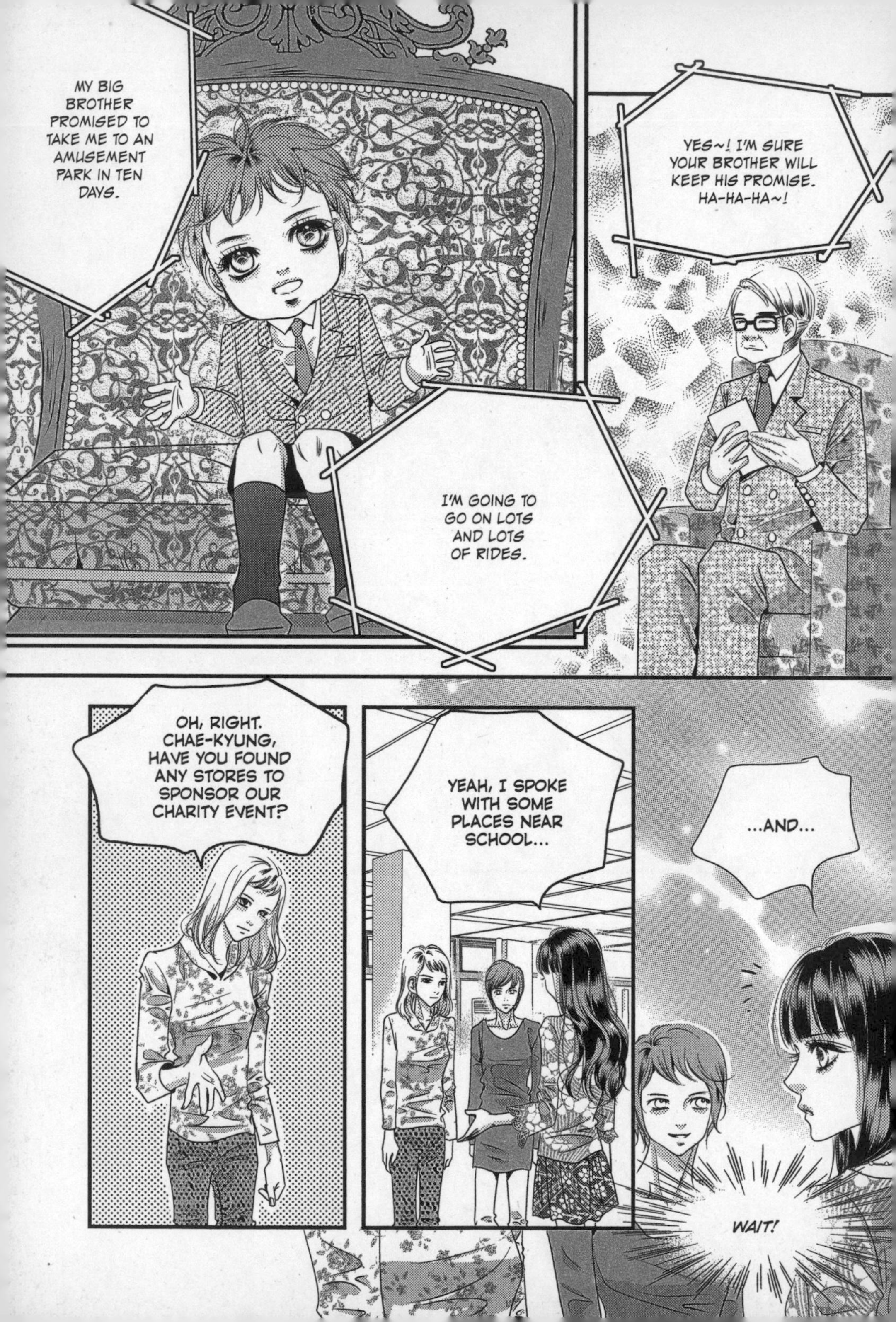
MY BIG BROTHER PROMISED TO TAKE ME TO AN AMUSEMENT PARK IN TEN DAYS.
YES~! I'M SURE YOUR BROTHER WILL KEEP HIS PROMISE. HA-HA-HA~!
I'M GOING TO GO ON LOTS AND LOTS OF RIDES.
OH, RIGHT. CHAE-KYUNG, HAVE YOU FOUND ANY STORES TO SPONSOR OUR CHARITY EVENT?
YEAH, I SPOKE WITH SOME PLACES NEAR SCHOOL...
...AND...
WAIT!

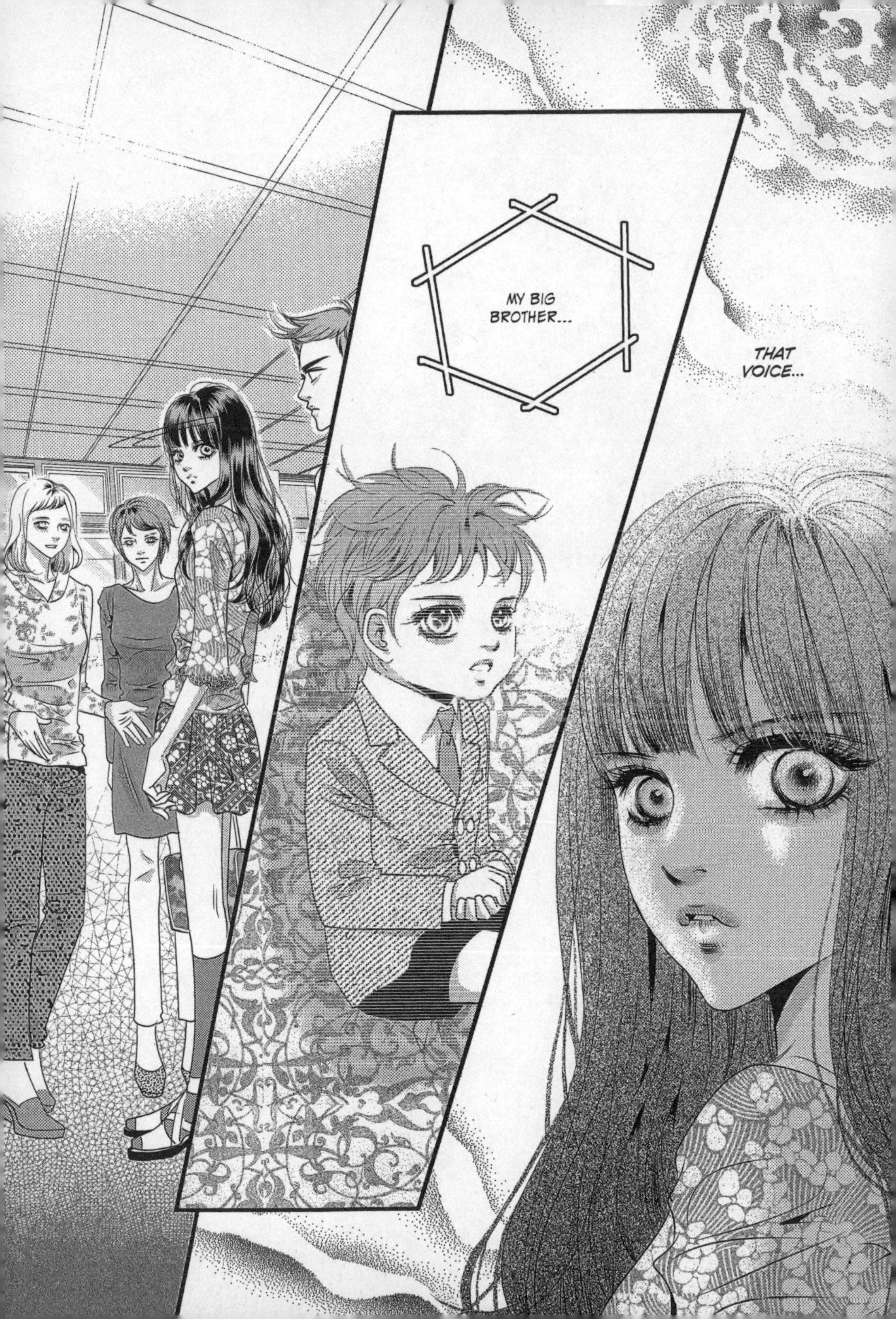
MY BIG
BROTHER...
THAT
VOICE...

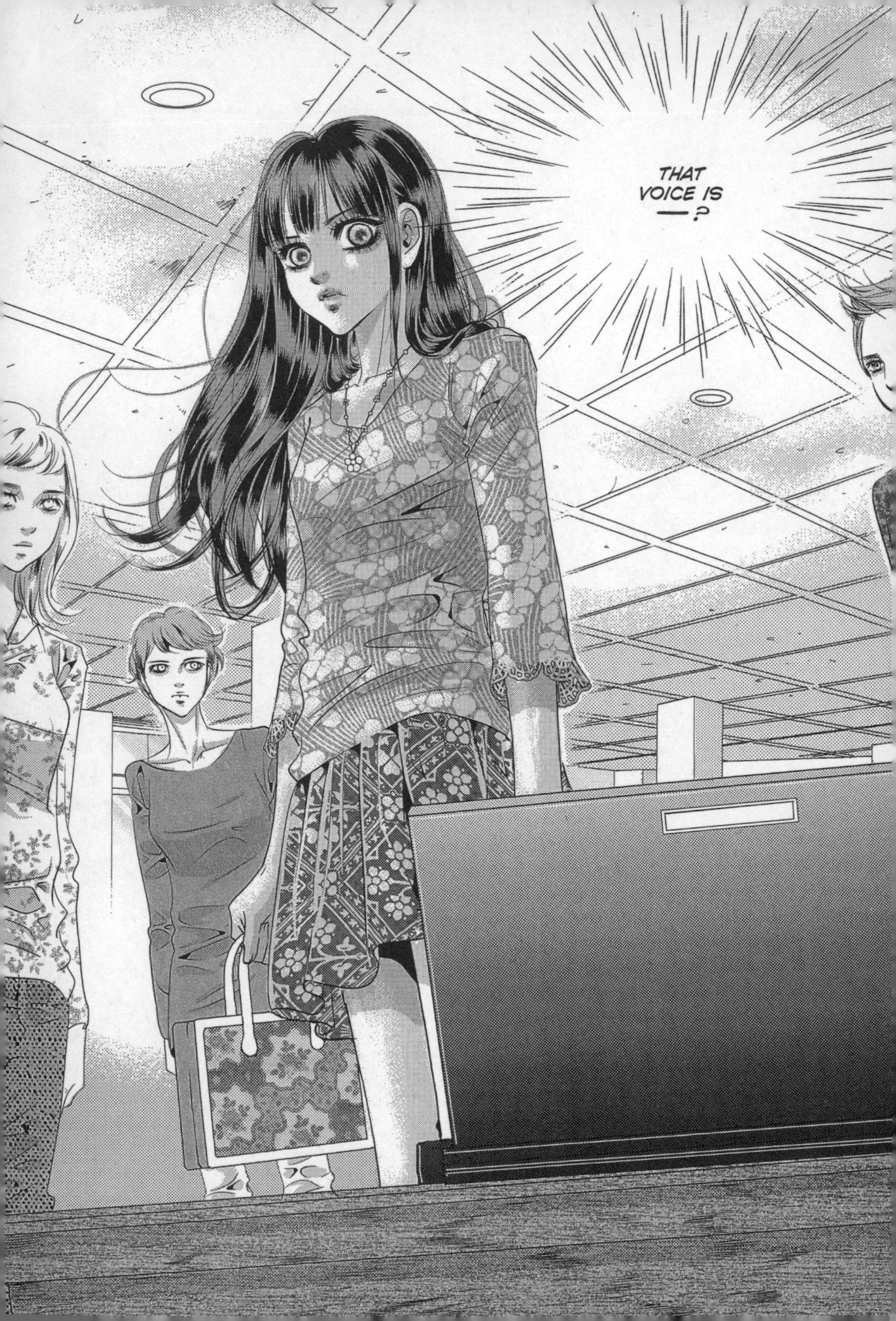
THAT VOICE IS —?

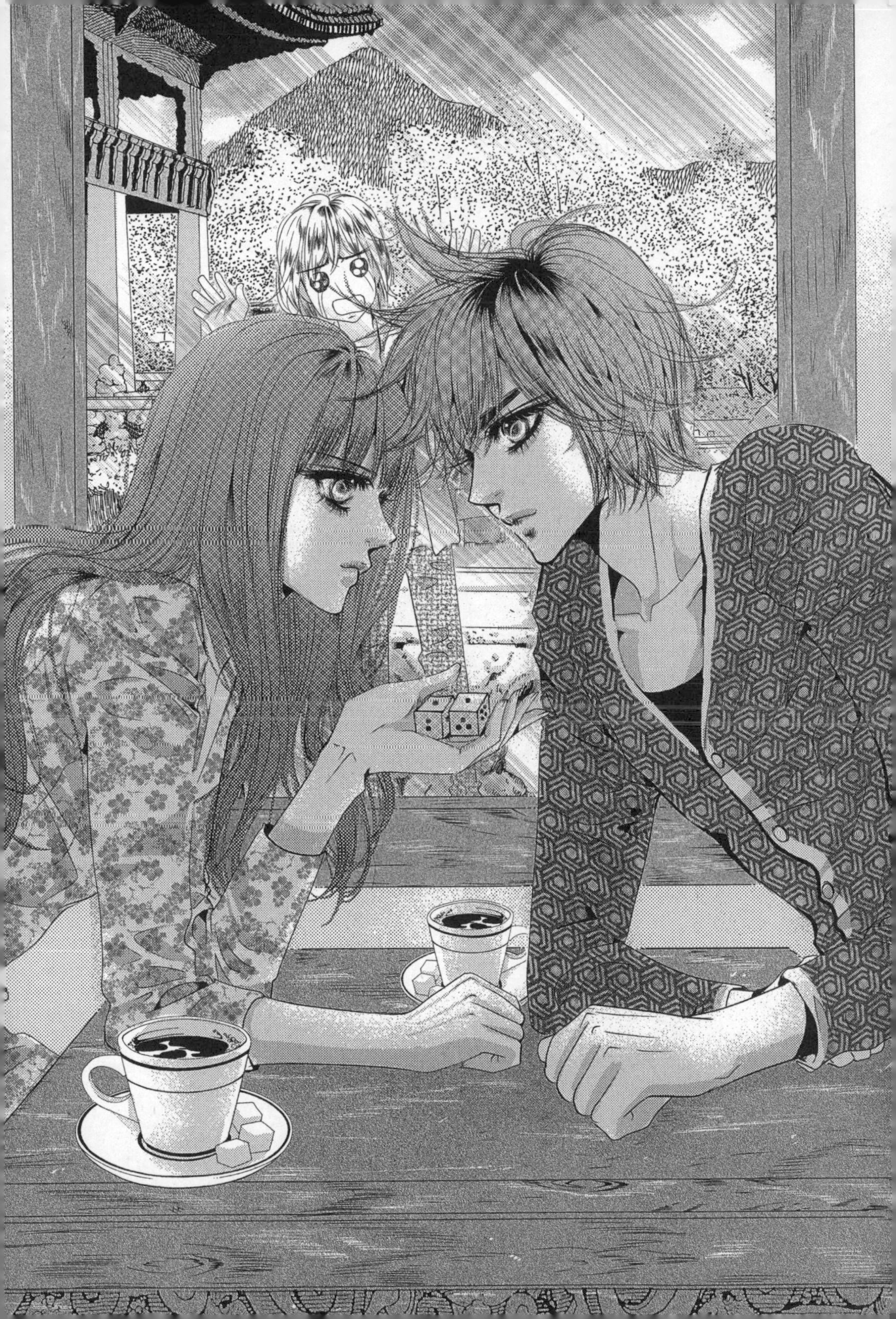

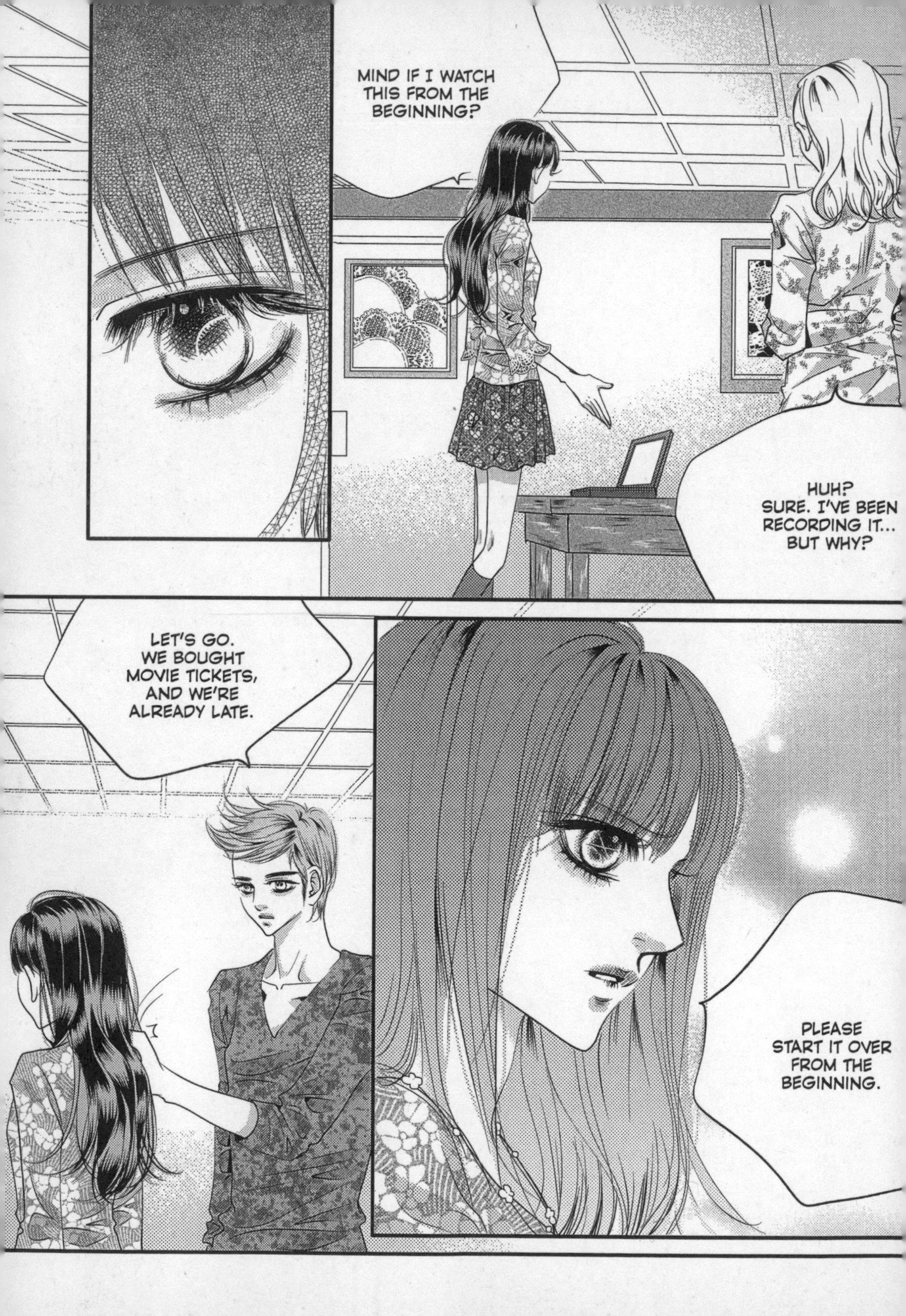
MIND IF I WATCH THIS FROM THE BEGINNING?
HUH? SURE. I'VE BEEN RECORDING IT... BUT WHY?
PLEASE START IT OVER FROM THE BEGINNING.
LET'S GO. WE BOUGHT MOVIE TICKETS, AND WE'RE ALREADY LATE.

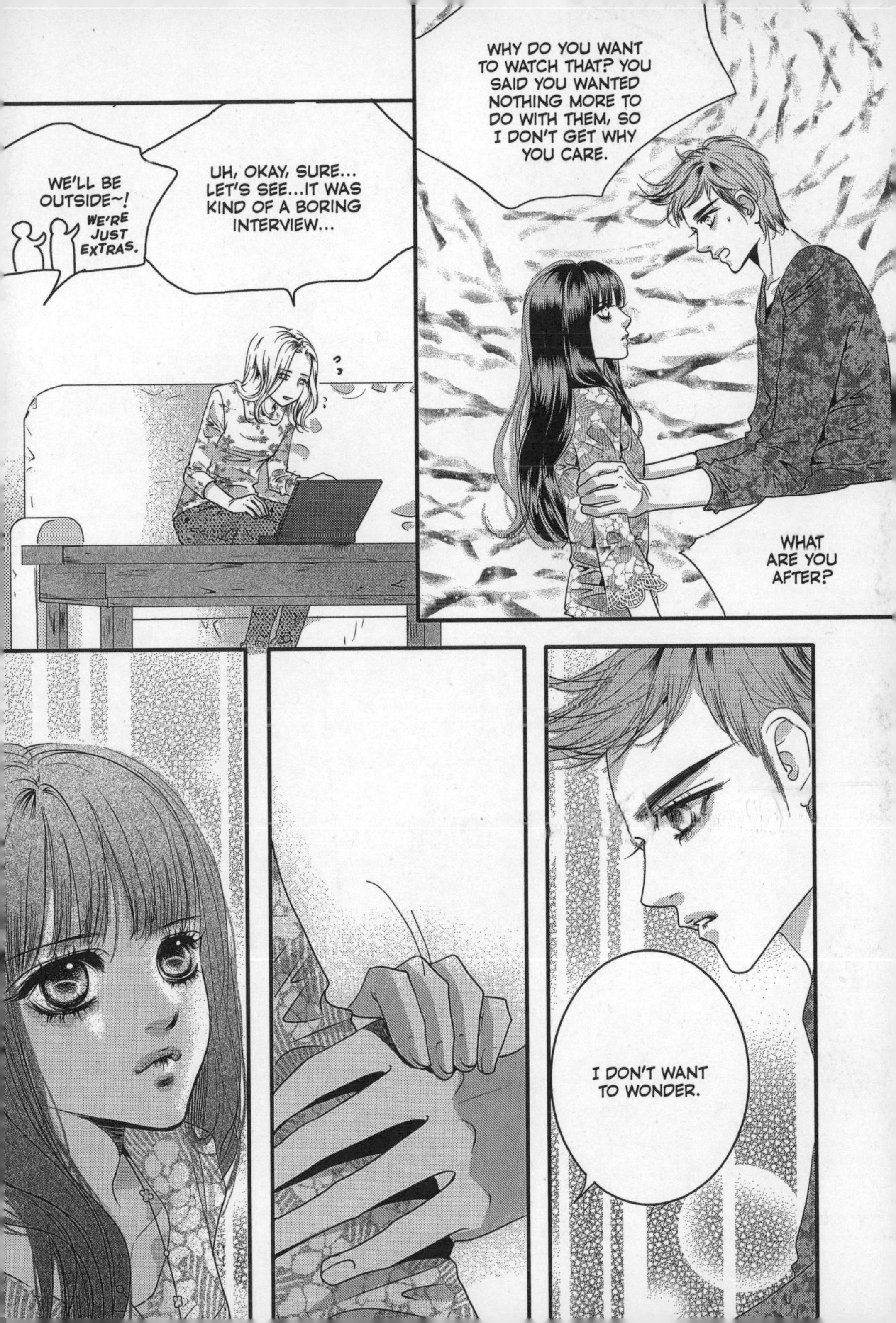
WE'LL BE OUTSIDE~!
WE'RE JUST EXTRAS.
UH, OKAY, SURE... LET'S SEE...IT WAS KIND OF A BORING INTERVIEW...
WHY DO YOU WANT TO WATCH THAT? YOU SAID YOU WANTED NOTHING MORE TO DO WITH THEM, SO I DON'T GET WHY YOU CARE.
WHAT ARE YOU AFTER?
I DON'T WANT TO WONDER.

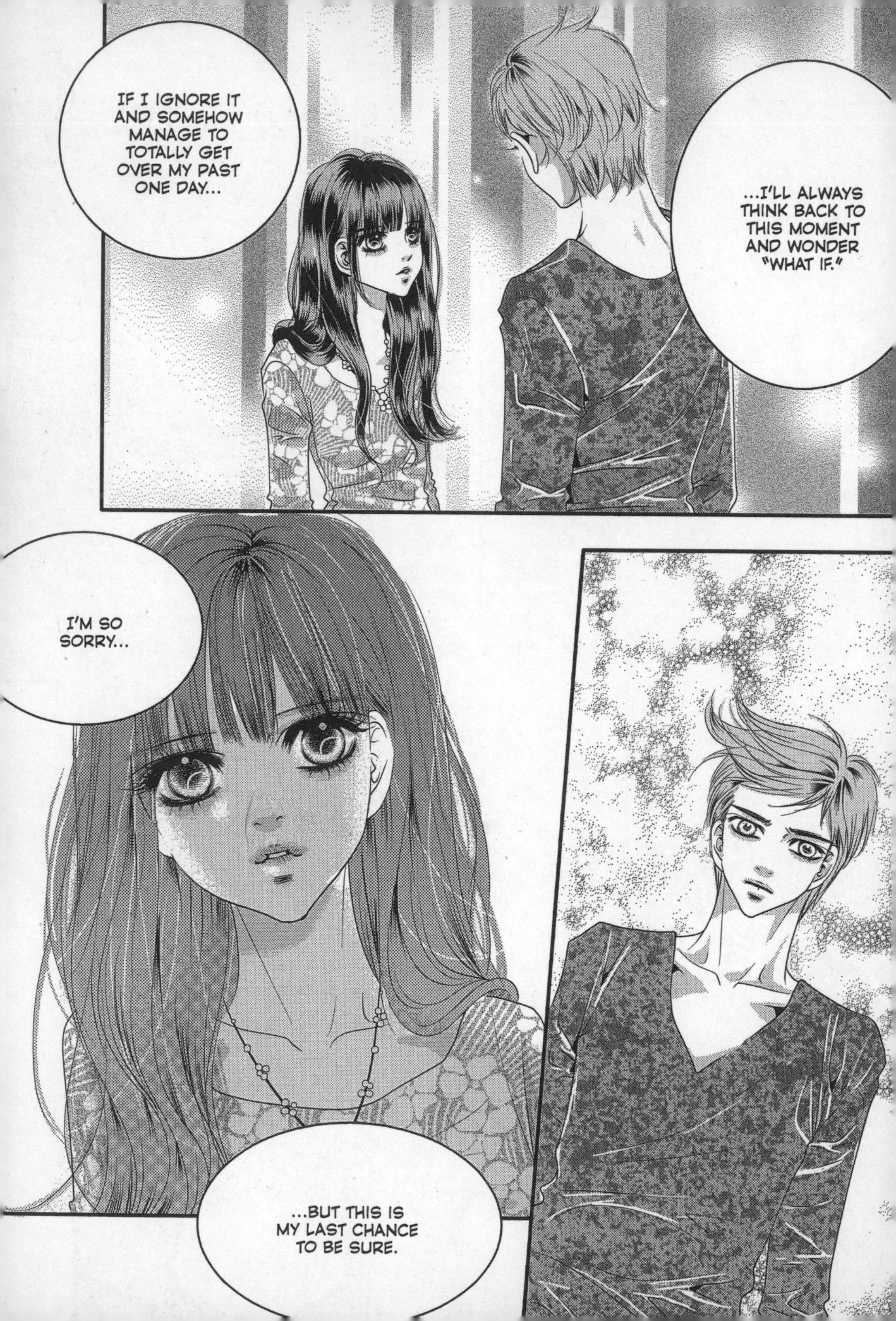
IF I IGNORE IT AND SOMEHOW MANAGE TO TOTALLY GET OVER MY PAST ONE DAY...
...I'LL ALWAYS THINK BACK TO THIS MOMENT AND WONDER "WHAT IF."
I'M SO SORRY...
...BUT THIS IS MY LAST CHANCE TO BE SURE.

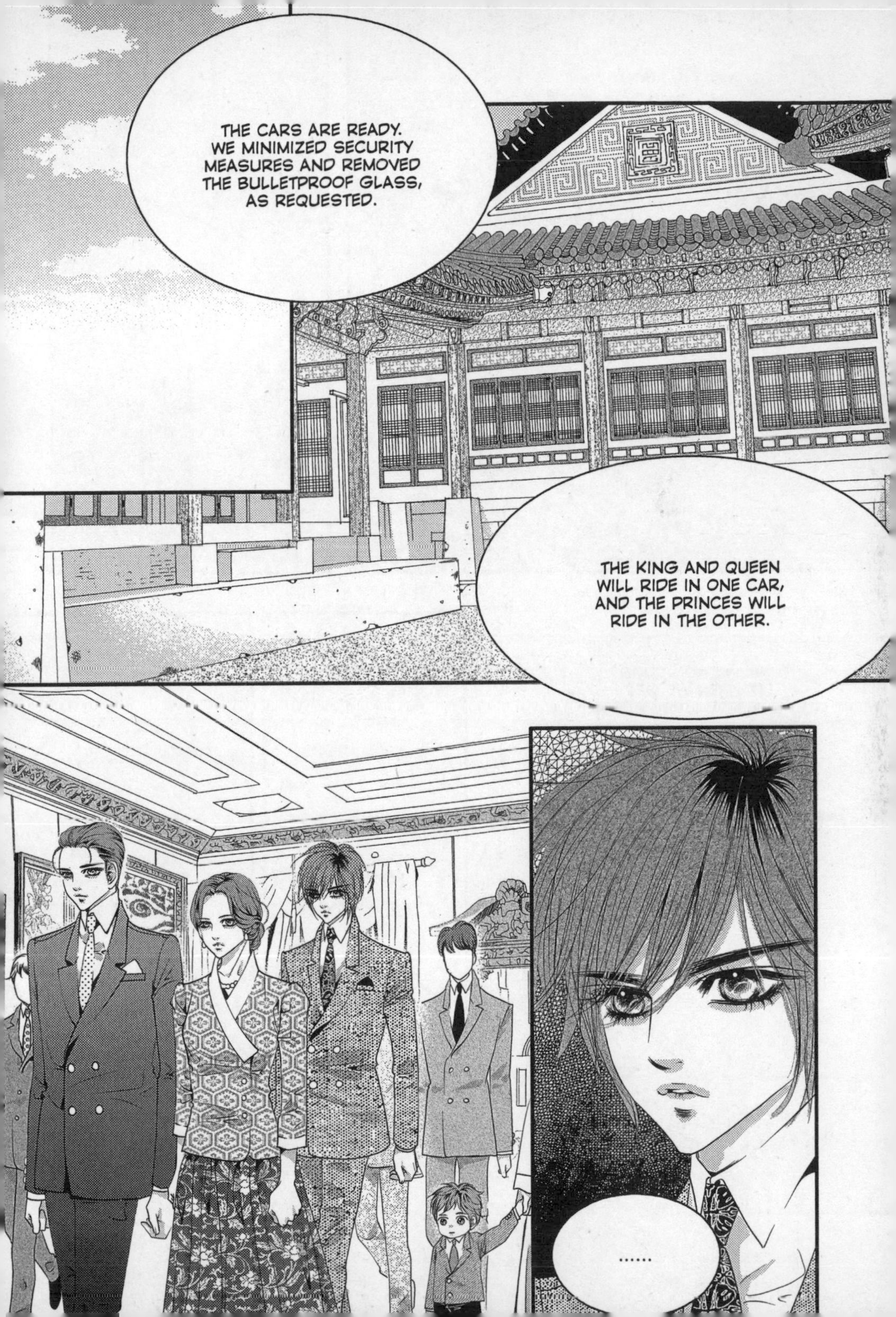
THE CARS ARE READY. WE MINIMIZED SECURITY MEASURES AND REMOVED THE BULLETPROOF GLASS, AS REQUESTED.
THE KING AND QUEEN WILL RIDE IN ONE CAR, AND THE PRINCES WILL RIDE IN THE OTHER.
......

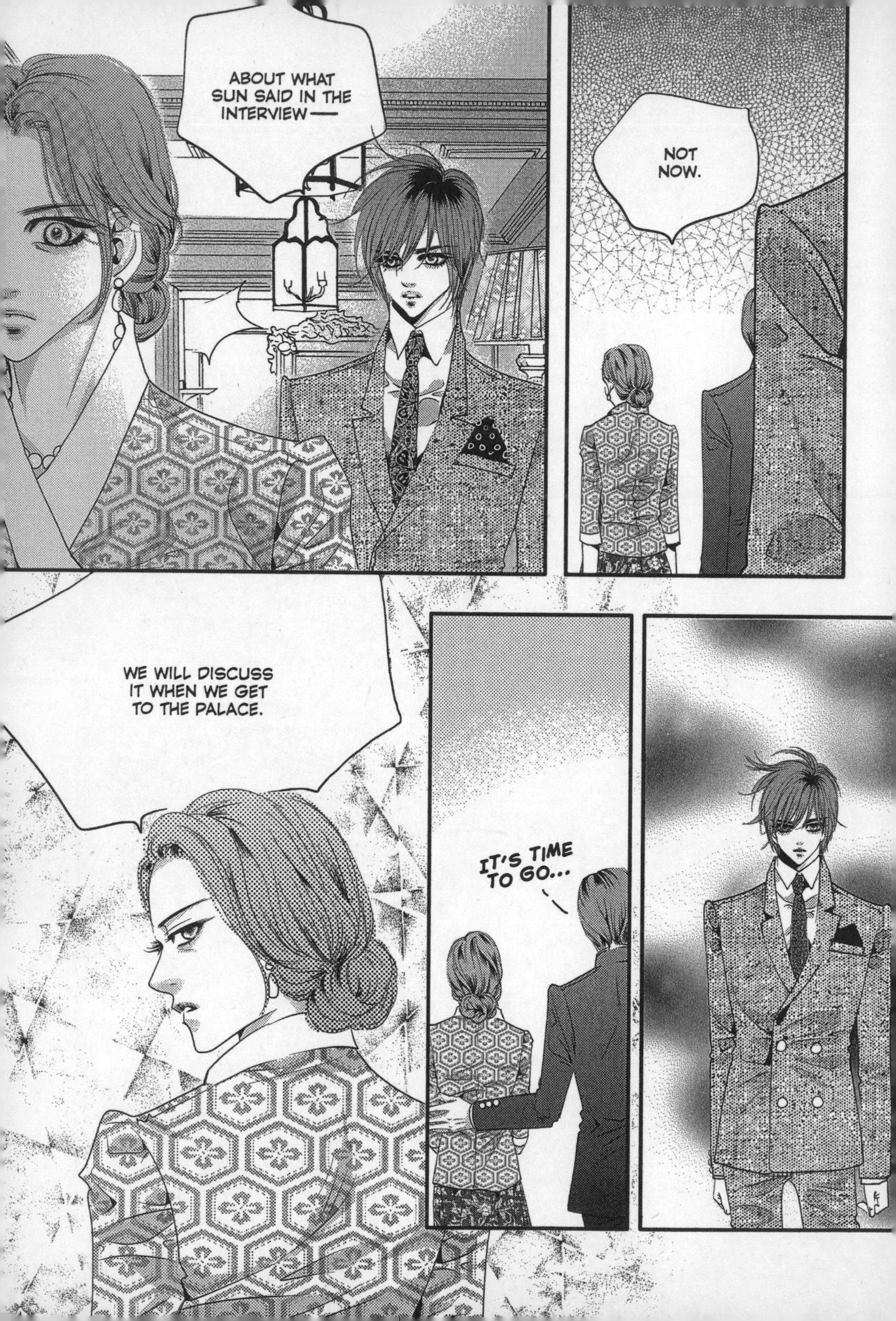
ABOUT WHAT SUN SAID IN THE INTERVIEW—
NOT NOW.
WE WILL DISCUSS IT WHEN WE GET TO THE PALACE.
IT'S TIME TO GO...

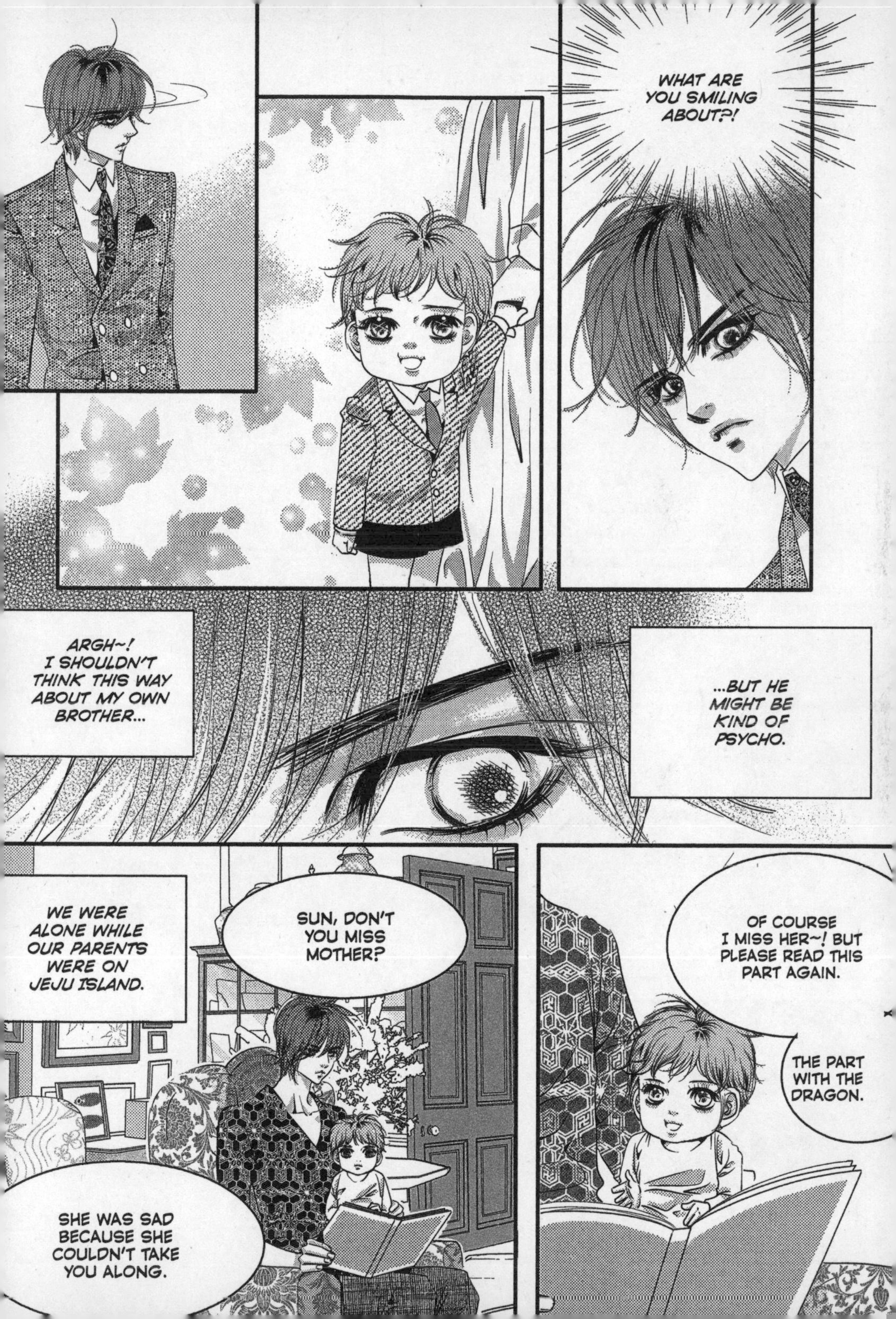
WHAT ARE YOU SMILING ABOUT?!
ARGH~! I SHOULDN'T THINK THIS WAY ABOUT MY OWN BROTHER...
...BUT HE MIGHT BE KIND OF PSYCHO.
WE WERE ALONE WHILE OUR PARENTS WERE ON JEJU ISLAND.
SUN, DON'T YOU MISS MOTHER?
SHE WAS SAD BECAUSE SHE COULDN'T TAKE YOU ALONG.
OF COURSE I MISS HER~! BUT PLEASE READ THIS PART AGAIN.
THE PART WITH THE DRAGON.

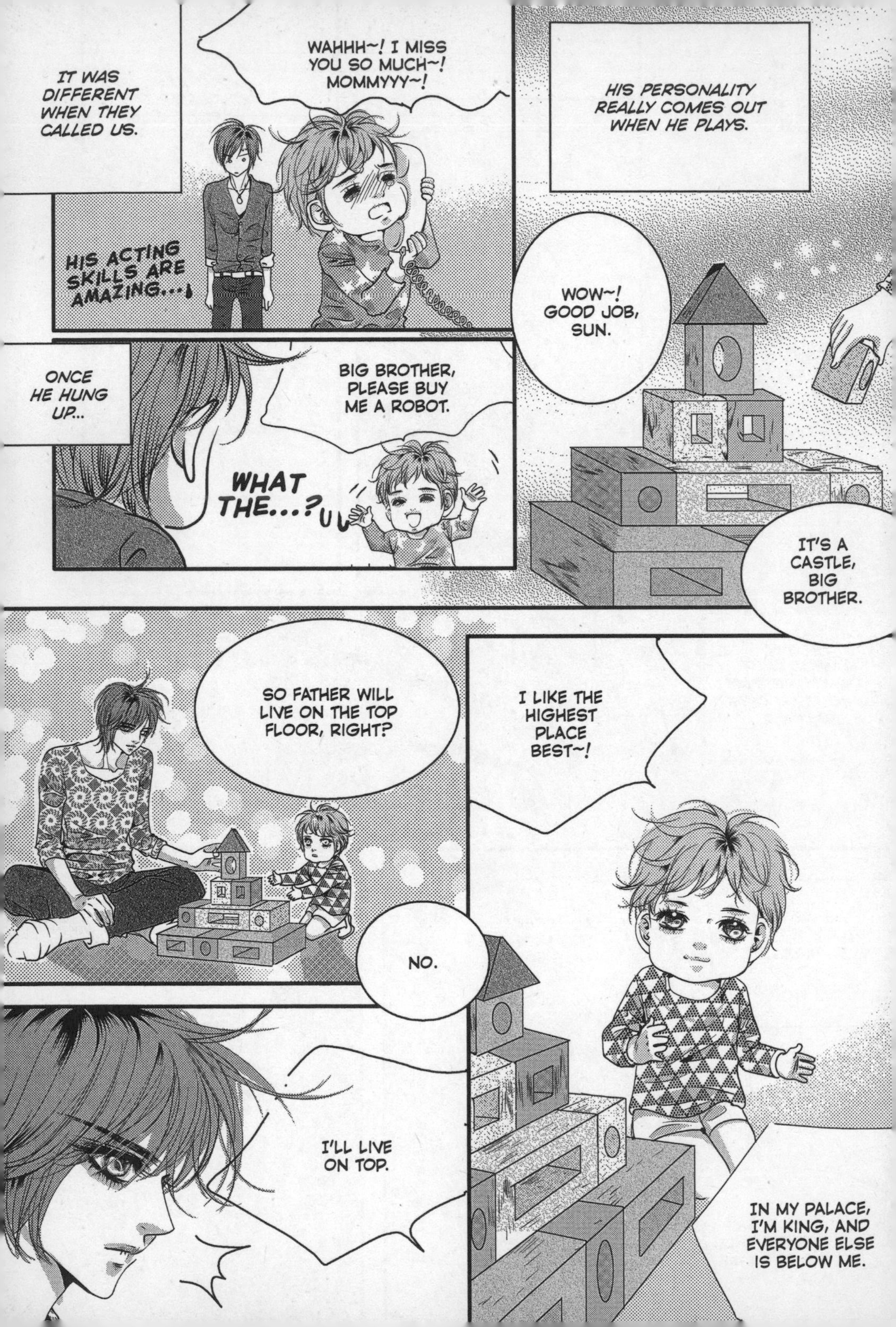
IT WAS DIFFERENT WHEN THEY CALLED US.
WAHHH~! I MISS YOU SO MUCH~! MOMMYYY~!
HIS ACTING SKILLS ARE AMAZING...
ONCE HE HUNG UP...
BIG BROTHER, PLEASE BUY ME A ROBOT.
WHAT THE...?
HIS PERSONALITY REALLY COMES OUT WHEN HE PLAYS.
WOW~! GOOD JOB, SUN.
IT'S A CASTLE, BIG BROTHER.
SO FATHER WILL LIVE ON THE TOP FLOOR, RIGHT?
NO.
I'LL LIVE ON TOP.
I LIKE THE HIGHEST PLACE BEST~!
IN MY PALACE, I'M KING, AND EVERYONE ELSE IS BELOW ME.

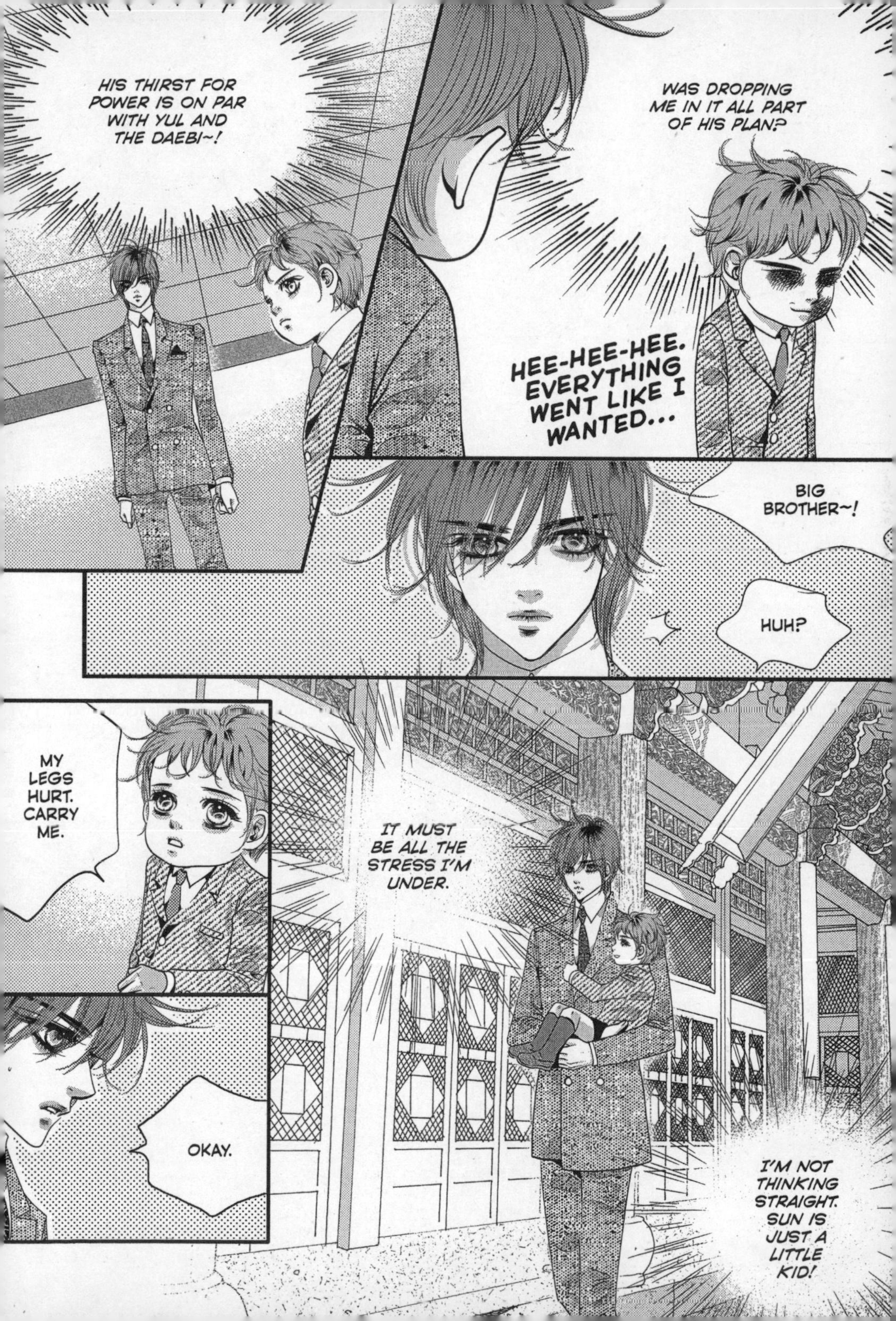
HIS THIRST FOR POWER IS ON PAR WITH YUL AND THE DAEBI~!
WAS DROPPING ME IN IT ALL PART OF HIS PLAN?
HEE-HEE-HEE. EVERYTHING WENT LIKE I WANTED...
BIG BROTHER~!
HUH?
MY LEGS HURT. CARRY ME.
OKAY.
IT MUST BE ALL THE STRESS I'M UNDER.
I'M NOT THINKING STRAIGHT. SUN IS JUST A LITTLE KID!

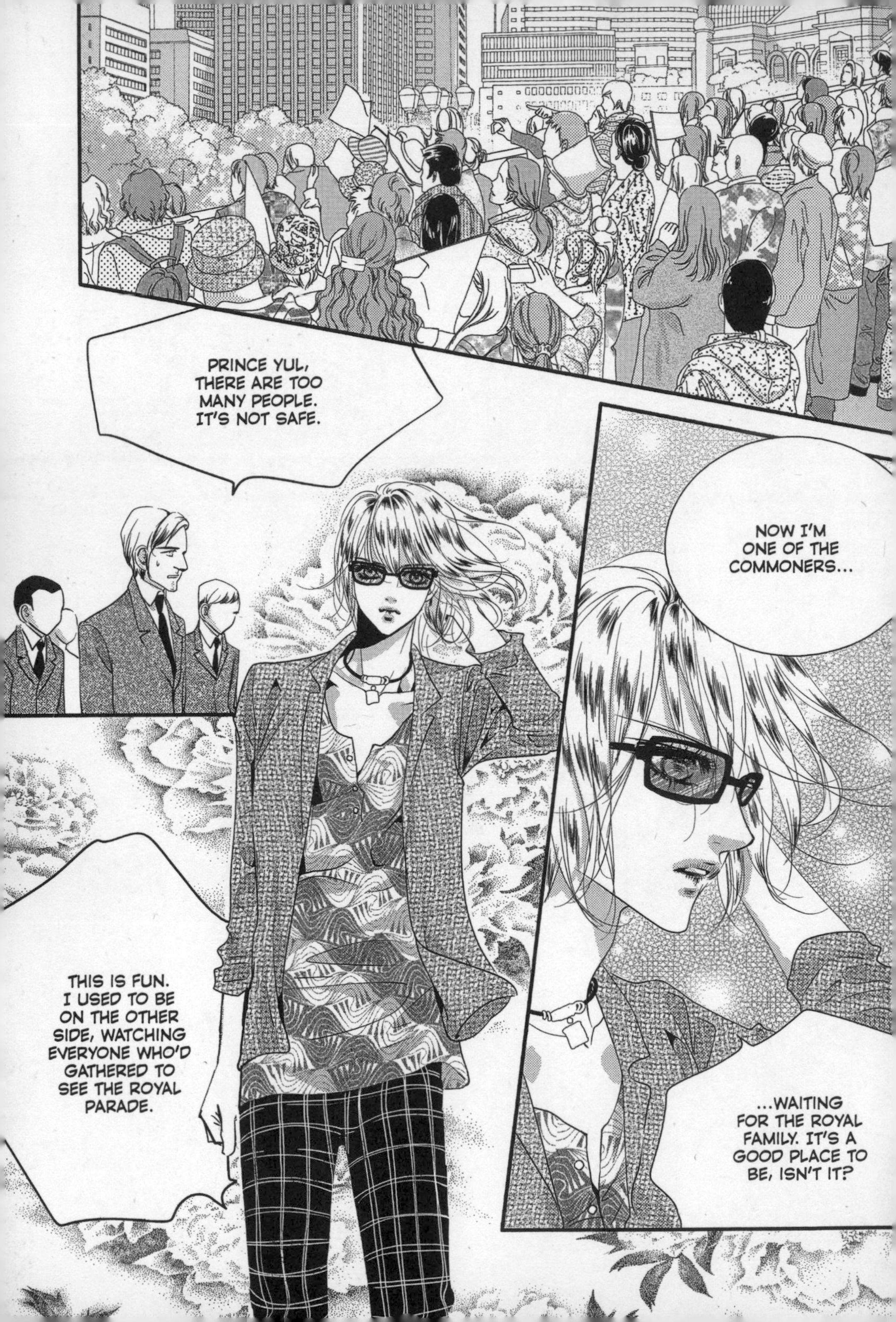
PRINCE YUL, THERE ARE TOO MANY PEOPLE. IT'S NOT SAFE.
NOW I'M ONE OF THE COMMONERS...
THIS IS FUN. I USED TO BE ON THE OTHER SIDE, WATCHING EVERYONE WHO'D GATHERED TO SEE THE ROYAL PARADE.
...WAITING FOR THE ROYAL FAMILY. IT'S A GOOD PLACE TO BE, ISN'T IT?

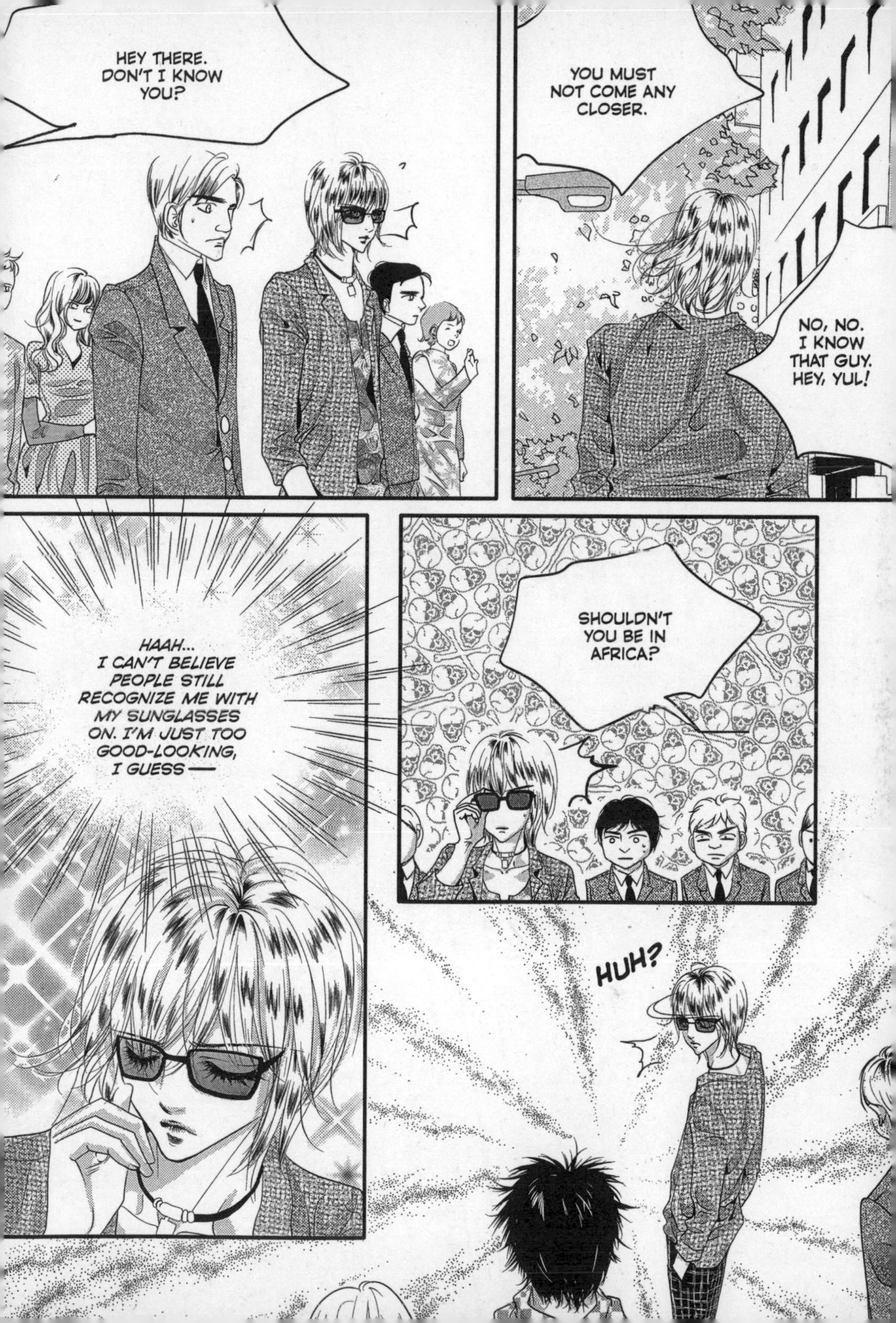
HEY THERE. DON'T I KNOW YOU?
YOU MUST NOT COME ANY CLOSER.
NO, NO. I KNOW THAT GUY. HEY, YUL!
HAAH... I CAN'T BELIEVE PEOPLE STILL RECOGNIZE ME WITH MY SUNGLASSES ON. I'M JUST TOO GOOD-LOOKING, I GUESS—
SHOULDN'T YOU BE IN AFRICA?
HUH?

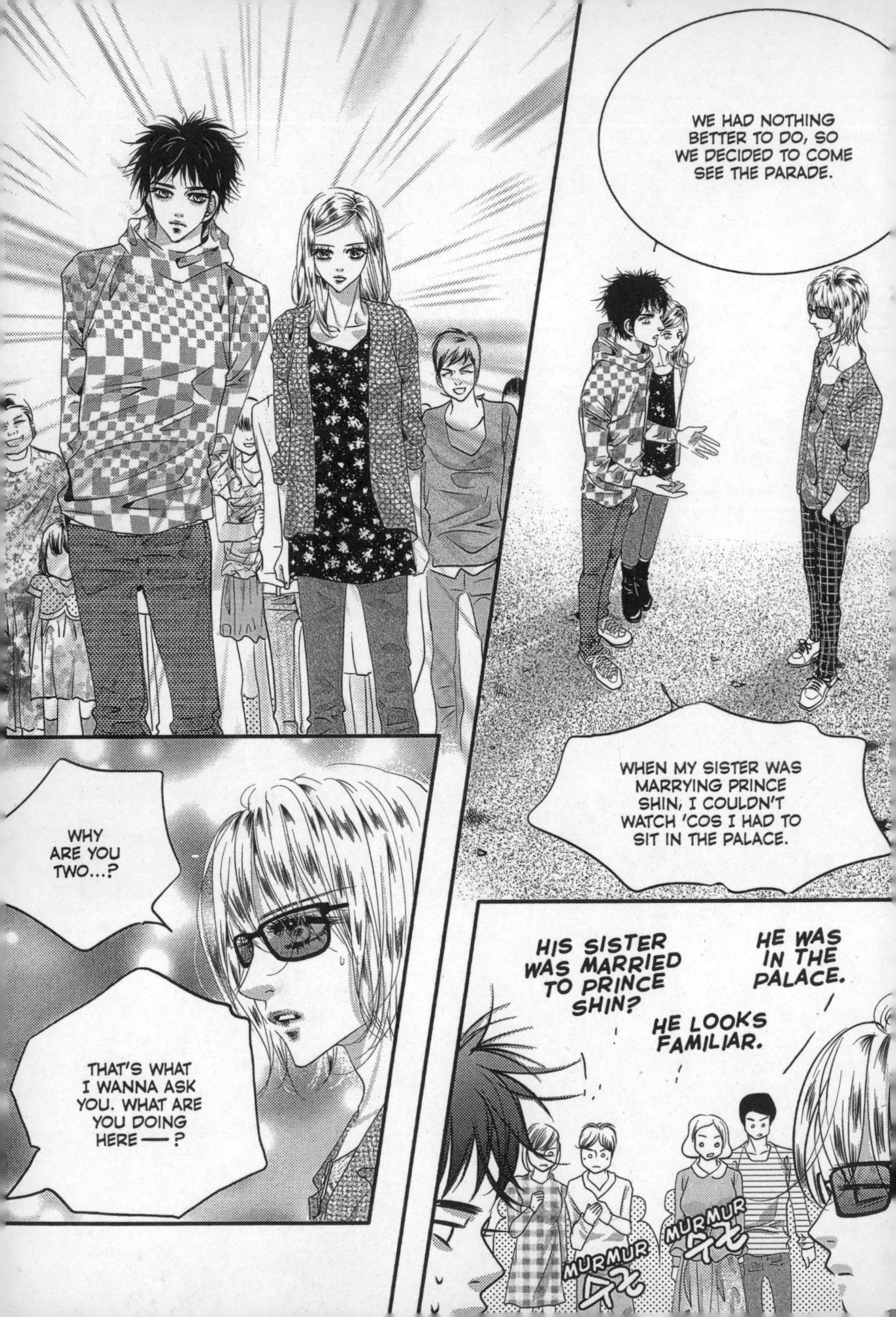
WHY ARE YOU TWO...?
THAT'S WHAT I WANNA ASK YOU. WHAT ARE YOU DOING HERE—?
WE HAD NOTHING BETTER TO DO, SO WE DECIDED TO COME SEE THE PARADE.
WHEN MY SISTER WAS MARRYING PRINCE SHIN, I COULDN'T WATCH 'COS I HAD TO SIT IN THE PALACE.
HIS SISTER WAS MARRIED TO PRINCE SHIN?
HE LOOKS FAMILIAR.
HE WAS IN THE PALACE.
MURMUR
MURMUR

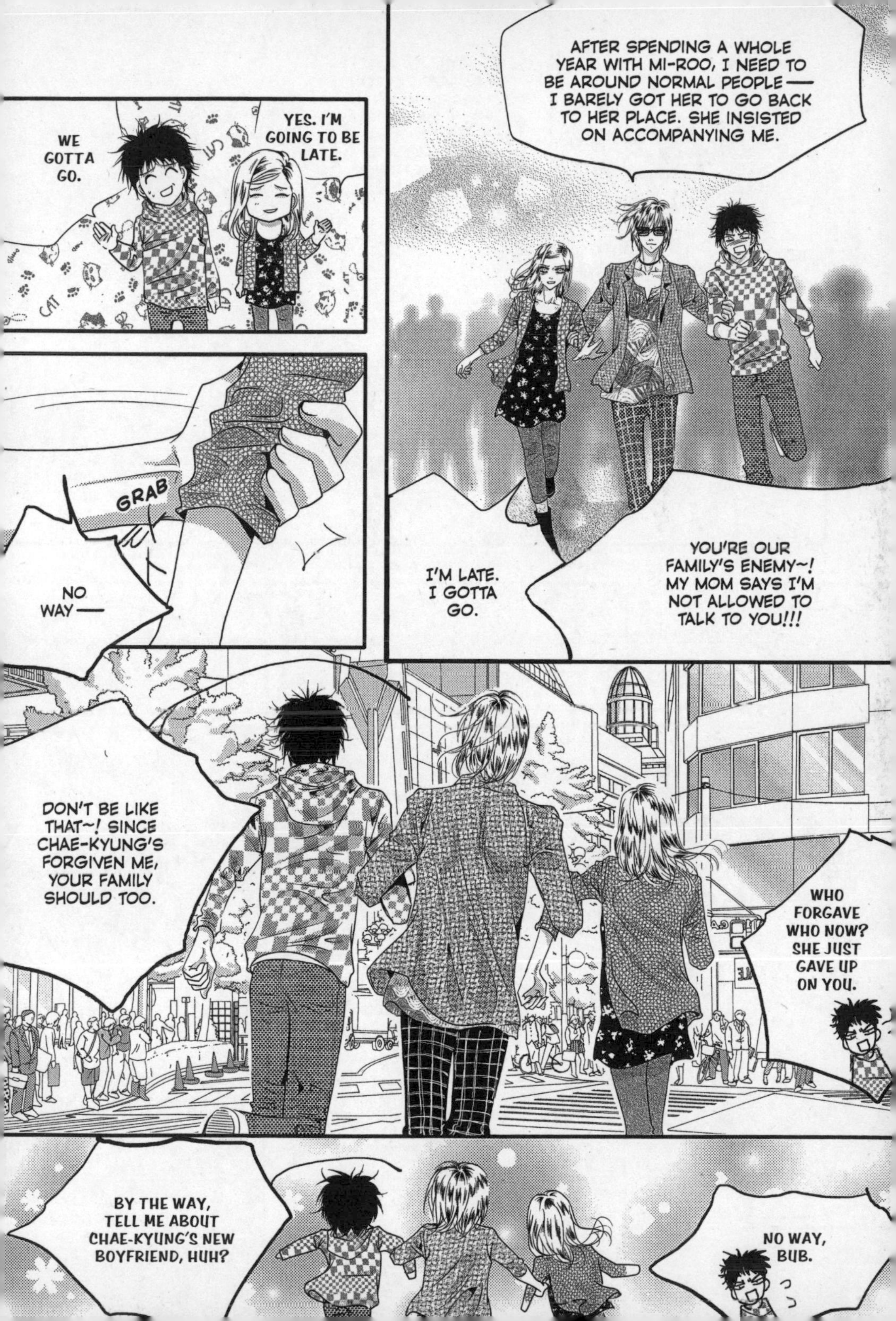
WE GOTTA GO.
YES. I'M GOING TO BE LATE.
GRAB
NO WAY—
AFTER SPENDING A WHOLE YEAR WITH MI-ROO, I NEED TO BE AROUND NORMAL PEOPLE— I BARELY GOT HER TO GO BACK TO HER PLACE. SHE INSISTED ON ACCOMPANYING ME.
I'M LATE. I GOTTA GO.
YOU'RE OUR FAMILY'S ENEMY~! MY MOM SAYS I'M NOT ALLOWED TO TALK TO YOU!!!
DON'T BE LIKE THAT~! SINCE CHAE-KYUNG'S FORGIVEN ME, YOUR FAMILY SHOULD TOO.
WHO FORGAVE WHO NOW? SHE JUST GAVE UP ON YOU.
BY THE WAY, TELL ME ABOUT CHAE-KYUNG'S NEW BOYFRIEND, HUH?
NO WAY, BUB.

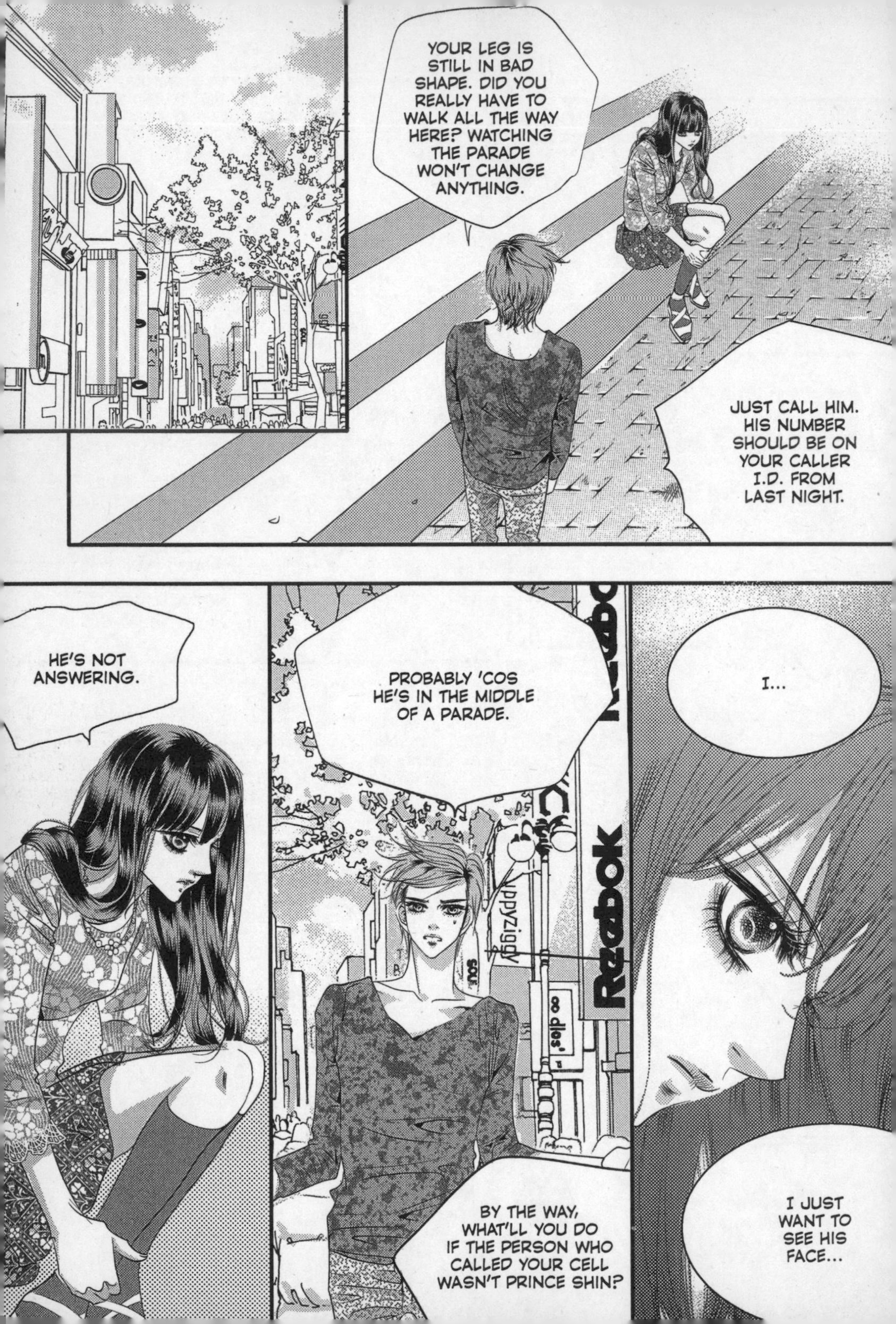
YOUR LEG IS STILL IN BAD SHAPE. DID YOU REALLY HAVE TO WALK ALL THE WAY HERE? WATCHING THE PARADE WON'T CHANGE ANYTHING.
JUST CALL HIM. HIS NUMBER SHOULD BE ON YOUR CALLER I.D. FROM LAST NIGHT.
HE'S NOT ANSWERING.
PROBABLY 'COS HE'S IN THE MIDDLE OF A PARADE.
Reebok
BY THE WAY, WHAT'LL YOU DO IF THE PERSON WHO CALLED YOUR CELL WASN'T PRINCE SHIN?
I...
I JUST WANT TO SEE HIS FACE...

......

SOMETIMES WE'RE COMPELLED TO ACTION WITHOUT EVEN KNOWING WHAT IT IS WE SHOULD DO.

SEEING HIS FACE WON'T TELL YOU WHAT YOU NEED TO KNOW, BUT I UNDERSTAND THAT YOU FEEL LIKE YOU'LL GO CRAZY IF YOU DON'T.

WHAT IS SITTING HERE GOING TO ACCOMPLISH?

THE THING IS... IF YOU HAVE TO DO THIS, DO IT RIGHT, OR DON'T EVEN BOTHER.

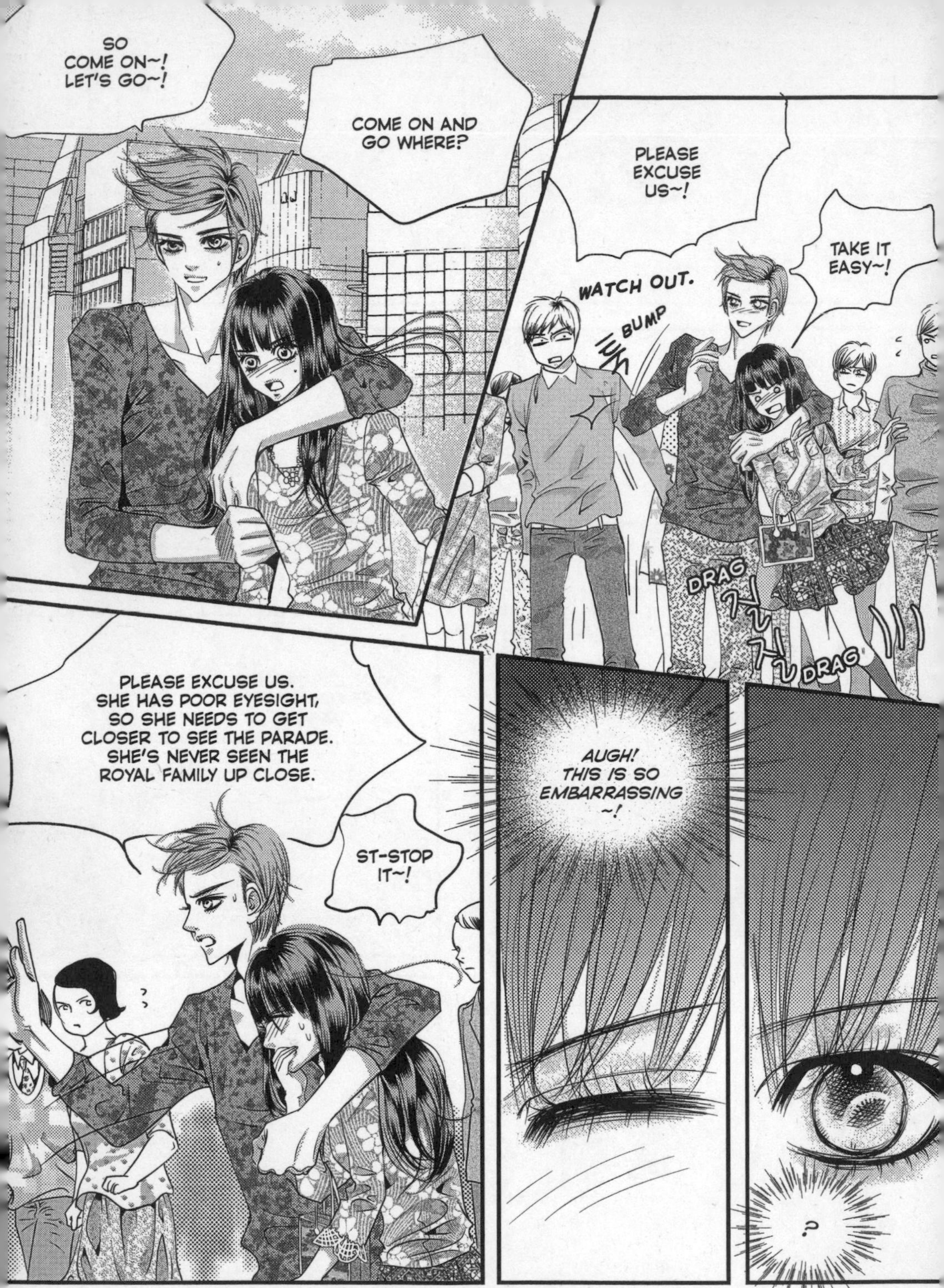
SO COME ON~! LET'S GO~!
COME ON AND GO WHERE?
PLEASE EXCUSE US~!
TAKE IT EASY~!
WATCH OUT.
BUMP
DRAG
DRAG
PLEASE EXCUSE US. SHE HAS POOR EYESIGHT, SO SHE NEEDS TO GET CLOSER TO SEE THE PARADE. SHE'S NEVER SEEN THE ROYAL FAMILY UP CLOSE.
ST-STOP IT~!
AUGH! THIS IS SO EMBARRASSING ~!
?

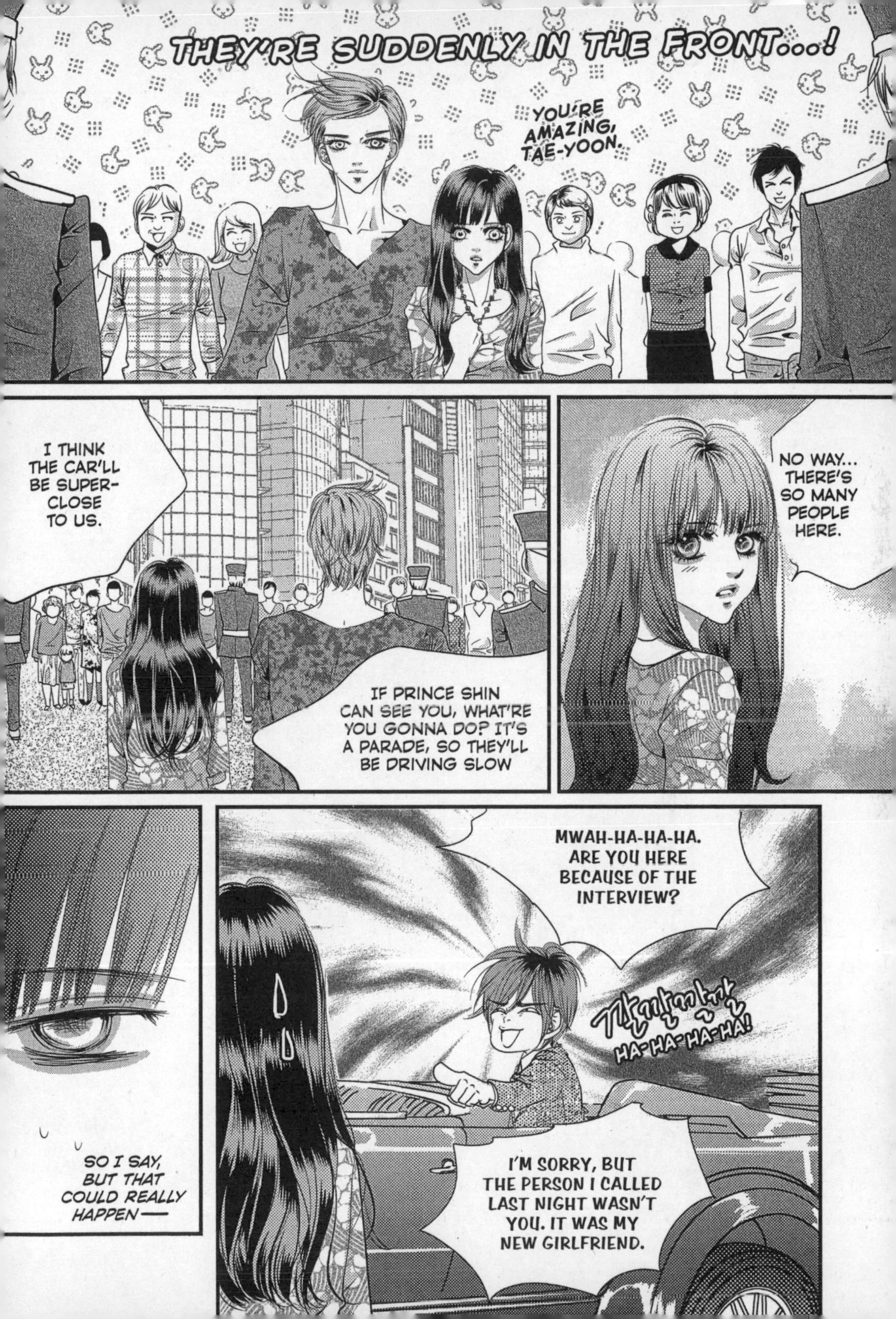
THEY'RE SUDDENLY IN THE FRONT...!
YOU'RE AMAZING, TAE-YOON.
I THINK THE CAR'LL BE SUPER-CLOSE TO US.
IF PRINCE SHIN CAN SEE YOU, WHAT'RE YOU GONNA DO? IT'S A PARADE, SO THEY'LL BE DRIVING SLOW
NO WAY... THERE'S SO MANY PEOPLE HERE.
SO I SAY, BUT THAT COULD REALLY HAPPEN—
MWAH-HA-HA-HA. ARE YOU HERE BECAUSE OF THE INTERVIEW?
HA-HA-HA-HA!
I'M SORRY, BUT THE PERSON I CALLED LAST NIGHT WASN'T YOU. IT WAS MY NEW GIRLFRIEND.

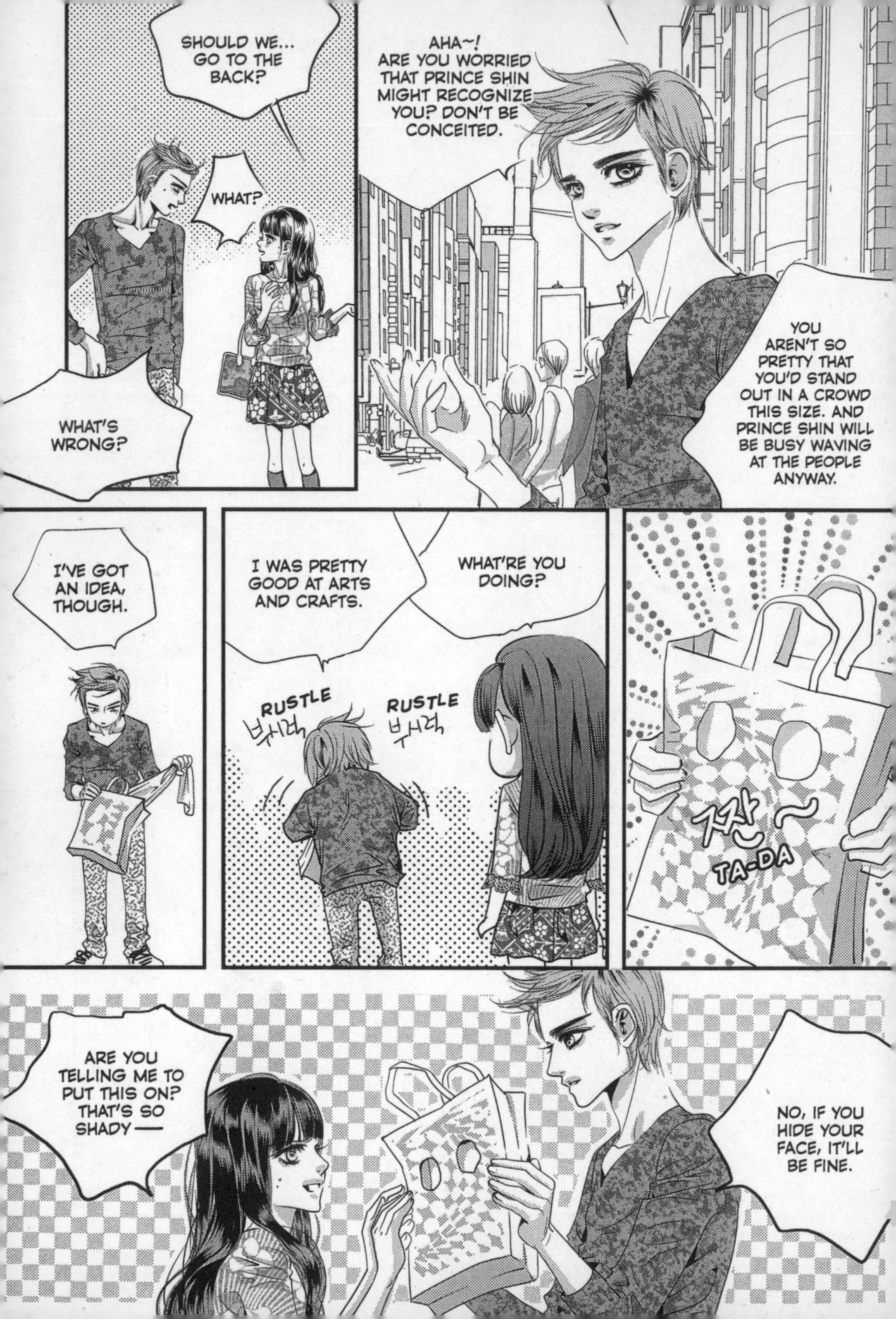
SHOULD WE... GO TO THE BACK?
WHAT?
WHAT'S WRONG?
AHA~! ARE YOU WORRIED THAT PRINCE SHIN MIGHT RECOGNIZE YOU? DON'T BE CONCEITED.
YOU AREN'T SO PRETTY THAT YOU'D STAND OUT IN A CROWD THIS SIZE. AND PRINCE SHIN WILL BE BUSY WAVING AT THE PEOPLE ANYWAY.
I'VE GOT AN IDEA, THOUGH.
I WAS PRETTY GOOD AT ARTS AND CRAFTS.
WHAT'RE YOU DOING?
RUSTLE
부스럭
RUSTLE
부스럭
짜잔~
TA-DA
ARE YOU TELLING ME TO PUT THIS ON? THAT'S SO SHADY—
NO, IF YOU HIDE YOUR FACE, IT'LL BE FINE.

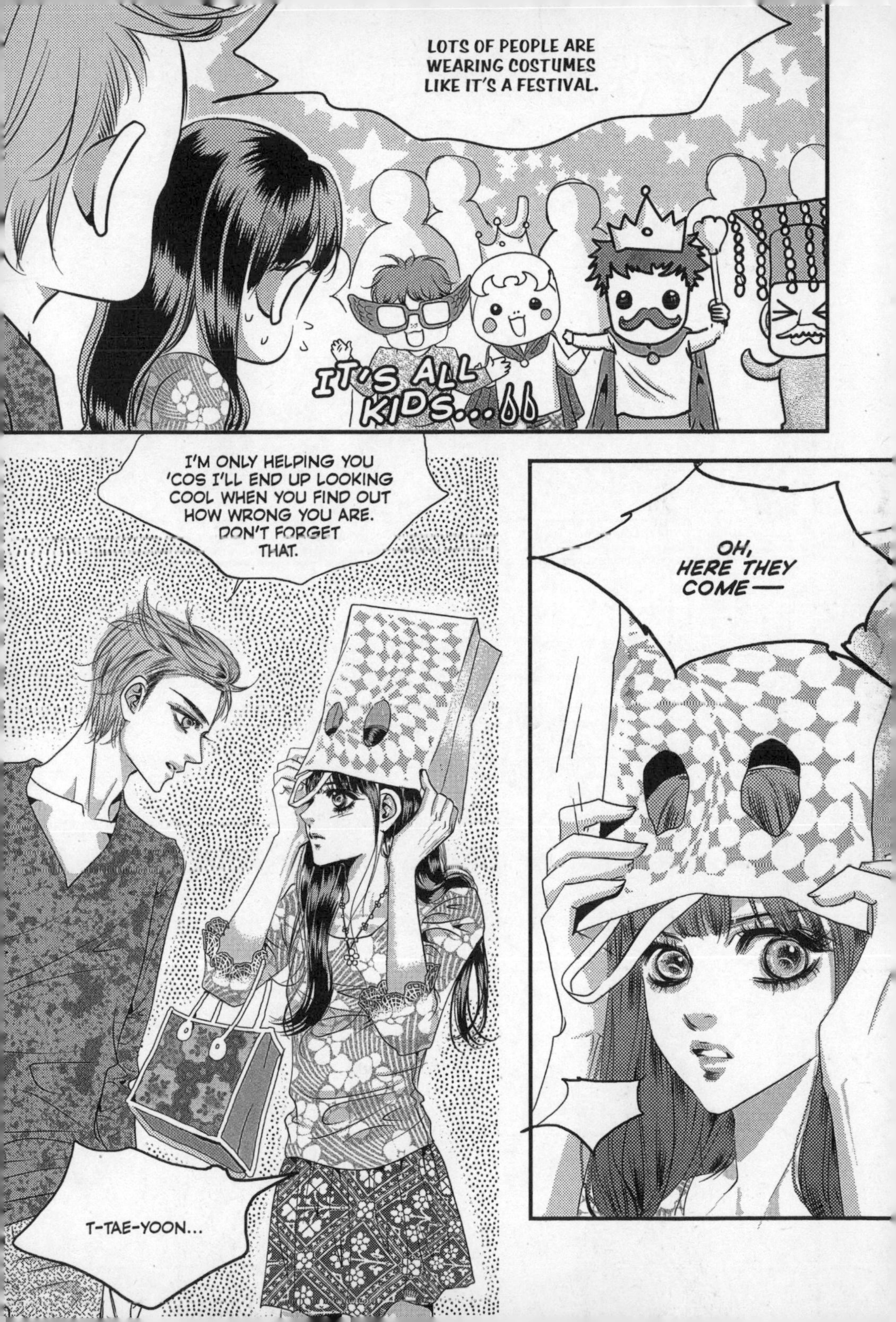
LOTS OF PEOPLE ARE WEARING COSTUMES LIKE IT'S A FESTIVAL.
IT'S ALL KIDS...
I'M ONLY HELPING YOU 'COS I'LL END UP LOOKING COOL WHEN YOU FIND OUT HOW WRONG YOU ARE. DON'T FORGET THAT.
T-TAE-YOON...
OH, HERE THEY COME—

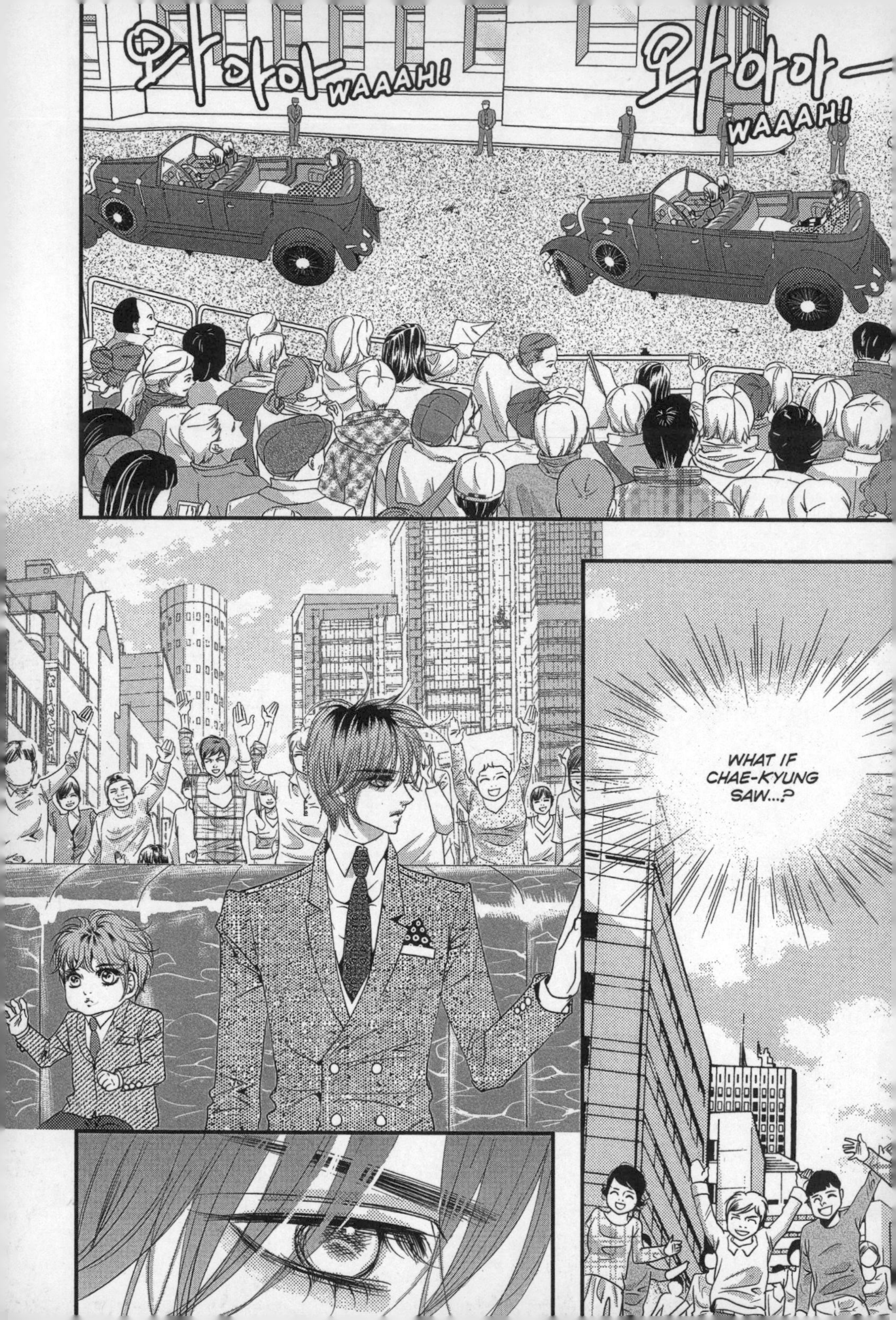
와아아
WAAAH!
와아아—
WAAAH!
WHAT IF CHAE-KYUNG SAW...?

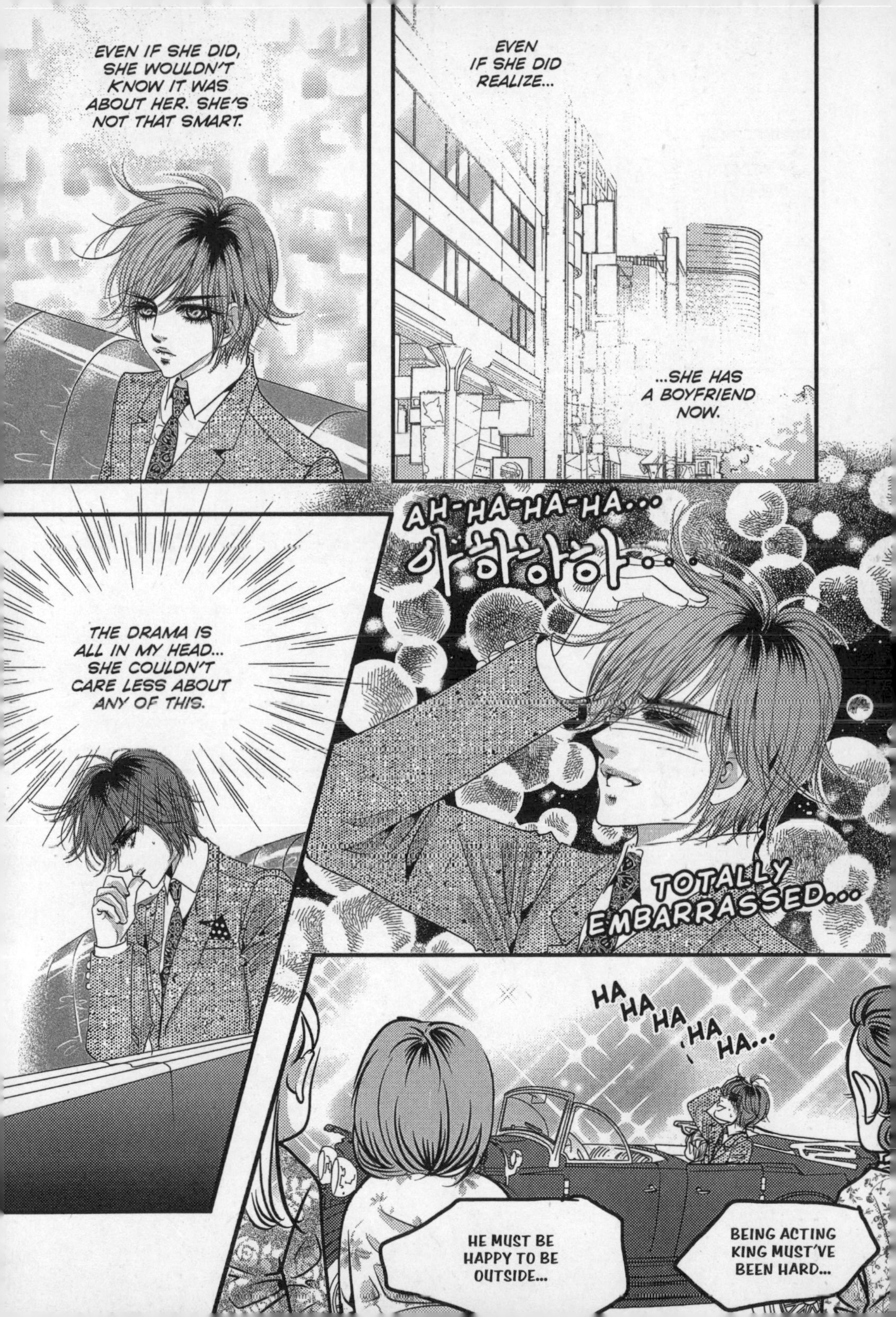
EVEN IF SHE DID, SHE WOULDN'T KNOW IT WAS ABOUT HER. SHE'S NOT THAT SMART.
EVEN IF SHE DID REALIZE...
...SHE HAS A BOYFRIEND NOW.
THE DRAMA IS ALL IN MY HEAD... SHE COULDN'T CARE LESS ABOUT ANY OF THIS.
AH-HA-HA-HA...
아하하하...
TOTALLY EMBARRASSED...
HA HA HA HA HA...
HE MUST BE HAPPY TO BE OUTSIDE...
BEING ACTING KING MUST'VE BEEN HARD...

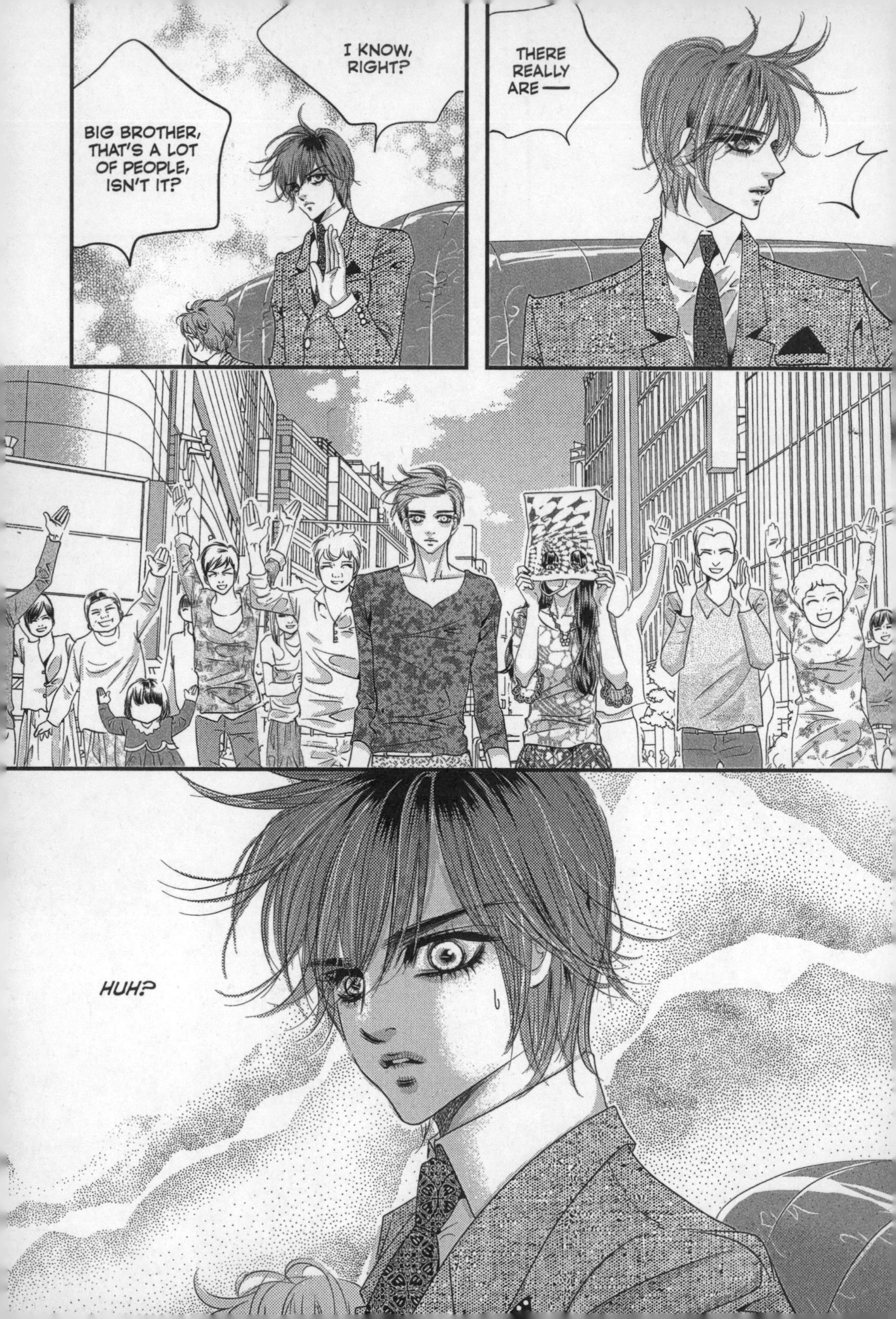
BIG BROTHER, THAT'S A LOT OF PEOPLE, ISN'T IT?
I KNOW, RIGHT?
THERE REALLY ARE—
HUH?

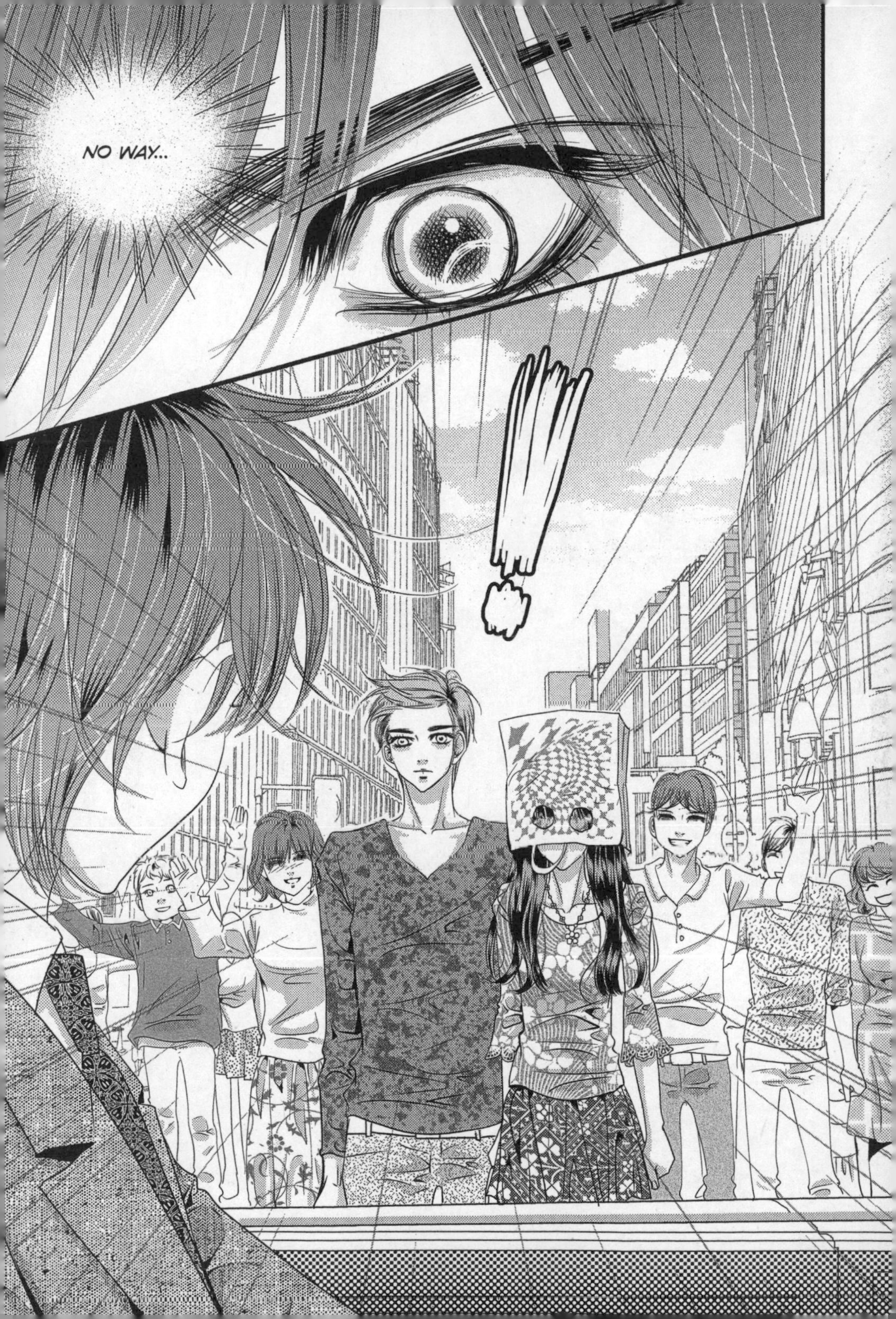
NO WAY...

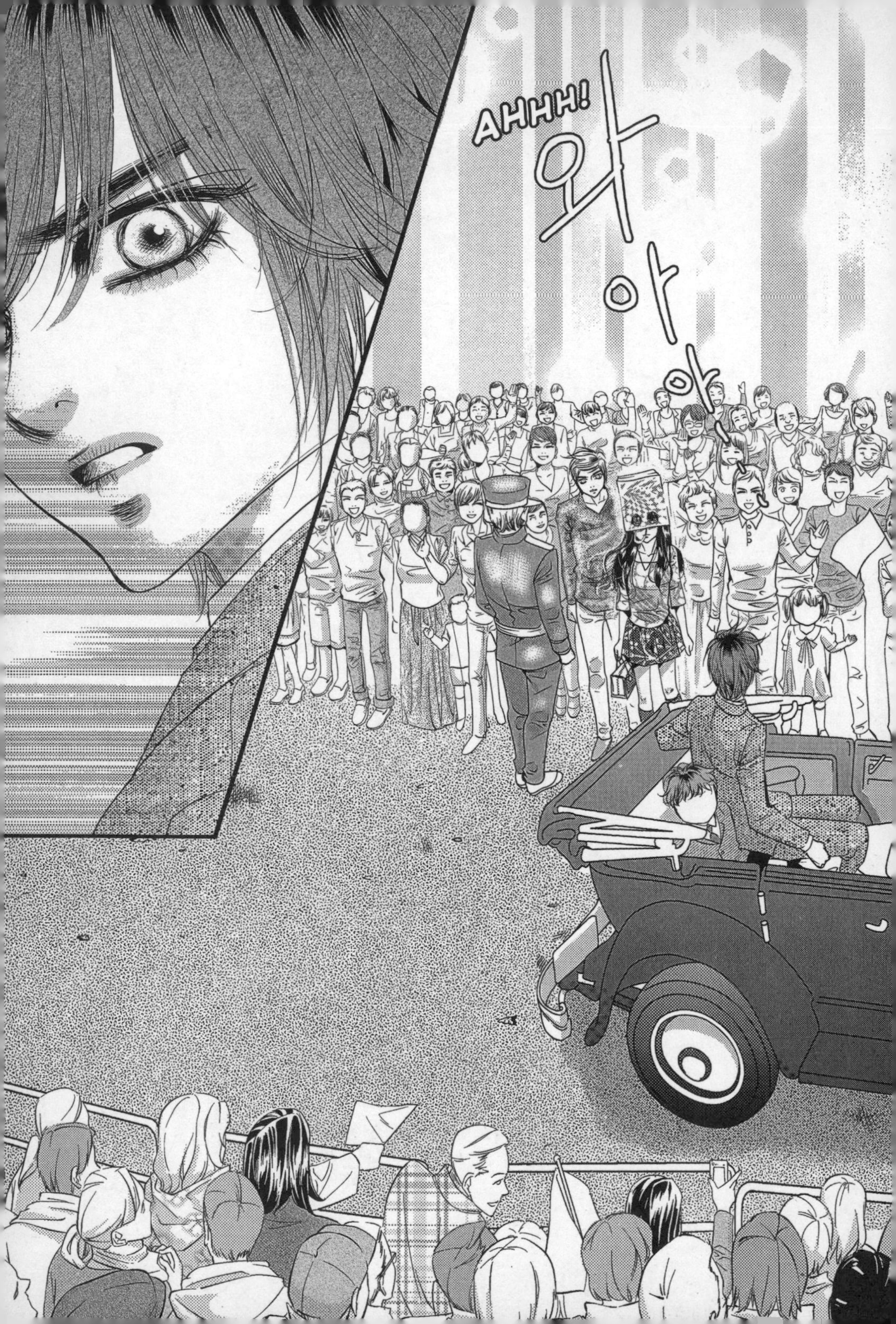
AHHH!
와아아

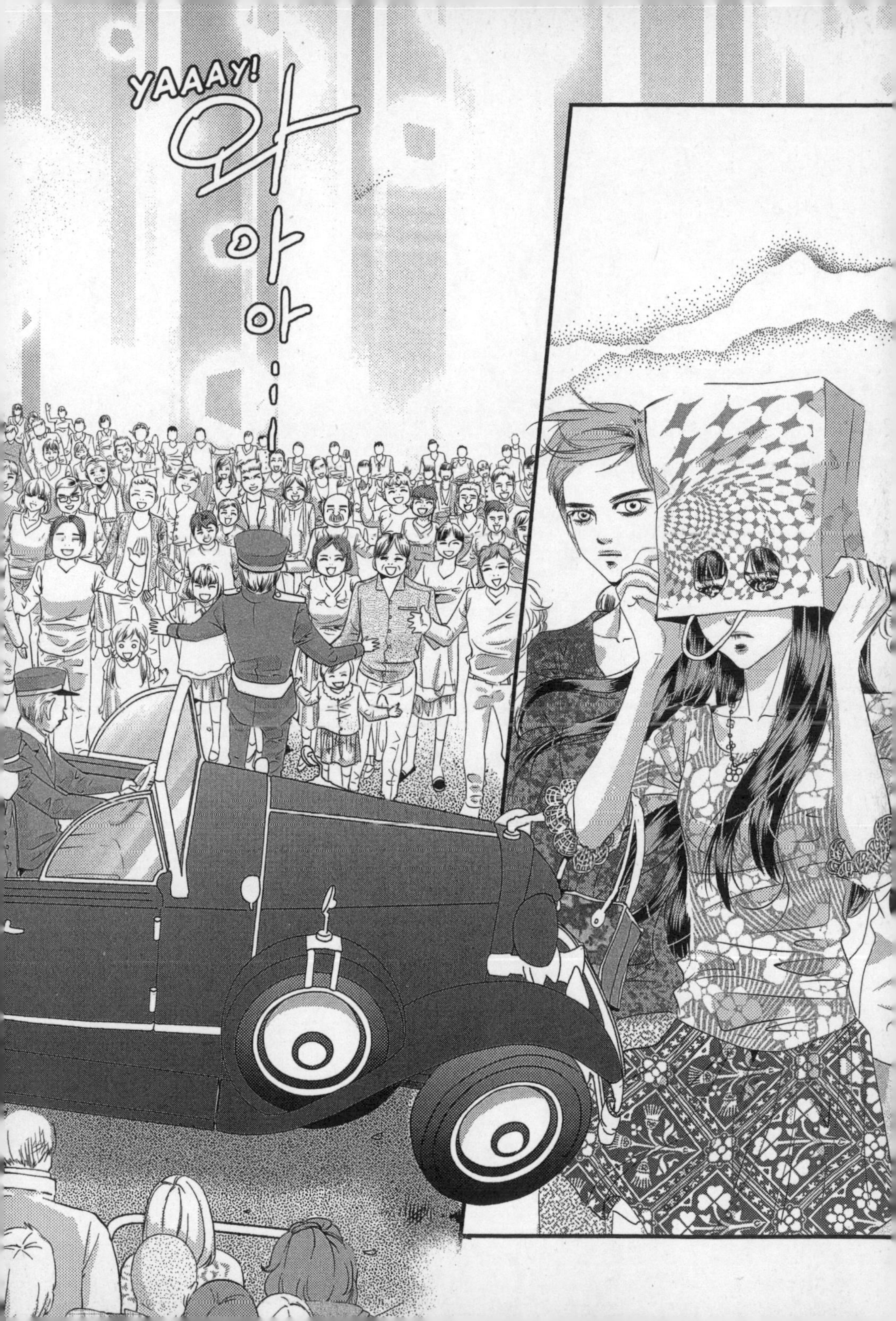
YAAAY!
와아아아…

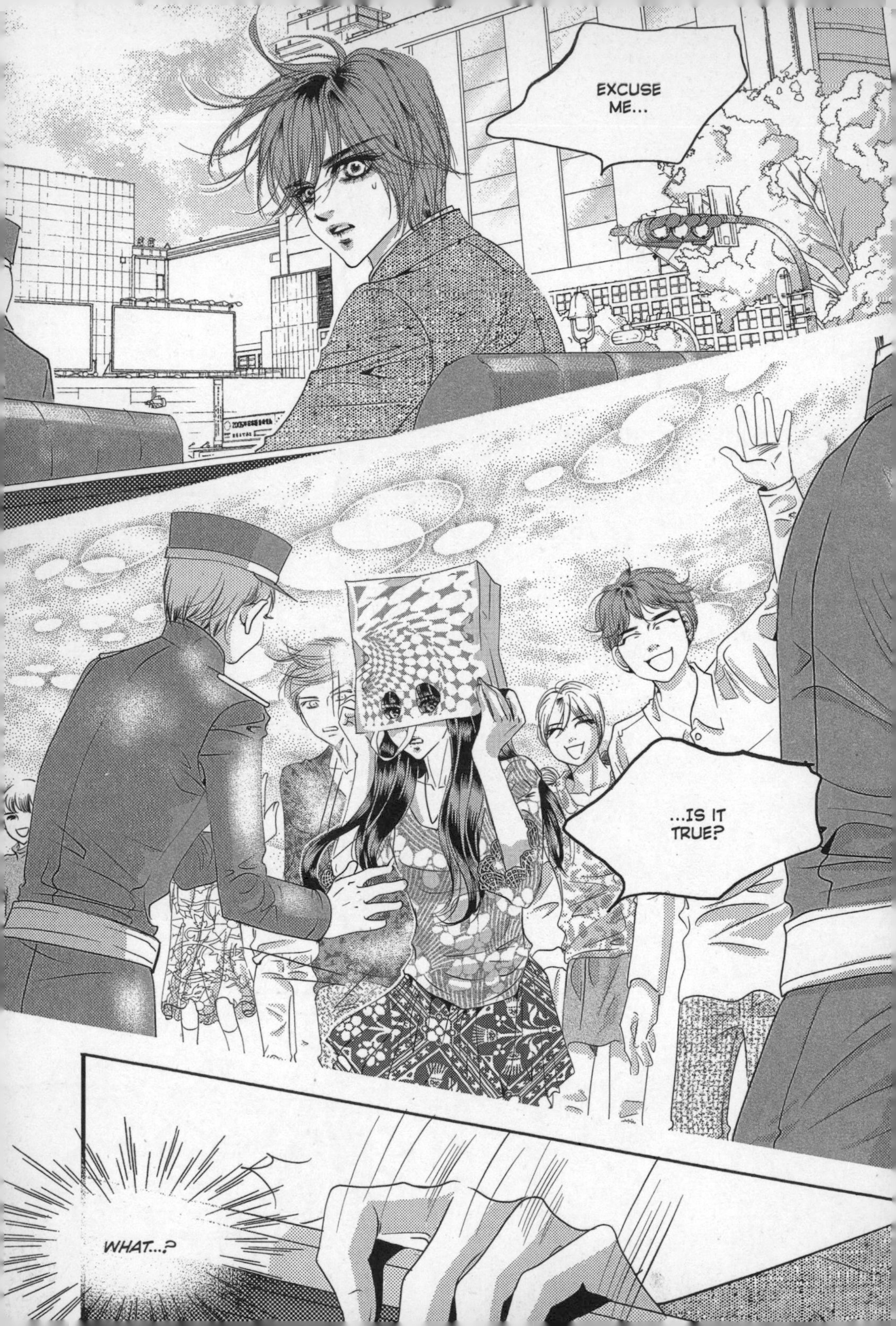
EXCUSE ME...
...IS IT TRUE?
WHAT...?

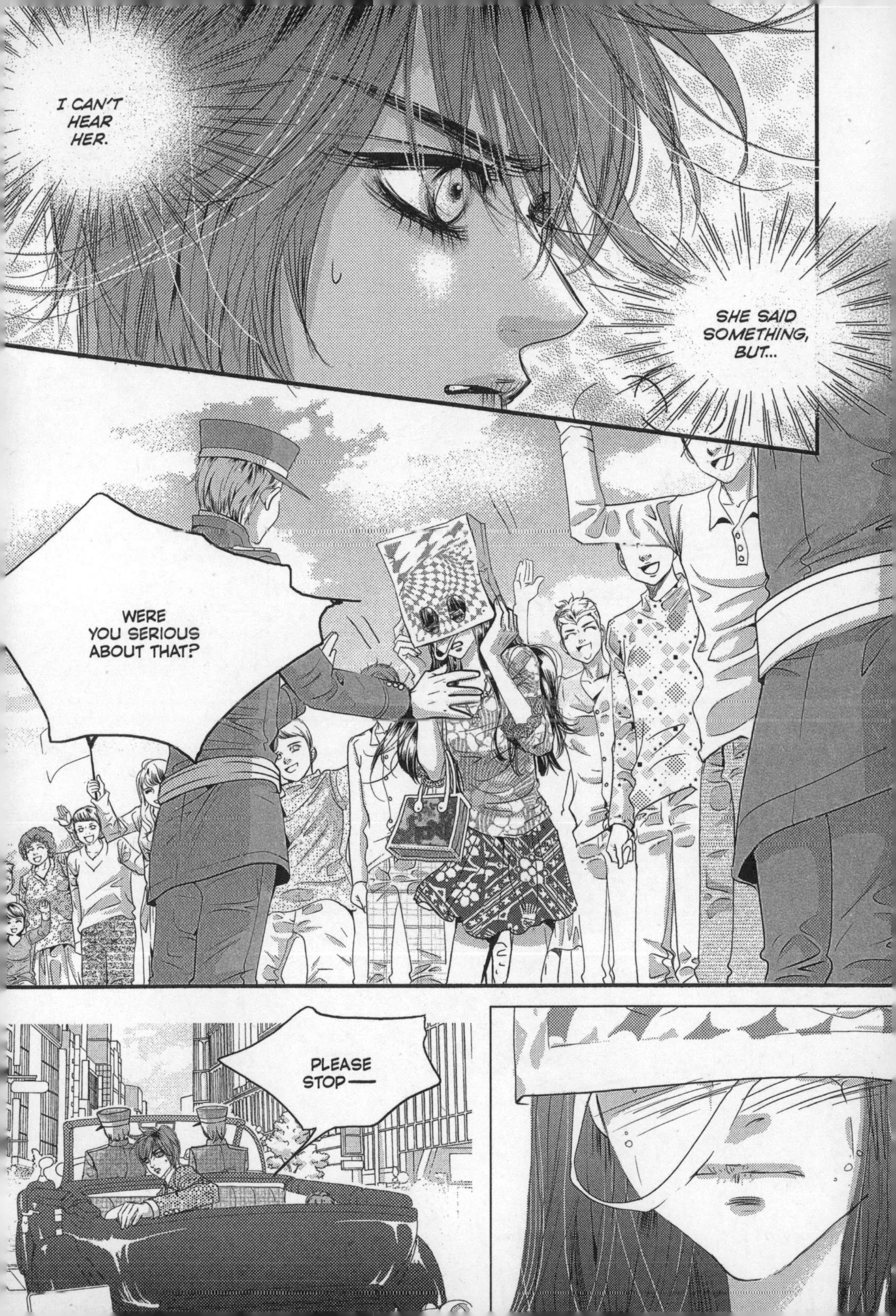
I CAN'T HEAR HER.
SHE SAID SOMETHING, BUT...
WERE YOU SERIOUS ABOUT THAT?
PLEASE STOP—

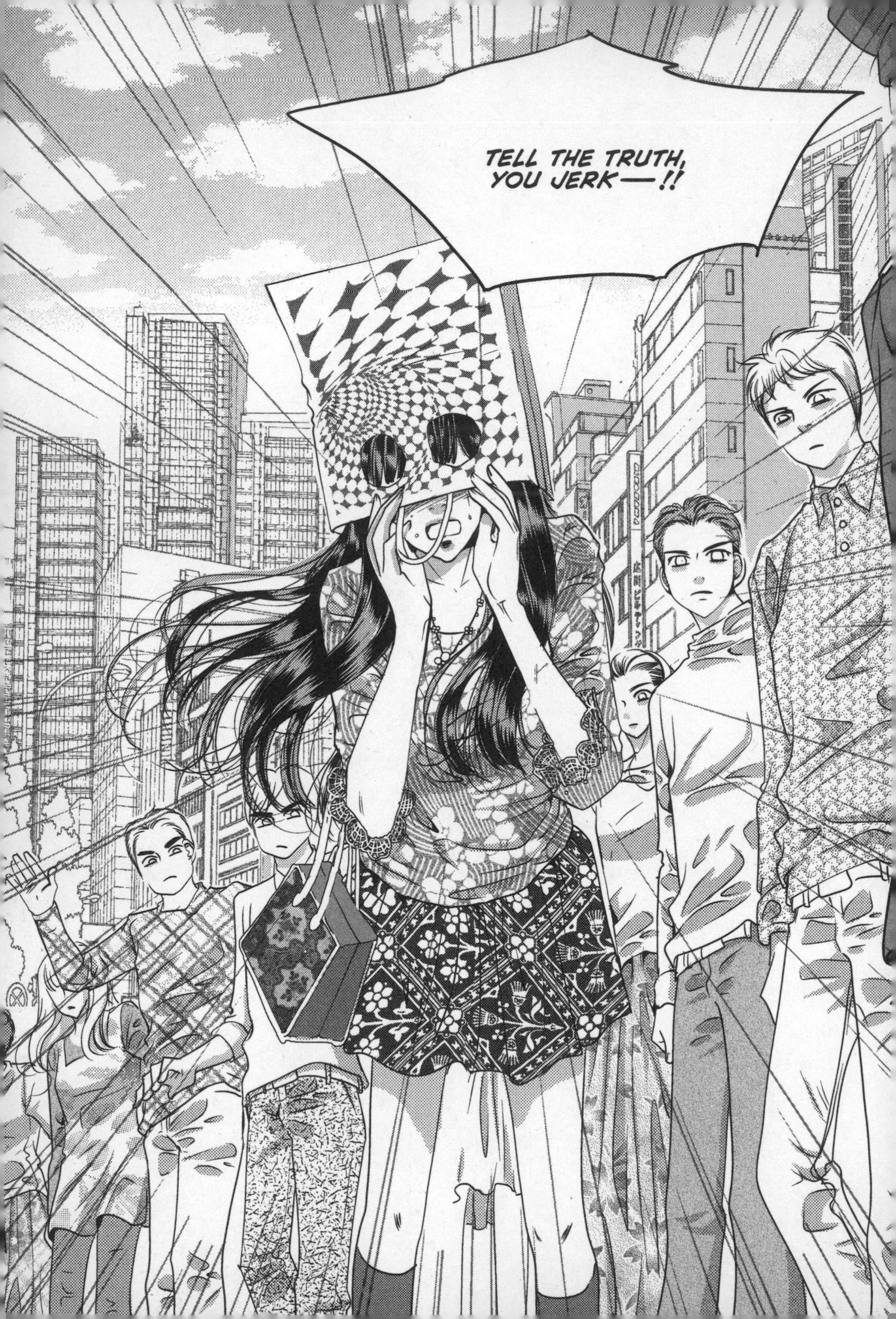
TELL THE TRUTH, YOU JERK—!!

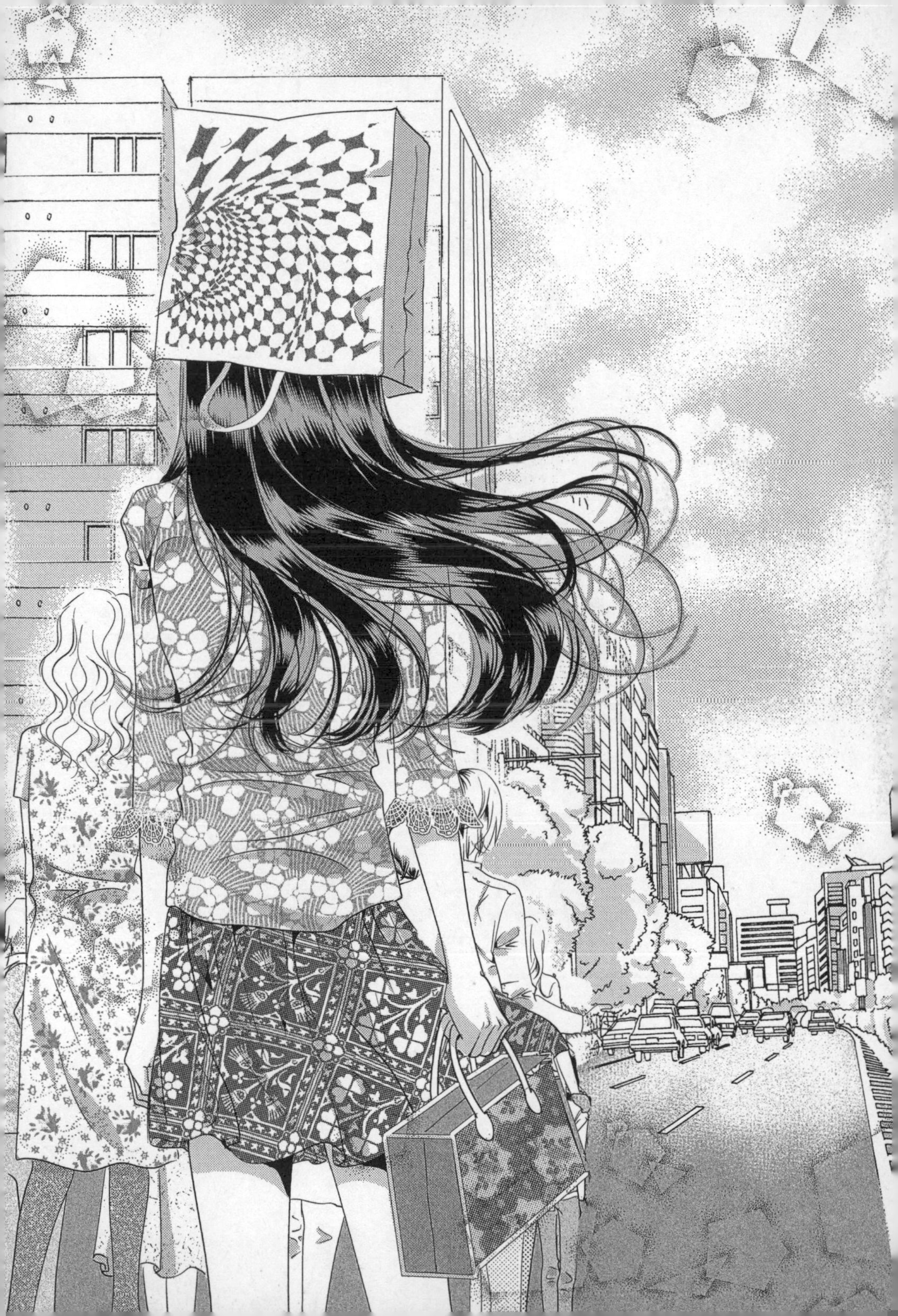

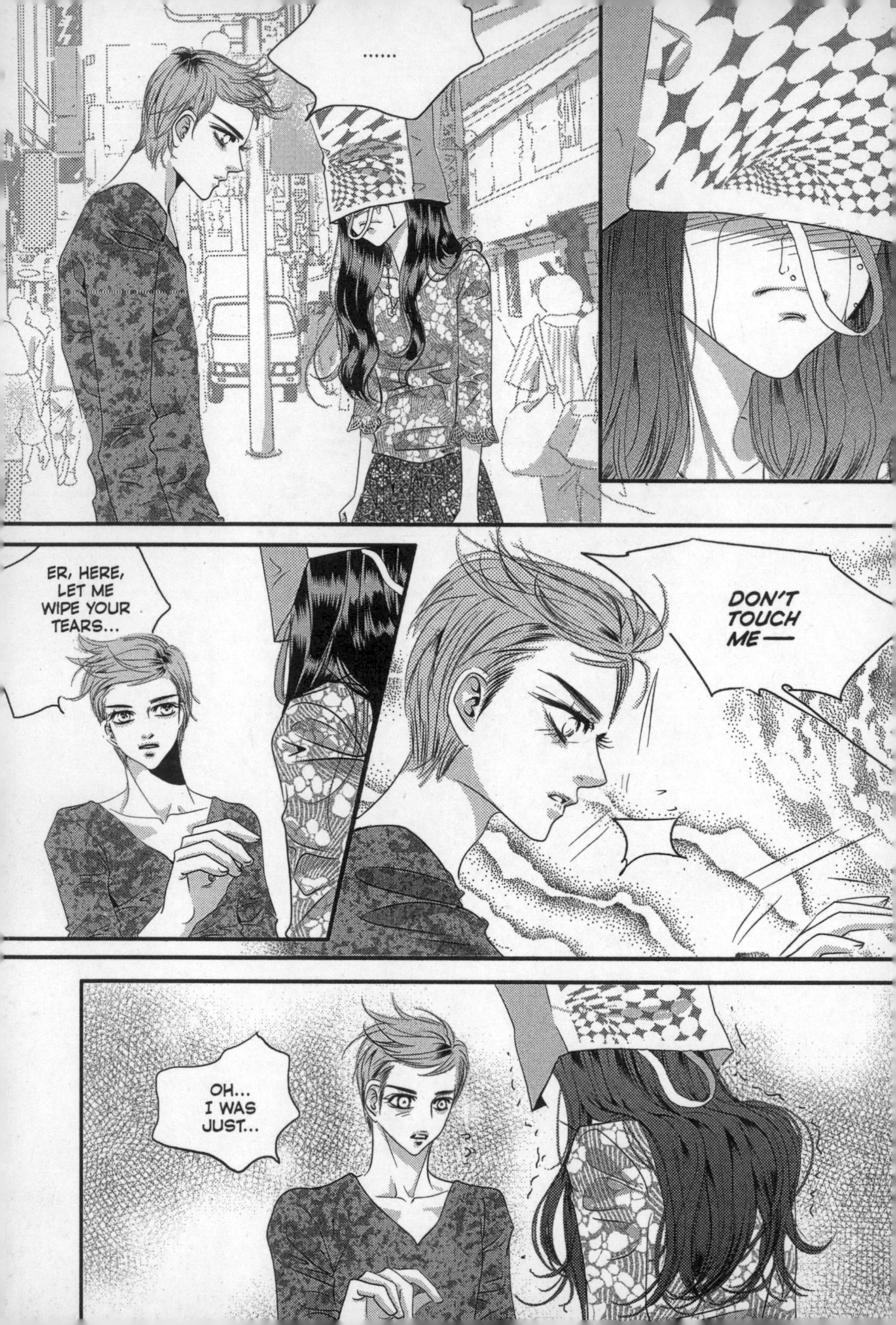
......
ER, HERE, LET ME WIPE YOUR TEARS...
DON'T TOUCH ME—
OH... I WAS JUST...

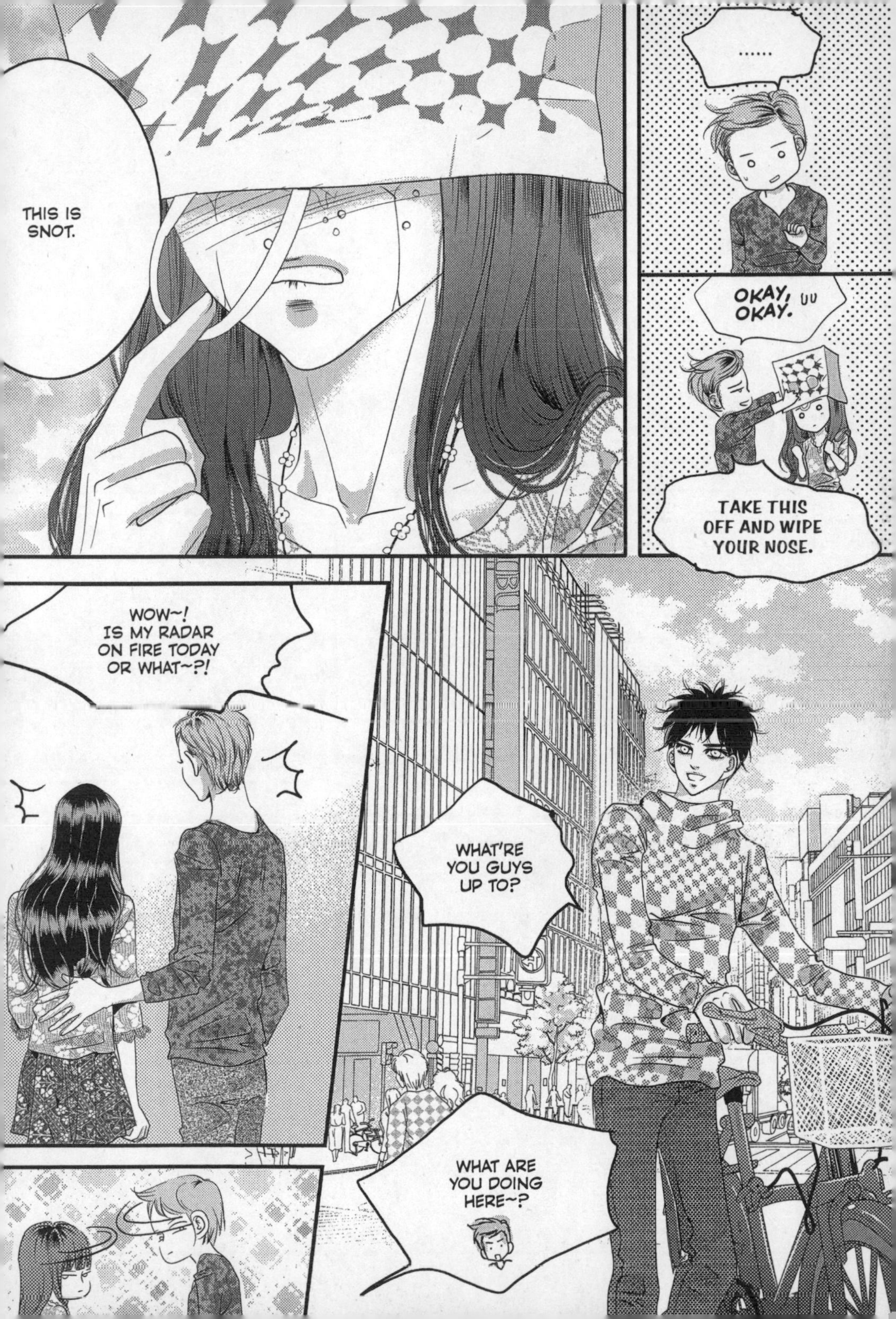
THIS IS SNOT.
......
OKAY, OKAY.
TAKE THIS OFF AND WIPE YOUR NOSE.
WOW~! IS MY RADAR ON FIRE TODAY OR WHAT~?!
WHAT'RE YOU GUYS UP TO?
WHAT ARE YOU DOING HERE~?

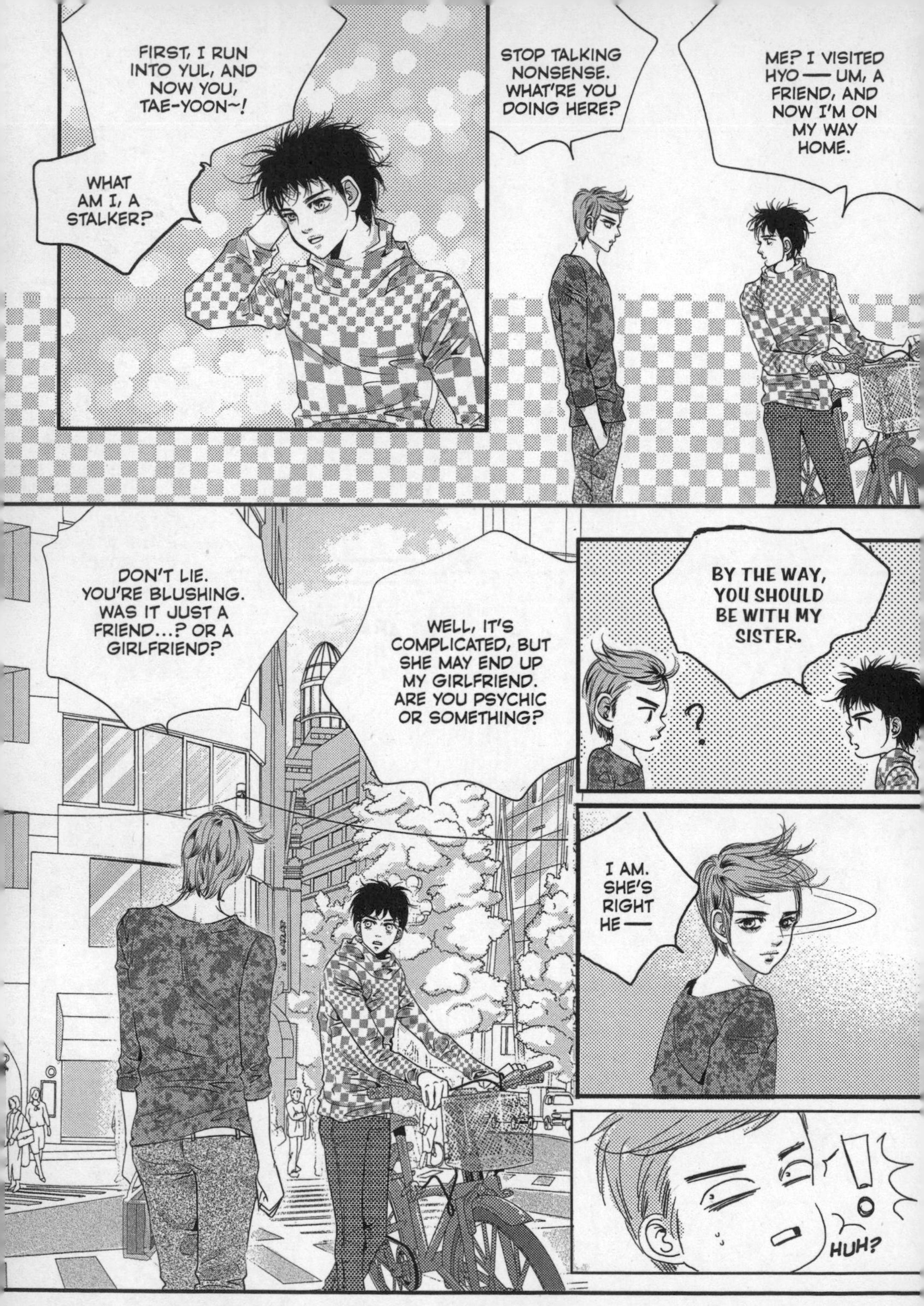
FIRST, I RUN INTO YUL, AND NOW YOU, TAE-YOON~!
WHAT AM I, A STALKER?
STOP TALKING NONSENSE. WHAT'RE YOU DOING HERE?
ME? I VISITED HYO— UM, A FRIEND, AND NOW I'M ON MY WAY HOME.
DON'T LIE. YOU'RE BLUSHING. WAS IT JUST A FRIEND...? OR A GIRLFRIEND?
WELL, IT'S COMPLICATED, BUT SHE MAY END UP MY GIRLFRIEND. ARE YOU PSYCHIC OR SOMETHING?
BY THE WAY, YOU SHOULD BE WITH MY SISTER.
I AM. SHE'S RIGHT HE—
HUH?

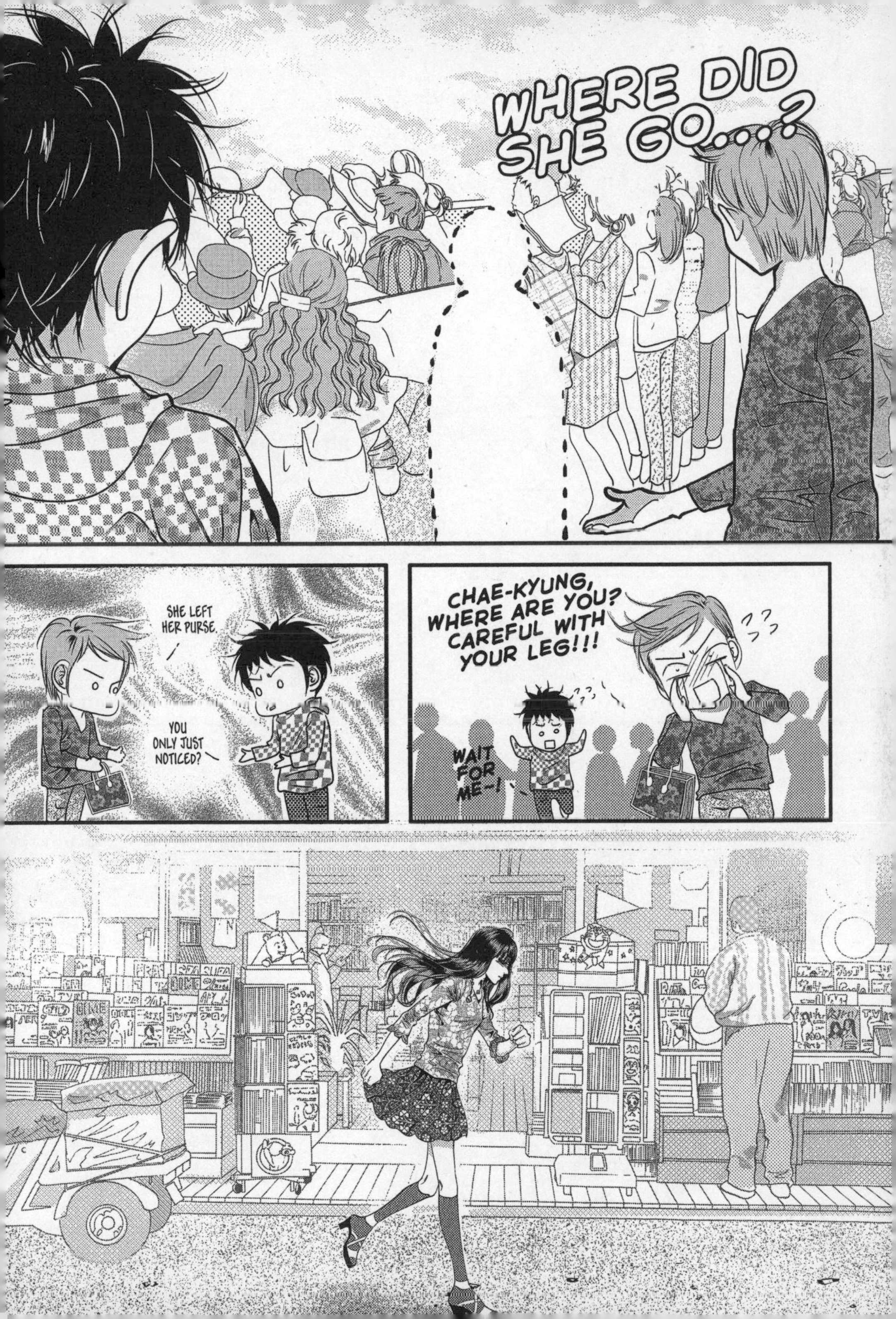
WHERE DID SHE GO...?
SHE LEFT HER PURSE.
YOU ONLY JUST NOTICED?
CHAE-KYUNG, WHERE ARE YOU? CAREFUL WITH YOUR LEG!!!
WAIT FOR ME—!

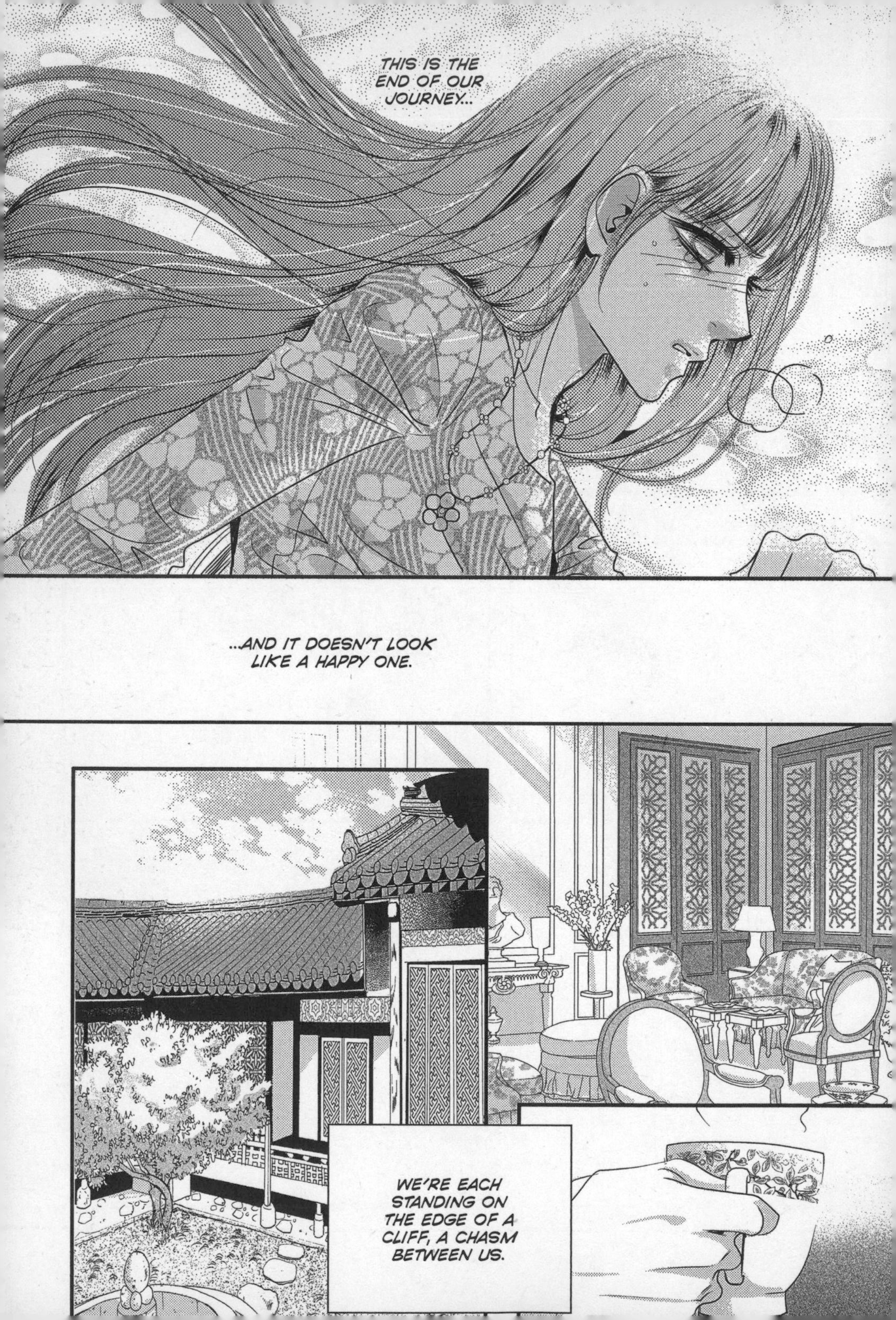
THIS IS THE END OF OUR JOURNEY...
...AND IT DOESN'T LOOK LIKE A HAPPY ONE.
WE'RE EACH STANDING ON THE EDGE OF A CLIFF, A CHASM BETWEEN US.

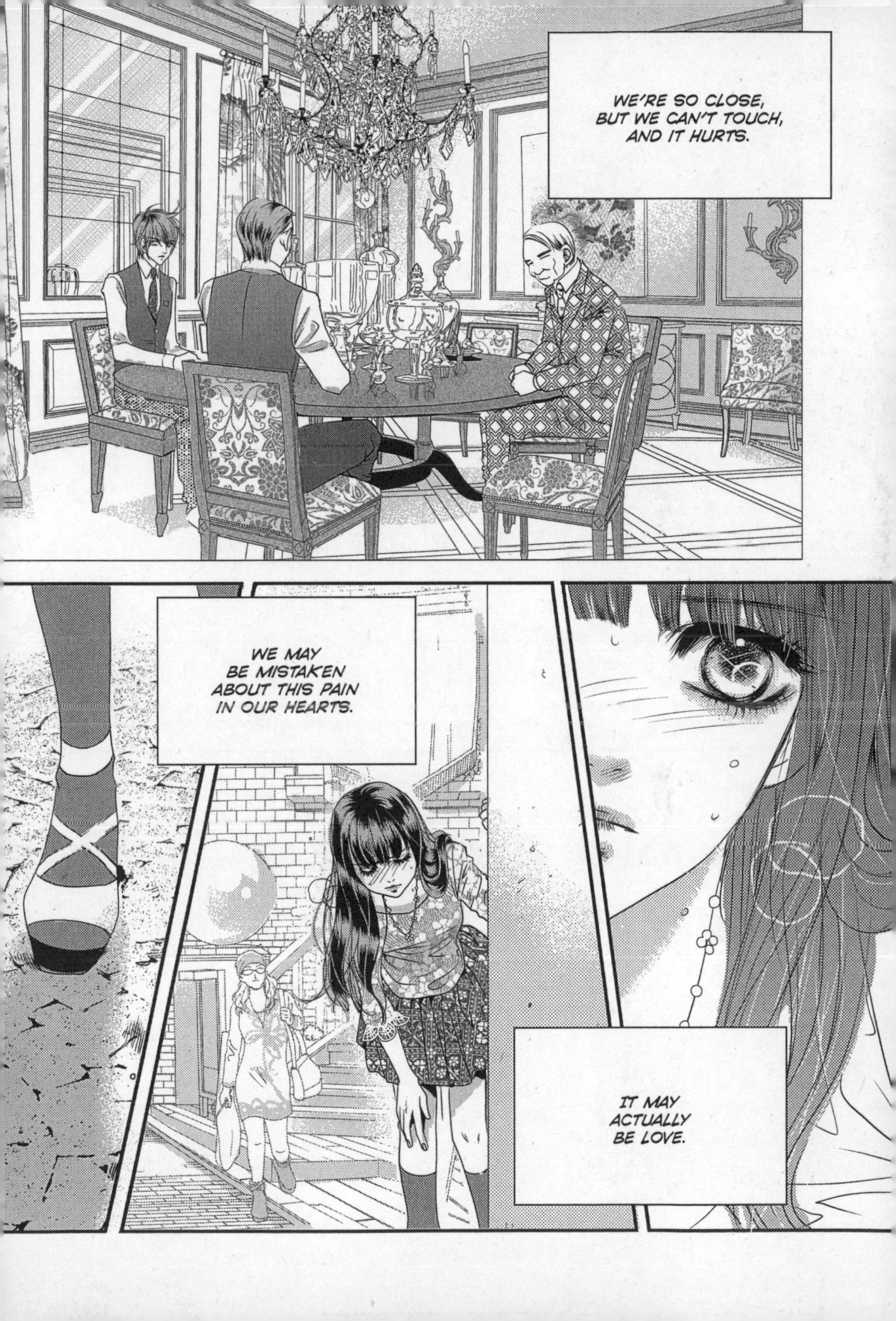
WE'RE SO CLOSE, BUT WE CAN'T TOUCH, AND IT HURTS.
WE MAY BE MISTAKEN ABOUT THIS PAIN IN OUR HEARTS.
IT MAY ACTUALLY BE LOVE.

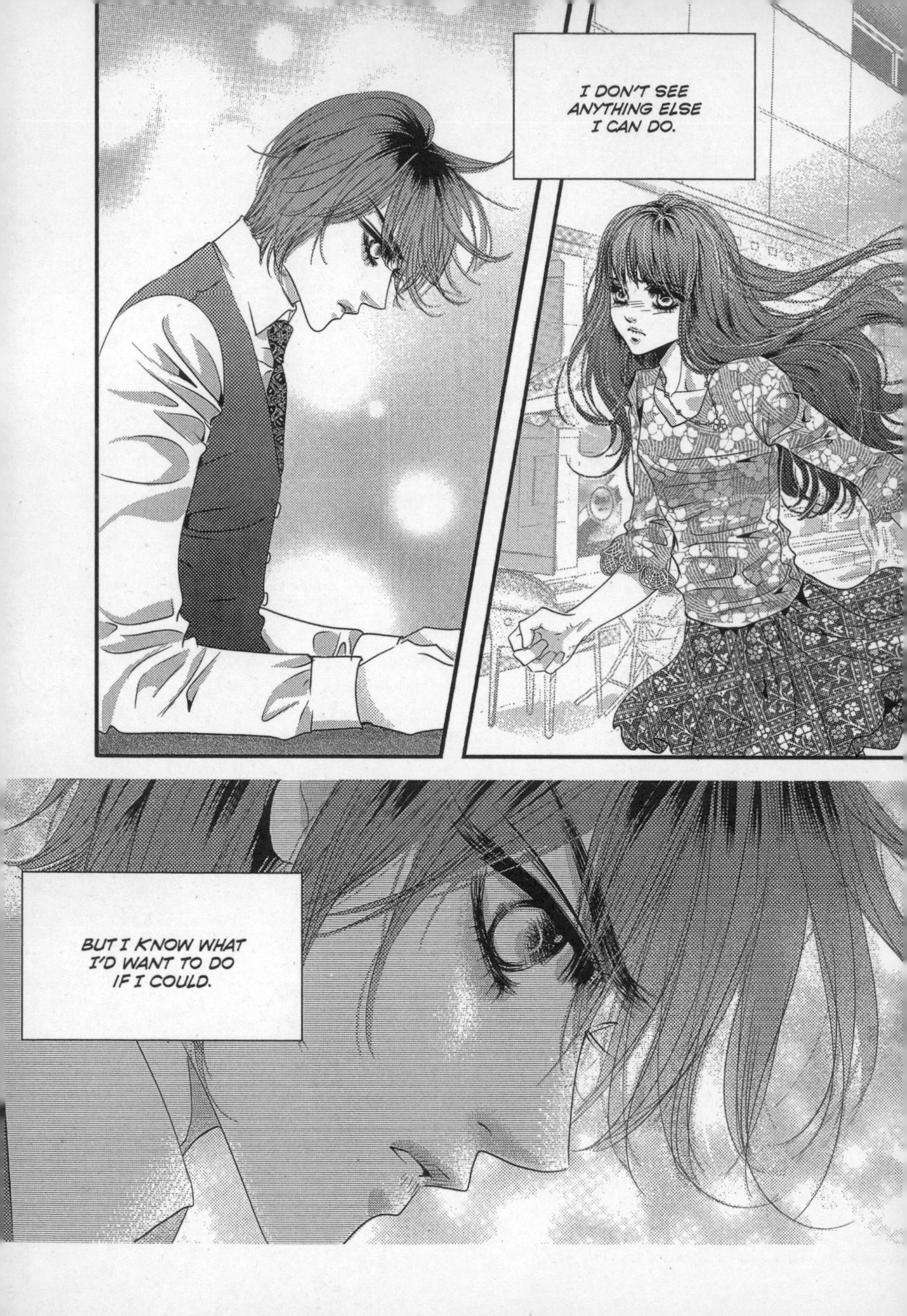
I DON'T SEE ANYTHING ELSE I CAN DO.
BUT I KNOW WHAT I'D WANT TO DO IF I COULD.

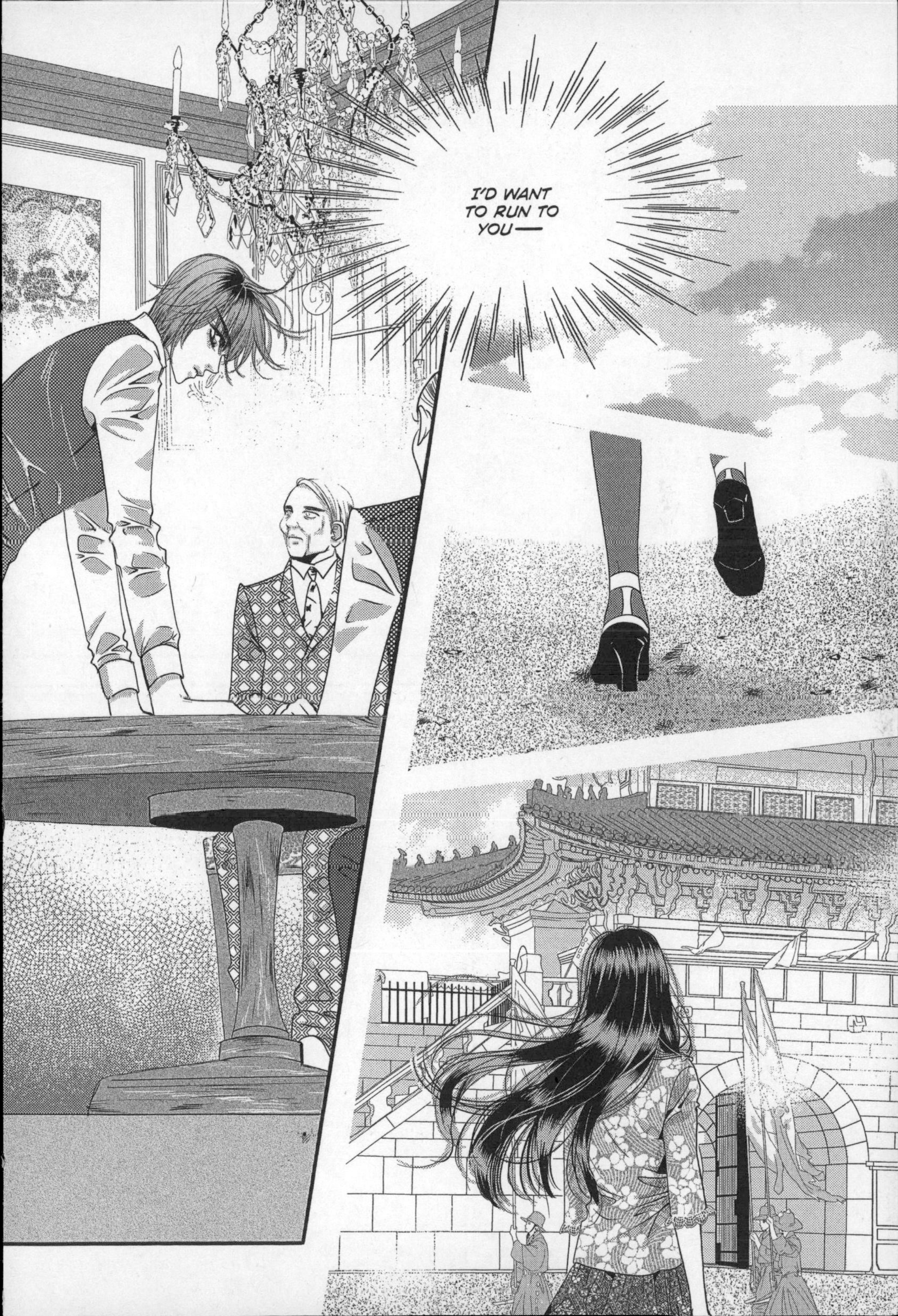
I'D WANT TO RUN TO YOU—

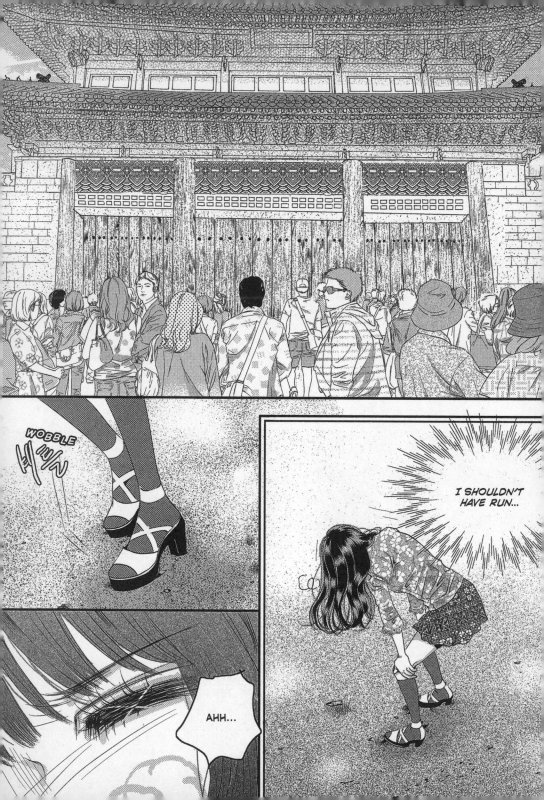

WOBBLE

I SHOULDN'T HAVE RUN...

AHH...

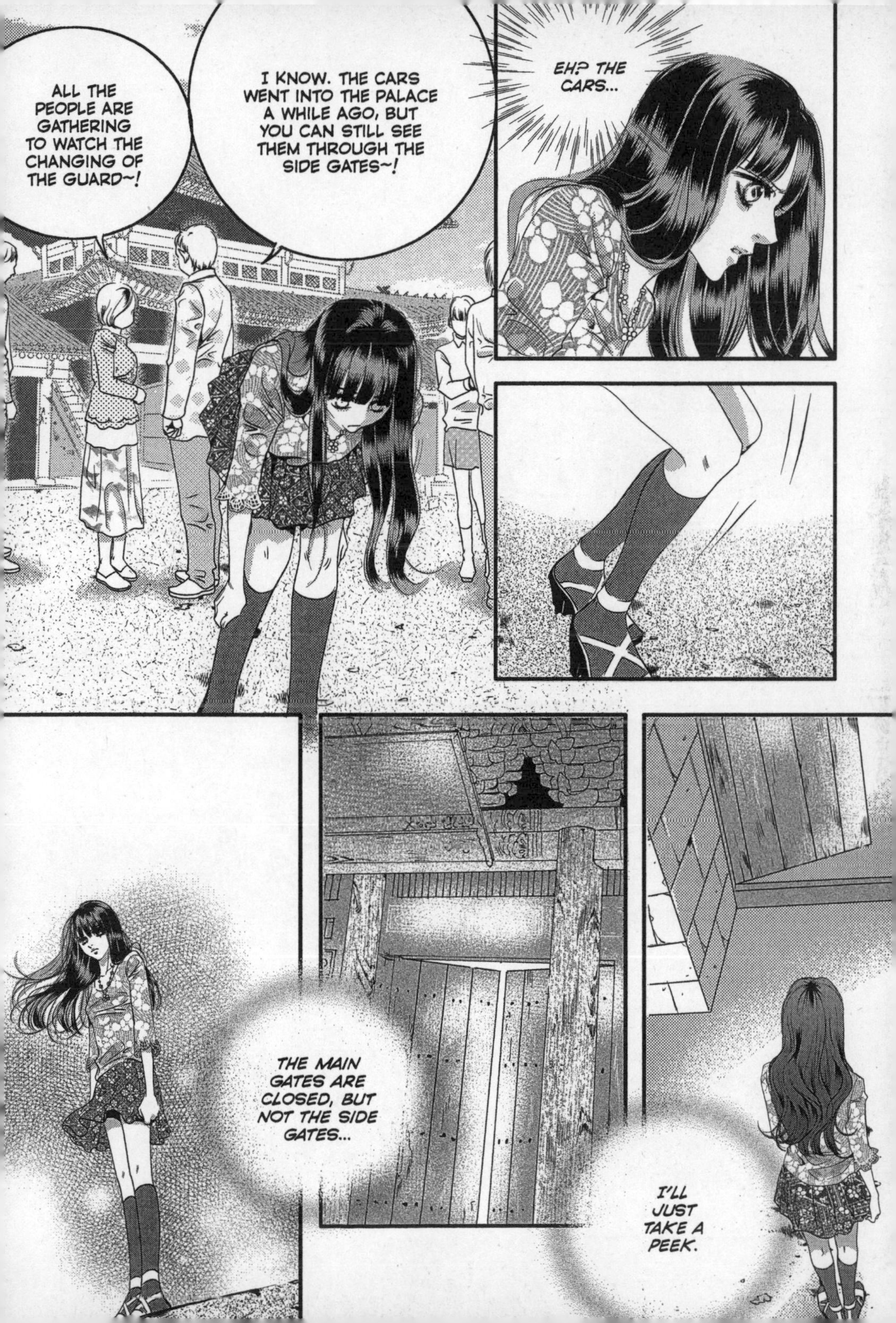
ALL THE PEOPLE ARE GATHERING TO WATCH THE CHANGING OF THE GUARD~!
I KNOW. THE CARS WENT INTO THE PALACE A WHILE AGO, BUT YOU CAN STILL SEE THEM THROUGH THE SIDE GATES~!
EH? THE CARS...
THE MAIN GATES ARE CLOSED, BUT NOT THE SIDE GATES...
I'LL JUST TAKE A PEEK.

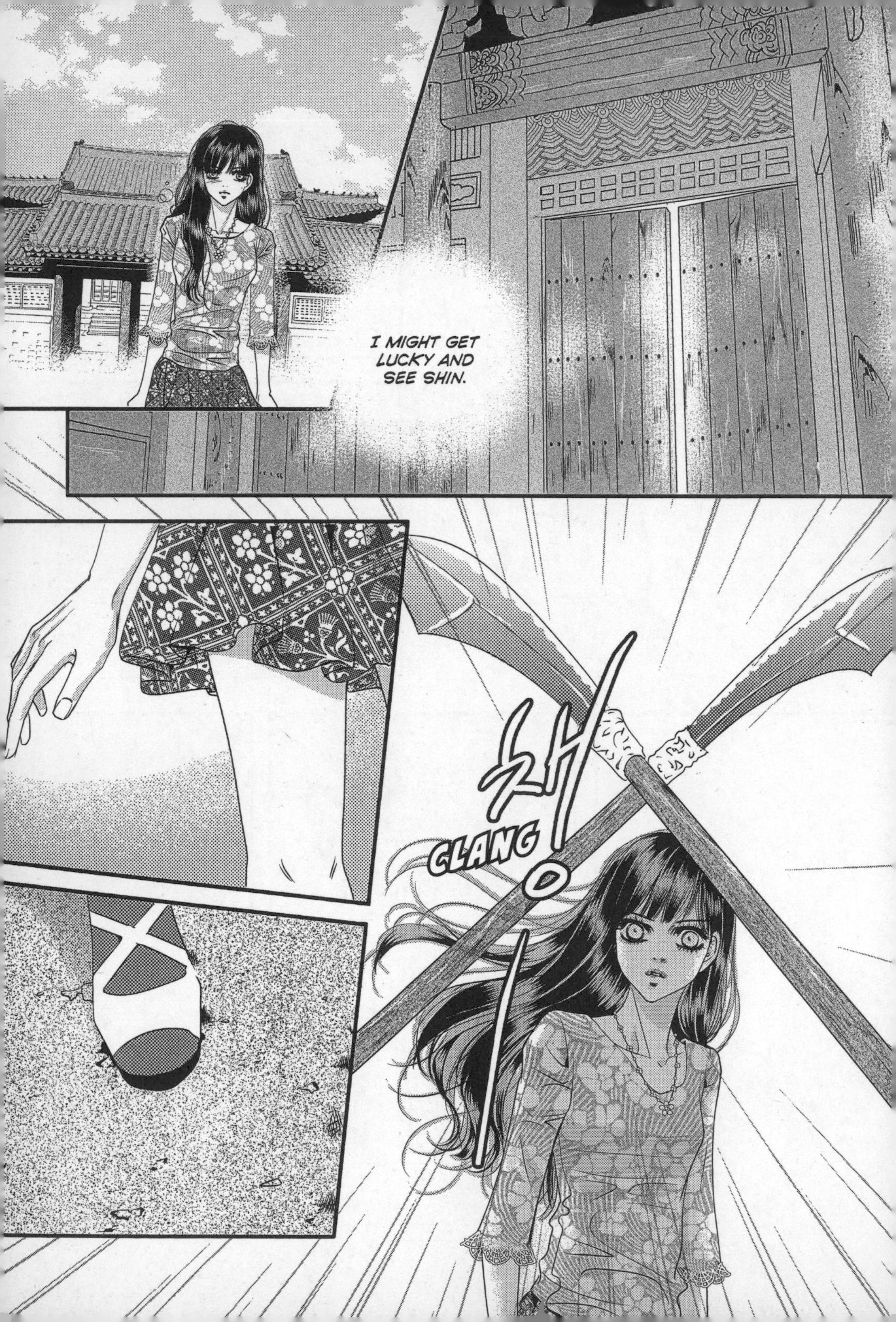
I MIGHT GET LUCKY AND SEE SHIN.
CLANG

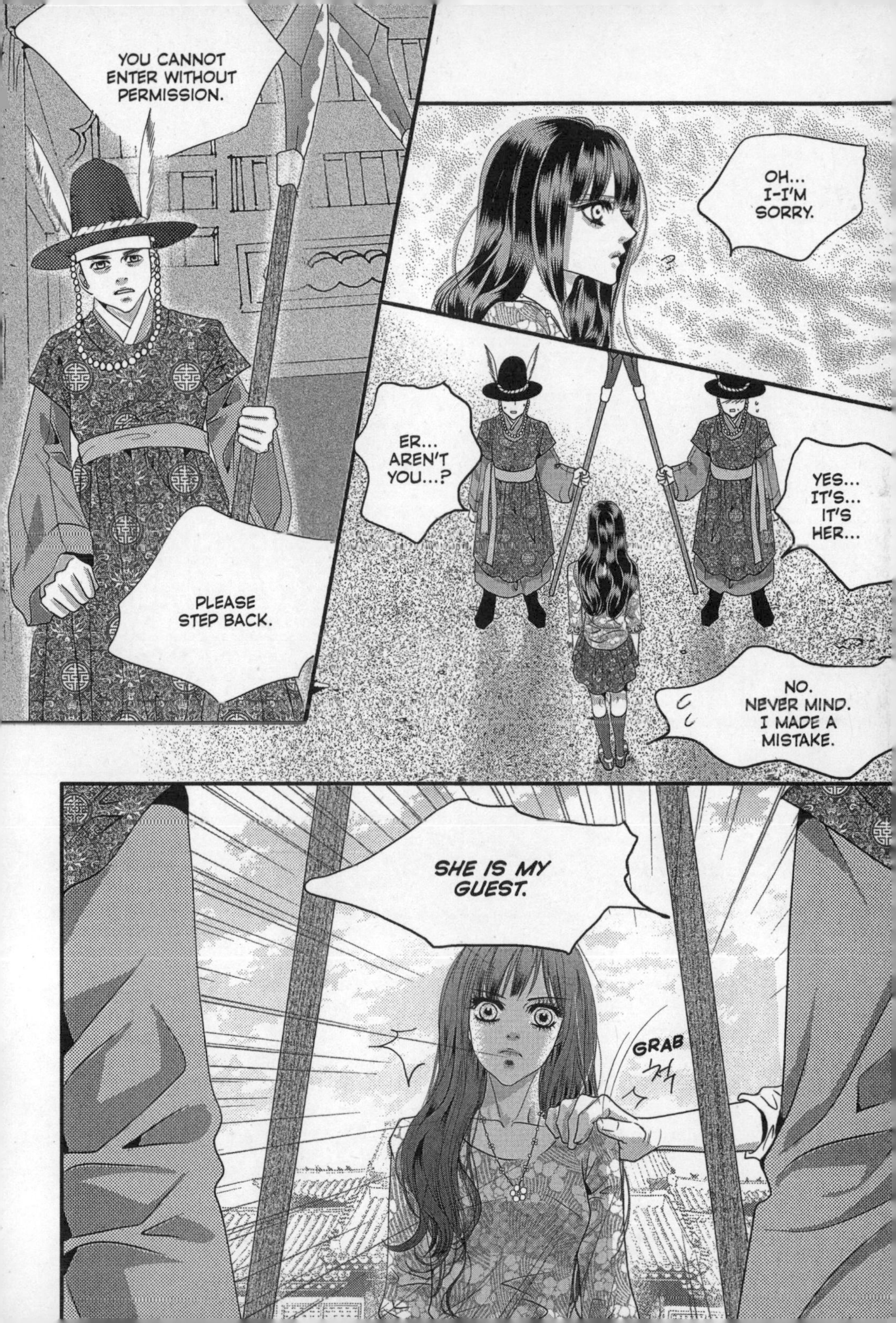
YOU CANNOT ENTER WITHOUT PERMISSION.
PLEASE STEP BACK.
OH... I-I'M SORRY.
ER... AREN'T YOU...?
YES... IT'S... IT'S HER...
NO. NEVER MIND. I MADE A MISTAKE.
SHE IS MY GUEST.
GRAB

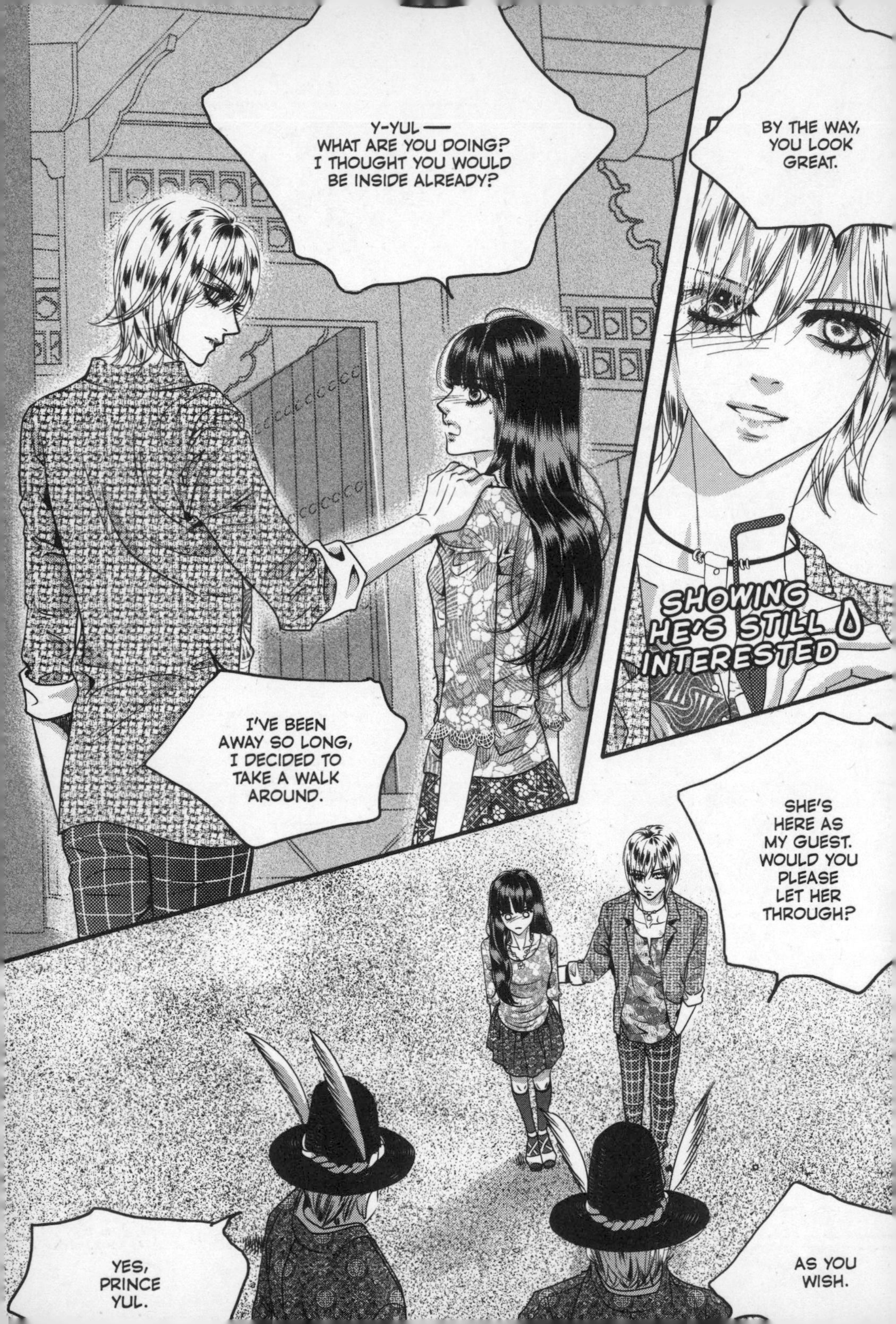
Y-YUL — WHAT ARE YOU DOING? I THOUGHT YOU WOULD BE INSIDE ALREADY?
I'VE BEEN AWAY SO LONG, I DECIDED TO TAKE A WALK AROUND.
BY THE WAY, YOU LOOK GREAT.
SHOWING HE'S STILL INTERESTED
SHE'S HERE AS MY GUEST. WOULD YOU PLEASE LET HER THROUGH?
YES, PRINCE YUL.
AS YOU WISH.

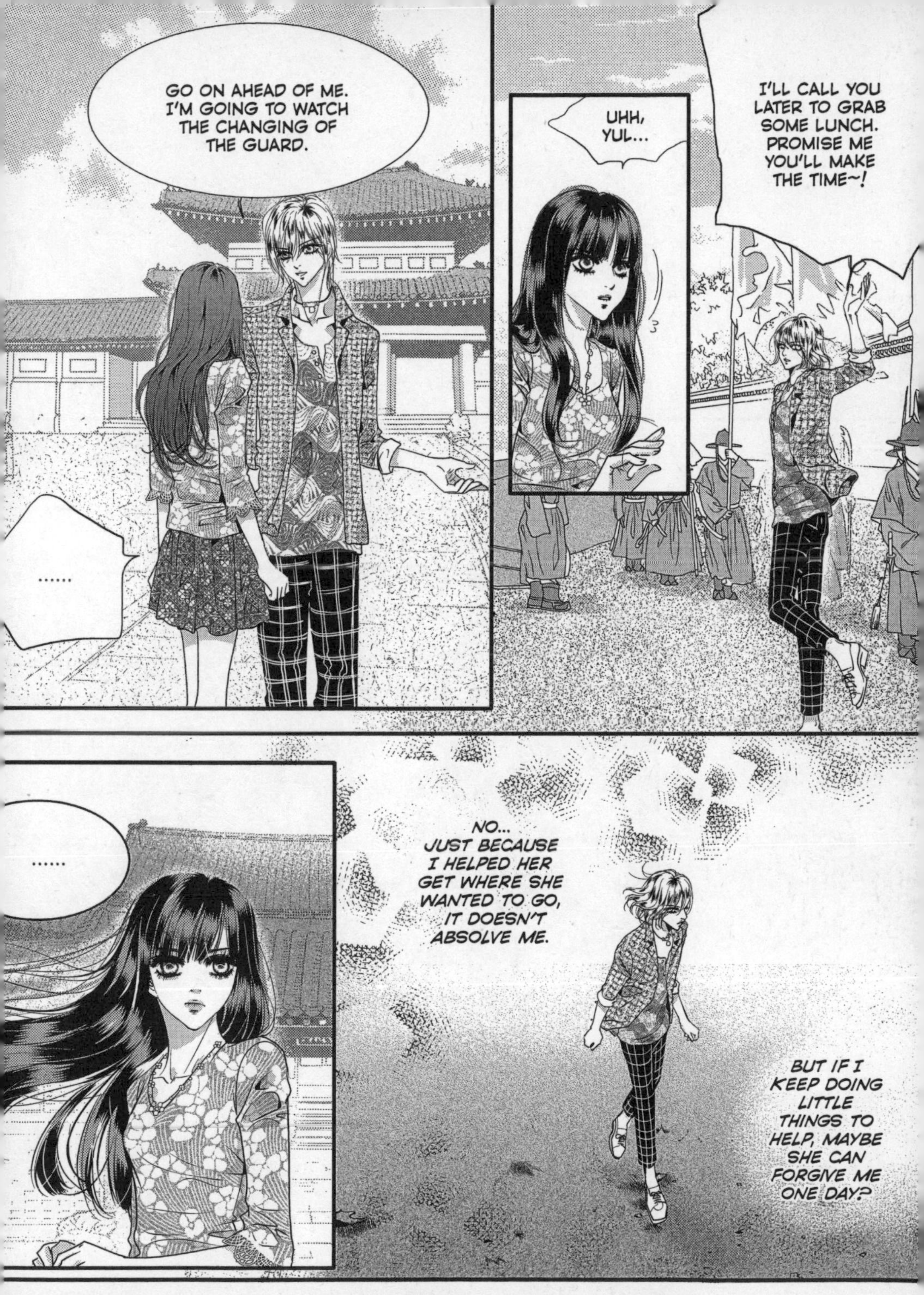
GO ON AHEAD OF ME. I'M GOING TO WATCH THE CHANGING OF THE GUARD.
......
UHH, YUL...
I'LL CALL YOU LATER TO GRAB SOME LUNCH. PROMISE ME YOU'LL MAKE THE TIME~!
......
NO... JUST BECAUSE I HELPED HER GET WHERE SHE WANTED TO GO, IT DOESN'T ABSOLVE ME.
BUT IF I KEEP DOING LITTLE THINGS TO HELP, MAYBE SHE CAN FORGIVE ME ONE DAY?

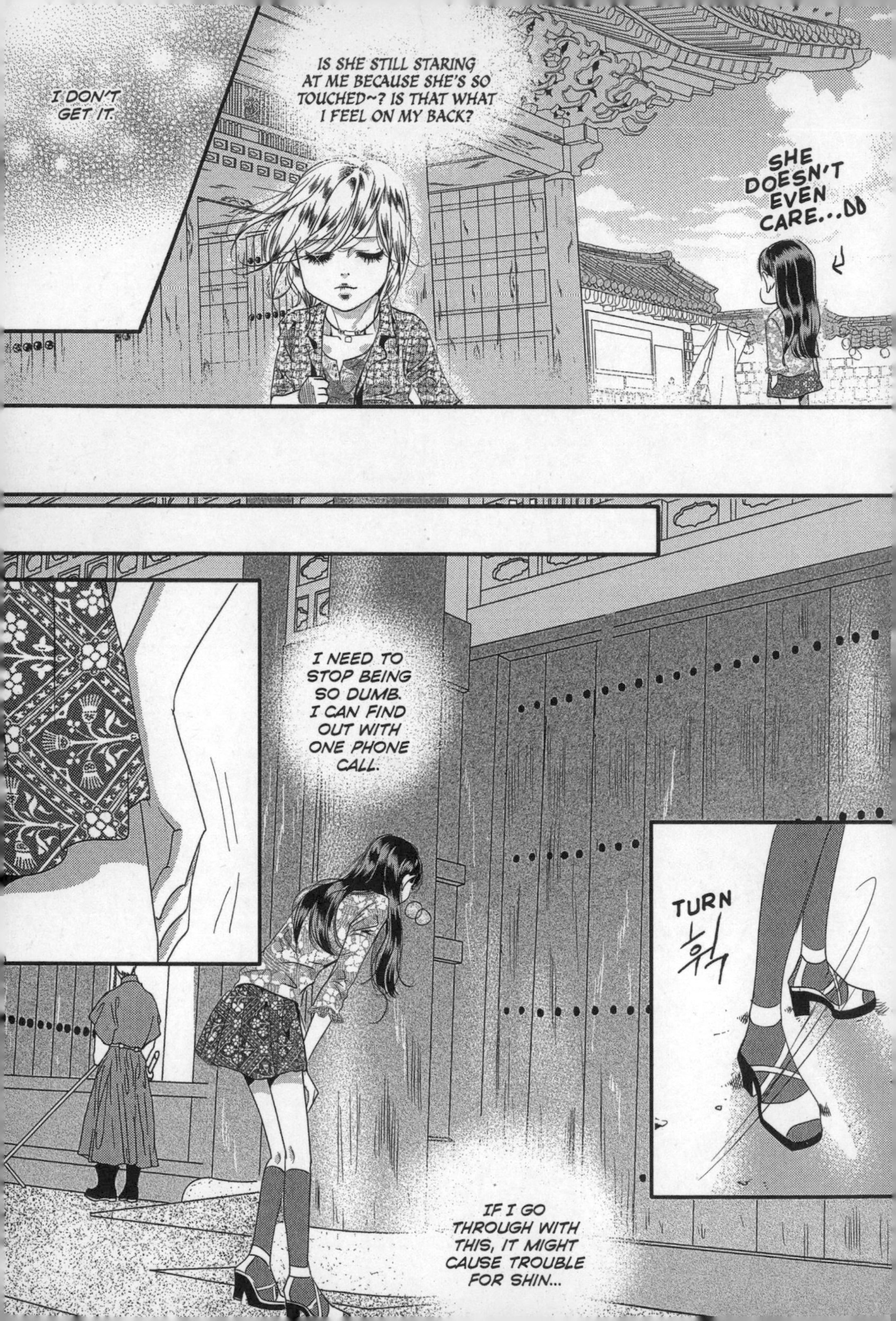
I DON'T GET IT.
IS SHE STILL STARING AT ME BECAUSE SHE'S SO TOUCHED~? IS THAT WHAT I FEEL ON MY BACK?
SHE DOESN'T EVEN CARE...
I NEED TO STOP BEING SO DUMB. I CAN FIND OUT WITH ONE PHONE CALL.
TURN
휙
IF I GO THROUGH WITH THIS, IT MIGHT CAUSE TROUBLE FOR SHIN...

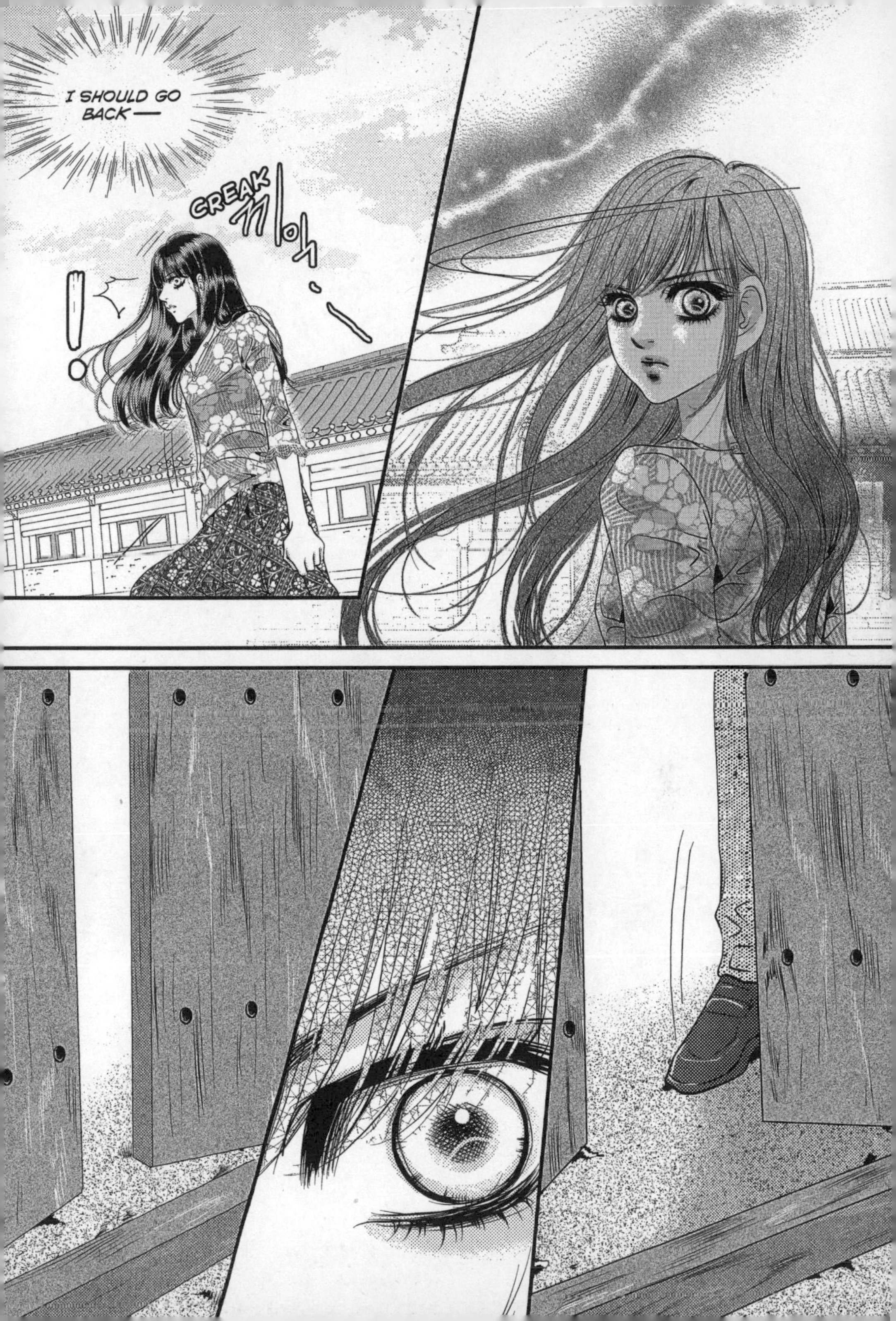
I SHOULD GO BACK—
CREAK
끼익
!

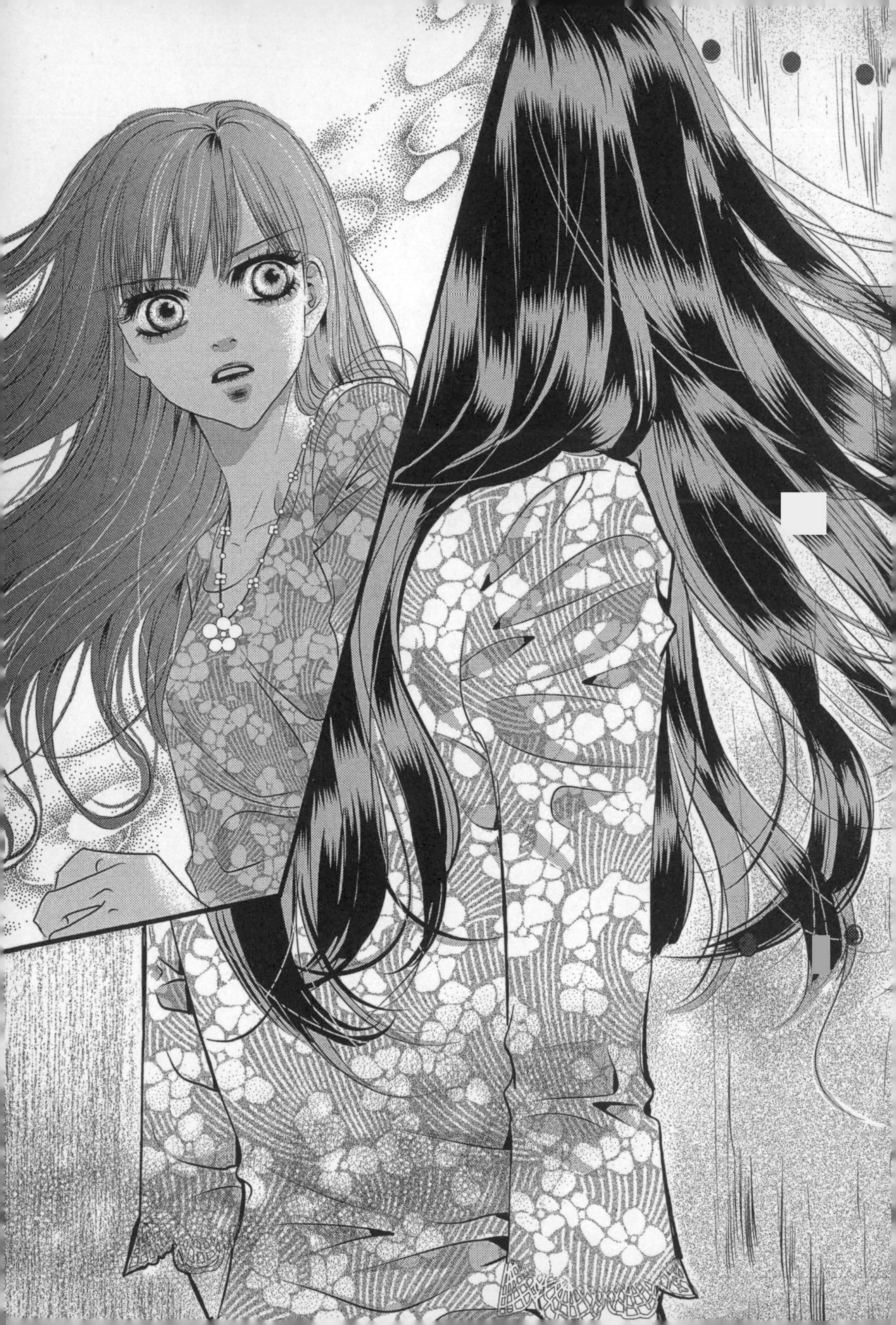

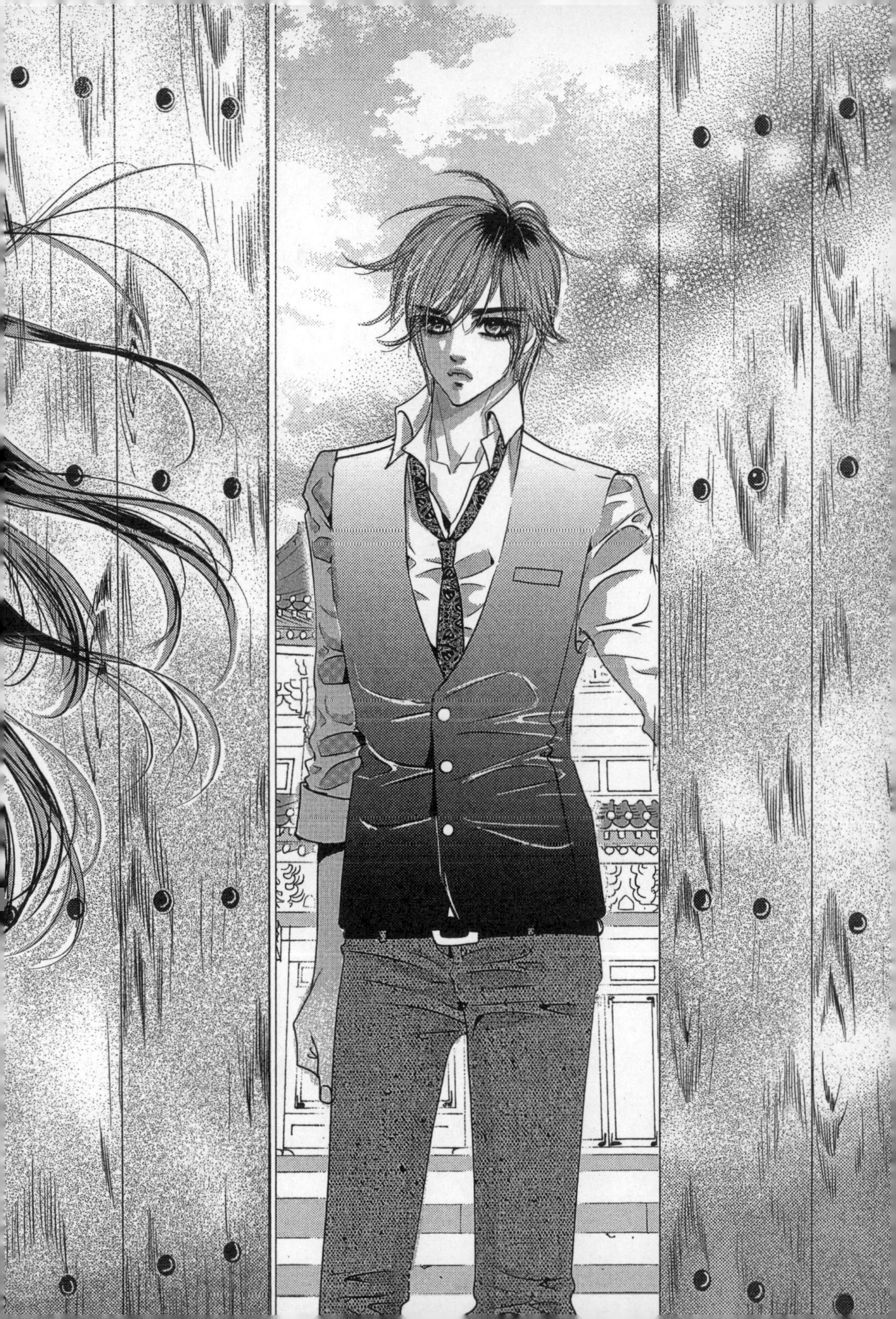

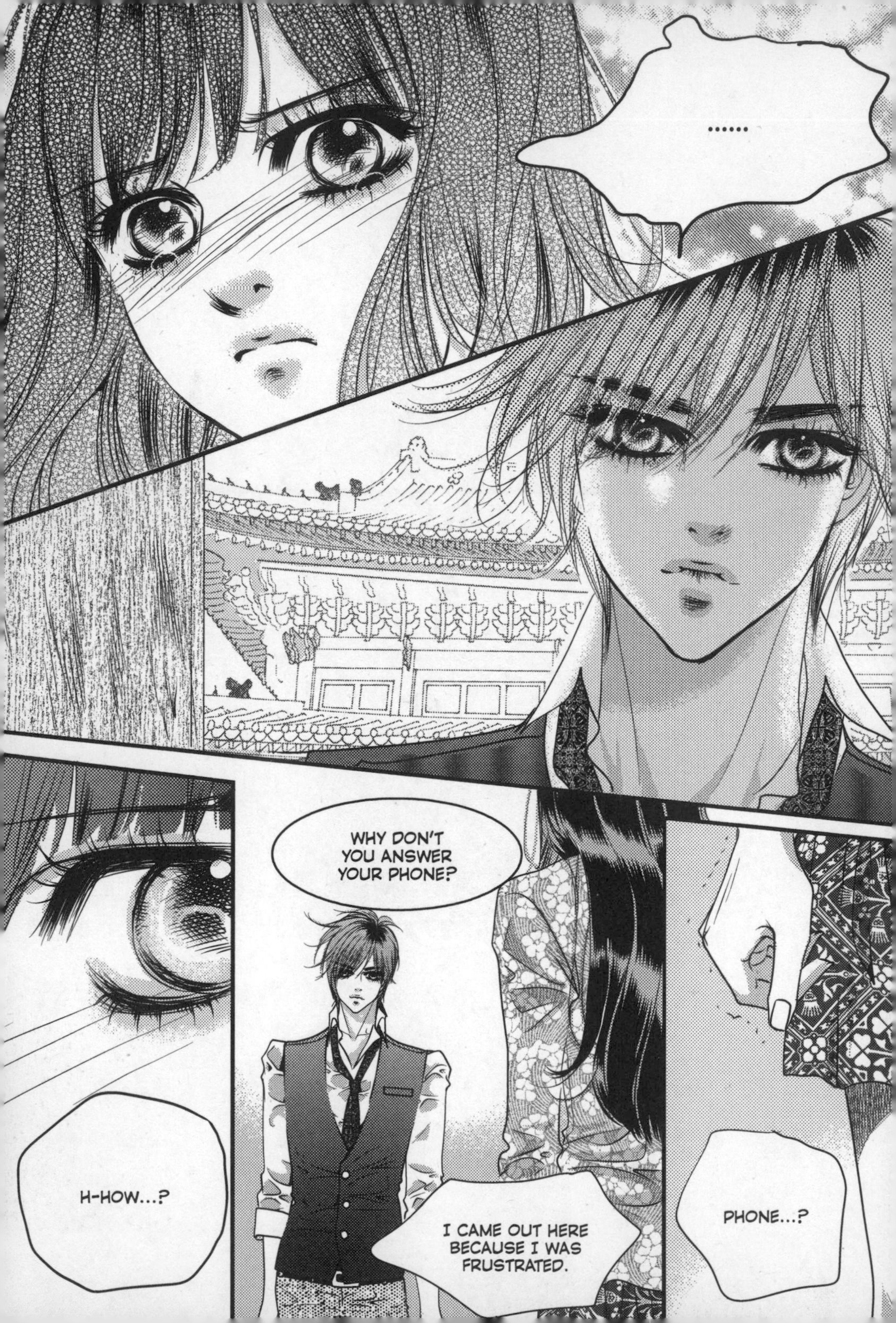
......
H-HOW...?
WHY DON'T YOU ANSWER YOUR PHONE?
I CAME OUT HERE BECAUSE I WAS FRUSTRATED.
PHONE...?

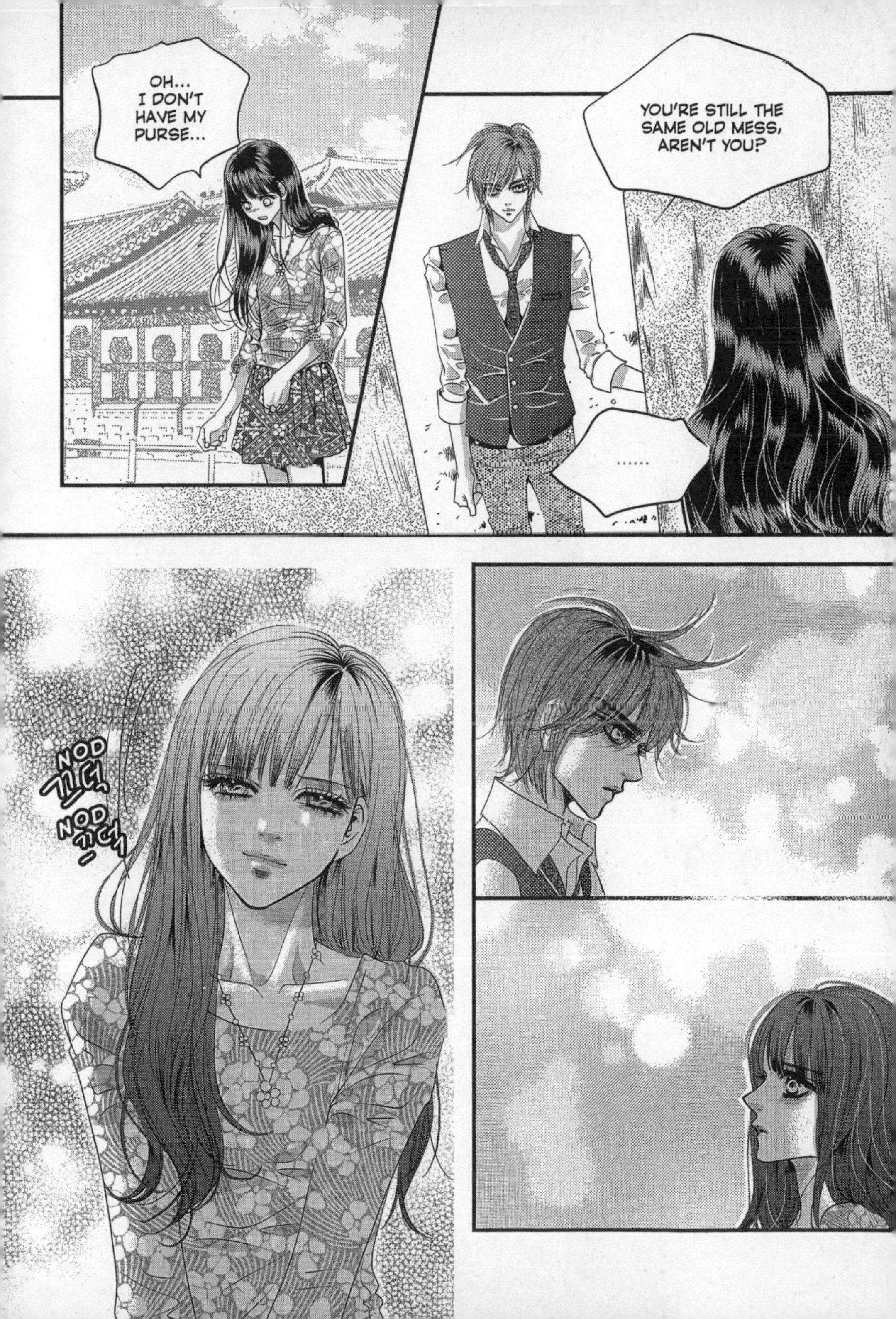
OH... I DON'T HAVE MY PURSE...
YOU'RE STILL THE SAME OLD MESS, AREN'T YOU?
......
NOD
NOD

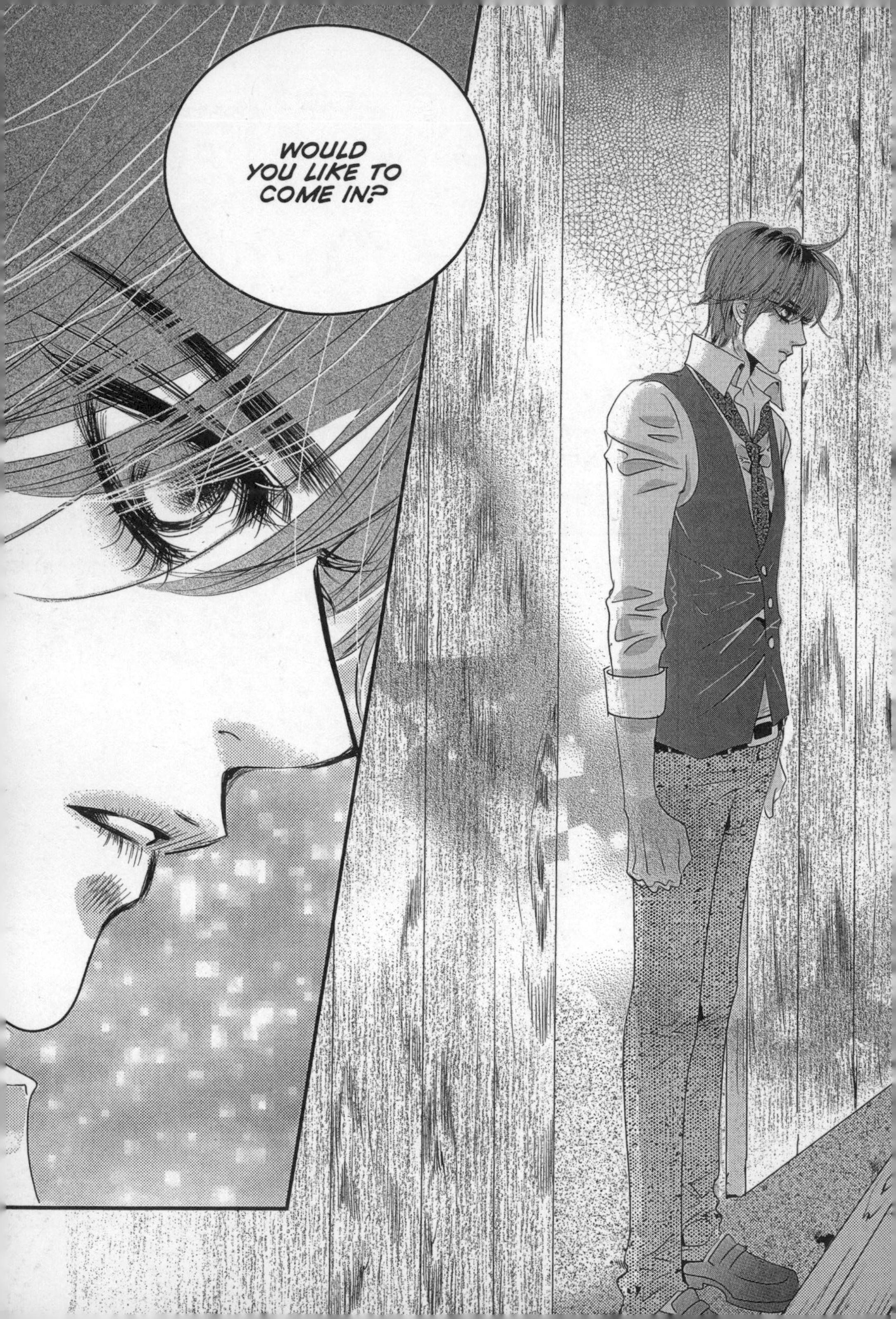
WOULD YOU LIKE TO COME IN?

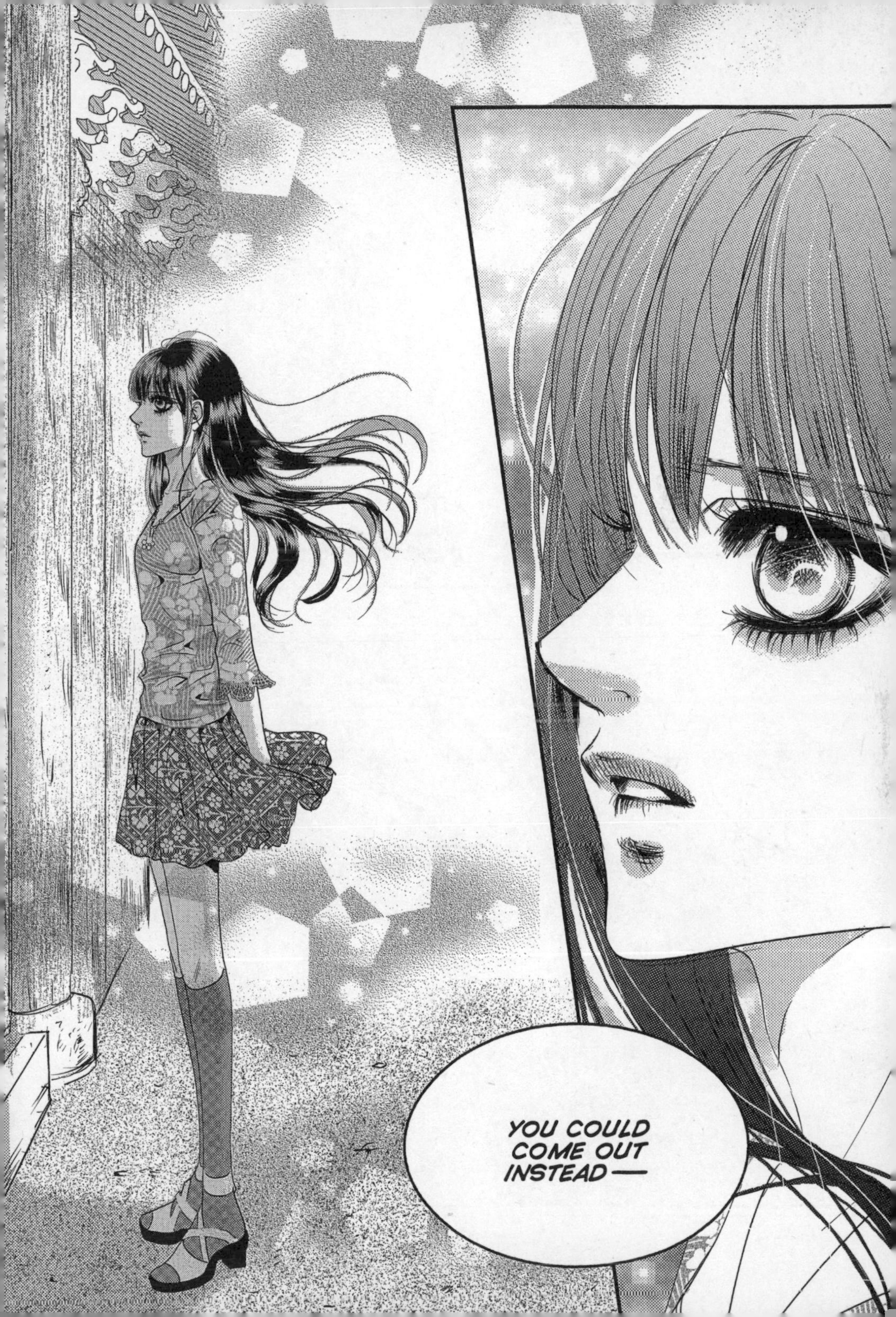
YOU COULD COME OUT INSTEAD—

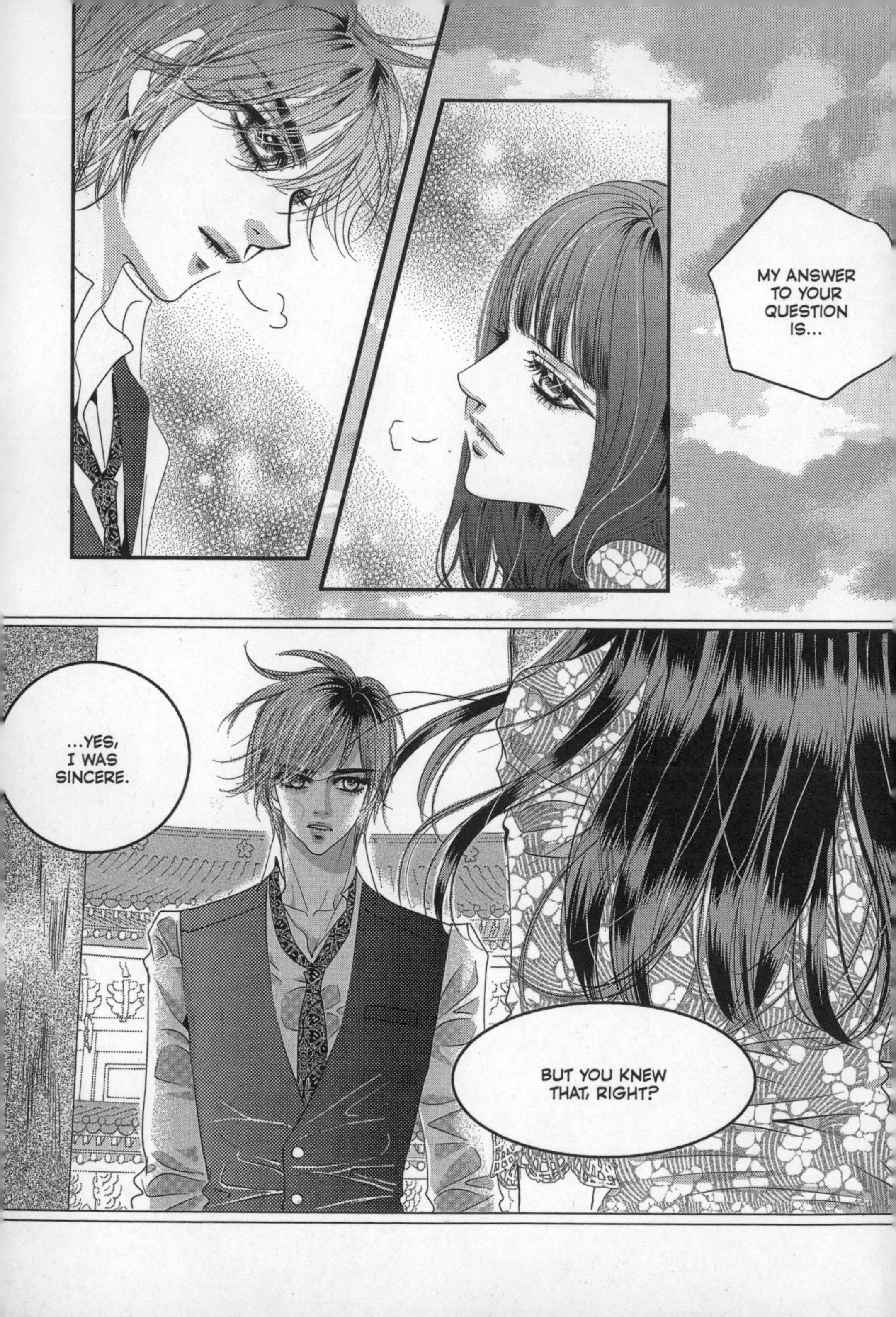
MY ANSWER TO YOUR QUESTION IS...
...YES, I WAS SINCERE.
BUT YOU KNEW THAT, RIGHT?

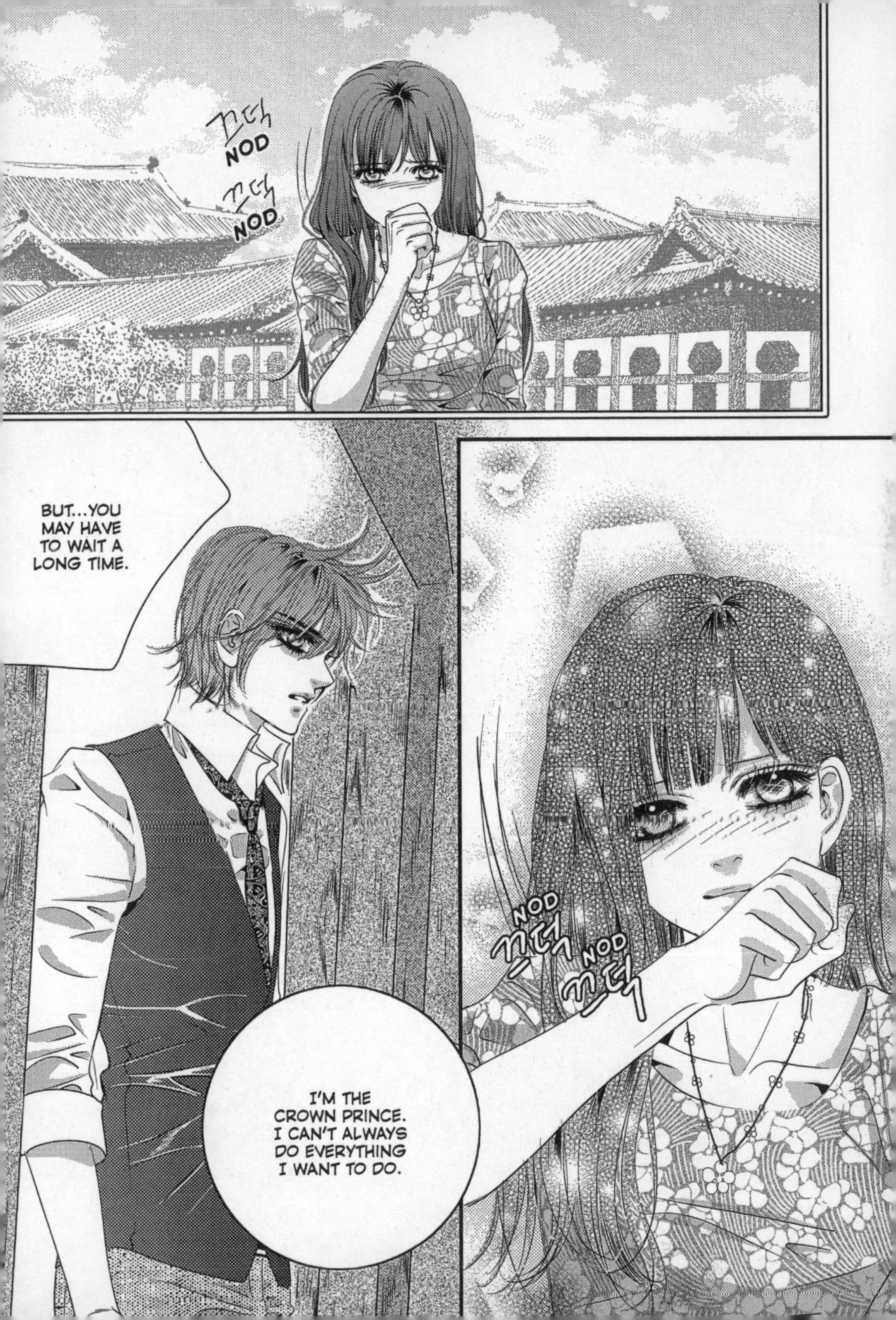
끄덕
NOD
끄덕
NOD
BUT...YOU MAY HAVE TO WAIT A LONG TIME.
I'M THE CROWN PRINCE. I CAN'T ALWAYS DO EVERYTHING I WANT TO DO.
NOD
끄덕
NOD
끄덕

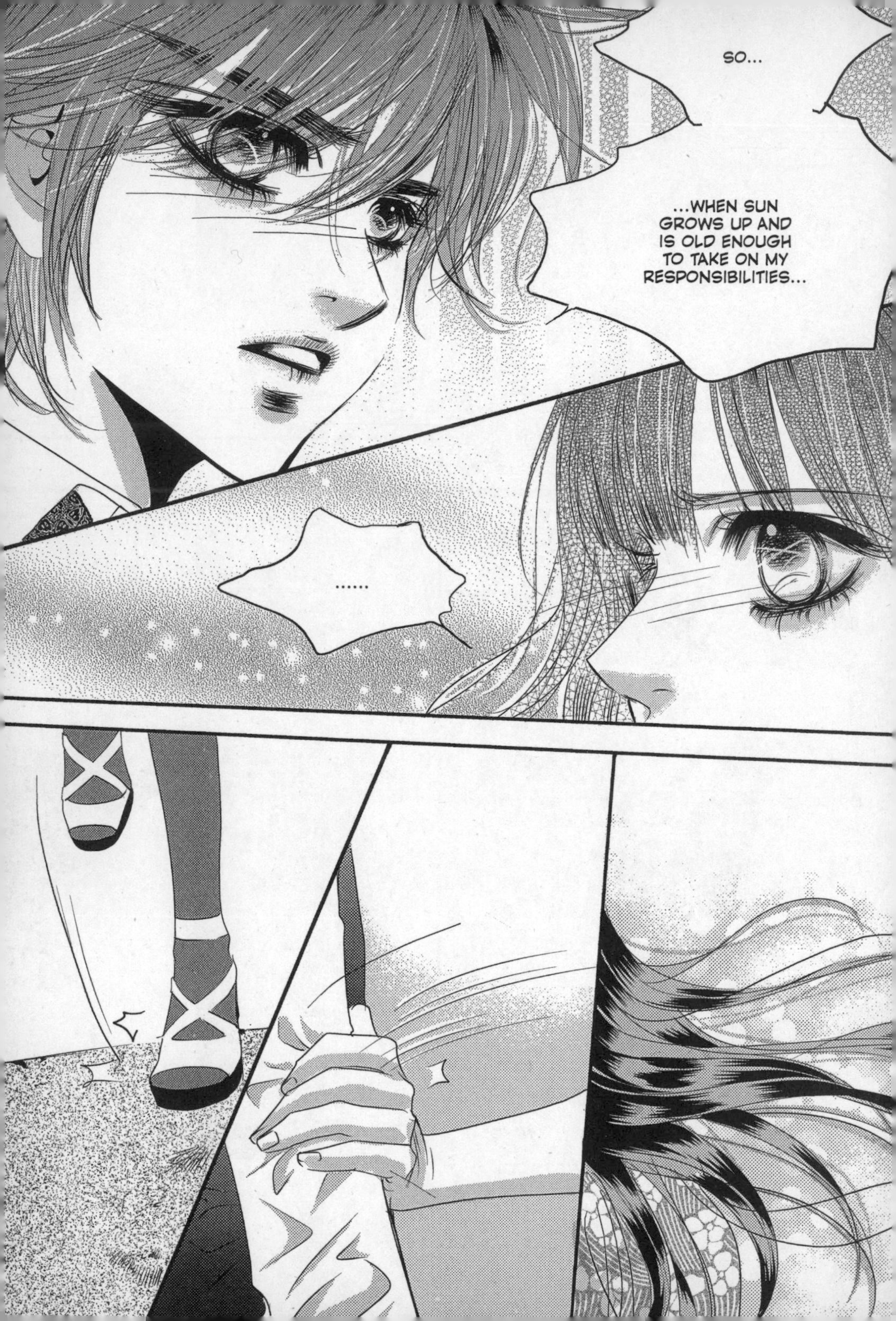
SO...
...WHEN SUN GROWS UP AND IS OLD ENOUGH TO TAKE ON MY RESPONSIBILITIES...
......

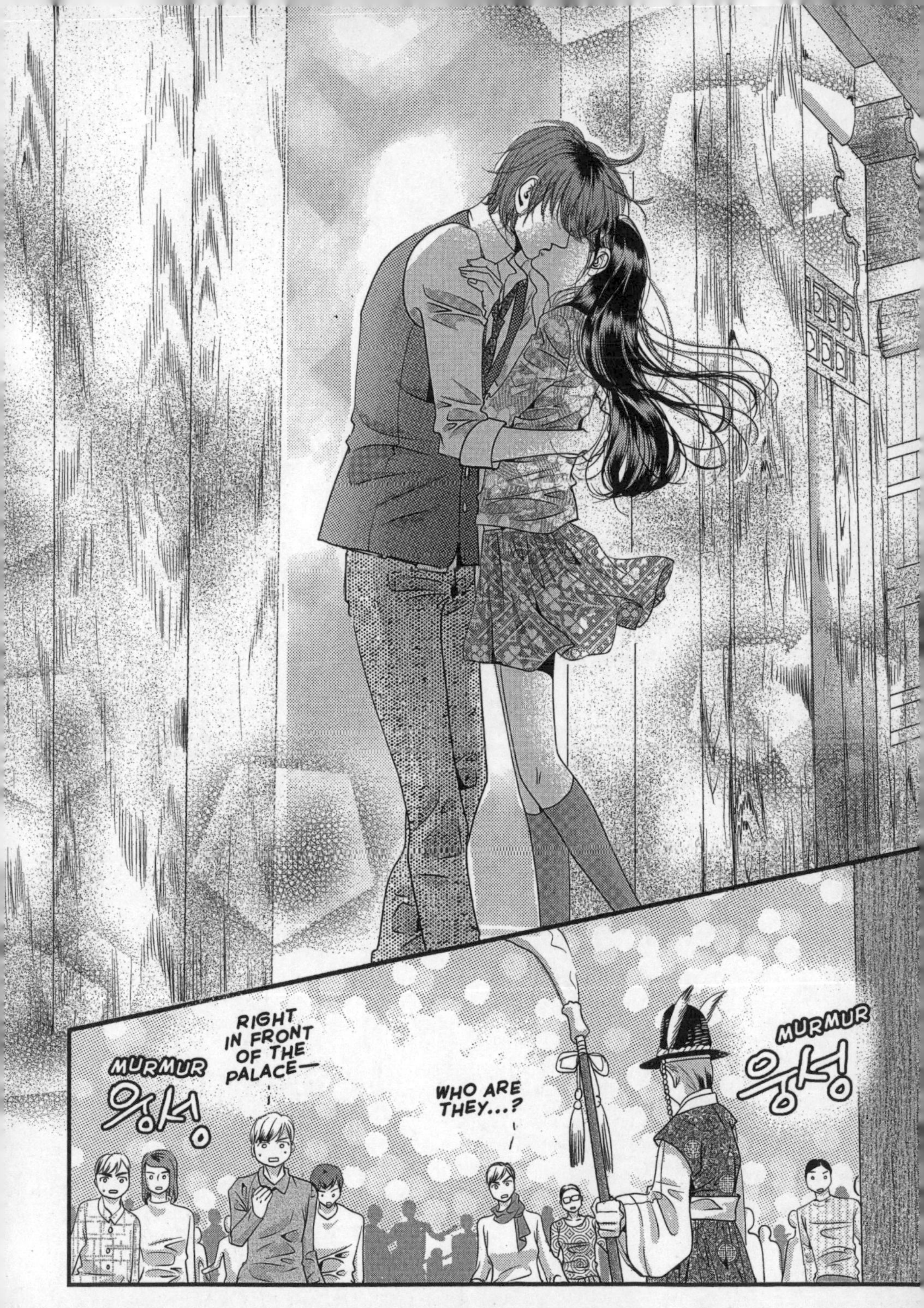
MURMUR
웅성
RIGHT IN FRONT OF THE PALACE—
WHO ARE THEY...?
MURMUR
웅성

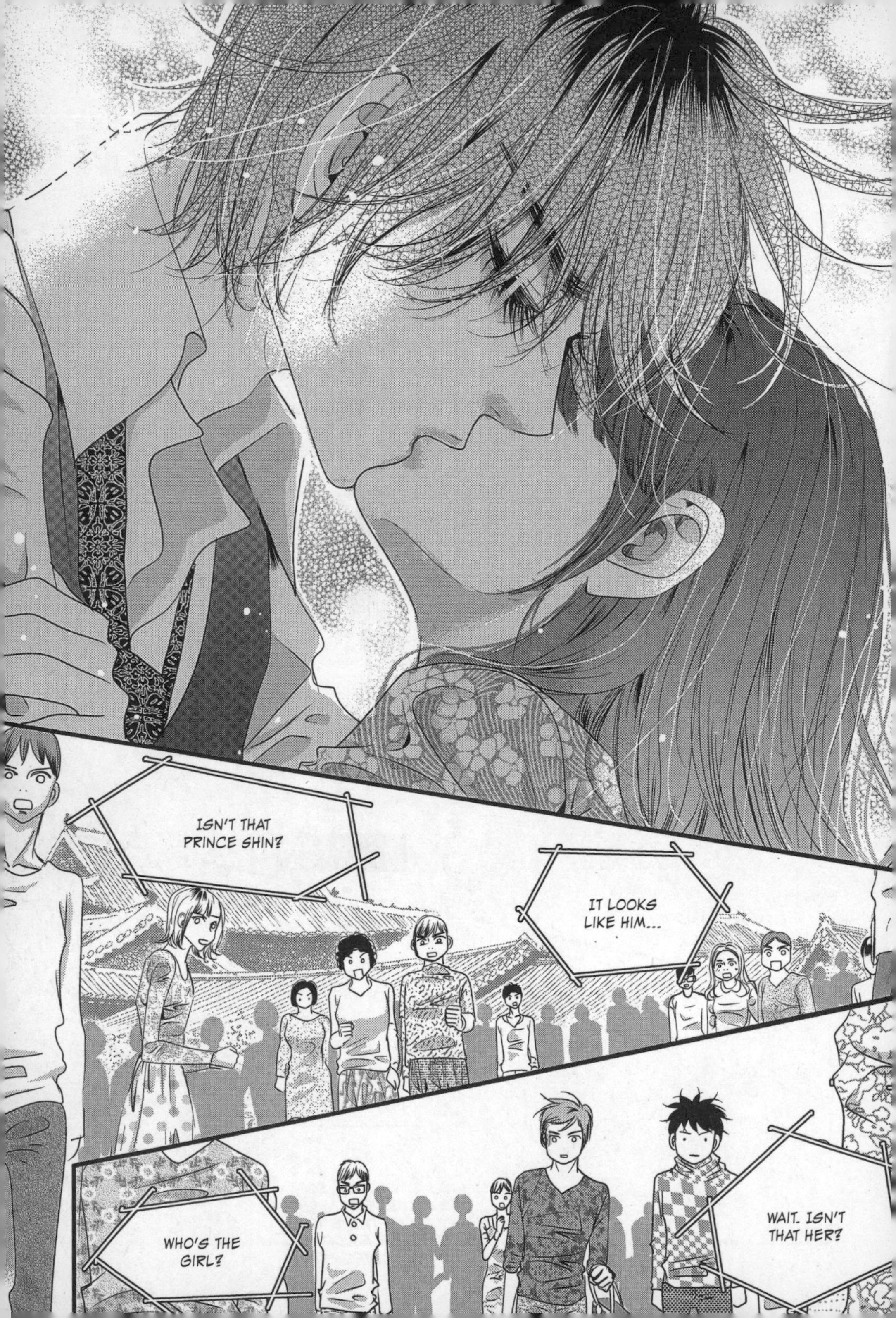
ISN'T THAT PRINCE SHIN?
IT LOOKS LIKE HIM...
WHO'S THE GIRL?
WAIT. ISN'T THAT HER?

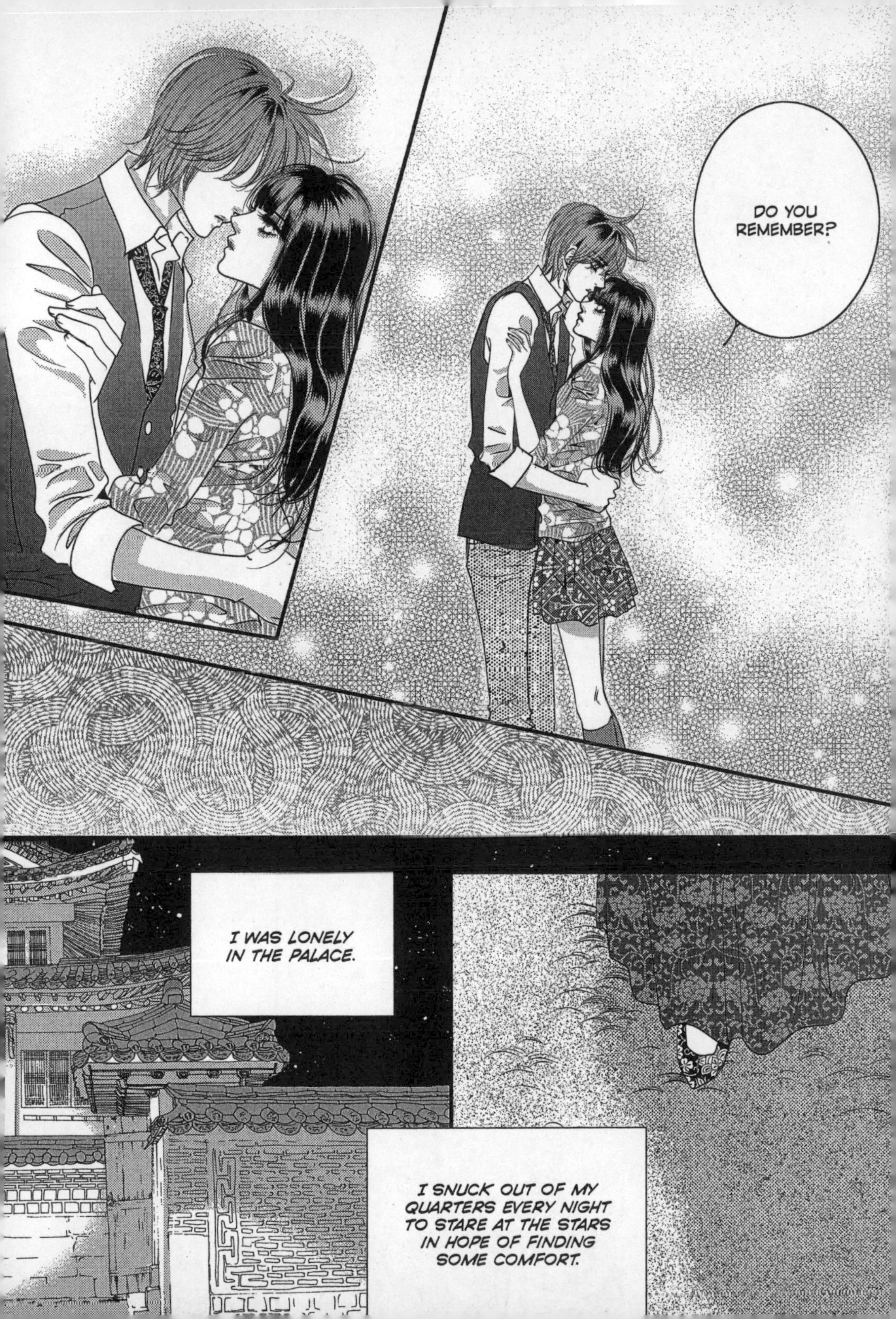
DO YOU REMEMBER?
I WAS LONELY IN THE PALACE.
I SNUCK OUT OF MY QUARTERS EVERY NIGHT TO STARE AT THE STARS IN HOPE OF FINDING SOME COMFORT.

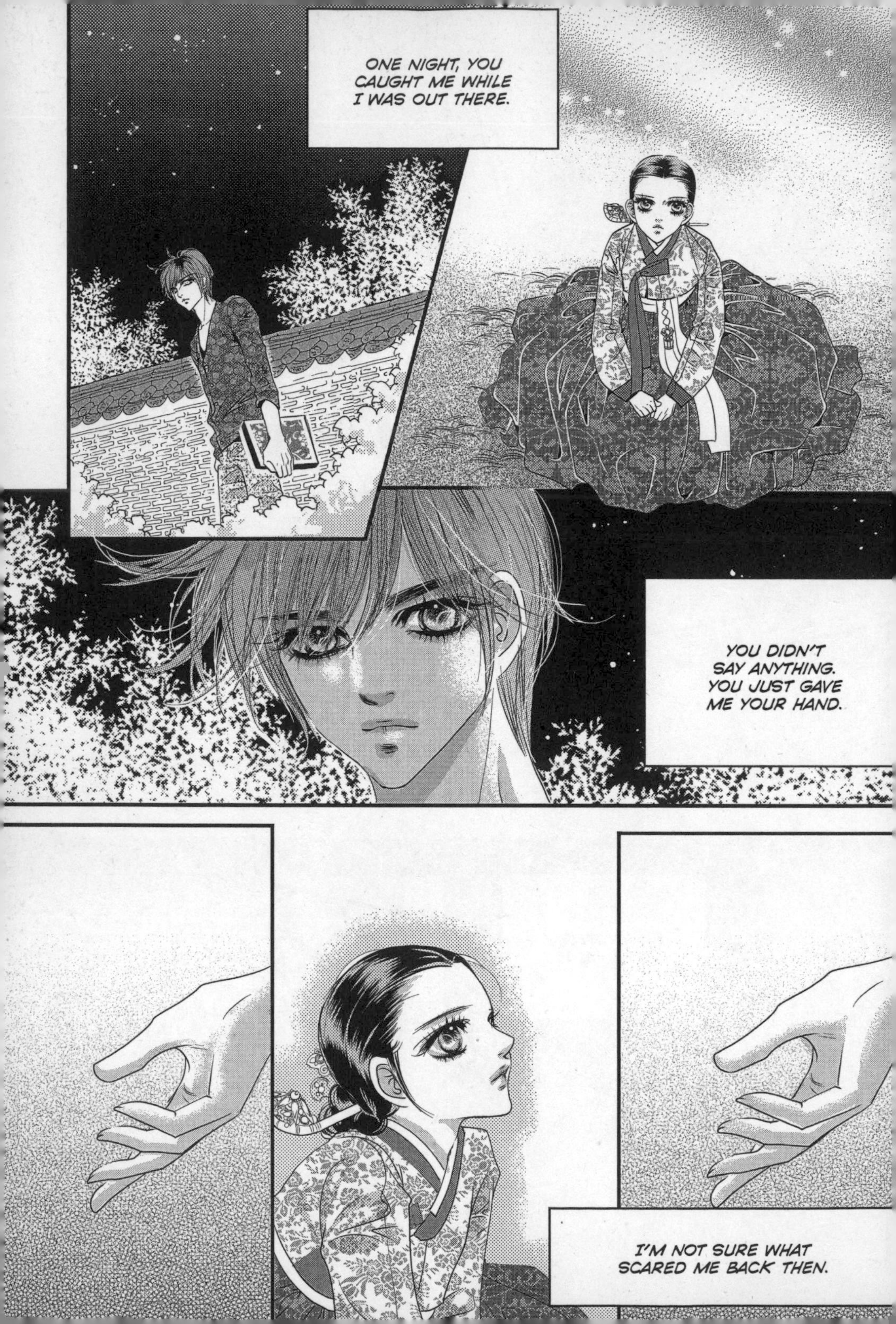
ONE NIGHT, YOU CAUGHT ME WHILE I WAS OUT THERE.
YOU DIDN'T SAY ANYTHING. YOU JUST GAVE ME YOUR HAND.
I'M NOT SURE WHAT SCARED ME BACK THEN.

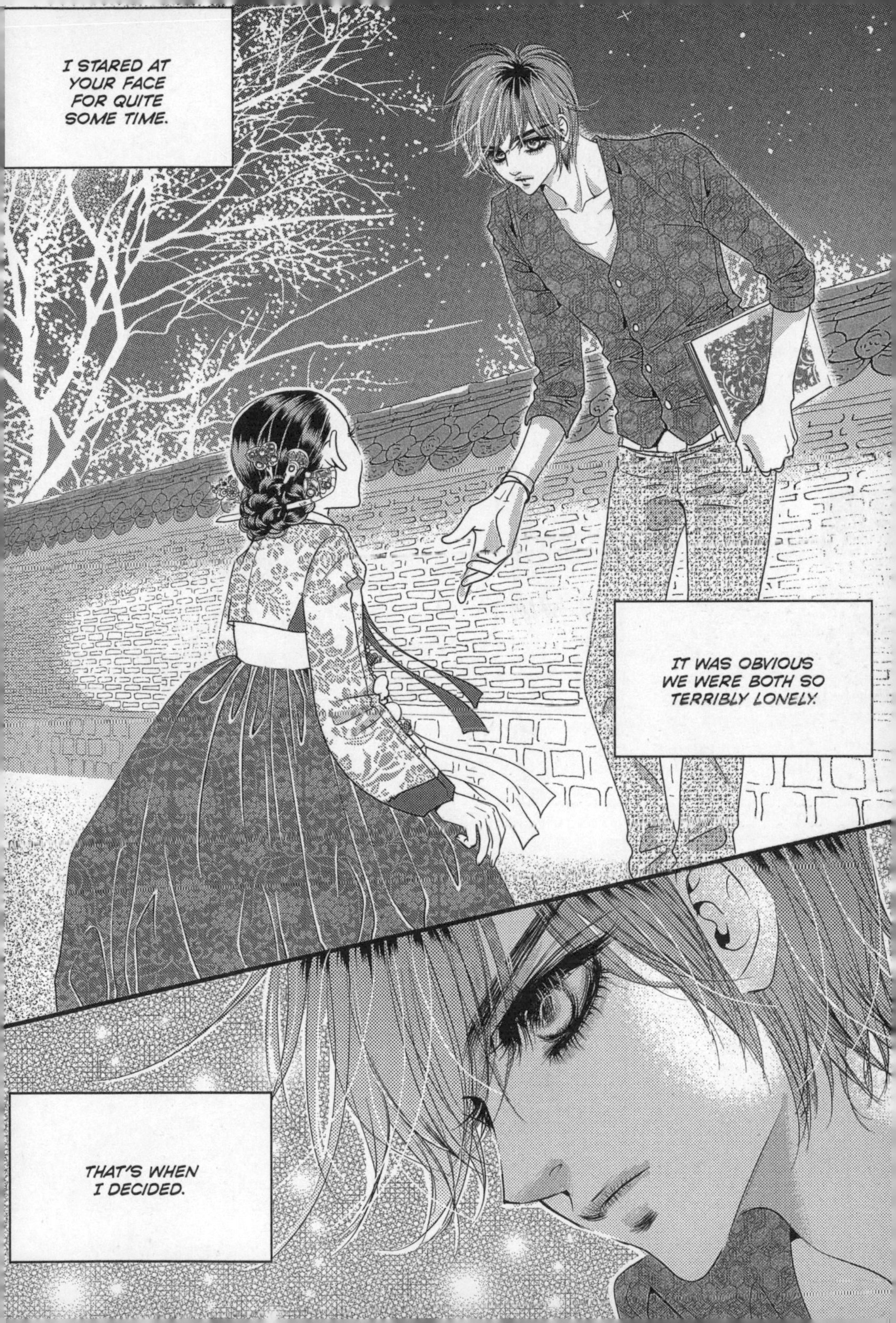
I STARED AT YOUR FACE FOR QUITE SOME TIME.
IT WAS OBVIOUS WE WERE BOTH SO TERRIBLY LONELY.
THAT'S WHEN I DECIDED.

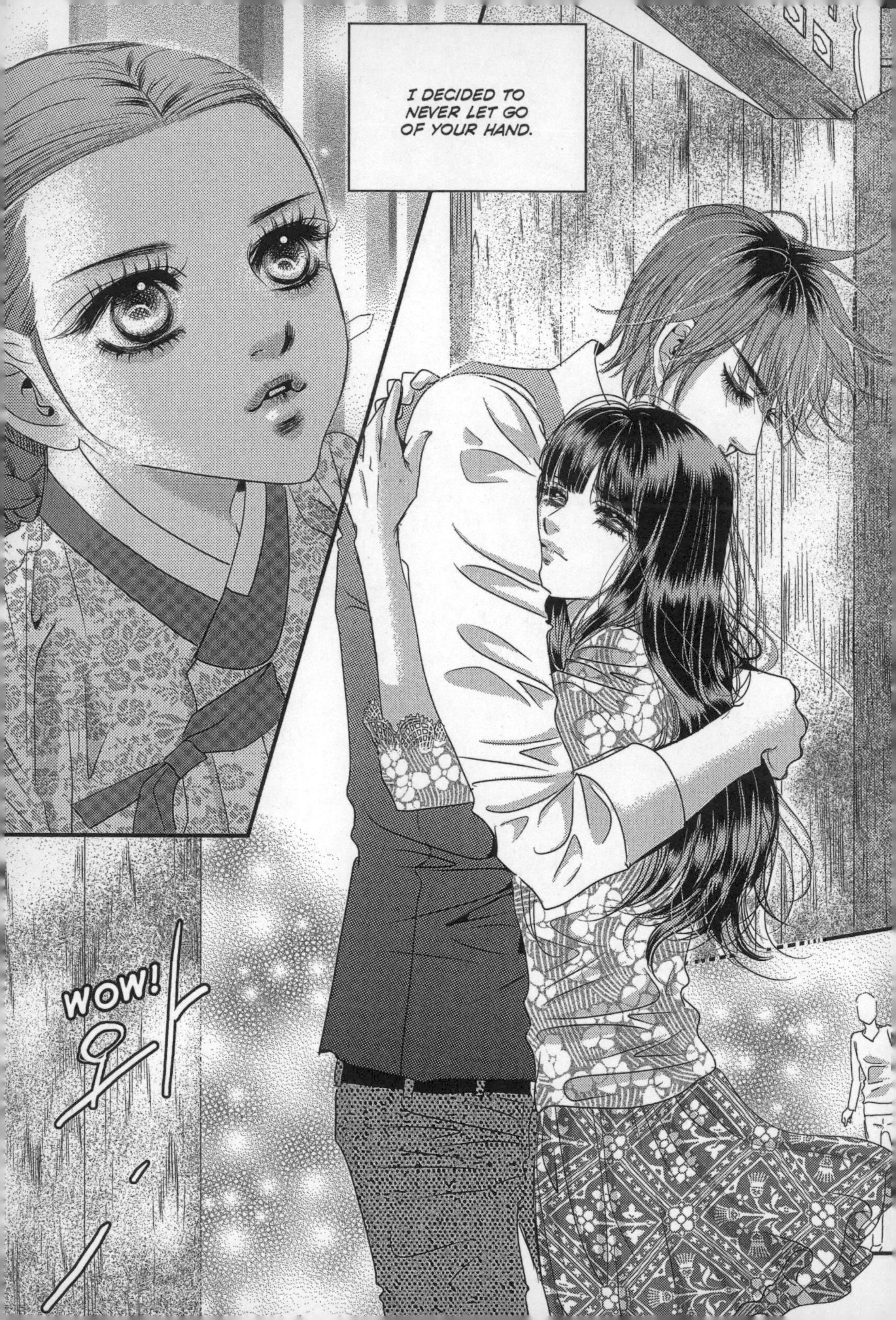
I DECIDED TO NEVER LET GO OF YOUR HAND.
WOW!

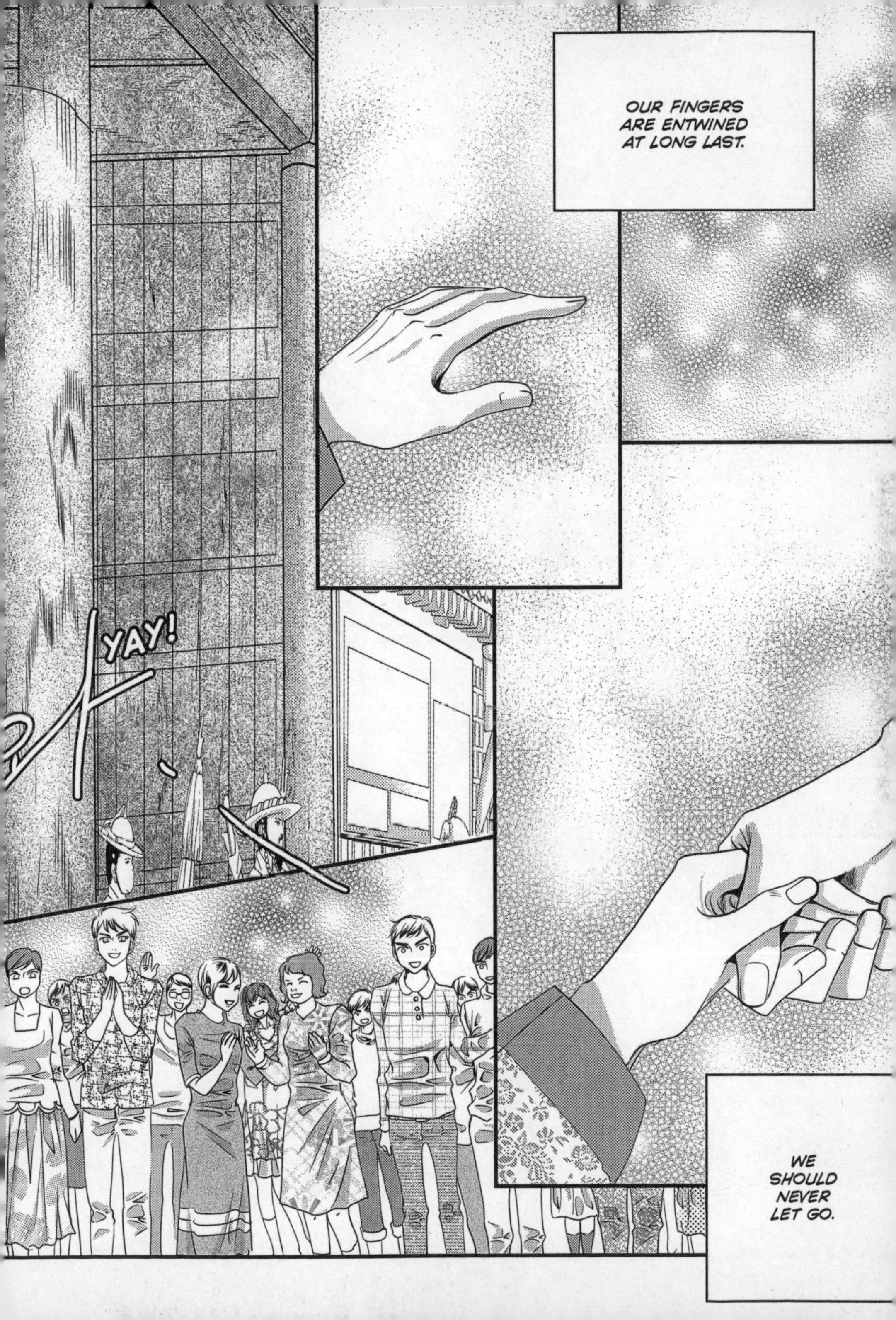

YAY!
OUR FINGERS ARE ENTWINED AT LONG LAST.
WE SHOULD NEVER LET GO.

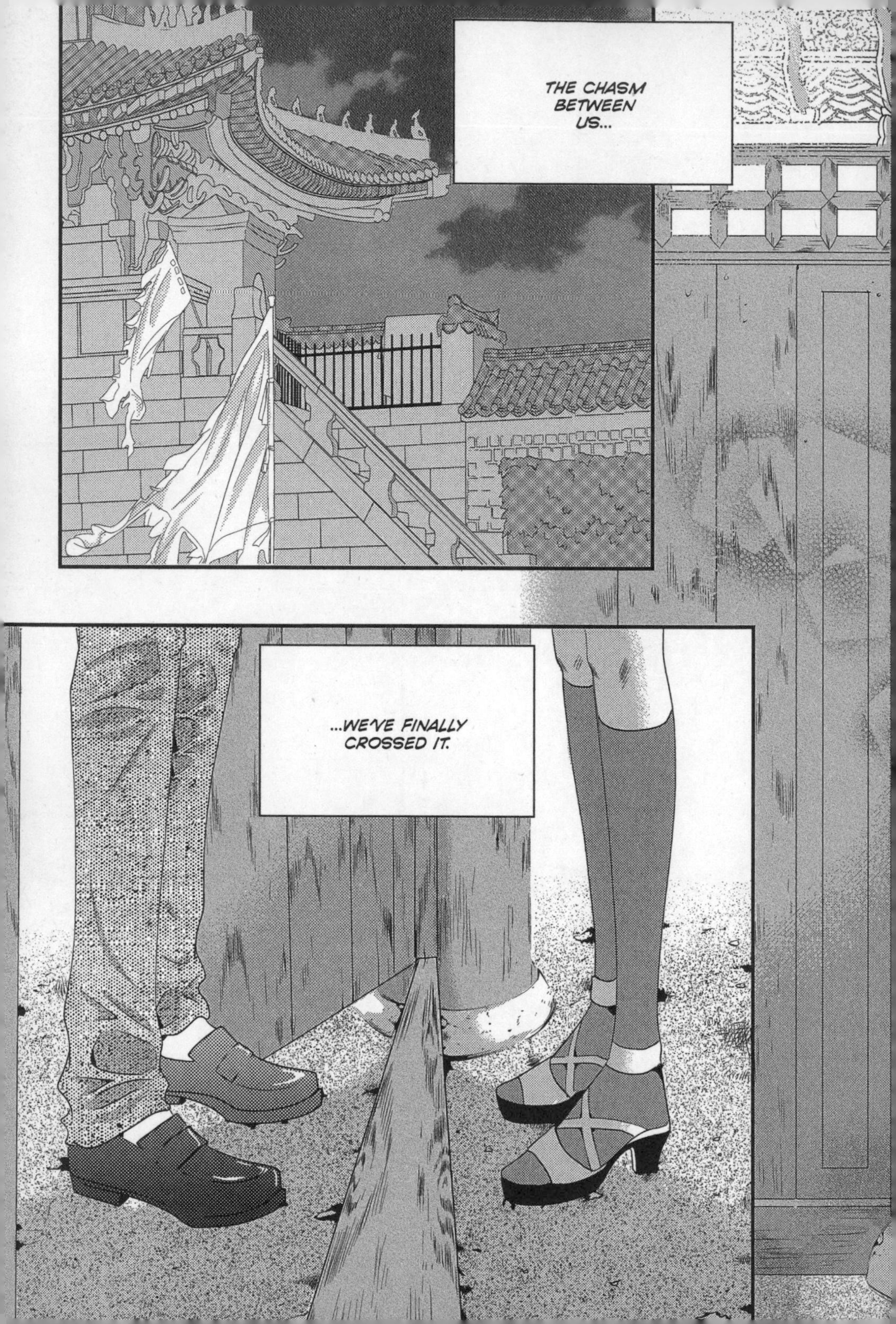
THE CHASM BETWEEN US...
...WE'VE FINALLY CROSSED IT.

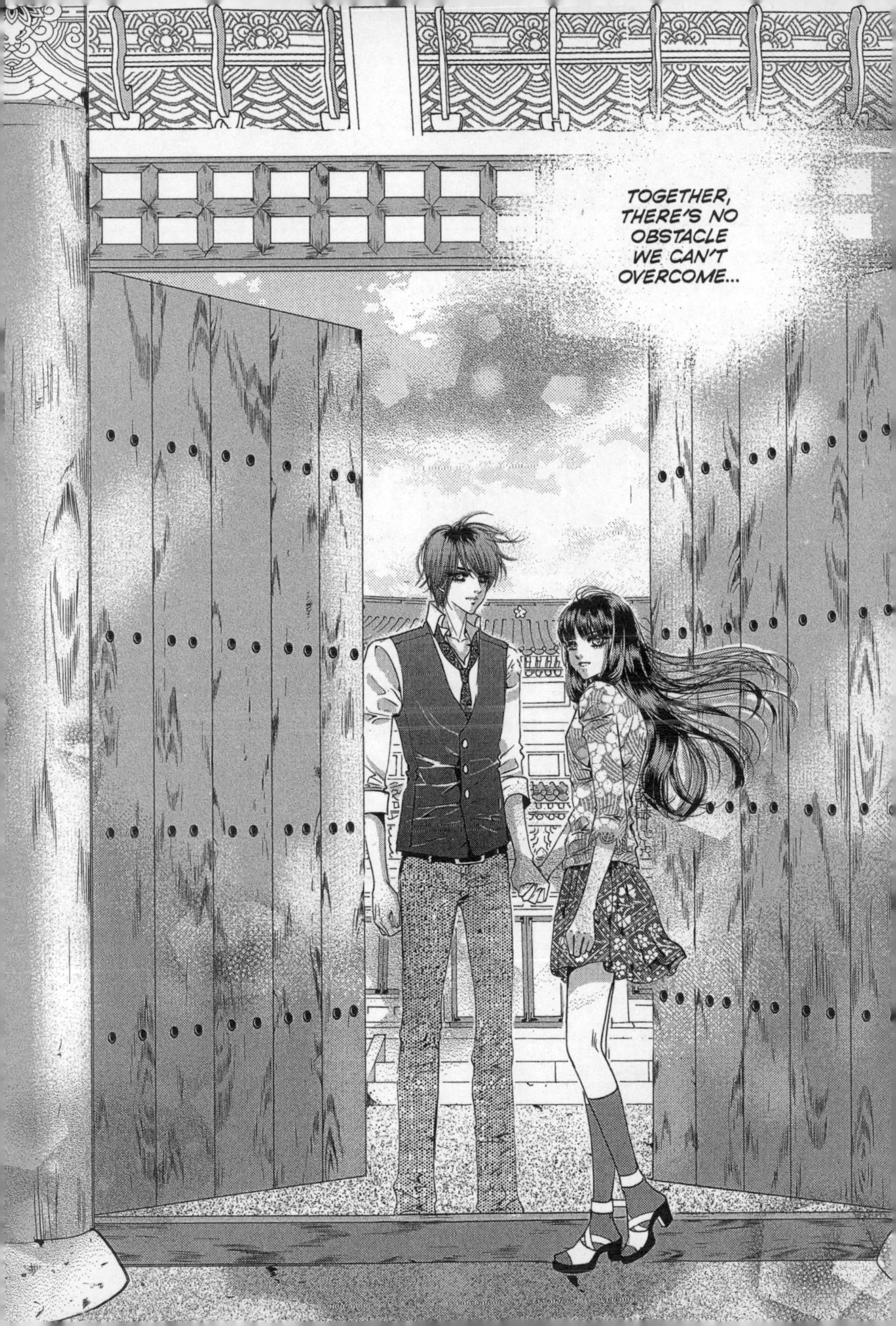
TOGETHER, THERE'S NO OBSTACLE WE CAN'T OVERCOME...

NO ONE REALLY CARES, BUT...

GOONG STARTED LIKE THIS!!!

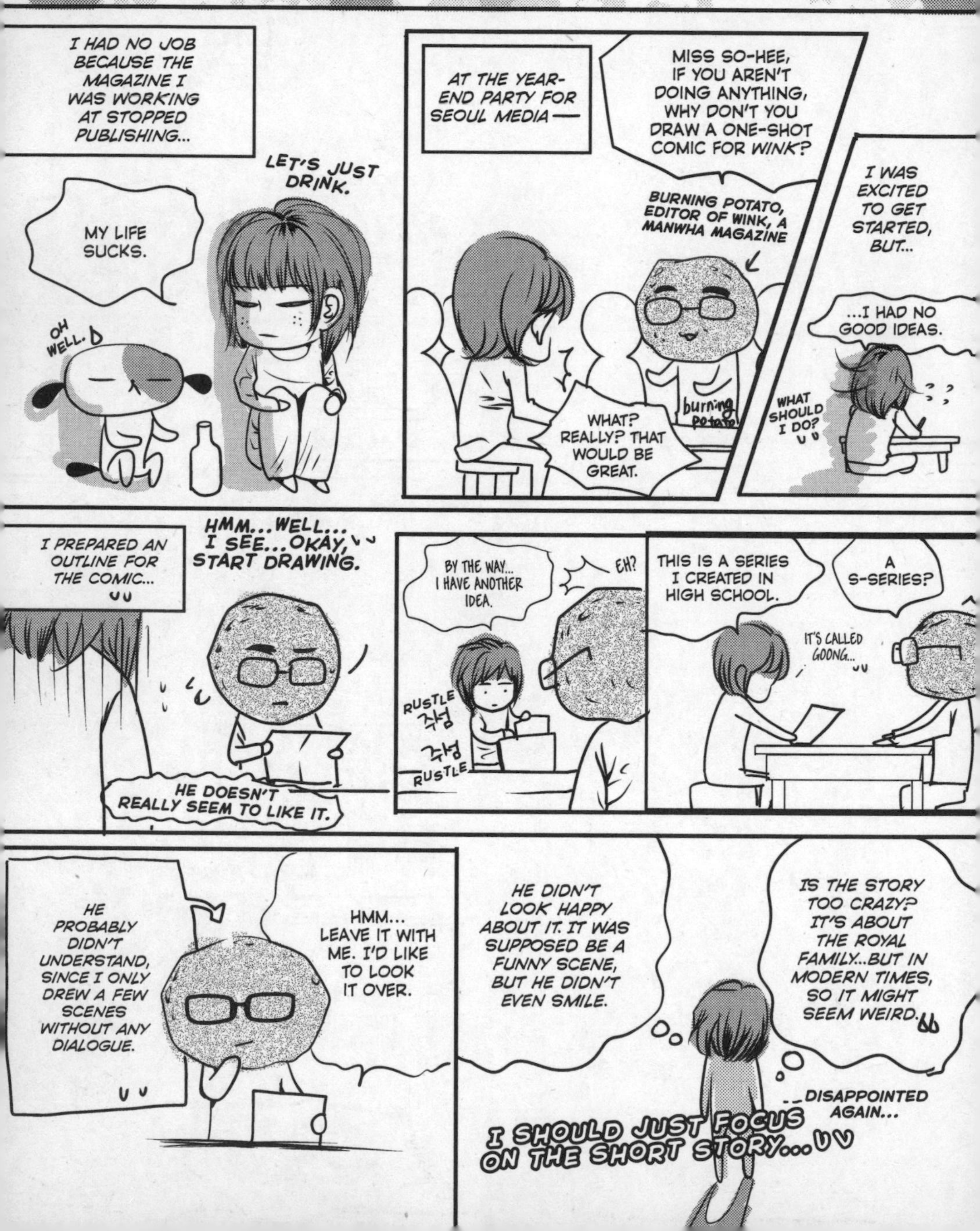
I HAD NO JOB BECAUSE THE MAGAZINE I WAS WORKING AT STOPPED PUBLISHING...
LET'S JUST DRINK.
MY LIFE SUCKS.
OH WELL.
AT THE YEAR-END PARTY FOR SEOUL MEDIA—
MISS SO-HEE, IF YOU AREN'T DOING ANYTHING, WHY DON'T YOU DRAW A ONE-SHOT COMIC FOR *WINK*?
BURNING POTATO, EDITOR OF WINK, A MANWHA MAGAZINE
burning potato
WHAT? REALLY? THAT WOULD BE GREAT.
I WAS EXCITED TO GET STARTED, BUT...
...I HAD NO GOOD IDEAS.
WHAT SHOULD I DO?
I PREPARED AN OUTLINE FOR THE COMIC...
HMM...WELL... I SEE...OKAY, START DRAWING.
HE DOESN'T REALLY SEEM TO LIKE IT.
BY THE WAY... I HAVE ANOTHER IDEA.
EH?
RUSTLE
RUSTLE
THIS IS A SERIES I CREATED IN HIGH SCHOOL.
A S-SERIES?
IT'S CALLED GOONG...
HE PROBABLY DIDN'T UNDERSTAND, SINCE I ONLY DREW A FEW SCENES WITHOUT ANY DIALOGUE.
HMM... LEAVE IT WITH ME. I'D LIKE TO LOOK IT OVER.
HE DIDN'T LOOK HAPPY ABOUT IT. IT WAS SUPPOSED BE A FUNNY SCENE, BUT HE DIDN'T EVEN SMILE.
IS THE STORY TOO CRAZY? IT'S ABOUT THE ROYAL FAMILY...BUT IN MODERN TIMES, SO IT MIGHT SEEM WEIRD.
DISAPPOINTED AGAIN...
I SHOULD JUST FOCUS ON THE SHORT STORY...

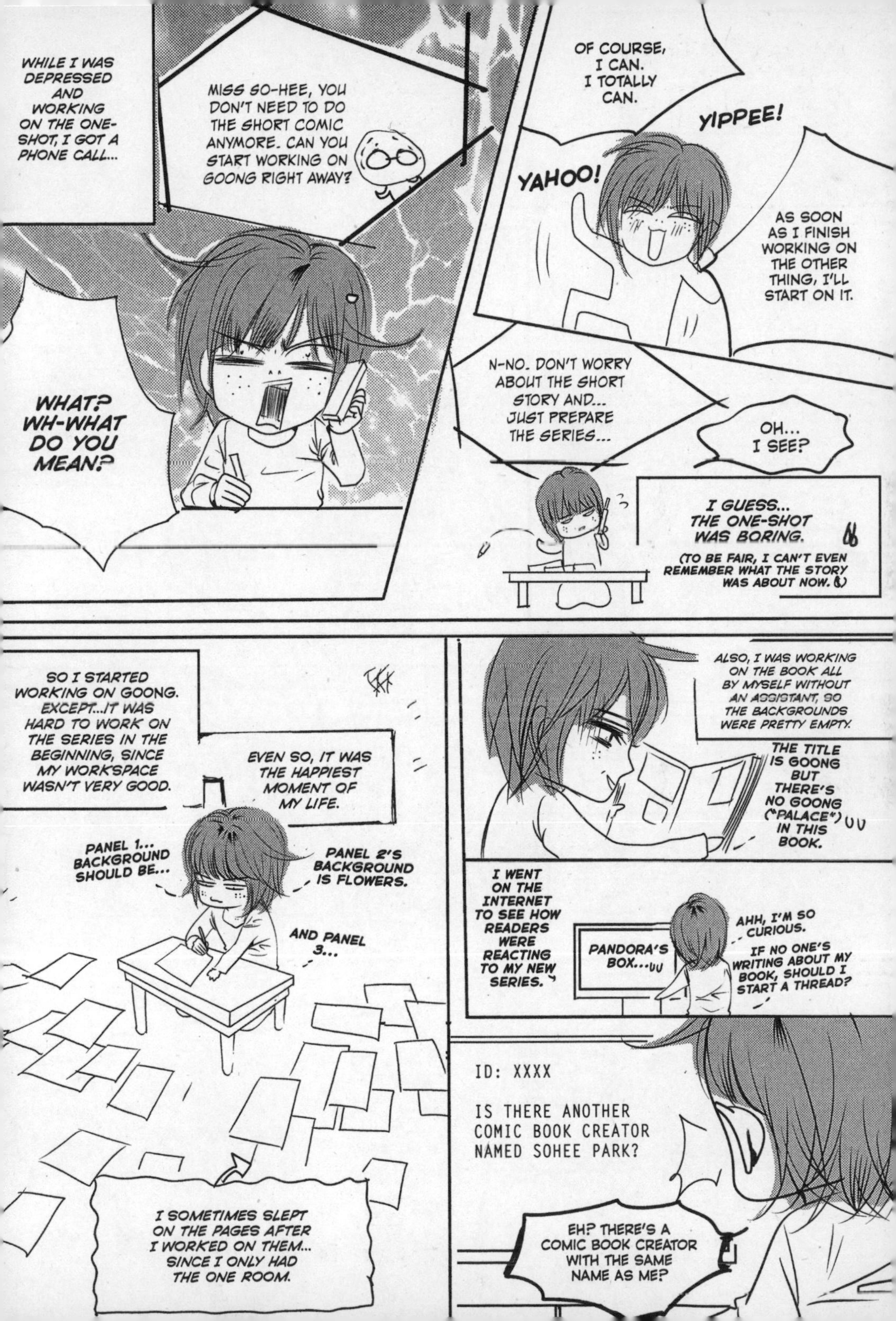
WHILE I WAS DEPRESSED AND WORKING ON THE ONE-SHOT, I GOT A PHONE CALL...
MISS SO-HEE, YOU DON'T NEED TO DO THE SHORT COMIC ANYMORE. CAN YOU START WORKING ON GOONG RIGHT AWAY?
WHAT? WH-WHAT DO YOU MEAN?
OF COURSE, I CAN. I TOTALLY CAN.
YIPPEE!
YAHOO!
AS SOON AS I FINISH WORKING ON THE OTHER THING, I'LL START ON IT.
N-NO. DON'T WORRY ABOUT THE SHORT STORY AND... JUST PREPARE THE SERIES...
OH... I SEE?
I GUESS... THE ONE-SHOT WAS BORING.
(TO BE FAIR, I CAN'T EVEN REMEMBER WHAT THE STORY WAS ABOUT NOW.)
SO I STARTED WORKING ON GOONG. EXCEPT...IT WAS HARD TO WORK ON THE SERIES IN THE BEGINNING, SINCE MY WORKSPACE WASN'T VERY GOOD.
EVEN SO, IT WAS THE HAPPIEST MOMENT OF MY LIFE.
PANEL 1... BACKGROUND SHOULD BE...
PANEL 2'S BACKGROUND IS FLOWERS.
AND PANEL 3...
I SOMETIMES SLEPT ON THE PAGES AFTER I WORKED ON THEM... SINCE I ONLY HAD THE ONE ROOM.
ALSO, I WAS WORKING ON THE BOOK ALL BY MYSELF WITHOUT AN ASSISTANT, SO THE BACKGROUNDS WERE PRETTY EMPTY.
THE TITLE IS GOONG BUT THERE'S NO GOONG ("PALACE") IN THIS BOOK.
I WENT ON THE INTERNET TO SEE HOW READERS WERE REACTING TO MY NEW SERIES.
PANDORA'S BOX...
AHH, I'M SO CURIOUS.
IF NO ONE'S WRITING ABOUT MY BOOK, SHOULD I START A THREAD?
ID: XXXX
IS THERE ANOTHER COMIC BOOK CREATOR NAMED SOHEE PARK?
EH? THERE'S A COMIC BOOK CREATOR WITH THE SAME NAME AS ME?

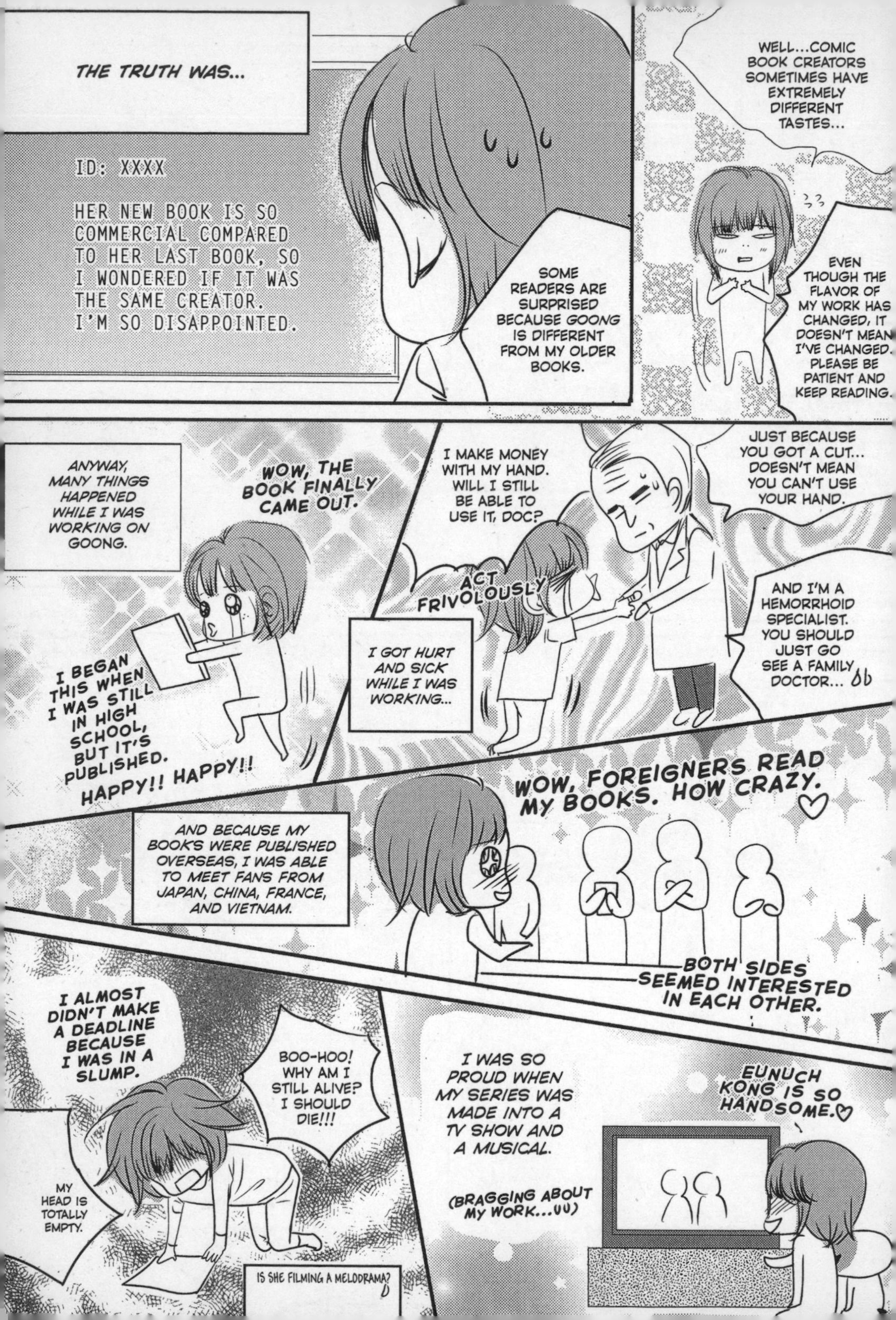
THE TRUTH WAS...
ID: XXXX
HER NEW BOOK IS SO COMMERCIAL COMPARED TO HER LAST BOOK, SO I WONDERED IF IT WAS THE SAME CREATOR. I'M SO DISAPPOINTED.
SOME READERS ARE SURPRISED BECAUSE GOONG IS DIFFERENT FROM MY OLDER BOOKS.
WELL...COMIC BOOK CREATORS SOMETIMES HAVE EXTREMELY DIFFERENT TASTES...
EVEN THOUGH THE FLAVOR OF MY WORK HAS CHANGED, IT DOESN'T MEAN I'VE CHANGED. PLEASE BE PATIENT AND KEEP READING.
ANYWAY, MANY THINGS HAPPENED WHILE I WAS WORKING ON GOONG.
WOW, THE BOOK FINALLY CAME OUT.
I BEGAN THIS WHEN I WAS STILL IN HIGH SCHOOL, BUT IT'S PUBLISHED.
HAPPY!! HAPPY!!
I GOT HURT AND SICK WHILE I WAS WORKING...
I MAKE MONEY WITH MY HAND. WILL I STILL BE ABLE TO USE IT, DOC?
ACT FRIVOLOUSLY
JUST BECAUSE YOU GOT A CUT... DOESN'T MEAN YOU CAN'T USE YOUR HAND.
AND I'M A HEMORRHOID SPECIALIST. YOU SHOULD JUST GO SEE A FAMILY DOCTOR...
AND BECAUSE MY BOOKS WERE PUBLISHED OVERSEAS, I WAS ABLE TO MEET FANS FROM JAPAN, CHINA, FRANCE, AND VIETNAM.
WOW, FOREIGNERS READ MY BOOKS. HOW CRAZY.
BOTH SIDES SEEMED INTERESTED IN EACH OTHER.
I ALMOST DIDN'T MAKE A DEADLINE BECAUSE I WAS IN A SLUMP.
BOO-HOO! WHY AM I STILL ALIVE? I SHOULD DIE!!!
MY HEAD IS TOTALLY EMPTY.
IS SHE FILMING A MELODRAMA?
I WAS SO PROUD WHEN MY SERIES WAS MADE INTO A TV SHOW AND A MUSICAL.
EUNUCH KONG IS SO HANDSOME.
(BRAGGING ABOUT MY WORK...)

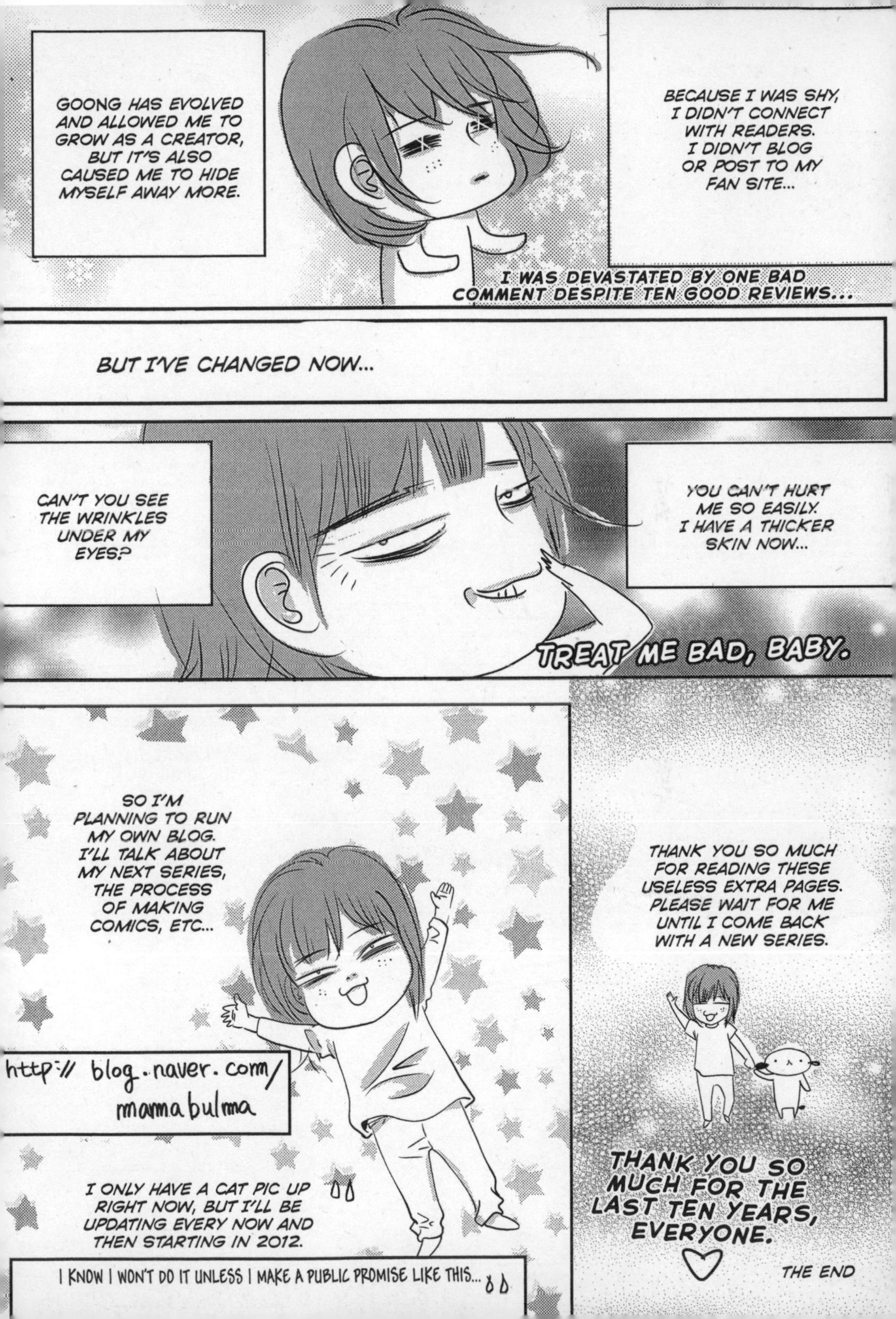
GOONG HAS EVOLVED AND ALLOWED ME TO GROW AS A CREATOR, BUT IT'S ALSO CAUSED ME TO HIDE MYSELF AWAY MORE.
BECAUSE I WAS SHY, I DIDN'T CONNECT WITH READERS. I DIDN'T BLOG OR POST TO MY FAN SITE...
I WAS DEVASTATED BY ONE BAD COMMENT DESPITE TEN GOOD REVIEWS...
BUT I'VE CHANGED NOW...
CAN'T YOU SEE THE WRINKLES UNDER MY EYES?
YOU CAN'T HURT ME SO EASILY. I HAVE A THICKER SKIN NOW...
TREAT ME BAD, BABY.
SO I'M PLANNING TO RUN MY OWN BLOG. I'LL TALK ABOUT MY NEXT SERIES, THE PROCESS OF MAKING COMICS, ETC...
http:// blog.naver.com/ mamabulma
I ONLY HAVE A CAT PIC UP RIGHT NOW, BUT I'LL BE UPDATING EVERY NOW AND THEN STARTING IN 2012.
I KNOW I WON'T DO IT UNLESS I MAKE A PUBLIC PROMISE LIKE THIS...
THANK YOU SO MUCH FOR READING THESE USELESS EXTRA PAGES. PLEASE WAIT FOR ME UNTIL I COME BACK WITH A NEW SERIES.
THANK YOU SO MUCH FOR THE LAST TEN YEARS, EVERYONE.
THE END

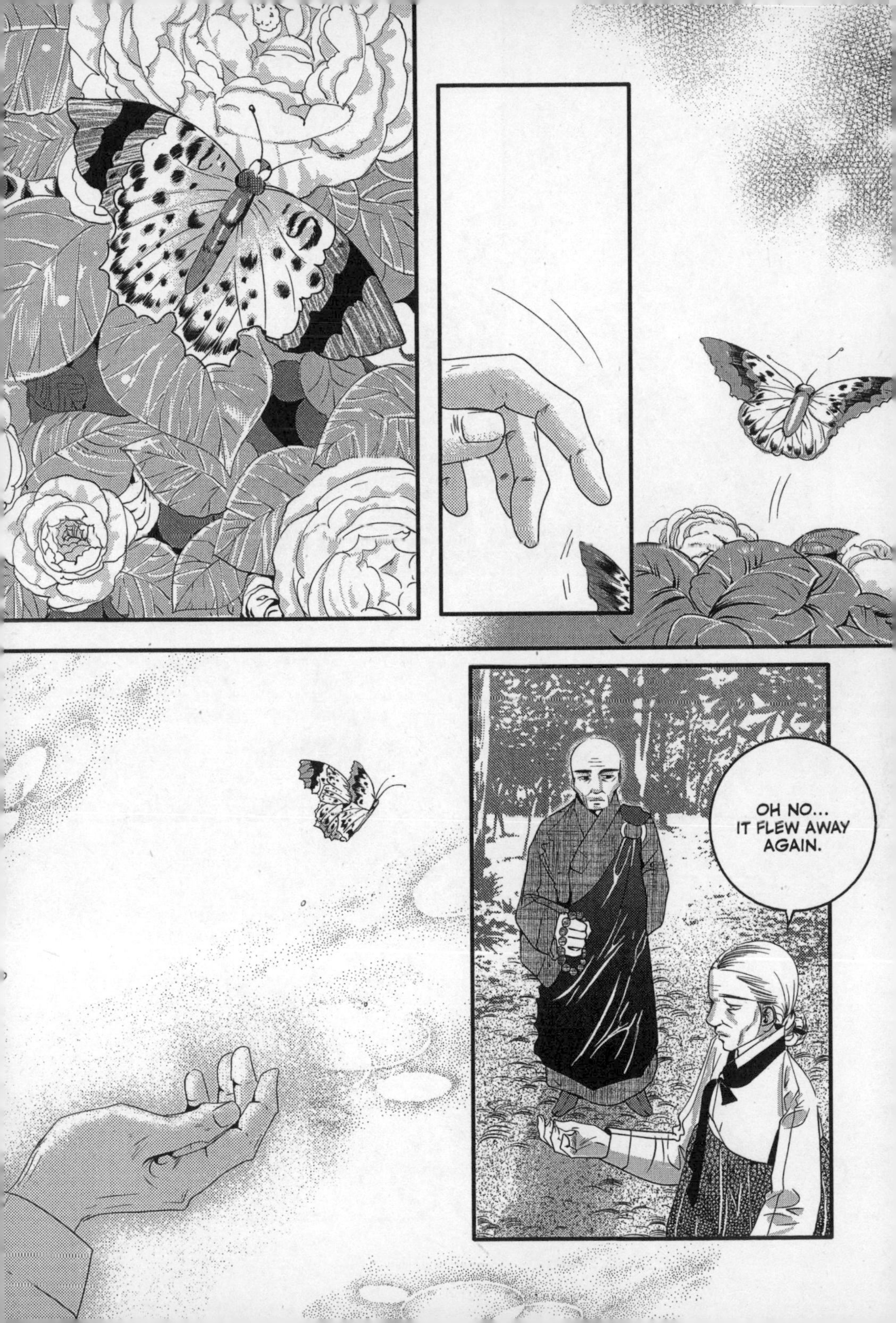
OH NO... IT FLEW AWAY AGAIN.

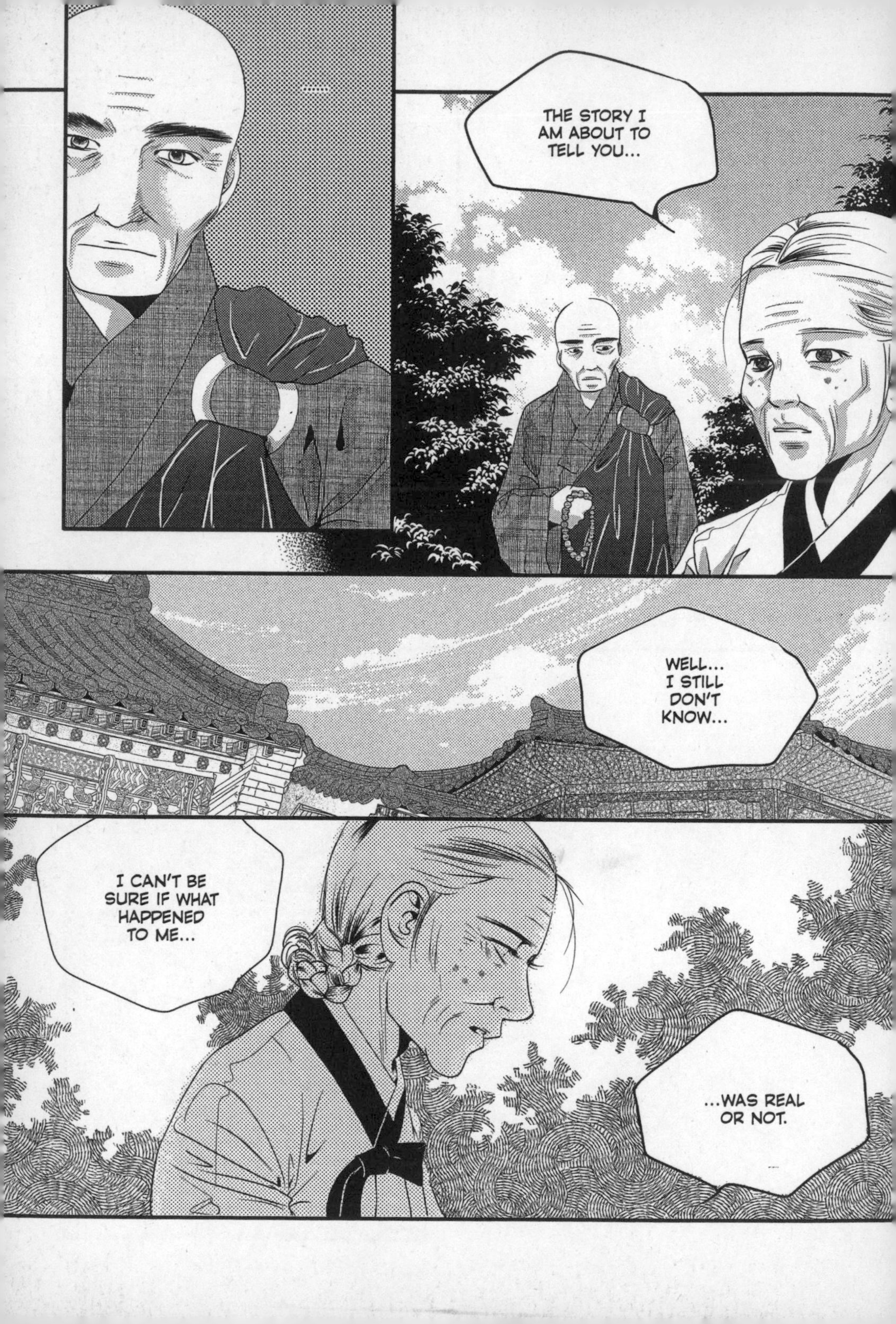
THE STORY I AM ABOUT TO TELL YOU...
WELL... I STILL DON'T KNOW...
I CAN'T BE SURE IF WHAT HAPPENED TO ME...
...WAS REAL OR NOT.

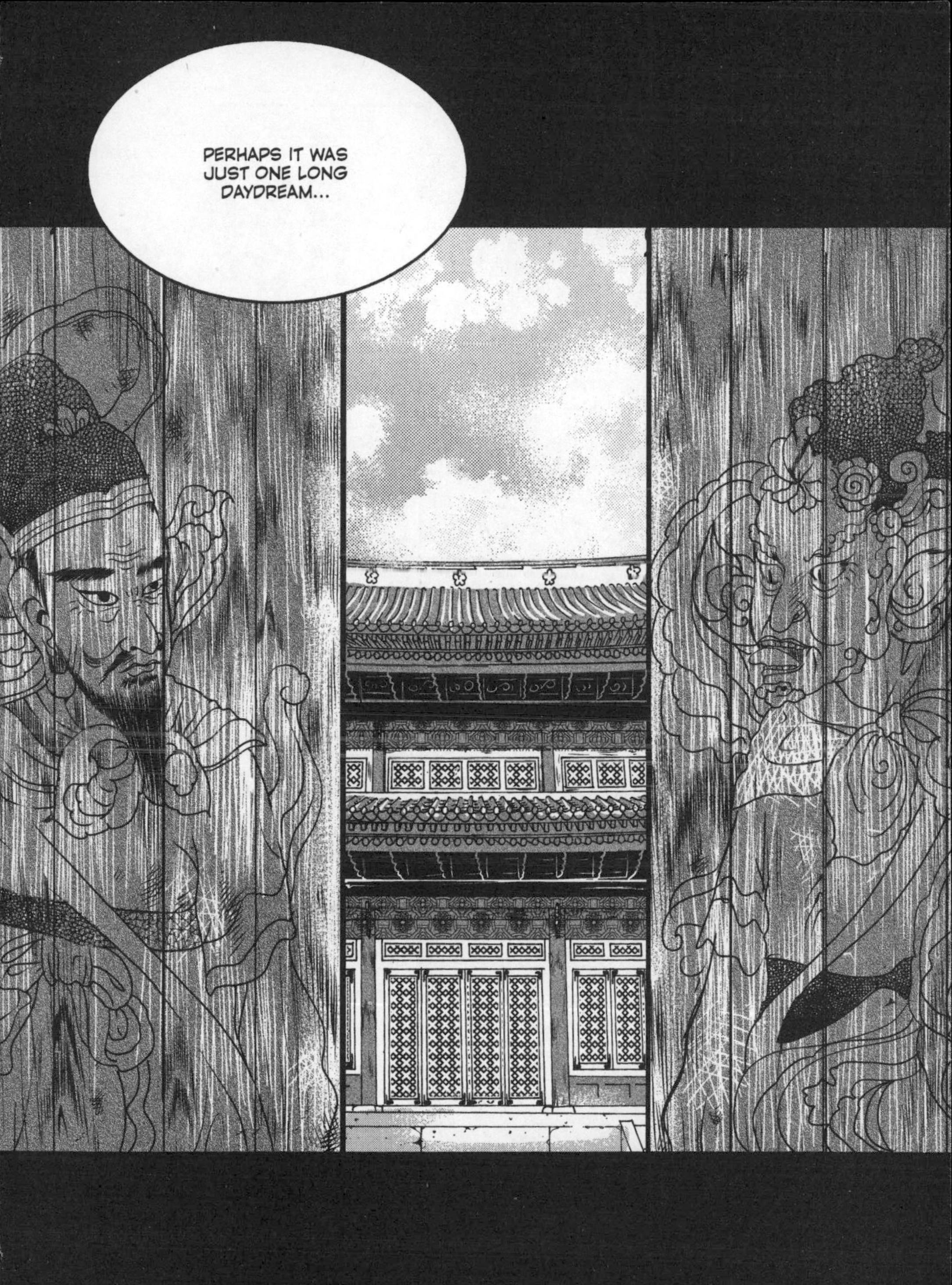
PERHAPS IT WAS JUST ONE LONG DAYDREAM...

A CONCUBINE'S CONFESSION

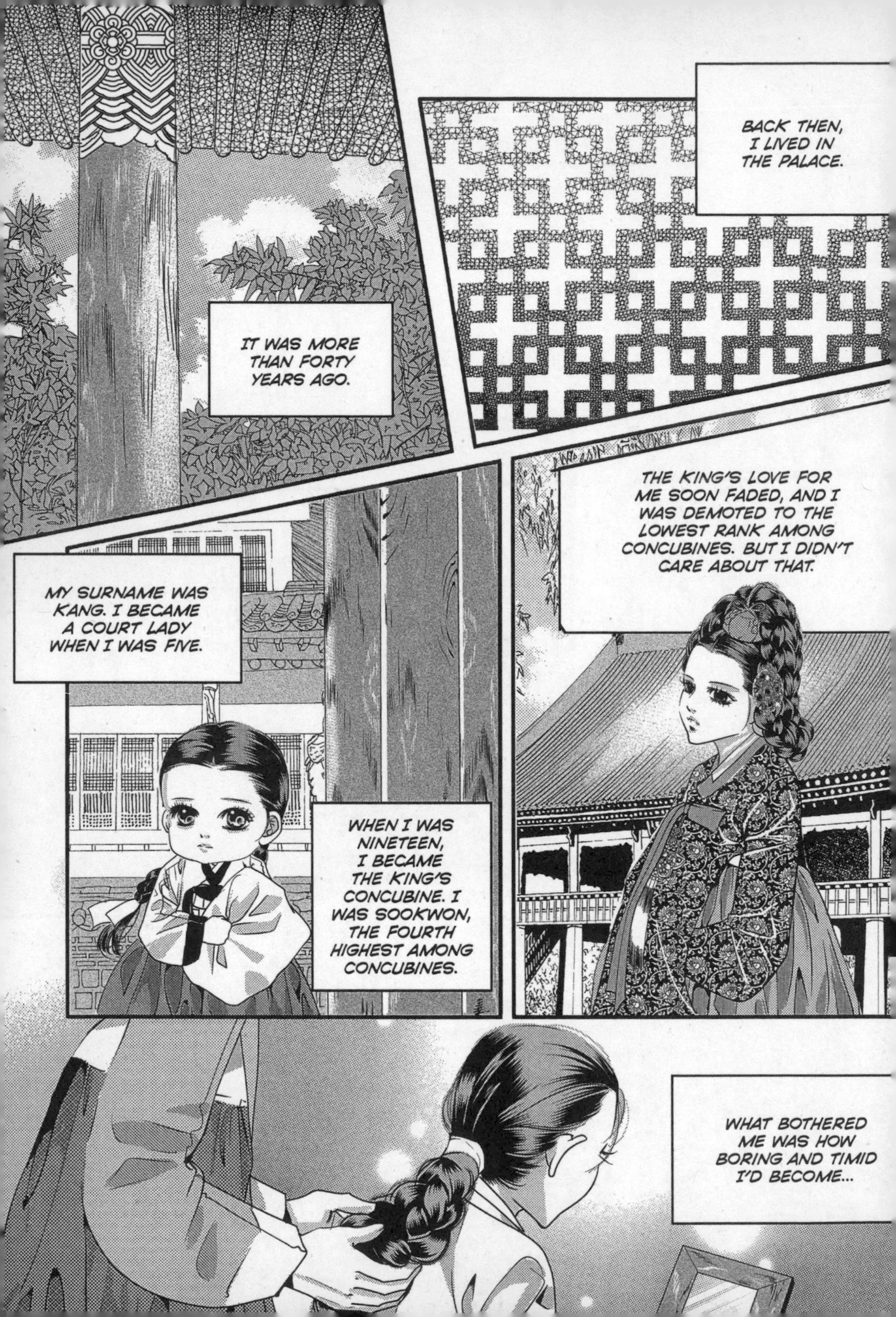
IT WAS MORE THAN FORTY YEARS AGO.
BACK THEN, I LIVED IN THE PALACE.
MY SURNAME WAS KANG. I BECAME A COURT LADY WHEN I WAS FIVE.
WHEN I WAS NINETEEN, I BECAME THE KING'S CONCUBINE. I WAS SOOKWON, THE FOURTH HIGHEST AMONG CONCUBINES.
THE KING'S LOVE FOR ME SOON FADED, AND I WAS DEMOTED TO THE LOWEST RANK AMONG CONCUBINES. BUT I DIDN'T CARE ABOUT THAT.
WHAT BOTHERED ME WAS HOW BORING AND TIMID I'D BECOME...

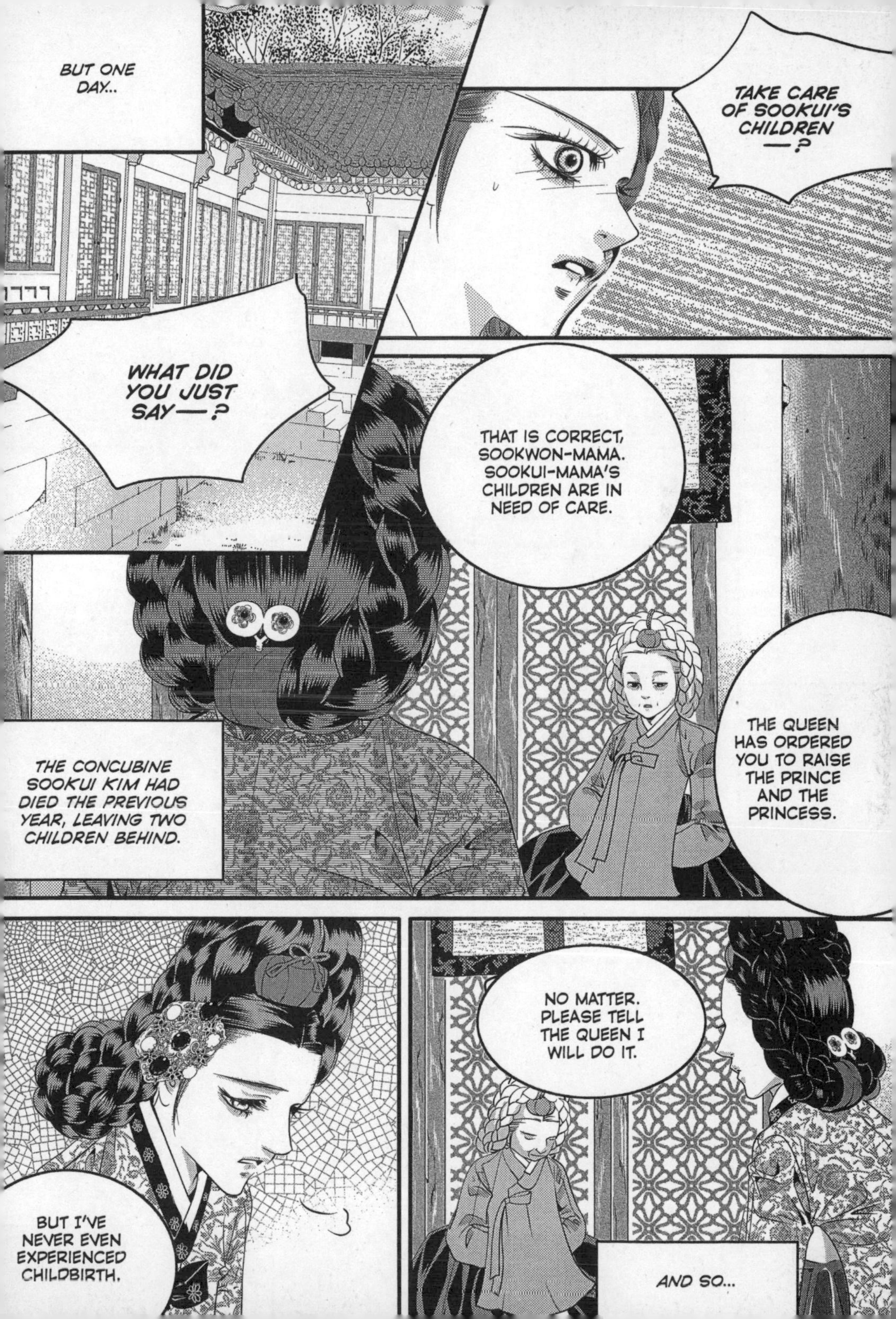
BUT ONE DAY...
TAKE CARE OF SOOKUI'S CHILDREN —?
WHAT DID YOU JUST SAY—?
THAT IS CORRECT, SOOKWON-MAMA. SOOKUI-MAMA'S CHILDREN ARE IN NEED OF CARE.
THE CONCUBINE SOOKUI KIM HAD DIED THE PREVIOUS YEAR, LEAVING TWO CHILDREN BEHIND.
THE QUEEN HAS ORDERED YOU TO RAISE THE PRINCE AND THE PRINCESS.
BUT I'VE NEVER EVEN EXPERIENCED CHILDBIRTH.
NO MATTER. PLEASE TELL THE QUEEN I WILL DO IT.
AND SO...

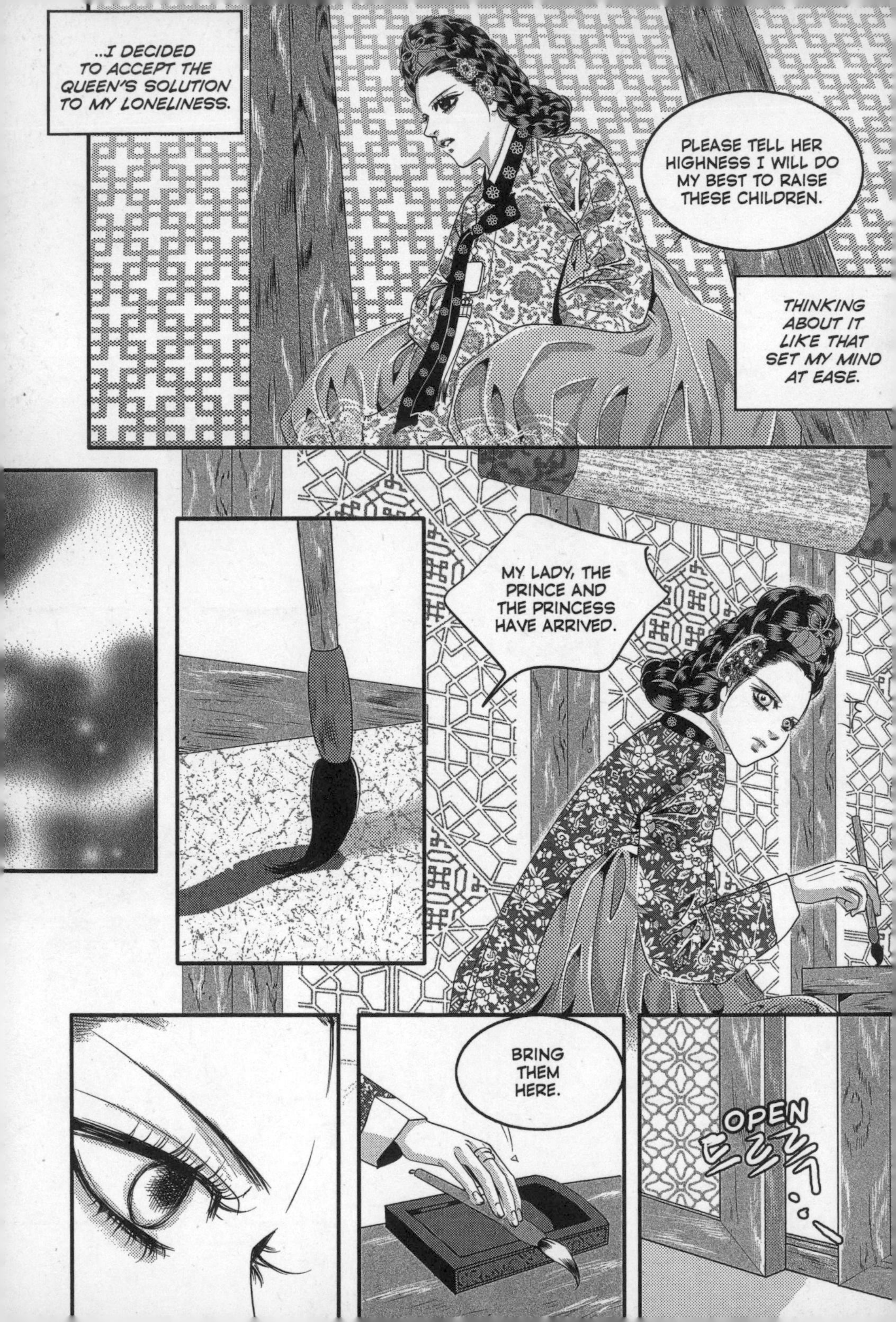
...I DECIDED TO ACCEPT THE QUEEN'S SOLUTION TO MY LONELINESS.
PLEASE TELL HER HIGHNESS I WILL DO MY BEST TO RAISE THESE CHILDREN.
THINKING ABOUT IT LIKE THAT SET MY MIND AT EASE.
MY LADY, THE PRINCE AND THE PRINCESS HAVE ARRIVED.
BRING THEM HERE.
OPEN

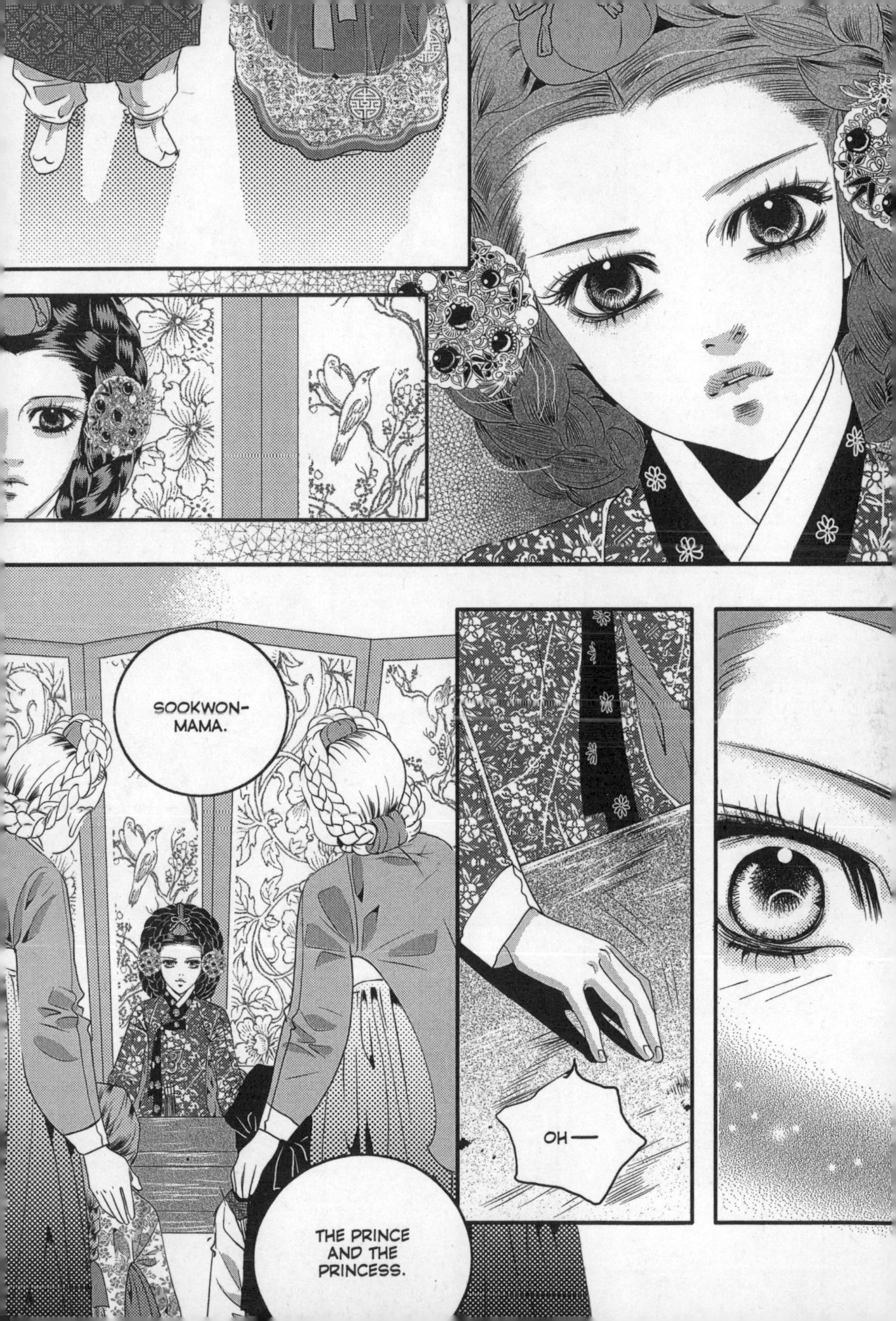
SOOKWON-MAMA.
THE PRINCE AND THE PRINCESS.
OH—

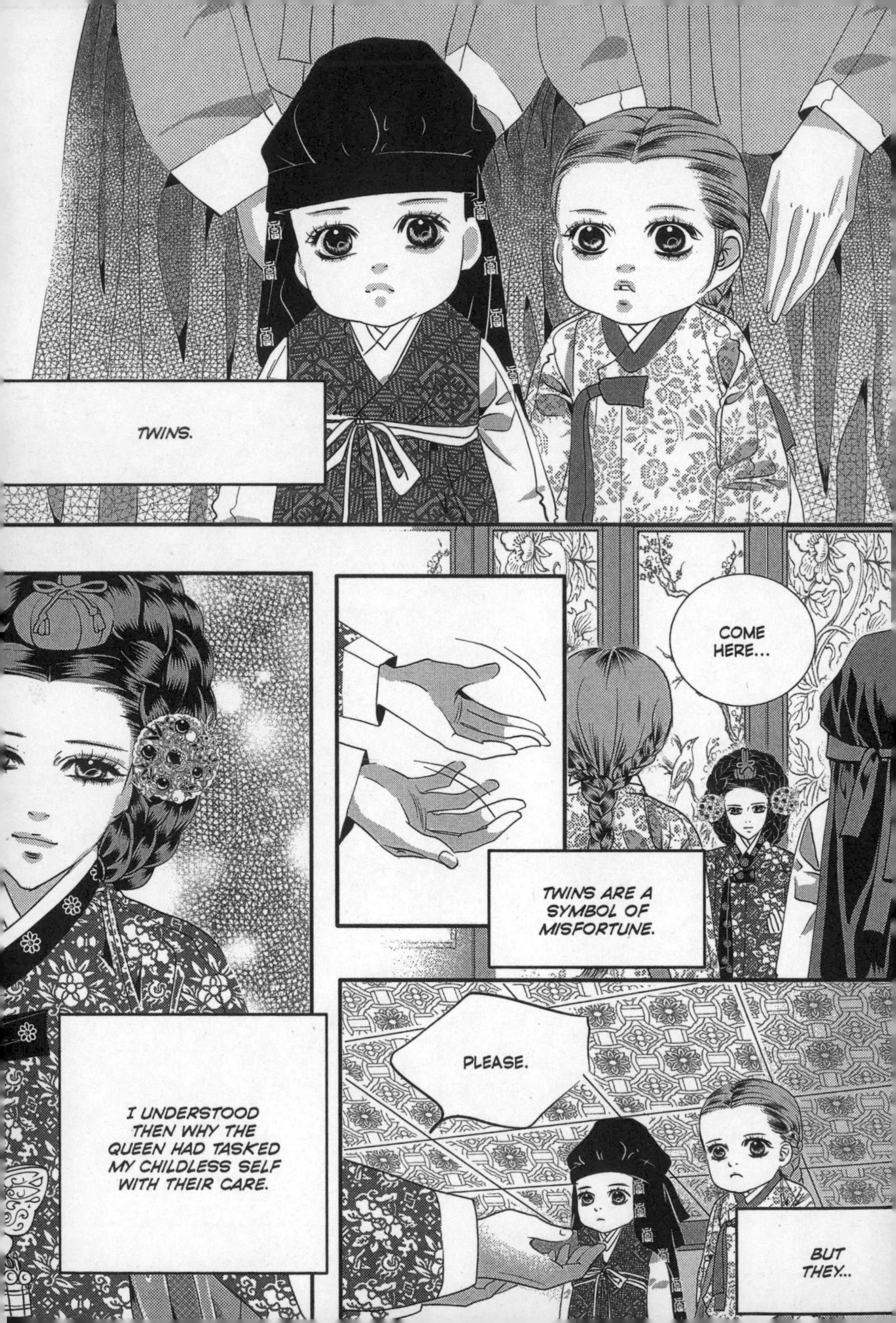
TWINS.
COME HERE...
TWINS ARE A SYMBOL OF MISFORTUNE.
I UNDERSTOOD THEN WHY THE QUEEN HAD TASKED MY CHILDLESS SELF WITH THEIR CARE.
PLEASE.
BUT THEY...

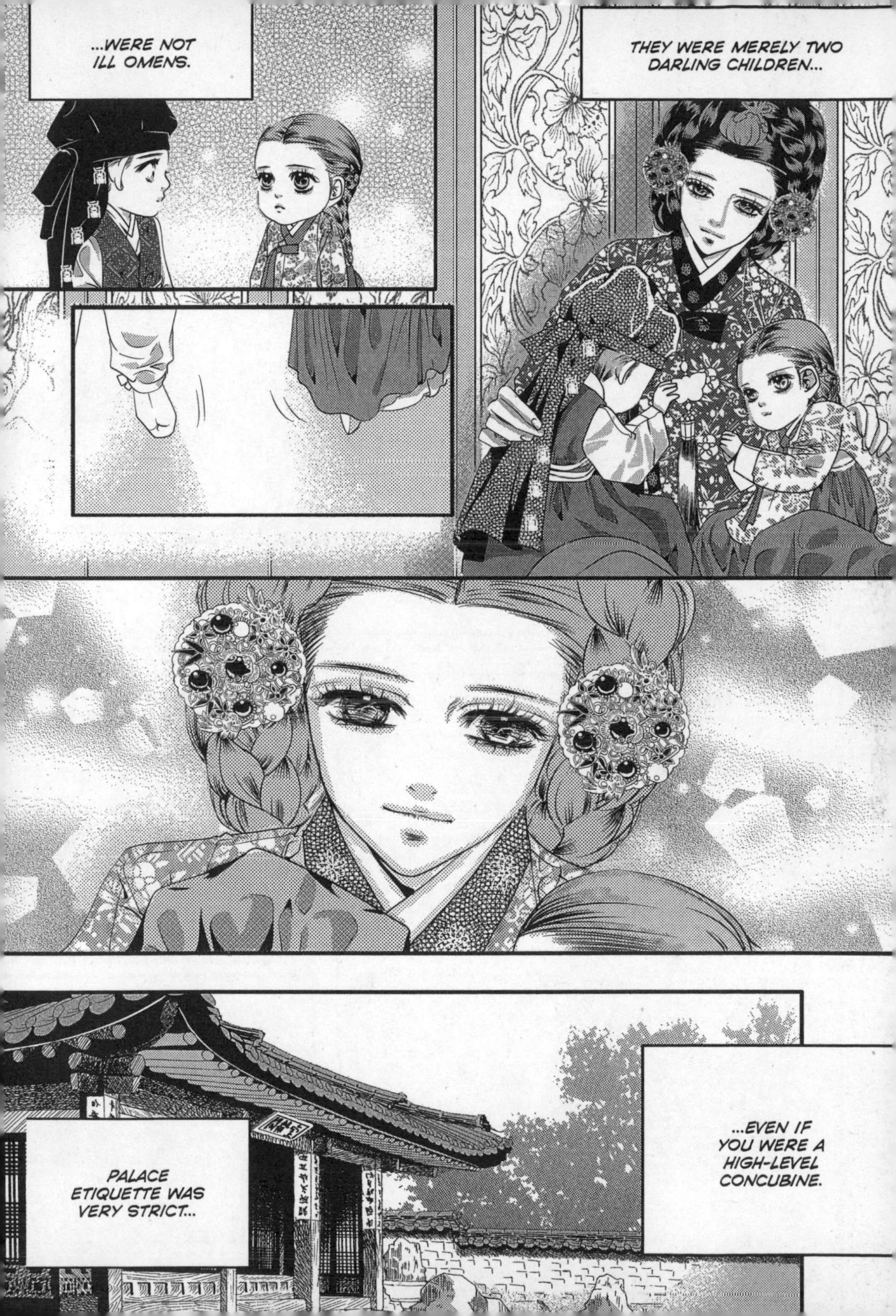
...WERE NOT ILL OMENS.
THEY WERE MERELY TWO DARLING CHILDREN...
PALACE ETIQUETTE WAS VERY STRICT...
...EVEN IF YOU WERE A HIGH-LEVEL CONCUBINE.

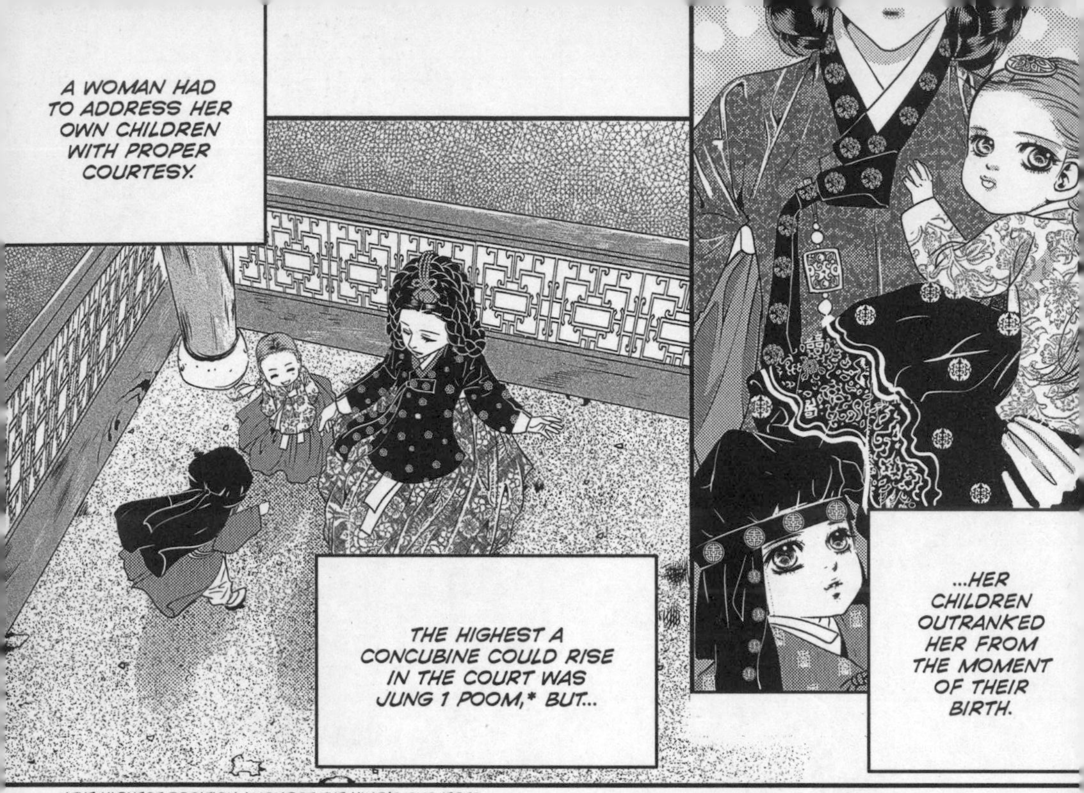
A WOMAN HAD TO ADDRESS HER OWN CHILDREN WITH PROPER COURTESY.
THE HIGHEST A CONCUBINE COULD RISE IN THE COURT WAS JUNG 1 POOM,* BUT...
...HER CHILDREN OUTRANKED HER FROM THE MOMENT OF THEIR BIRTH.

*THE HIGHEST POSITION AMONGST THE KING'S SUBJECTS.

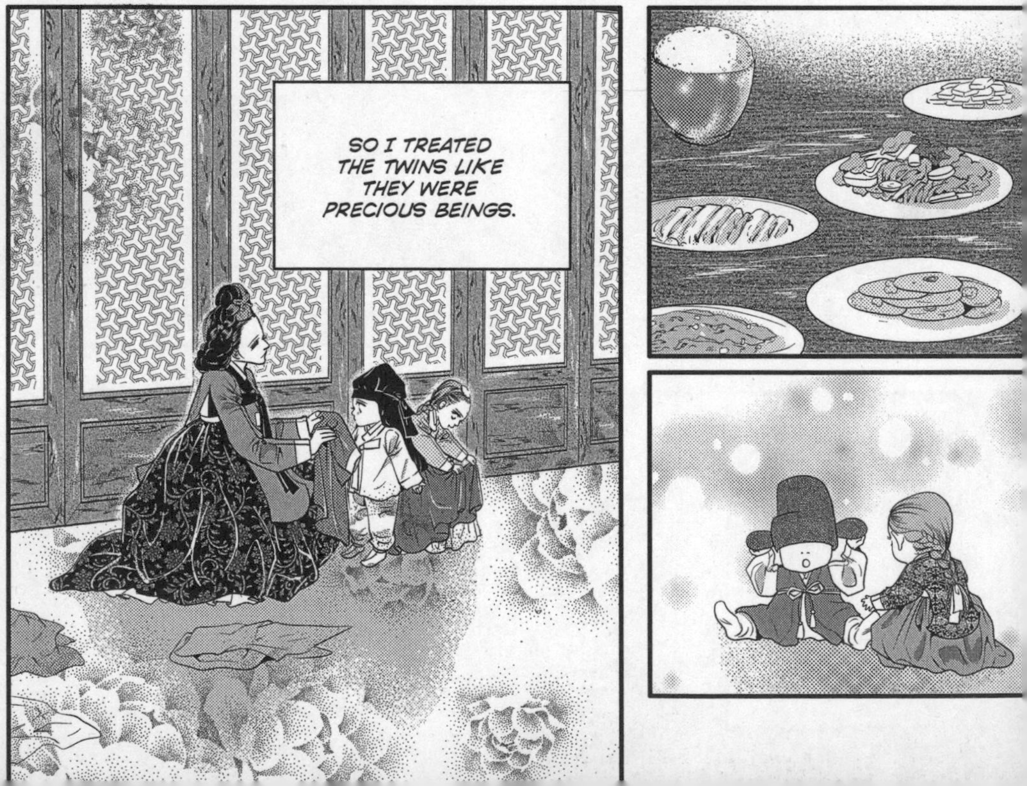
SO I TREATED THE TWINS LIKE THEY WERE PRECIOUS BEINGS.

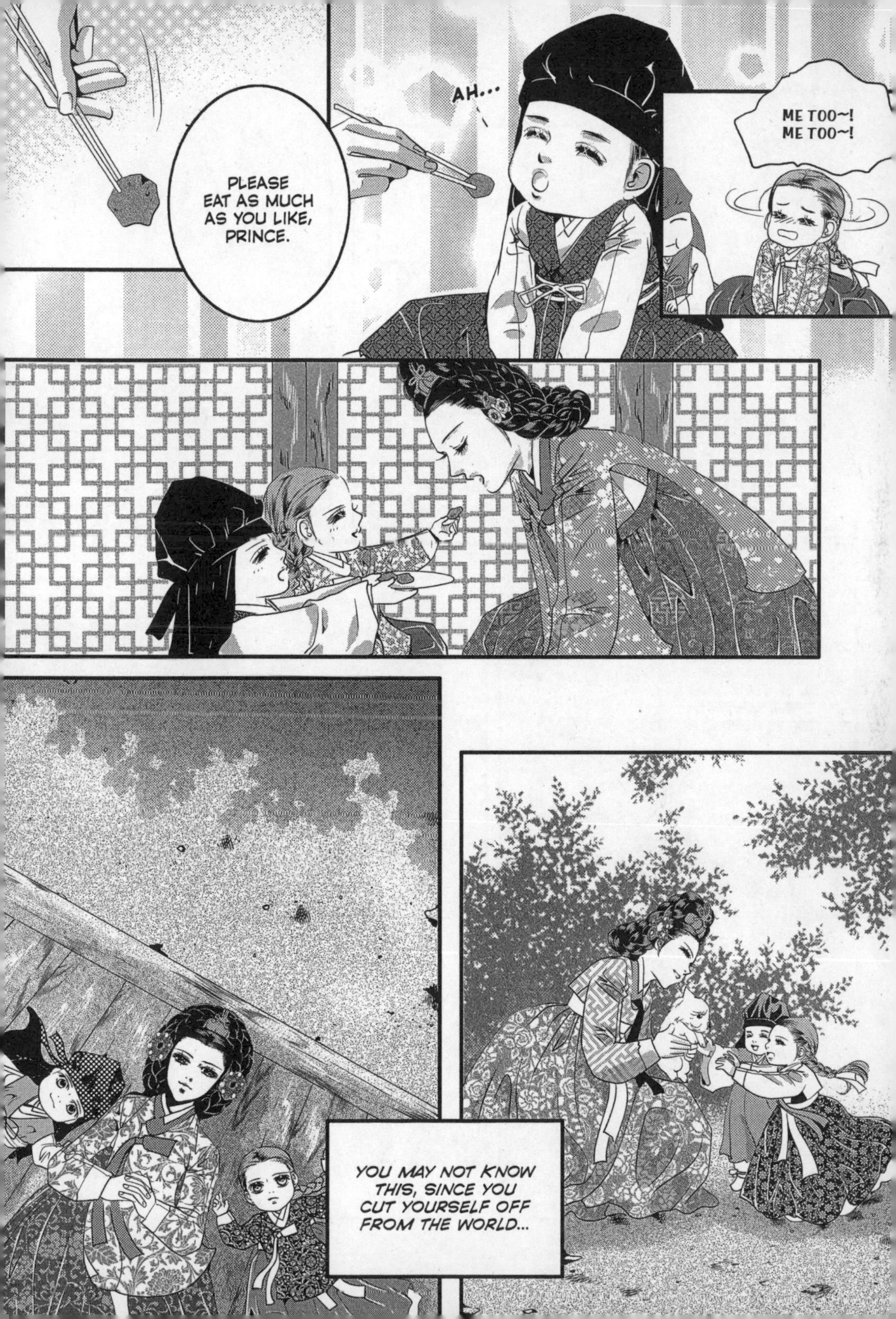
PLEASE EAT AS MUCH AS YOU LIKE, PRINCE.
AH...
ME TOO~! ME TOO~!
YOU MAY NOT KNOW THIS, SINCE YOU CUT YOURSELF OFF FROM THE WORLD...

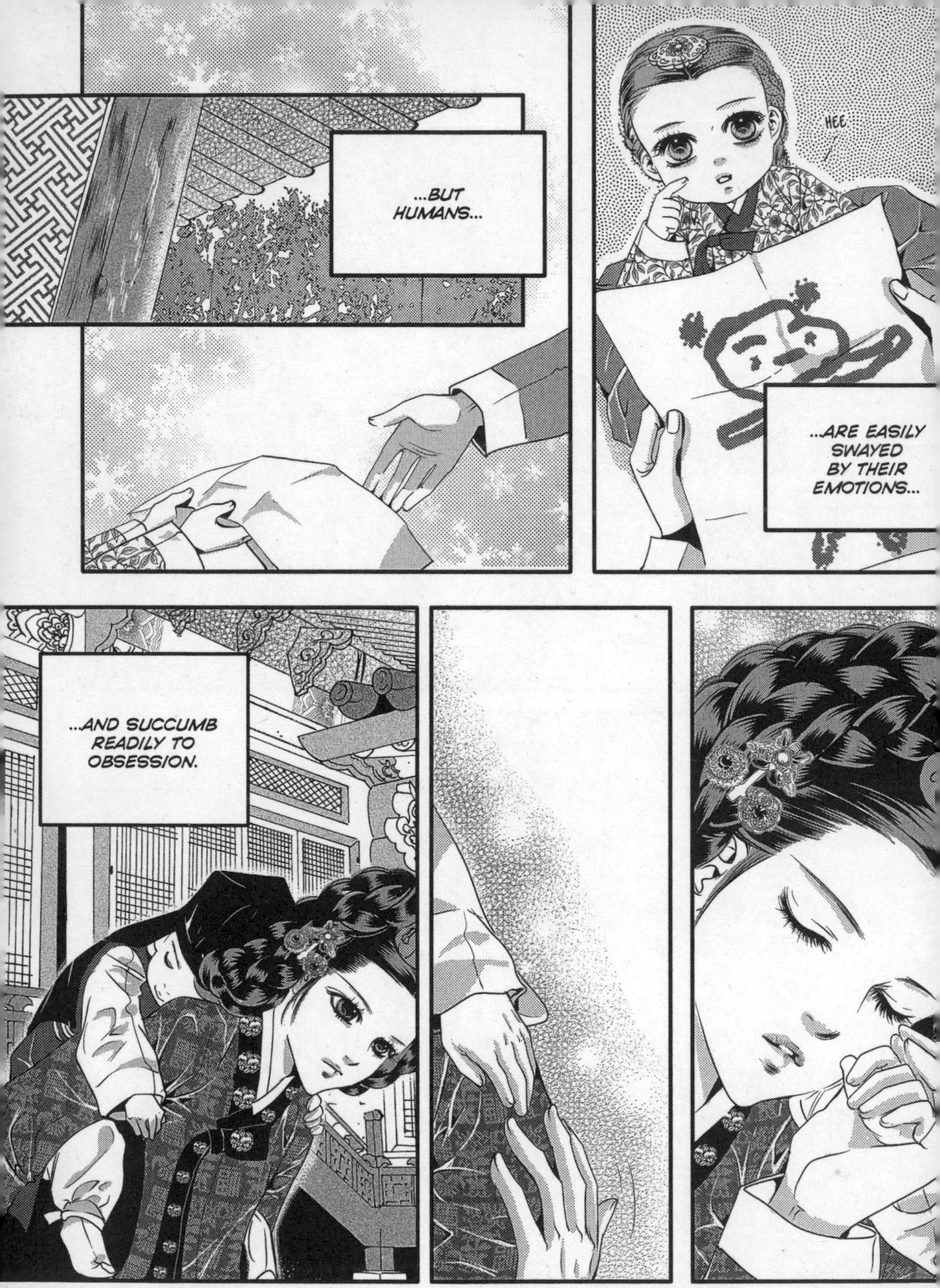
...BUT HUMANS...
HEE
...ARE EASILY SWAYED BY THEIR EMOTIONS...
...AND SUCCUMB READILY TO OBSESSION.

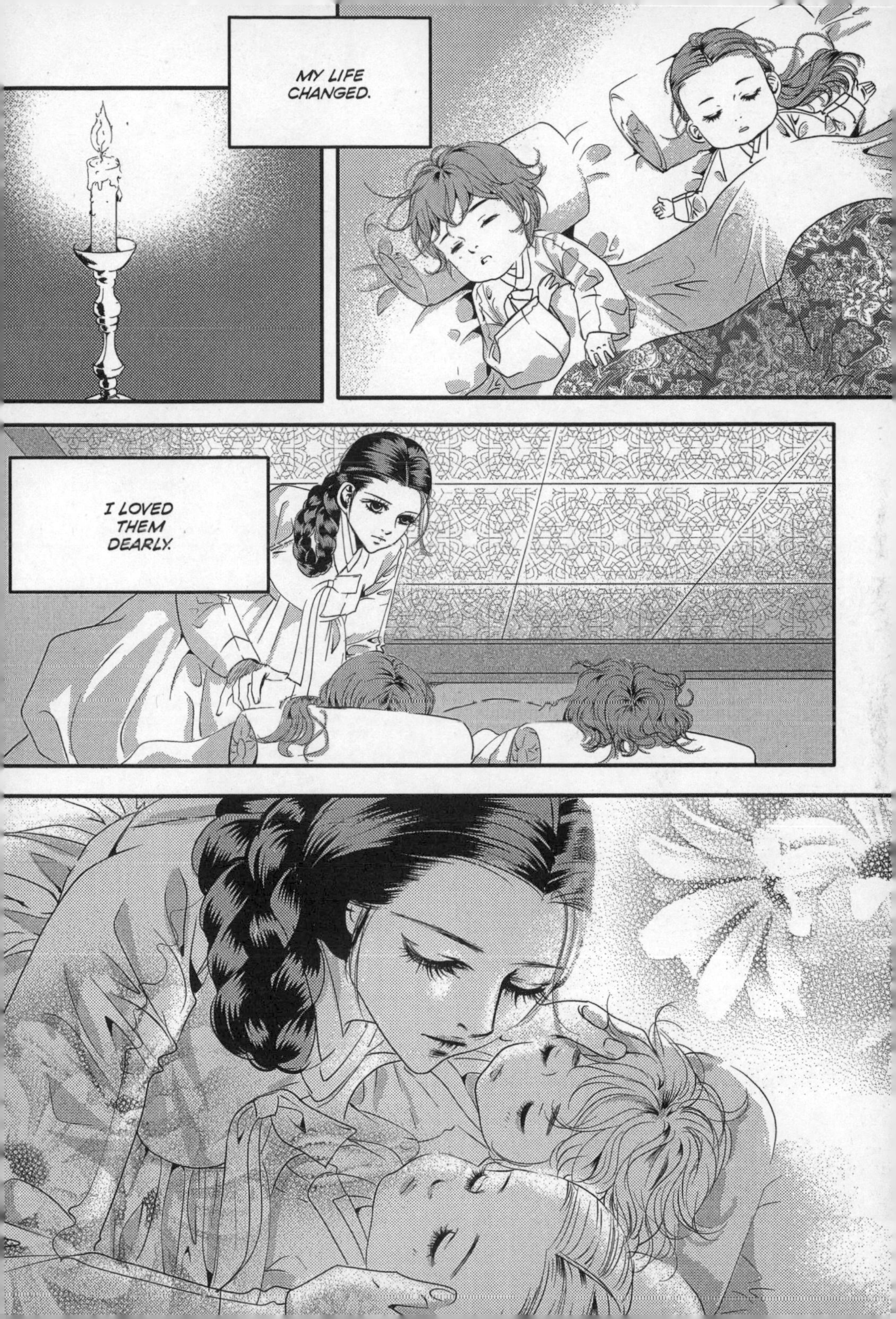
MY LIFE CHANGED.
I LOVED THEM DEARLY.

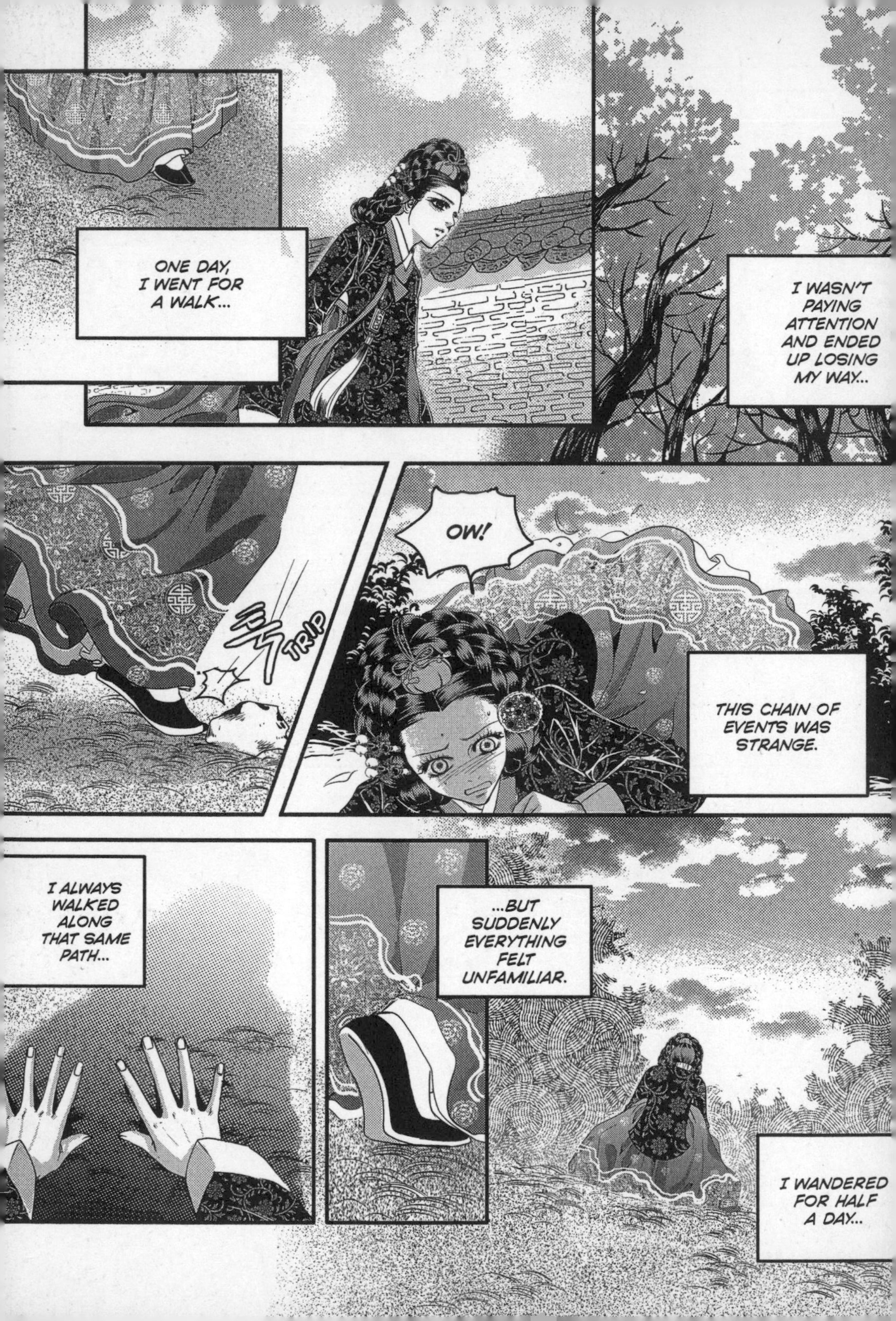
ONE DAY, I WENT FOR A WALK...
I WASN'T PAYING ATTENTION AND ENDED UP LOSING MY WAY...
TRIP
OW!
THIS CHAIN OF EVENTS WAS STRANGE.
I ALWAYS WALKED ALONG THAT SAME PATH...
...BUT SUDDENLY EVERYTHING FELT UNFAMILIAR.
I WANDERED FOR HALF A DAY...

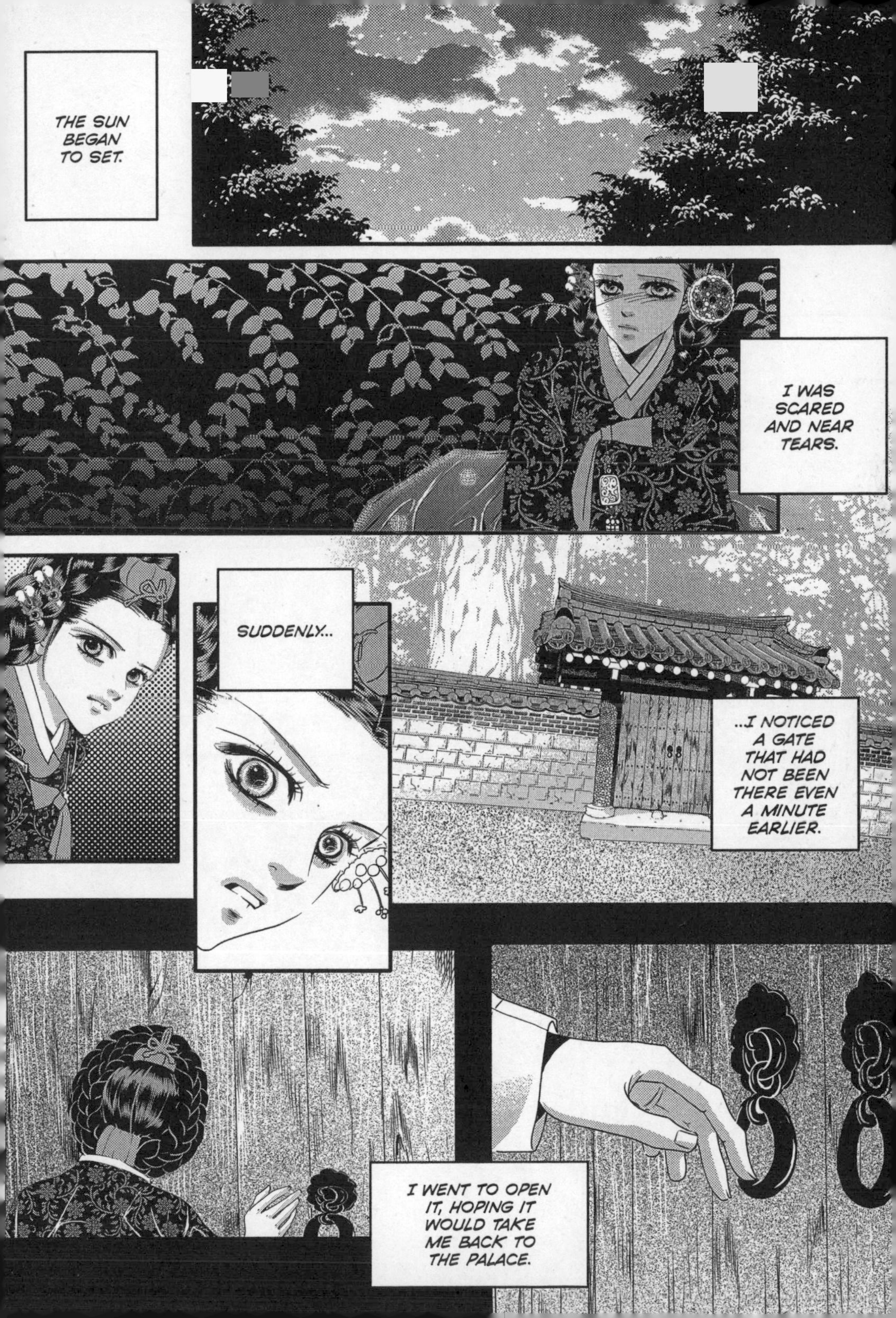
THE SUN BEGAN TO SET.
I WAS SCARED AND NEAR TEARS.
SUDDENLY...
...I NOTICED A GATE THAT HAD NOT BEEN THERE EVEN A MINUTE EARLIER.
I WENT TO OPEN IT, HOPING IT WOULD TAKE ME BACK TO THE PALACE.

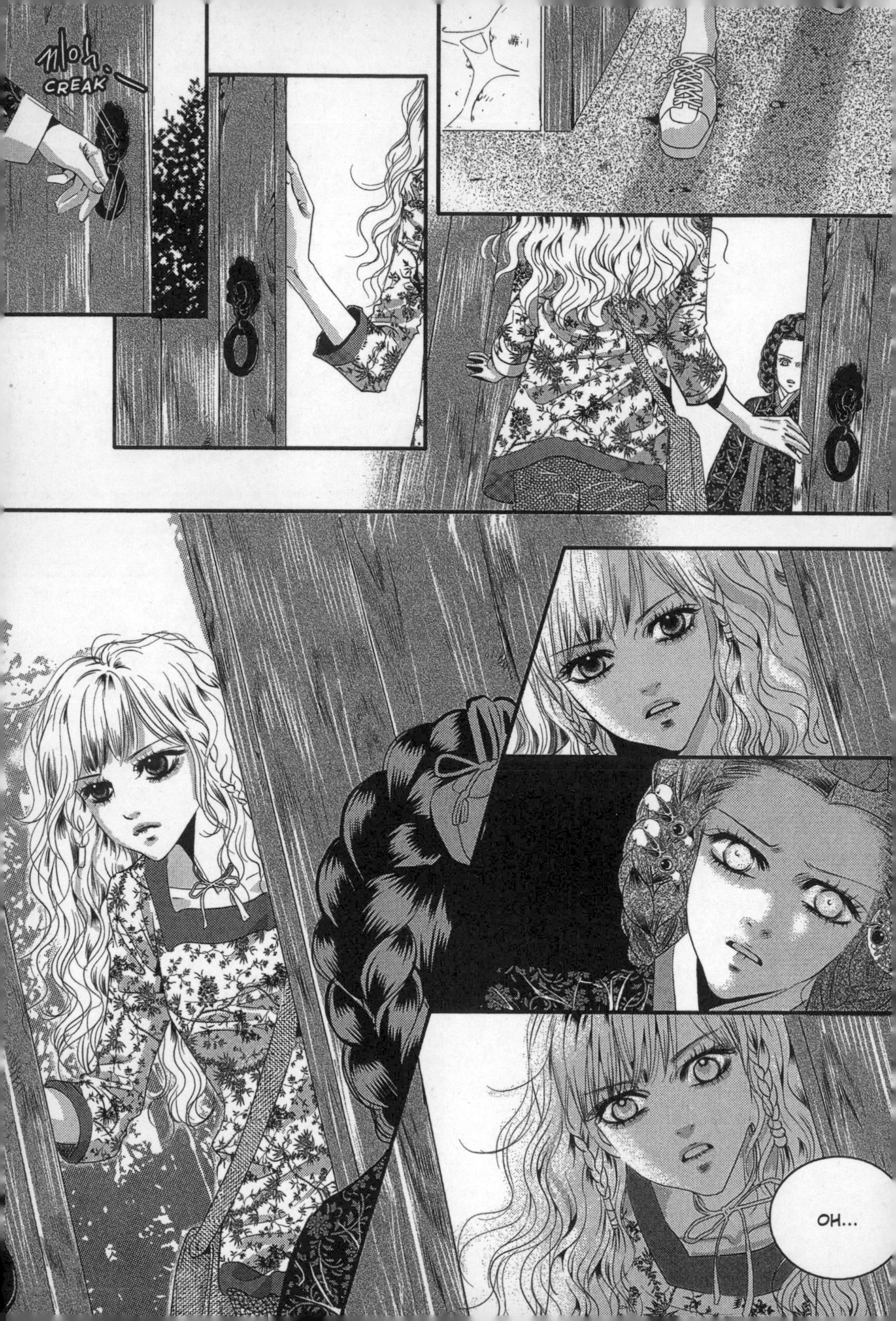
끼익
CREAK
OH...

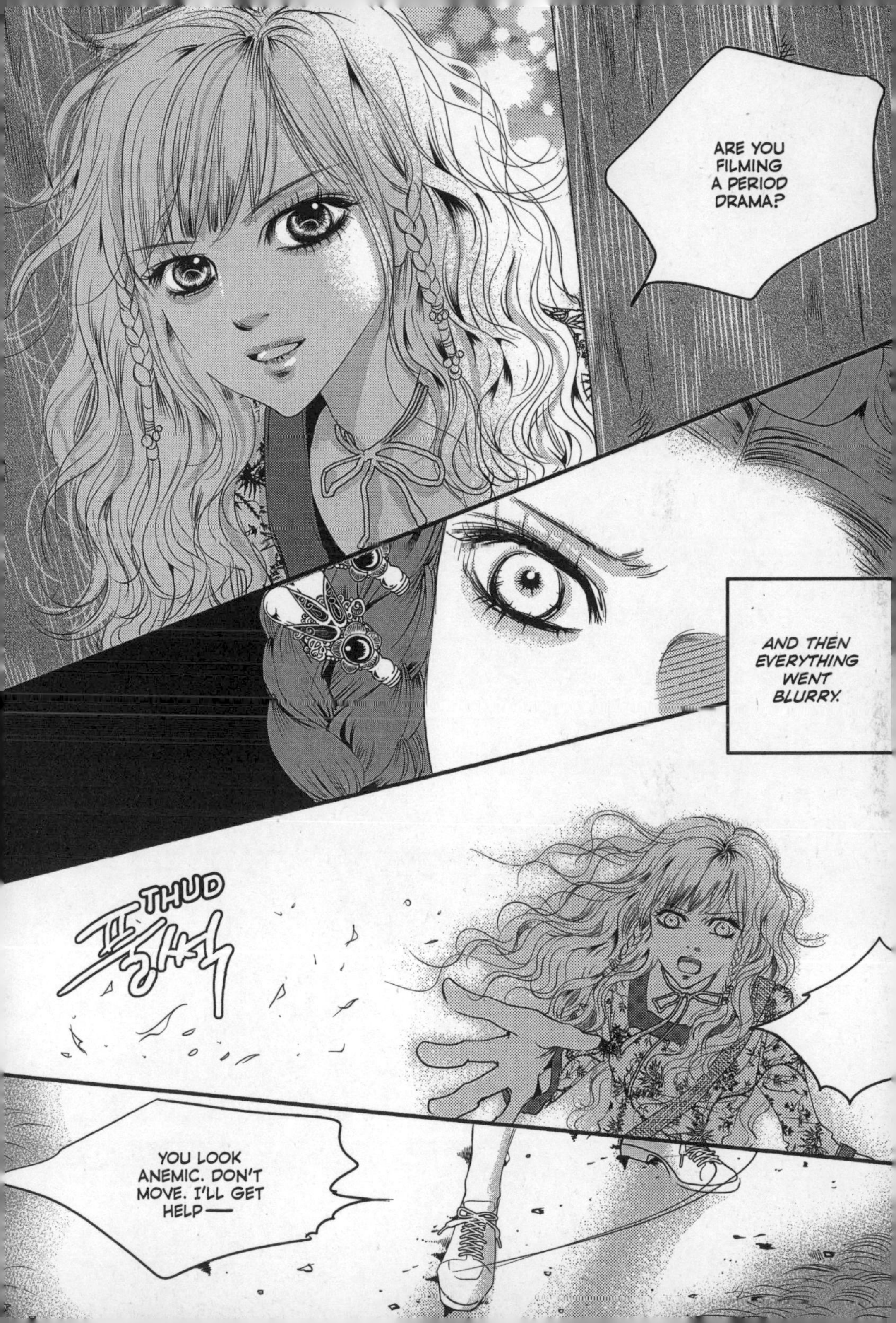
ARE YOU FILMING A PERIOD DRAMA?
AND THEN EVERYTHING WENT BLURRY.
THUD
YOU LOOK ANEMIC. DON'T MOVE. I'LL GET HELP—

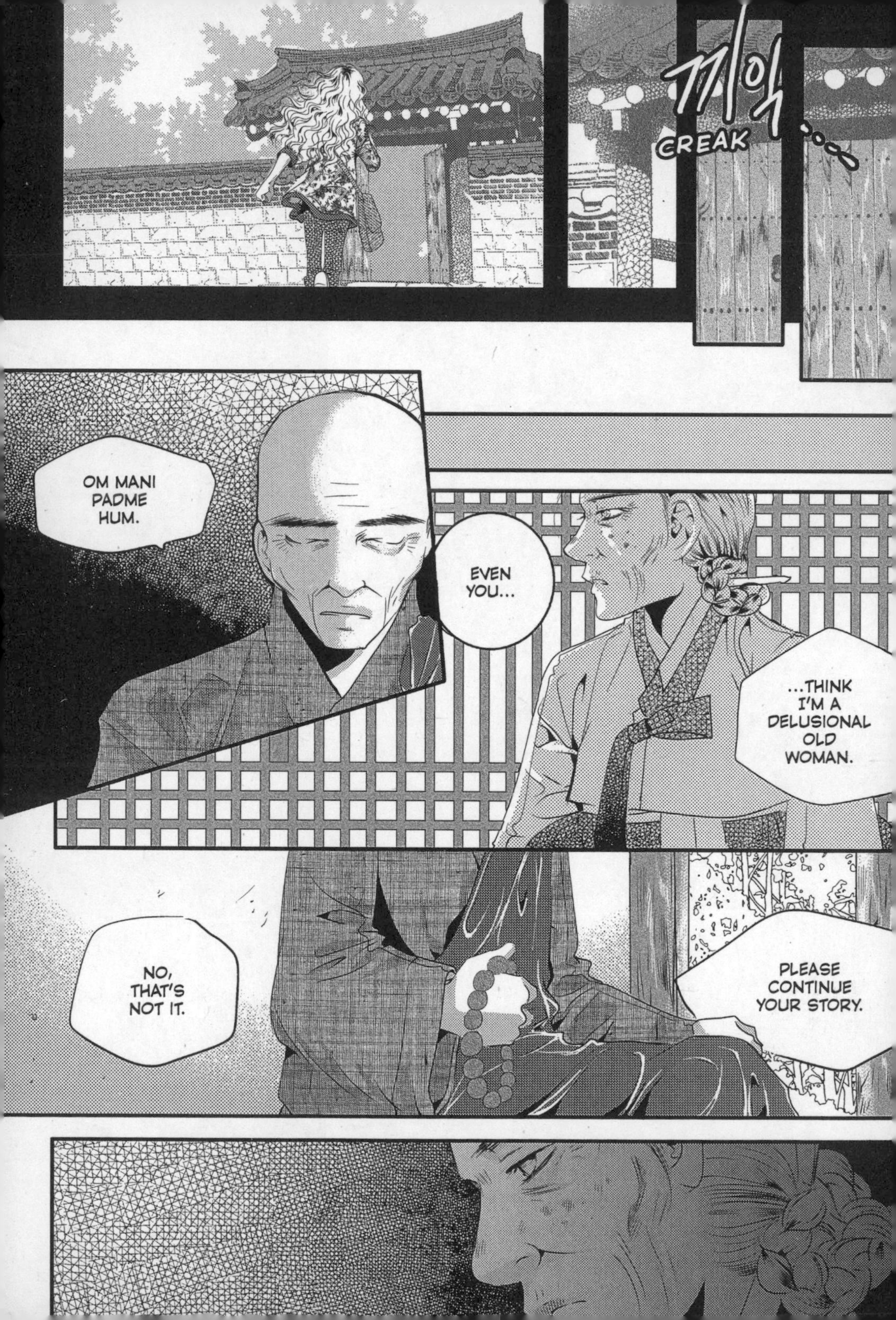
끼익
CREAK
OM MANI PADME HUM.
EVEN YOU...
...THINK I'M A DELUSIONAL OLD WOMAN.
NO, THAT'S NOT IT.
PLEASE CONTINUE YOUR STORY.

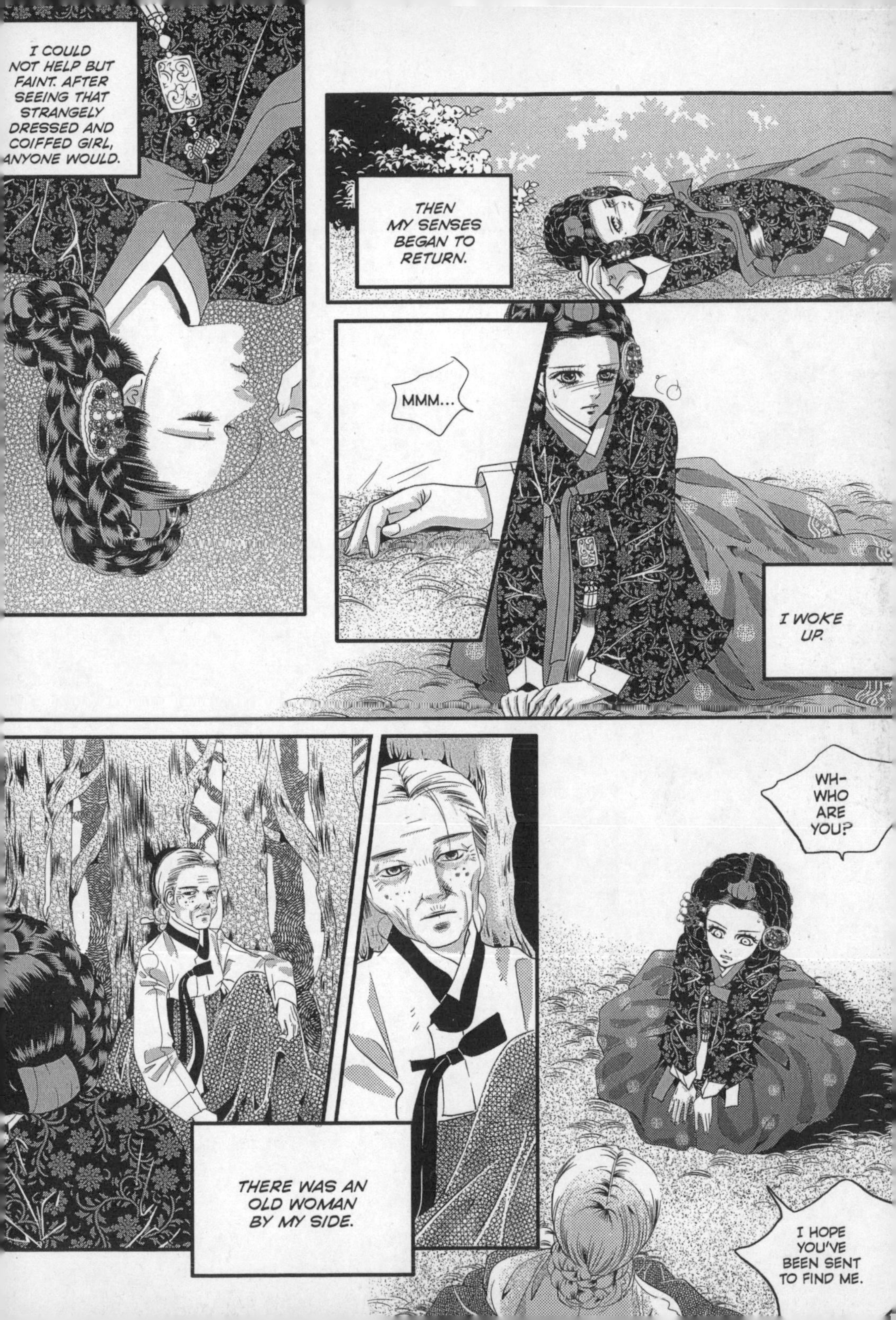
I COULD NOT HELP BUT FAINT. AFTER SEEING THAT STRANGELY DRESSED AND COIFFED GIRL, ANYONE WOULD.
THEN MY SENSES BEGAN TO RETURN.
MMM...
I WOKE UP.
THERE WAS AN OLD WOMAN BY MY SIDE.
WH- WHO ARE YOU?
I HOPE YOU'VE BEEN SENT TO FIND ME.

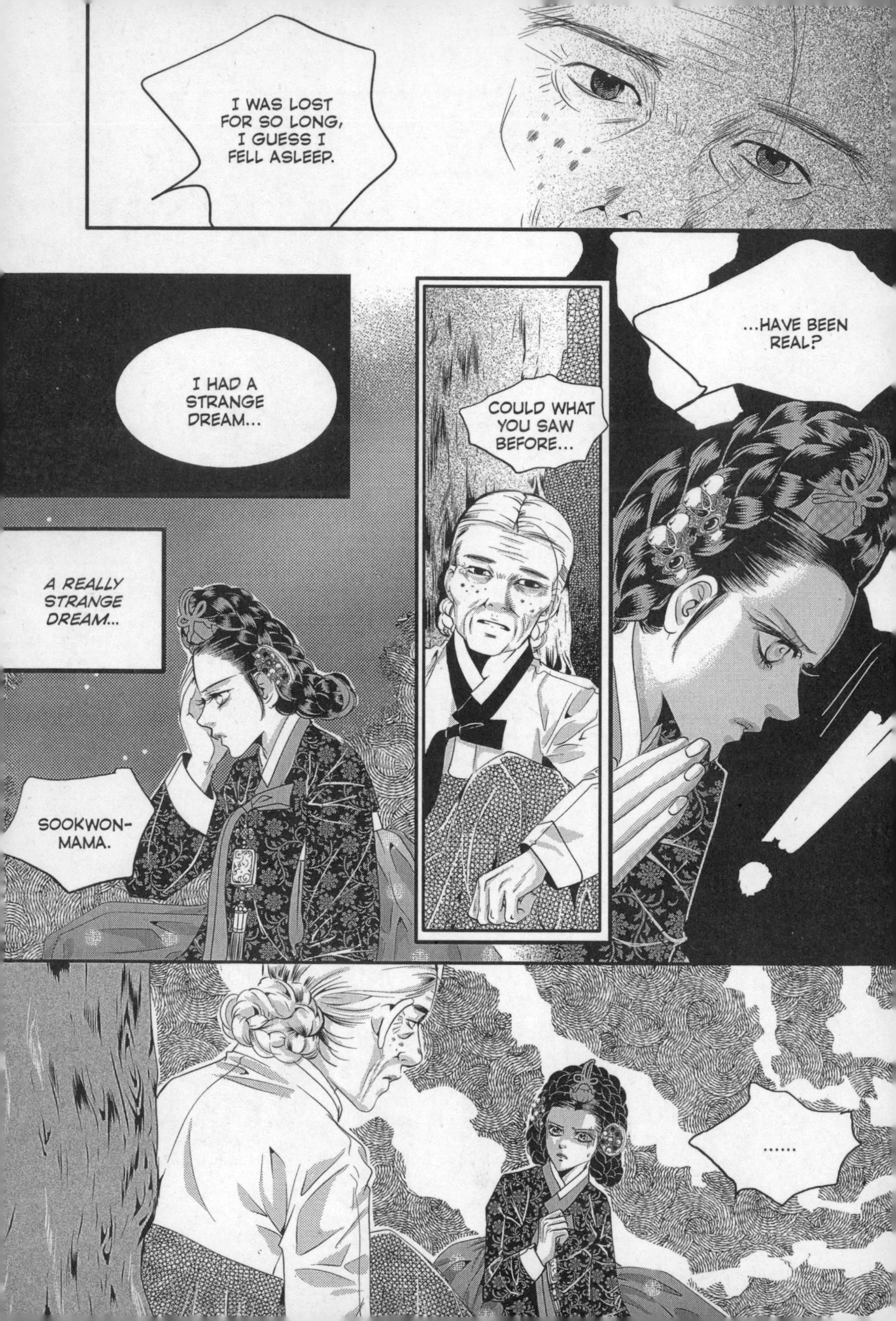
I WAS LOST FOR SO LONG, I GUESS I FELL ASLEEP.
I HAD A STRANGE DREAM...
A REALLY STRANGE DREAM...
SOOKWON-MAMA.
COULD WHAT YOU SAW BEFORE...
...HAVE BEEN REAL?
......

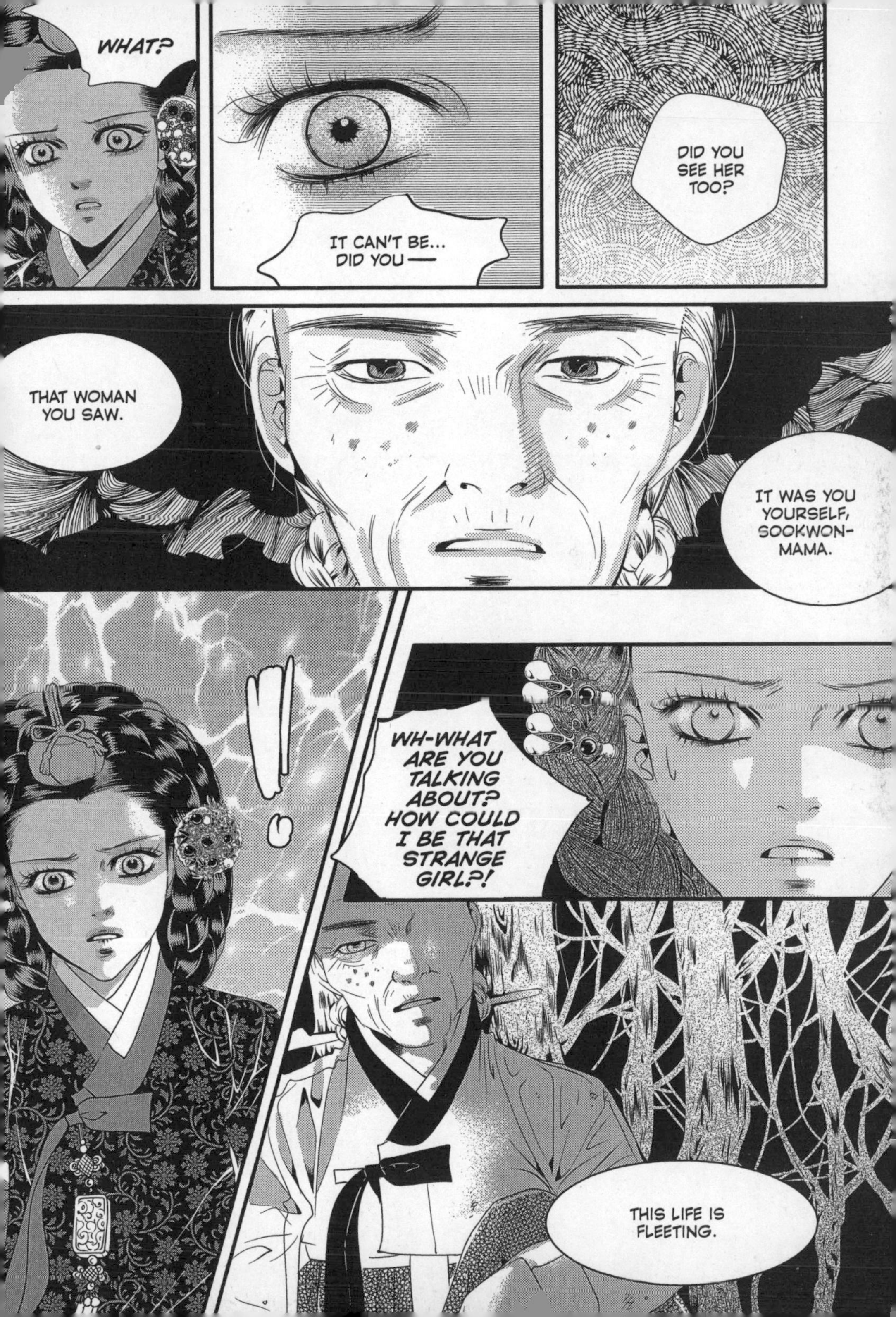
WHAT?
IT CAN'T BE... DID YOU—
DID YOU SEE HER TOO?
THAT WOMAN YOU SAW.
IT WAS YOU YOURSELF, SOOKWON-MAMA.
!
WH-WHAT ARE YOU TALKING ABOUT? HOW COULD I BE THAT STRANGE GIRL?!
THIS LIFE IS FLEETING.

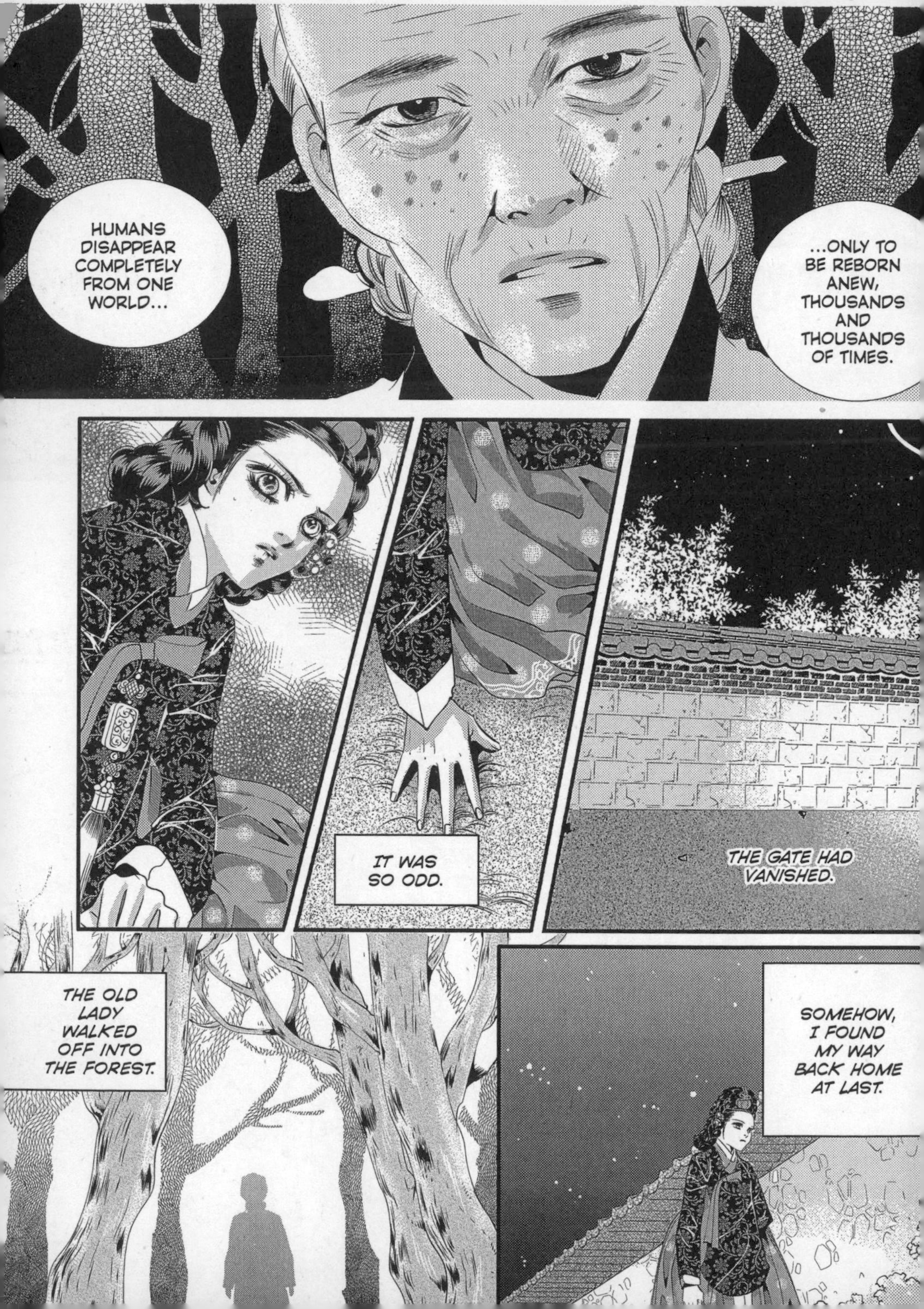
HUMANS DISAPPEAR COMPLETELY FROM ONE WORLD...
...ONLY TO BE REBORN ANEW, THOUSANDS AND THOUSANDS OF TIMES.
IT WAS SO ODD.
THE GATE HAD VANISHED.
THE OLD LADY WALKED OFF INTO THE FOREST.
SOMEHOW, I FOUND MY WAY BACK HOME AT LAST.

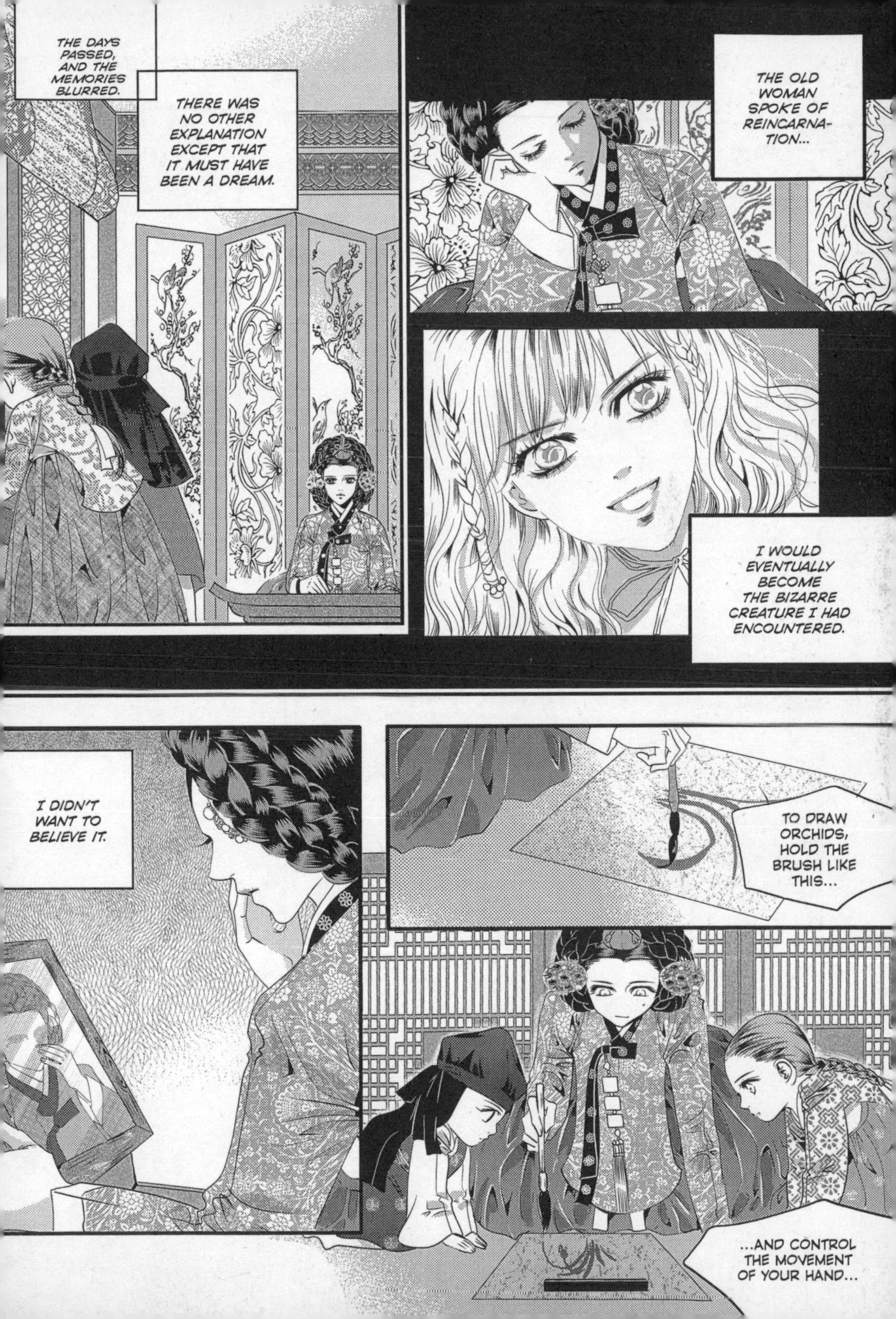
THE DAYS PASSED, AND THE MEMORIES BLURRED.
THERE WAS NO OTHER EXPLANATION EXCEPT THAT IT MUST HAVE BEEN A DREAM.
THE OLD WOMAN SPOKE OF REINCARNA-TION...
I WOULD EVENTUALLY BECOME THE BIZARRE CREATURE I HAD ENCOUNTERED.
I DIDN'T WANT TO BELIEVE IT.
TO DRAW ORCHIDS, HOLD THE BRUSH LIKE THIS...
...AND CONTROL THE MOVEMENT OF YOUR HAND...

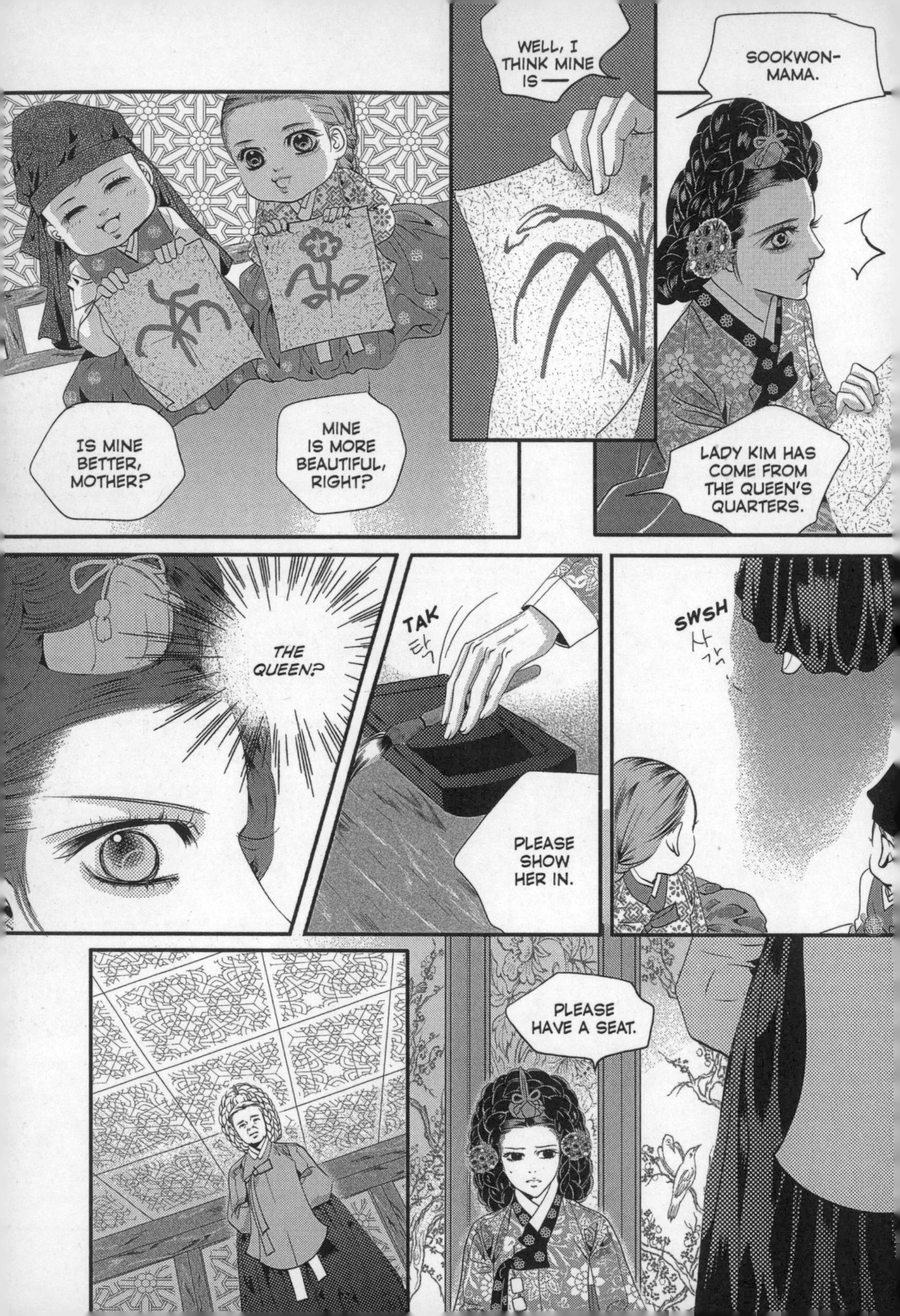
IS MINE BETTER, MOTHER?
MINE IS MORE BEAUTIFUL, RIGHT?
WELL, I THINK MINE IS—
SOOKWON-MAMA.
LADY KIM HAS COME FROM THE QUEEN'S QUARTERS.
THE QUEEN?
TAK
탁
PLEASE SHOW HER IN.
SWSH
PLEASE HAVE A SEAT.

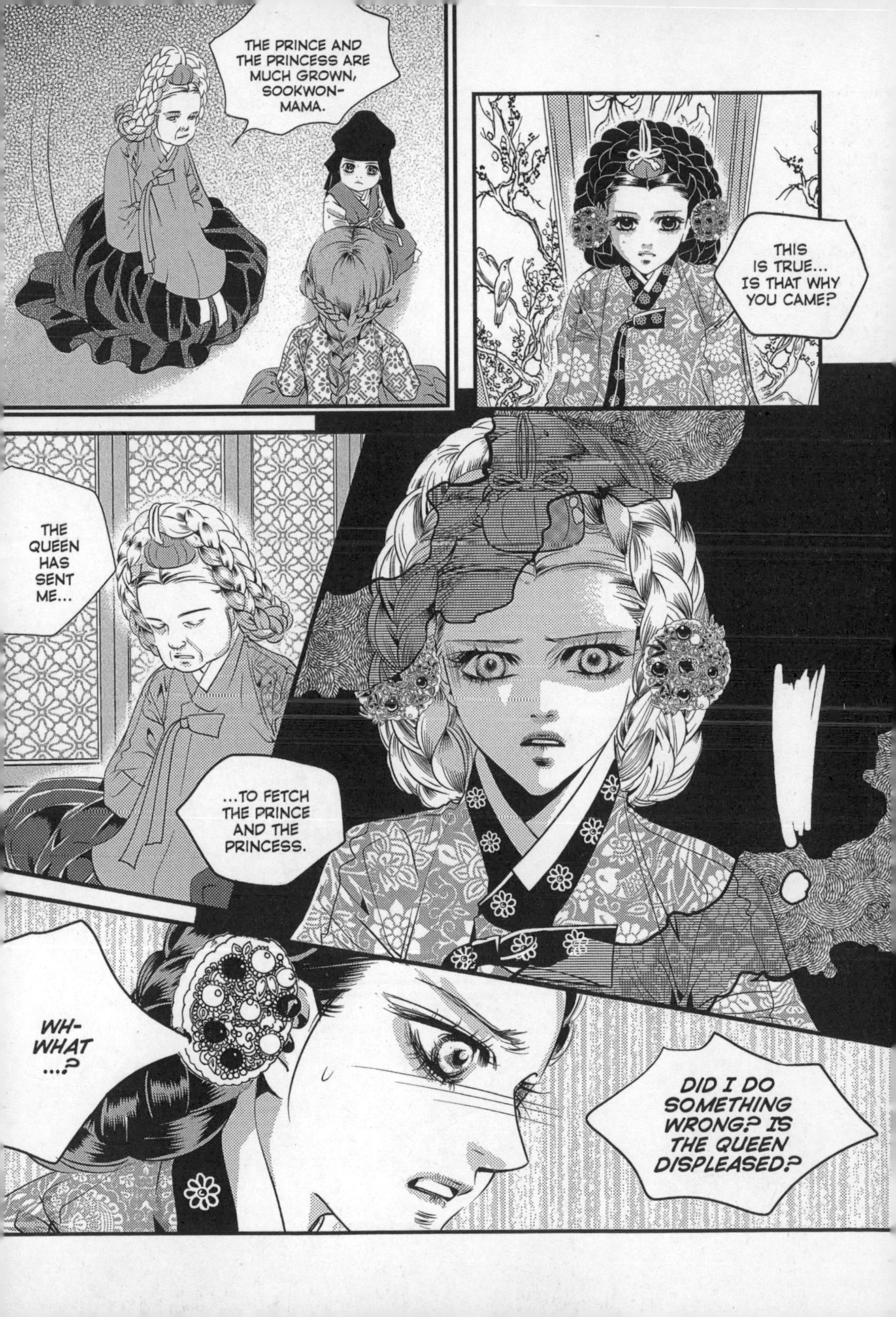
THE PRINCE AND THE PRINCESS ARE MUCH GROWN, SOOKWON-MAMA.
THIS IS TRUE... IS THAT WHY YOU CAME?
THE QUEEN HAS SENT ME...
...TO FETCH THE PRINCE AND THE PRINCESS.
!
WH-WHAT ...?
DID I DO SOMETHING WRONG? IS THE QUEEN DISPLEASED?

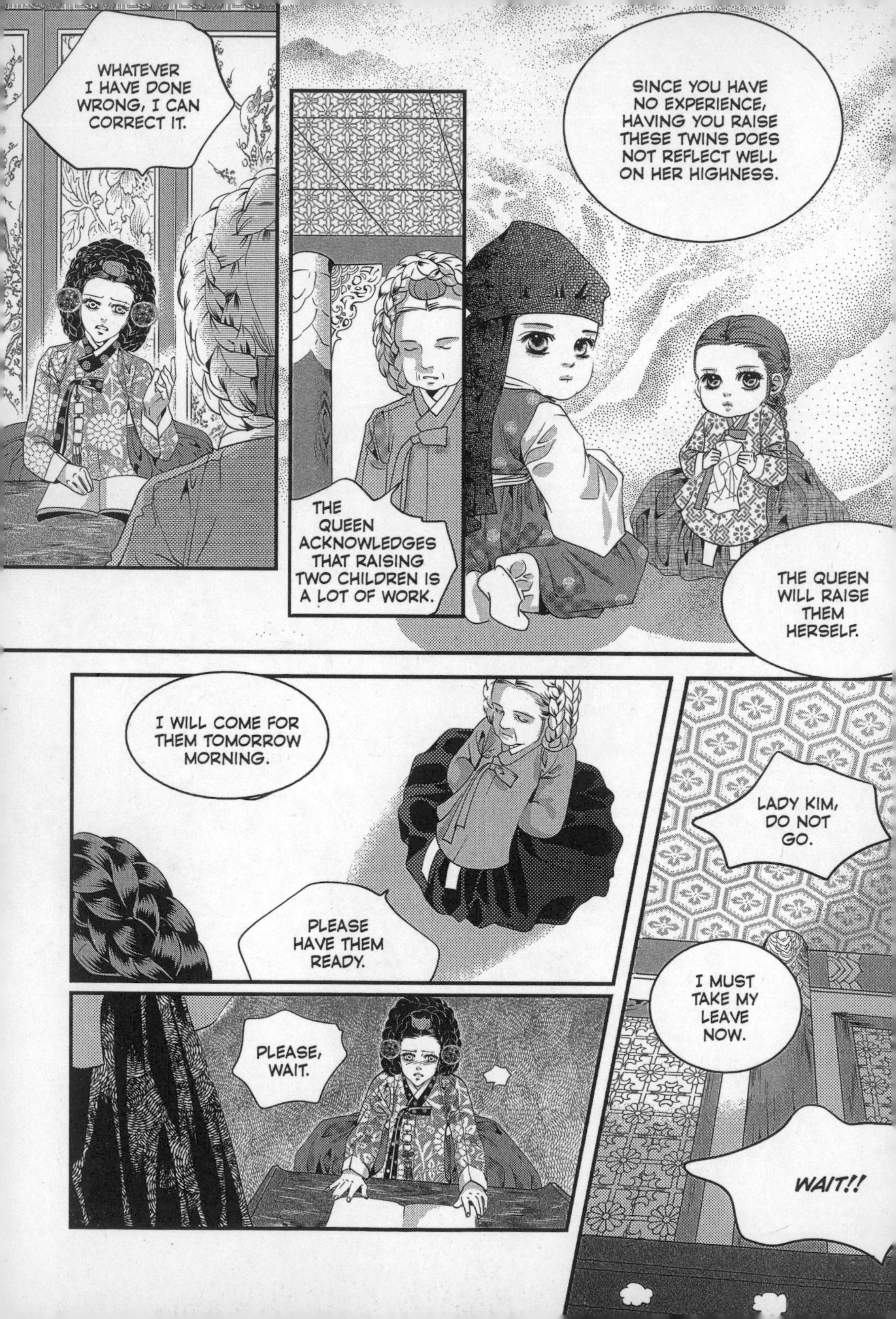
WHATEVER I HAVE DONE WRONG, I CAN CORRECT IT.
SINCE YOU HAVE NO EXPERIENCE, HAVING YOU RAISE THESE TWINS DOES NOT REFLECT WELL ON HER HIGHNESS.
THE QUEEN ACKNOWLEDGES THAT RAISING TWO CHILDREN IS A LOT OF WORK.
THE QUEEN WILL RAISE THEM HERSELF.
I WILL COME FOR THEM TOMORROW MORNING.
PLEASE HAVE THEM READY.
LADY KIM, DO NOT GO.
PLEASE, WAIT.
I MUST TAKE MY LEAVE NOW.
WAIT!!

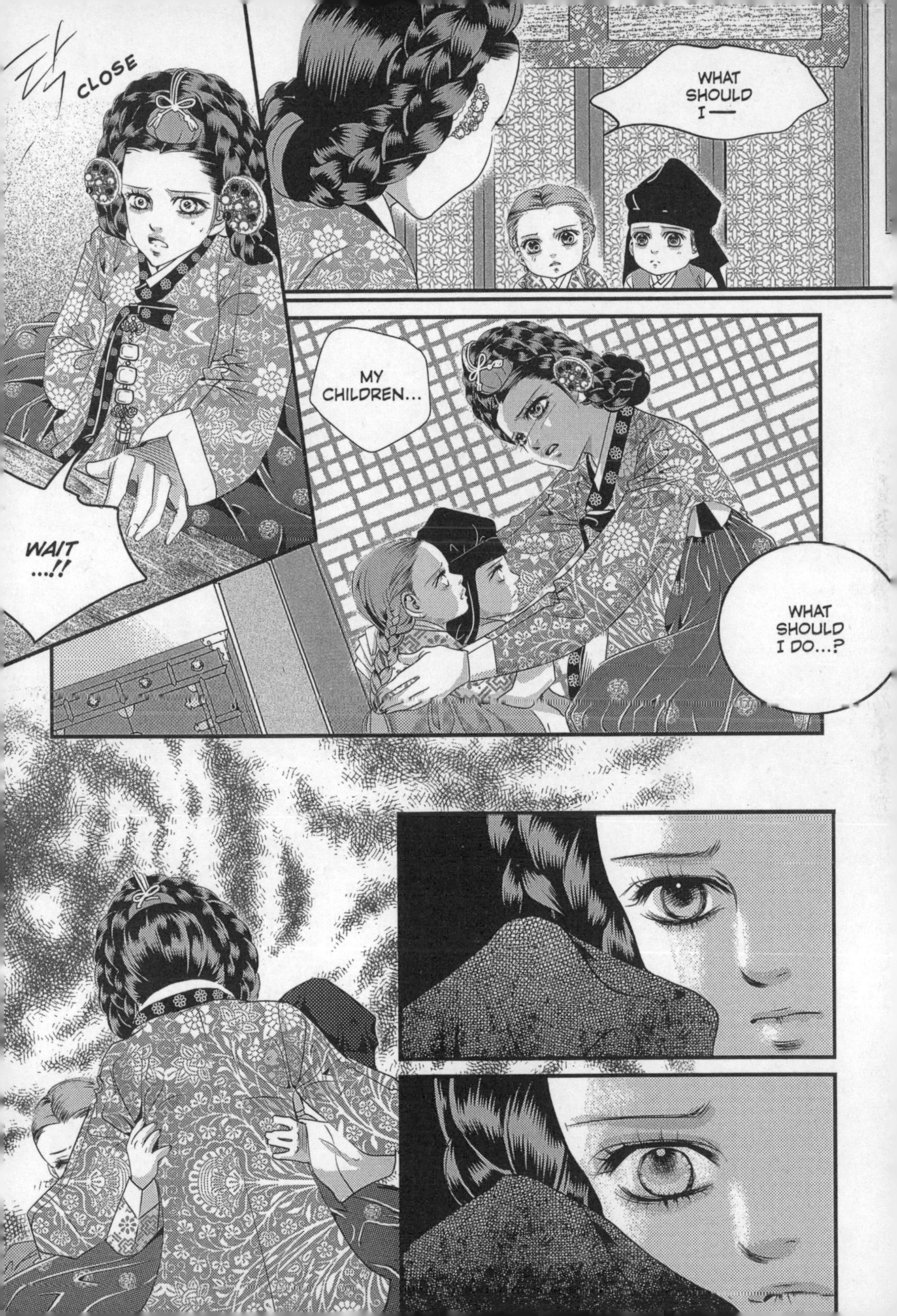
CLOSE
WHAT SHOULD I—
WAIT...!!
MY CHILDREN...
WHAT SHOULD I DO...?

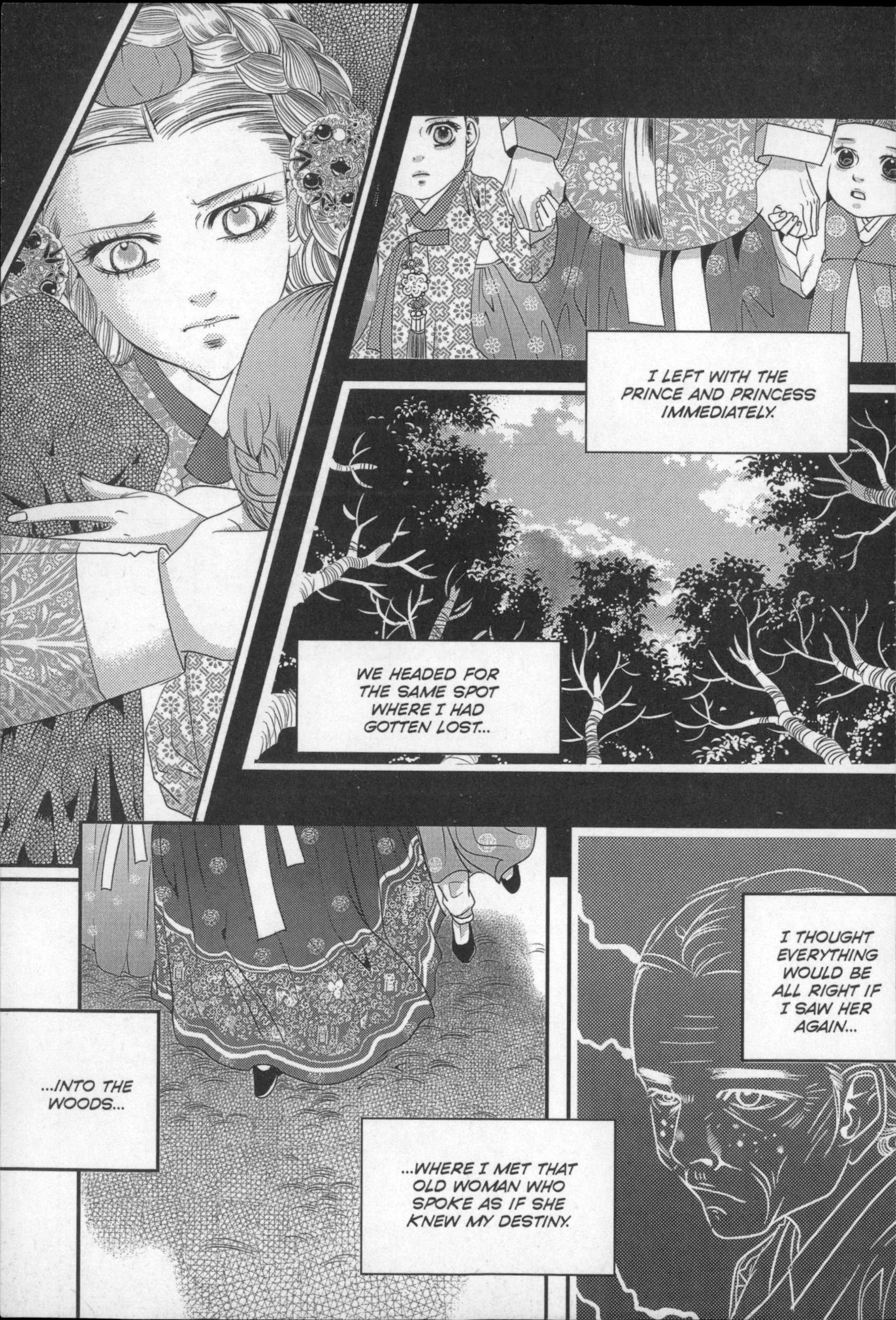
I LEFT WITH THE PRINCE AND PRINCESS IMMEDIATELY.
WE HEADED FOR THE SAME SPOT WHERE I HAD GOTTEN LOST...
...INTO THE WOODS...
...WHERE I MET THAT OLD WOMAN WHO SPOKE AS IF SHE KNEW MY DESTINY.
I THOUGHT EVERYTHING WOULD BE ALL RIGHT IF I SAW HER AGAIN...

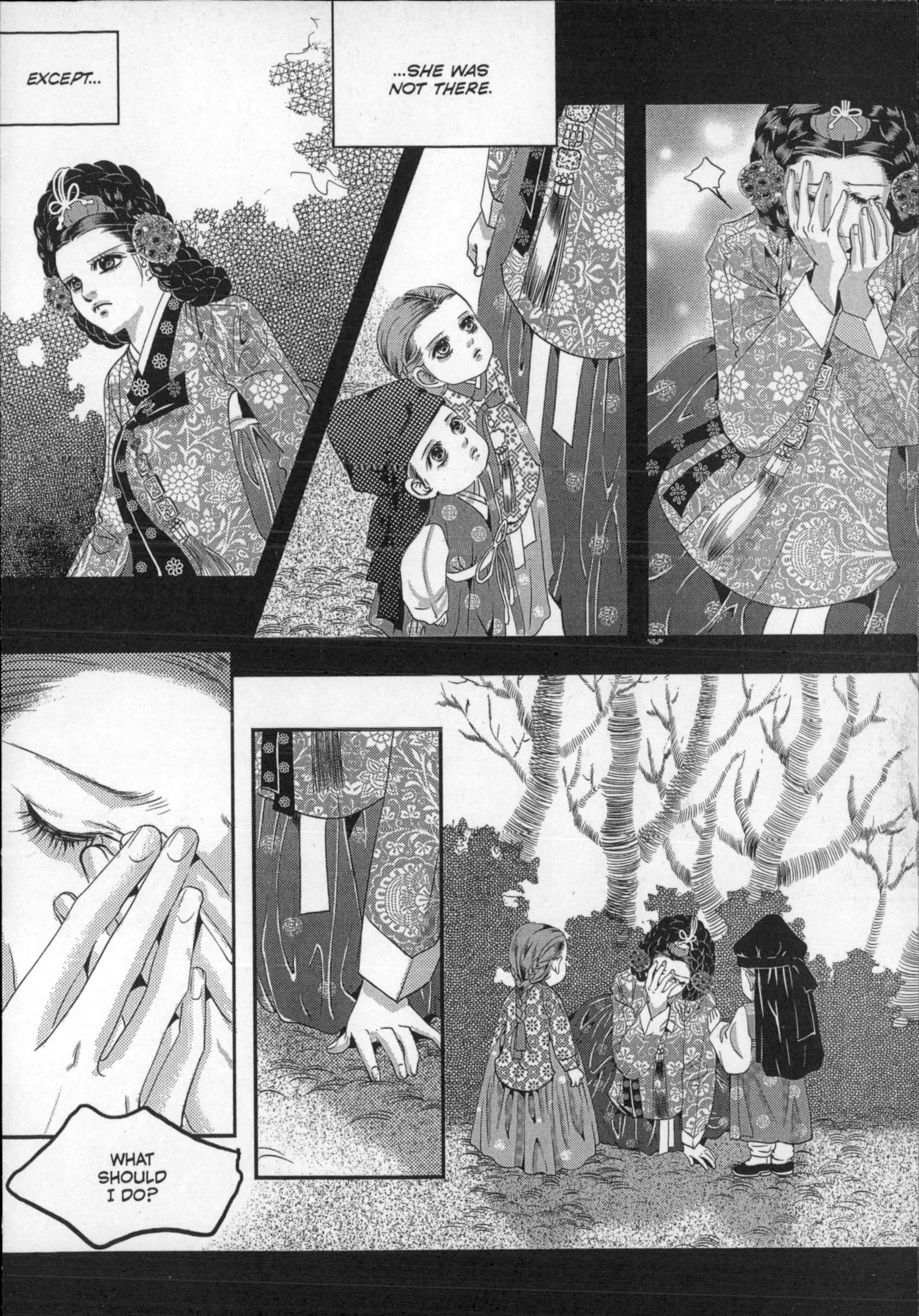
EXCEPT...
...SHE WAS NOT THERE.
WHAT SHOULD I DO?

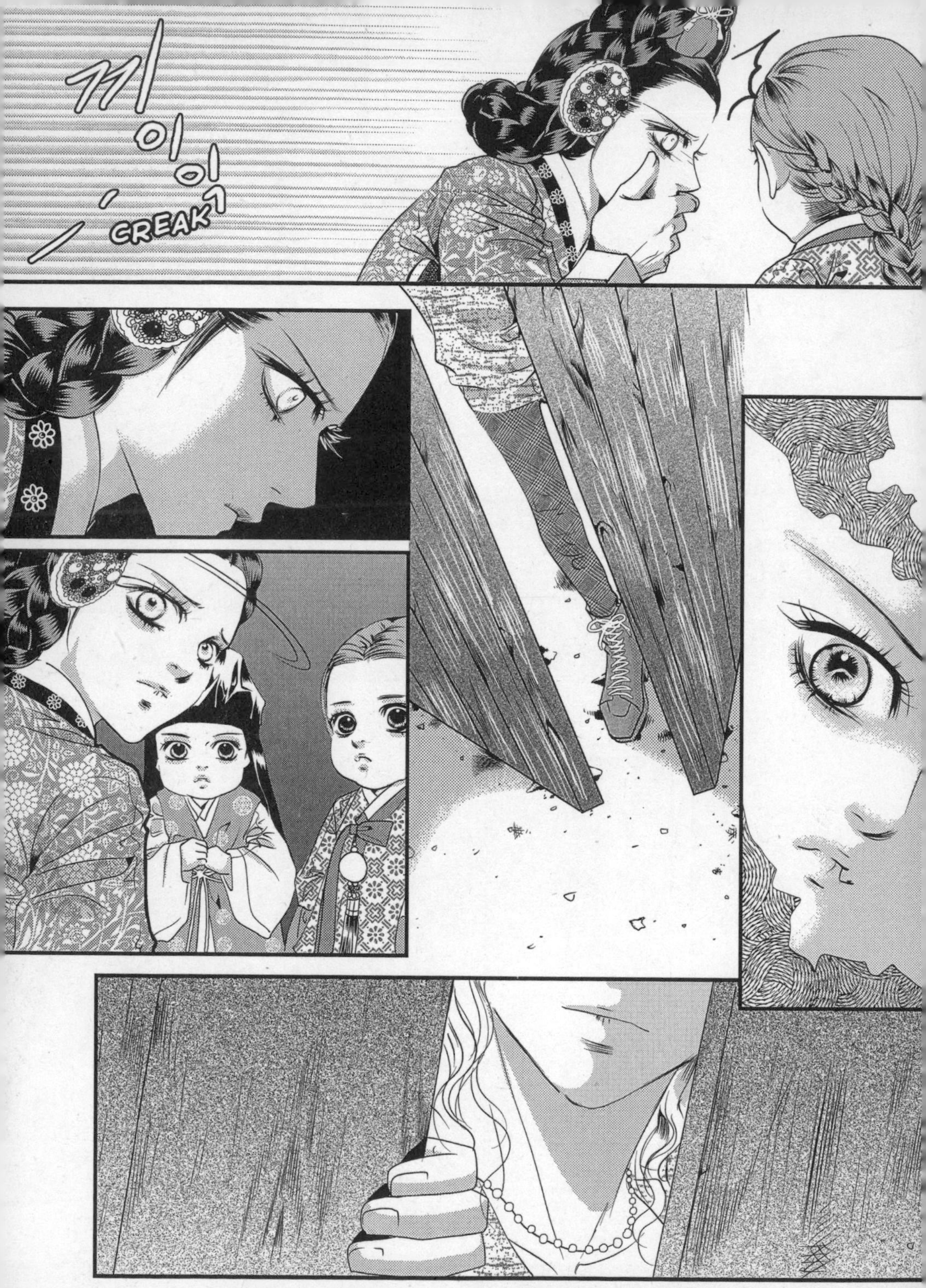
끼이익
CREAK

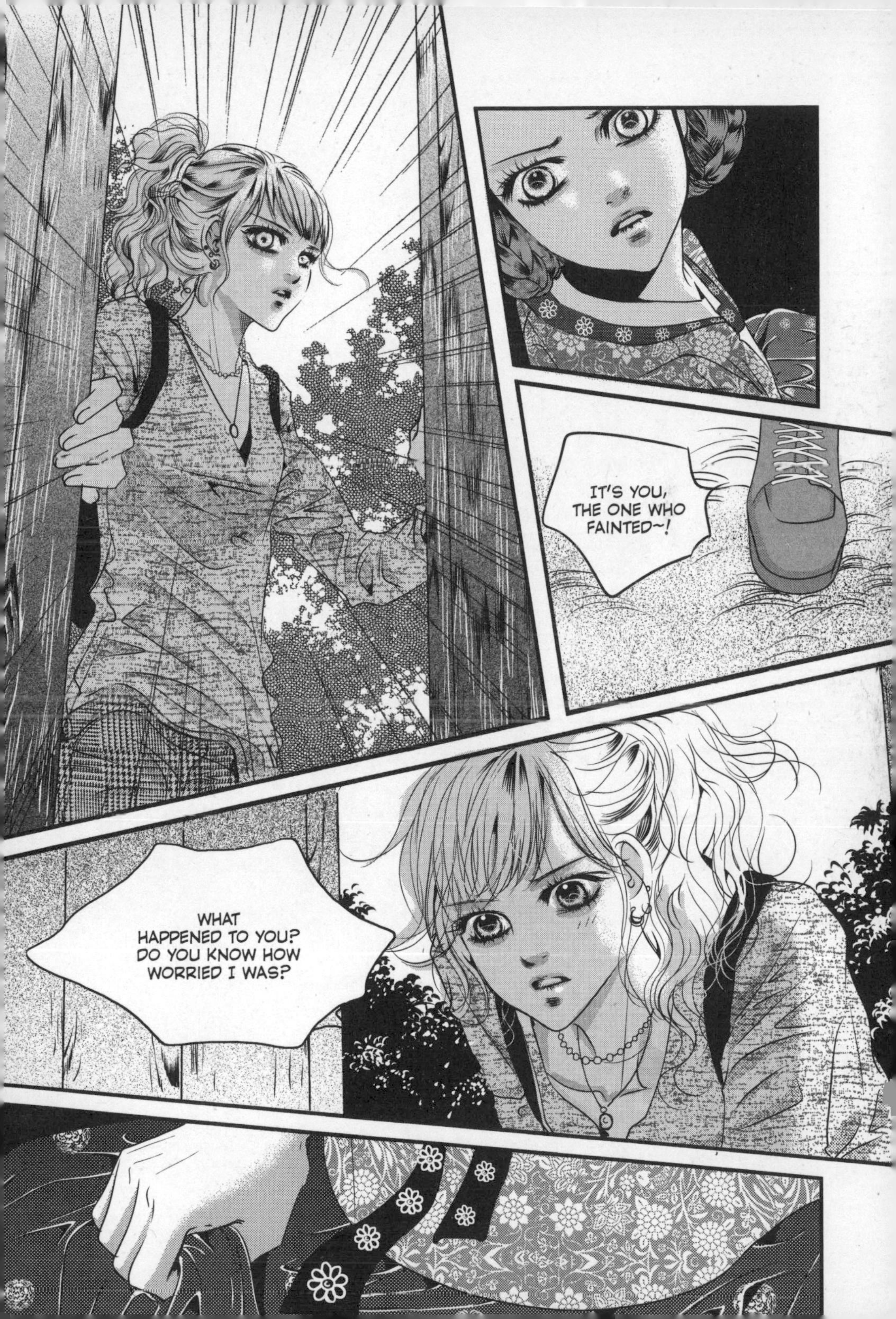
IT'S YOU, THE ONE WHO FAINTED~!
WHAT HAPPENED TO YOU? DO YOU KNOW HOW WORRIED I WAS?

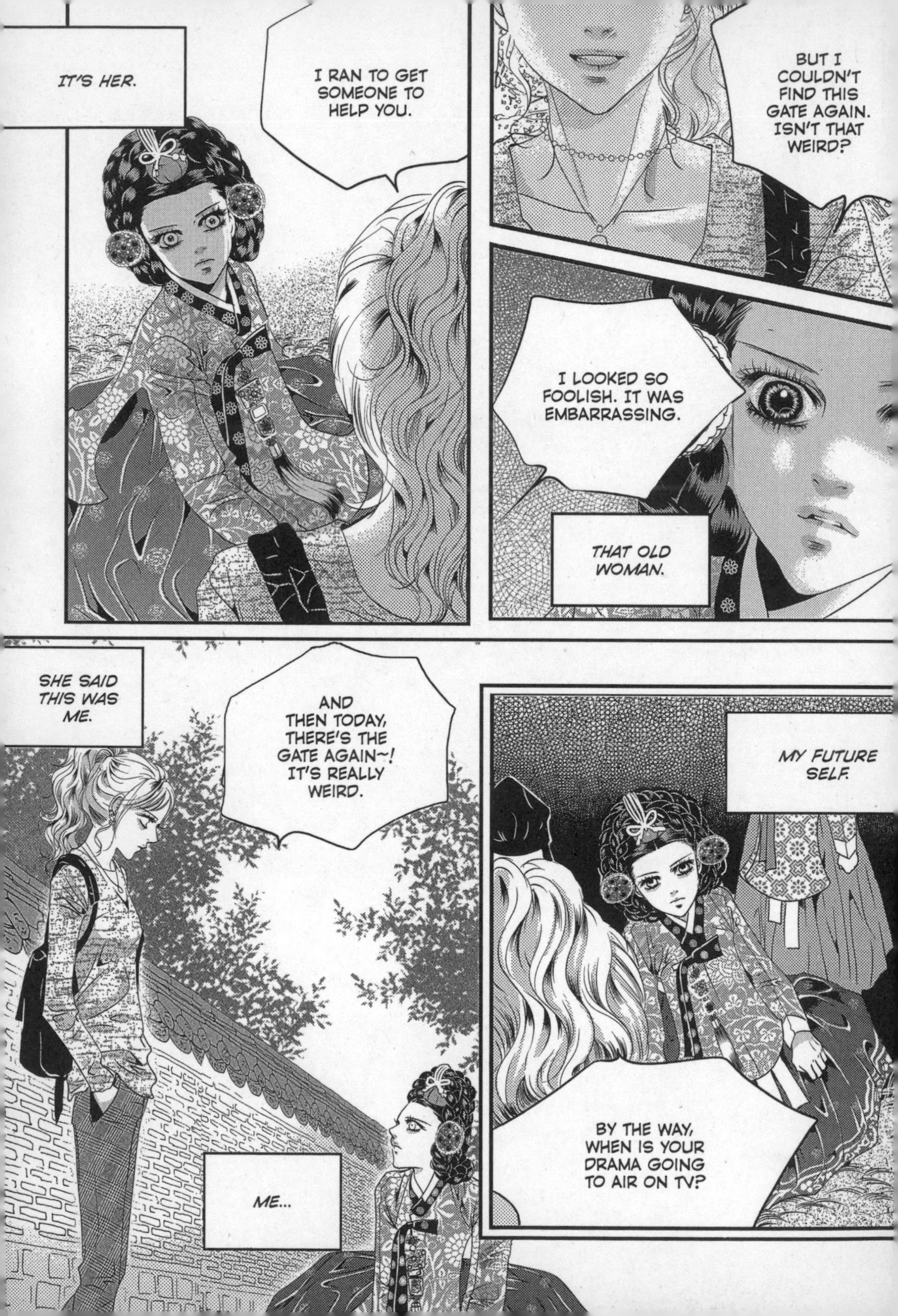
IT'S HER.
I RAN TO GET SOMEONE TO HELP YOU.
BUT I COULDN'T FIND THIS GATE AGAIN. ISN'T THAT WEIRD?
I LOOKED SO FOOLISH. IT WAS EMBARRASSING.
THAT OLD WOMAN.
SHE SAID THIS WAS ME.
AND THEN TODAY, THERE'S THE GATE AGAIN~! IT'S REALLY WEIRD.
ME...
MY FUTURE SELF.
BY THE WAY, WHEN IS YOUR DRAMA GOING TO AIR ON TV?

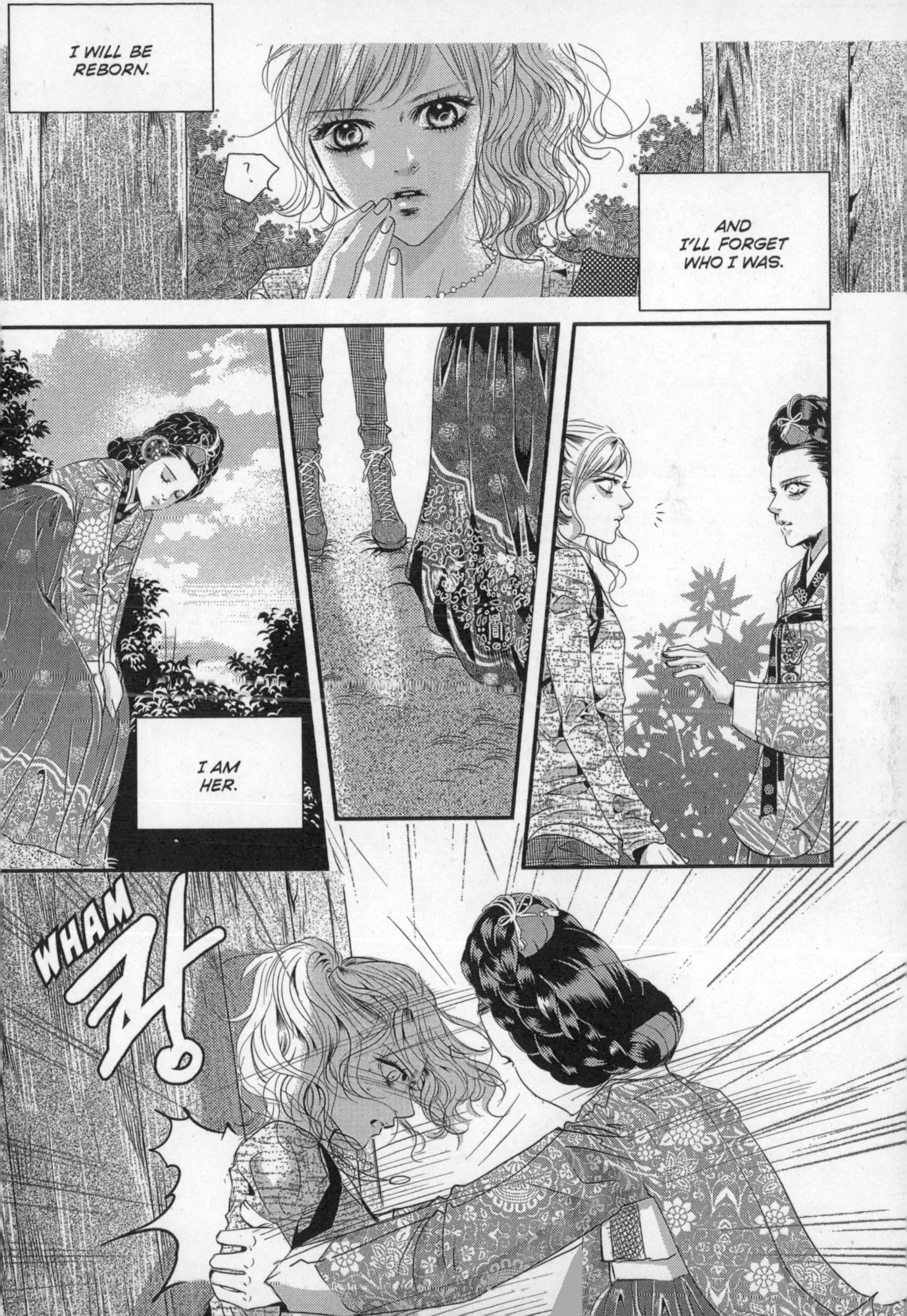
I WILL BE REBORN.
?
AND I'LL FORGET WHO I WAS.
I AM HER.
WHAM
쾅

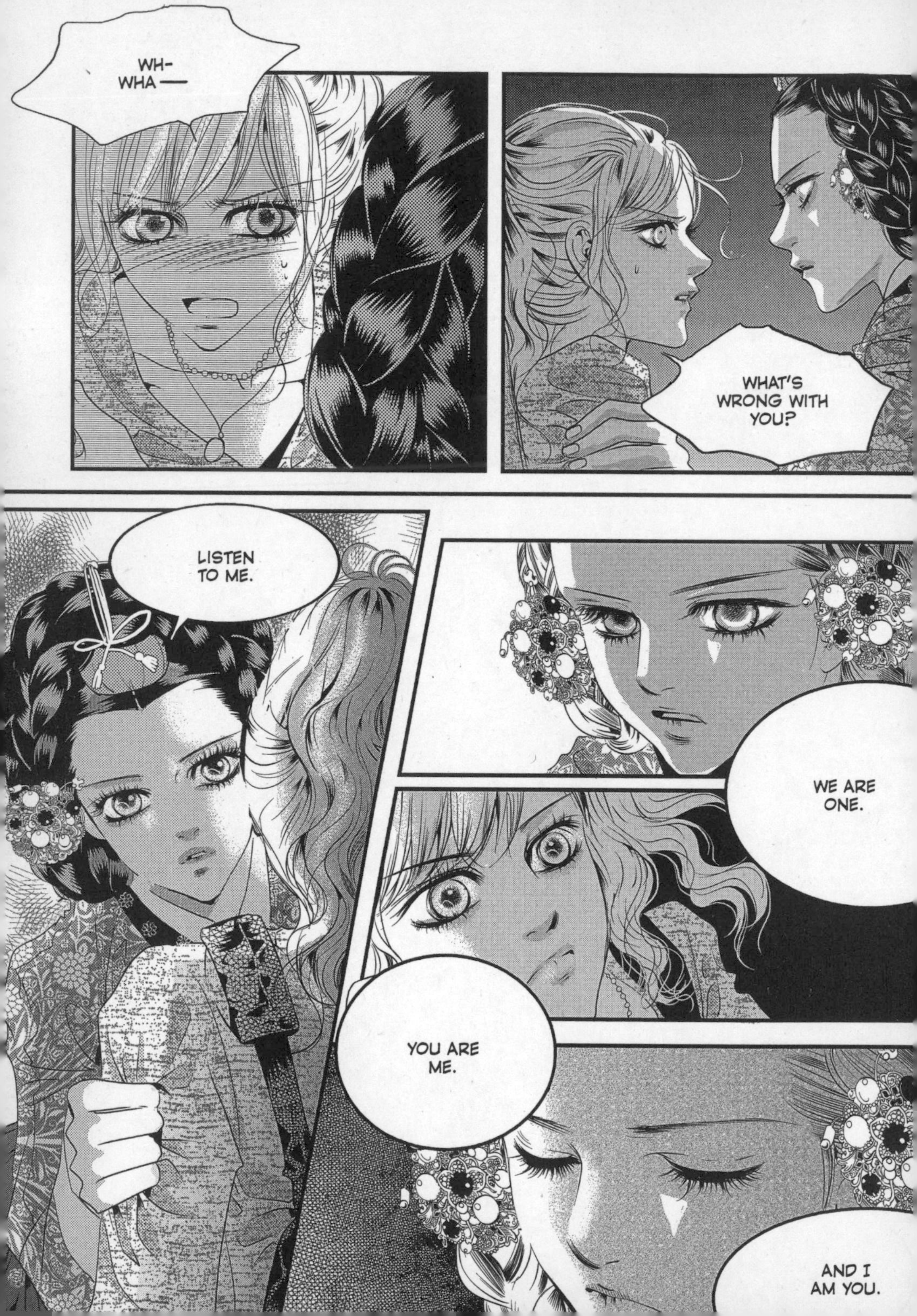
WH-
WHA—
WHAT'S WRONG WITH YOU?
LISTEN TO ME.
WE ARE ONE.
YOU ARE ME.
AND I AM YOU.

SO...

...THE CHILDREN I LOVE SO DEARLY...

...WERE BELOVED BY YOU IN A PAST LIFE.

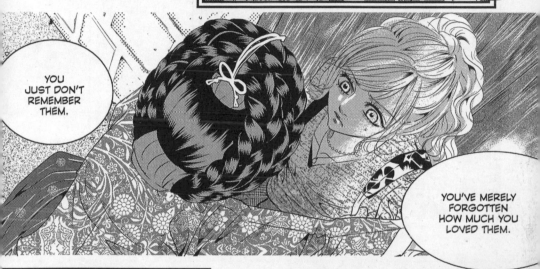

YOU JUST DON'T REMEMBER THEM.

YOU'VE MERELY FORGOTTEN HOW MUCH YOU LOVED THEM.

THIS IS THE MOMENT...

...WE MEET AGAIN.

THIS MOMENT IS OUR DESTINY.

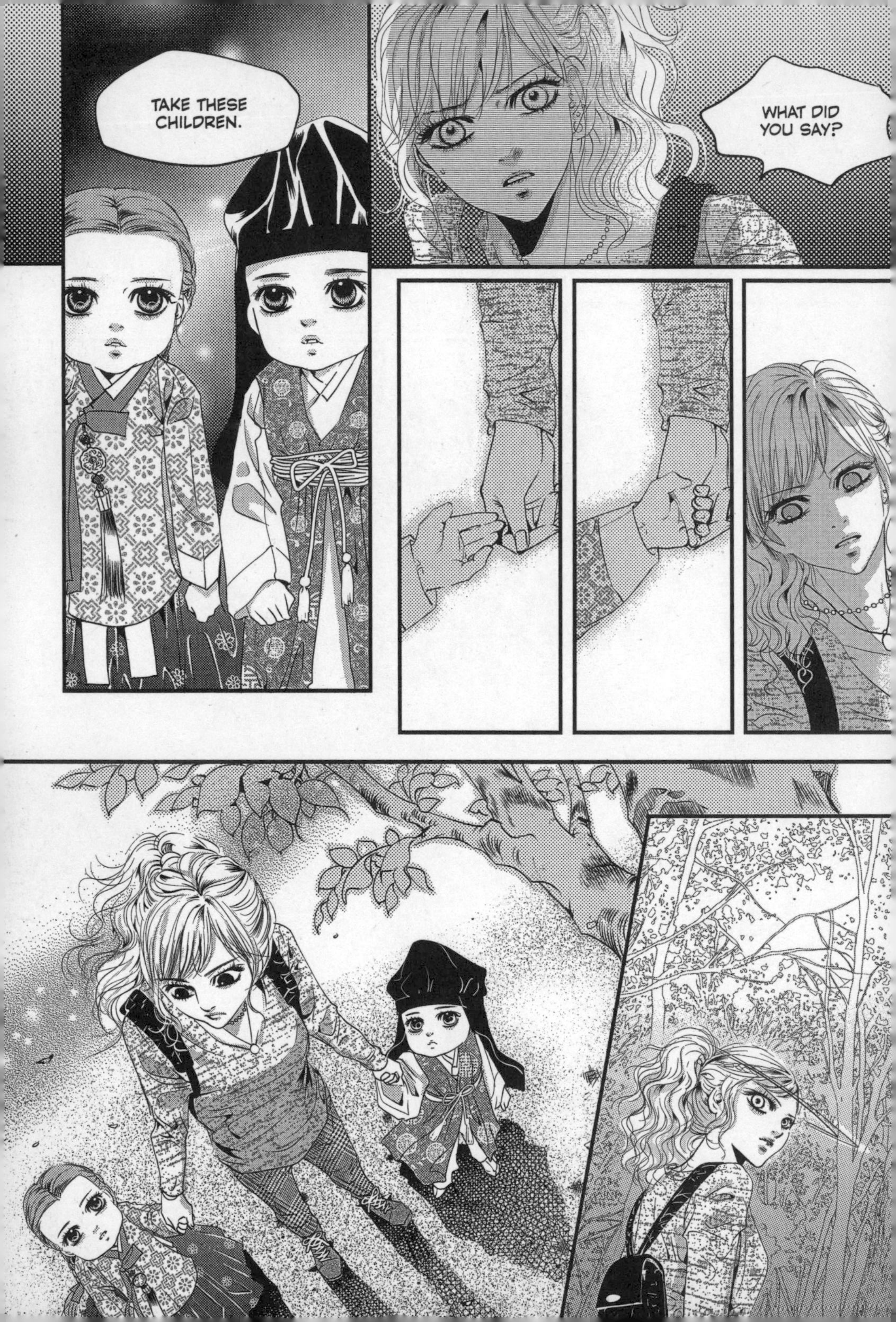
TAKE THESE CHILDREN.
WHAT DID YOU SAY?

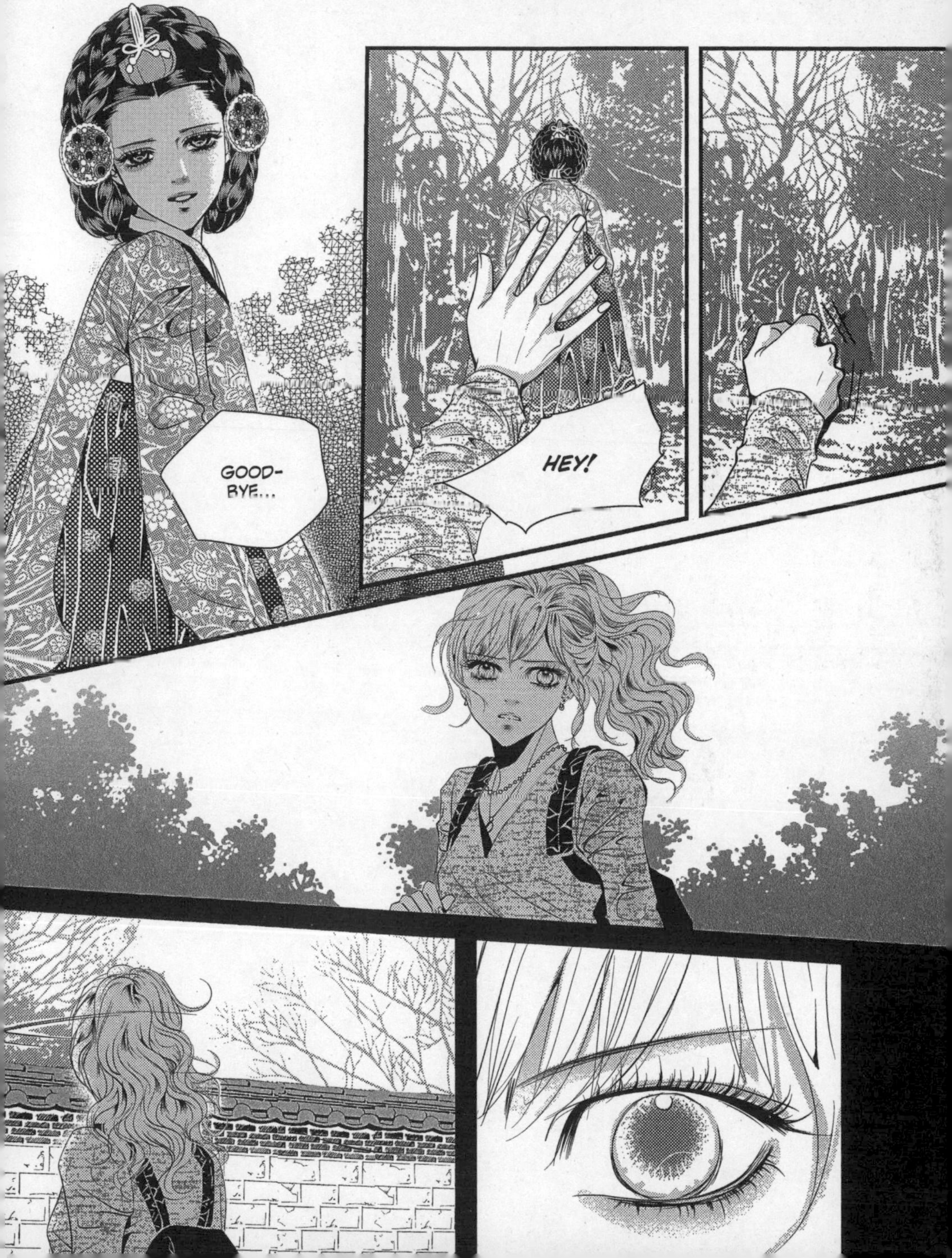
GOOD-BYE...
HEY!

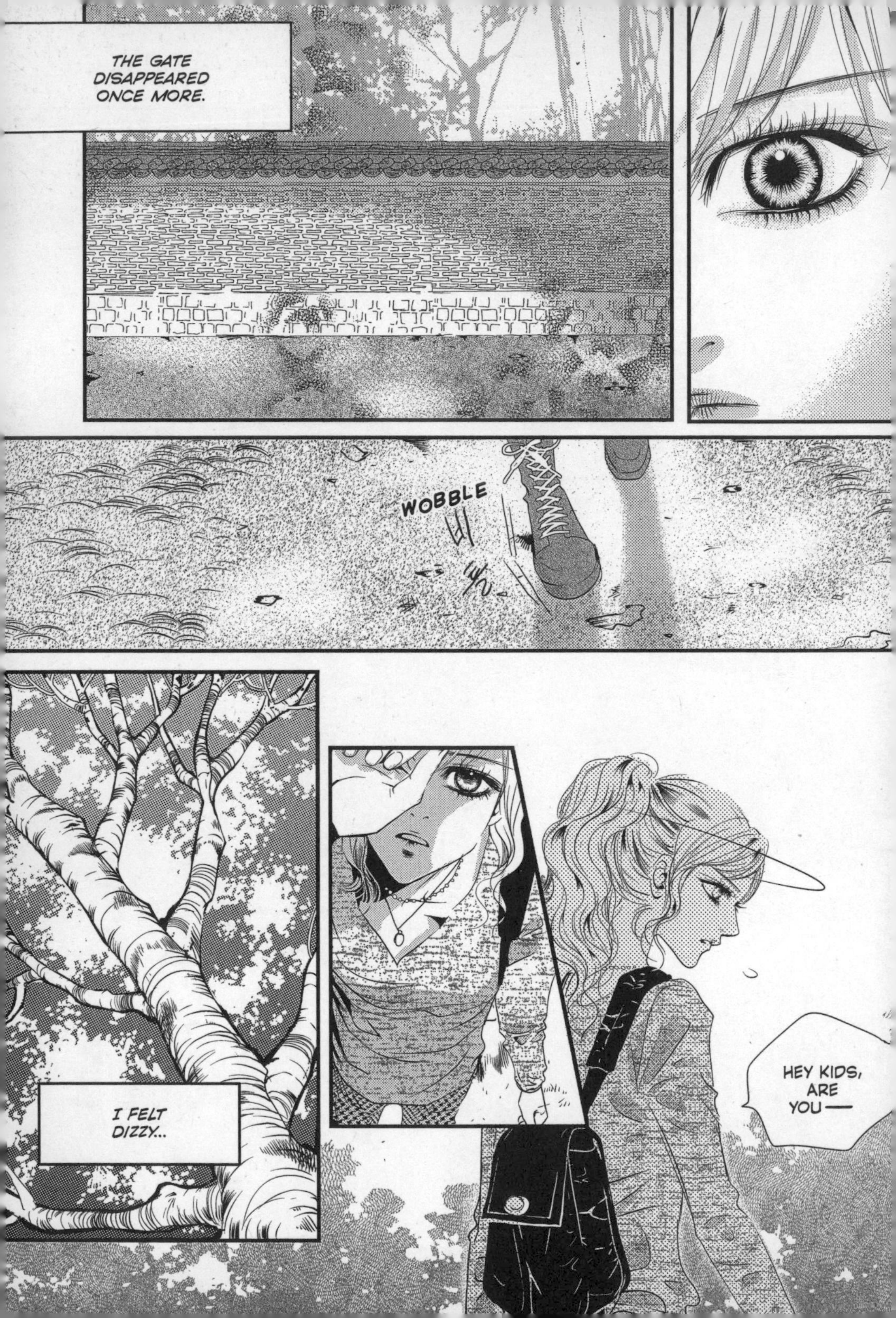
THE GATE DISAPPEARED ONCE MORE.
WOBBLE
I FELT DIZZY...
HEY KIDS, ARE YOU—

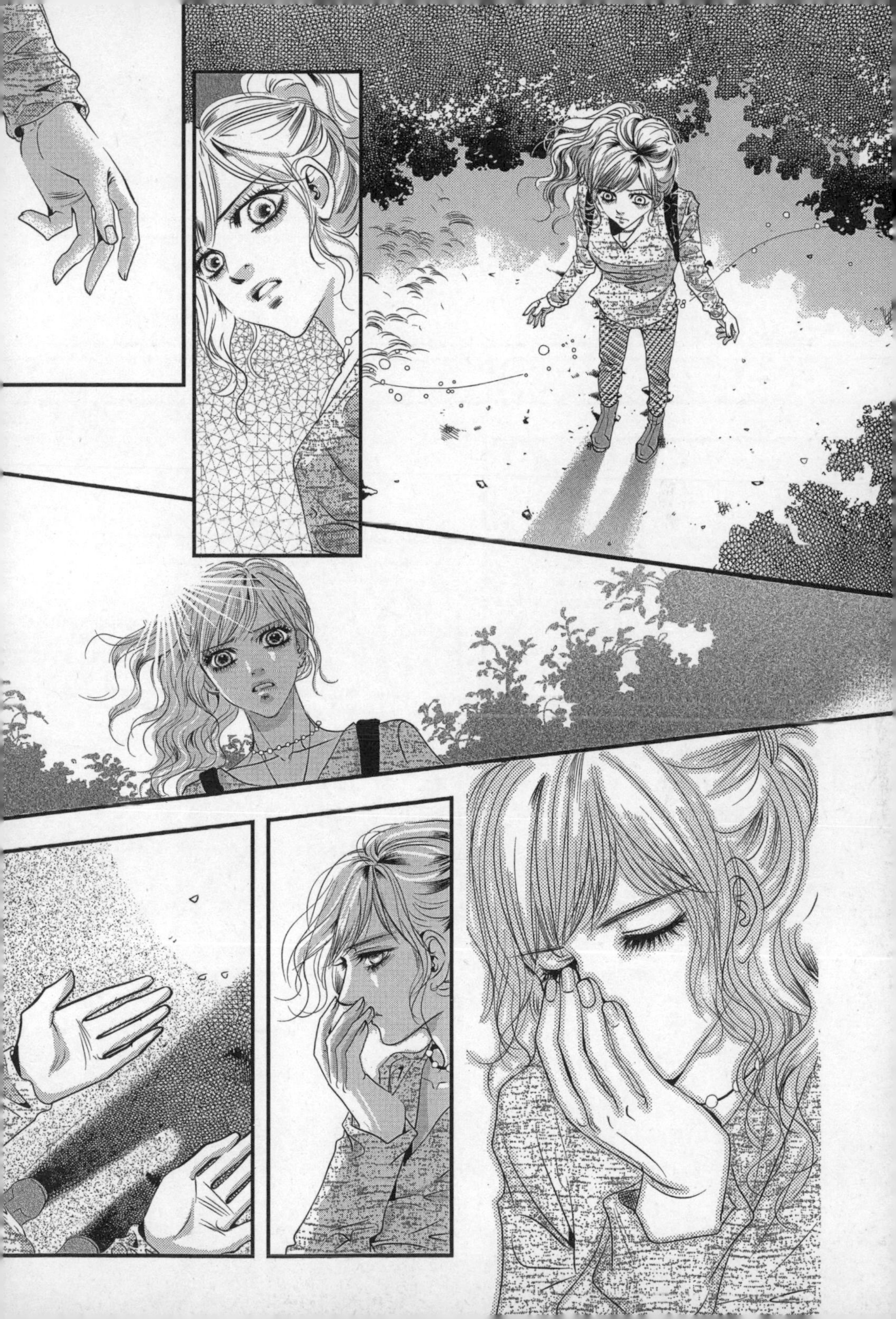

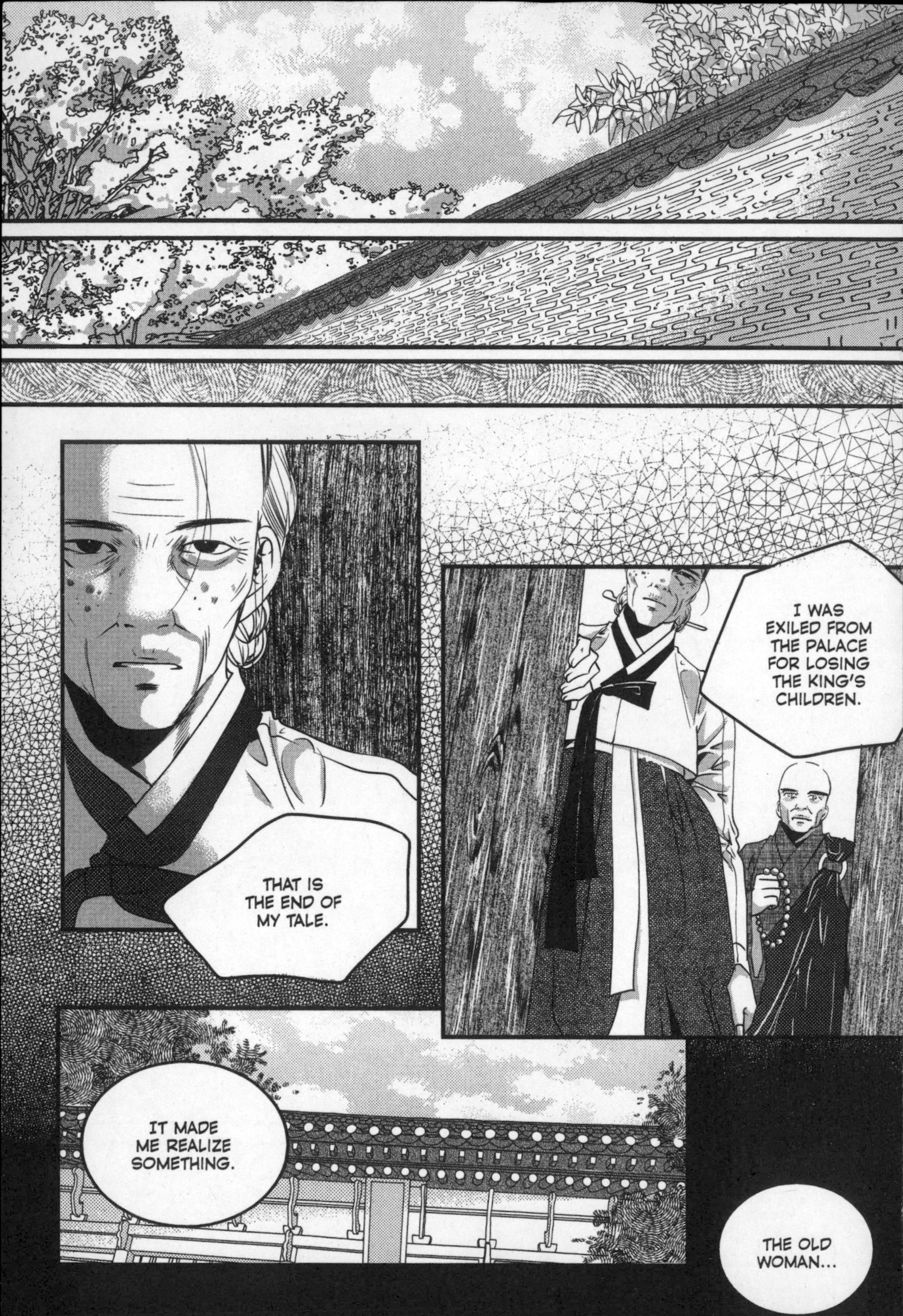

THAT IS THE END OF MY TALE.
I WAS EXILED FROM THE PALACE FOR LOSING THE KING'S CHILDREN.
IT MADE ME REALIZE SOMETHING.
THE OLD WOMAN...

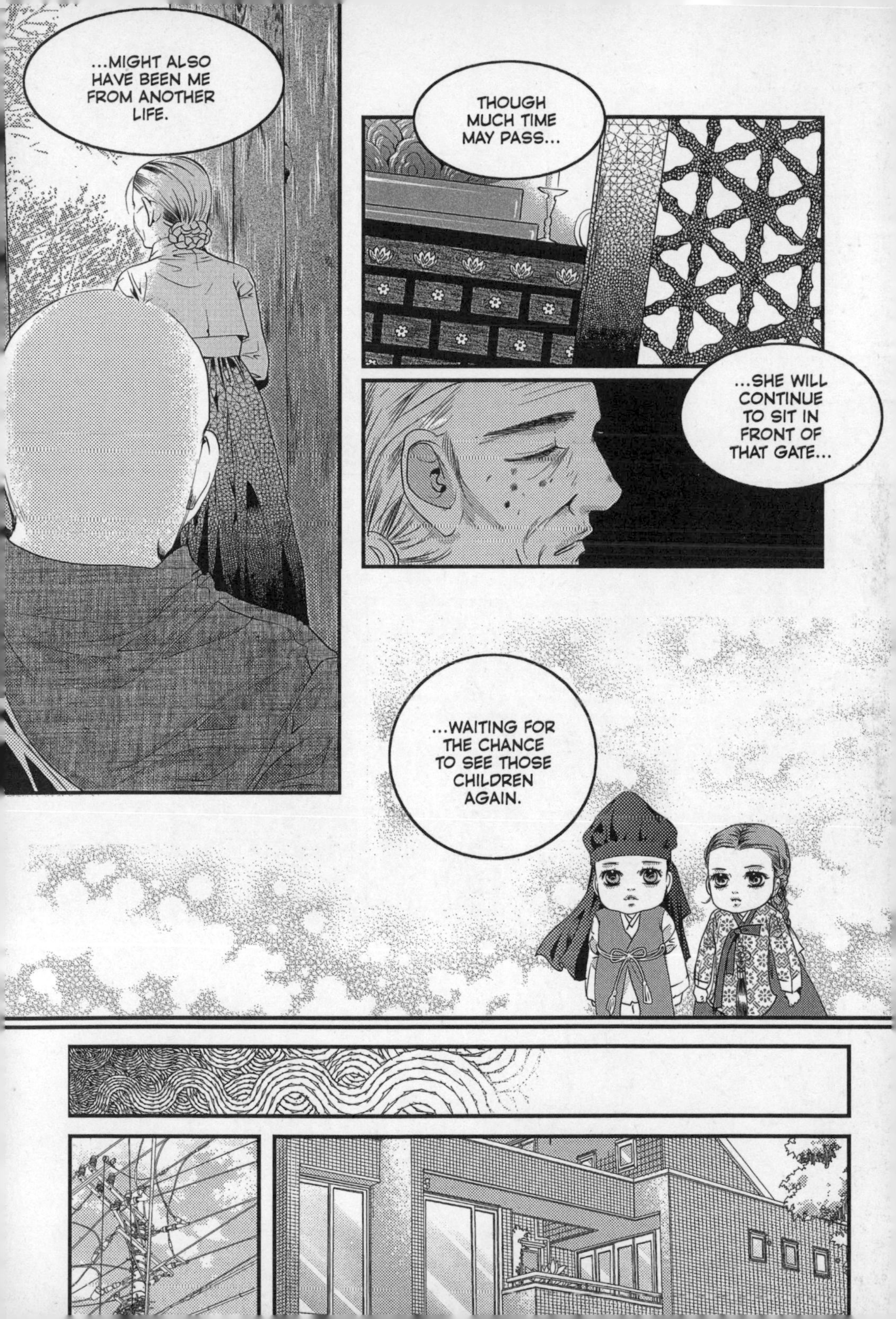
...MIGHT ALSO HAVE BEEN ME FROM ANOTHER LIFE.
THOUGH MUCH TIME MAY PASS...
...SHE WILL CONTINUE TO SIT IN FRONT OF THAT GATE...
...WAITING FOR THE CHANCE TO SEE THOSE CHILDREN AGAIN.

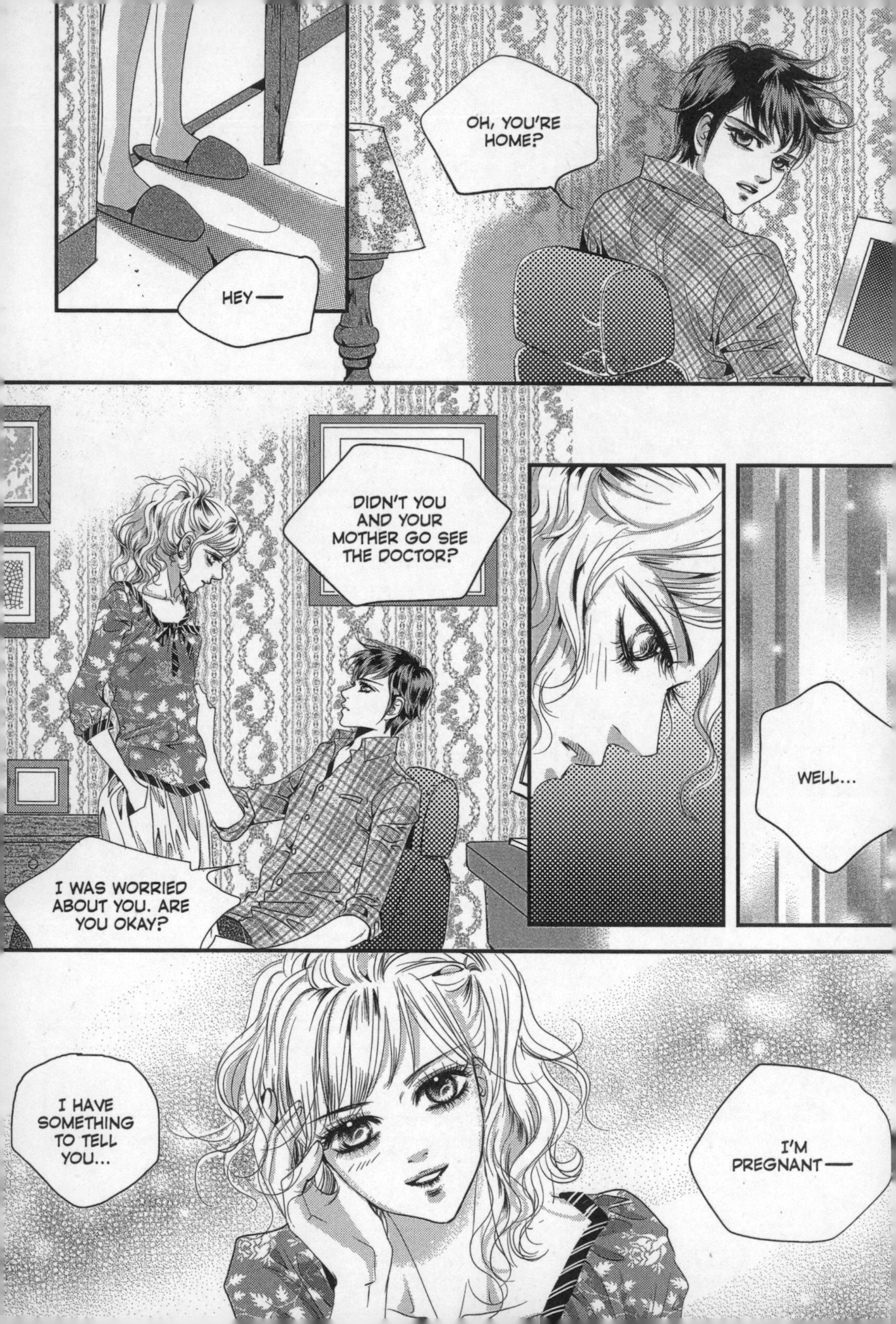
HEY—
OH, YOU'RE HOME?
DIDN'T YOU AND YOUR MOTHER GO SEE THE DOCTOR?
I WAS WORRIED ABOUT YOU. ARE YOU OKAY?
WELL...
I HAVE SOMETHING TO TELL YOU...
I'M PREGNANT—

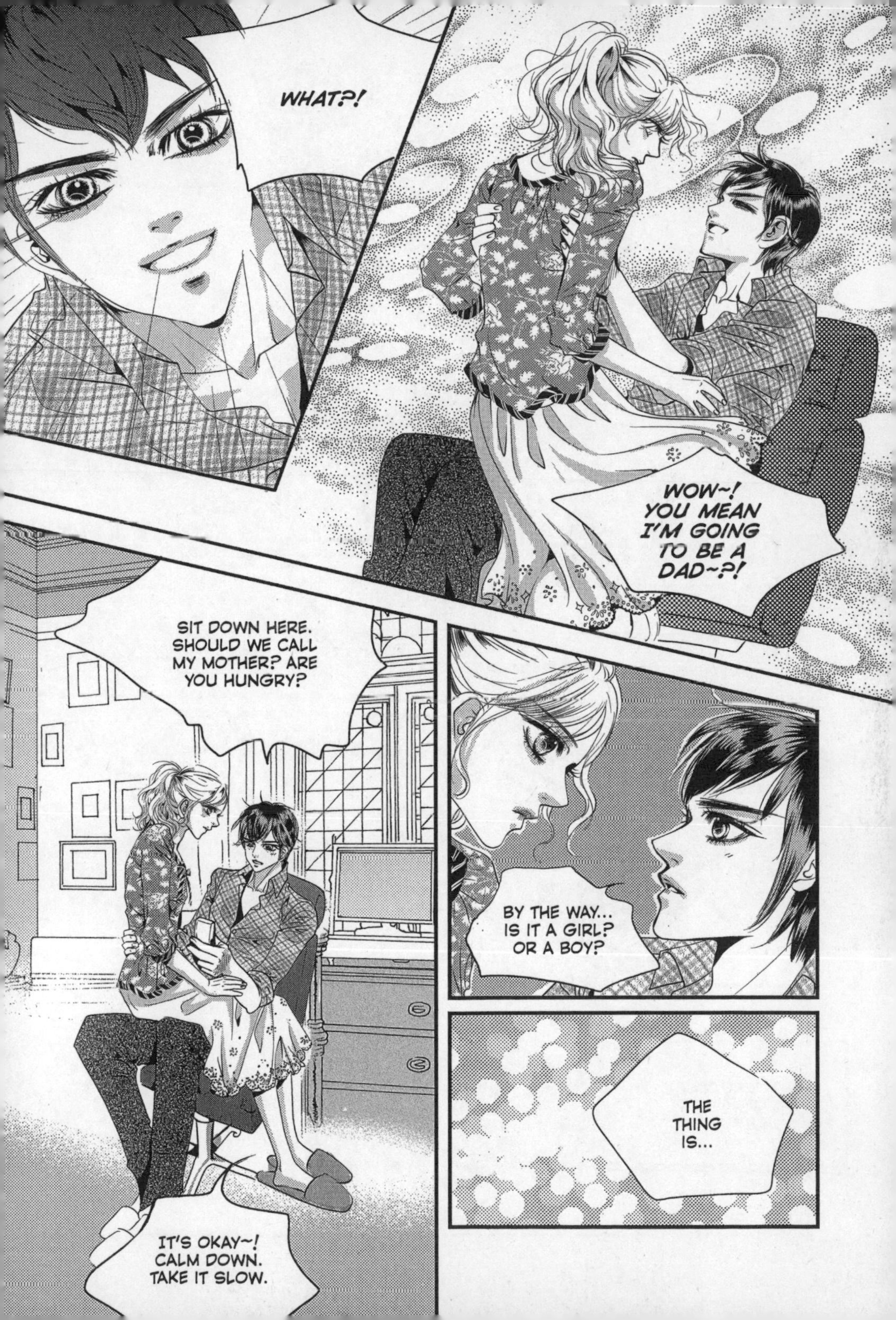
WHAT?!
WOW~! YOU MEAN I'M GOING TO BE A DAD~?!
SIT DOWN HERE. SHOULD WE CALL MY MOTHER? ARE YOU HUNGRY?
IT'S OKAY~! CALM DOWN. TAKE IT SLOW.
BY THE WAY... IS IT A GIRL? OR A BOY?
THE THING IS...

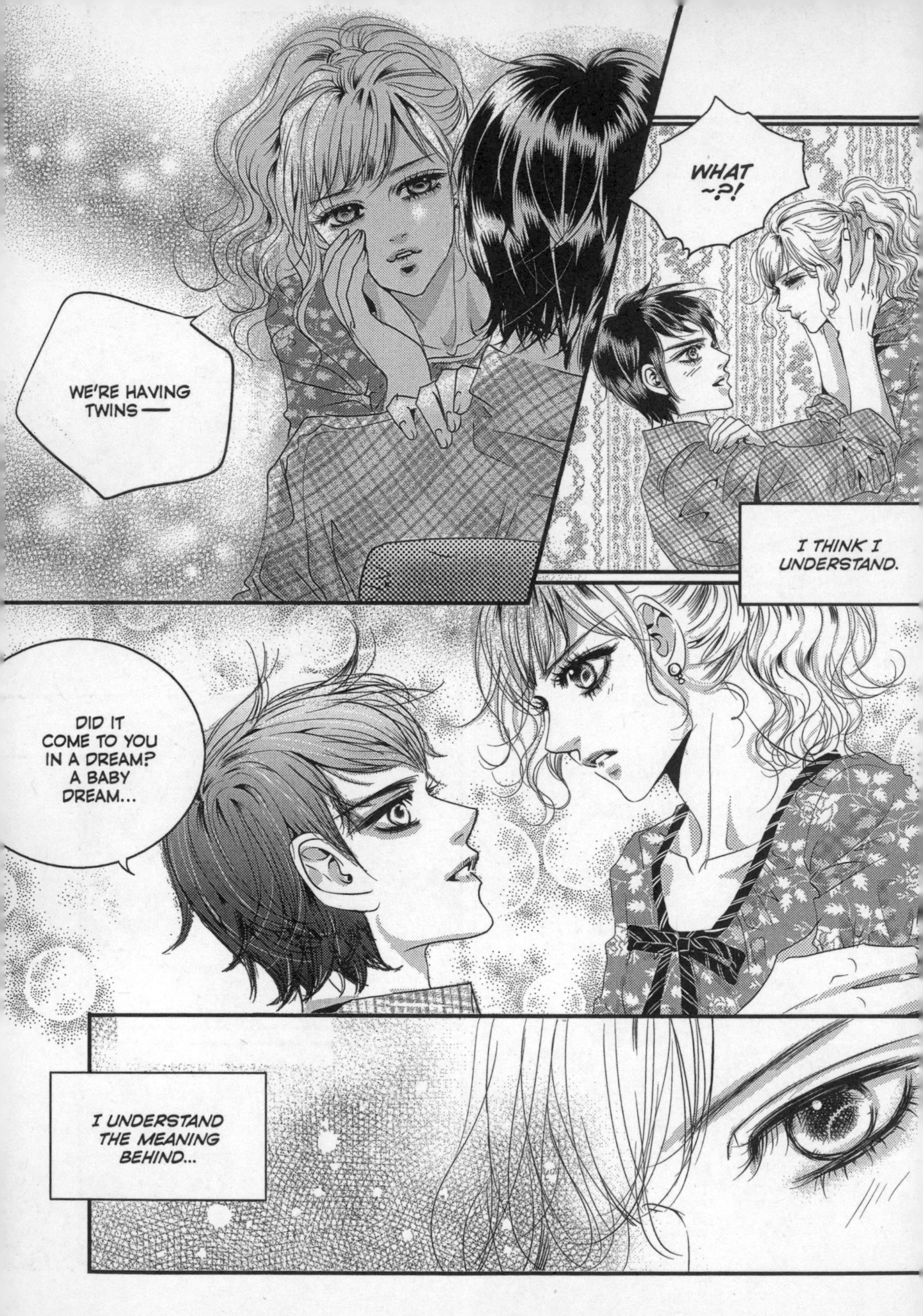
WE'RE HAVING TWINS—
WHAT ~?!
I THINK I UNDERSTAND.
DID IT COME TO YOU IN A DREAM? A BABY DREAM...
I UNDERSTAND THE MEANING BEHIND...

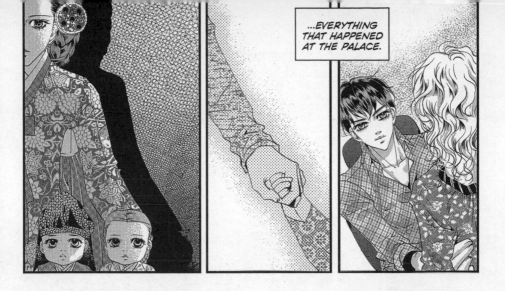

...EVERYTHING THAT HAPPENED AT THE PALACE.

IT DID.

I HAD THE BEST BABY DREAM EVER.

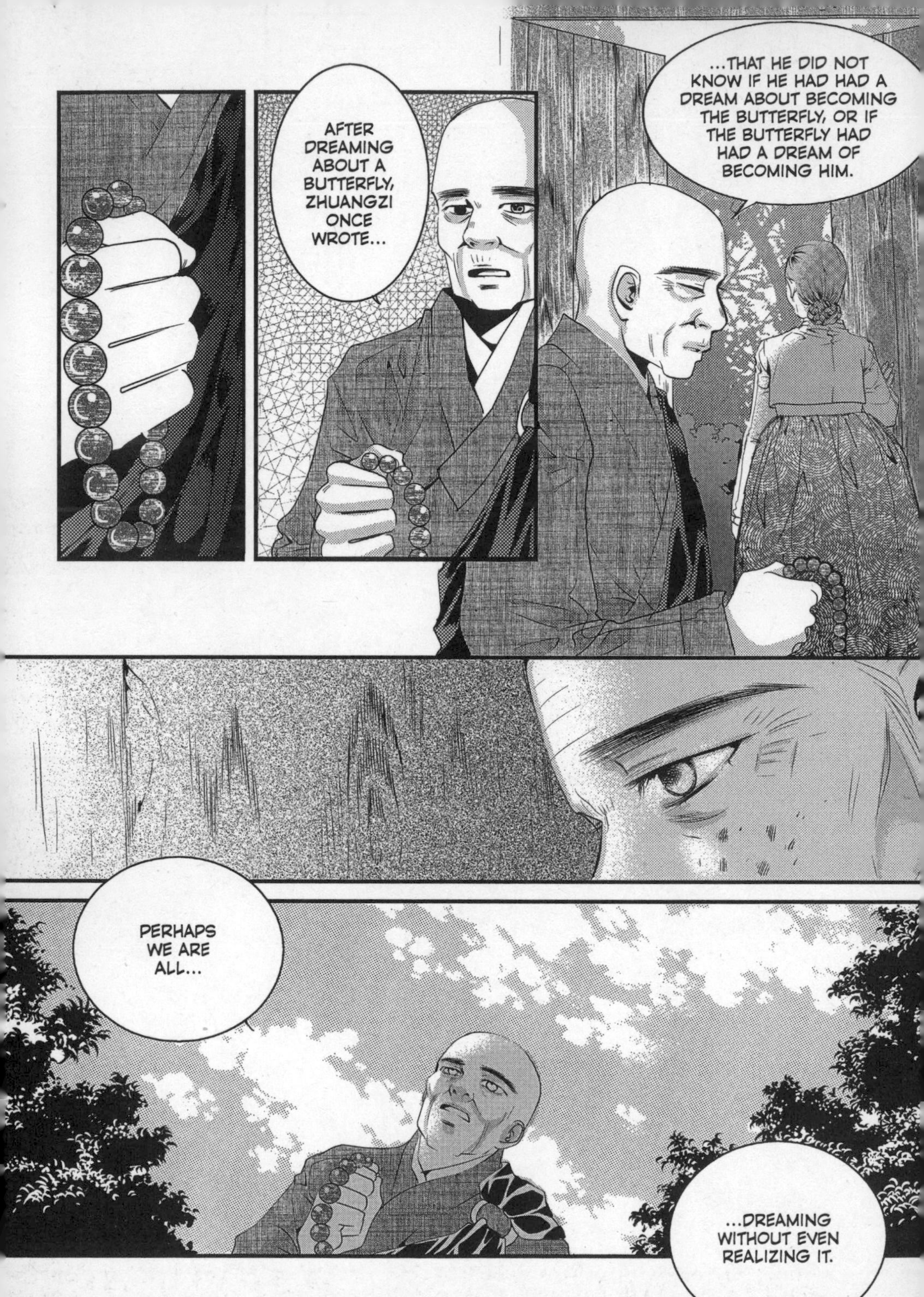
AFTER DREAMING ABOUT A BUTTERFLY, ZHUANGZI ONCE WROTE...
...THAT HE DID NOT KNOW IF HE HAD HAD A DREAM ABOUT BECOMING THE BUTTERFLY, OR IF THE BUTTERFLY HAD HAD A DREAM OF BECOMING HIM.
PERHAPS WE ARE ALL...
...DREAMING WITHOUT EVEN REALIZING IT.

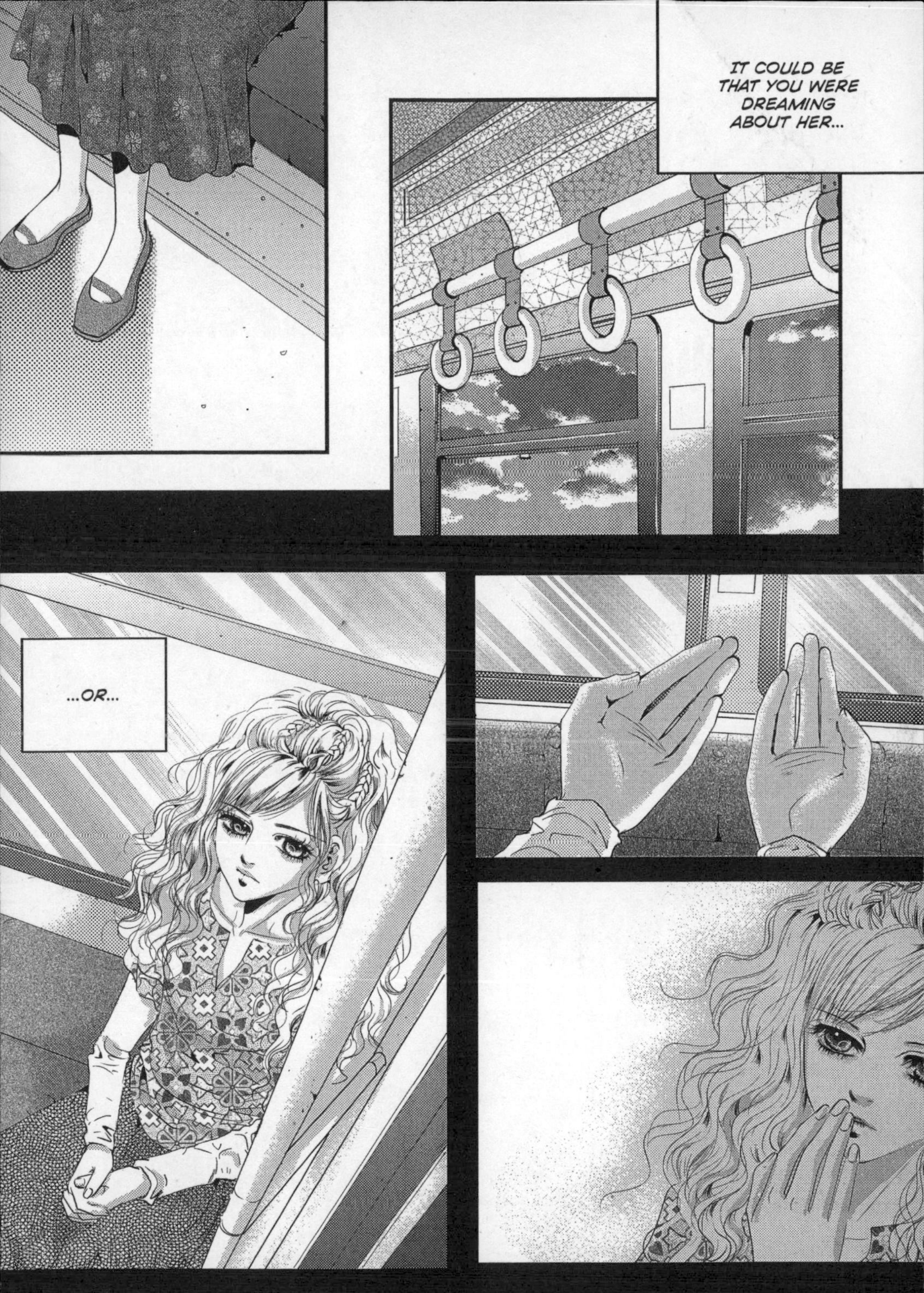
IT COULD BE THAT YOU WERE DREAMING ABOUT HER...
...OR...

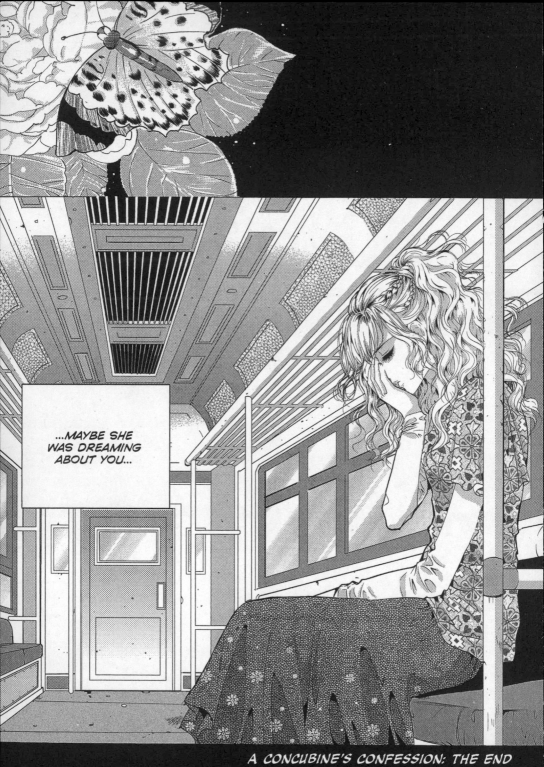

...MAYBE SHE
WAS DREAMING
ABOUT YOU...

A CONCUBINE'S CONFESSION: THE END

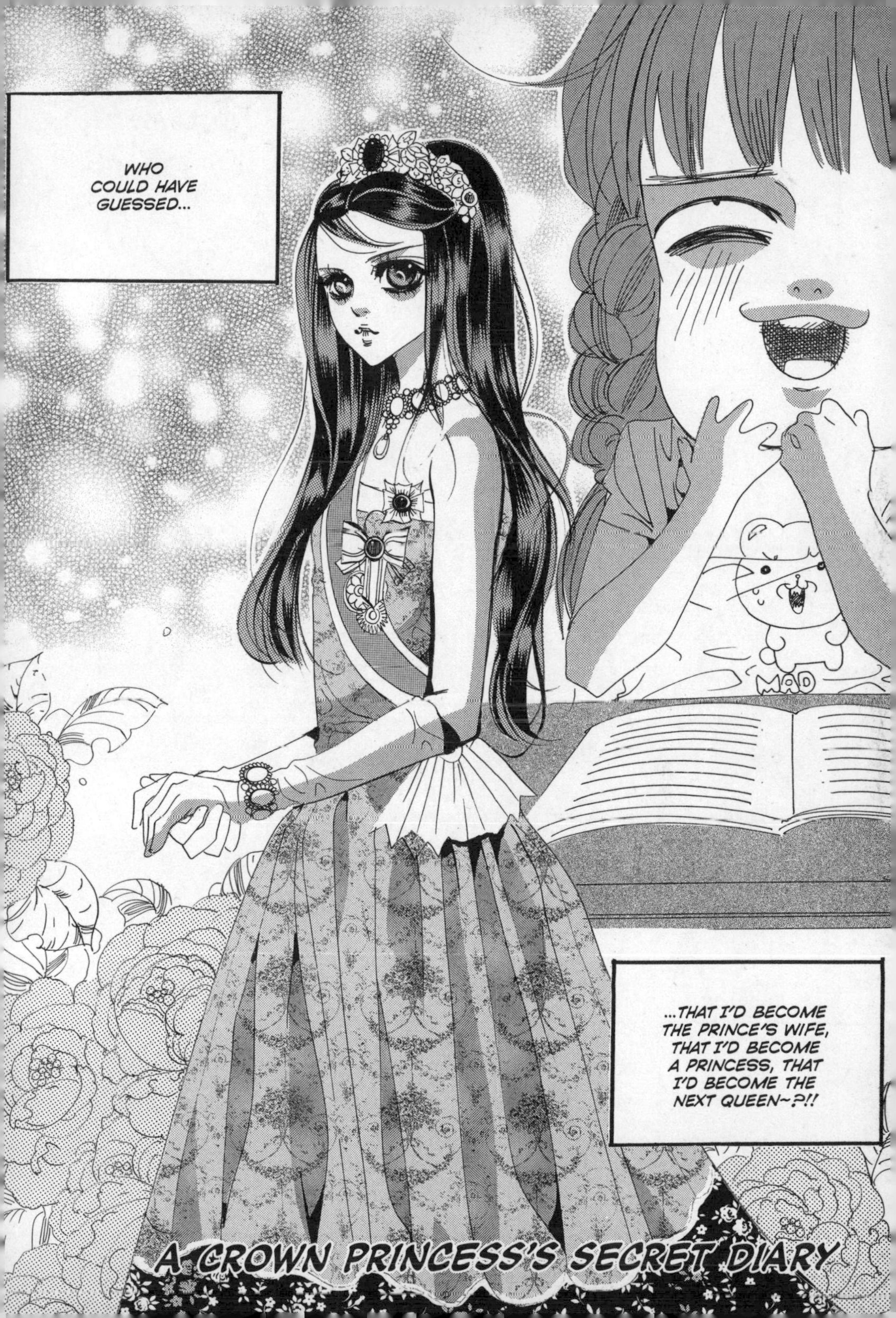

WHO COULD HAVE GUESSED...
MAD
...THAT I'D BECOME THE PRINCE'S WIFE, THAT I'D BECOME A PRINCESS, THAT I'D BECOME THE NEXT QUEEN~?!!
A CROWN PRINCESS'S SECRET DIARY

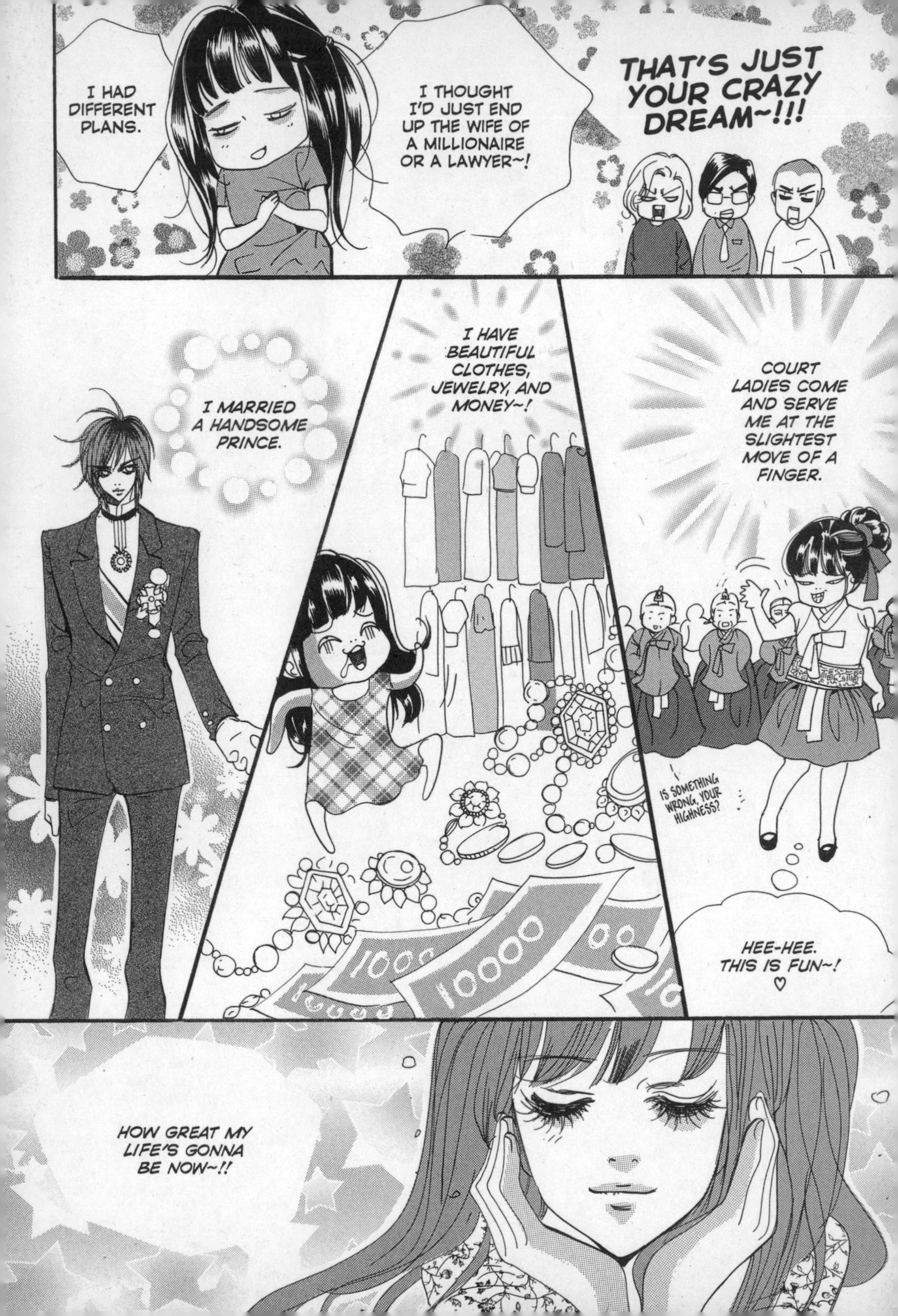

I HAD DIFFERENT PLANS.
I THOUGHT I'D JUST END UP THE WIFE OF A MILLIONAIRE OR A LAWYER~!
THAT'S JUST YOUR CRAZY DREAM~!!!
I MARRIED A HANDSOME PRINCE.
I HAVE BEAUTIFUL CLOTHES, JEWELRY, AND MONEY~!
COURT LADIES COME AND SERVE ME AT THE SLIGHTEST MOVE OF A FINGER.
IS SOMETHING WRONG, YOUR HIGHNESS?
HEE-HEE. THIS IS FUN~! ♡
HOW GREAT MY LIFE'S GONNA BE NOW~!!

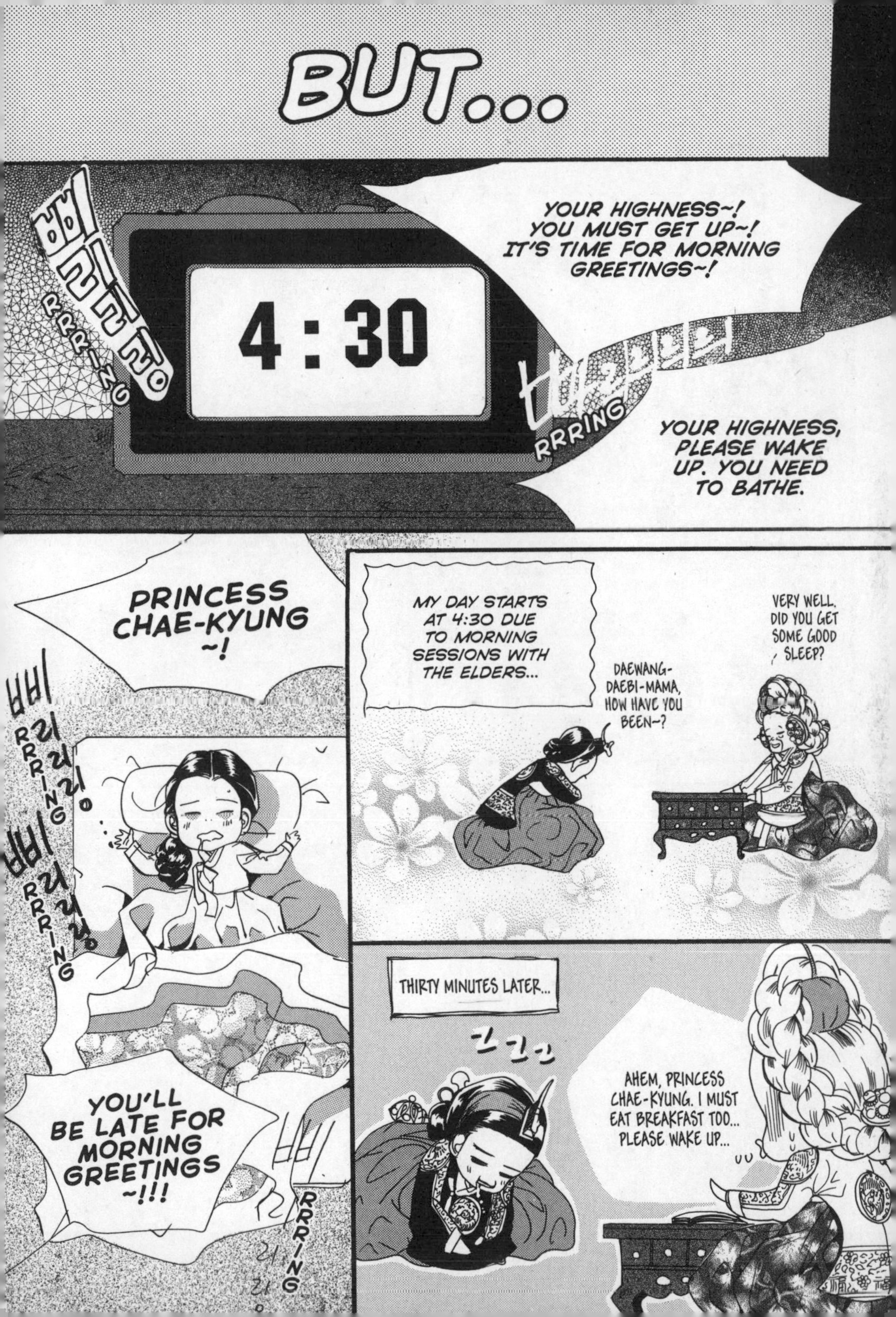
BUT...
RRRING
4:30
YOUR HIGHNESS~! YOU MUST GET UP~! IT'S TIME FOR MORNING GREETINGS~!
RRRING
YOUR HIGHNESS, PLEASE WAKE UP. YOU NEED TO BATHE.
PRINCESS CHAE-KYUNG ~!
RRRING
RRRING
YOU'LL BE LATE FOR MORNING GREETINGS ~!!!
RRRING
MY DAY STARTS AT 4:30 DUE TO MORNING SESSIONS WITH THE ELDERS...
DAEWANG-DAEBI-MAMA, HOW HAVE YOU BEEN~?
VERY WELL. DID YOU GET SOME GOOD SLEEP?
THIRTY MINUTES LATER...
AHEM, PRINCESS CHAE-KYUNG. I MUST EAT BREAKFAST TOO... PLEASE WAKE UP...

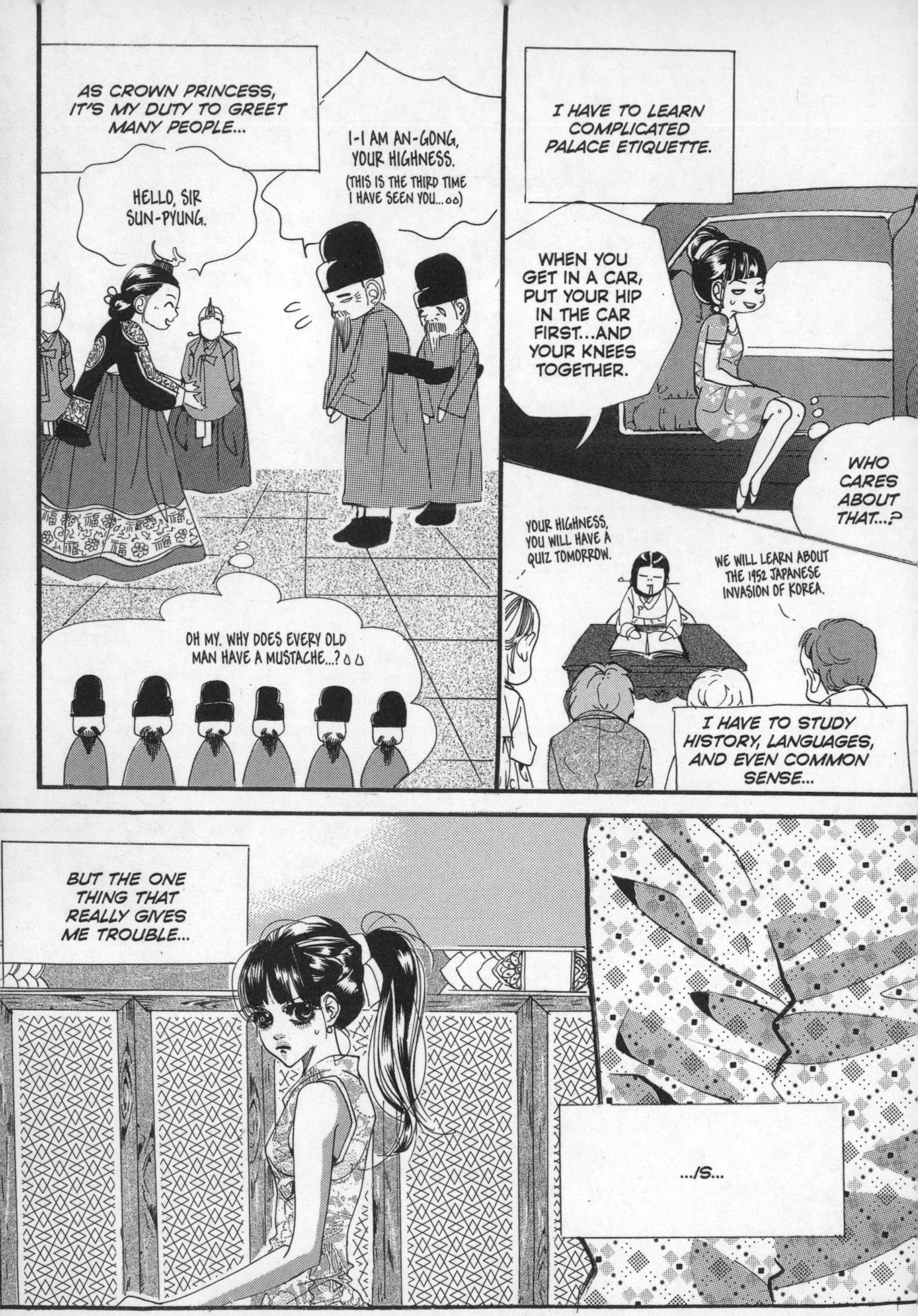
AS CROWN PRINCESS, IT'S MY DUTY TO GREET MANY PEOPLE...
HELLO, SIR SUN-PYUNG.
I-I AM AN-GONG, YOUR HIGHNESS.
(THIS IS THE THIRD TIME I HAVE SEEN YOU...)
OH MY. WHY DOES EVERY OLD MAN HAVE A MUSTACHE...?
I HAVE TO LEARN COMPLICATED PALACE ETIQUETTE.
WHEN YOU GET IN A CAR, PUT YOUR HIP IN THE CAR FIRST...AND YOUR KNEES TOGETHER.
WHO CARES ABOUT THAT...?
YOUR HIGHNESS, YOU WILL HAVE A QUIZ TOMORROW.
WE WILL LEARN ABOUT THE 1952 JAPANESE INVASION OF KOREA.
I HAVE TO STUDY HISTORY, LANGUAGES, AND EVEN COMMON SENSE...
BUT THE ONE THING THAT REALLY GIVES ME TROUBLE...
...IS...

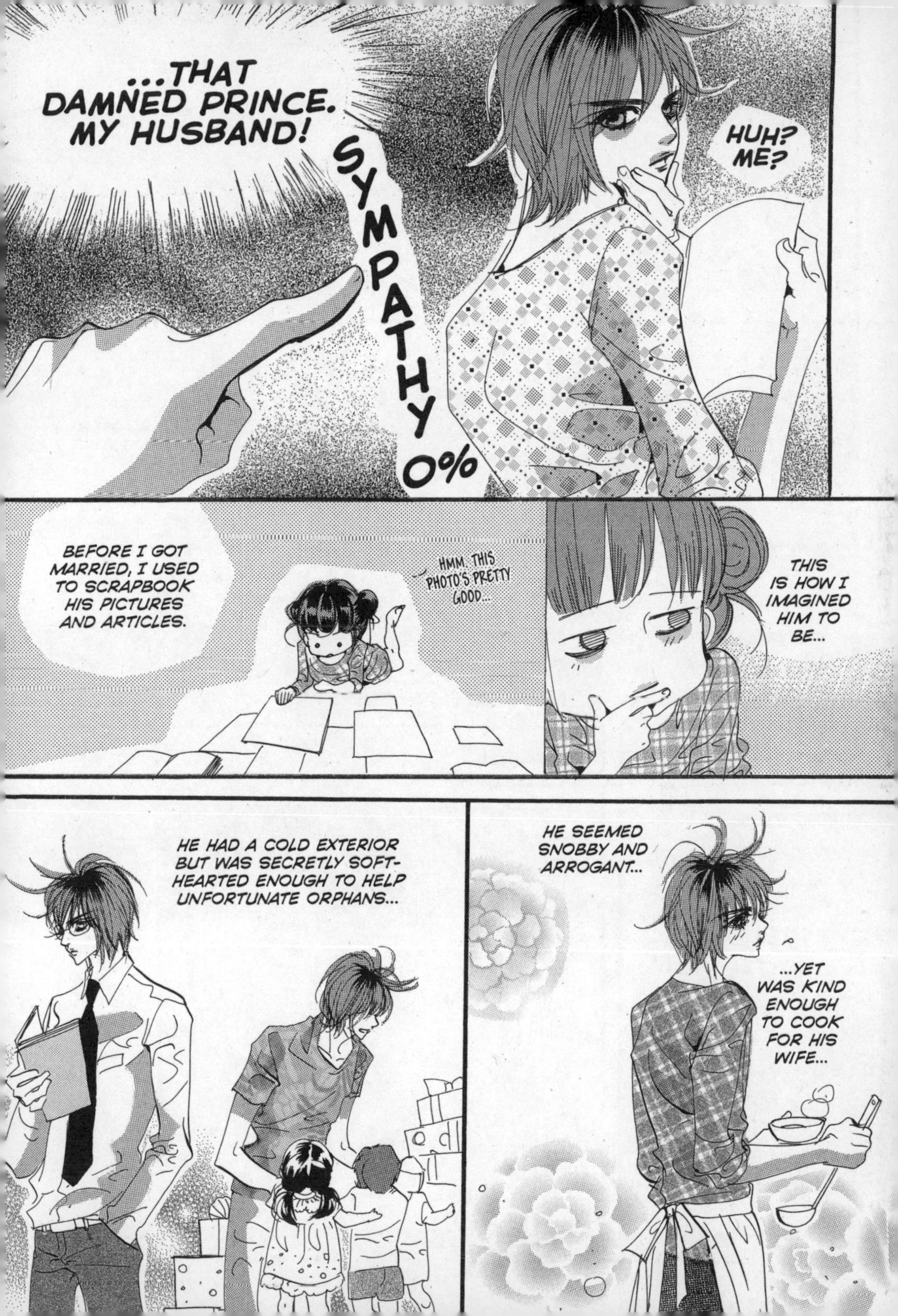
...THAT DAMNED PRINCE. MY HUSBAND!
SYMPATHY 0%
HUH? ME?
BEFORE I GOT MARRIED, I USED TO SCRAPBOOK HIS PICTURES AND ARTICLES.
HMM. THIS PHOTO'S PRETTY GOOD...
THIS IS HOW I IMAGINED HIM TO BE...
HE HAD A COLD EXTERIOR BUT WAS SECRETLY SOFT-HEARTED ENOUGH TO HELP UNFORTUNATE ORPHANS...
HE SEEMED SNOBBY AND ARROGANT...
...YET WAS KIND ENOUGH TO COOK FOR HIS WIFE...

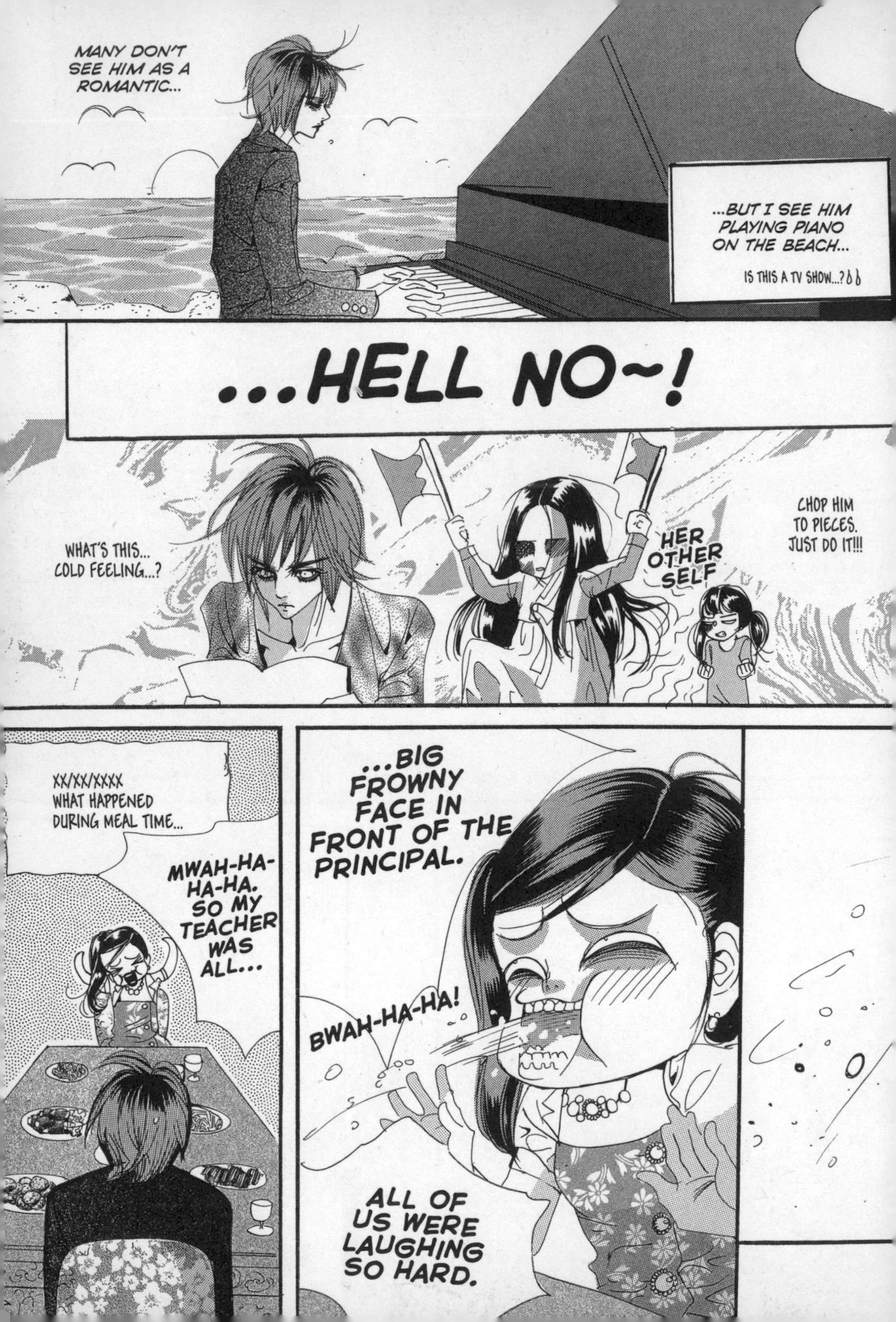
MANY DON'T SEE HIM AS A ROMANTIC...
...BUT I SEE HIM PLAYING PIANO ON THE BEACH...
IS THIS A TV SHOW...?
...HELL NO~!
WHAT'S THIS... COLD FEELING...?
HER OTHER SELF
CHOP HIM TO PIECES. JUST DO IT!!!
XX/XX/XXXX WHAT HAPPENED DURING MEAL TIME...
MWAH-HA-HA-HA. SO MY TEACHER WAS ALL...
...BIG FROWNY FACE IN FRONT OF THE PRINCIPAL.
BWAH-HA-HA!
ALL OF US WERE LAUGHING SO HARD.

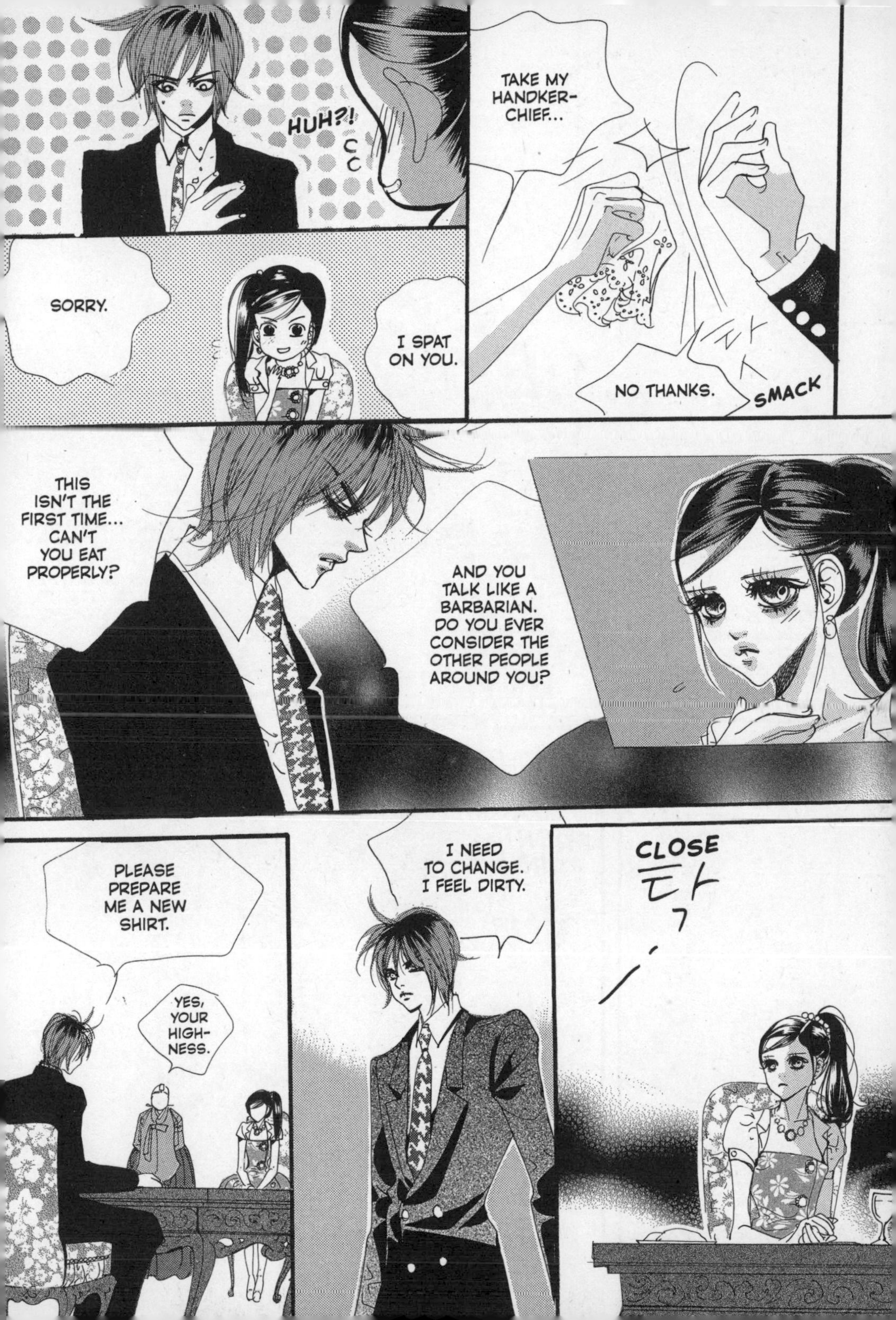
HUH?!
SORRY.
I SPAT ON YOU.
TAKE MY HANDKER-CHIEF...
NO THANKS.
SMACK
THIS ISN'T THE FIRST TIME... CAN'T YOU EAT PROPERLY?
AND YOU TALK LIKE A BARBARIAN. DO YOU EVER CONSIDER THE OTHER PEOPLE AROUND YOU?
PLEASE PREPARE ME A NEW SHIRT.
YES, YOUR HIGH-NESS.
I NEED TO CHANGE. I FEEL DIRTY.
CLOSE

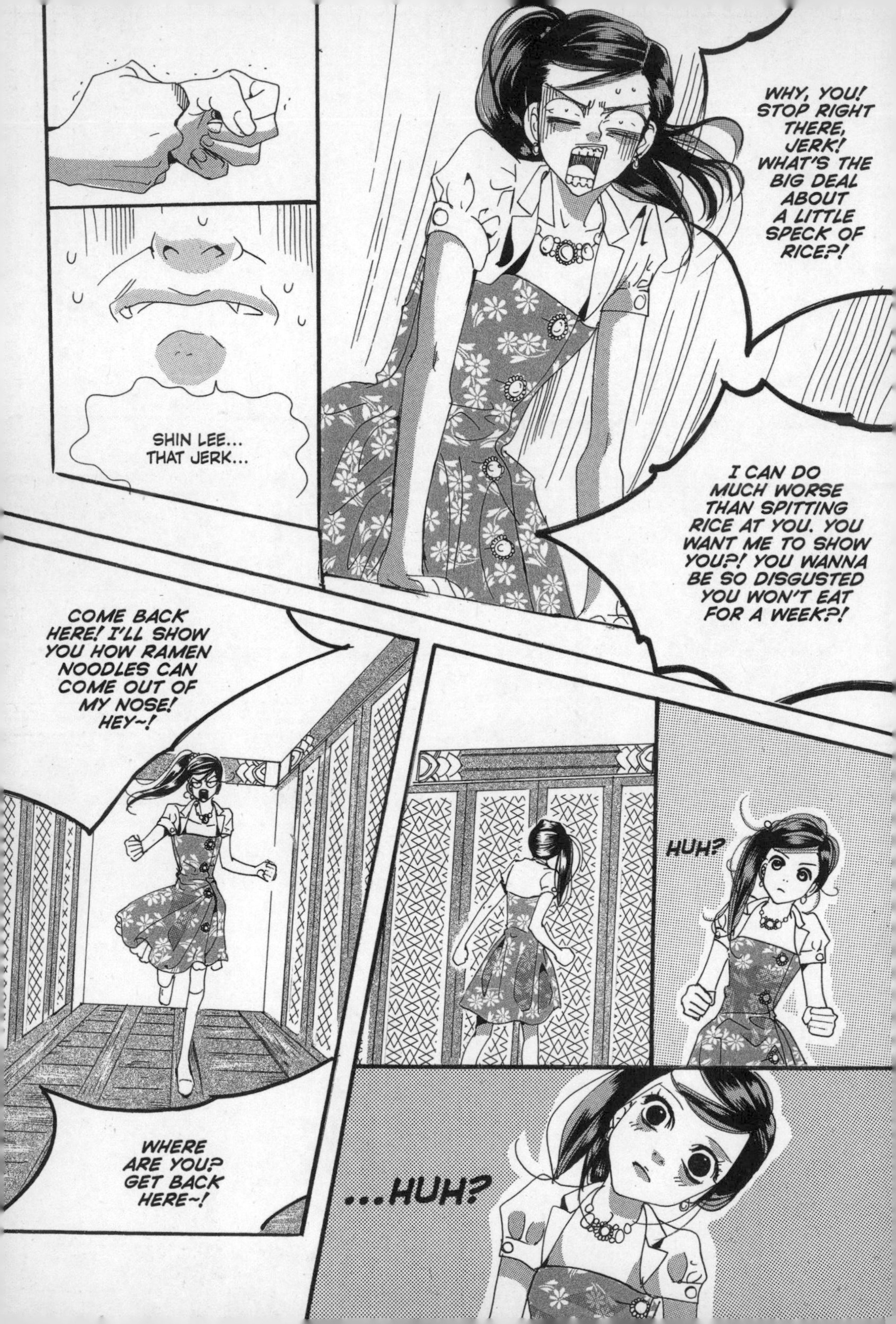

SHIN LEE... THAT JERK...
WHY, YOU! STOP RIGHT THERE, JERK! WHAT'S THE BIG DEAL ABOUT A LITTLE SPECK OF RICE?!
I CAN DO MUCH WORSE THAN SPITTING RICE AT YOU. YOU WANT ME TO SHOW YOU?! YOU WANNA BE SO DISGUSTED YOU WON'T EAT FOR A WEEK?!
COME BACK HERE! I'LL SHOW YOU HOW RAMEN NOODLES CAN COME OUT OF MY NOSE! HEY~!
WHERE ARE YOU? GET BACK HERE~!
HUH?
...HUH?

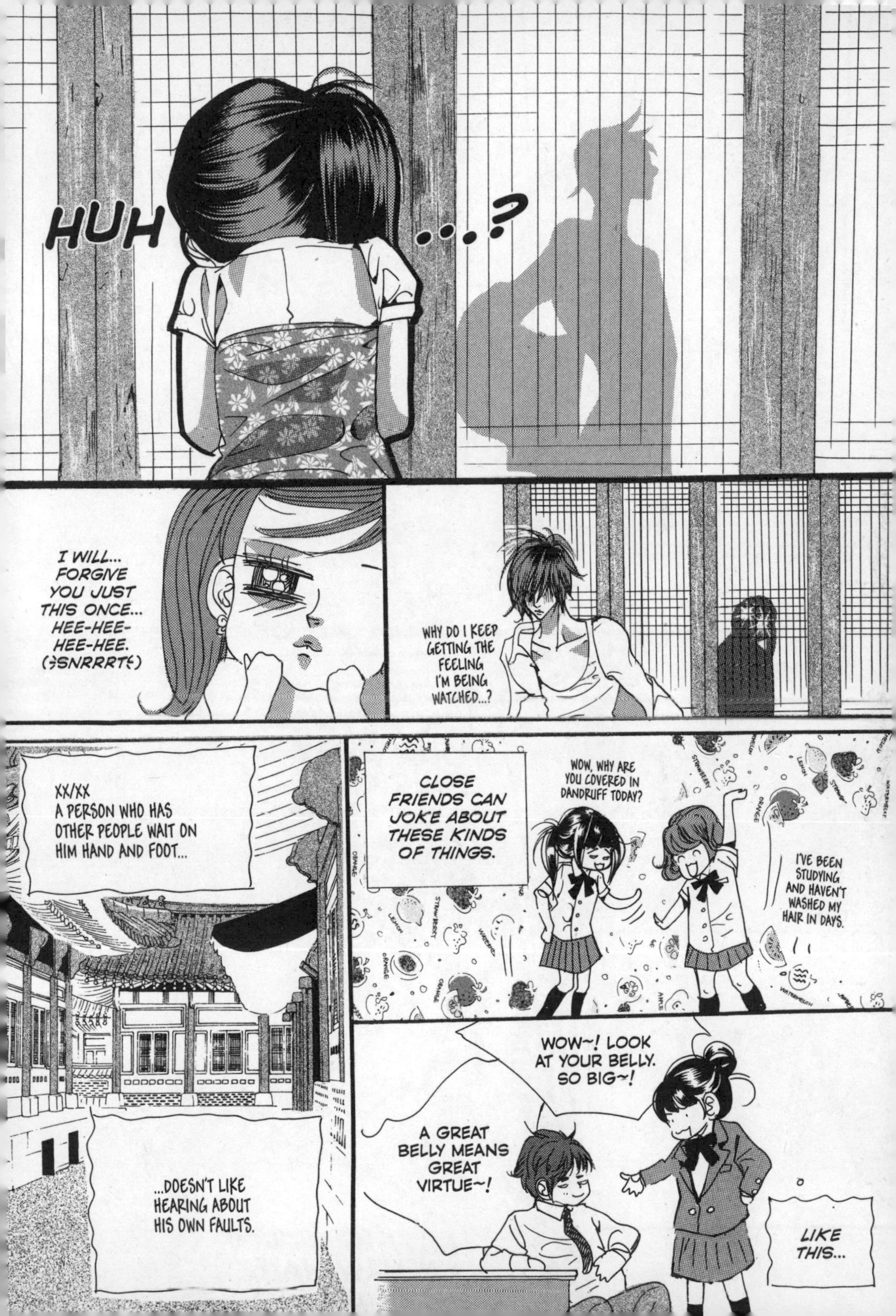
HUH ...?
I WILL... FORGIVE YOU JUST THIS ONCE... HEE-HEE-HEE-HEE. (SNRRRT)
WHY DO I KEEP GETTING THE FEELING I'M BEING WATCHED...?
XX/XX
A PERSON WHO HAS OTHER PEOPLE WAIT ON HIM HAND AND FOOT...
...DOESN'T LIKE HEARING ABOUT HIS OWN FAULTS.
CLOSE FRIENDS CAN JOKE ABOUT THESE KINDS OF THINGS.
WOW, WHY ARE YOU COVERED IN DANDRUFF TODAY?
I'VE BEEN STUDYING AND HAVEN'T WASHED MY HAIR IN DAYS.
WOW~! LOOK AT YOUR BELLY. SO BIG~!
A GREAT BELLY MEANS GREAT VIRTUE~!
LIKE THIS...

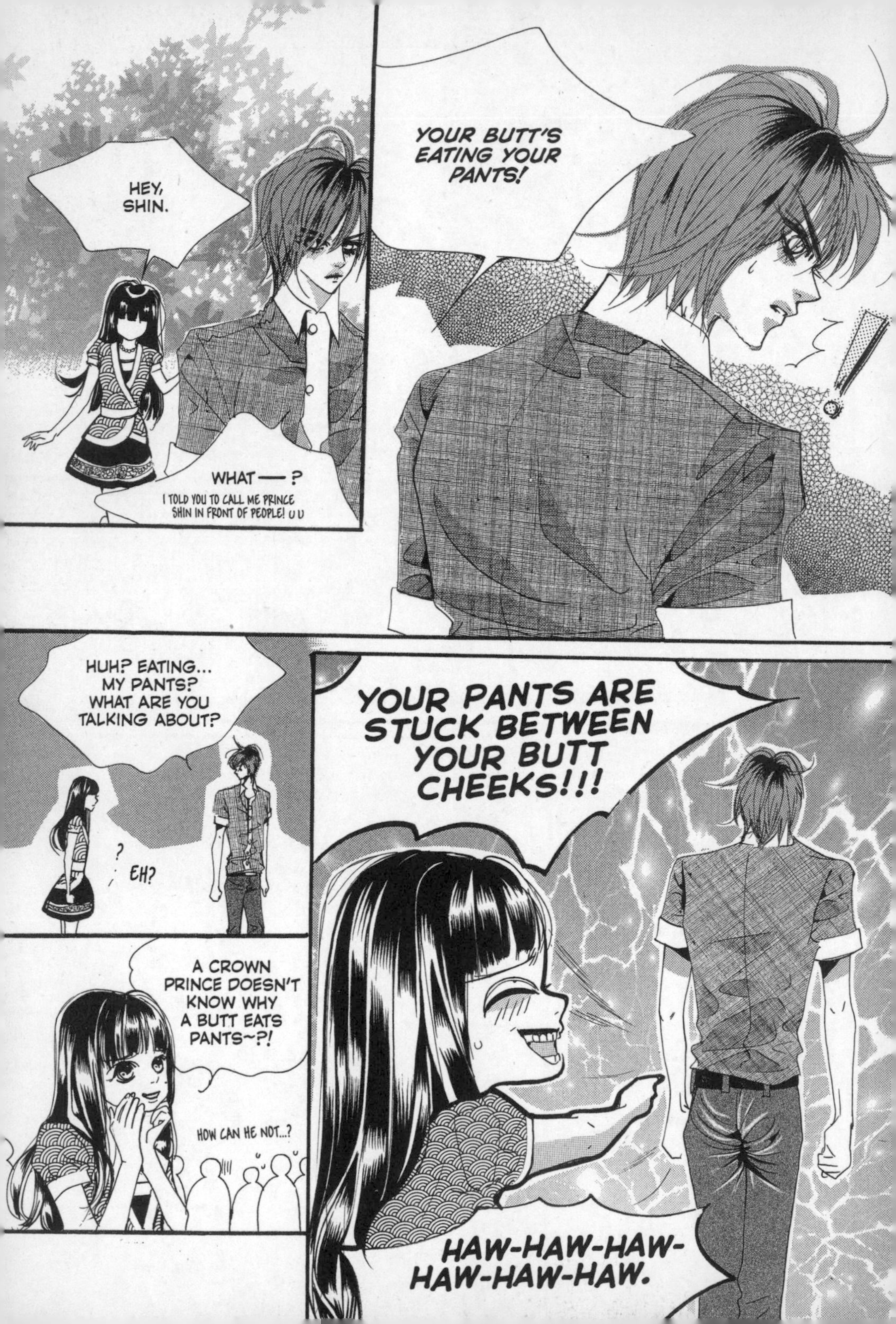
HEY, SHIN.
WHAT—?
I TOLD YOU TO CALL ME PRINCE SHIN IN FRONT OF PEOPLE!
YOUR BUTT'S EATING YOUR PANTS!
HUH? EATING... MY PANTS? WHAT ARE YOU TALKING ABOUT?
EH?
YOUR PANTS ARE STUCK BETWEEN YOUR BUTT CHEEKS!!!
A CROWN PRINCE DOESN'T KNOW WHY A BUTT EATS PANTS~?!
HOW CAN HE NOT...?
HAW-HAW-HAW-HAW-HAW-HAW.

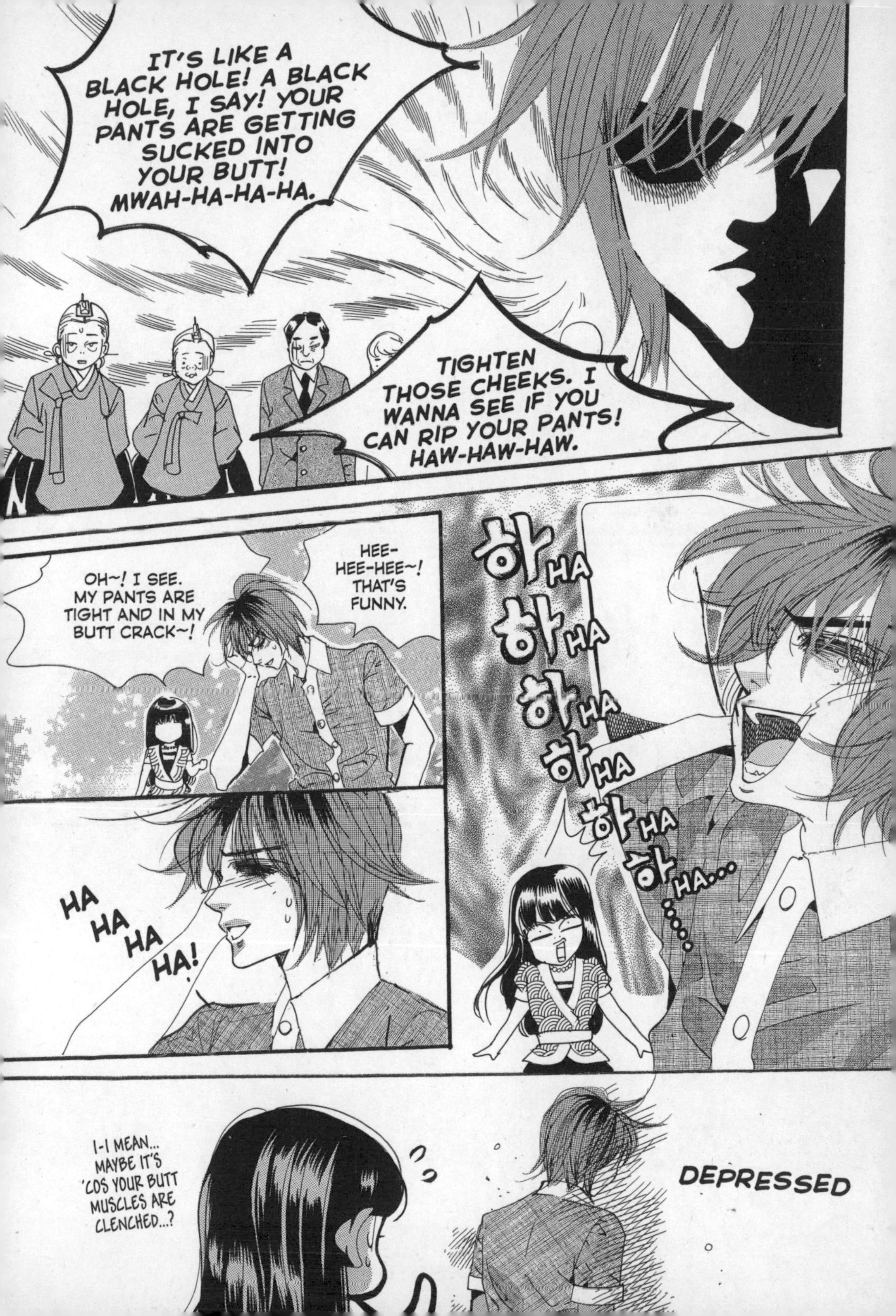
IT'S LIKE A BLACK HOLE! A BLACK HOLE, I SAY! YOUR PANTS ARE GETTING SUCKED INTO YOUR BUTT! MWAH-HA-HA-HA.
TIGHTEN THOSE CHEEKS. I WANNA SEE IF YOU CAN RIP YOUR PANTS! HAW-HAW-HAW.
OH~! I SEE. MY PANTS ARE TIGHT AND IN MY BUTT CRACK~!
HEE-HEE-HEE~! THAT'S FUNNY.
HA HA HA HA!
하 HA 하 HA 하 HA 하 HA 하 HA 하 HA...
.....
I-I MEAN... MAYBE IT'S 'COS YOUR BUTT MUSCLES ARE CLENCHED...?
DEPRESSED

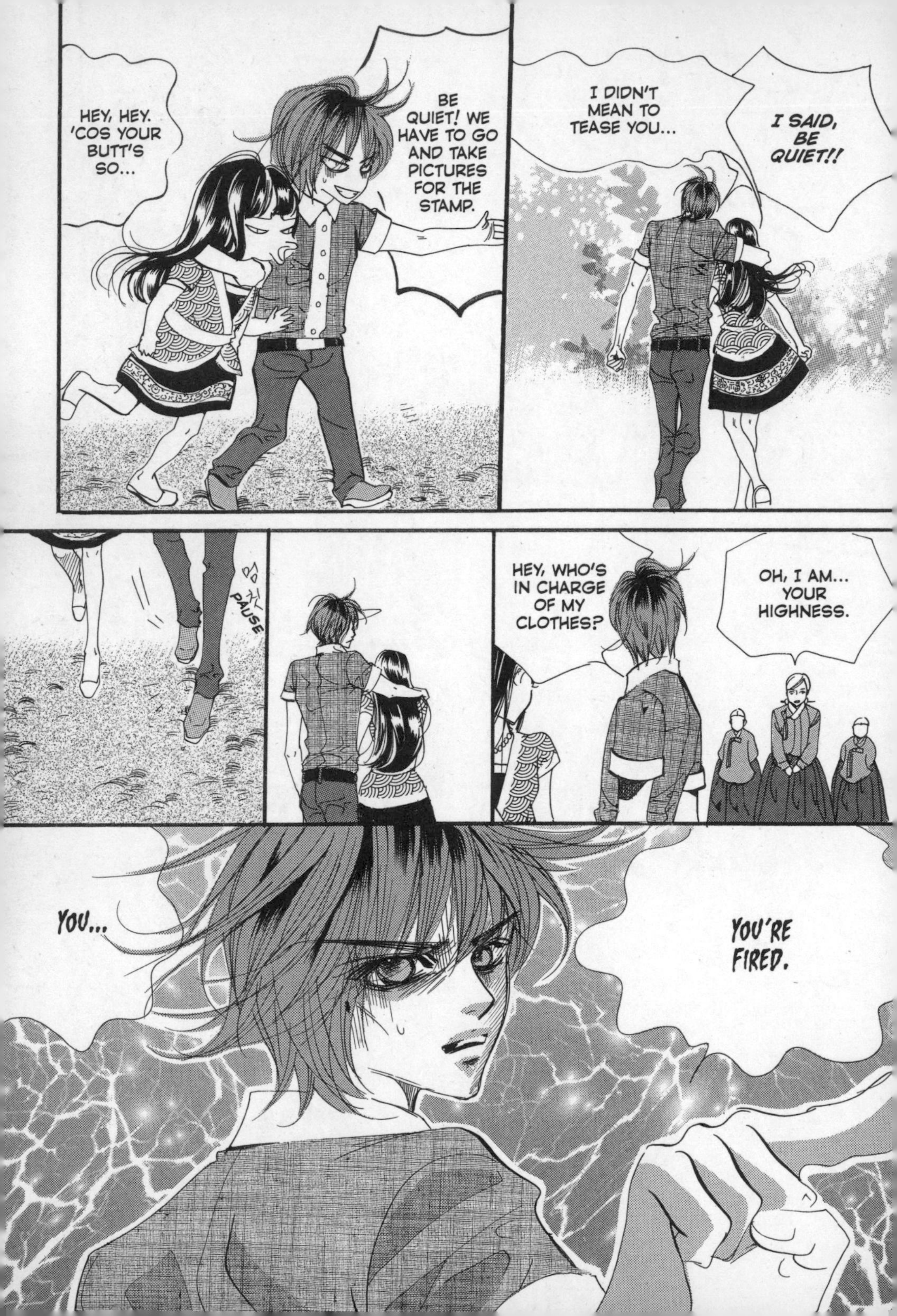
HEY, HEY. 'COS YOUR BUTT'S SO...
BE QUIET! WE HAVE TO GO AND TAKE PICTURES FOR THE STAMP.
I DIDN'T MEAN TO TEASE YOU...
I SAID, BE QUIET!!
PAUSE
HEY, WHO'S IN CHARGE OF MY CLOTHES?
OH, I AM... YOUR HIGHNESS.
YOU...
YOU'RE FIRED.

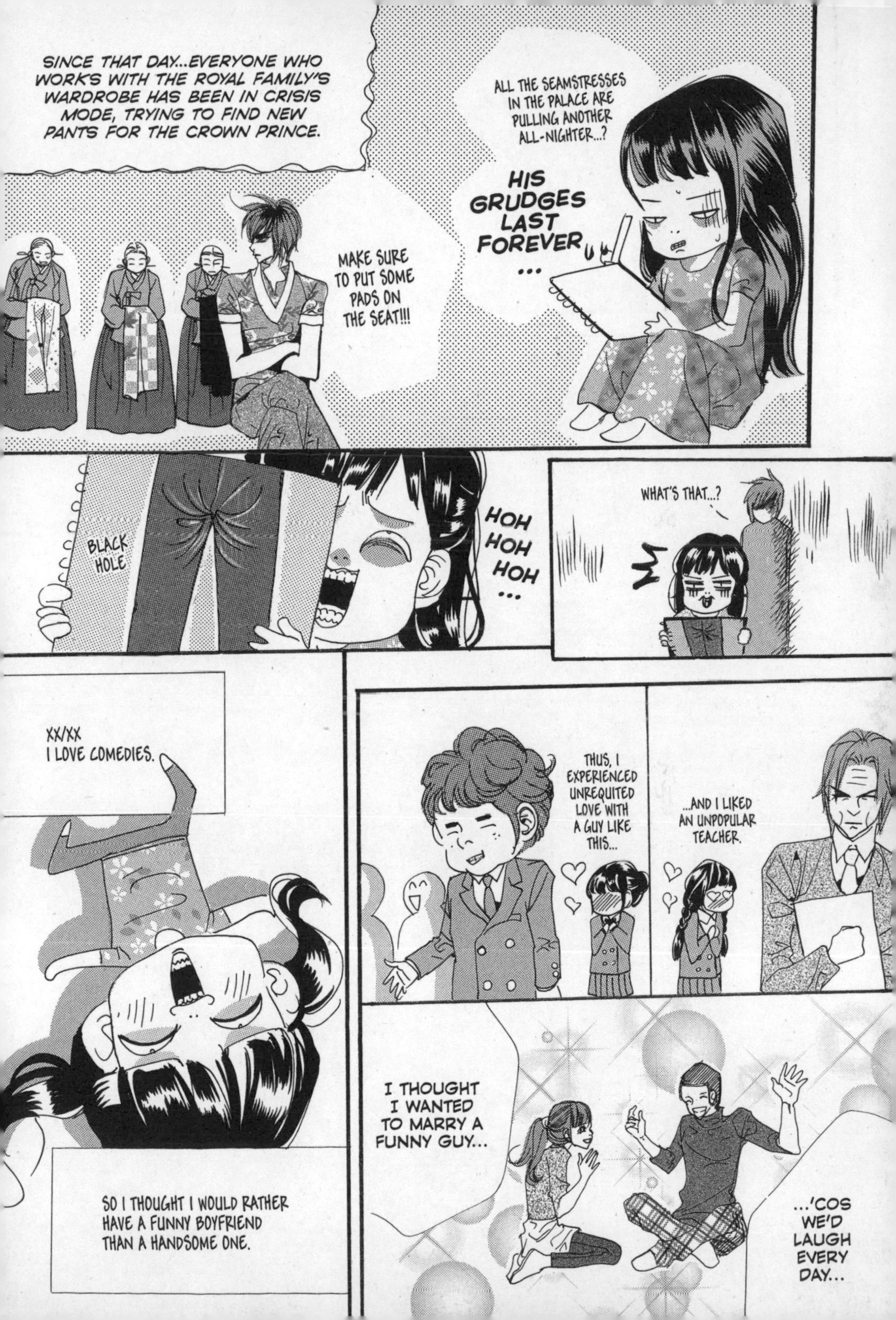
SINCE THAT DAY...EVERYONE WHO WORKS WITH THE ROYAL FAMILY'S WARDROBE HAS BEEN IN CRISIS MODE, TRYING TO FIND NEW PANTS FOR THE CROWN PRINCE.
ALL THE SEAMSTRESSES IN THE PALACE ARE PULLING ANOTHER ALL-NIGHTER...?
HIS GRUDGES LAST FOREVER...
MAKE SURE TO PUT SOME PADS ON THE SEAT!!!
BLACK HOLE
HOH HOH HOH...
WHAT'S THAT...?
XX/XX
I LOVE COMEDIES.
SO I THOUGHT I WOULD RATHER HAVE A FUNNY BOYFRIEND THAN A HANDSOME ONE.
THUS, I EXPERIENCED UNREQUITED LOVE WITH A GUY LIKE THIS...
...AND I LIKED AN UNPOPULAR TEACHER.
I THOUGHT I WANTED TO MARRY A FUNNY GUY...
...'COS WE'D LAUGH EVERY DAY...

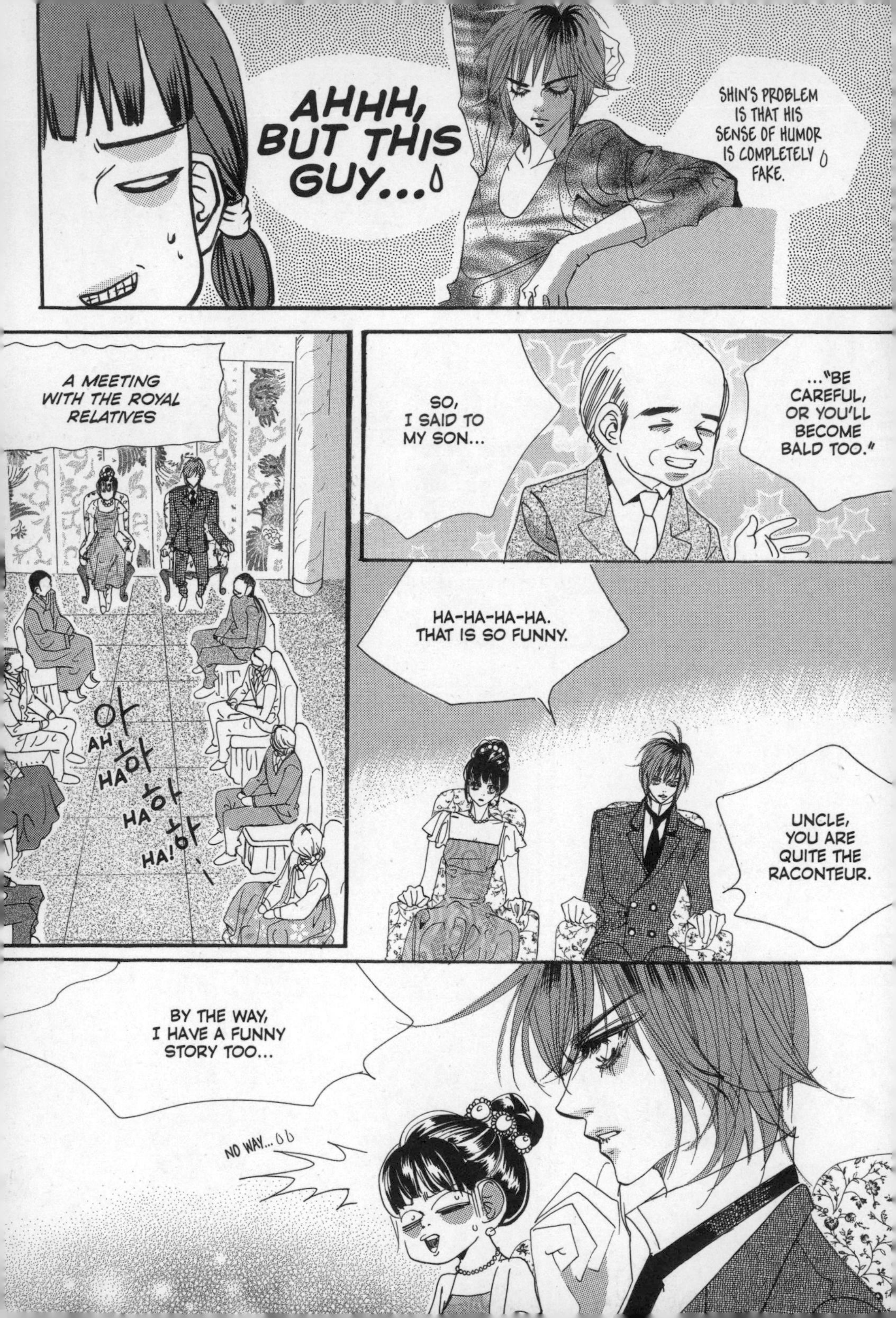
AHHH, BUT THIS GUY...
SHIN'S PROBLEM IS THAT HIS SENSE OF HUMOR IS COMPLETELY FAKE.
A MEETING WITH THE ROYAL RELATIVES
아하하하
AH HA HA HA!
SO, I SAID TO MY SON...
..."BE CAREFUL, OR YOU'LL BECOME BALD TOO."
HA-HA-HA-HA. THAT IS SO FUNNY.
UNCLE, YOU ARE QUITE THE RACONTEUR.
BY THE WAY, I HAVE A FUNNY STORY TOO...
NO WAY...

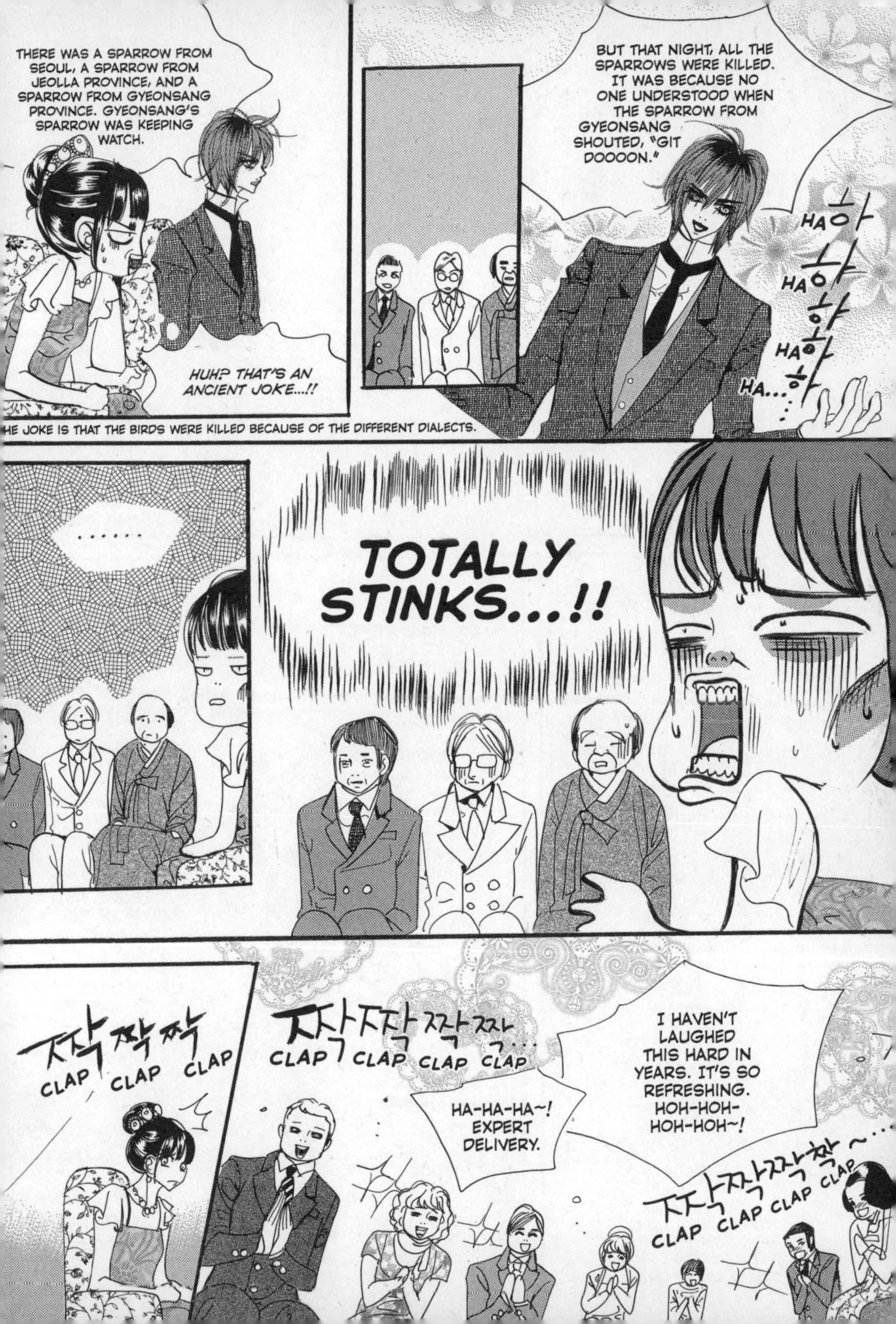

THERE WAS A SPARROW FROM SEOUL, A SPARROW FROM JEOLLA PROVINCE, AND A SPARROW FROM GYEONSANG PROVINCE. GYEONSANG'S SPARROW WAS KEEPING WATCH.
HUH? THAT'S AN ANCIENT JOKE...!!
HE JOKE IS THAT THE BIRDS WERE KILLED BECAUSE OF THE DIFFERENT DIALECTS.
BUT THAT NIGHT, ALL THE SPARROWS WERE KILLED. IT WAS BECAUSE NO ONE UNDERSTOOD WHEN THE SPARROW FROM GYEONSANG SHOUTED, "GIT DOOOON."
HA 하 HA 하 HA 하 HA... 하
......
TOTALLY STINKS...!!
짝작 짝작 짝
CLAP CLAP CLAP
짝작 짝작 작 짝
CLAP CLAP CLAP CLAP
HA-HA-HA~! EXPERT DELIVERY.
I HAVEN'T LAUGHED THIS HARD IN YEARS. IT'S SO REFRESHING. HOH-HOH-HOH-HOH~!
짝짝 작작 작 작~...
CLAP CLAP CLAP CLAP

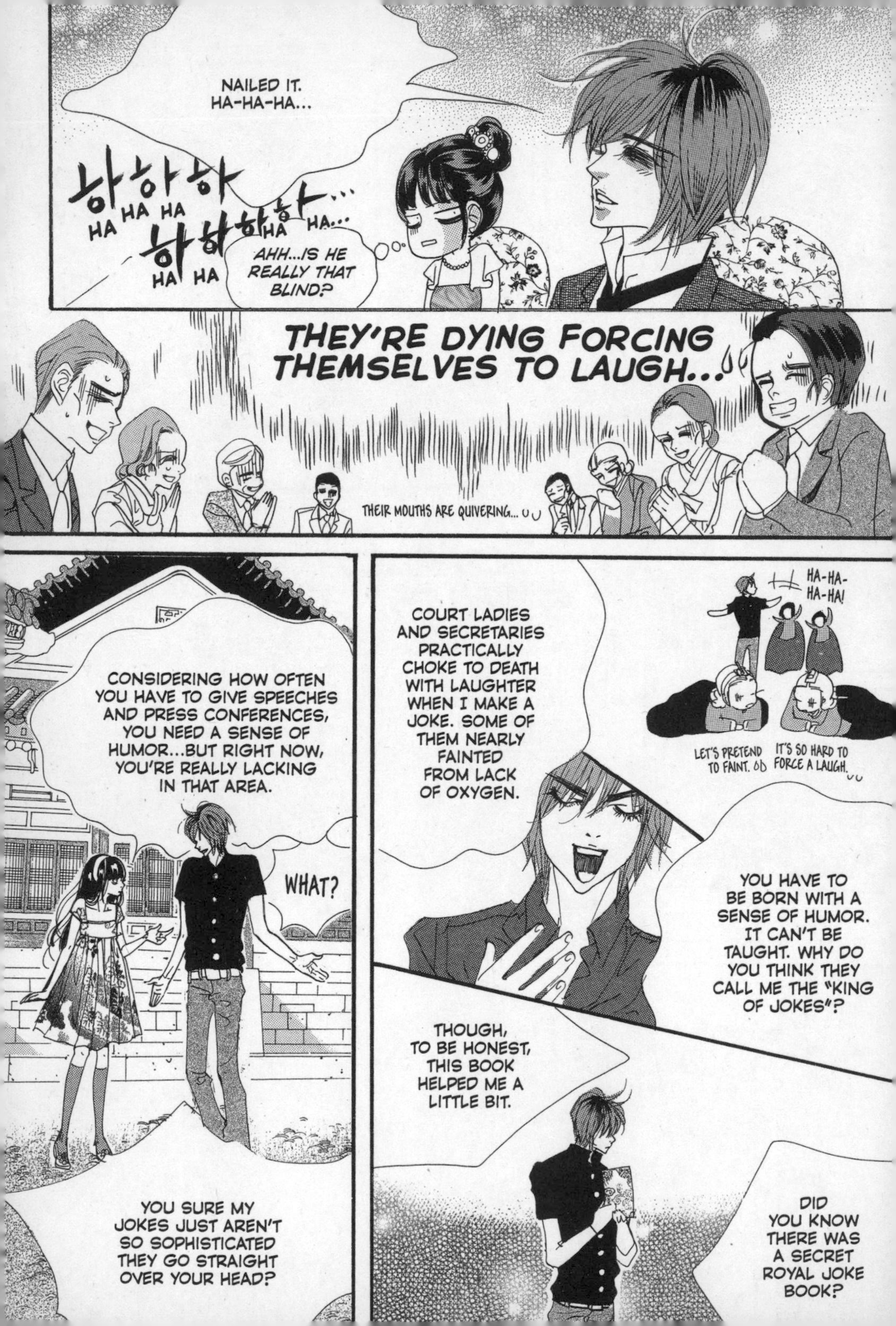
NAILED IT. HA-HA-HA...
하하하
HA HA HA
하하하하...
HA HA HA HA...
AHH...IS HE REALLY THAT BLIND?
THEY'RE DYING FORCING THEMSELVES TO LAUGH...
THEIR MOUTHS ARE QUIVERING...
CONSIDERING HOW OFTEN YOU HAVE TO GIVE SPEECHES AND PRESS CONFERENCES, YOU NEED A SENSE OF HUMOR...BUT RIGHT NOW, YOU'RE REALLY LACKING IN THAT AREA.
WHAT?
YOU SURE MY JOKES JUST AREN'T SO SOPHISTICATED THEY GO STRAIGHT OVER YOUR HEAD?
COURT LADIES AND SECRETARIES PRACTICALLY CHOKE TO DEATH WITH LAUGHTER WHEN I MAKE A JOKE. SOME OF THEM NEARLY FAINTED FROM LACK OF OXYGEN.
HA-HA-HA-HA!
LET'S PRETEND TO FAINT.
IT'S SO HARD TO FORCE A LAUGH.
YOU HAVE TO BE BORN WITH A SENSE OF HUMOR. IT CAN'T BE TAUGHT. WHY DO YOU THINK THEY CALL ME THE "KING OF JOKES"?
THOUGH, TO BE HONEST, THIS BOOK HELPED ME A LITTLE BIT.
DID YOU KNOW THERE WAS A SECRET ROYAL JOKE BOOK?

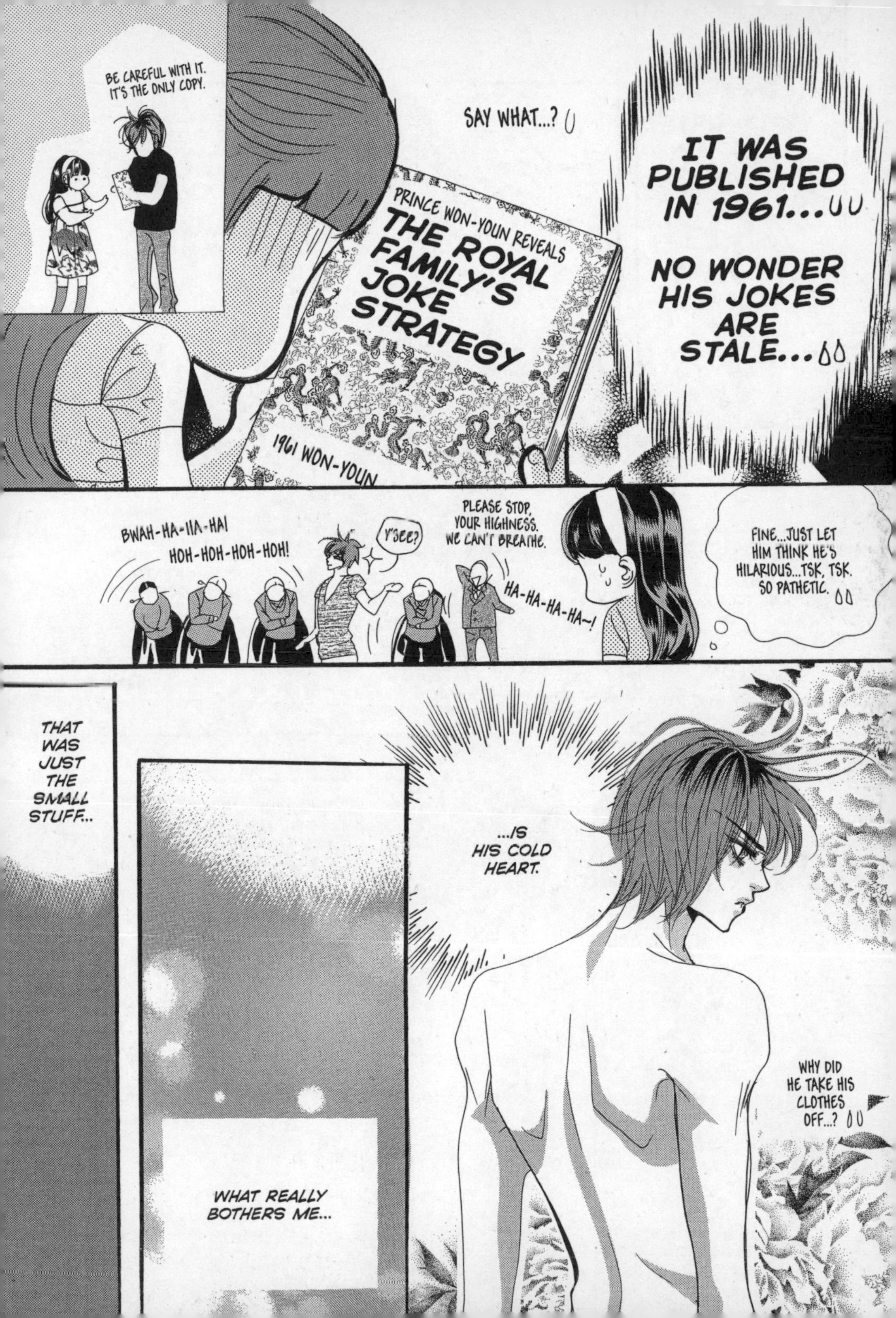
BE CAREFUL WITH IT. IT'S THE ONLY COPY.
SAY WHAT...?
PRINCE WON-YOUN REVEALS
THE ROYAL FAMILY'S JOKE STRATEGY
1961 WON-YOUN
IT WAS PUBLISHED IN 1961...
NO WONDER HIS JOKES ARE STALE...
BWAH-HA-HA-HA!
HOH-HOH-HOH-HOH!
Y'SEE?
PLEASE STOP, YOUR HIGHNESS. WE CAN'T BREATHE.
HA-HA-HA-HA~!
FINE...JUST LET HIM THINK HE'S HILARIOUS...TSK, TSK. SO PATHETIC.
THAT WAS JUST THE SMALL STUFF...
WHAT REALLY BOTHERS ME...
...IS HIS COLD HEART.
WHY DID HE TAKE HIS CLOTHES OFF...?

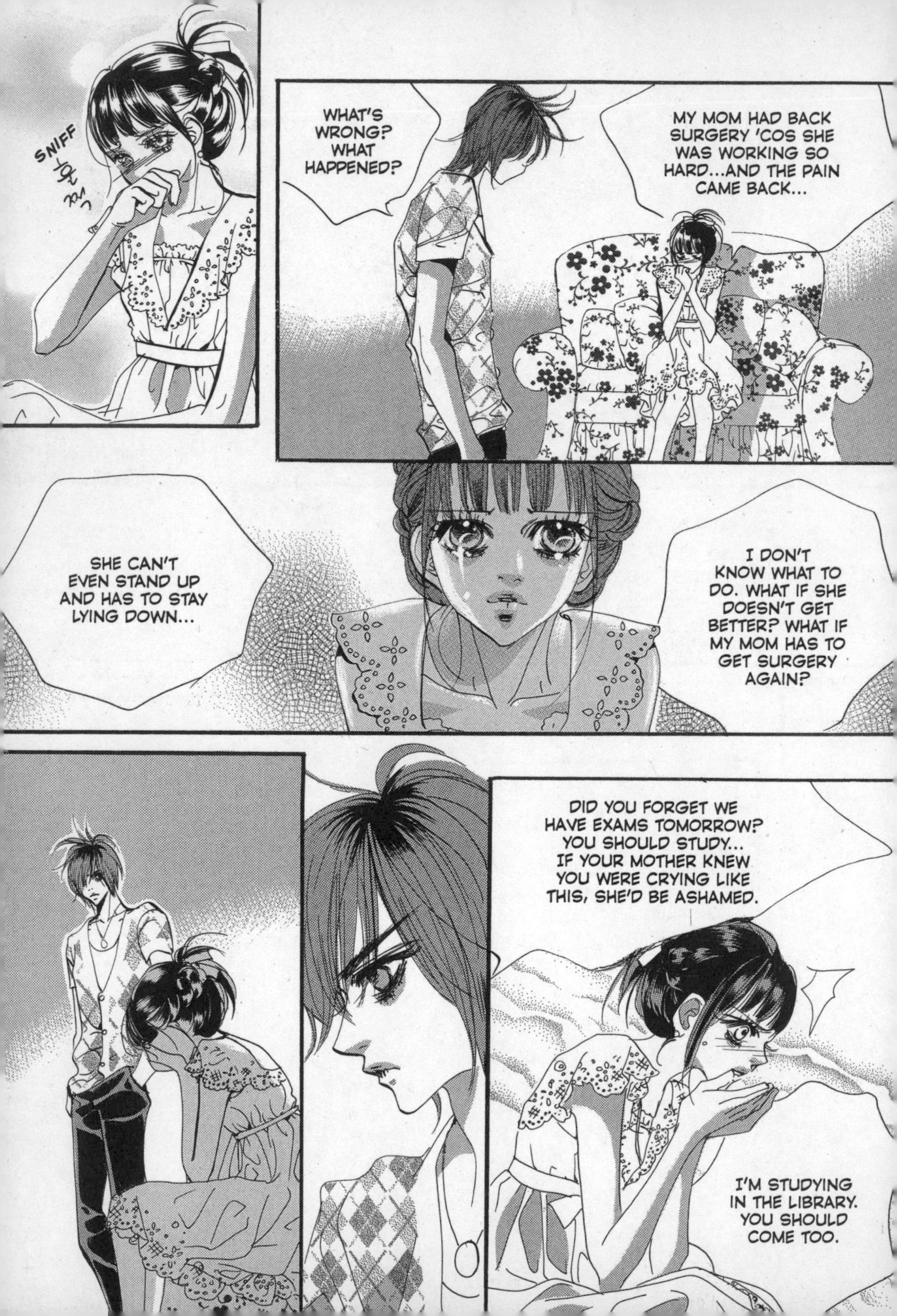
SNIFF
WHAT'S WRONG? WHAT HAPPENED?
MY MOM HAD BACK SURGERY 'COS SHE WAS WORKING SO HARD...AND THE PAIN CAME BACK...
SHE CAN'T EVEN STAND UP AND HAS TO STAY LYING DOWN...
I DON'T KNOW WHAT TO DO. WHAT IF SHE DOESN'T GET BETTER? WHAT IF MY MOM HAS TO GET SURGERY AGAIN?
DID YOU FORGET WE HAVE EXAMS TOMORROW? YOU SHOULD STUDY... IF YOUR MOTHER KNEW YOU WERE CRYING LIKE THIS, SHE'D BE ASHAMED.
I'M STUDYING IN THE LIBRARY. YOU SHOULD COME TOO.

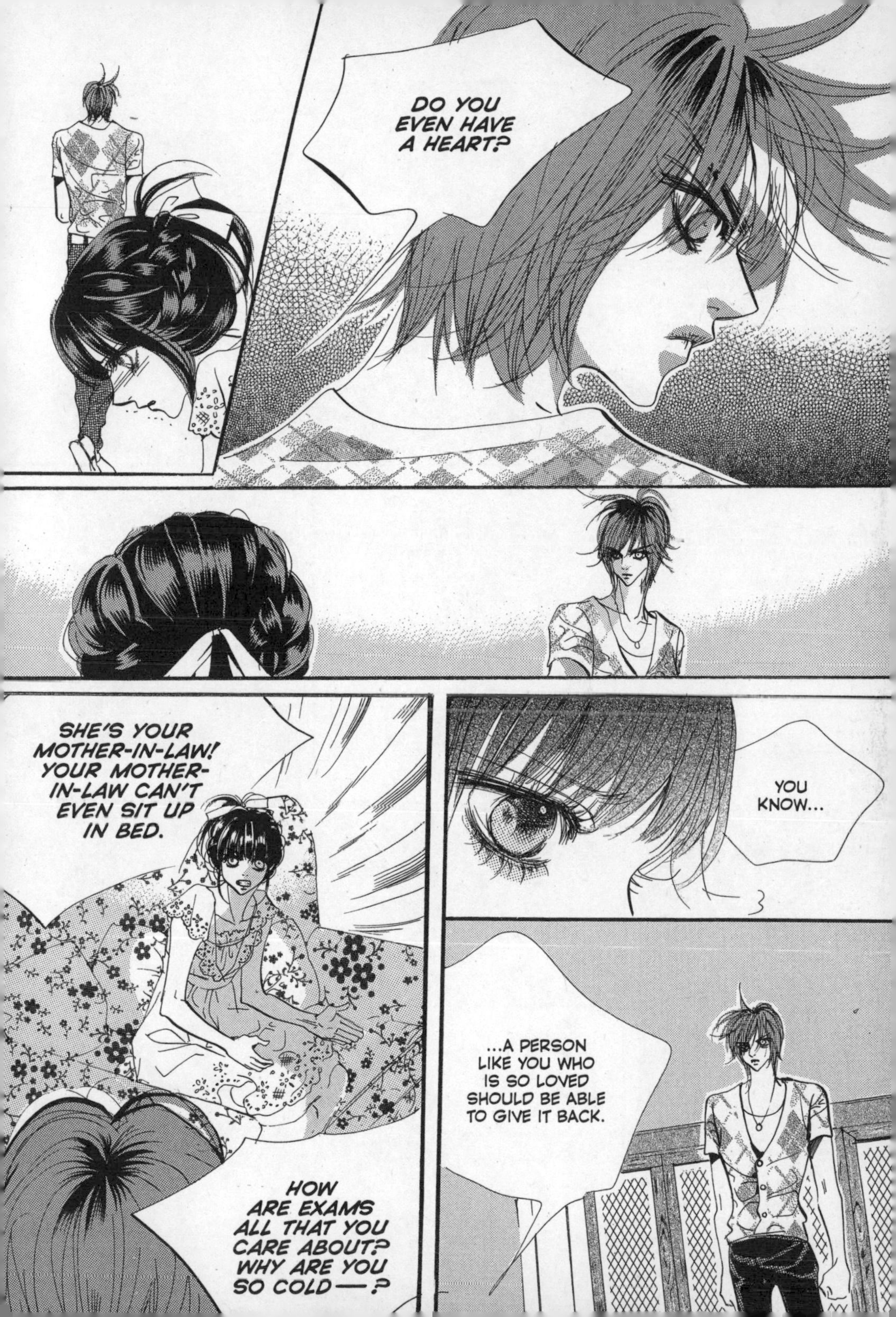
DO YOU EVEN HAVE A HEART?
SHE'S YOUR MOTHER-IN-LAW! YOUR MOTHER-IN-LAW CAN'T EVEN SIT UP IN BED.
HOW ARE EXAMS ALL THAT YOU CARE ABOUT? WHY ARE YOU SO COLD—?
YOU KNOW...
...A PERSON LIKE YOU WHO IS SO LOVED SHOULD BE ABLE TO GIVE IT BACK.

BUT BECAUSE YOU WERE RAISED BY NANNIES SINCE YOU WERE TWO, YOU PROBABLY DON'T EVEN KNOW WHAT IT'S LIKE TO HAVE A REAL FAMILY...

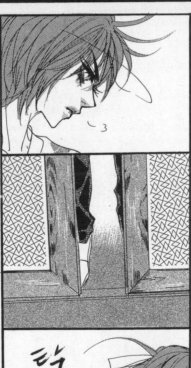

SHUT

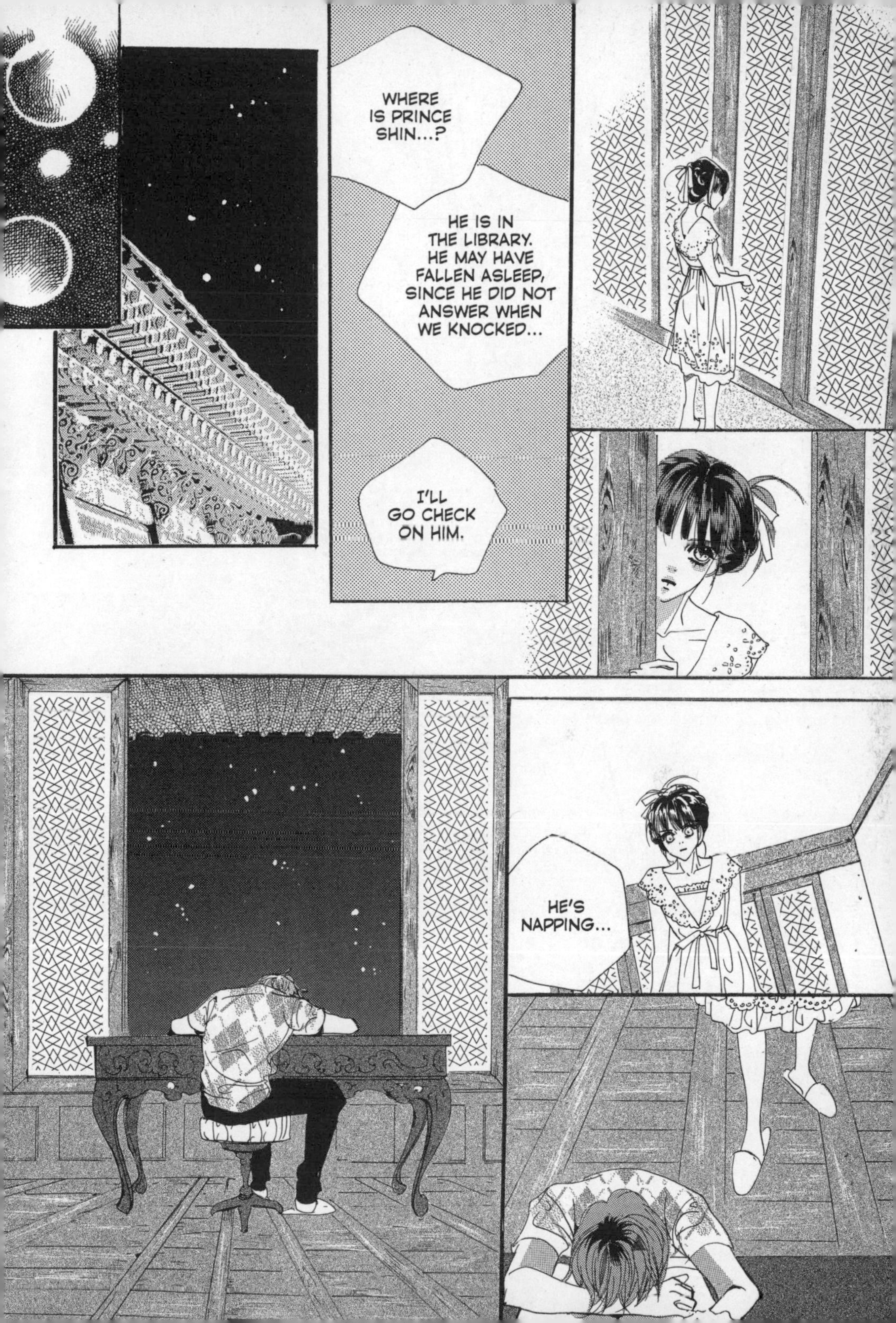
WHERE IS PRINCE SHIN...?
HE IS IN THE LIBRARY. HE MAY HAVE FALLEN ASLEEP, SINCE HE DID NOT ANSWER WHEN WE KNOCKED...
I'LL GO CHECK ON HIM.
HE'S NAPPING...

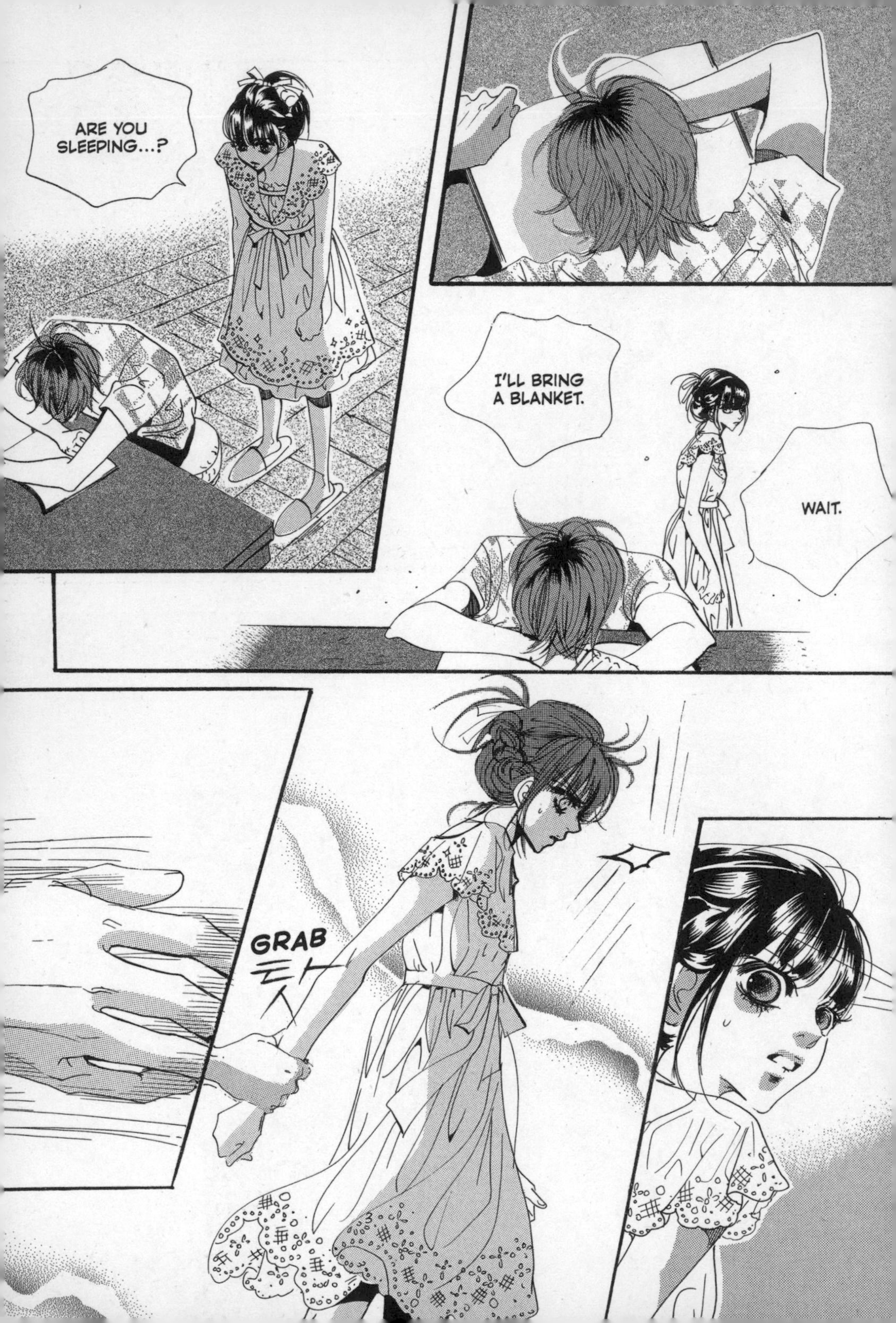
ARE YOU SLEEPING...?
I'LL BRING A BLANKET.
WAIT.
GRAB

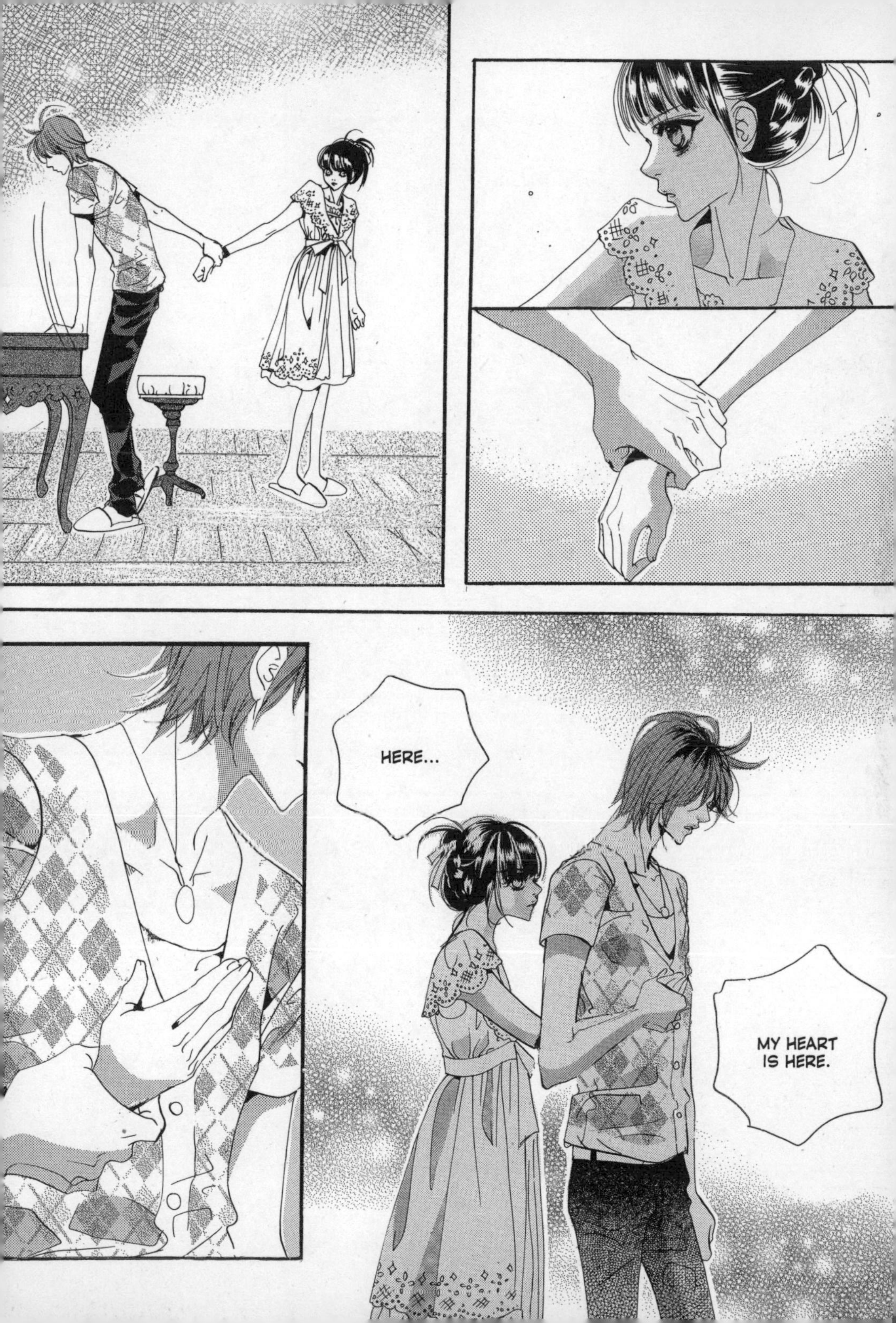
HERE...
MY HEART IS HERE.

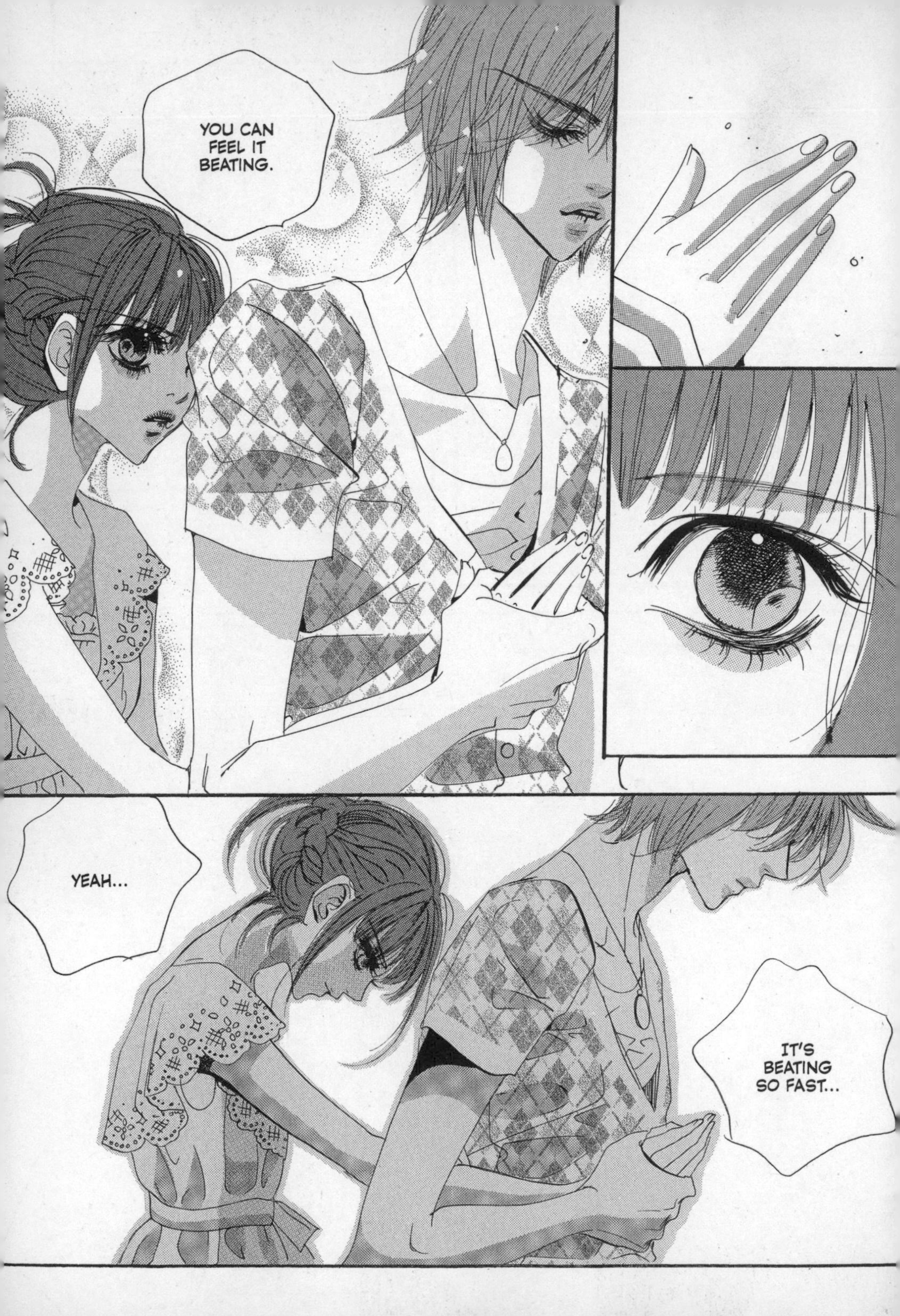
YOU CAN FEEL IT BEATING.
YEAH...
IT'S BEATING SO FAST...

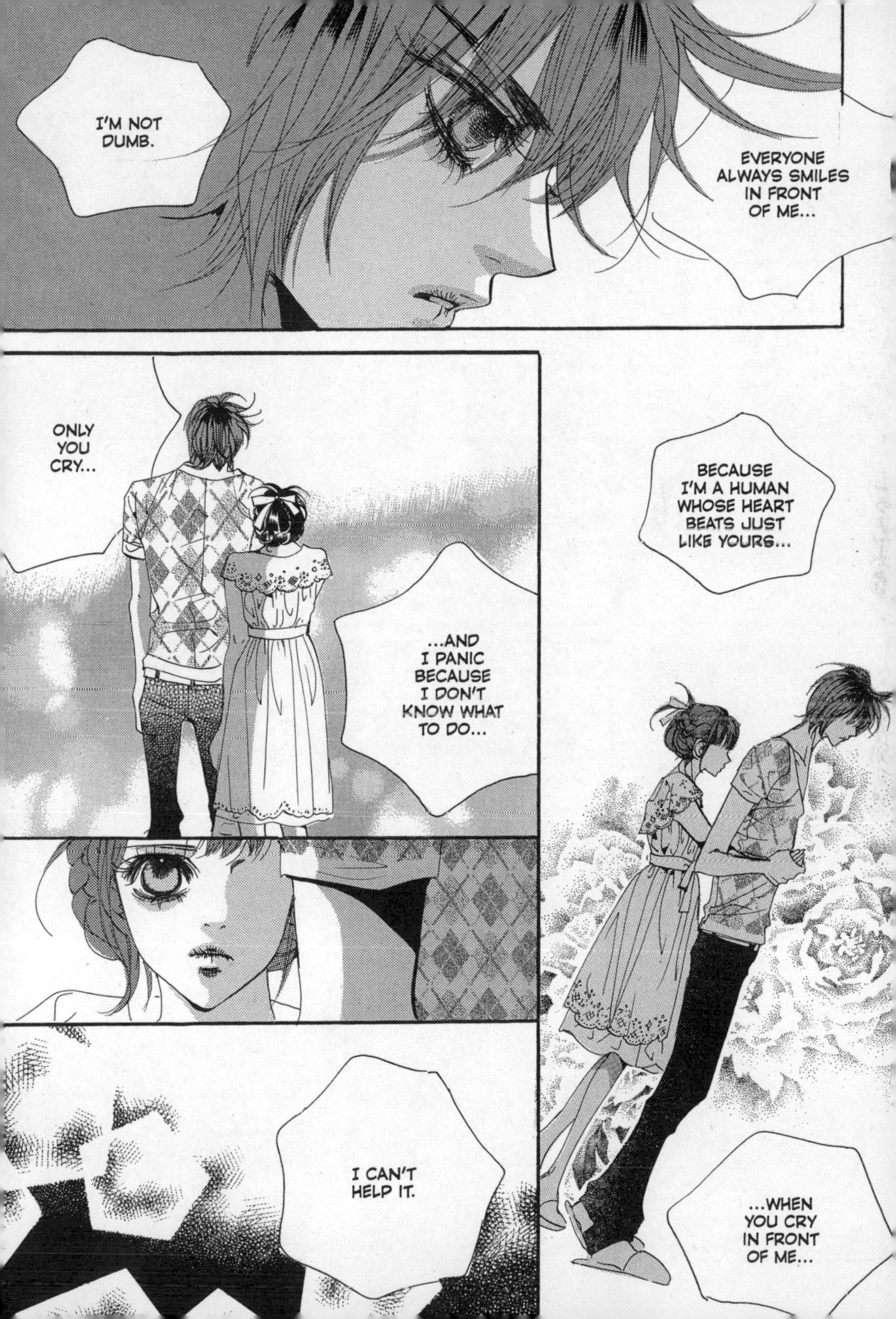
I'M NOT DUMB.
EVERYONE ALWAYS SMILES IN FRONT OF ME...
ONLY YOU CRY...
...AND I PANIC BECAUSE I DON'T KNOW WHAT TO DO...
I CAN'T HELP IT.
BECAUSE I'M A HUMAN WHOSE HEART BEATS JUST LIKE YOURS...
...WHEN YOU CRY IN FRONT OF ME...

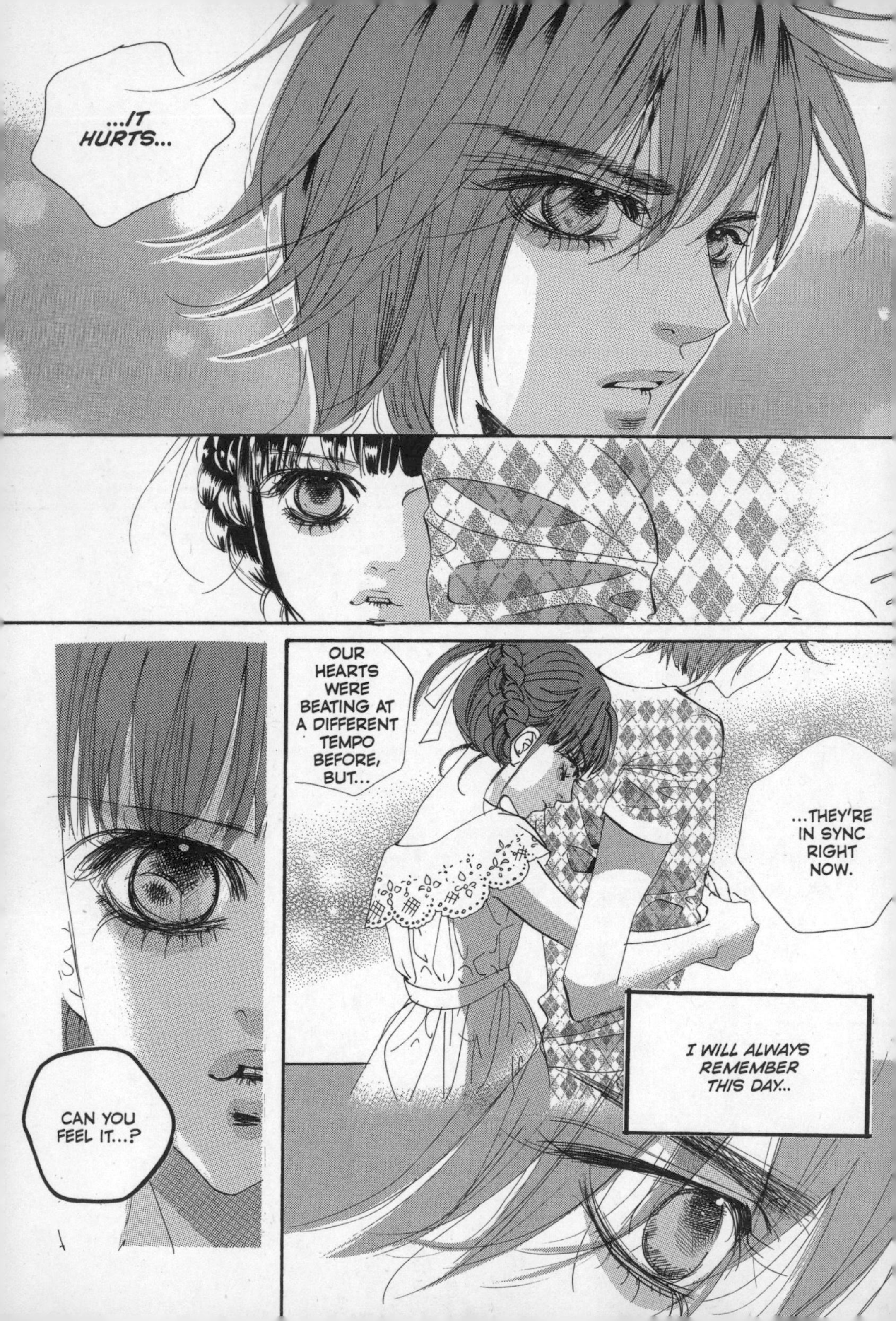
...IT HURTS...
CAN YOU FEEL IT...?
OUR HEARTS WERE BEATING AT A DIFFERENT TEMPO BEFORE, BUT...
...THEY'RE IN SYNC RIGHT NOW.
I WILL ALWAYS REMEMBER THIS DAY...

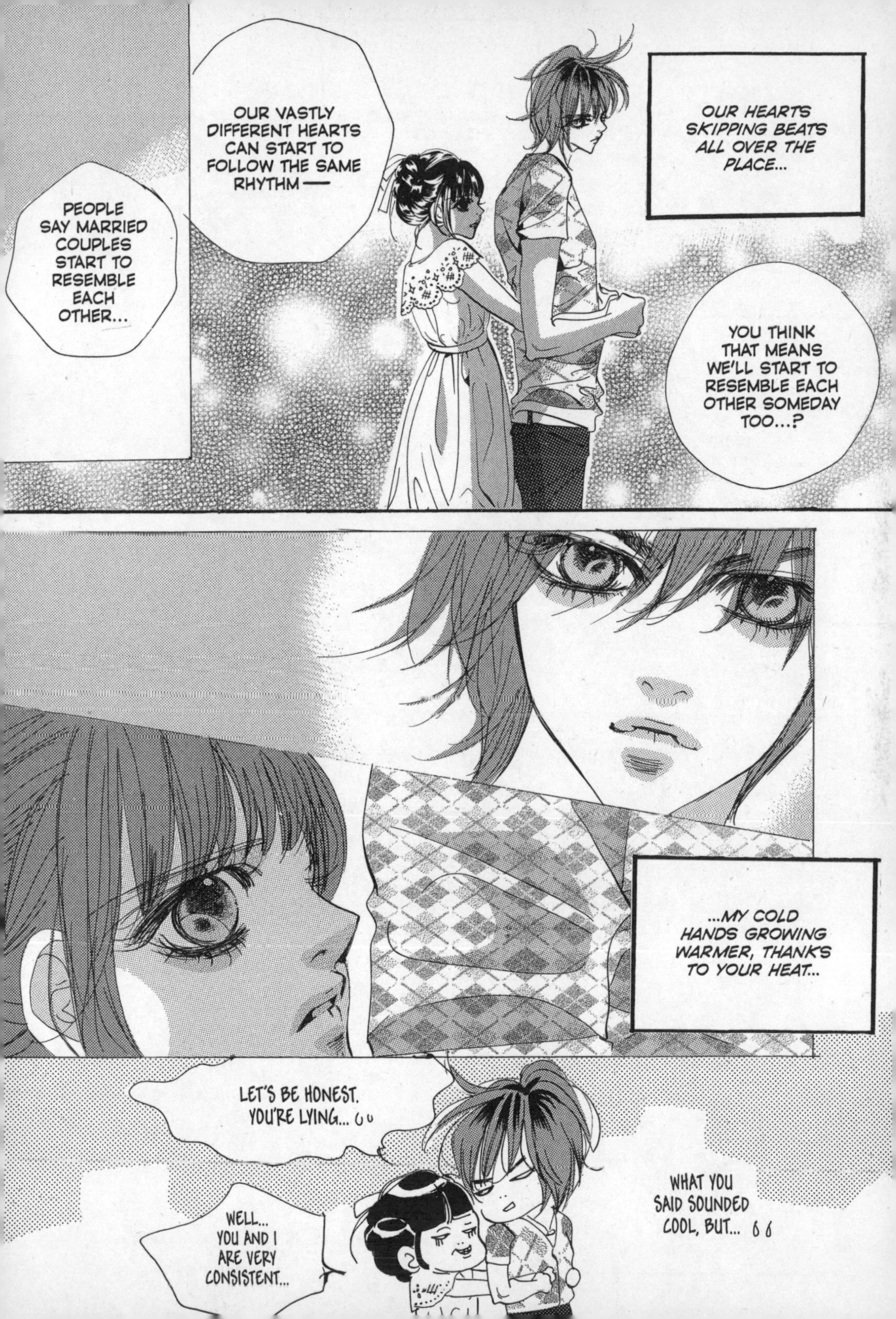
PEOPLE SAY MARRIED COUPLES START TO RESEMBLE EACH OTHER...
OUR VASTLY DIFFERENT HEARTS CAN START TO FOLLOW THE SAME RHYTHM—
OUR HEARTS SKIPPING BEATS ALL OVER THE PLACE...
YOU THINK THAT MEANS WE'LL START TO RESEMBLE EACH OTHER SOMEDAY TOO...?
...MY COLD HANDS GROWING WARMER, THANKS TO YOUR HEAT...
LET'S BE HONEST. YOU'RE LYING...
WELL... YOU AND I ARE VERY CONSISTENT...
WHAT YOU SAID SOUNDED COOL, BUT...

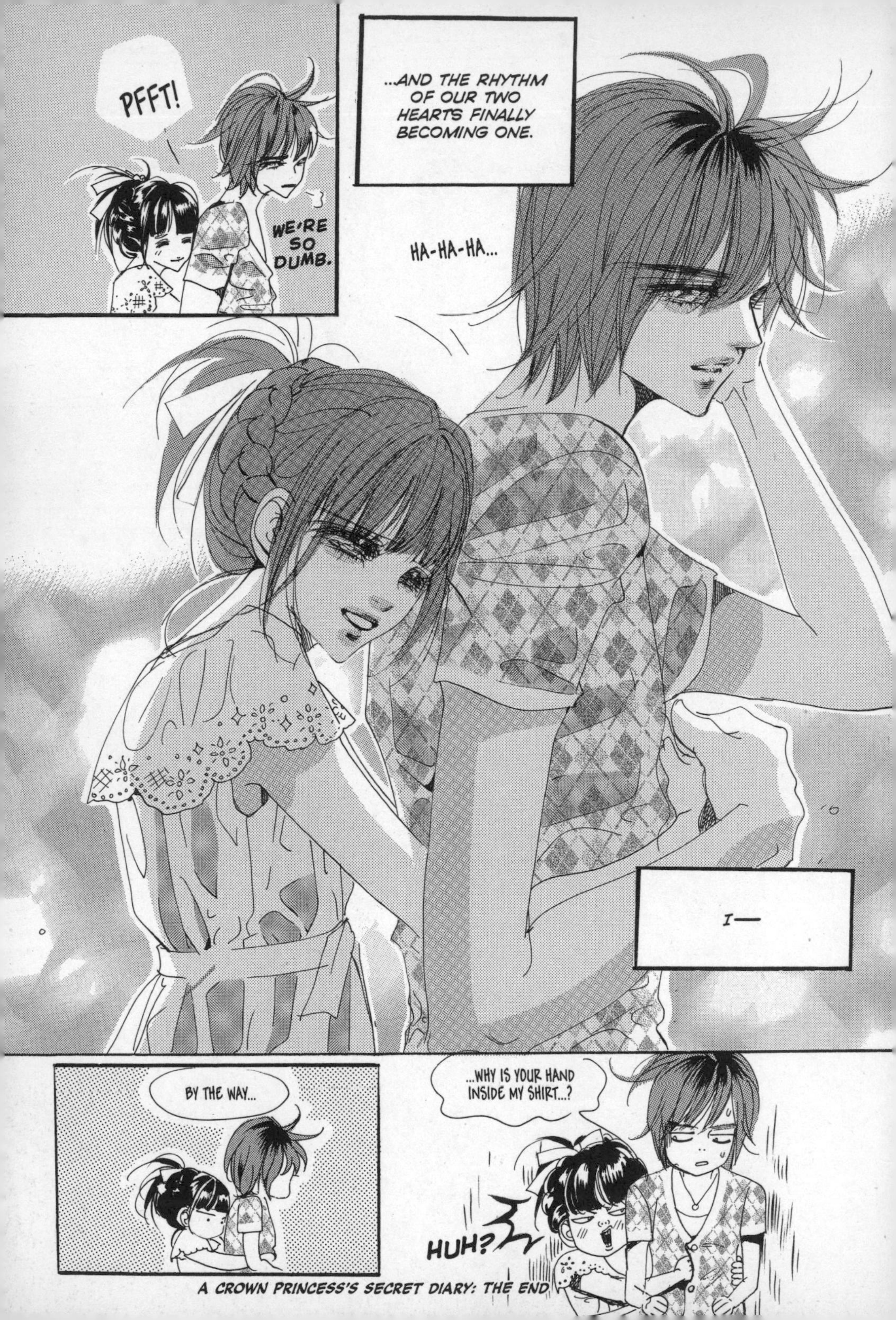
PFFT!
WE'RE SO DUMB.
...AND THE RHYTHM OF OUR TWO HEARTS FINALLY BECOMING ONE.
HA-HA-HA...
I—
BY THE WAY...
...WHY IS YOUR HAND INSIDE MY SHIRT...?
HUH?

A CROWN PRINCESS'S SECRET DIARY: THE END

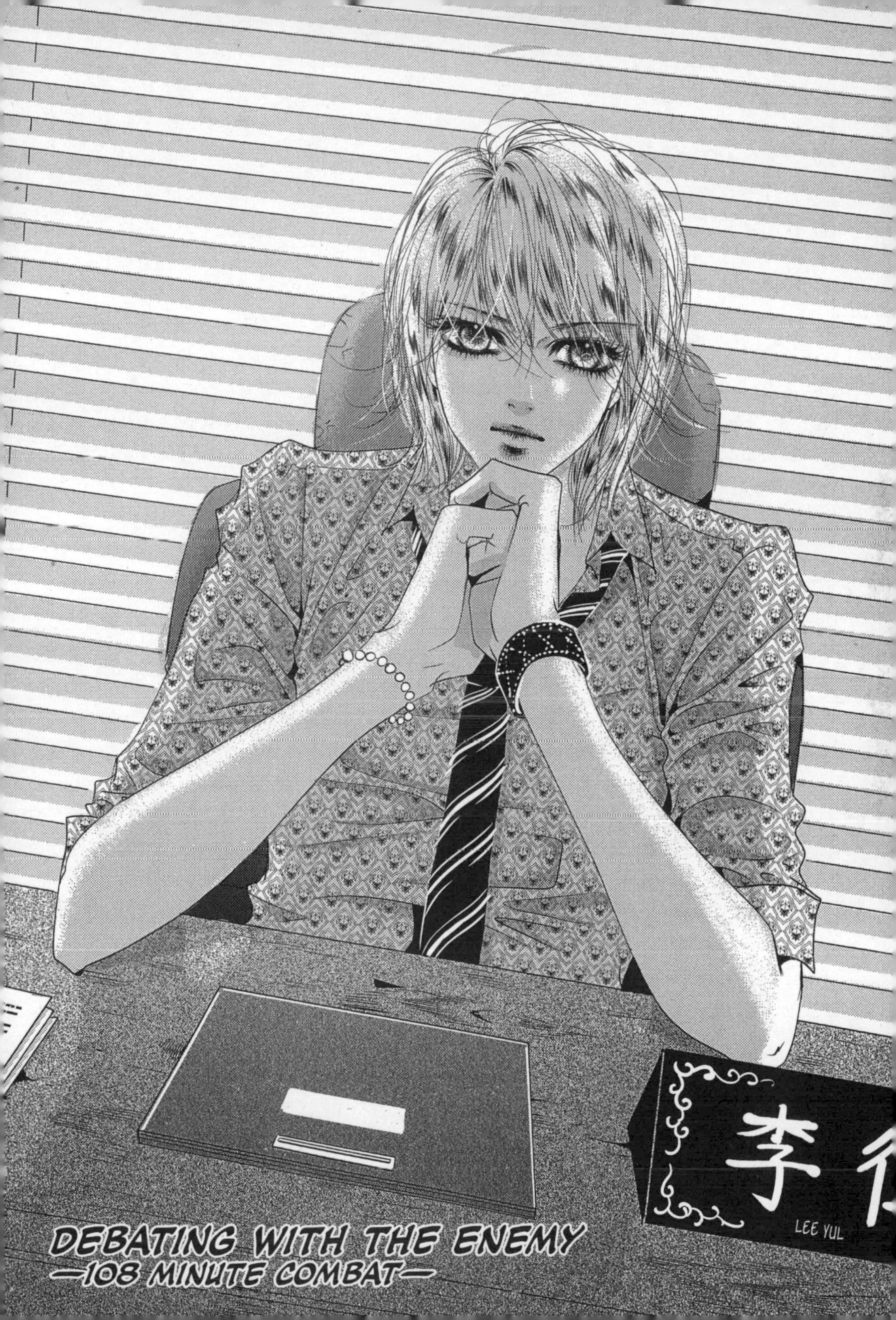
李
LEE YUL

DEBATING WITH THE ENEMY
—108 MINUTE COMBAT—

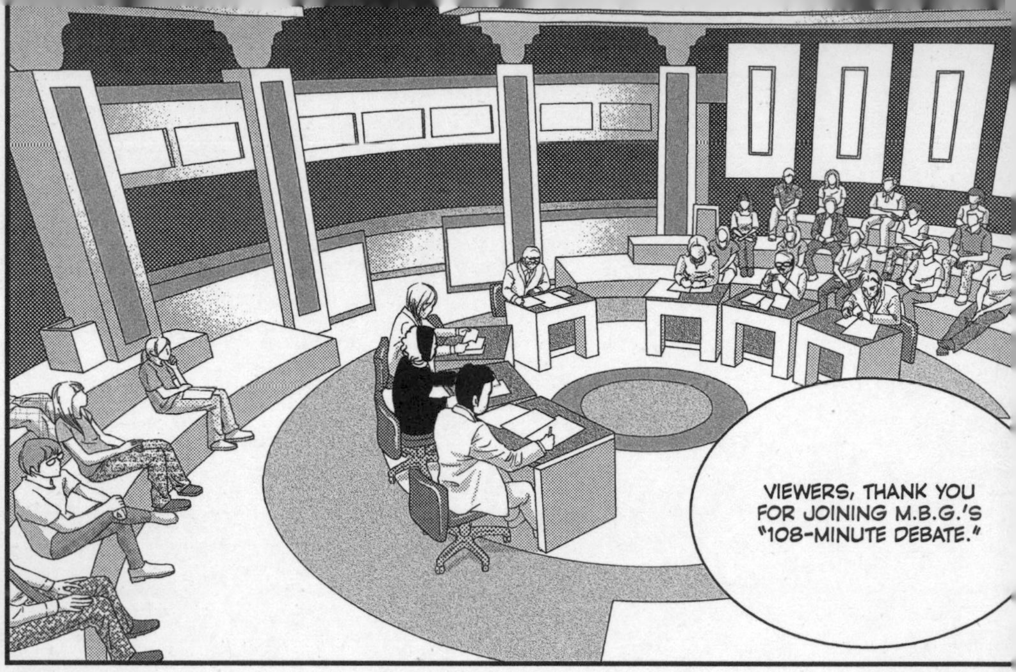
VIEWERS, THANK YOU FOR JOINING M.B.G.'S "108-MINUTE DEBATE."
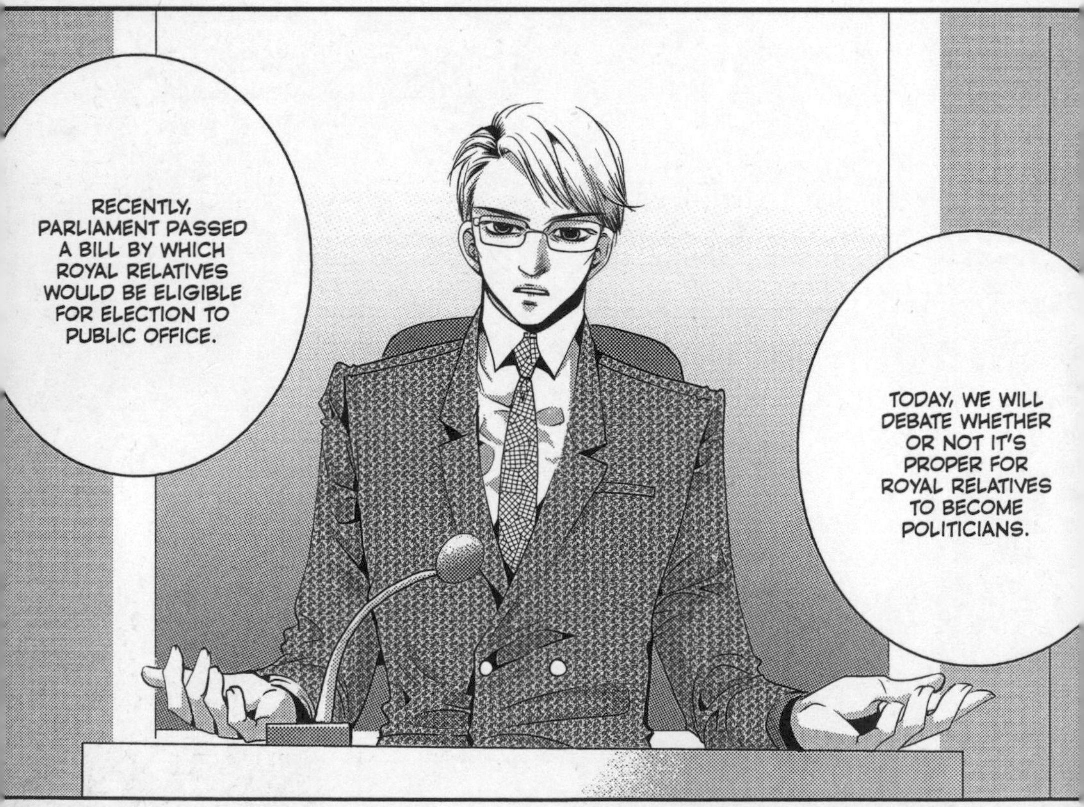
RECENTLY, PARLIAMENT PASSED A BILL BY WHICH ROYAL RELATIVES WOULD BE ELIGIBLE FOR ELECTION TO PUBLIC OFFICE.
TODAY, WE WILL DEBATE WHETHER OR NOT IT'S PROPER FOR ROYAL RELATIVES TO BECOME POLITICIANS.

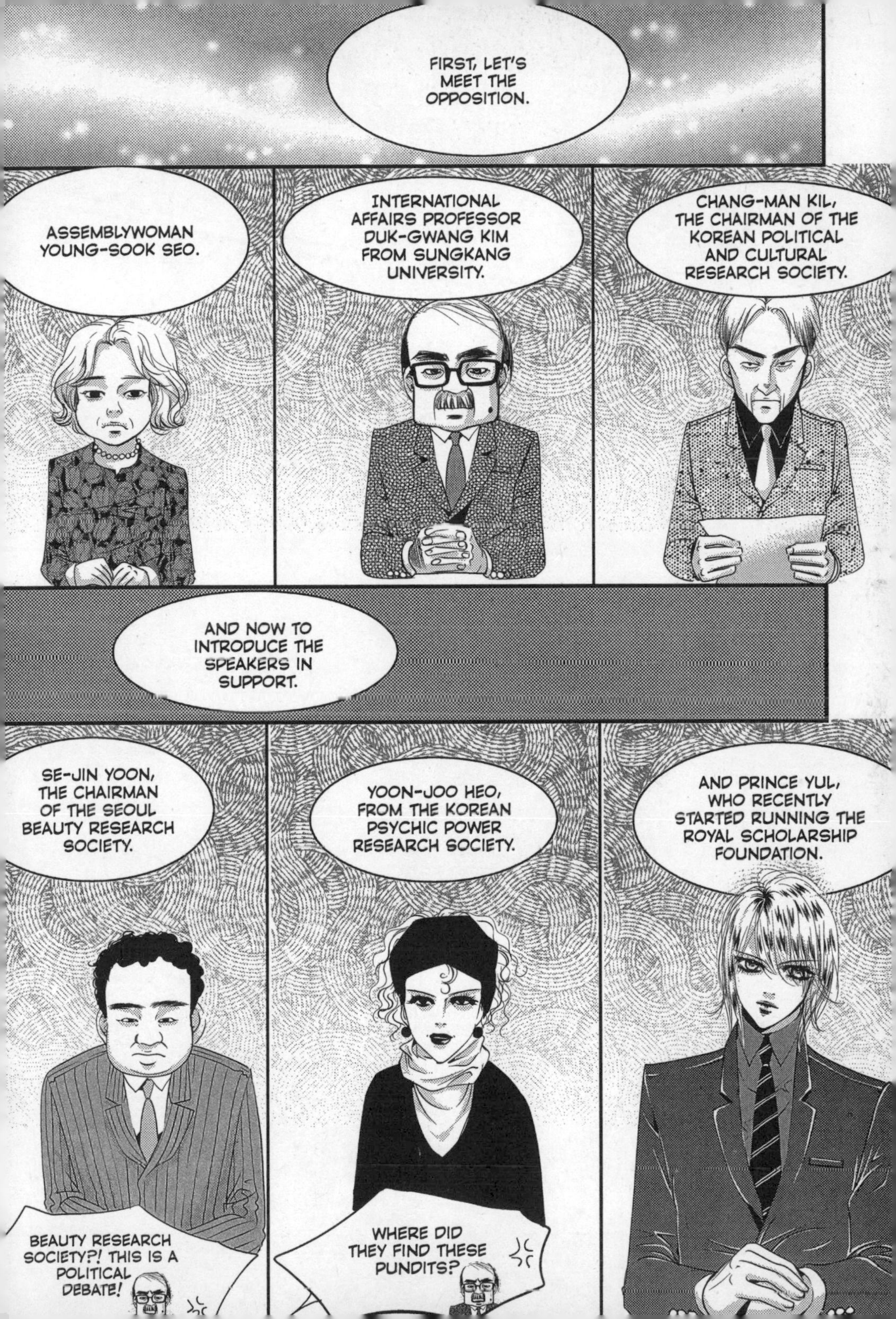
FIRST, LET'S MEET THE OPPOSITION.
ASSEMBLYWOMAN YOUNG-SOOK SEO.
INTERNATIONAL AFFAIRS PROFESSOR DUK-GWANG KIM FROM SUNGKANG UNIVERSITY.
CHANG-MAN KIL, THE CHAIRMAN OF THE KOREAN POLITICAL AND CULTURAL RESEARCH SOCIETY.
AND NOW TO INTRODUCE THE SPEAKERS IN SUPPORT.
SE-JIN YOON, THE CHAIRMAN OF THE SEOUL BEAUTY RESEARCH SOCIETY.
BEAUTY RESEARCH SOCIETY?! THIS IS A POLITICAL DEBATE!
YOON-JOO HEO, FROM THE KOREAN PSYCHIC POWER RESEARCH SOCIETY.
WHERE DID THEY FIND THESE PUNDITS?
AND PRINCE YUL, WHO RECENTLY STARTED RUNNING THE ROYAL SCHOLARSHIP FOUNDATION.

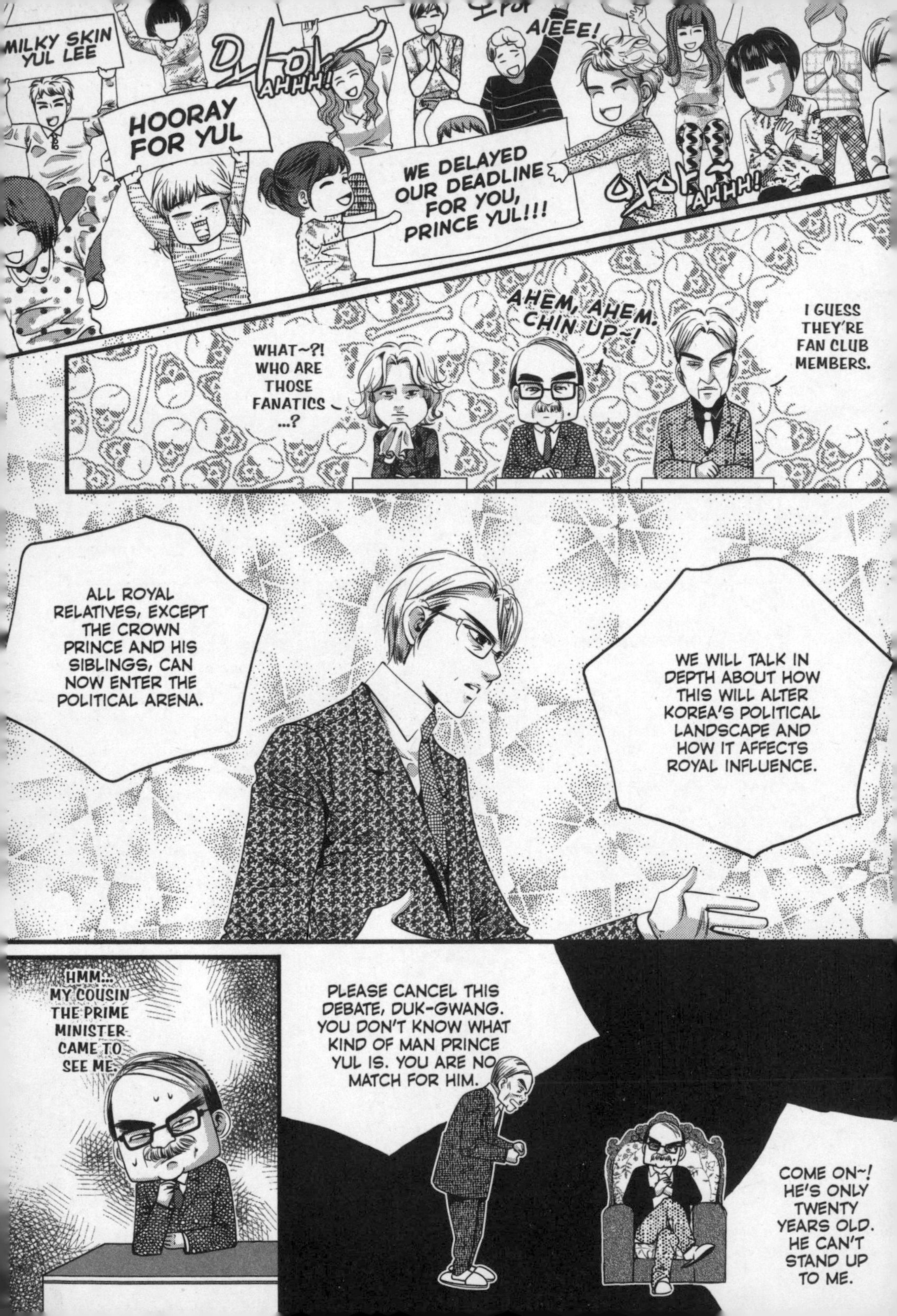
MILKY SKIN YUL LEE
AHHH!
AIEEE!
HOORAY FOR YUL
WE DELAYED OUR DEADLINE FOR YOU, PRINCE YUL!!!
AHHH!
WHAT~?! WHO ARE THOSE FANATICS ...?
AHEM, AHEM. CHIN UP~!
I GUESS THEY'RE FAN CLUB MEMBERS.
ALL ROYAL RELATIVES, EXCEPT THE CROWN PRINCE AND HIS SIBLINGS, CAN NOW ENTER THE POLITICAL ARENA.
WE WILL TALK IN DEPTH ABOUT HOW THIS WILL ALTER KOREA'S POLITICAL LANDSCAPE AND HOW IT AFFECTS ROYAL INFLUENCE.
HMM... MY COUSIN THE PRIME MINISTER CAME TO SEE ME.
PLEASE CANCEL THIS DEBATE, DUK-GWANG. YOU DON'T KNOW WHAT KIND OF MAN PRINCE YUL IS. YOU ARE NO MATCH FOR HIM.
COME ON~! HE'S ONLY TWENTY YEARS OLD. HE CAN'T STAND UP TO ME.

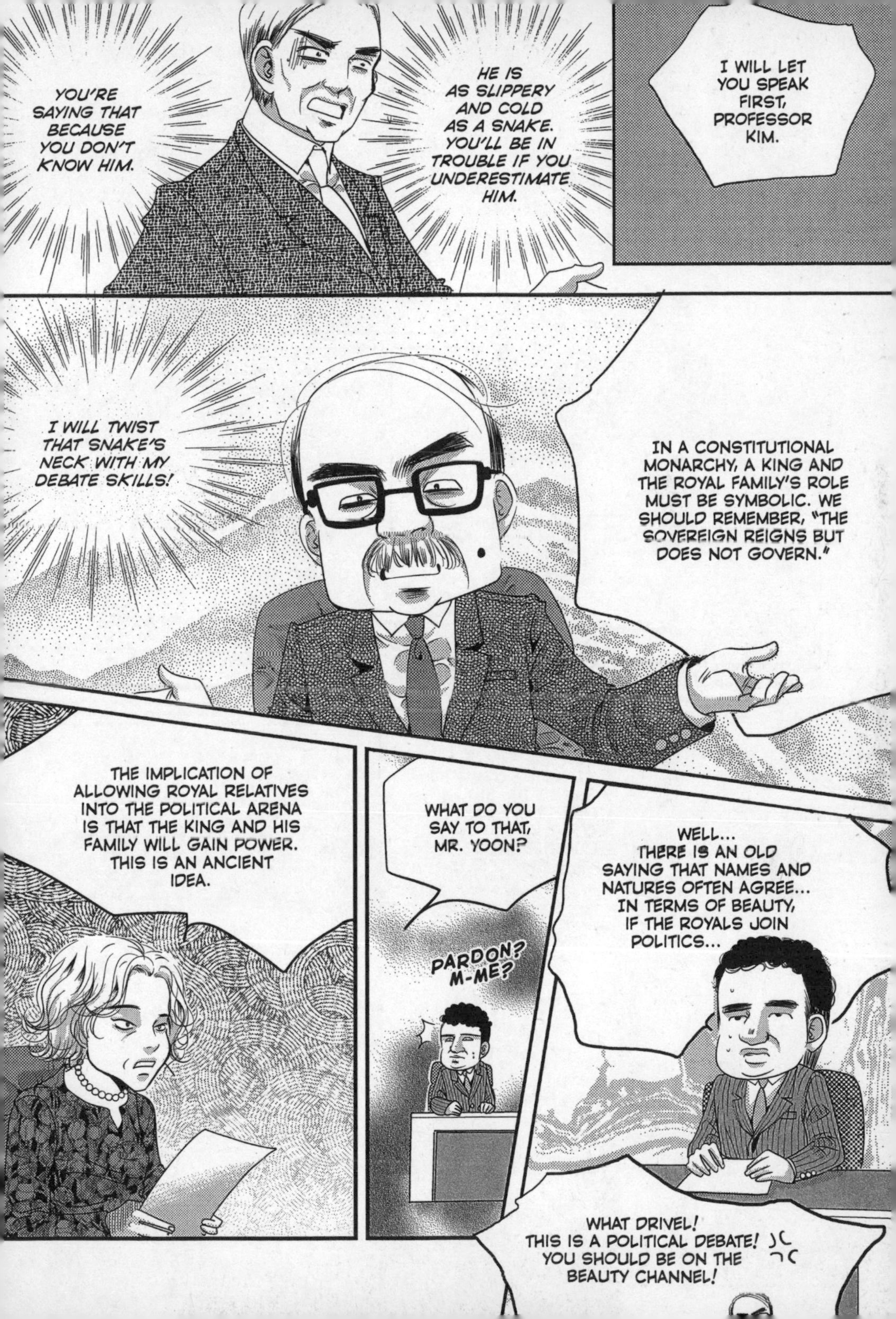
YOU'RE SAYING THAT BECAUSE YOU DON'T KNOW HIM.
HE IS AS SLIPPERY AND COLD AS A SNAKE. YOU'LL BE IN TROUBLE IF YOU UNDERESTIMATE HIM.
I WILL LET YOU SPEAK FIRST, PROFESSOR KIM.
I WILL TWIST THAT SNAKE'S NECK WITH MY DEBATE SKILLS!
IN A CONSTITUTIONAL MONARCHY, A KING AND THE ROYAL FAMILY'S ROLE MUST BE SYMBOLIC. WE SHOULD REMEMBER, "THE SOVEREIGN REIGNS BUT DOES NOT GOVERN."
THE IMPLICATION OF ALLOWING ROYAL RELATIVES INTO THE POLITICAL ARENA IS THAT THE KING AND HIS FAMILY WILL GAIN POWER. THIS IS AN ANCIENT IDEA.
WHAT DO YOU SAY TO THAT, MR. YOON?
PARDON? M-ME?
WELL... THERE IS AN OLD SAYING THAT NAMES AND NATURES OFTEN AGREE... IN TERMS OF BEAUTY, IF THE ROYALS JOIN POLITICS...
WHAT DRIVEL! THIS IS A POLITICAL DEBATE! YOU SHOULD BE ON THE BEAUTY CHANNEL!

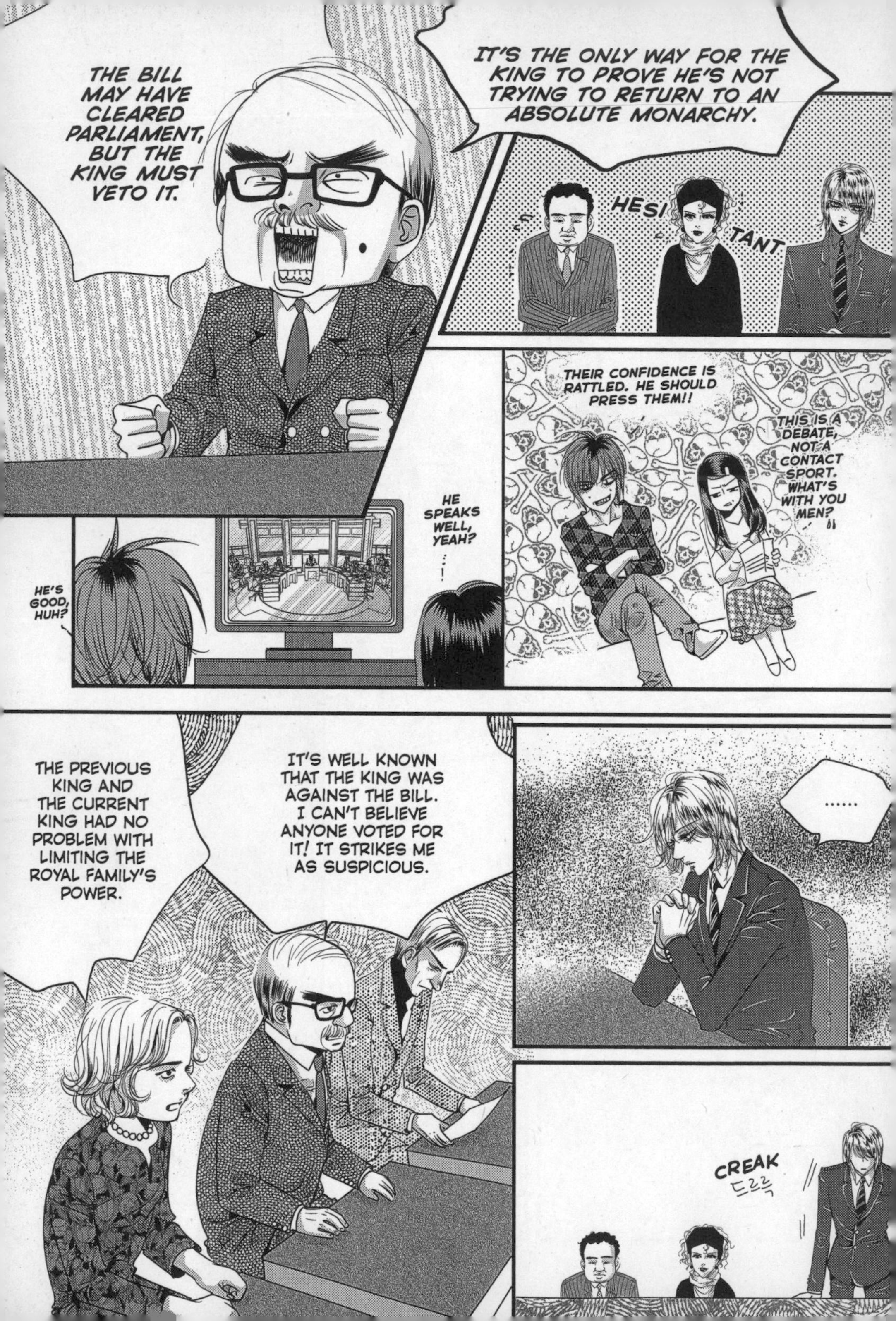
THE BILL MAY HAVE CLEARED PARLIAMENT, BUT THE KING MUST VETO IT.
IT'S THE ONLY WAY FOR THE KING TO PROVE HE'S NOT TRYING TO RETURN TO AN ABSOLUTE MONARCHY.
HESITANT.
HE'S GOOD, HUH?
HE SPEAKS WELL, YEAH?
...!
THEIR CONFIDENCE IS RATTLED. HE SHOULD PRESS THEM!!
THIS IS A DEBATE, NOT A CONTACT SPORT. WHAT'S WITH YOU MEN?
THE PREVIOUS KING AND THE CURRENT KING HAD NO PROBLEM WITH LIMITING THE ROYAL FAMILY'S POWER.
IT'S WELL KNOWN THAT THE KING WAS AGAINST THE BILL. I CAN'T BELIEVE ANYONE VOTED FOR IT! IT STRIKES ME AS SUSPICIOUS.
......
CREAK
드르륵

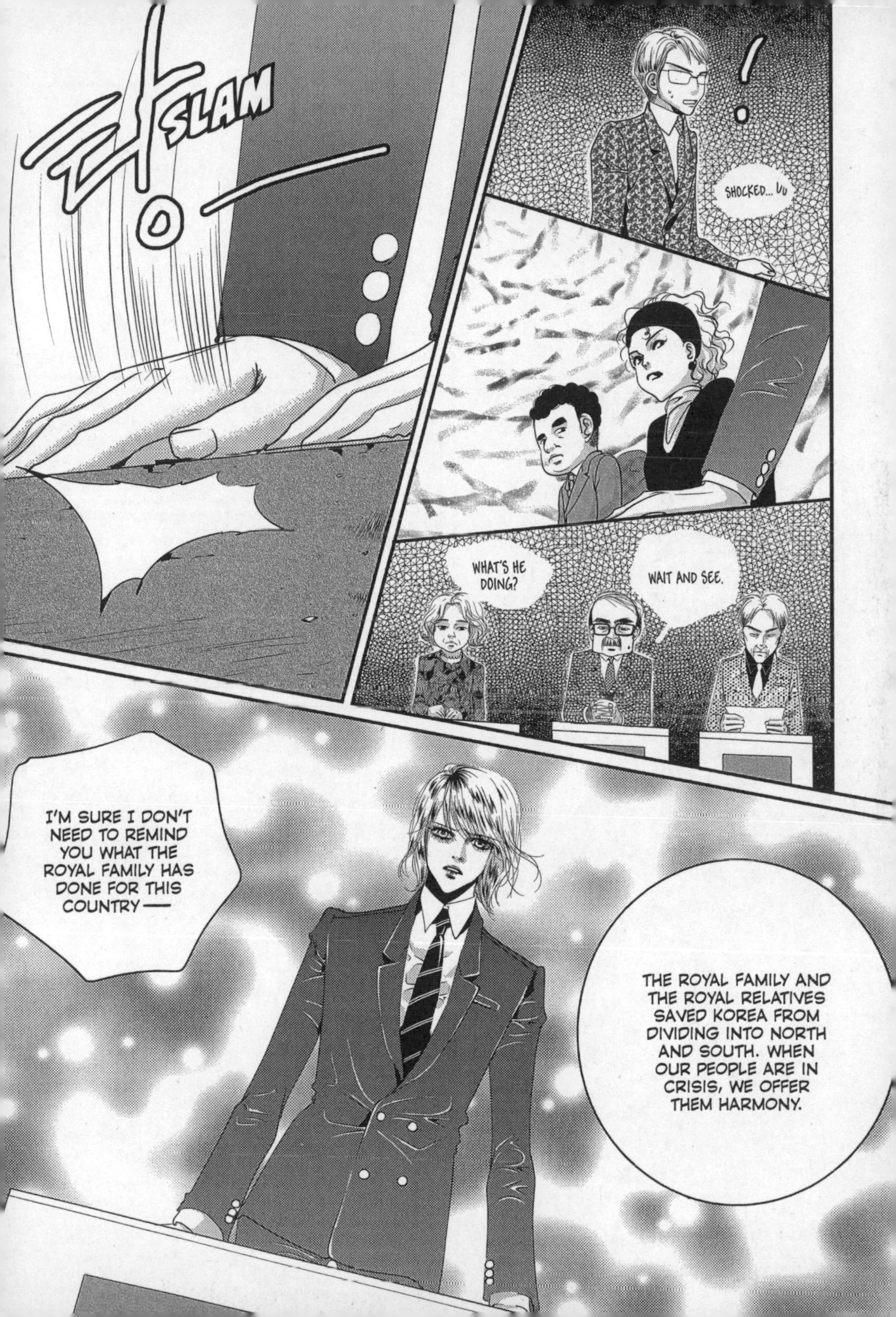
SLAM
!
SHOCKED... UU
WHAT'S HE DOING?
WAIT AND SEE.
I'M SURE I DON'T NEED TO REMIND YOU WHAT THE ROYAL FAMILY HAS DONE FOR THIS COUNTRY—
THE ROYAL FAMILY AND THE ROYAL RELATIVES SAVED KOREA FROM DIVIDING INTO NORTH AND SOUTH. WHEN OUR PEOPLE ARE IN CRISIS, WE OFFER THEM HARMONY.

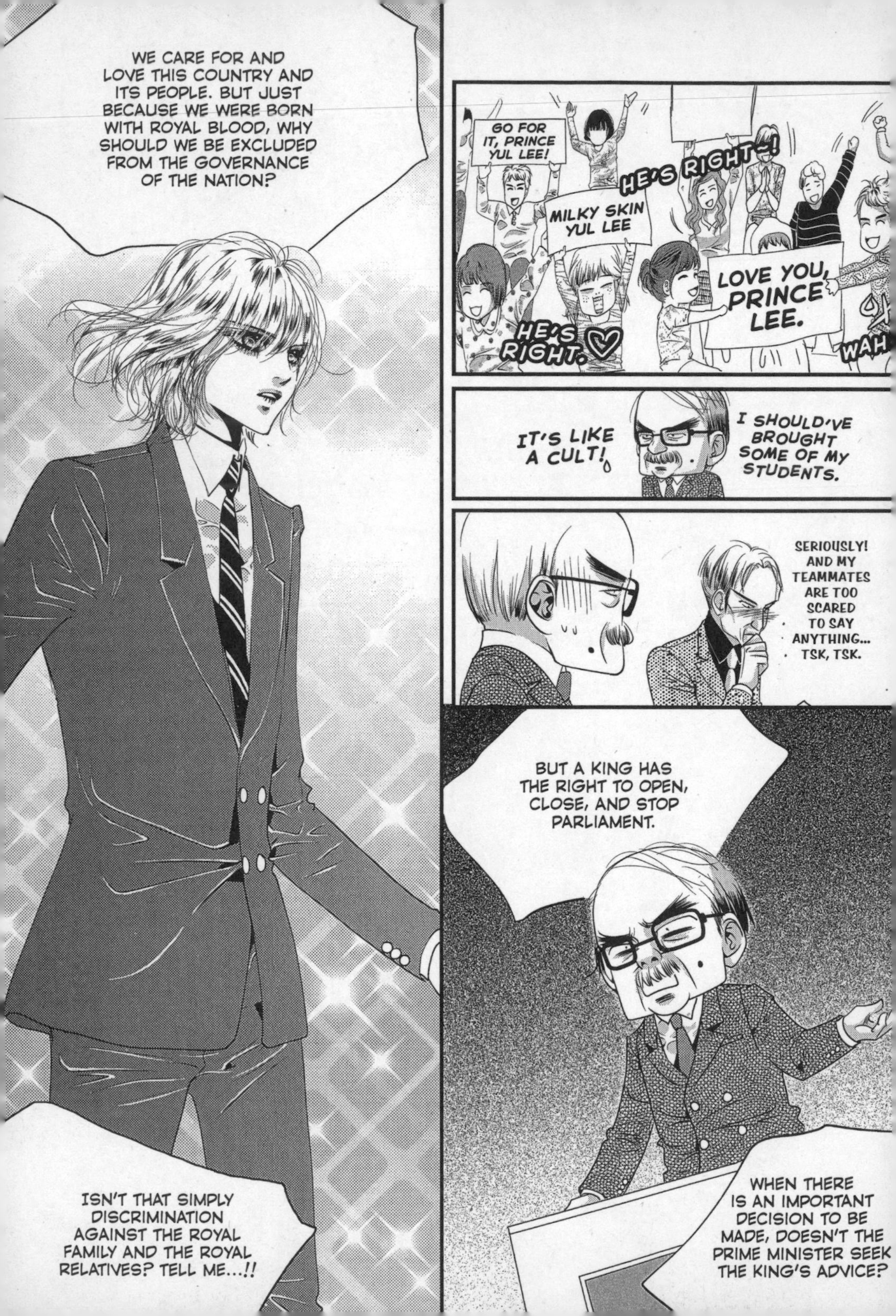
WE CARE FOR AND LOVE THIS COUNTRY AND ITS PEOPLE. BUT JUST BECAUSE WE WERE BORN WITH ROYAL BLOOD, WHY SHOULD WE BE EXCLUDED FROM THE GOVERNANCE OF THE NATION?
ISN'T THAT SIMPLY DISCRIMINATION AGAINST THE ROYAL FAMILY AND THE ROYAL RELATIVES? TELL ME...!!
GO FOR IT, PRINCE YUL LEE!
HE'S RIGHT~!
MILKY SKIN YUL LEE
LOVE YOU, PRINCE LEE.
HE'S RIGHT.
WAH
IT'S LIKE A CULT!
I SHOULD'VE BROUGHT SOME OF MY STUDENTS.
SERIOUSLY! AND MY TEAMMATES ARE TOO SCARED TO SAY ANYTHING... TSK, TSK.
BUT A KING HAS THE RIGHT TO OPEN, CLOSE, AND STOP PARLIAMENT.
WHEN THERE IS AN IMPORTANT DECISION TO BE MADE, DOESN'T THE PRIME MINISTER SEEK THE KING'S ADVICE?

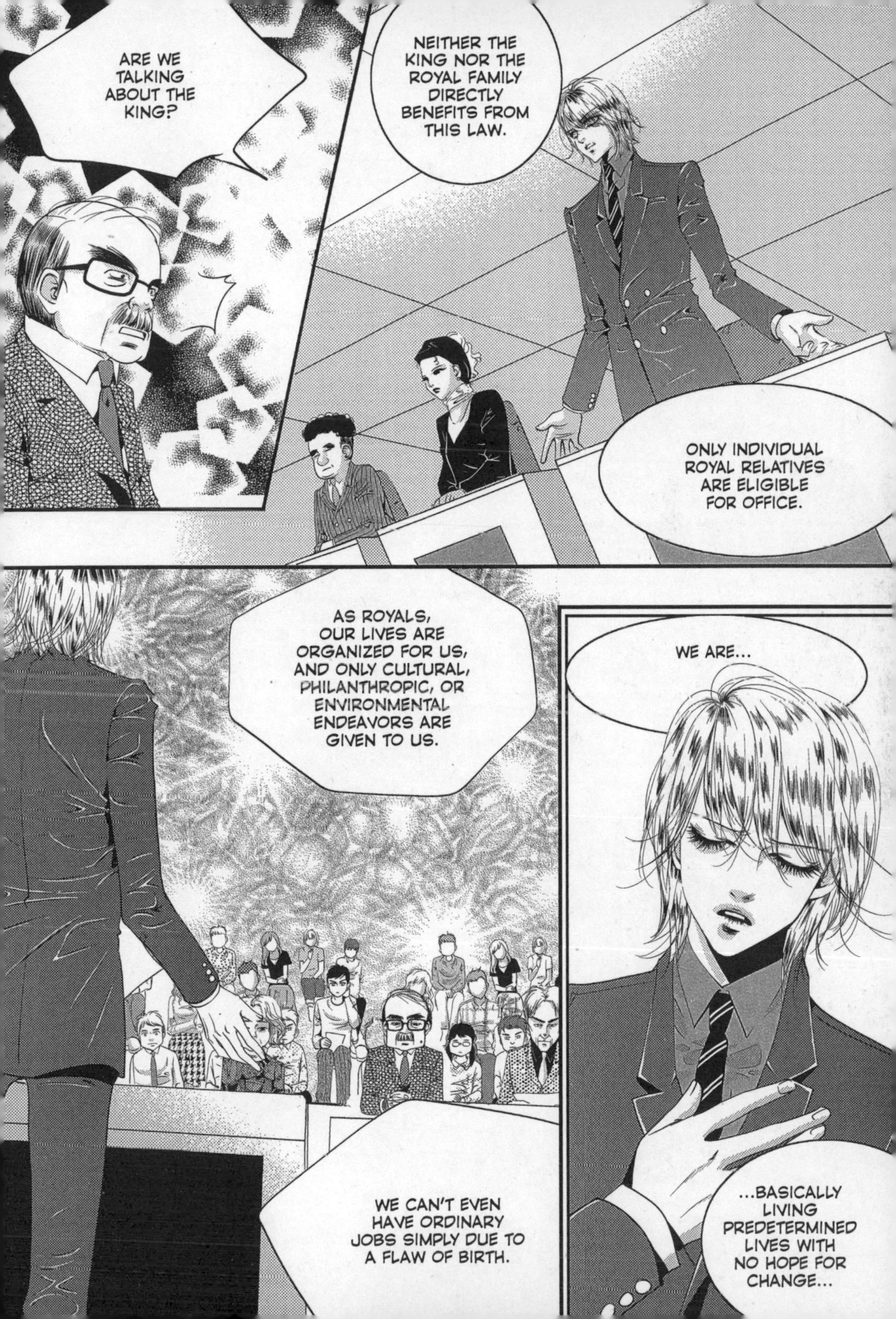
ARE WE TALKING ABOUT THE KING?
NEITHER THE KING NOR THE ROYAL FAMILY DIRECTLY BENEFITS FROM THIS LAW.
ONLY INDIVIDUAL ROYAL RELATIVES ARE ELIGIBLE FOR OFFICE.
AS ROYALS, OUR LIVES ARE ORGANIZED FOR US, AND ONLY CULTURAL, PHILANTHROPIC, OR ENVIRONMENTAL ENDEAVORS ARE GIVEN TO US.
WE CAN'T EVEN HAVE ORDINARY JOBS SIMPLY DUE TO A FLAW OF BIRTH.
WE ARE...
...BASICALLY LIVING PREDETERMINED LIVES WITH NO HOPE FOR CHANGE...

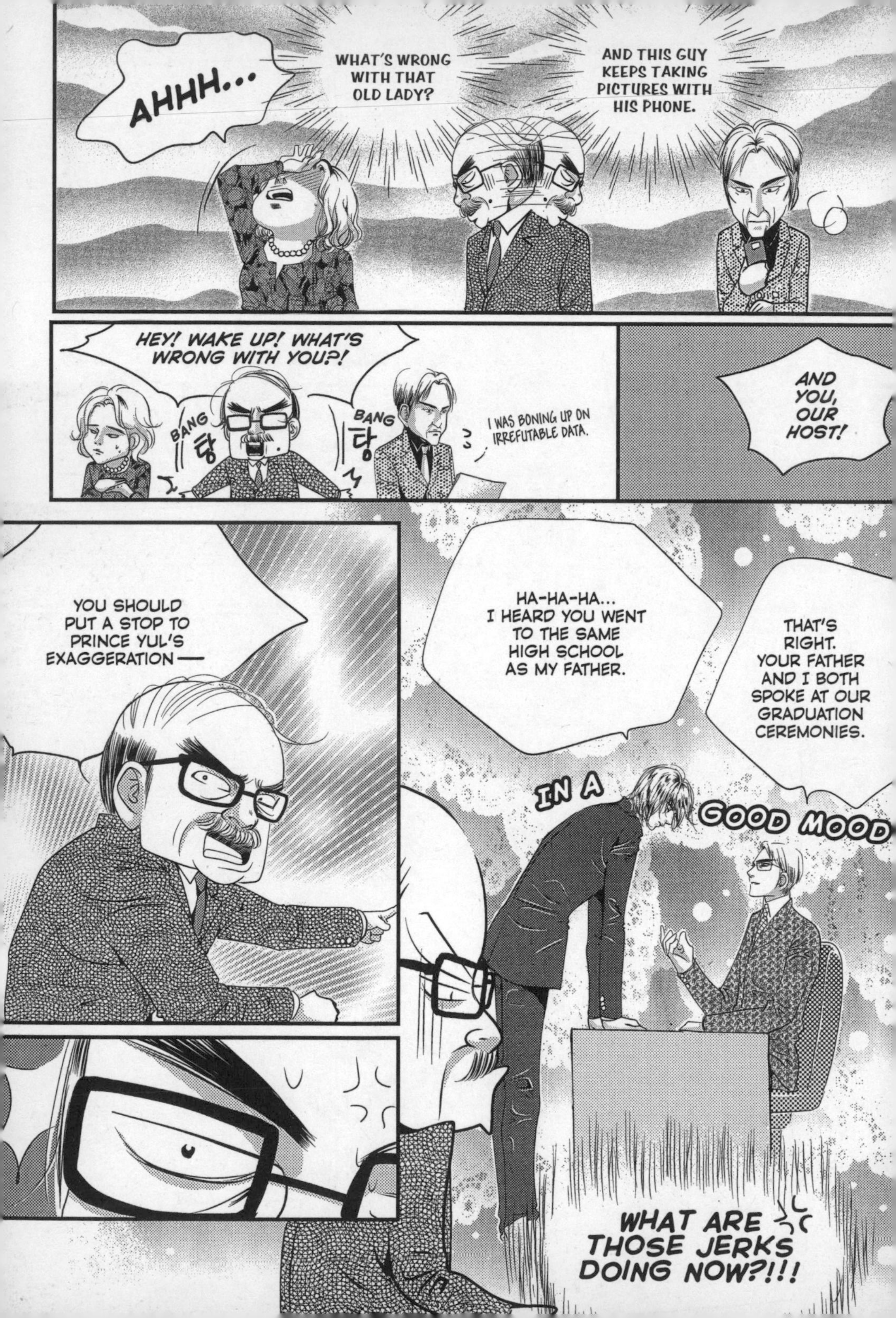
AHHH...
WHAT'S WRONG WITH THAT OLD LADY?
AND THIS GUY KEEPS TAKING PICTURES WITH HIS PHONE.
HEY! WAKE UP! WHAT'S WRONG WITH YOU?!
BANG 탕
BANG 탕
I WAS BONING UP ON IRREFUTABLE DATA.
AND YOU, OUR HOST!
YOU SHOULD PUT A STOP TO PRINCE YUL'S EXAGGERATION—
HA-HA-HA... I HEARD YOU WENT TO THE SAME HIGH SCHOOL AS MY FATHER.
THAT'S RIGHT. YOUR FATHER AND I BOTH SPOKE AT OUR GRADUATION CEREMONIES.
IN A GOOD MOOD
WHAT ARE THOSE JERKS DOING NOW?!!!

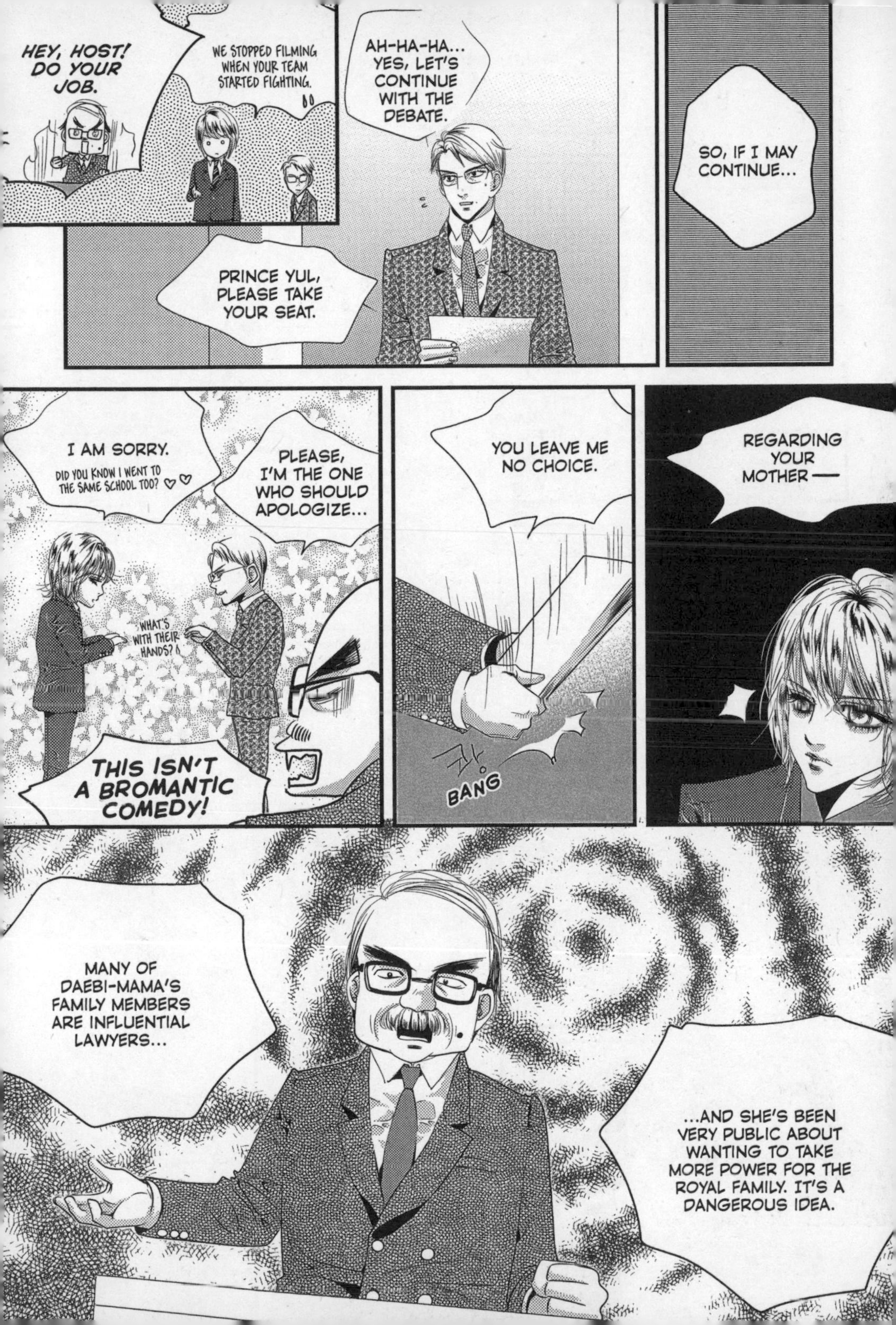
HEY, HOST! DO YOUR JOB.
WE STOPPED FILMING WHEN YOUR TEAM STARTED FIGHTING.
AH-HA-HA... YES, LET'S CONTINUE WITH THE DEBATE.
PRINCE YUL, PLEASE TAKE YOUR SEAT.
SO, IF I MAY CONTINUE...
I AM SORRY.
DID YOU KNOW I WENT TO THE SAME SCHOOL TOO?
PLEASE, I'M THE ONE WHO SHOULD APOLOGIZE...
WHAT'S WITH THEIR HANDS?
THIS ISN'T A BROMANTIC COMEDY!
YOU LEAVE ME NO CHOICE.
쾅
BANG
REGARDING YOUR MOTHER—
MANY OF DAEBI-MAMA'S FAMILY MEMBERS ARE INFLUENTIAL LAWYERS...
...AND SHE'S BEEN VERY PUBLIC ABOUT WANTING TO TAKE MORE POWER FOR THE ROYAL FAMILY. IT'S A DANGEROUS IDEA.

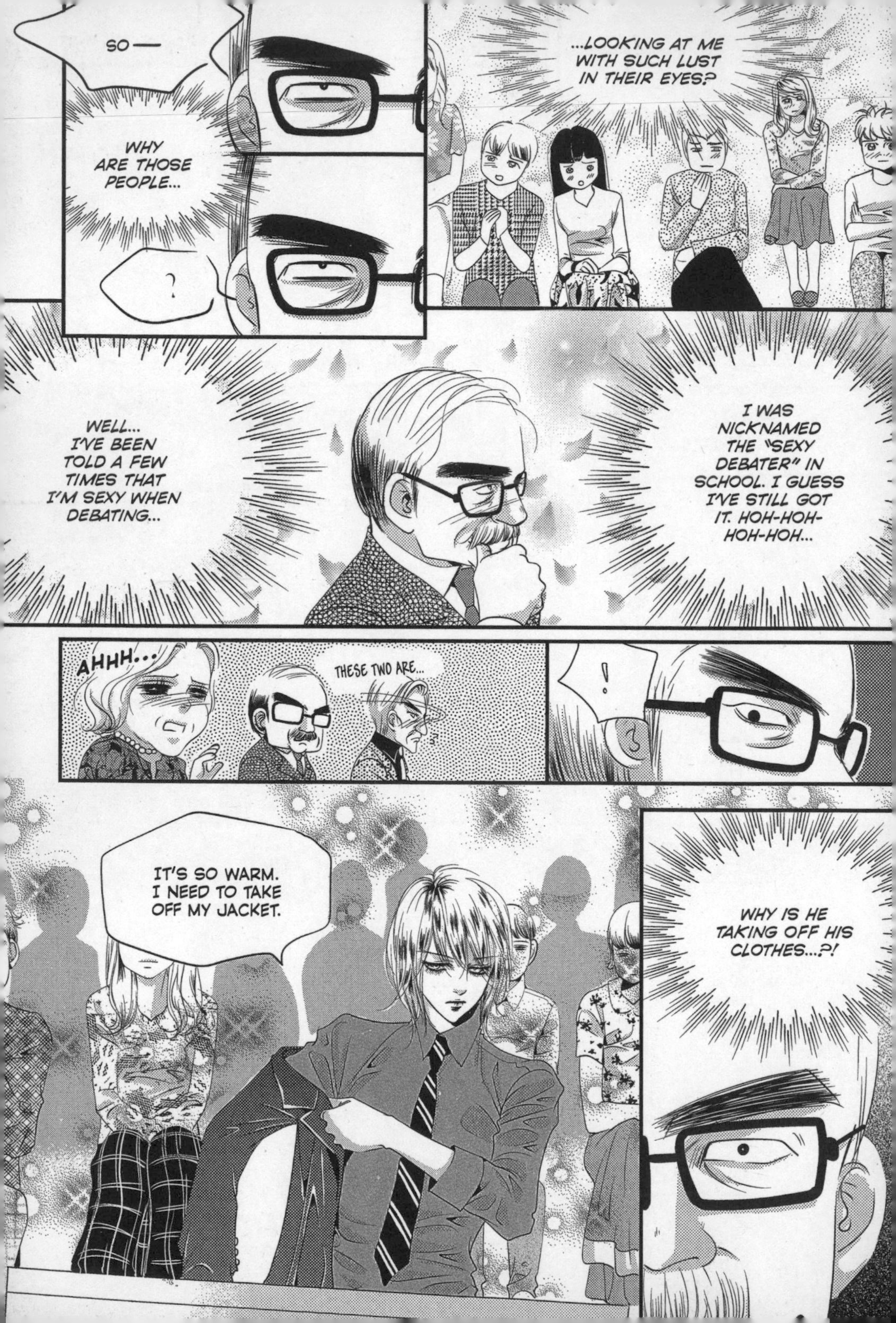
SO—
WHY ARE THOSE PEOPLE...
?
...LOOKING AT ME WITH SUCH LUST IN THEIR EYES?
WELL... I'VE BEEN TOLD A FEW TIMES THAT I'M SEXY WHEN DEBATING...
I WAS NICKNAMED THE "SEXY DEBATER" IN SCHOOL. I GUESS I'VE STILL GOT IT. HOH-HOH-HOH-HOH...
AHHH...
THESE TWO ARE...
!
IT'S SO WARM. I NEED TO TAKE OFF MY JACKET.
WHY IS HE TAKING OFF HIS CLOTHES...?!

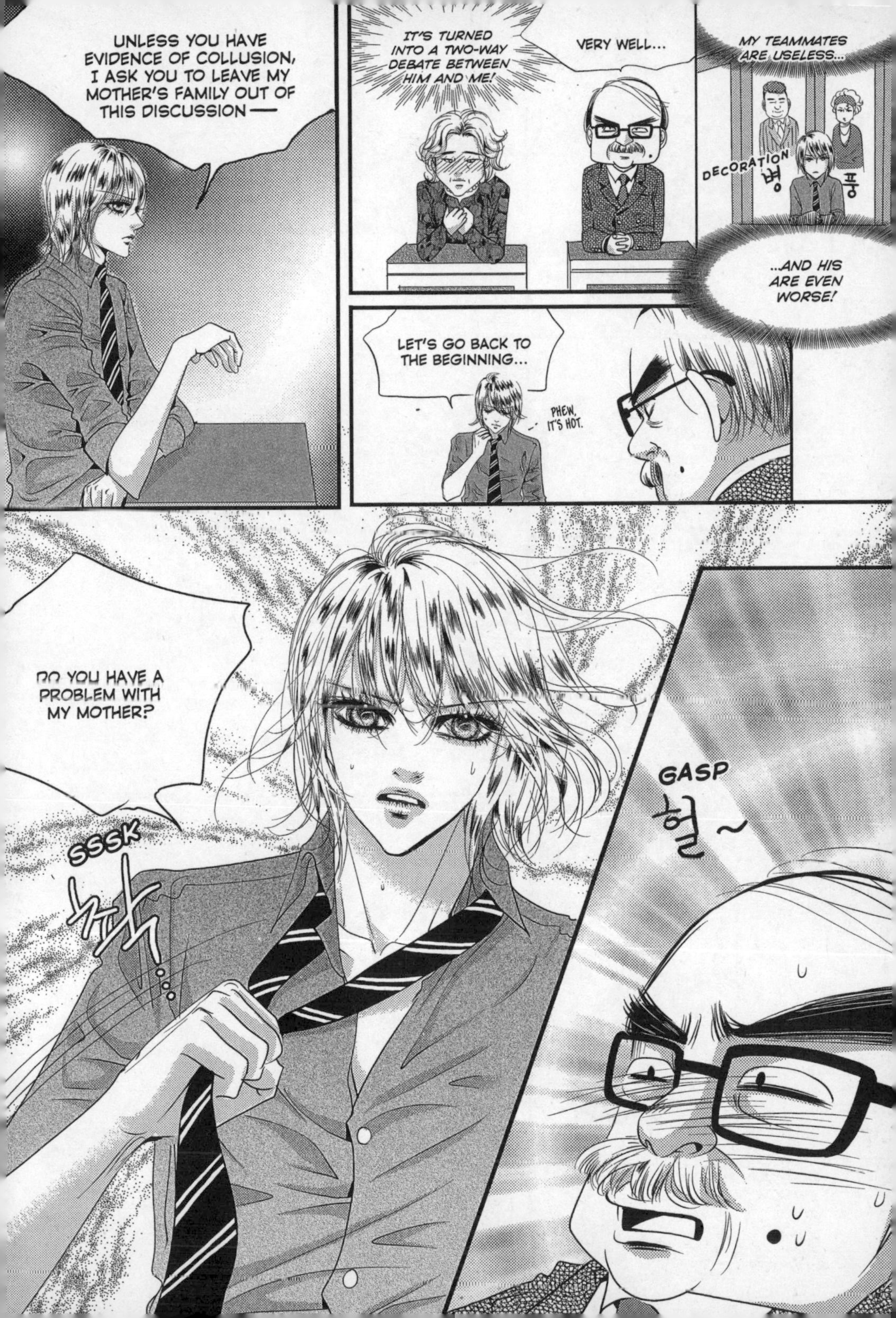
UNLESS YOU HAVE EVIDENCE OF COLLUSION, I ASK YOU TO LEAVE MY MOTHER'S FAMILY OUT OF THIS DISCUSSION—
IT'S TURNED INTO A TWO-WAY DEBATE BETWEEN HIM AND ME!
VERY WELL...
MY TEAMMATES ARE USELESS...
DECORATION
병
풍
...AND HIS ARE EVEN WORSE!
LET'S GO BACK TO THE BEGINNING...
PHEW, IT'S HOT.
DO YOU HAVE A PROBLEM WITH MY MOTHER?
SSSK
GASP
헐~

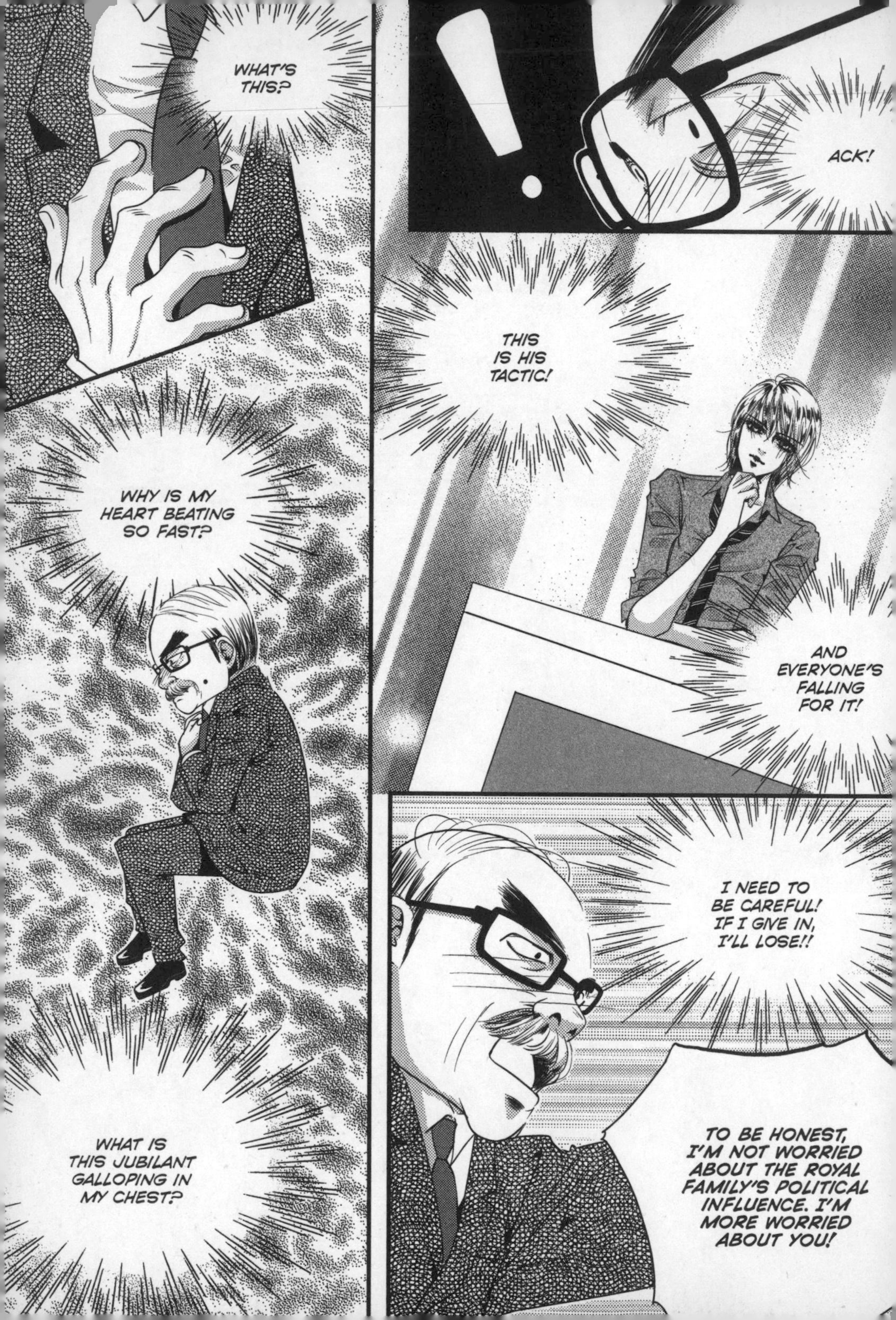
WHAT'S THIS?
ACK!
WHY IS MY HEART BEATING SO FAST?
WHAT IS THIS JUBILANT GALLOPING IN MY CHEST?
THIS IS HIS TACTIC!
AND EVERYONE'S FALLING FOR IT!
I NEED TO BE CAREFUL! IF I GIVE IN, I'LL LOSE!!
TO BE HONEST, I'M NOT WORRIED ABOUT THE ROYAL FAMILY'S POLITICAL INFLUENCE. I'M MORE WORRIED ABOUT YOU!

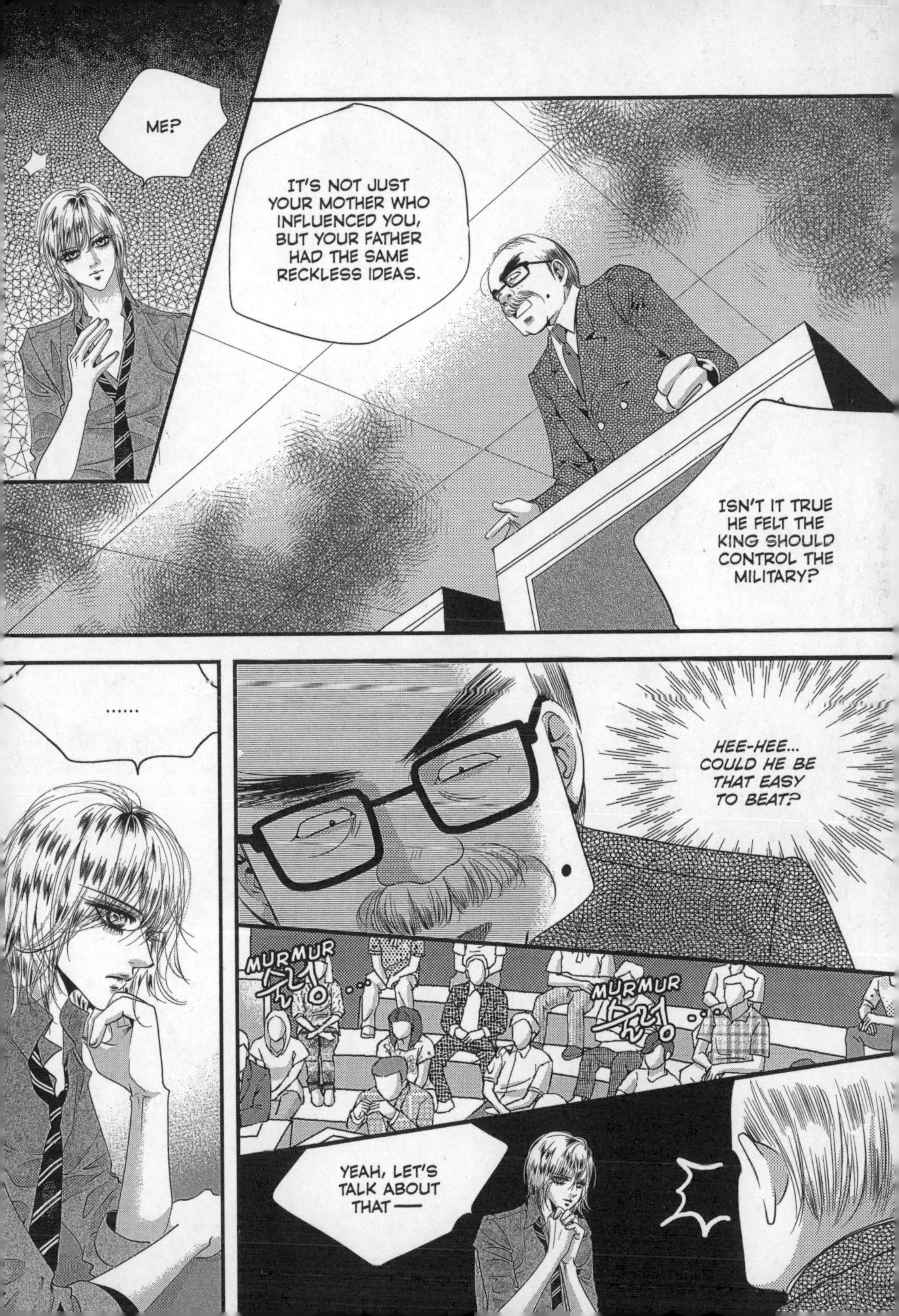
ME?
IT'S NOT JUST YOUR MOTHER WHO INFLUENCED YOU, BUT YOUR FATHER HAD THE SAME RECKLESS IDEAS.
ISN'T IT TRUE HE FELT THE KING SHOULD CONTROL THE MILITARY?
......
HEE-HEE... COULD HE BE THAT EASY TO BEAT?
MURMUR
MURMUR
YEAH, LET'S TALK ABOUT THAT—

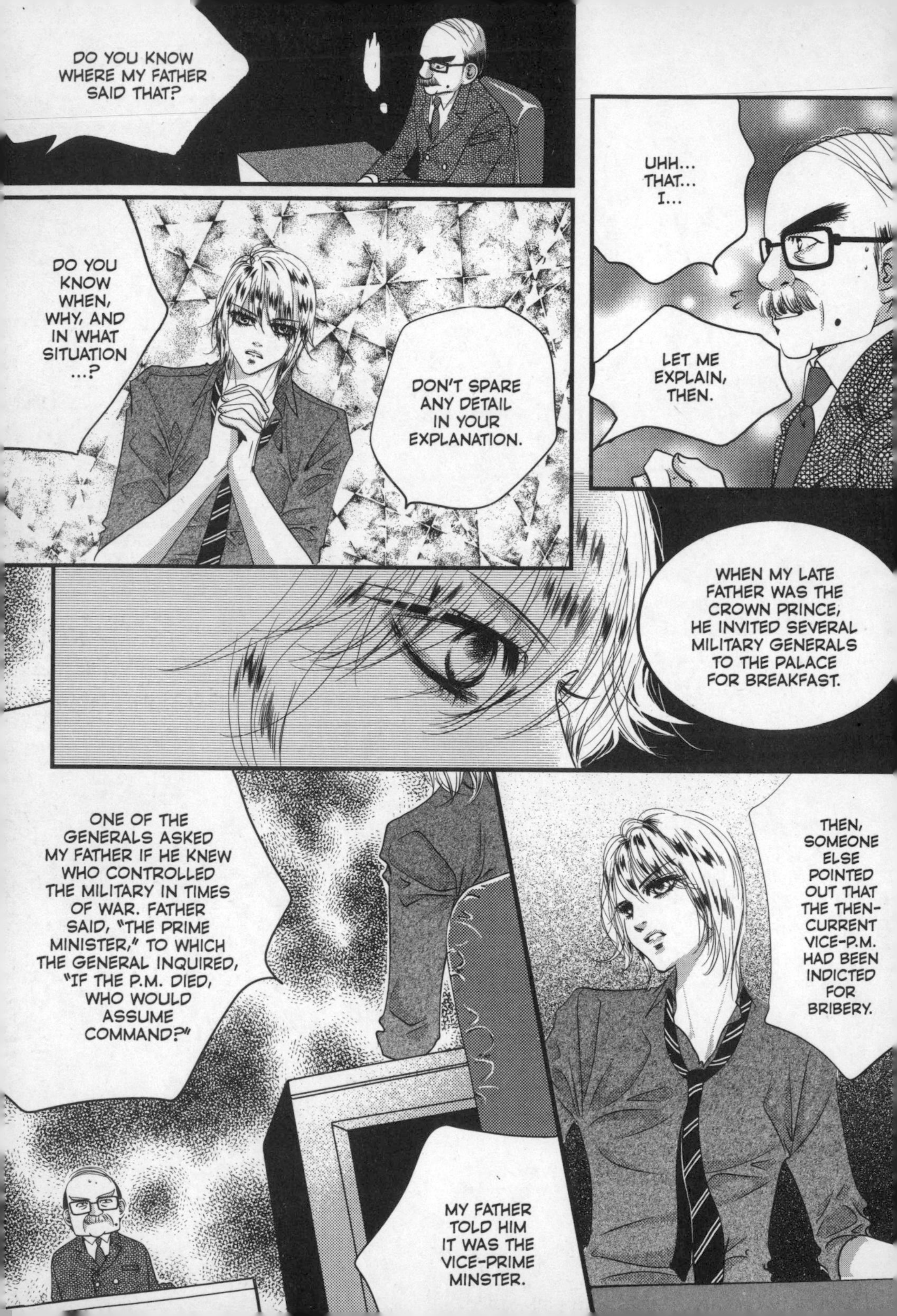
DO YOU KNOW WHERE MY FATHER SAID THAT?
DO YOU KNOW WHEN, WHY, AND IN WHAT SITUATION ...?
DON'T SPARE ANY DETAIL IN YOUR EXPLANATION.
UHH... THAT... I...
LET ME EXPLAIN, THEN.
WHEN MY LATE FATHER WAS THE CROWN PRINCE, HE INVITED SEVERAL MILITARY GENERALS TO THE PALACE FOR BREAKFAST.
ONE OF THE GENERALS ASKED MY FATHER IF HE KNEW WHO CONTROLLED THE MILITARY IN TIMES OF WAR. FATHER SAID, "THE PRIME MINISTER," TO WHICH THE GENERAL INQUIRED, "IF THE P.M. DIED, WHO WOULD ASSUME COMMAND?"
THEN, SOMEONE ELSE POINTED OUT THAT THE THEN-CURRENT VICE-P.M. HAD BEEN INDICTED FOR BRIBERY.
MY FATHER TOLD HIM IT WAS THE VICE-PRIME MINSTER.

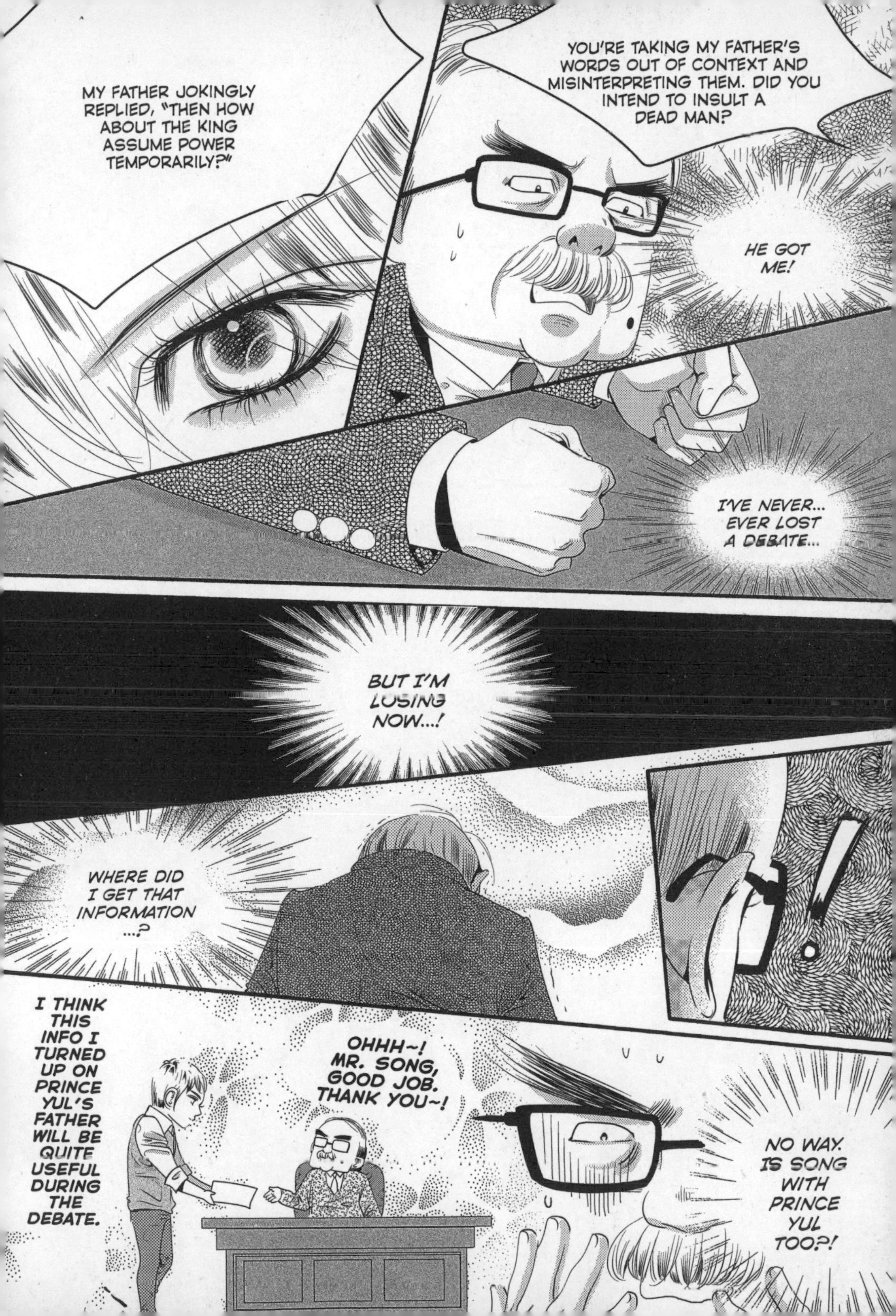
MY FATHER JOKINGLY REPLIED, "THEN HOW ABOUT THE KING ASSUME POWER TEMPORARILY?"
YOU'RE TAKING MY FATHER'S WORDS OUT OF CONTEXT AND MISINTERPRETING THEM. DID YOU INTEND TO INSULT A DEAD MAN?
HE GOT ME!
I'VE NEVER... EVER LOST A DEBATE...
BUT I'M LOSING NOW...!
WHERE DID I GET THAT INFORMATION ...?
I THINK THIS INFO I TURNED UP ON PRINCE YUL'S FATHER WILL BE QUITE USEFUL DURING THE DEBATE.
OHHH~! MR. SONG, GOOD JOB. THANK YOU~!
NO WAY. IS SONG WITH PRINCE YUL TOO?!

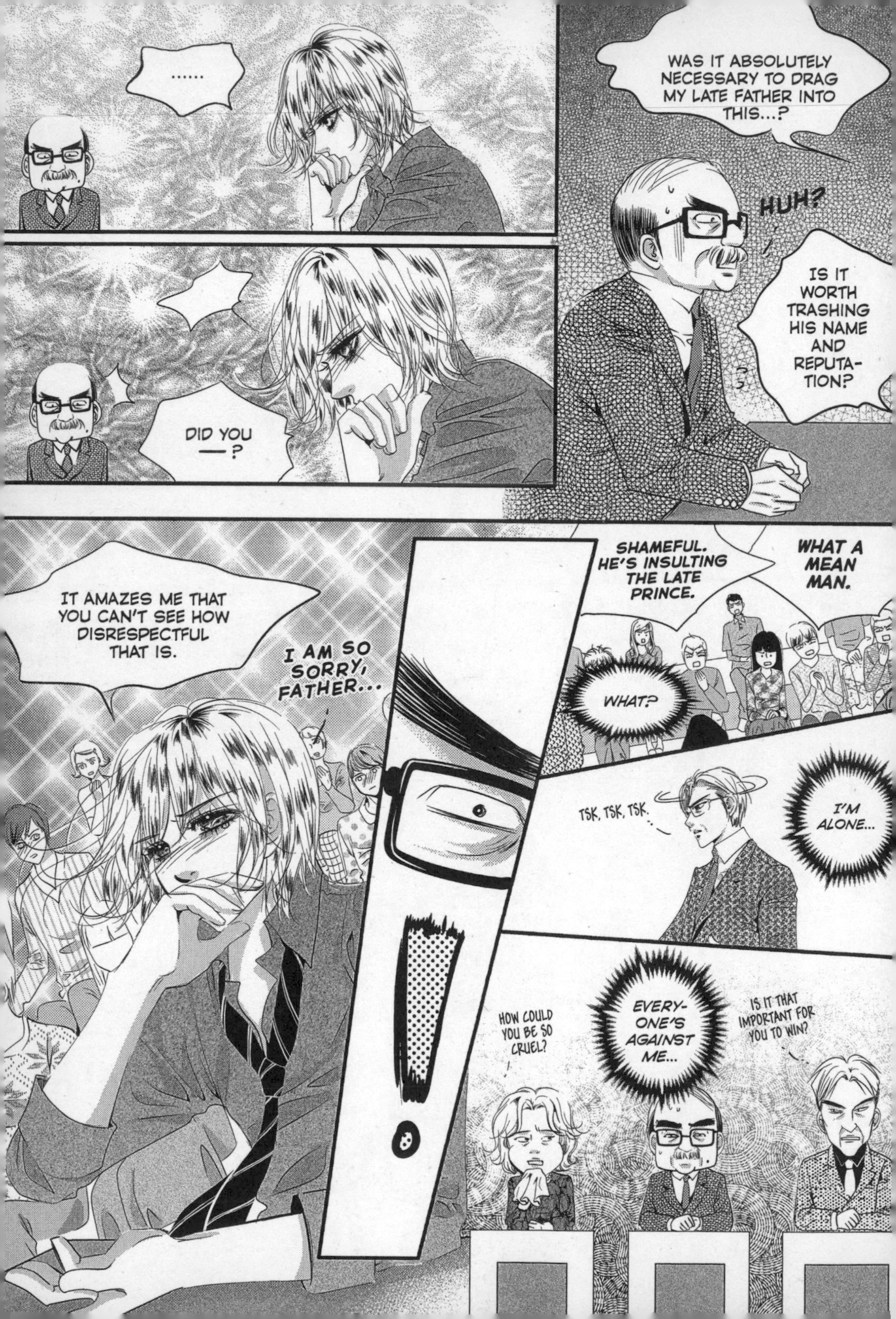
......
DID YOU —?
WAS IT ABSOLUTELY NECESSARY TO DRAG MY LATE FATHER INTO THIS...?
HUH?
IS IT WORTH TRASHING HIS NAME AND REPUTATION?
IT AMAZES ME THAT YOU CAN'T SEE HOW DISRESPECTFUL THAT IS.
I AM SO SORRY, FATHER...
SHAMEFUL. HE'S INSULTING THE LATE PRINCE.
WHAT A MEAN MAN.
WHAT?
TSK, TSK, TSK.
I'M ALONE...
HOW COULD YOU BE SO CRUEL?
EVERYONE'S AGAINST ME...
IS IT THAT IMPORTANT FOR YOU TO WIN?

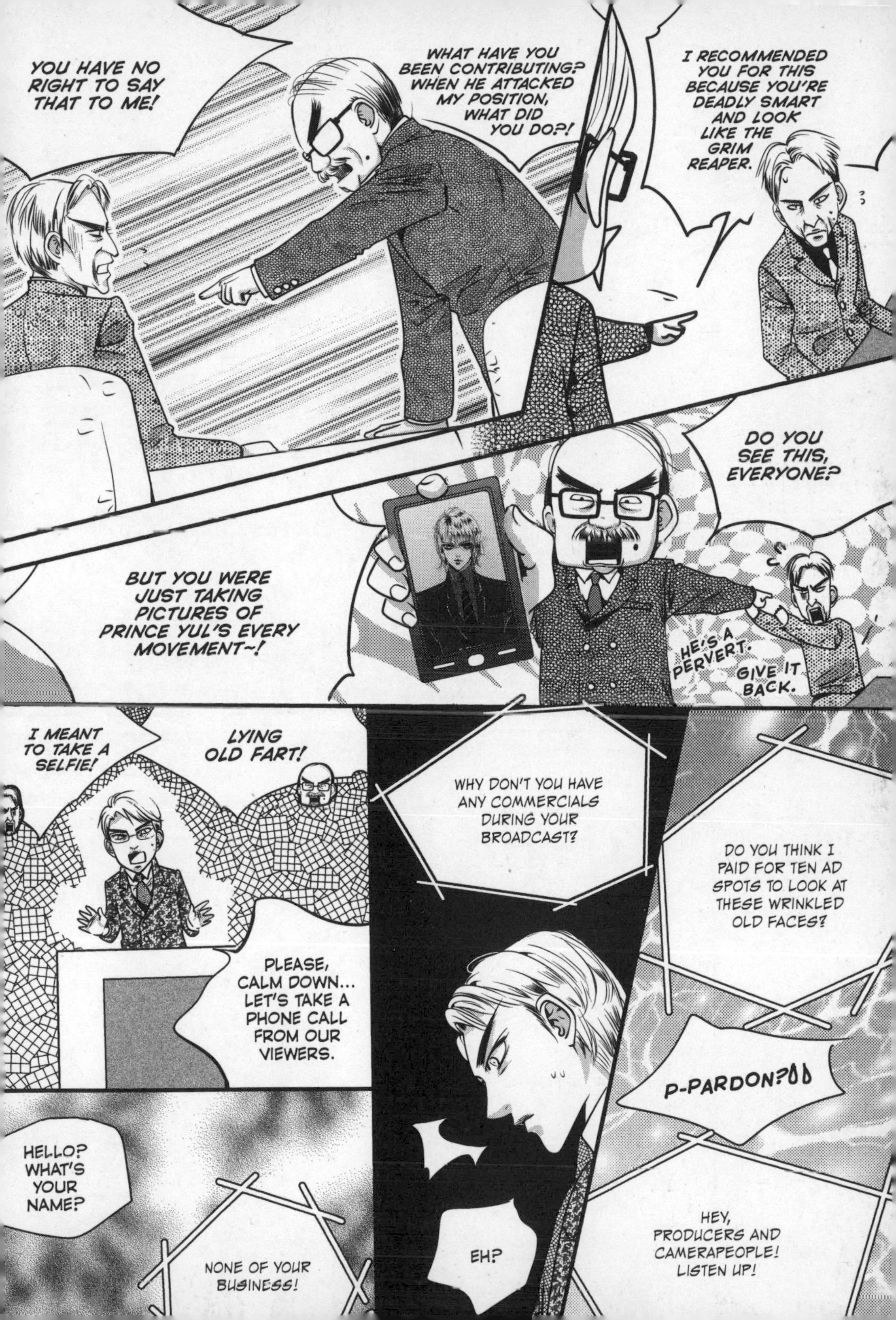

YOU HAVE NO RIGHT TO SAY THAT TO ME!
WHAT HAVE YOU BEEN CONTRIBUTING? WHEN HE ATTACKED MY POSITION, WHAT DID YOU DO?!
I RECOMMENDED YOU FOR THIS BECAUSE YOU'RE DEADLY SMART AND LOOK LIKE THE GRIM REAPER.
BUT YOU WERE JUST TAKING PICTURES OF PRINCE YUL'S EVERY MOVEMENT~!
DO YOU SEE THIS, EVERYONE?
HE'S A PERVERT.
GIVE IT BACK.
I MEANT TO TAKE A SELFIE!
LYING OLD FART!
PLEASE, CALM DOWN... LET'S TAKE A PHONE CALL FROM OUR VIEWERS.
WHY DON'T YOU HAVE ANY COMMERCIALS DURING YOUR BROADCAST?
DO YOU THINK I PAID FOR TEN AD SPOTS TO LOOK AT THESE WRINKLED OLD FACES?
P-PARDON?
HELLO? WHAT'S YOUR NAME?
NONE OF YOUR BUSINESS!
EH?
HEY, PRODUCERS AND CAMERAPEOPLE! LISTEN UP!

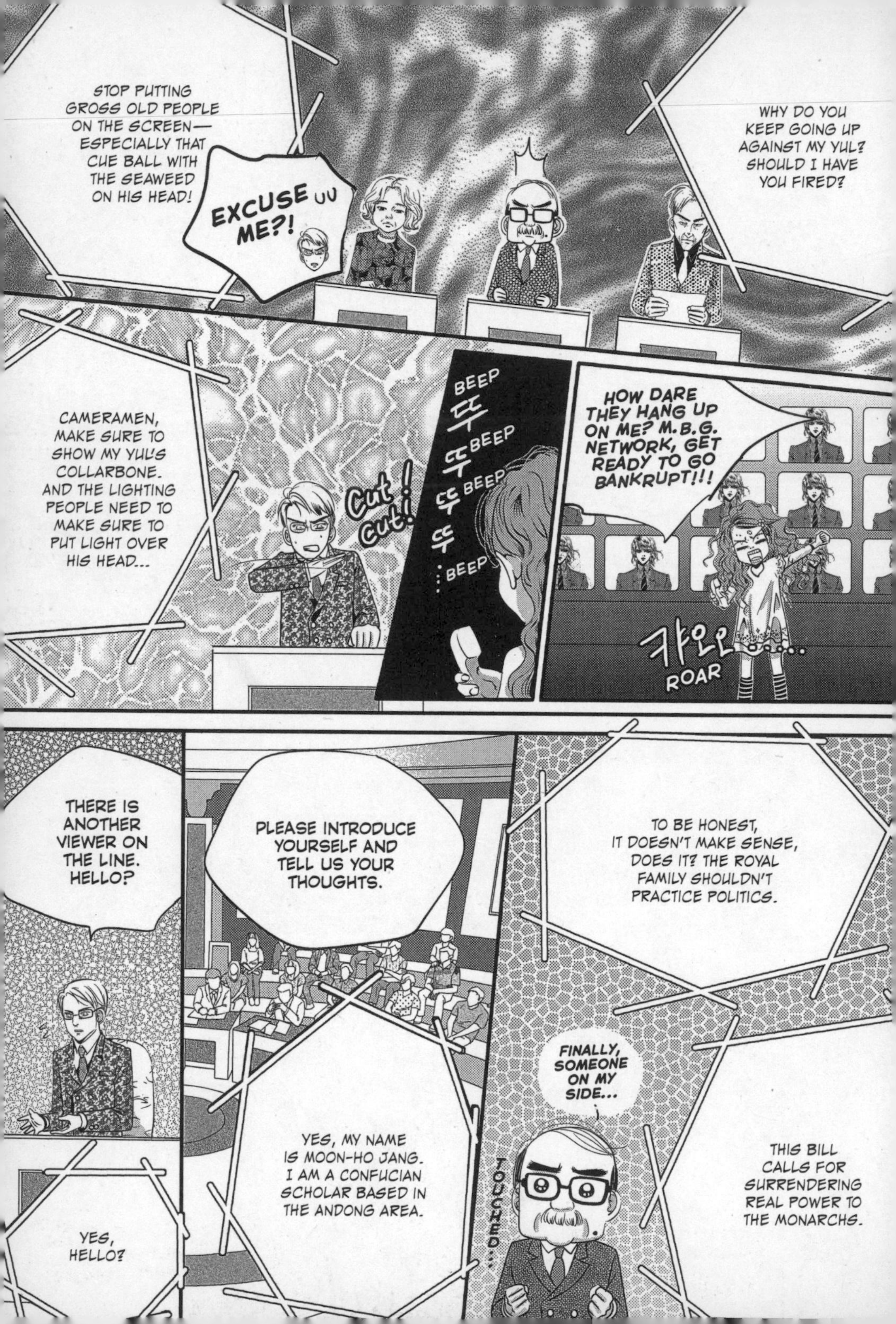
STOP PUTTING GROSS OLD PEOPLE ON THE SCREEN—ESPECIALLY THAT CUE BALL WITH THE SEAWEED ON HIS HEAD!
EXCUSE ME?!
WHY DO YOU KEEP GOING UP AGAINST MY YUL? SHOULD I HAVE YOU FIRED?
CAMERAMEN, MAKE SURE TO SHOW MY YUL'S COLLARBONE. AND THE LIGHTING PEOPLE NEED TO MAKE SURE TO PUT LIGHT OVER HIS HEAD...
Cut! cut!
뚜 BEEP
뚜 BEEP
뚜 BEEP
뚜 BEEP
HOW DARE THEY HANG UP ON ME? M.B.G. NETWORK, GET READY TO GO BANKRUPT!!!
캬오오...
ROAR
THERE IS ANOTHER VIEWER ON THE LINE. HELLO?
YES, HELLO?
PLEASE INTRODUCE YOURSELF AND TELL US YOUR THOUGHTS.
YES, MY NAME IS MOON-HO JANG. I AM A CONFUCIAN SCHOLAR BASED IN THE ANDONG AREA.
TO BE HONEST, IT DOESN'T MAKE SENSE, DOES IT? THE ROYAL FAMILY SHOULDN'T PRACTICE POLITICS.
FINALLY, SOMEONE ON MY SIDE...
TOUCHED...
THIS BILL CALLS FOR SURRENDERING REAL POWER TO THE MONARCHS.

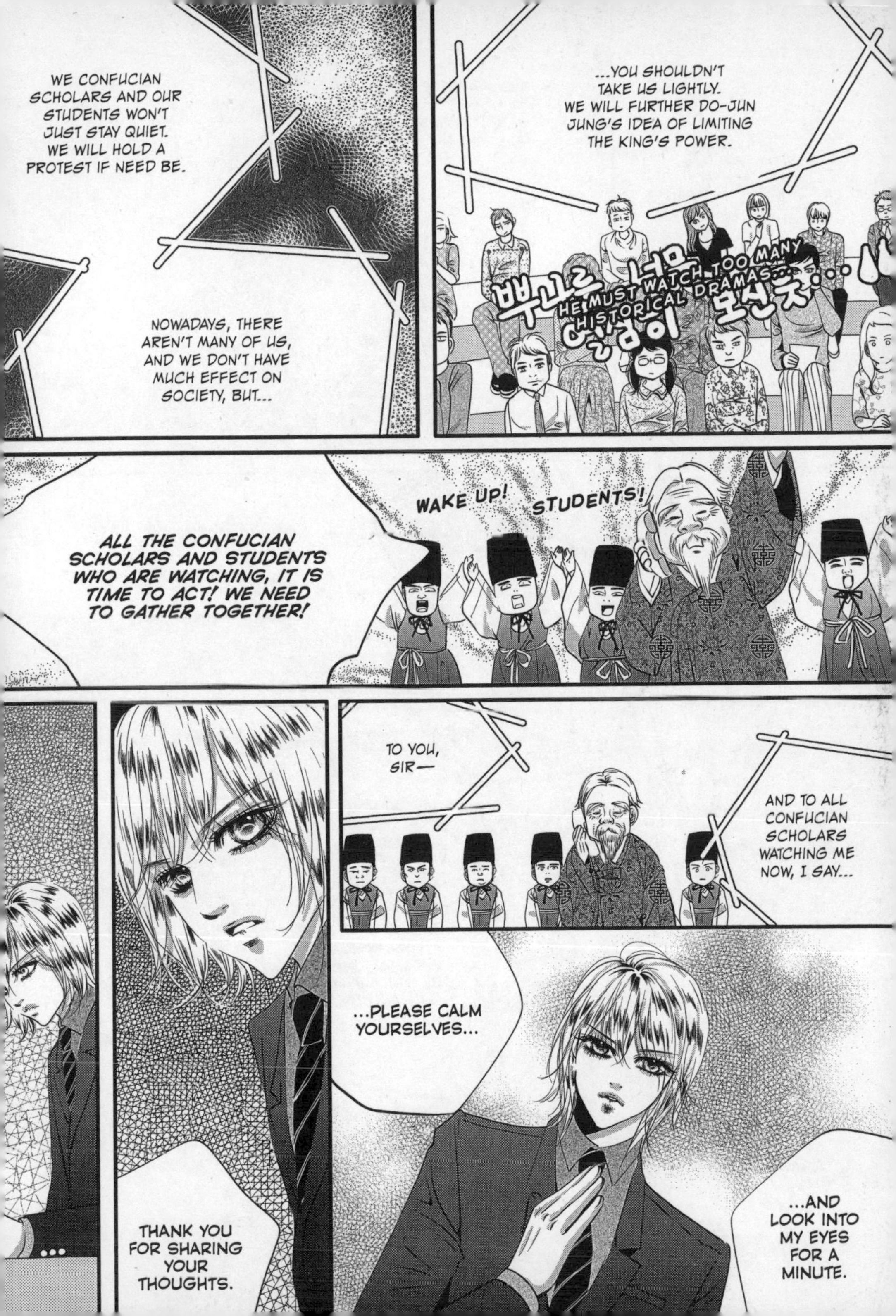
WE CONFUCIAN SCHOLARS AND OUR STUDENTS WON'T JUST STAY QUIET. WE WILL HOLD A PROTEST IF NEED BE.
NOWADAYS, THERE AREN'T MANY OF US, AND WE DON'T HAVE MUCH EFFECT ON SOCIETY, BUT...
...YOU SHOULDN'T TAKE US LIGHTLY. WE WILL FURTHER DO-JUN JUNG'S IDEA OF LIMITING THE KING'S POWER.
HE MUST WATCH TOO MANY HISTORICAL DRAMAS...
ALL THE CONFUCIAN SCHOLARS AND STUDENTS WHO ARE WATCHING, IT IS TIME TO ACT! WE NEED TO GATHER TOGETHER!
WAKE UP!
STUDENTS!
...
THANK YOU FOR SHARING YOUR THOUGHTS.
TO YOU, SIR—
AND TO ALL CONFUCIAN SCHOLARS WATCHING ME NOW, I SAY...
...PLEASE CALM YOURSELVES...
...AND LOOK INTO MY EYES FOR A MINUTE.

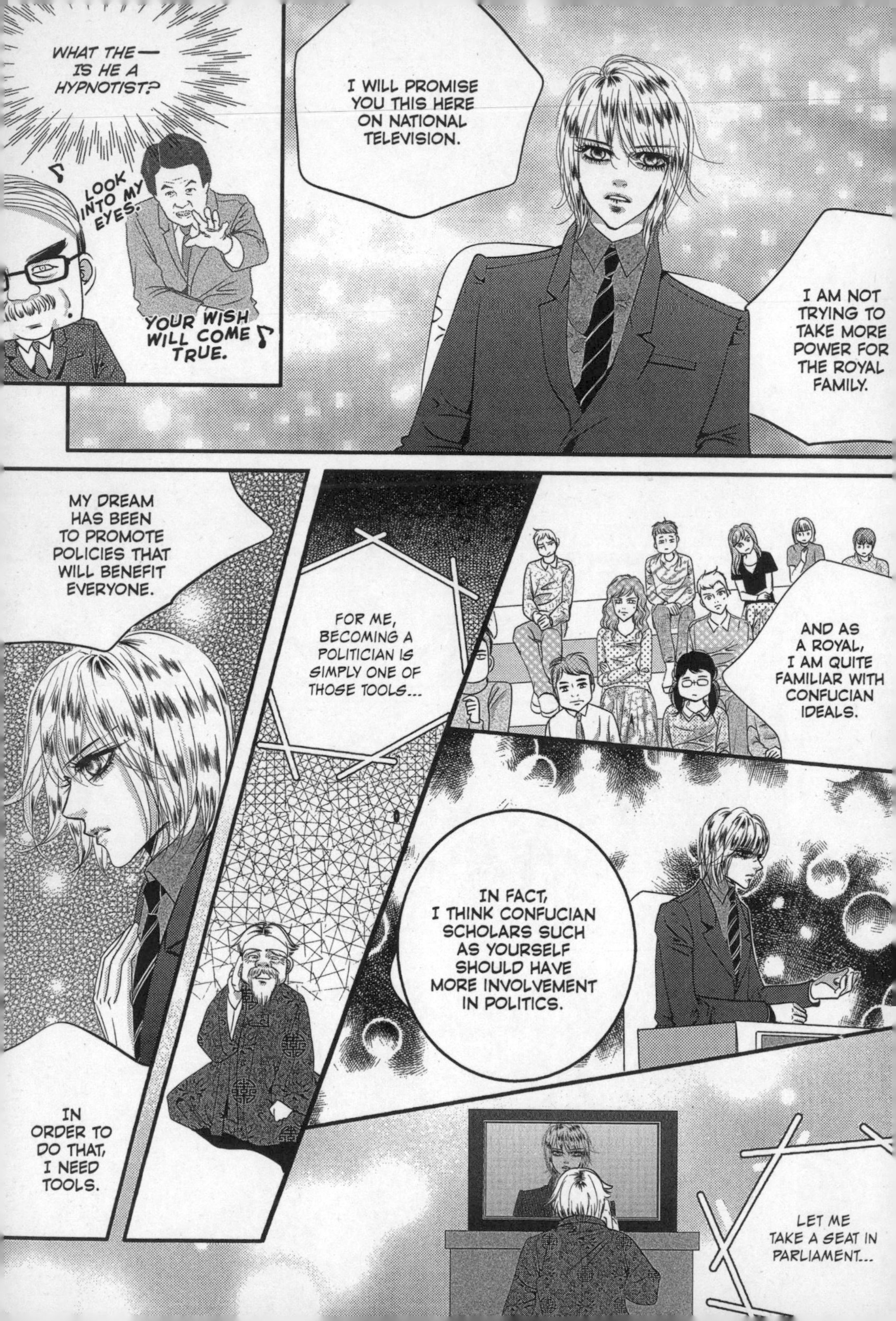
WHAT THE— IS HE A HYPNOTIST?
LOOK INTO MY EYES.
YOUR WISH WILL COME TRUE.
I WILL PROMISE YOU THIS HERE ON NATIONAL TELEVISION.
I AM NOT TRYING TO TAKE MORE POWER FOR THE ROYAL FAMILY.
MY DREAM HAS BEEN TO PROMOTE POLICIES THAT WILL BENEFIT EVERYONE.
IN ORDER TO DO THAT, I NEED TOOLS.
FOR ME, BECOMING A POLITICIAN IS SIMPLY ONE OF THOSE TOOLS...
AND AS A ROYAL, I AM QUITE FAMILIAR WITH CONFUCIAN IDEALS.
IN FACT, I THINK CONFUCIAN SCHOLARS SUCH AS YOURSELF SHOULD HAVE MORE INVOLVEMENT IN POLITICS.
LET ME TAKE A SEAT IN PARLIAMENT...

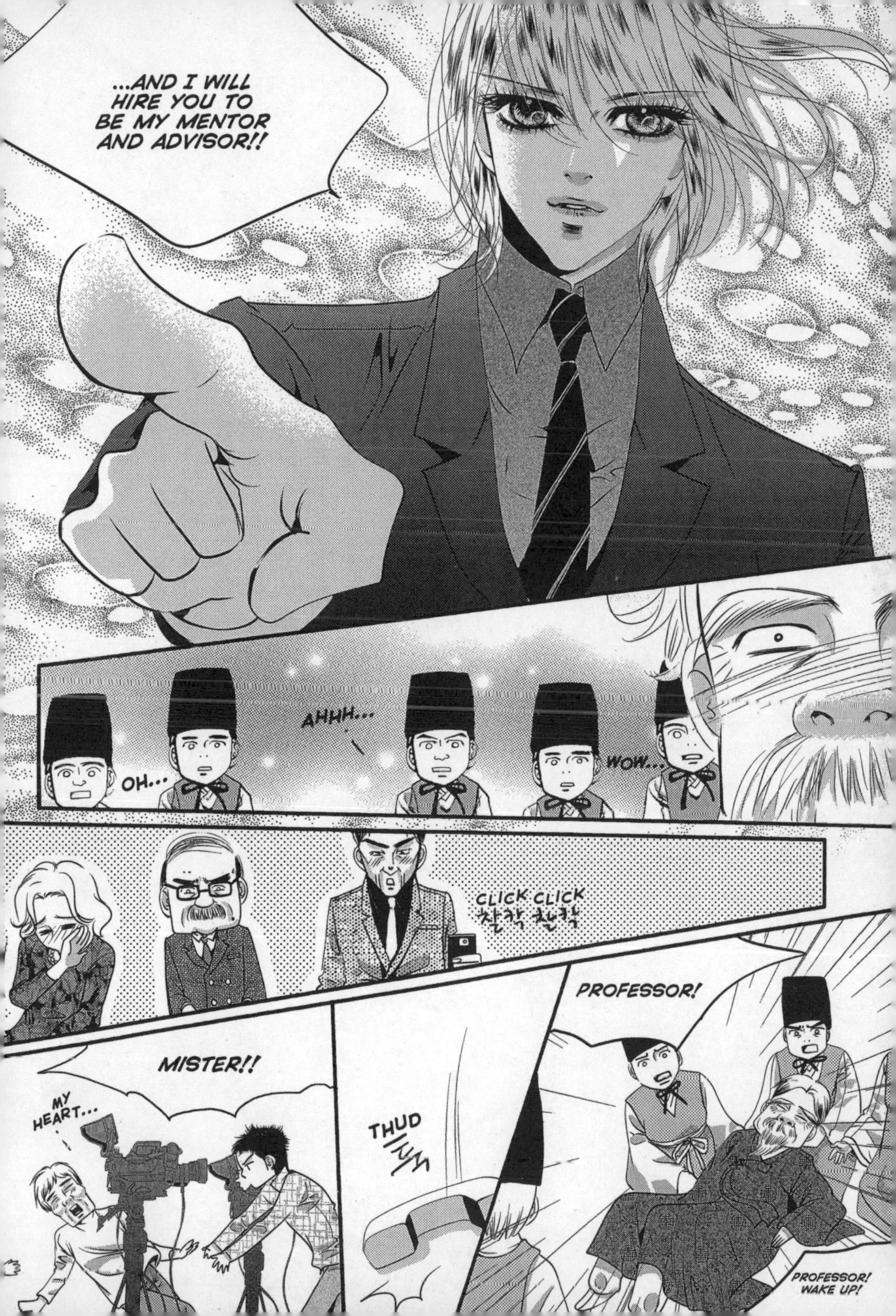
...AND I WILL HIRE YOU TO BE MY MENTOR AND ADVISOR!!
OH...
AHHH...
WOW...
CLICK CLICK
찰칵 찰칵
MISTER!!
MY HEART...
THUD
PROFESSOR!
PROFESSOR! WAKE UP!

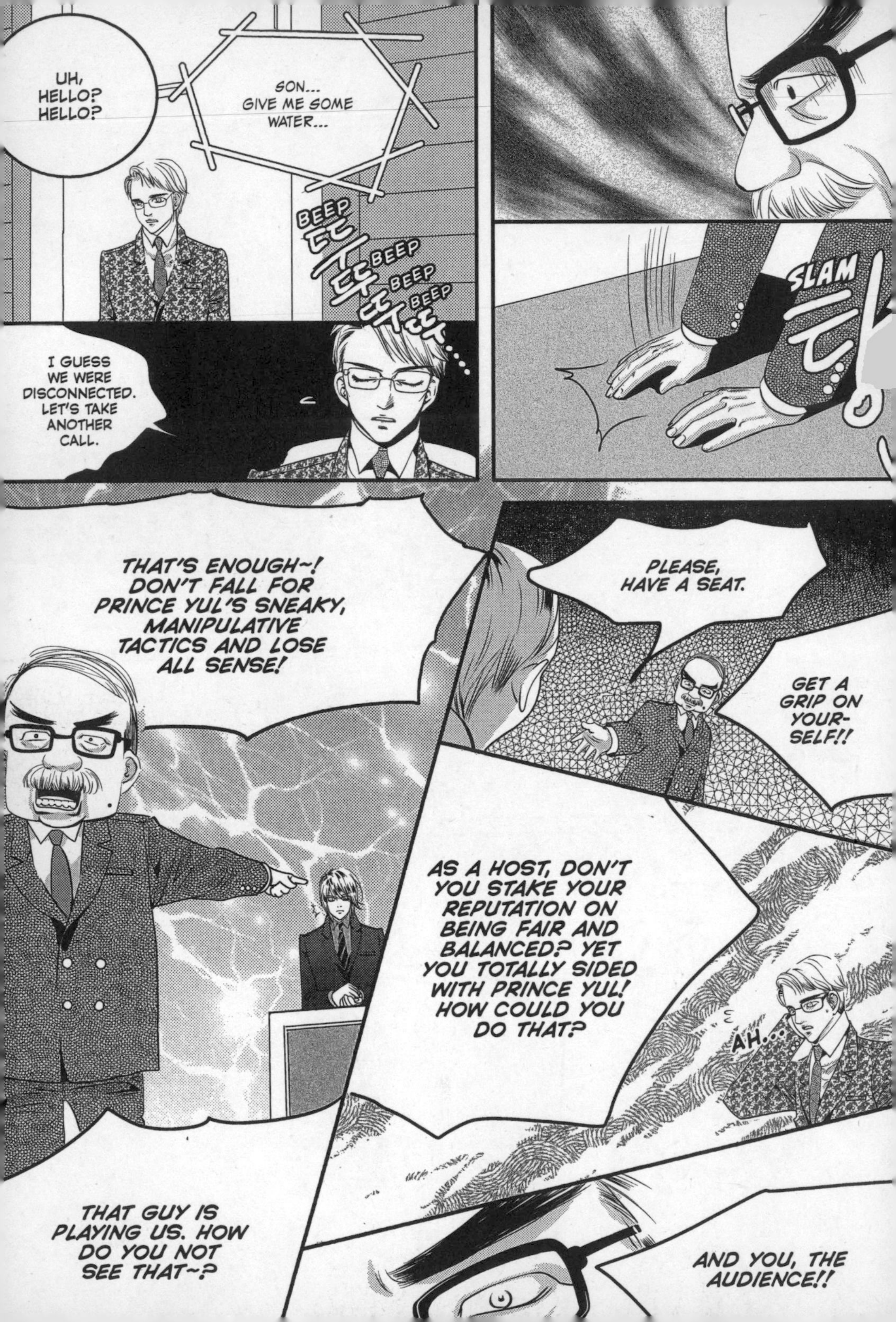
UH, HELLO? HELLO?
SON... GIVE ME SOME WATER...
BEEP
BEEP
BEEP
BEEP
I GUESS WE WERE DISCONNECTED. LET'S TAKE ANOTHER CALL.
SLAM
THAT'S ENOUGH~! DON'T FALL FOR PRINCE YUL'S SNEAKY, MANIPULATIVE TACTICS AND LOSE ALL SENSE!
THAT GUY IS PLAYING US. HOW DO YOU NOT SEE THAT~?
PLEASE, HAVE A SEAT.
GET A GRIP ON YOURSELF!!
AS A HOST, DON'T YOU STAKE YOUR REPUTATION ON BEING FAIR AND BALANCED? YET YOU TOTALLY SIDED WITH PRINCE YUL! HOW COULD YOU DO THAT?
AH...
AND YOU, THE AUDIENCE!!

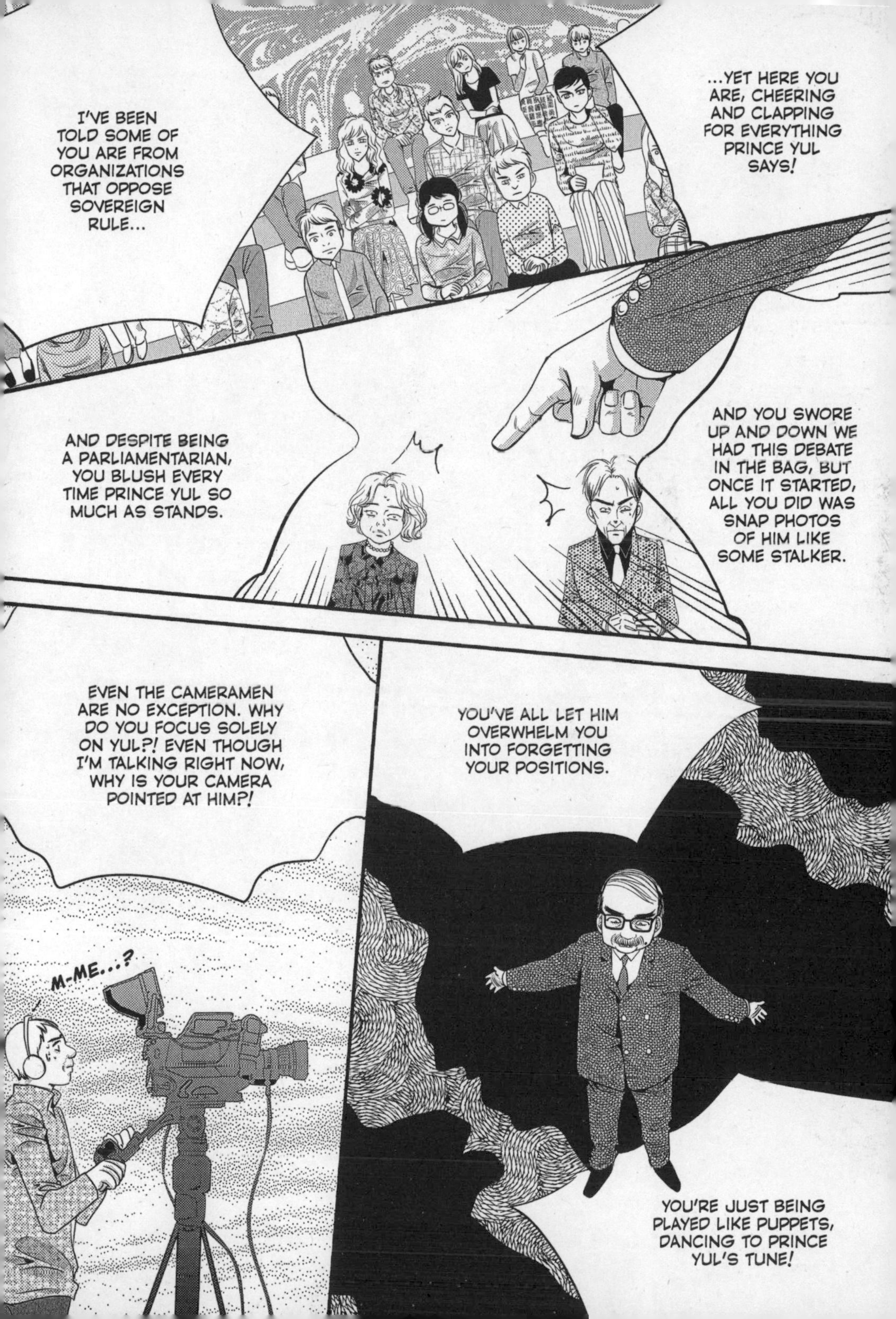
I'VE BEEN TOLD SOME OF YOU ARE FROM ORGANIZATIONS THAT OPPOSE SOVEREIGN RULE...
...YET HERE YOU ARE, CHEERING AND CLAPPING FOR EVERYTHING PRINCE YUL SAYS!
AND DESPITE BEING A PARLIAMENTARIAN, YOU BLUSH EVERY TIME PRINCE YUL SO MUCH AS STANDS.
AND YOU SWORE UP AND DOWN WE HAD THIS DEBATE IN THE BAG, BUT ONCE IT STARTED, ALL YOU DID WAS SNAP PHOTOS OF HIM LIKE SOME STALKER.
EVEN THE CAMERAMEN ARE NO EXCEPTION. WHY DO YOU FOCUS SOLELY ON YUL?! EVEN THOUGH I'M TALKING RIGHT NOW, WHY IS YOUR CAMERA POINTED AT HIM?!
M-ME...?
YOU'VE ALL LET HIM OVERWHELM YOU INTO FORGETTING YOUR POSITIONS.
YOU'RE JUST BEING PLAYED LIKE PUPPETS, DANCING TO PRINCE YUL'S TUNE!

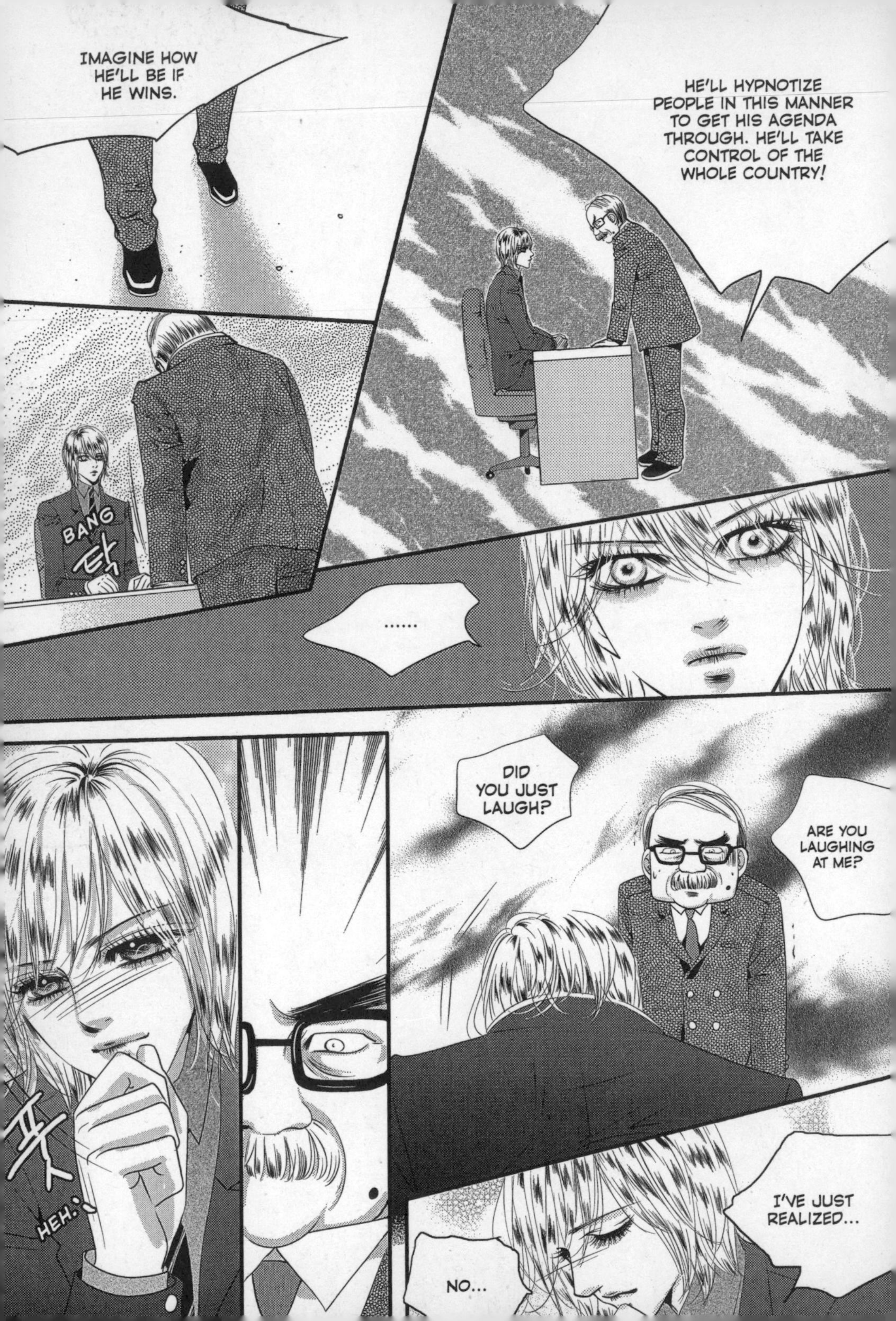
IMAGINE HOW HE'LL BE IF HE WINS.
HE'LL HYPNOTIZE PEOPLE IN THIS MANNER TO GET HIS AGENDA THROUGH. HE'LL TAKE CONTROL OF THE WHOLE COUNTRY!
BANG
탁
......
HEH.
DID YOU JUST LAUGH?
ARE YOU LAUGHING AT ME?
NO...
I'VE JUST REALIZED...

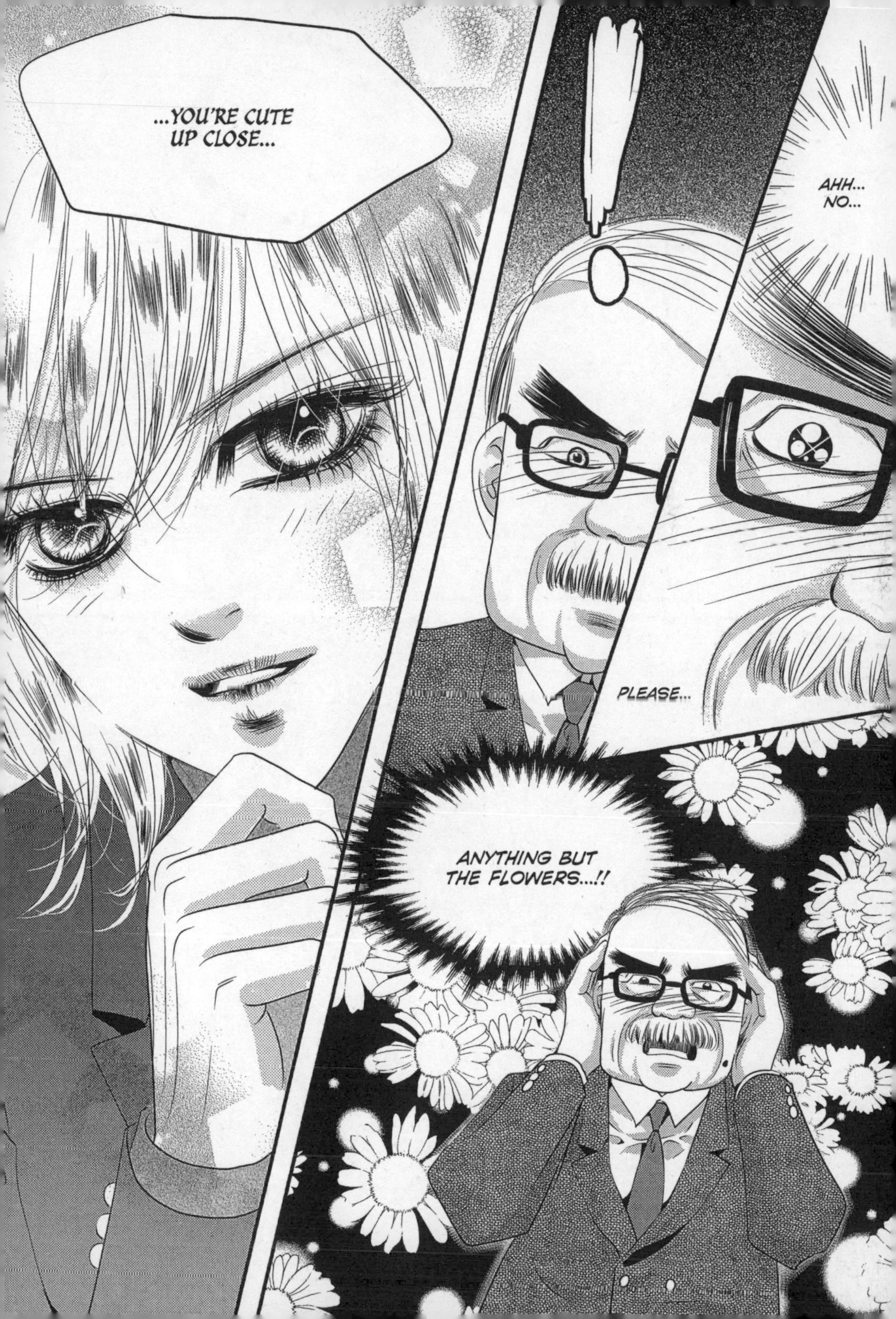
...YOU'RE CUTE UP CLOSE...
!
AHH... NO...
PLEASE...
ANYTHING BUT THE FLOWERS...!!

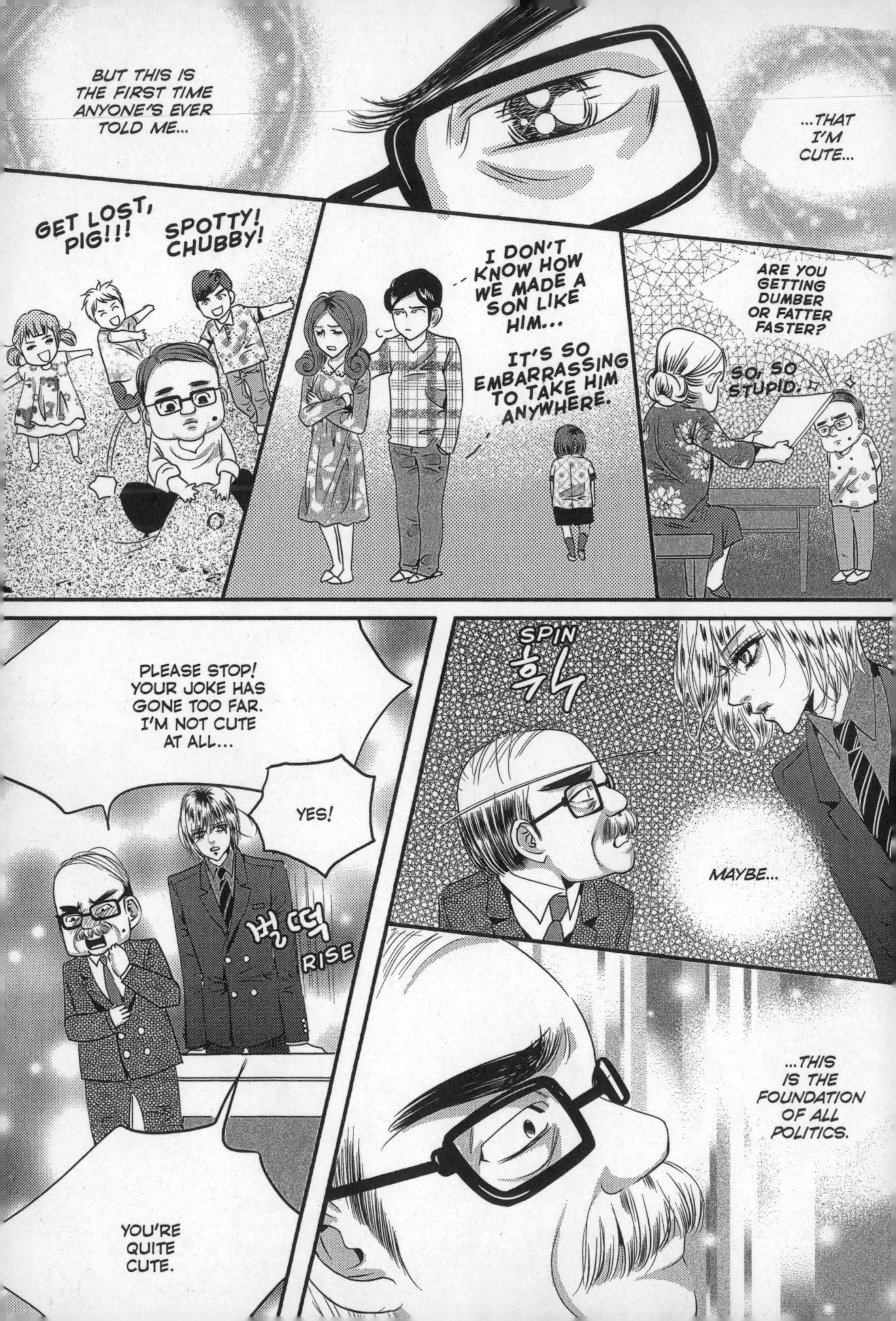
BUT THIS IS THE FIRST TIME ANYONE'S EVER TOLD ME...
...THAT I'M CUTE...
GET LOST, PIG!!!
SPOTTY! CHUBBY!
I DON'T KNOW HOW WE MADE A SON LIKE HIM...
IT'S SO EMBARRASSING TO TAKE HIM ANYWHERE.
ARE YOU GETTING DUMBER OR FATTER FASTER?
SO, SO STUPID.
PLEASE STOP! YOUR JOKE HAS GONE TOO FAR. I'M NOT CUTE AT ALL...
YES!
벌떡
RISE
YOU'RE QUITE CUTE.
SPIN
MAYBE...
...THIS IS THE FOUNDATION OF ALL POLITICS.

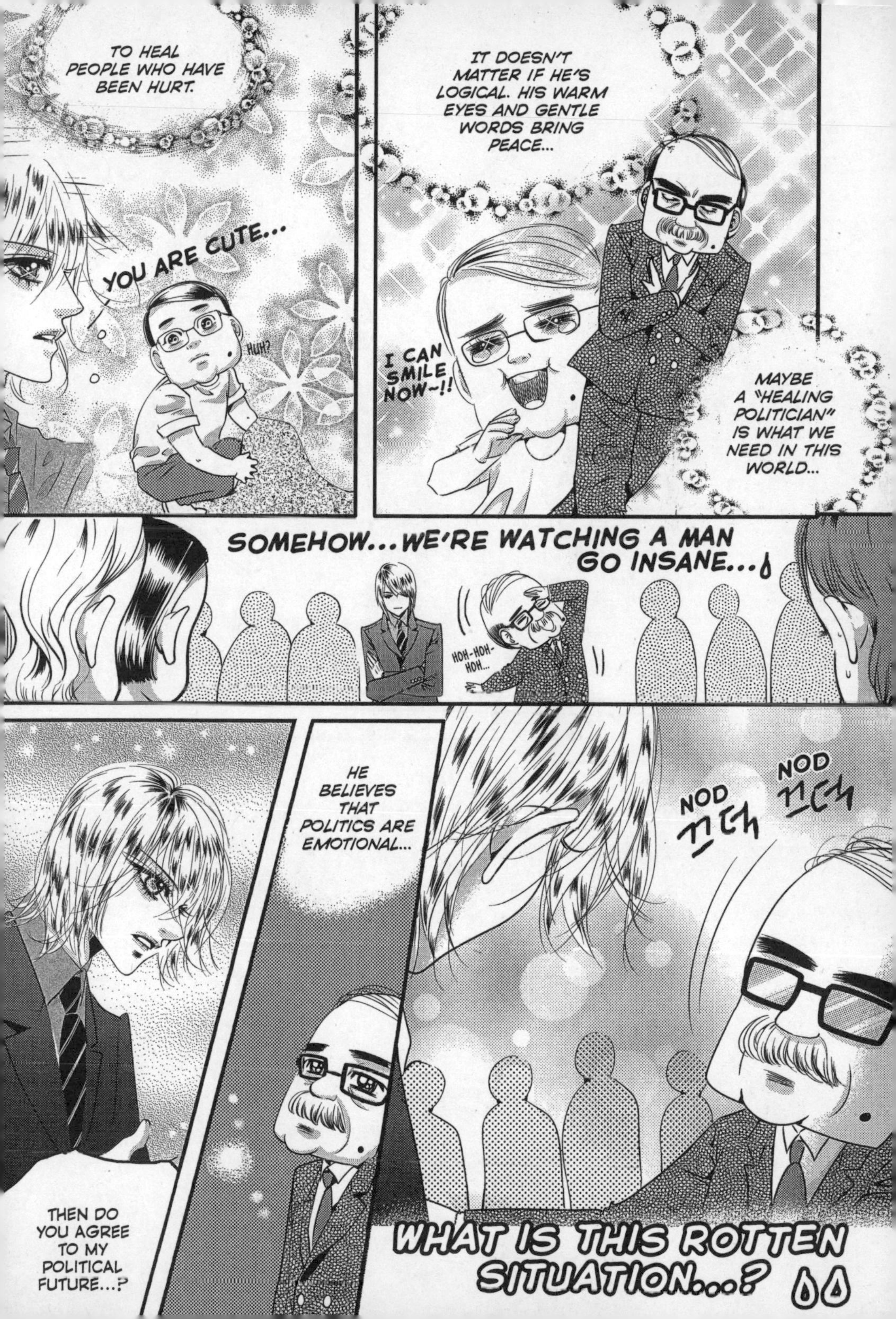
TO HEAL PEOPLE WHO HAVE BEEN HURT.
YOU ARE CUTE...
HUH?
IT DOESN'T MATTER IF HE'S LOGICAL. HIS WARM EYES AND GENTLE WORDS BRING PEACE...
I CAN SMILE NOW~!!
MAYBE A "HEALING POLITICIAN" IS WHAT WE NEED IN THIS WORLD...
SOMEHOW...WE'RE WATCHING A MAN GO INSANE...
HOH-HOH-HOH...
THEN DO YOU AGREE TO MY POLITICAL FUTURE...?
HE BELIEVES THAT POLITICS ARE EMOTIONAL...
NOD
끄덕
NOD
끄덕
WHAT IS THIS ROTTEN SITUATION...?

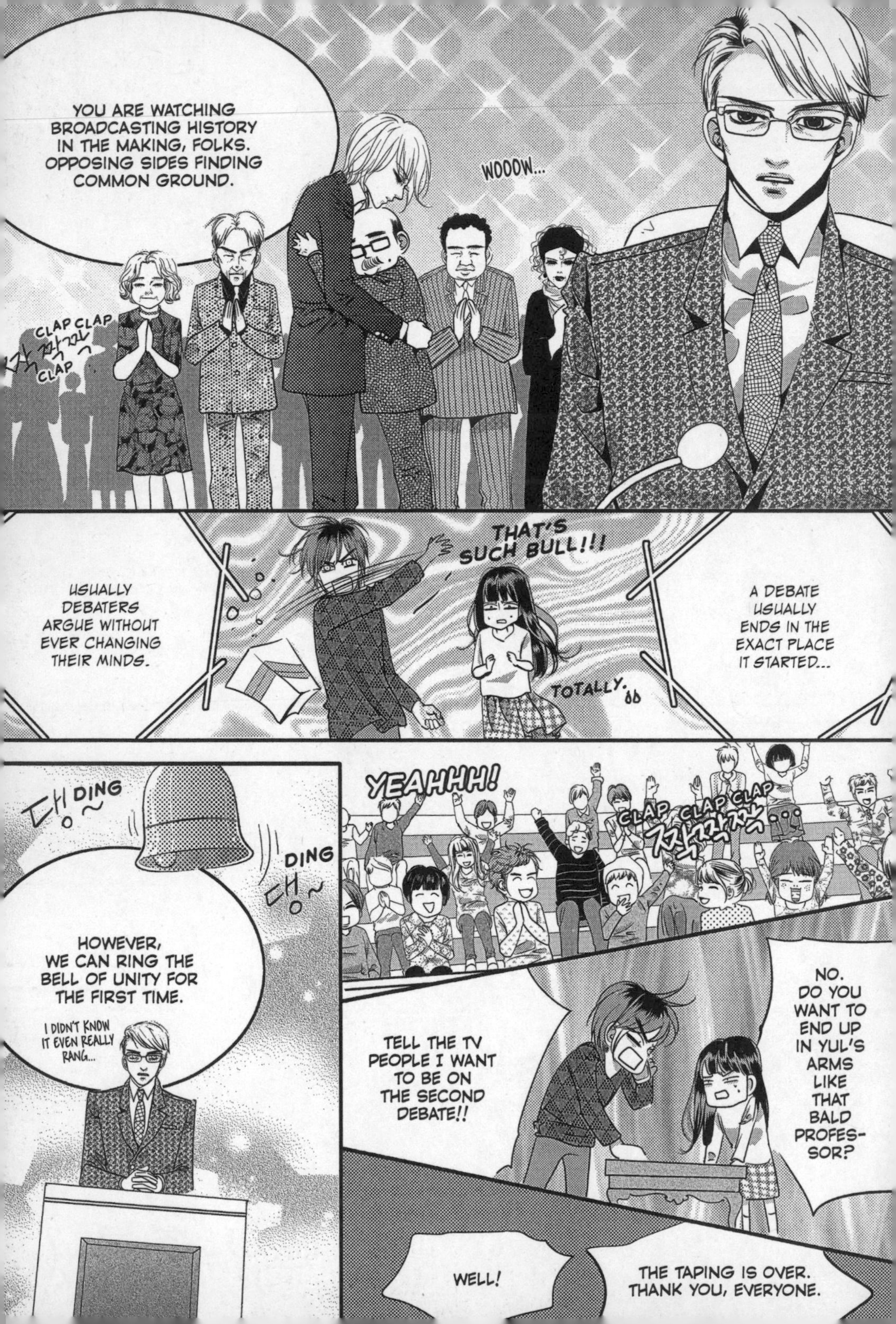
YOU ARE WATCHING BROADCASTING HISTORY IN THE MAKING, FOLKS. OPPOSING SIDES FINDING COMMON GROUND.
CLAP CLAP
CLAP
WOOOW...
USUALLY DEBATERS ARGUE WITHOUT EVER CHANGING THEIR MINDS.
THAT'S SUCH BULL!!!
TOTALLY.
A DEBATE USUALLY ENDS IN THE EXACT PLACE IT STARTED...
DING
DING
HOWEVER, WE CAN RING THE BELL OF UNITY FOR THE FIRST TIME.
I DIDN'T KNOW IT EVEN REALLY RANG...
YEAHHH!
CLAP CLAP CLAP
TELL THE TV PEOPLE I WANT TO BE ON THE SECOND DEBATE!!
NO. DO YOU WANT TO END UP IN YUL'S ARMS LIKE THAT BALD PROFES-SOR?
WELL!
THE TAPING IS OVER. THANK YOU, EVERYONE.

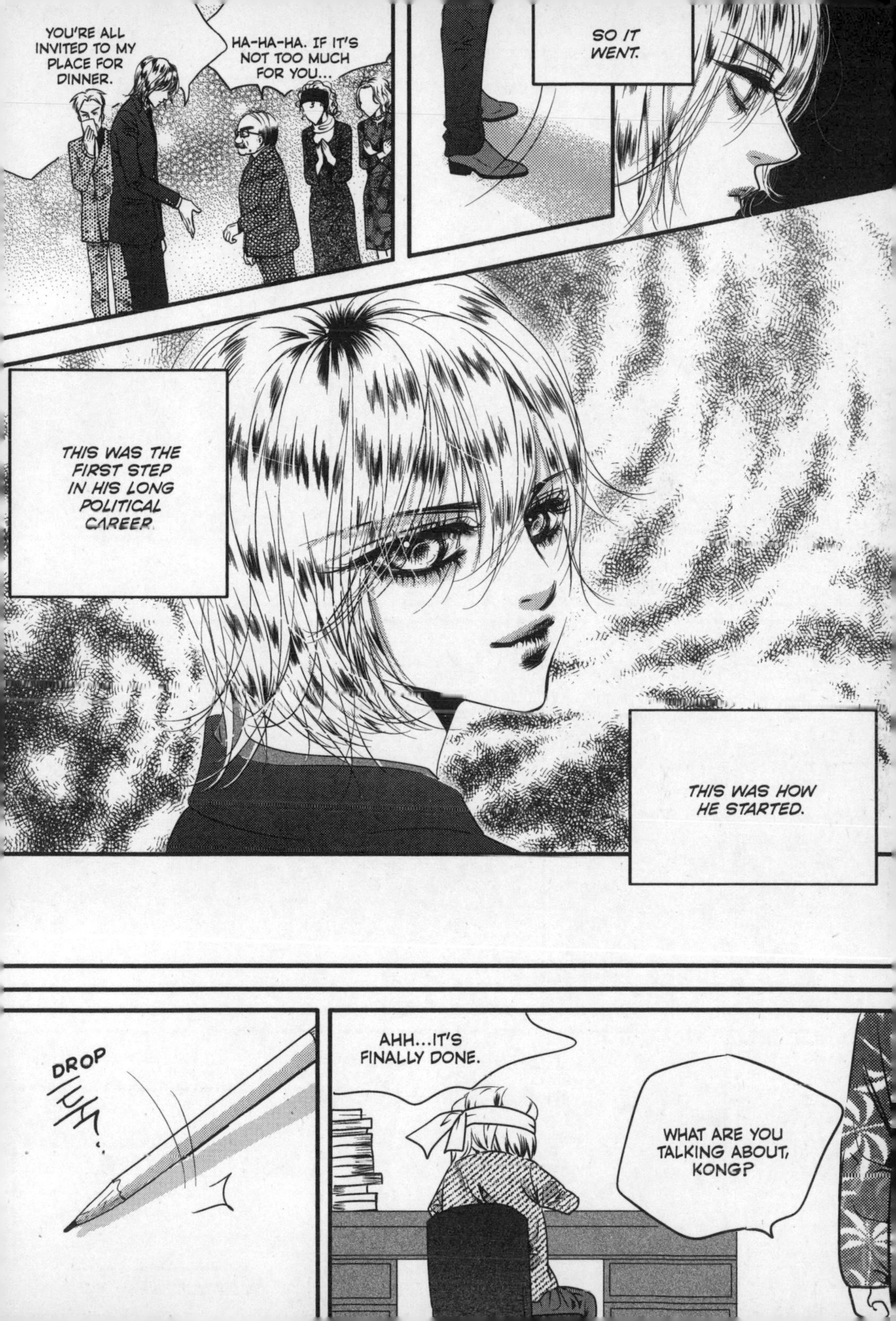
YOU'RE ALL INVITED TO MY PLACE FOR DINNER.
HA-HA-HA. IF IT'S NOT TOO MUCH FOR YOU...
SO IT WENT.
THIS WAS THE FIRST STEP IN HIS LONG POLITICAL CAREER.
THIS WAS HOW HE STARTED.
DROP
AHH...IT'S FINALLY DONE.
WHAT ARE YOU TALKING ABOUT, KONG?

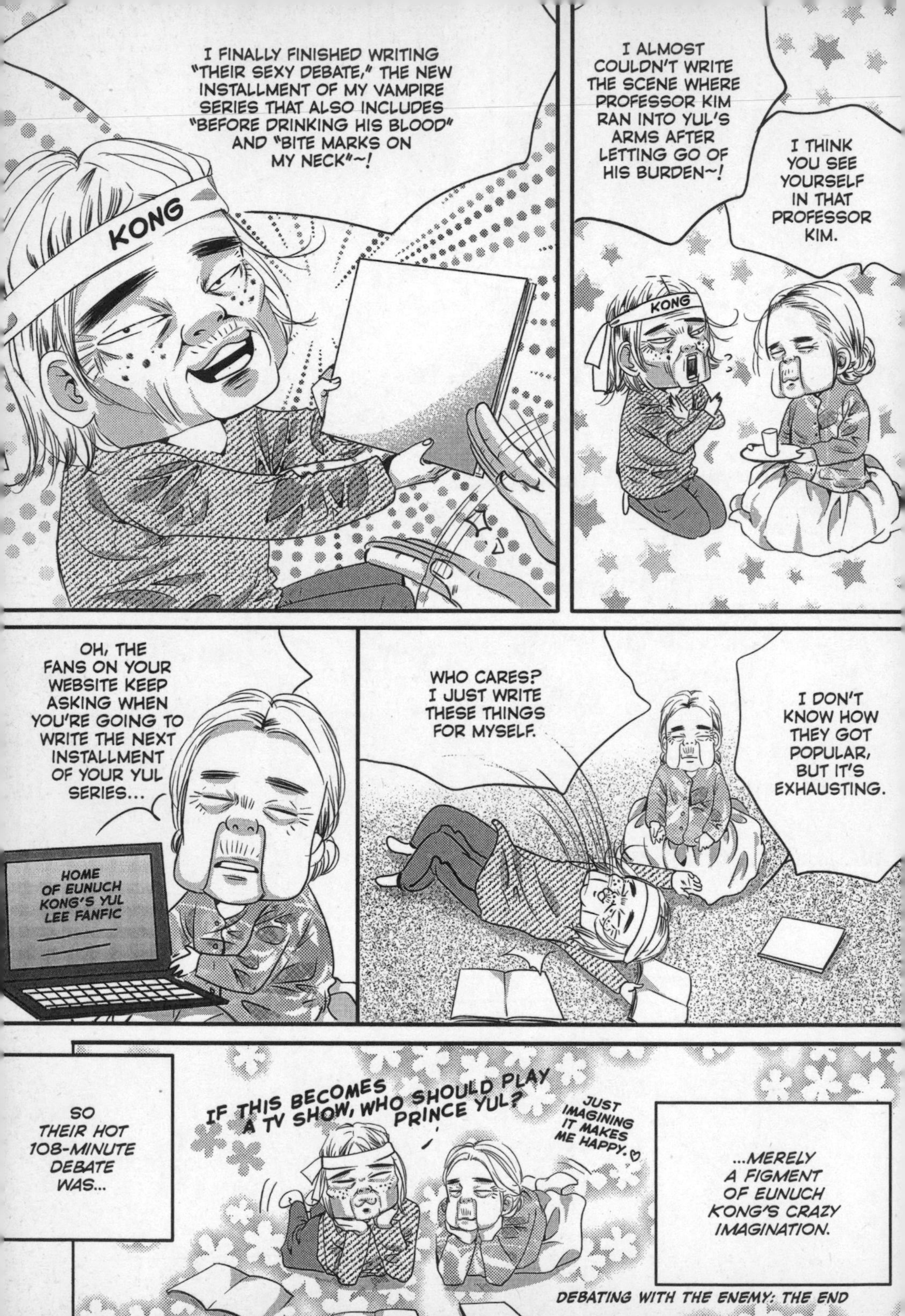
I FINALLY FINISHED WRITING "THEIR SEXY DEBATE," THE NEW INSTALLMENT OF MY VAMPIRE SERIES THAT ALSO INCLUDES "BEFORE DRINKING HIS BLOOD" AND "BITE MARKS ON MY NECK"~!
KONG
I ALMOST COULDN'T WRITE THE SCENE WHERE PROFESSOR KIM RAN INTO YUL'S ARMS AFTER LETTING GO OF HIS BURDEN~!
I THINK YOU SEE YOURSELF IN THAT PROFESSOR KIM.
KONG
OH, THE FANS ON YOUR WEBSITE KEEP ASKING WHEN YOU'RE GOING TO WRITE THE NEXT INSTALLMENT OF YOUR YUL SERIES...
HOME OF EUNUCH KONG'S YUL LEE FANFIC
WHO CARES? I JUST WRITE THESE THINGS FOR MYSELF.
I DON'T KNOW HOW THEY GOT POPULAR, BUT IT'S EXHAUSTING.
SO THEIR HOT 108-MINUTE DEBATE WAS...
IF THIS BECOMES A TV SHOW, WHO SHOULD PLAY PRINCE YUL?
JUST IMAGINING IT MAKES ME HAPPY.♡
...MERELY A FIGMENT OF EUNUCH KONG'S CRAZY IMAGINATION.

DEBATING WITH THE ENEMY: THE END

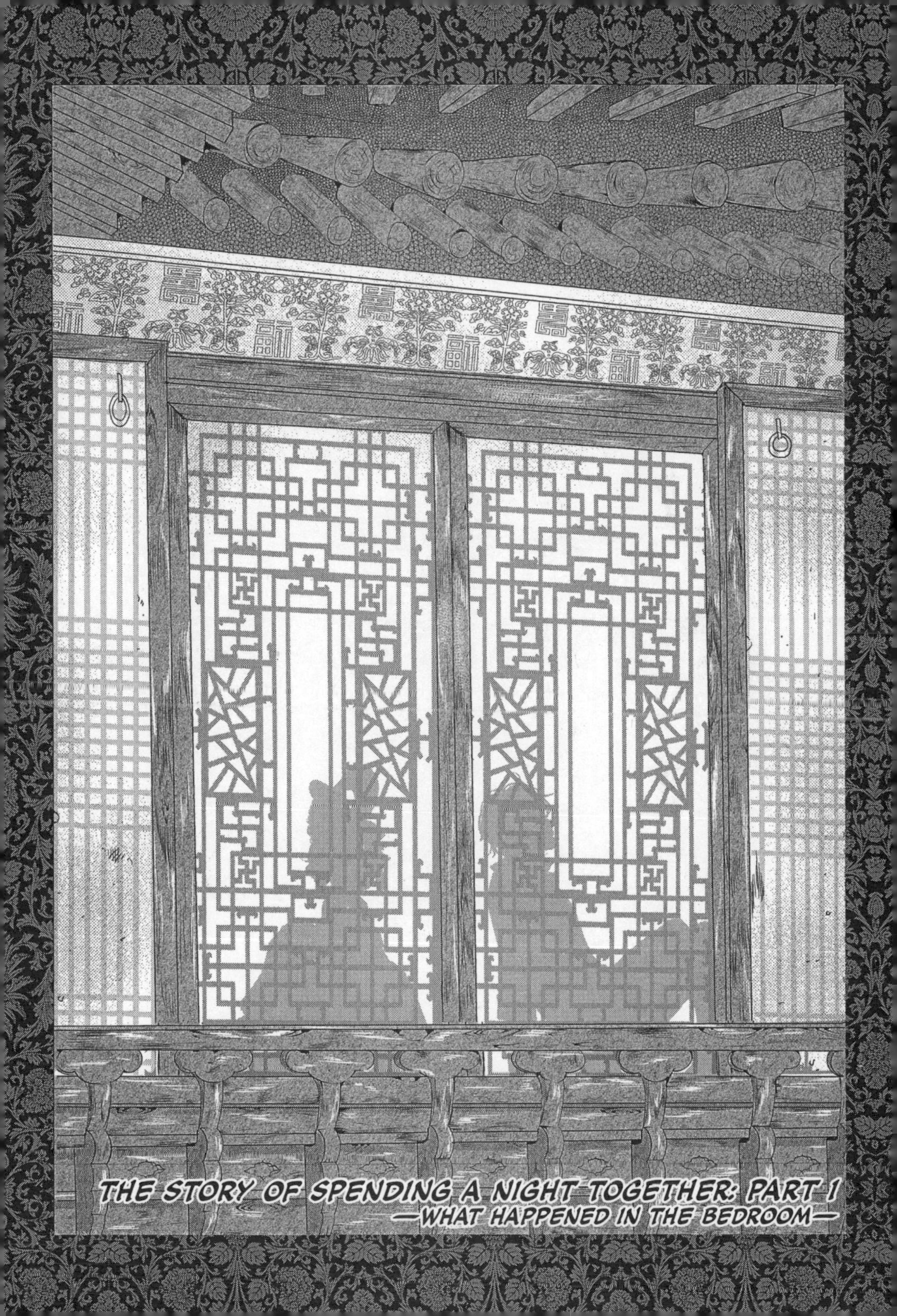
THE STORY OF SPENDING A NIGHT TOGETHER: PART 1
—WHAT HAPPENED IN THE BEDROOM—

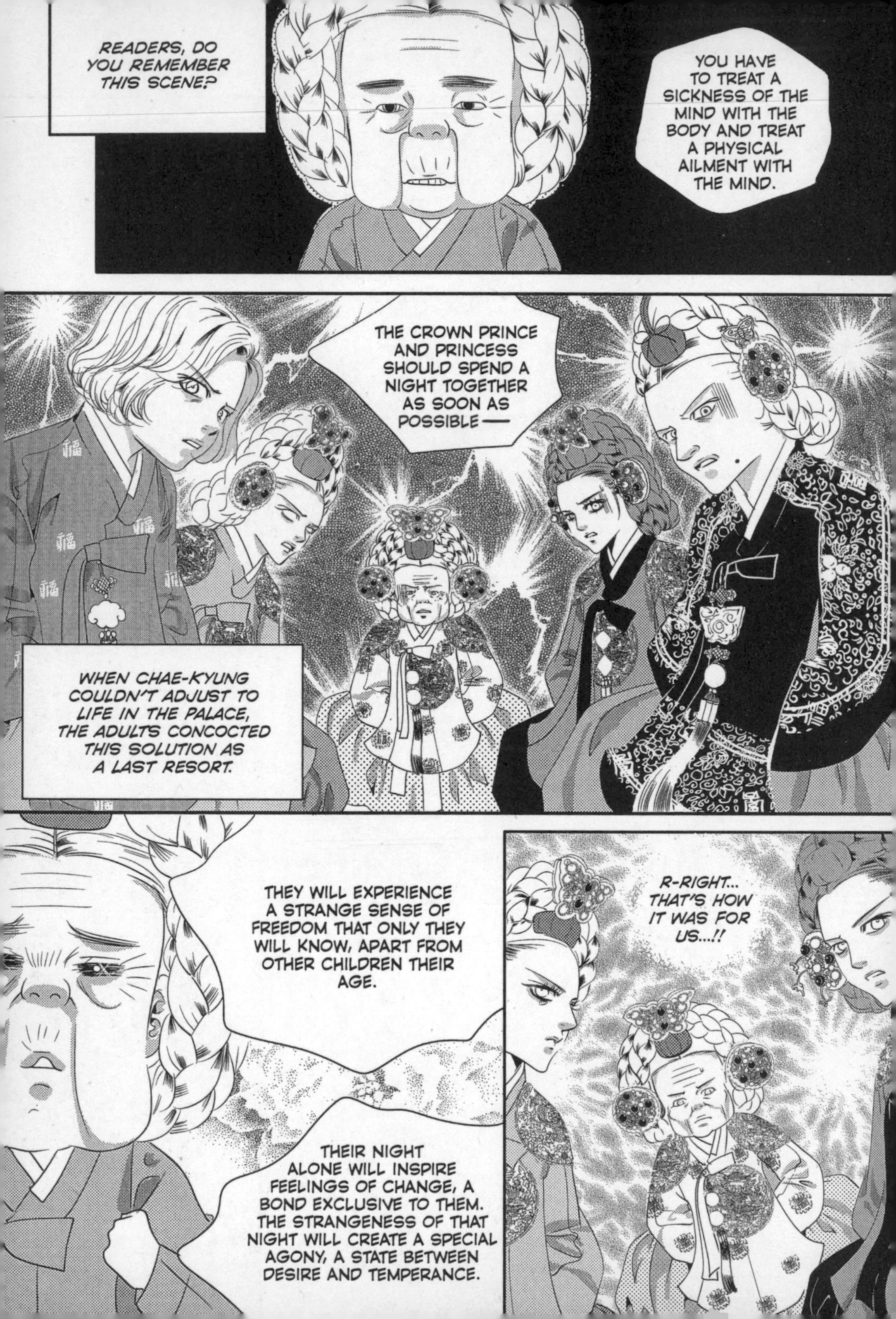
READERS, DO YOU REMEMBER THIS SCENE?
YOU HAVE TO TREAT A SICKNESS OF THE MIND WITH THE BODY AND TREAT A PHYSICAL AILMENT WITH THE MIND.
THE CROWN PRINCE AND PRINCESS SHOULD SPEND A NIGHT TOGETHER AS SOON AS POSSIBLE—
WHEN CHAE-KYUNG COULDN'T ADJUST TO LIFE IN THE PALACE, THE ADULTS CONCOCTED THIS SOLUTION AS A LAST RESORT.
THEY WILL EXPERIENCE A STRANGE SENSE OF FREEDOM THAT ONLY THEY WILL KNOW, APART FROM OTHER CHILDREN THEIR AGE.
THEIR NIGHT ALONE WILL INSPIRE FEELINGS OF CHANGE, A BOND EXCLUSIVE TO THEM. THE STRANGENESS OF THAT NIGHT WILL CREATE A SPECIAL AGONY, A STATE BETWEEN DESIRE AND TEMPERANCE.
R-RIGHT... THAT'S HOW IT WAS FOR US...!!

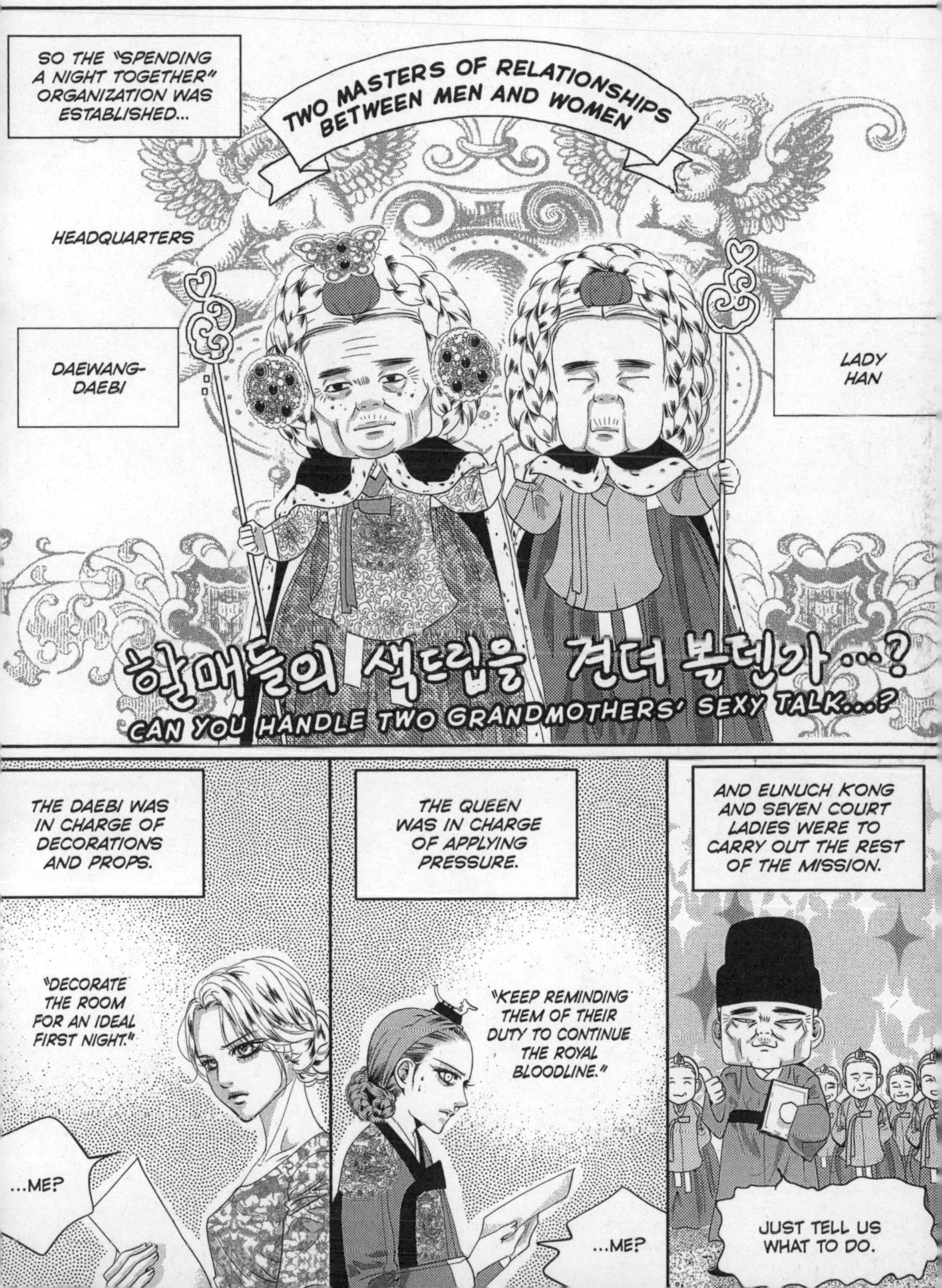
SO THE "SPENDING A NIGHT TOGETHER" ORGANIZATION WAS ESTABLISHED...
TWO MASTERS OF RELATIONSHIPS BETWEEN MEN AND WOMEN
HEADQUARTERS
DAEWANG-DAEBI
LADY HAN
할매들의 색드립을 견뎌 볼텐가 …?
CAN YOU HANDLE TWO GRANDMOTHERS' SEXY TALK...?
THE DAEBI WAS IN CHARGE OF DECORATIONS AND PROPS.
"DECORATE THE ROOM FOR AN IDEAL FIRST NIGHT."
...ME?
THE QUEEN WAS IN CHARGE OF APPLYING PRESSURE.
"KEEP REMINDING THEM OF THEIR DUTY TO CONTINUE THE ROYAL BLOODLINE."
...ME?
AND EUNUCH KONG AND SEVEN COURT LADIES WERE TO CARRY OUT THE REST OF THE MISSION.
JUST TELL US WHAT TO DO.

YOU'RE MISSING THE POINT. SHOULDN'T THEY SET A GOOD EXAMPLE FOR OTHER KIDS? THEY'RE STILL IN HIGH SCHOOL!!

NO ONE NEEDS SPECIAL DECORATIONS TO SPEND A NIGHT TOGETHER. IT'S A WASTE OF MY TIME—

......

DON'T WORRY. THERE AREN'T ENOUGH PROPS IN THE WORLD...

...TO MAKE A COLD STIFF LIKE PRINCE SHIN GET IN BED WITH SOMEONE AS UNATTRACTIVE AS CHAE-KYUNG.

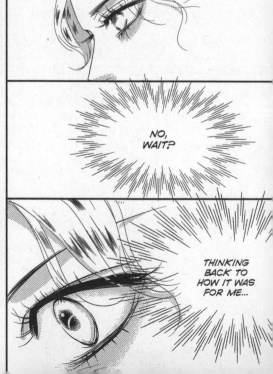

NO, WAIT?

...

THINKING BACK TO HOW IT WAS FOR ME...

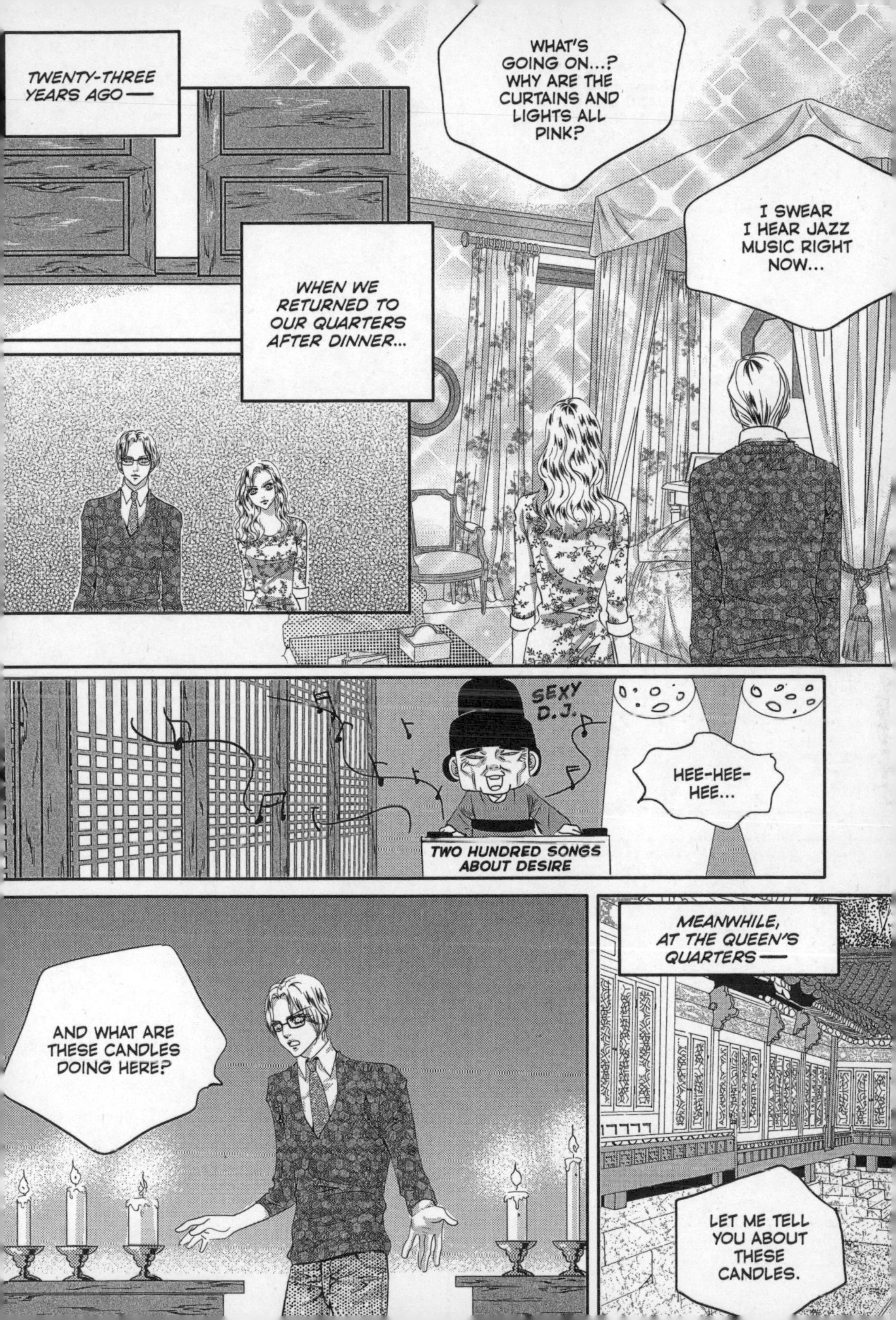
TWENTY-THREE YEARS AGO—
WHAT'S GOING ON...? WHY ARE THE CURTAINS AND LIGHTS ALL PINK?
WHEN WE RETURNED TO OUR QUARTERS AFTER DINNER...
I SWEAR I HEAR JAZZ MUSIC RIGHT NOW...
SEXY D.J.
TWO HUNDRED SONGS ABOUT DESIRE
HEE-HEE-HEE...
AND WHAT ARE THESE CANDLES DOING HERE?
MEANWHILE, AT THE QUEEN'S QUARTERS—
LET ME TELL YOU ABOUT THESE CANDLES.

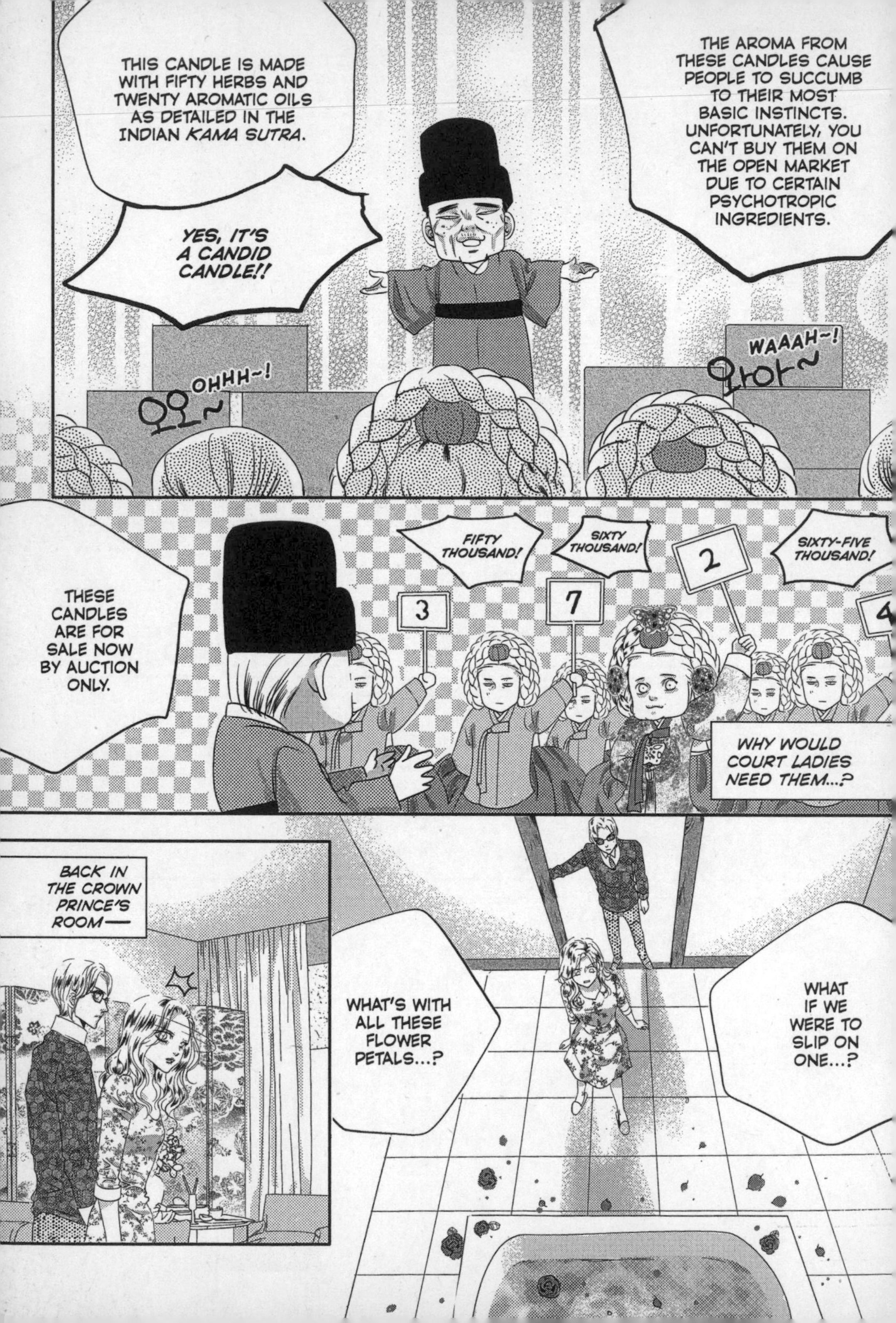
THIS CANDLE IS MADE WITH FIFTY HERBS AND TWENTY AROMATIC OILS AS DETAILED IN THE INDIAN *KAMA SUTRA*.
YES, IT'S A CANDID CANDLE!!
THE AROMA FROM THESE CANDLES CAUSE PEOPLE TO SUCCUMB TO THEIR MOST BASIC INSTINCTS. UNFORTUNATELY, YOU CAN'T BUY THEM ON THE OPEN MARKET DUE TO CERTAIN PSYCHOTROPIC INGREDIENTS.
오오~
OHHH~!
와아~
WAAAH~!
THESE CANDLES ARE FOR SALE NOW BY AUCTION ONLY.
3
FIFTY THOUSAND!
7
SIXTY THOUSAND!
2
SIXTY-FIVE THOUSAND!
4
WHY WOULD COURT LADIES NEED THEM...?
BACK IN THE CROWN PRINCE'S ROOM—
WHAT'S WITH ALL THESE FLOWER PETALS...?
WHAT IF WE WERE TO SLIP ON ONE...?

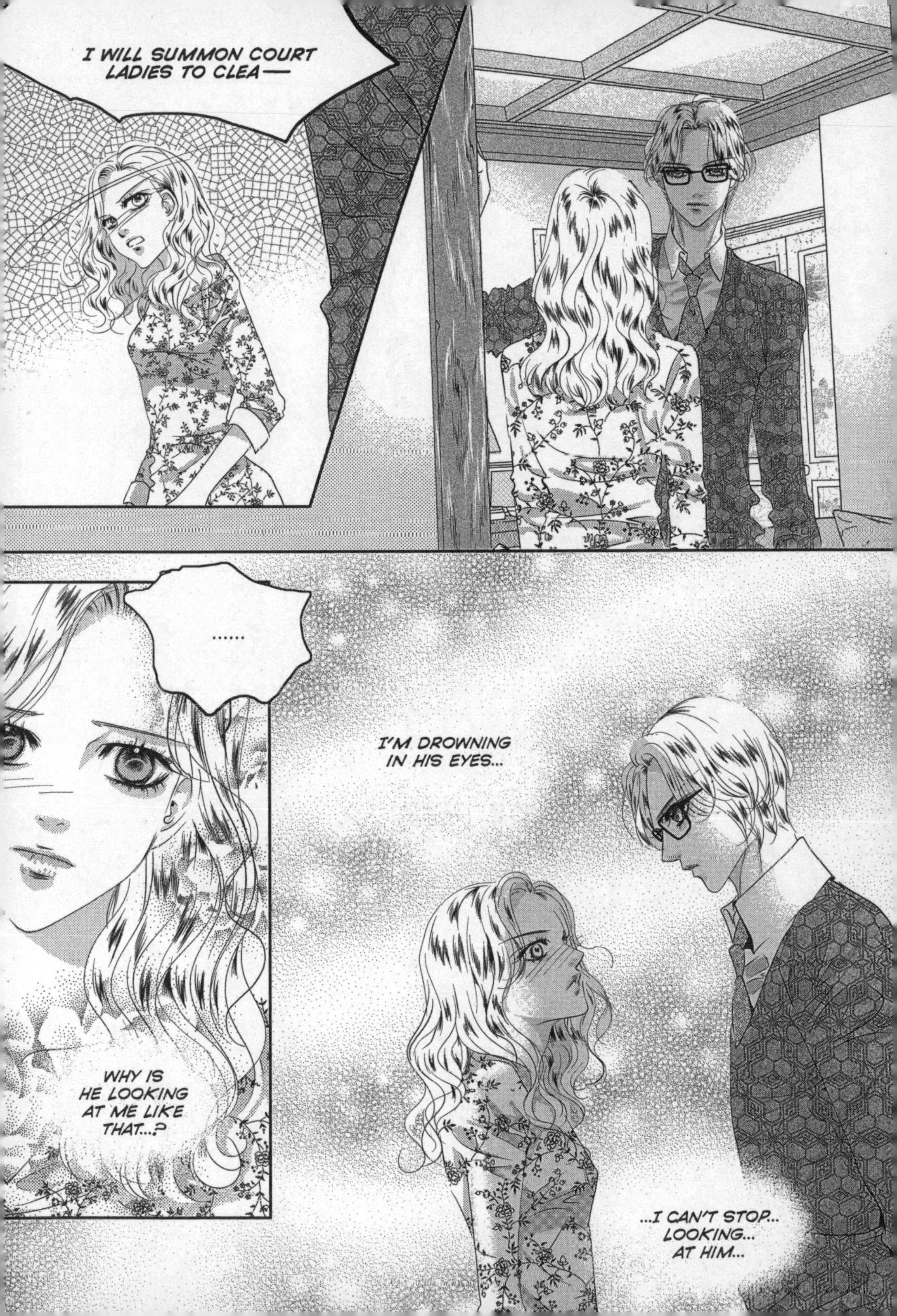
I WILL SUMMON COURT LADIES TO CLEA—
......
WHY IS HE LOOKING AT ME LIKE THAT...?
I'M DROWNING IN HIS EYES...
...I CAN'T STOP... LOOKING... AT HIM...

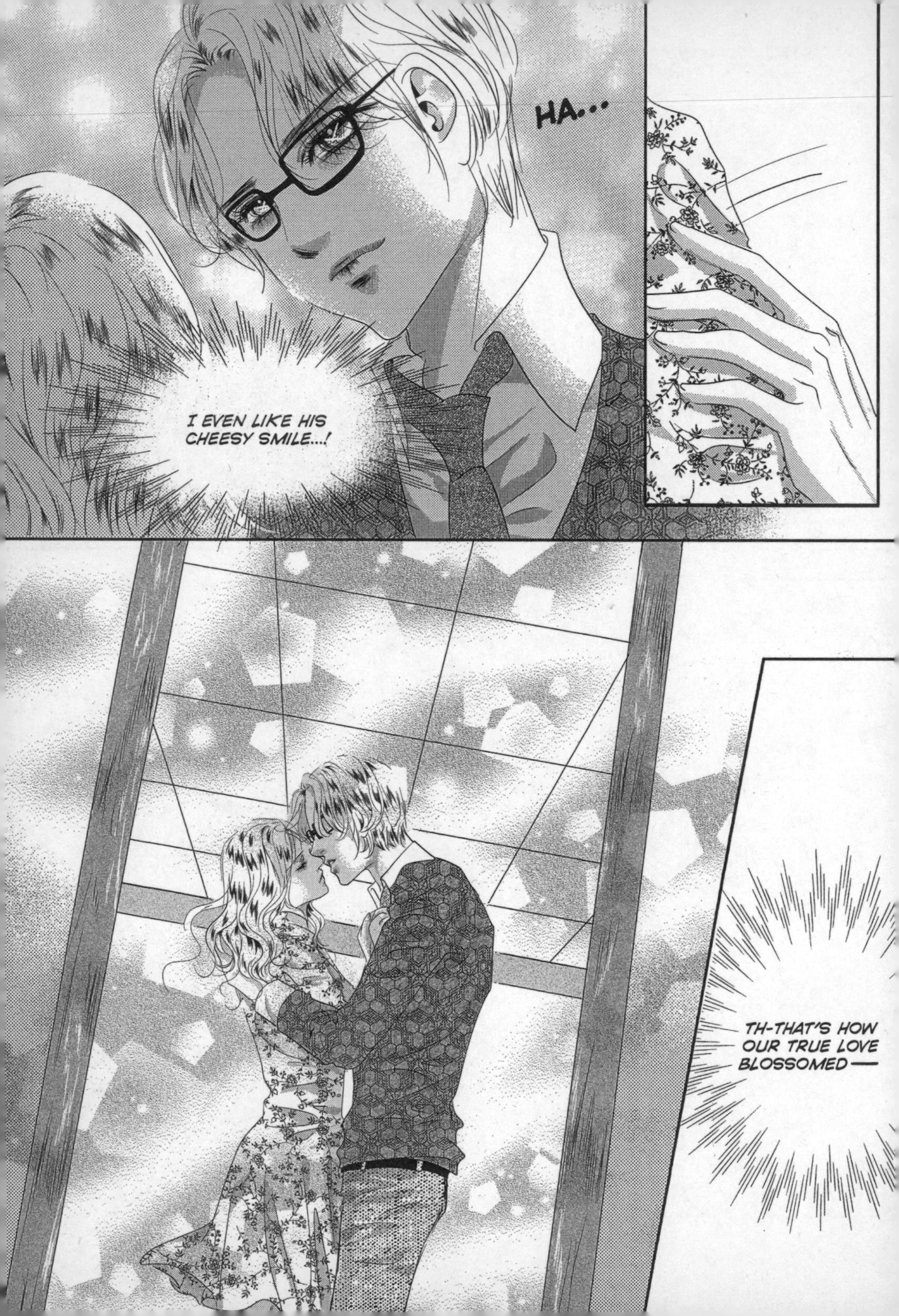
HA...
I EVEN LIKE HIS CHEESY SMILE...!
TH-THAT'S HOW OUR TRUE LOVE BLOSSOMED—

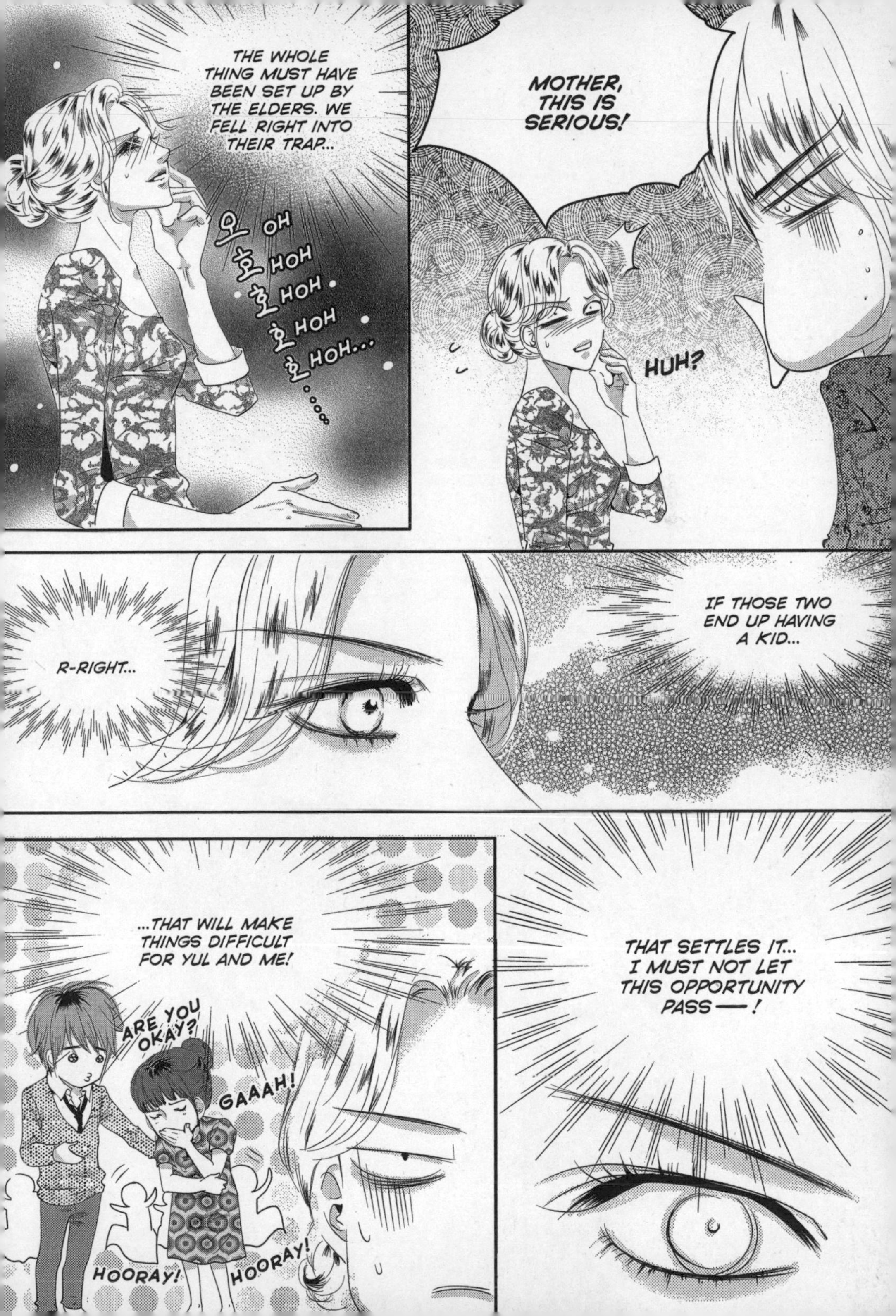
THE WHOLE THING MUST HAVE BEEN SET UP BY THE ELDERS. WE FELL RIGHT INTO THEIR TRAP...
오 OH
호 HOH
호 HOH
호 HOH
호 HOH...
MOTHER, THIS IS SERIOUS!
HUH?
R-RIGHT...
IF THOSE TWO END UP HAVING A KID...
...THAT WILL MAKE THINGS DIFFICULT FOR YUL AND ME!
ARE YOU OKAY?
GAAAH!
HOORAY!
HOORAY!
THAT SETTLES IT... I MUST NOT LET THIS OPPORTUNITY PASS—!

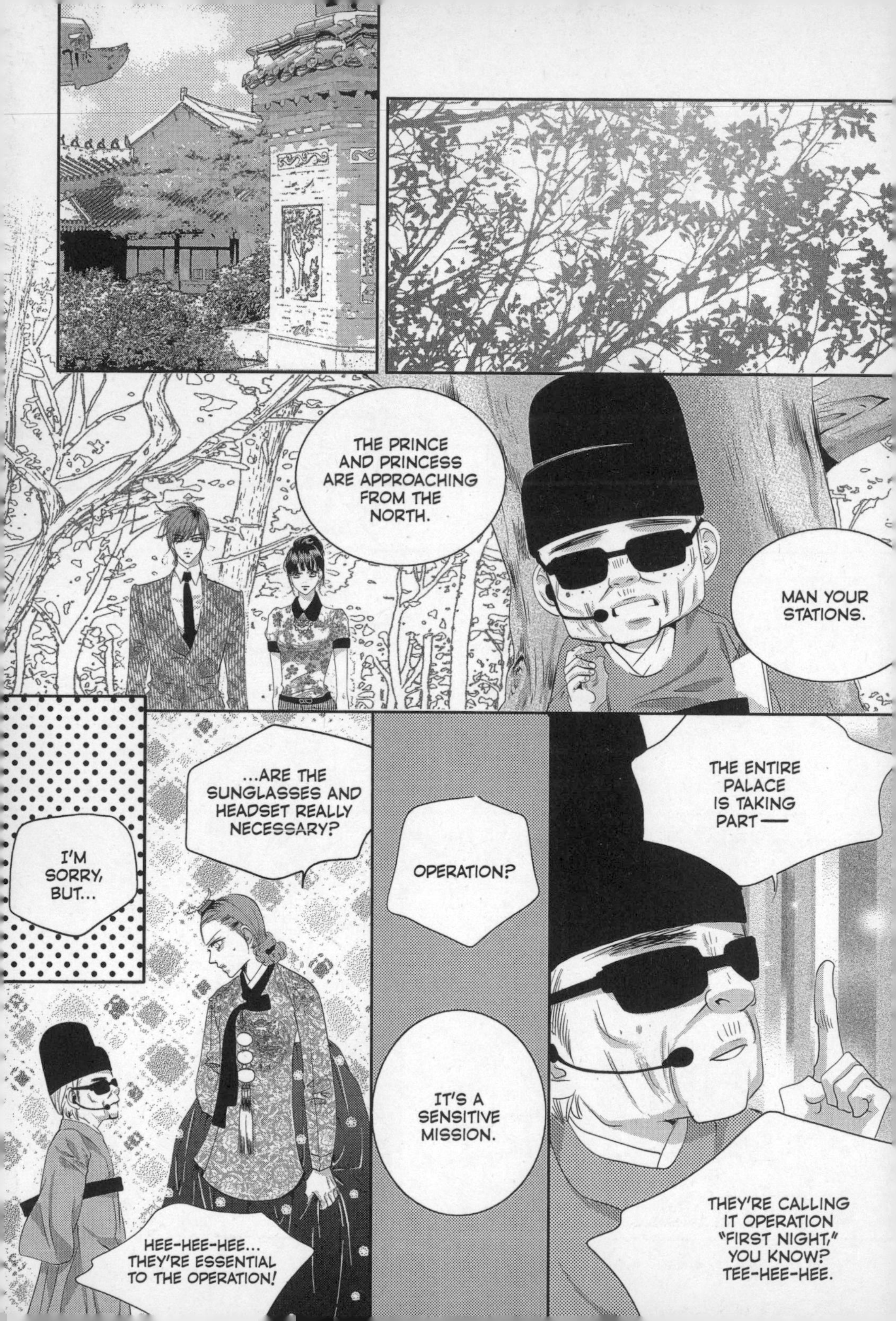
THE PRINCE AND PRINCESS ARE APPROACHING FROM THE NORTH.
MAN YOUR STATIONS.
I'M SORRY, BUT...
...ARE THE SUNGLASSES AND HEADSET REALLY NECESSARY?
HEE-HEE-HEE... THEY'RE ESSENTIAL TO THE OPERATION!
OPERATION?
IT'S A SENSITIVE MISSION.
THE ENTIRE PALACE IS TAKING PART—
THEY'RE CALLING IT OPERATION "FIRST NIGHT," YOU KNOW? TEE-HEE-HEE.

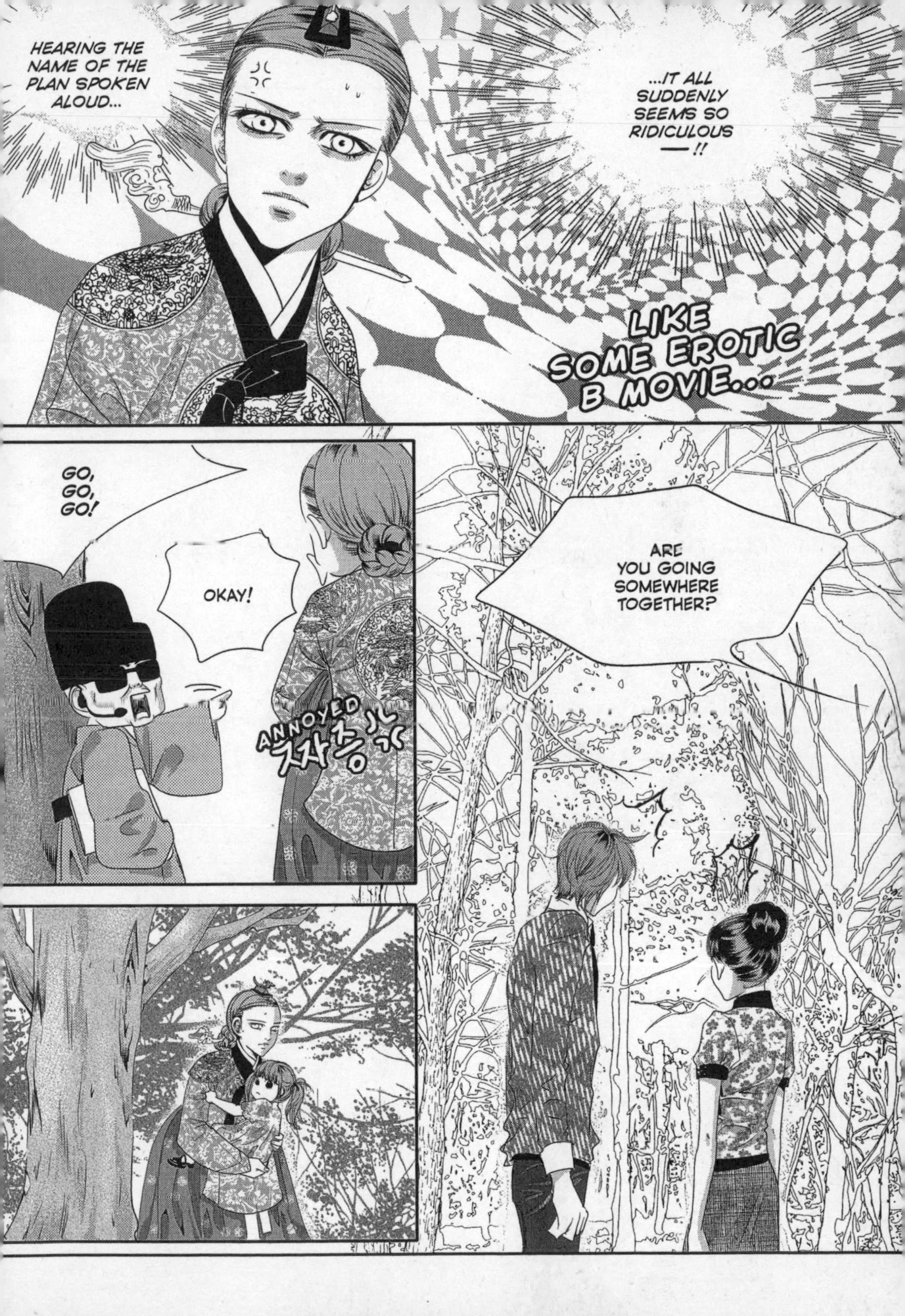
HEARING THE NAME OF THE PLAN SPOKEN ALOUD...
...IT ALL SUDDENLY SEEMS SO RIDICULOUS—!!
LIKE SOME EROTIC B MOVIE...
GO, GO, GO!
OKAY!
ANNOYED
ARE YOU GOING SOMEWHERE TOGETHER?

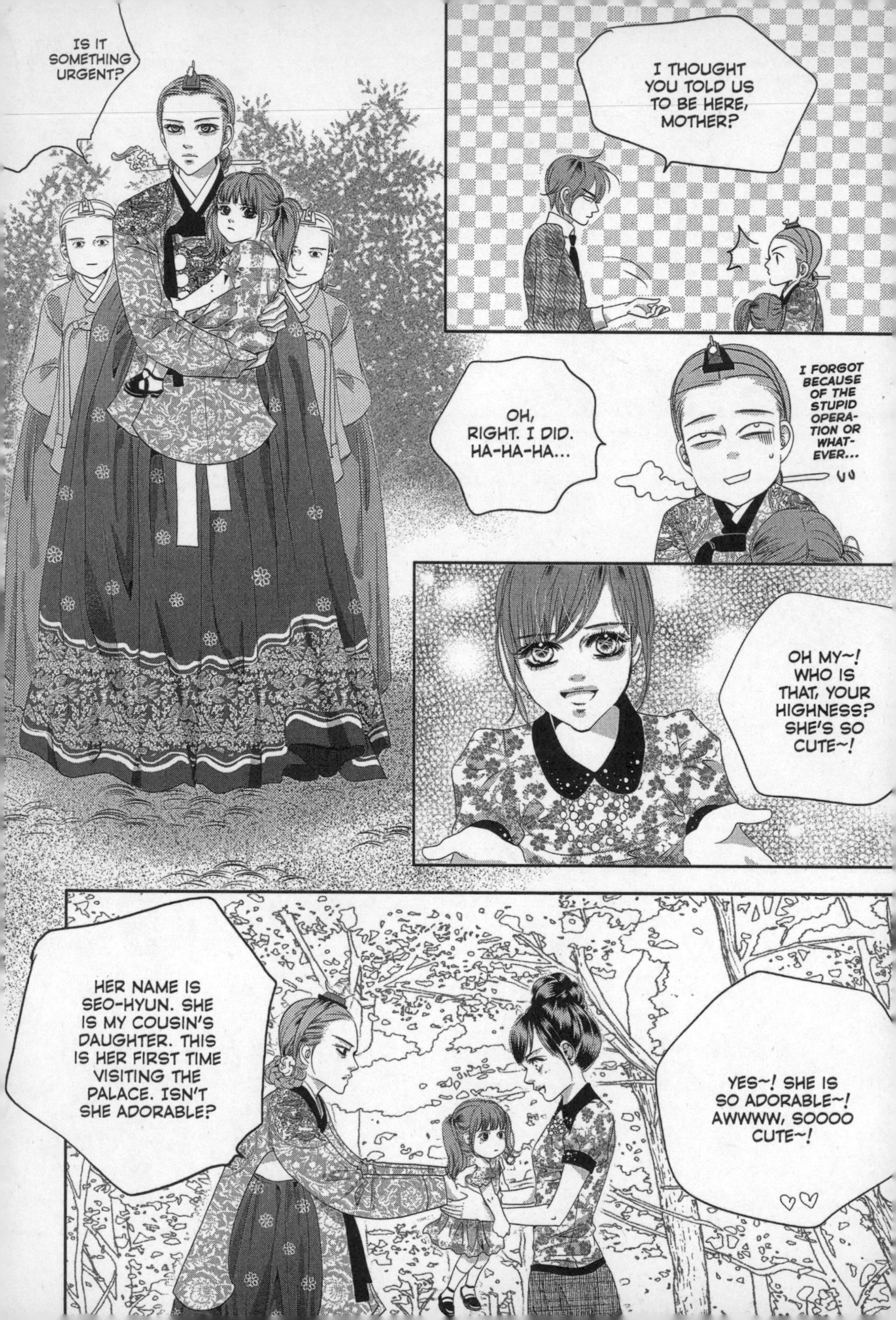
IS IT SOMETHING URGENT?
I THOUGHT YOU TOLD US TO BE HERE, MOTHER?
OH, RIGHT. I DID. HA-HA-HA...
I FORGOT BECAUSE OF THE STUPID OPERA-TION OR WHAT-EVER...
OH MY~! WHO IS THAT, YOUR HIGHNESS? SHE'S SO CUTE~!
HER NAME IS SEO-HYUN. SHE IS MY COUSIN'S DAUGHTER. THIS IS HER FIRST TIME VISITING THE PALACE. ISN'T SHE ADORABLE?
YES~! SHE IS SO ADORABLE~! AWWWW, SOOOO CUTE~!

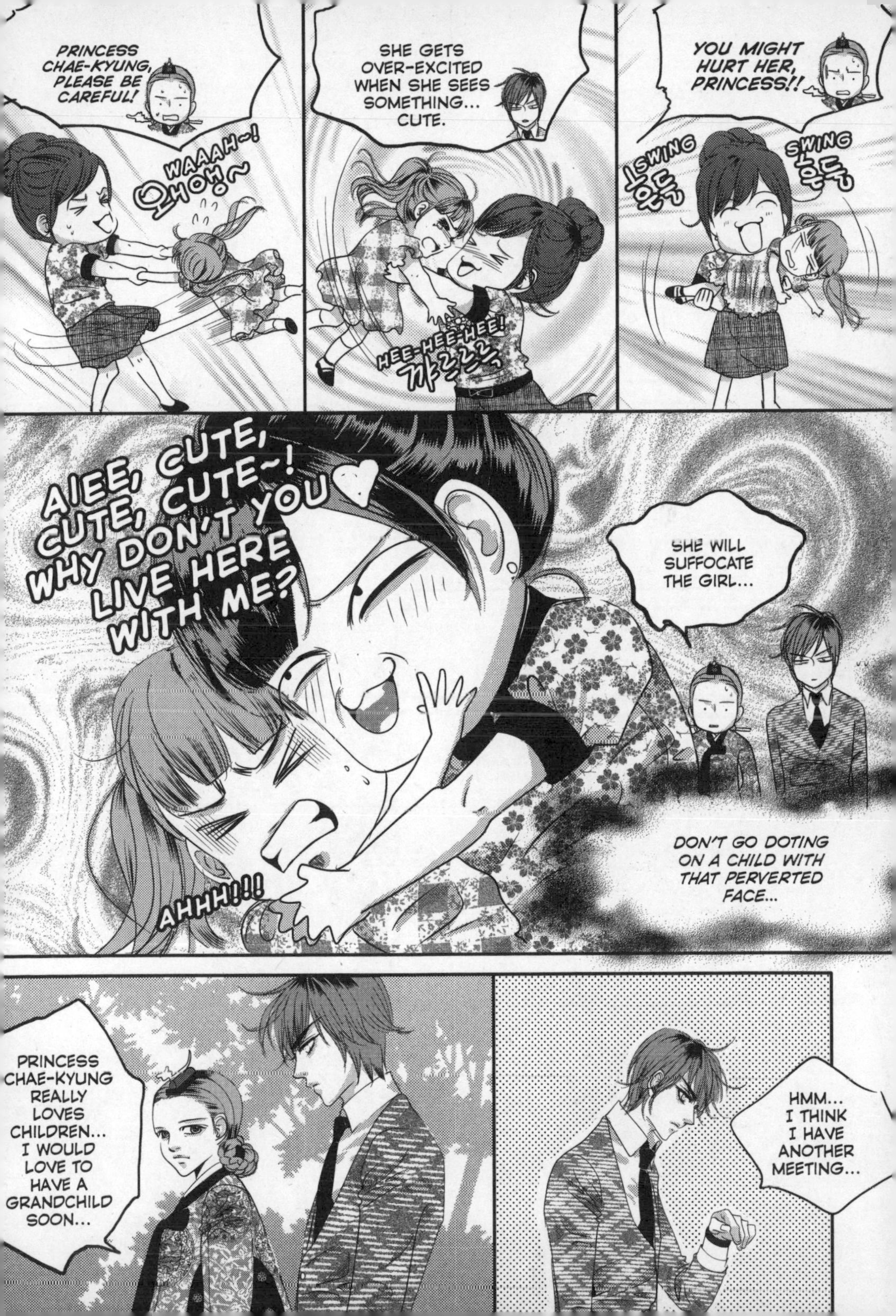
PRINCESS CHAE-KYUNG, PLEASE BE CAREFUL!
WAAAH~!
SHE GETS OVER-EXCITED WHEN SHE SEES SOMETHING... CUTE.
HEE-HEE-HEE!
YOU MIGHT HURT HER, PRINCESS!!
SWING!
SWING
AIEE, CUTE, CUTE, CUTE~! WHY DON'T YOU LIVE HERE WITH ME?
SHE WILL SUFFOCATE THE GIRL...
AHHH!!!
DON'T GO DOTING ON A CHILD WITH THAT PERVERTED FACE...
PRINCESS CHAE-KYUNG REALLY LOVES CHILDREN... I WOULD LOVE TO HAVE A GRANDCHILD SOON...
HMM... I THINK I HAVE ANOTHER MEETING...

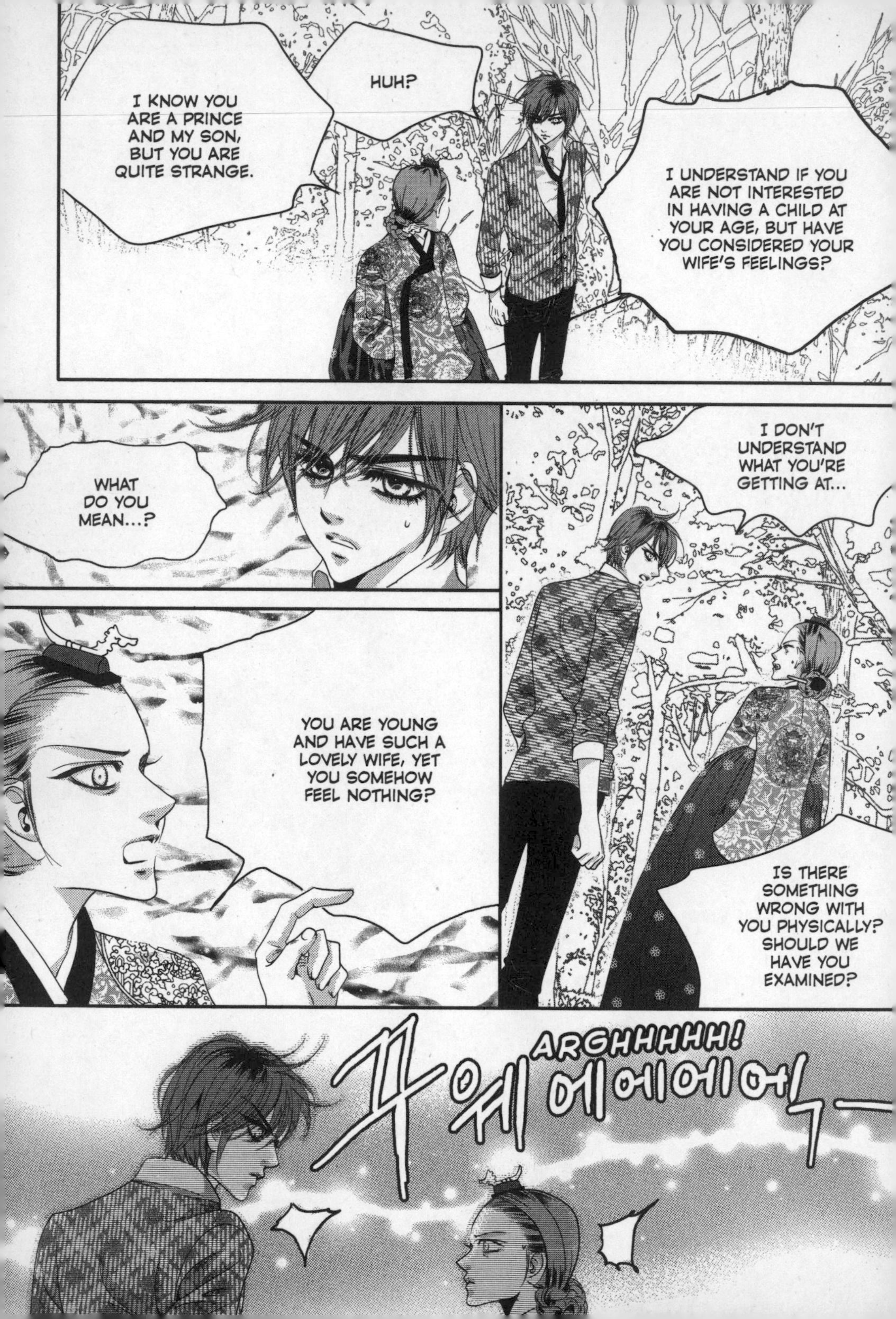
I KNOW YOU ARE A PRINCE AND MY SON, BUT YOU ARE QUITE STRANGE.
HUH?
I UNDERSTAND IF YOU ARE NOT INTERESTED IN HAVING A CHILD AT YOUR AGE, BUT HAVE YOU CONSIDERED YOUR WIFE'S FEELINGS?
WHAT DO YOU MEAN...?
YOU ARE YOUNG AND HAVE SUCH A LOVELY WIFE, YET YOU SOMEHOW FEEL NOTHING?
I DON'T UNDERSTAND WHAT YOU'RE GETTING AT...
IS THERE SOMETHING WRONG WITH YOU PHYSICALLY? SHOULD WE HAVE YOU EXAMINED?
ARGHHHHH!

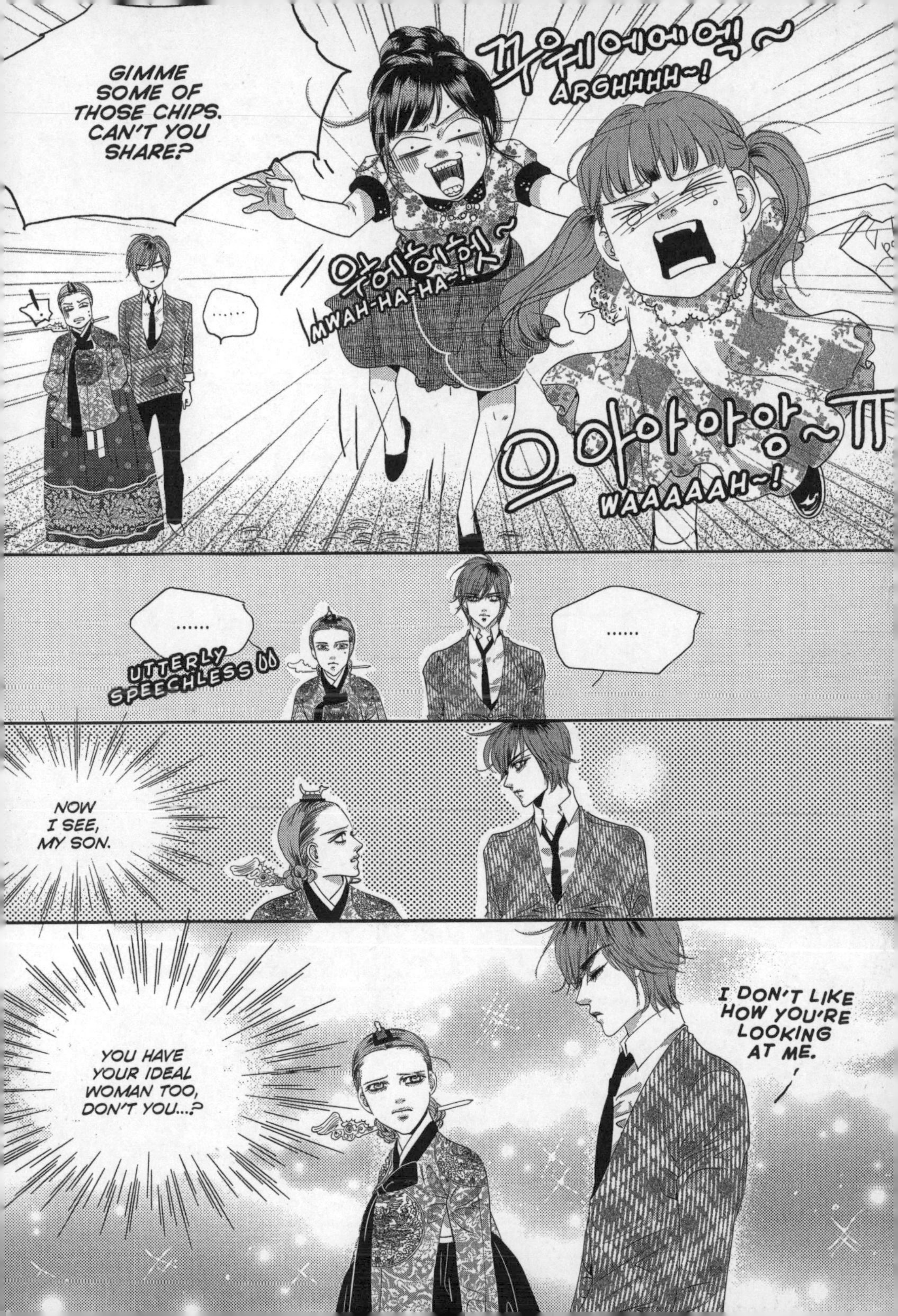
GIMME SOME OF THOSE CHIPS. CAN'T YOU SHARE?
끄우웨에에엑! ~
ARGHHHH~!
우에헤헷~
MWAH-HA-HA~!
......
으아아앙~ㅠ
WAAAAAH~!
......
UTTERLY SPEECHLESS
......
NOW I SEE, MY SON.
YOU HAVE YOUR IDEAL WOMAN TOO, DON'T YOU...?
I DON'T LIKE HOW YOU'RE LOOKING AT ME.

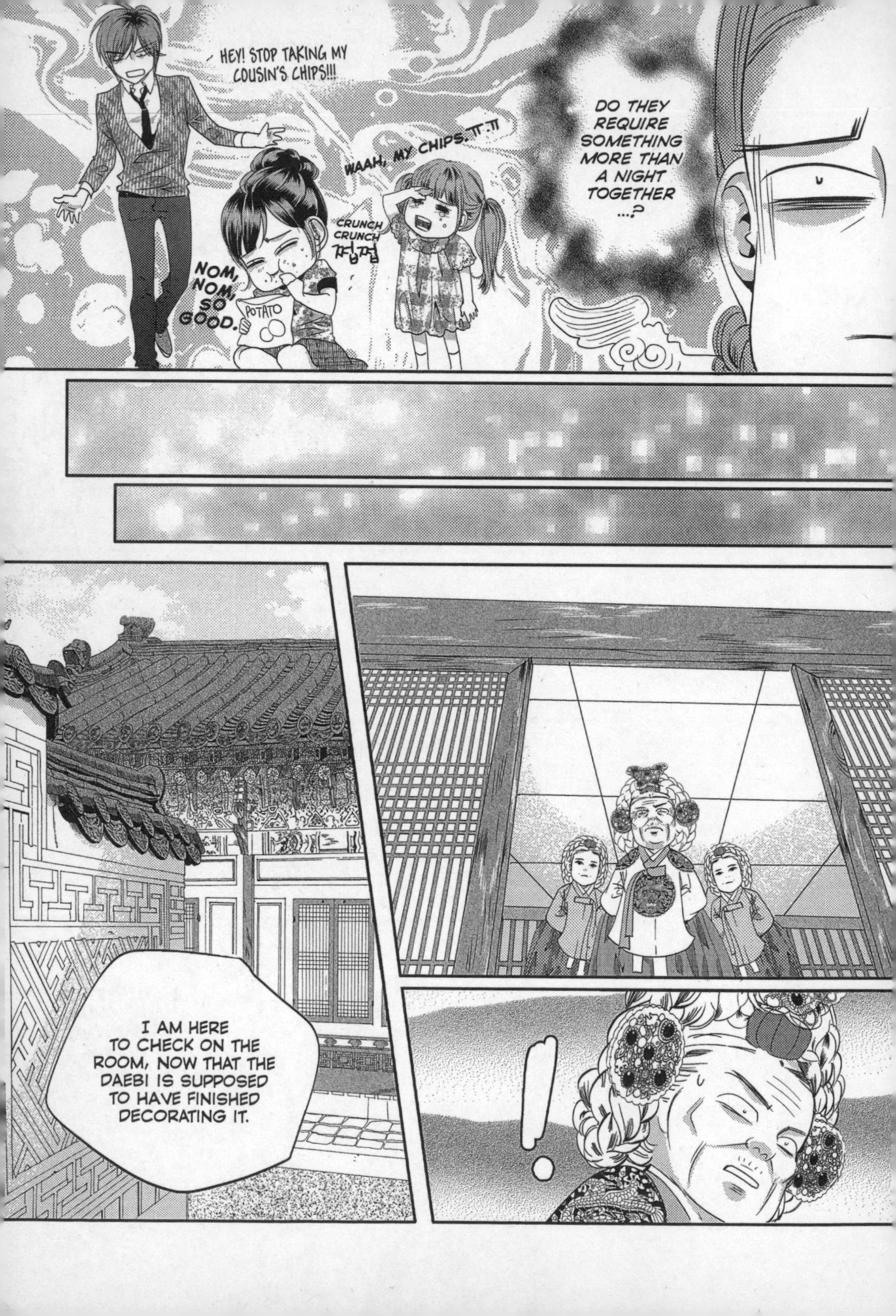
HEY! STOP TAKING MY COUSIN'S CHIPS!!!
WAAH, MY CHIPS. ㅠ.ㅠ
CRUNCH CRUNCH
NOM, NOM, SO GOOD.
POTATO
DO THEY REQUIRE SOMETHING MORE THAN A NIGHT TOGETHER ...?
I AM HERE TO CHECK ON THE ROOM, NOW THAT THE DAEBI IS SUPPOSED TO HAVE FINISHED DECORATING IT.
!

WHAT IS THIS? WHY IS THE WALLPAPER SO DARK AND GLOOMY, AND WHY IS THERE A ROOM DIVIDER?

AND THERE ARE PICTURES OF THE TOP FIVE MOST WANTED KILLERS AND ALL THESE MONSTER MASKS!!

SHE CREATED A LOVERS' HELL, NOT HEAVEN. IT LOOKS LIKE THE GRIM REAPER IS GOING TO APPEAR AT ANY SECOND!!

THE SHELVES ARE FULL OF TEXTBOOKS AND DICTIONARIES.

THE SIGHT OF THESE WILL ONLY STRESS THEM OUT...

TEENAGE PARENTS RUIN OUR SOCIETY

TEENAGE PREGNANCY DEEPENS SICKNESS OF MIND AND BODY

TEENAGE PARENTS: THE END OF WORLD

DIFFICULTIES ALL TEENAGE PARENTS MUST OVERCOME

IMMATURE PARENTS AND THE EDUCATION OF CHILDREN

AND JUST LOOK AT THESE TERRIBLE BOOKS ALL OVER THE FLOOR!!!

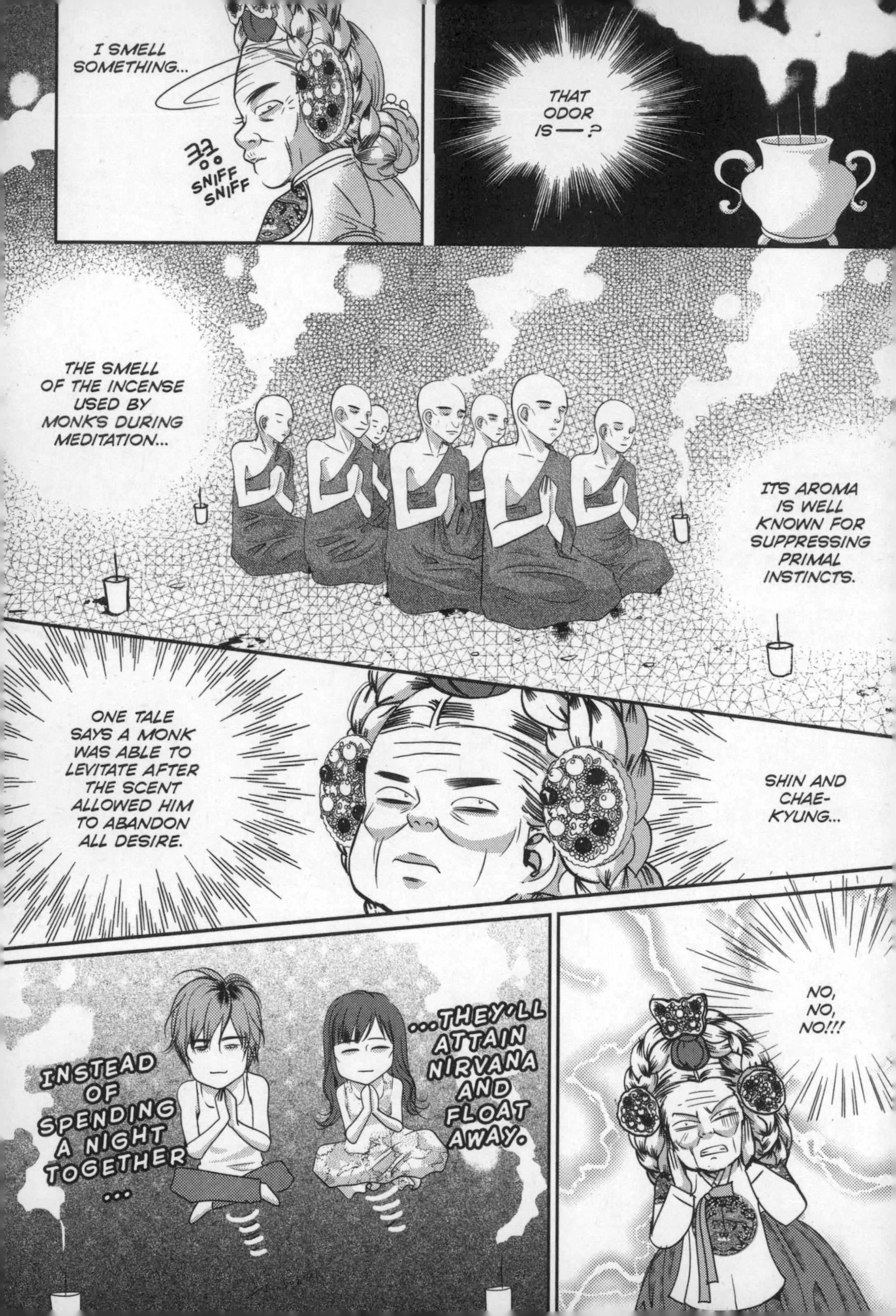
I SMELL SOMETHING...
킁킁
SNIFF SNIFF
THAT ODOR IS—?
THE SMELL OF THE INCENSE USED BY MONKS DURING MEDITATION...
ITS AROMA IS WELL KNOWN FOR SUPPRESSING PRIMAL INSTINCTS.
ONE TALE SAYS A MONK WAS ABLE TO LEVITATE AFTER THE SCENT ALLOWED HIM TO ABANDON ALL DESIRE.
SHIN AND CHAE-KYUNG...
INSTEAD OF SPENDING A NIGHT TOGETHER...
...THEY'LL ATTAIN NIRVANA AND FLOAT AWAY.
NO, NO, NO!!!

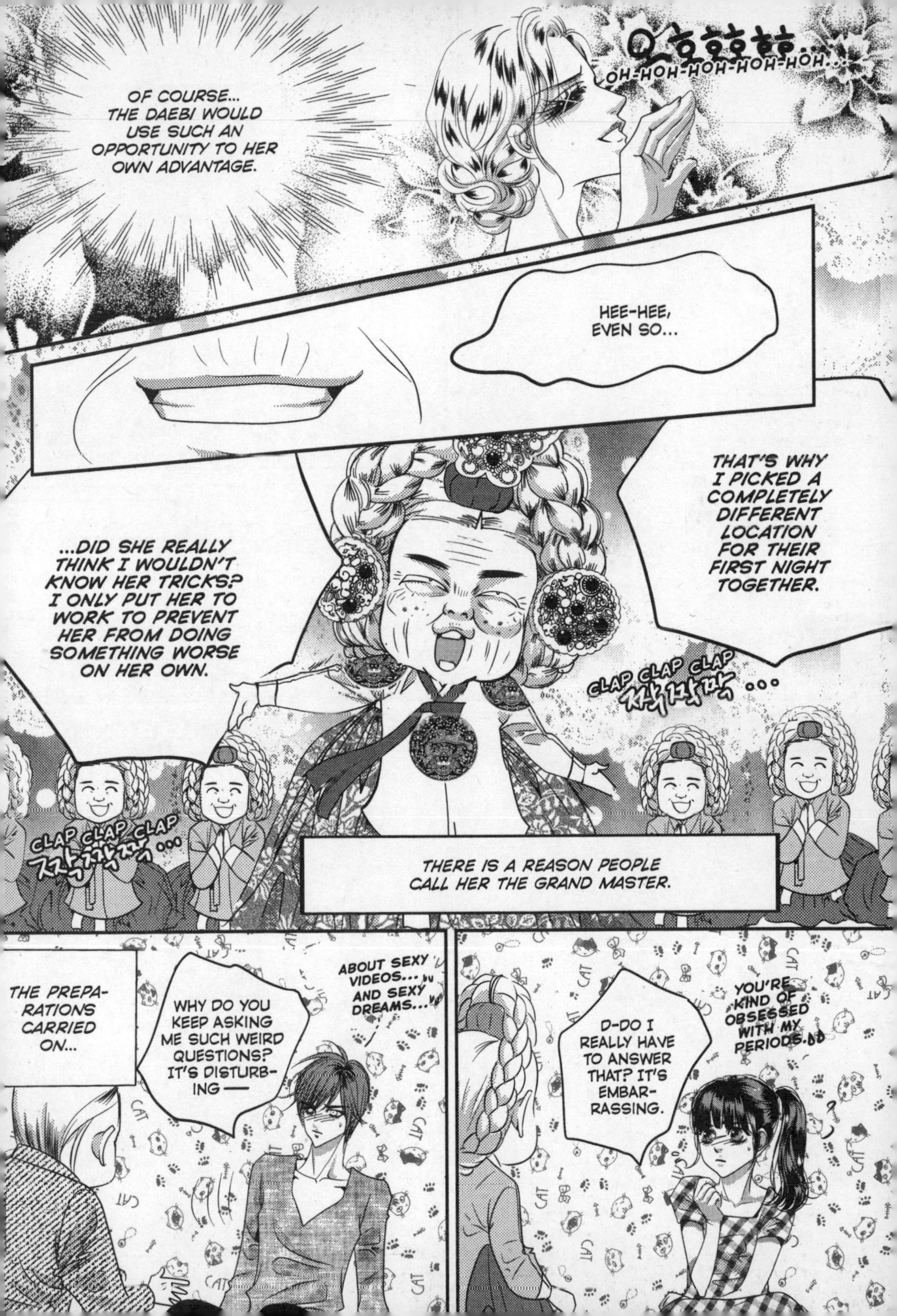
OF COURSE... THE DAEBI WOULD USE SUCH AN OPPORTUNITY TO HER OWN ADVANTAGE.
OH-HOH-HOH-HOH-HOH...
HEE-HEE, EVEN SO...
...DID SHE REALLY THINK I WOULDN'T KNOW HER TRICKS? I ONLY PUT HER TO WORK TO PREVENT HER FROM DOING SOMETHING WORSE ON HER OWN.
THAT'S WHY I PICKED A COMPLETELY DIFFERENT LOCATION FOR THEIR FIRST NIGHT TOGETHER.
CLAP CLAP CLAP...
CLAP CLAP CLAP...
THERE IS A REASON PEOPLE CALL HER THE GRAND MASTER.
THE PREPARATIONS CARRIED ON...
WHY DO YOU KEEP ASKING ME SUCH WEIRD QUESTIONS? IT'S DISTURBING—
ABOUT SEXY VIDEOS... AND SEXY DREAMS...
D-DO I REALLY HAVE TO ANSWER THAT? IT'S EMBARRASSING.
YOU'RE KIND OF OBSESSED WITH MY PERIODS.

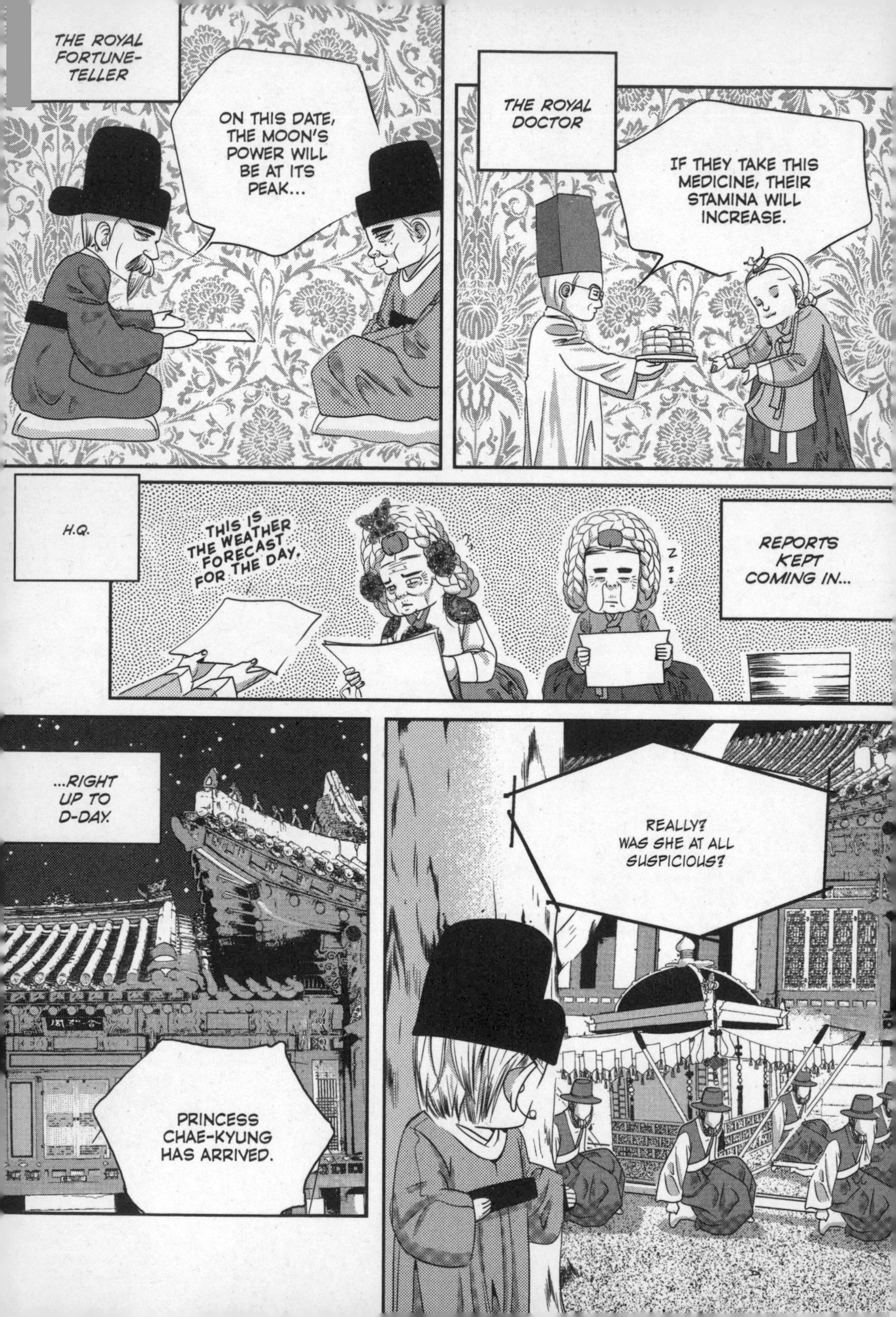
THE ROYAL FORTUNE-TELLER
ON THIS DATE, THE MOON'S POWER WILL BE AT ITS PEAK...
THE ROYAL DOCTOR
IF THEY TAKE THIS MEDICINE, THEIR STAMINA WILL INCREASE.
H.Q.
THIS IS THE WEATHER FORECAST FOR THE DAY.
REPORTS KEPT COMING IN...
...RIGHT UP TO D-DAY.
PRINCESS CHAE-KYUNG HAS ARRIVED.
REALLY? WAS SHE AT ALL SUSPICIOUS?

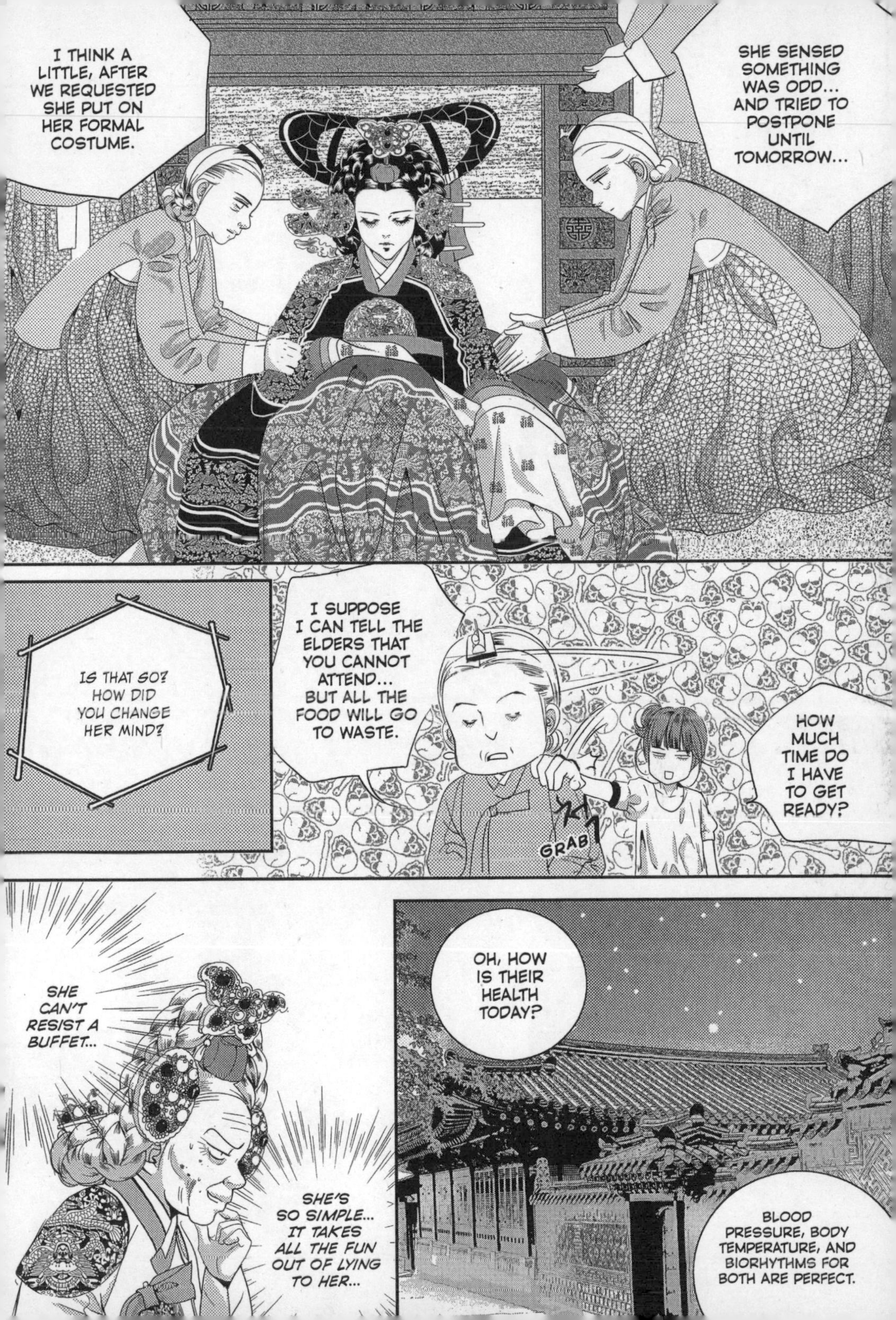
I THINK A LITTLE, AFTER WE REQUESTED SHE PUT ON HER FORMAL COSTUME.
SHE SENSED SOMETHING WAS ODD... AND TRIED TO POSTPONE UNTIL TOMORROW...
IS THAT SO? HOW DID YOU CHANGE HER MIND?
I SUPPOSE I CAN TELL THE ELDERS THAT YOU CANNOT ATTEND... BUT ALL THE FOOD WILL GO TO WASTE.
GRAB
HOW MUCH TIME DO I HAVE TO GET READY?
SHE CAN'T RESIST A BUFFET...
SHE'S SO SIMPLE... IT TAKES ALL THE FUN OUT OF LYING TO HER...
OH, HOW IS THEIR HEALTH TODAY?
BLOOD PRESSURE, BODY TEMPERATURE, AND BIORHYTHMS FOR BOTH ARE PERFECT.

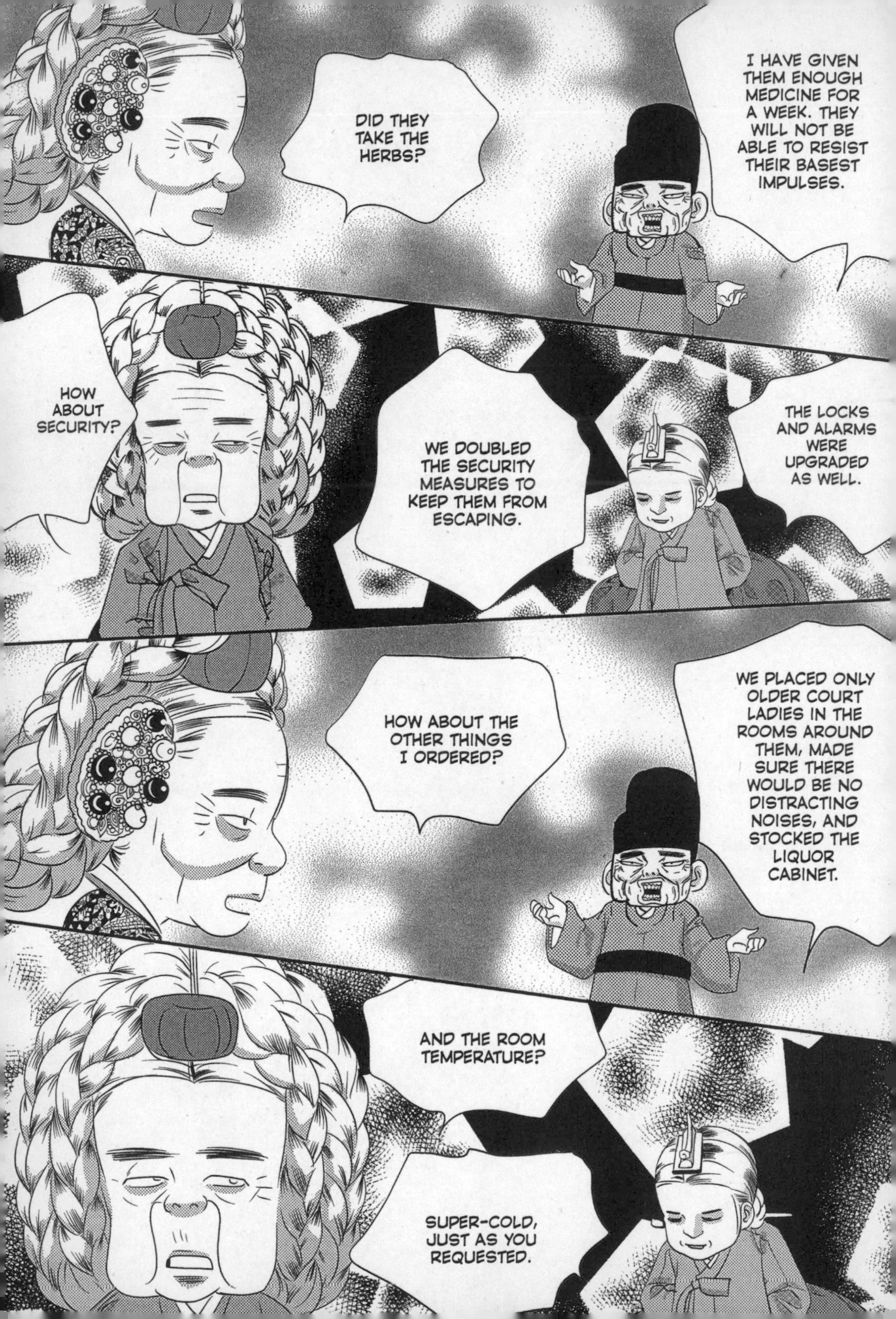

DID THEY TAKE THE HERBS?
I HAVE GIVEN THEM ENOUGH MEDICINE FOR A WEEK. THEY WILL NOT BE ABLE TO RESIST THEIR BASEST IMPULSES.
HOW ABOUT SECURITY?
WE DOUBLED THE SECURITY MEASURES TO KEEP THEM FROM ESCAPING.
THE LOCKS AND ALARMS WERE UPGRADED AS WELL.
HOW ABOUT THE OTHER THINGS I ORDERED?
WE PLACED ONLY OLDER COURT LADIES IN THE ROOMS AROUND THEM, MADE SURE THERE WOULD BE NO DISTRACTING NOISES, AND STOCKED THE LIQUOR CABINET.
AND THE ROOM TEMPERATURE?
SUPER-COLD, JUST AS YOU REQUESTED.

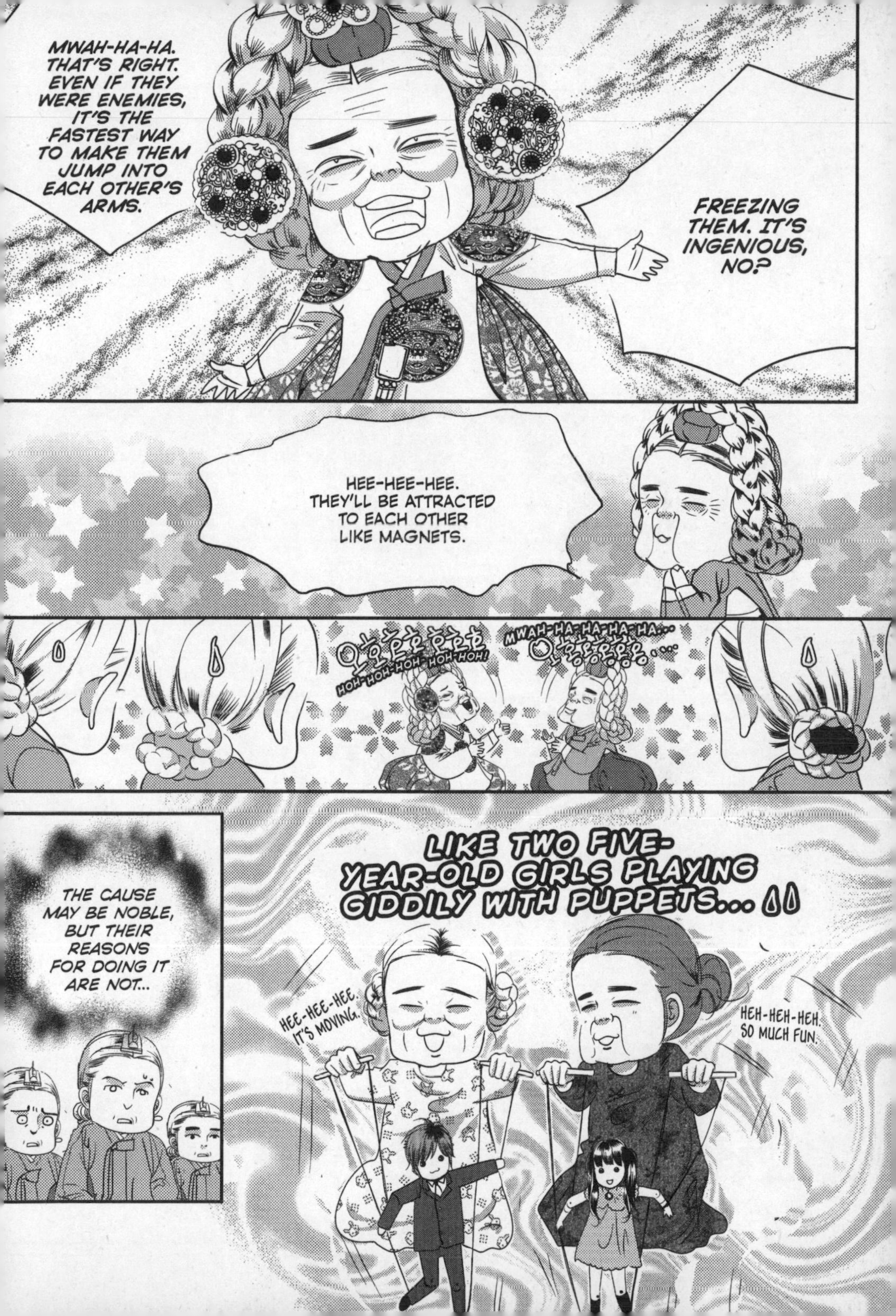
MWAH-HA-HA. THAT'S RIGHT. EVEN IF THEY WERE ENEMIES, IT'S THE FASTEST WAY TO MAKE THEM JUMP INTO EACH OTHER'S ARMS.
FREEZING THEM. IT'S INGENIOUS, NO?
HEE-HEE-HEE. THEY'LL BE ATTRACTED TO EACH OTHER LIKE MAGNETS.
HOH-HOH-HOH-HOH-HOH-HOH!
MWAH-HA-HA-HA-HA...
THE CAUSE MAY BE NOBLE, BUT THEIR REASONS FOR DOING IT ARE NOT...
LIKE TWO FIVE-YEAR-OLD GIRLS PLAYING GIDDILY WITH PUPPETS...
HEE-HEE-HEE. IT'S MOVING.
HEH-HEH-HEH. SO MUCH FUN.

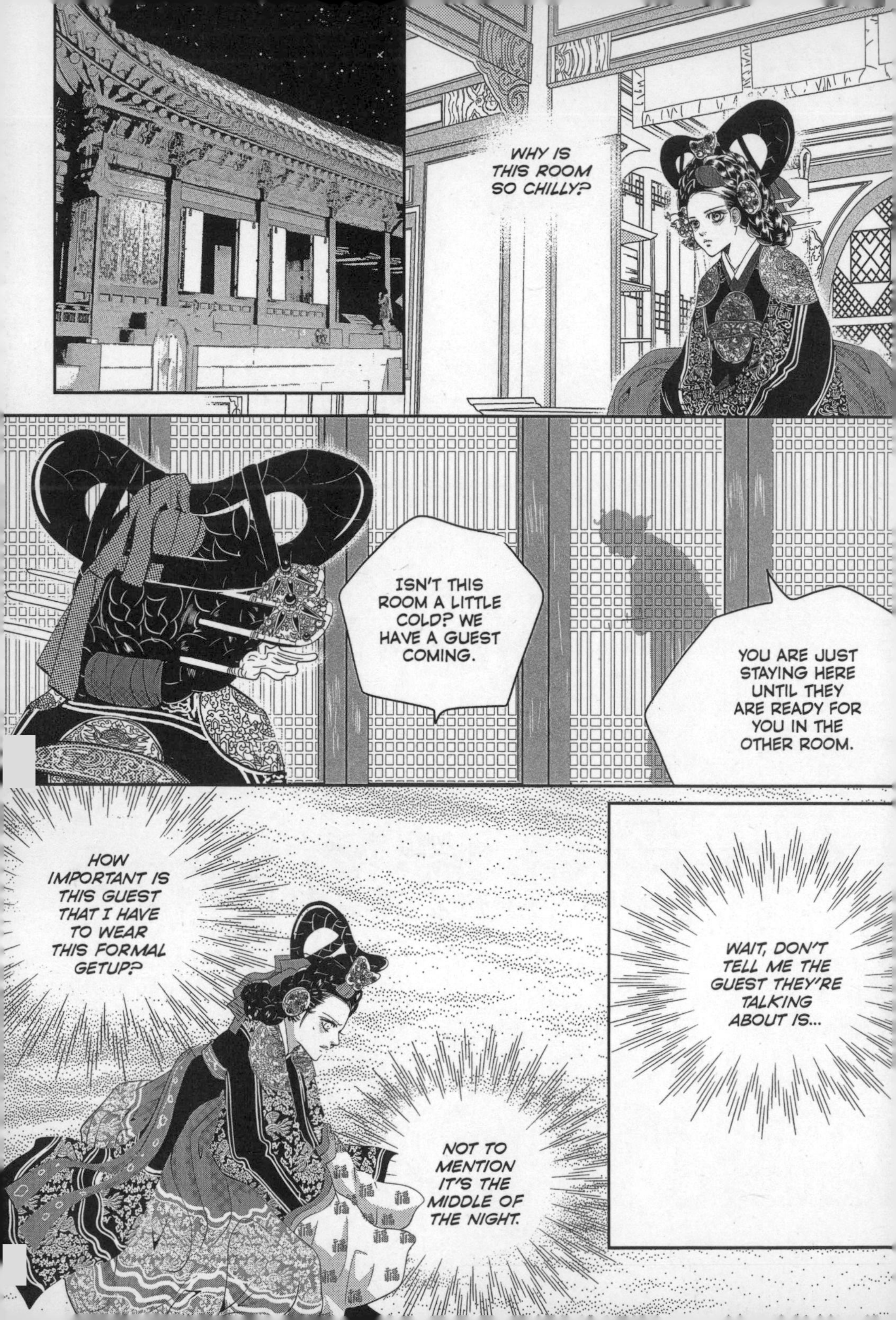
WHY IS THIS ROOM SO CHILLY?
ISN'T THIS ROOM A LITTLE COLD? WE HAVE A GUEST COMING.
YOU ARE JUST STAYING HERE UNTIL THEY ARE READY FOR YOU IN THE OTHER ROOM.
HOW IMPORTANT IS THIS GUEST THAT I HAVE TO WEAR THIS FORMAL GETUP?
NOT TO MENTION IT'S THE MIDDLE OF THE NIGHT.
WAIT, DON'T TELL ME THE GUEST THEY'RE TALKING ABOUT IS...

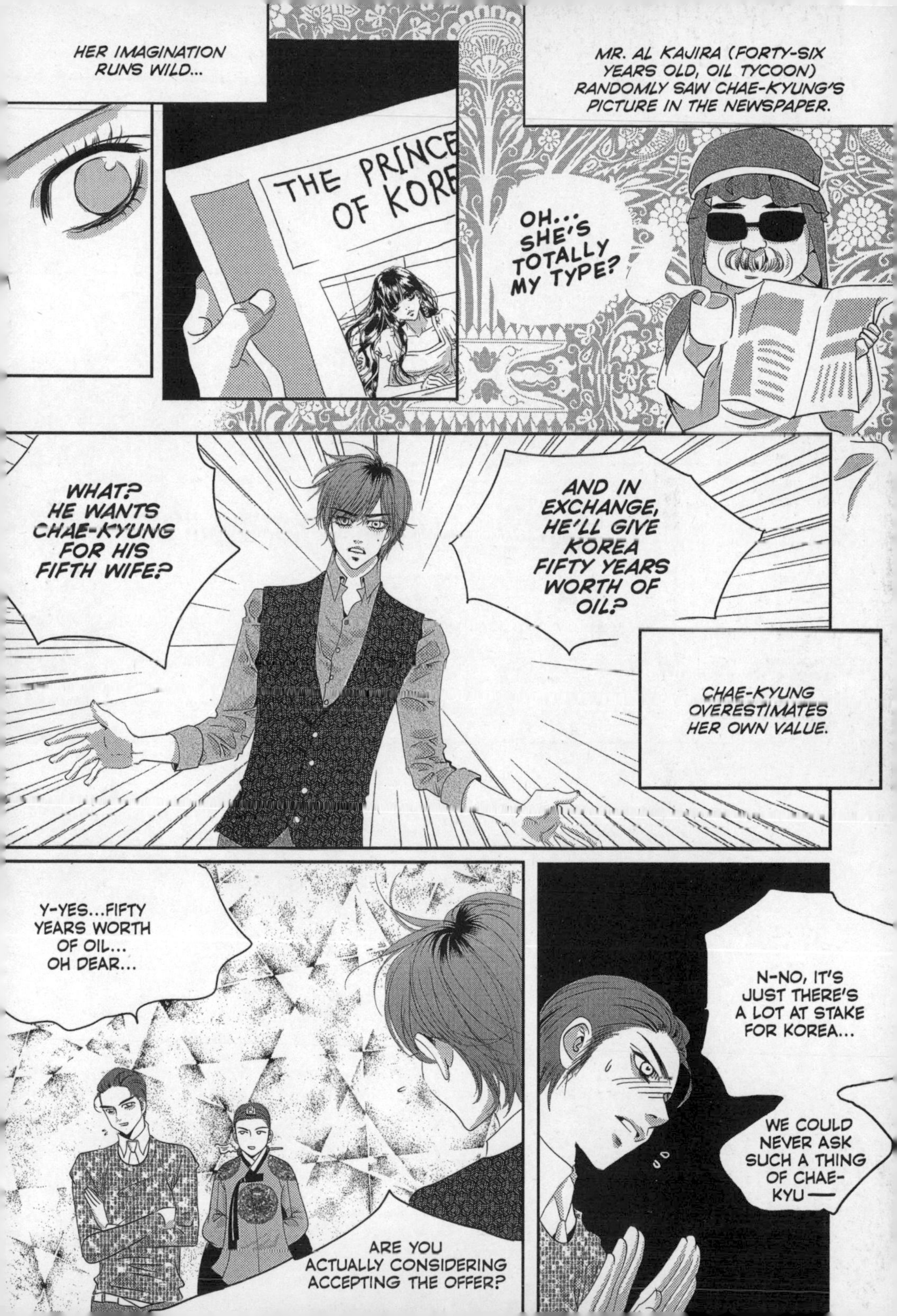
HER IMAGINATION RUNS WILD...
MR. AL KAJIRA (FORTY-SIX YEARS OLD, OIL TYCOON) RANDOMLY SAW CHAE-KYUNG'S PICTURE IN THE NEWSPAPER.
THE PRINCE OF KORE
OH... SHE'S TOTALLY MY TYPE?
WHAT? HE WANTS CHAE-KYUNG FOR HIS FIFTH WIFE?
AND IN EXCHANGE, HE'LL GIVE KOREA FIFTY YEARS WORTH OF OIL?
CHAE-KYUNG OVERESTIMATES HER OWN VALUE.
Y-YES...FIFTY YEARS WORTH OF OIL... OH DEAR...
ARE YOU ACTUALLY CONSIDERING ACCEPTING THE OFFER?
N-NO, IT'S JUST THERE'S A LOT AT STAKE FOR KOREA...
WE COULD NEVER ASK SUCH A THING OF CHAE-KYU—

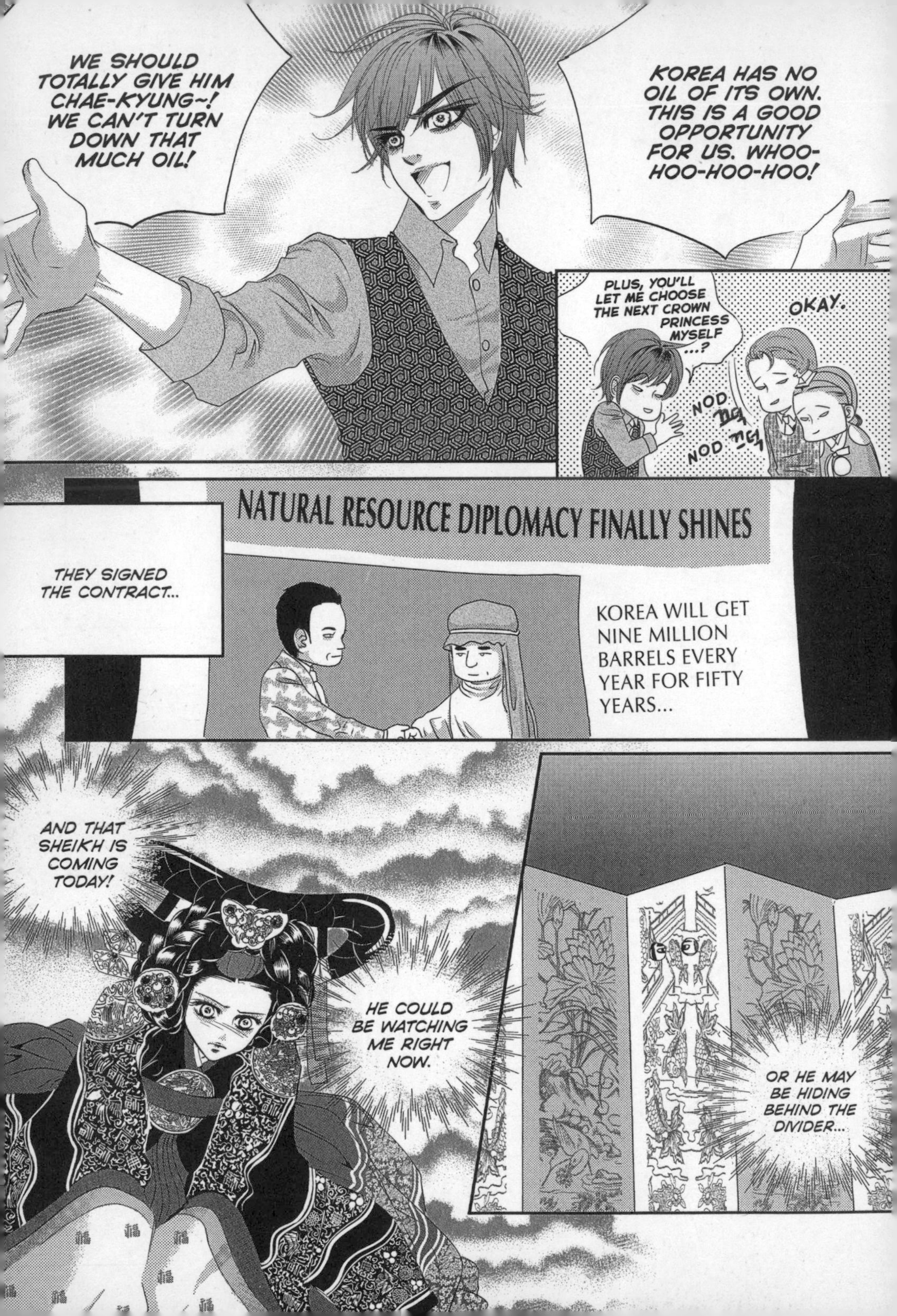
WE SHOULD TOTALLY GIVE HIM CHAE-KYUNG~! WE CAN'T TURN DOWN THAT MUCH OIL!
KOREA HAS NO OIL OF ITS OWN. THIS IS A GOOD OPPORTUNITY FOR US. WHOO-HOO-HOO-HOO!
PLUS, YOU'LL LET ME CHOOSE THE NEXT CROWN PRINCESS MYSELF ...?
OKAY.
NOD
NOD
THEY SIGNED THE CONTRACT...
NATURAL RESOURCE DIPLOMACY FINALLY SHINES
KOREA WILL GET NINE MILLION BARRELS EVERY YEAR FOR FIFTY YEARS...
AND THAT SHEIKH IS COMING TODAY!
HE COULD BE WATCHING ME RIGHT NOW.
OR HE MAY BE HIDING BEHIND THE DIVIDER...

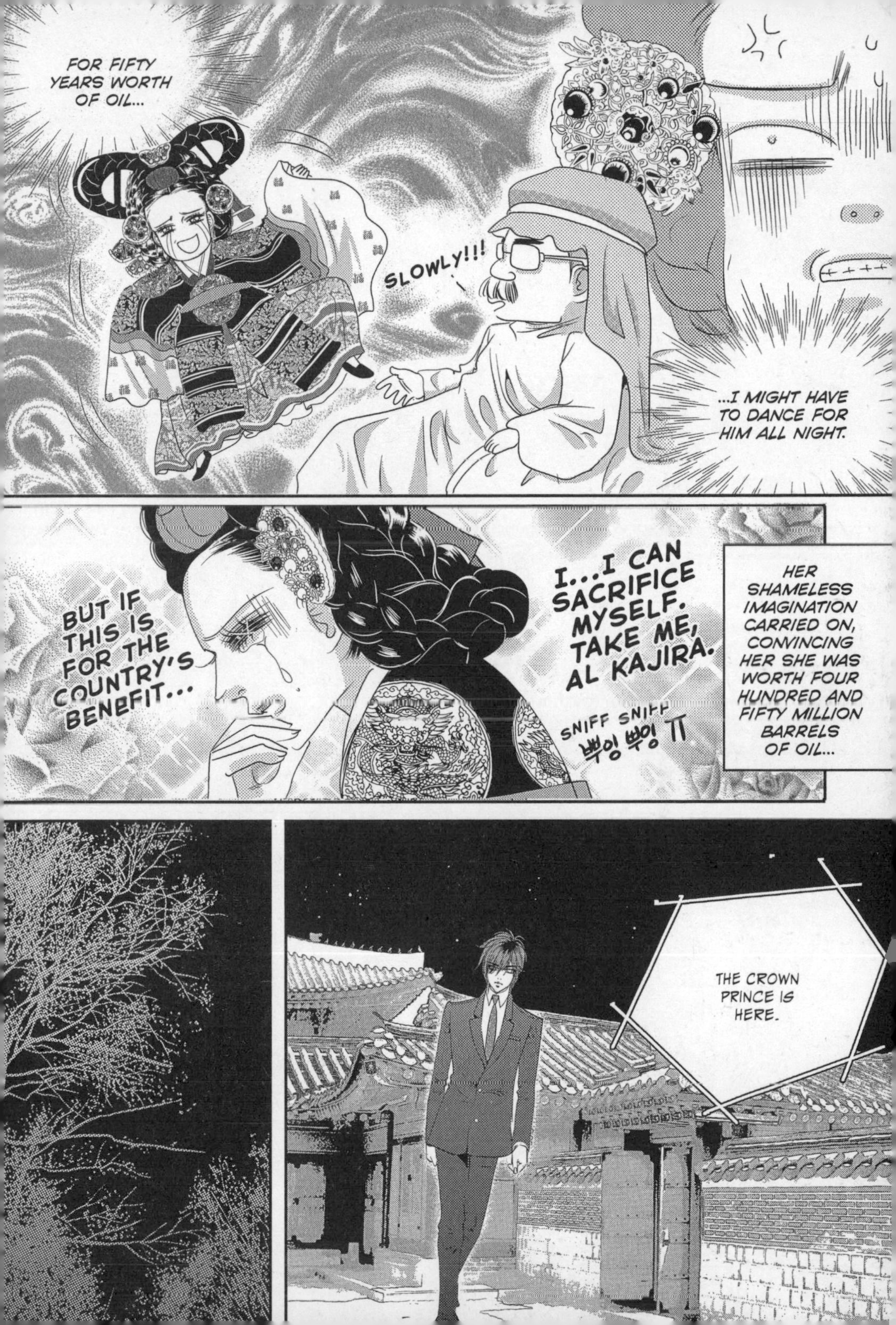
FOR FIFTY YEARS WORTH OF OIL...
SLOWLY!!!
...I MIGHT HAVE TO DANCE FOR HIM ALL NIGHT.
BUT IF THIS IS FOR THE COUNTRY'S BENEFIT...
I...I CAN SACRIFICE MYSELF. TAKE ME, AL KAJIRA.
SNIFF SNIFF
뿌잉 뿌잉 ㅠ
HER SHAMELESS IMAGINATION CARRIED ON, CONVINCING HER SHE WAS WORTH FOUR HUNDRED AND FIFTY MILLION BARRELS OF OIL...
THE CROWN PRINCE IS HERE.

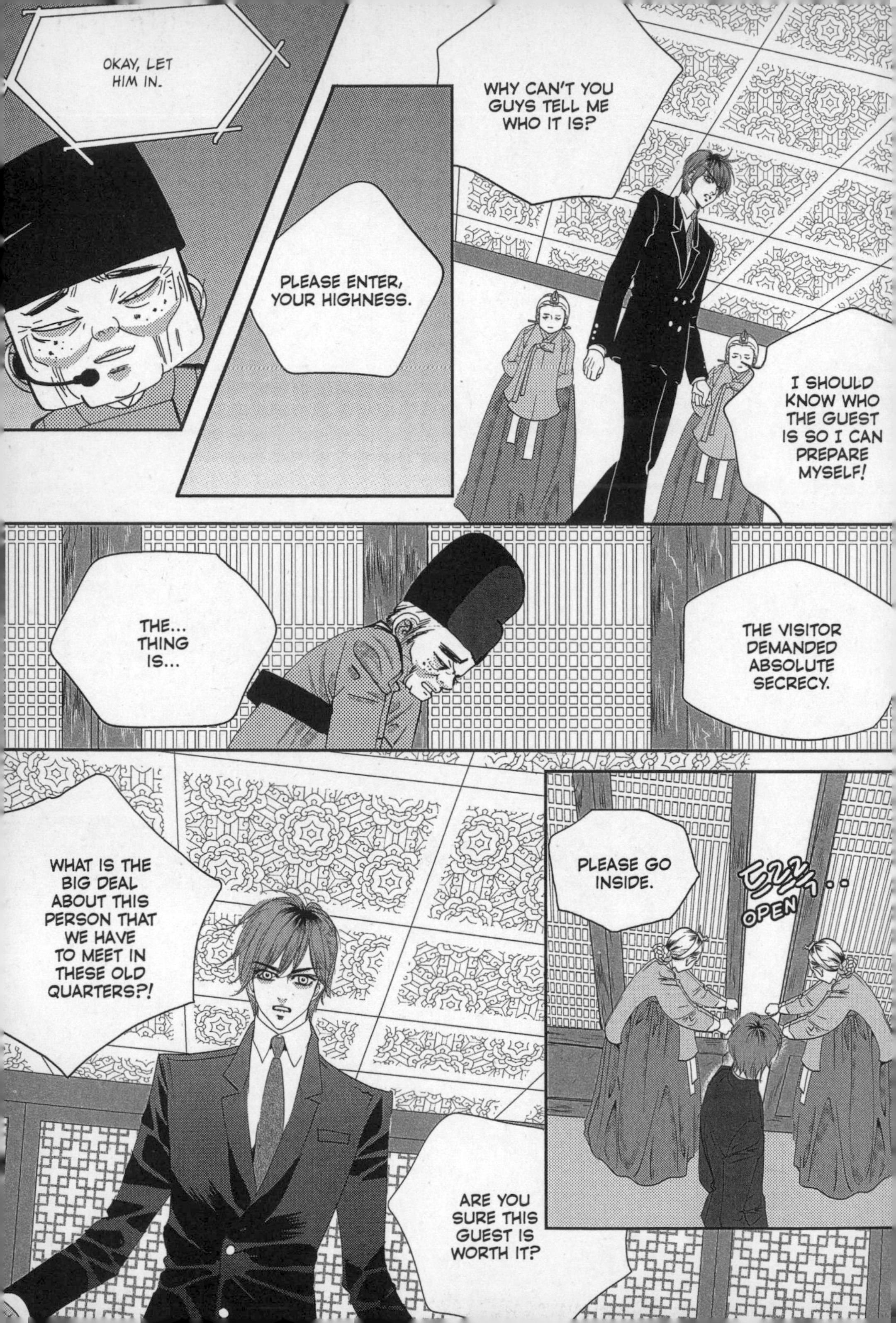
OKAY, LET HIM IN.
PLEASE ENTER, YOUR HIGHNESS.
WHY CAN'T YOU GUYS TELL ME WHO IT IS?
I SHOULD KNOW WHO THE GUEST IS SO I CAN PREPARE MYSELF!
THE... THING IS...
THE VISITOR DEMANDED ABSOLUTE SECRECY.
WHAT IS THE BIG DEAL ABOUT THIS PERSON THAT WE HAVE TO MEET IN THESE OLD QUARTERS?!
ARE YOU SURE THIS GUEST IS WORTH IT?
PLEASE GO INSIDE.
OPEN

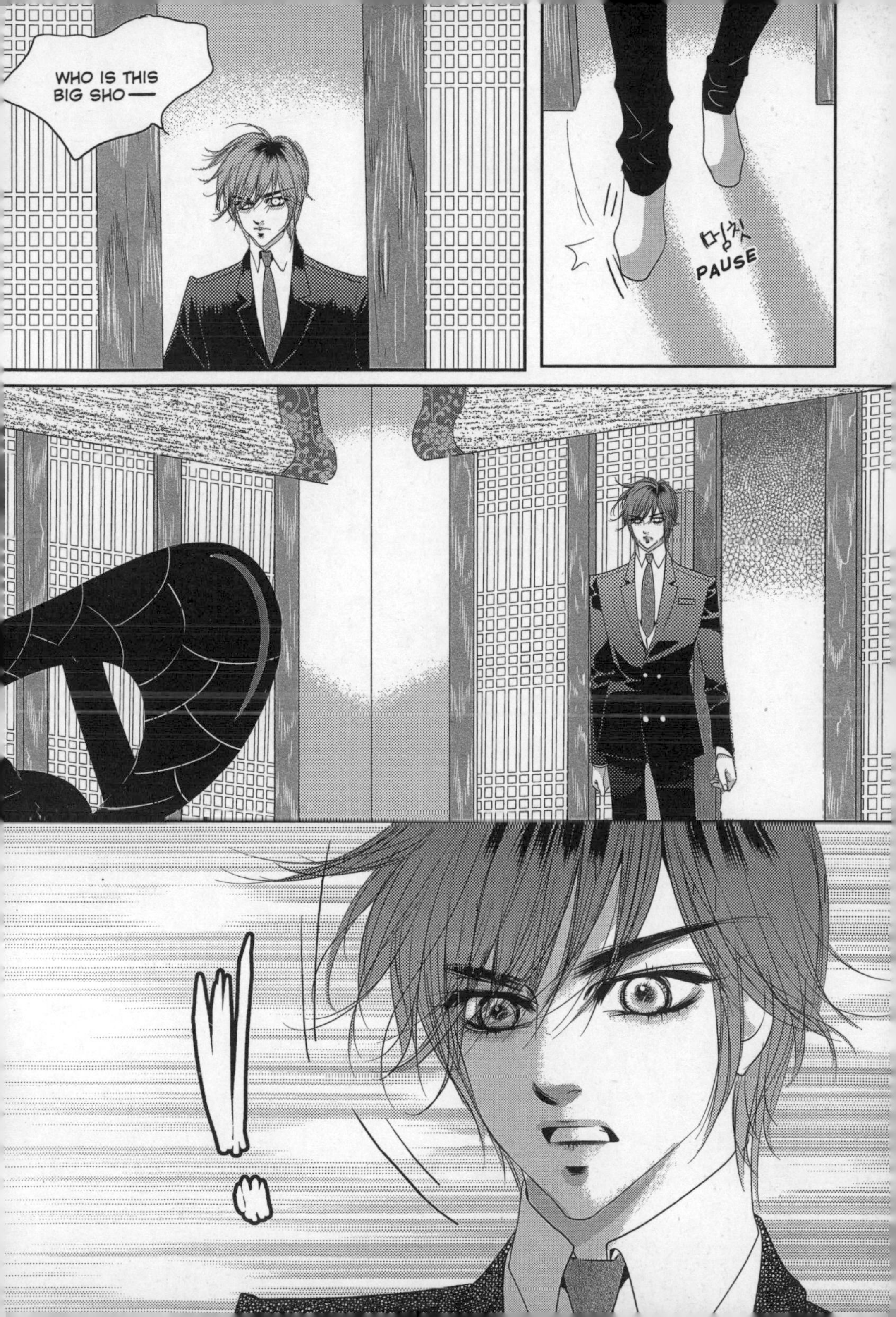
WHO IS THIS BIG SHO—
멈칫
PAUSE

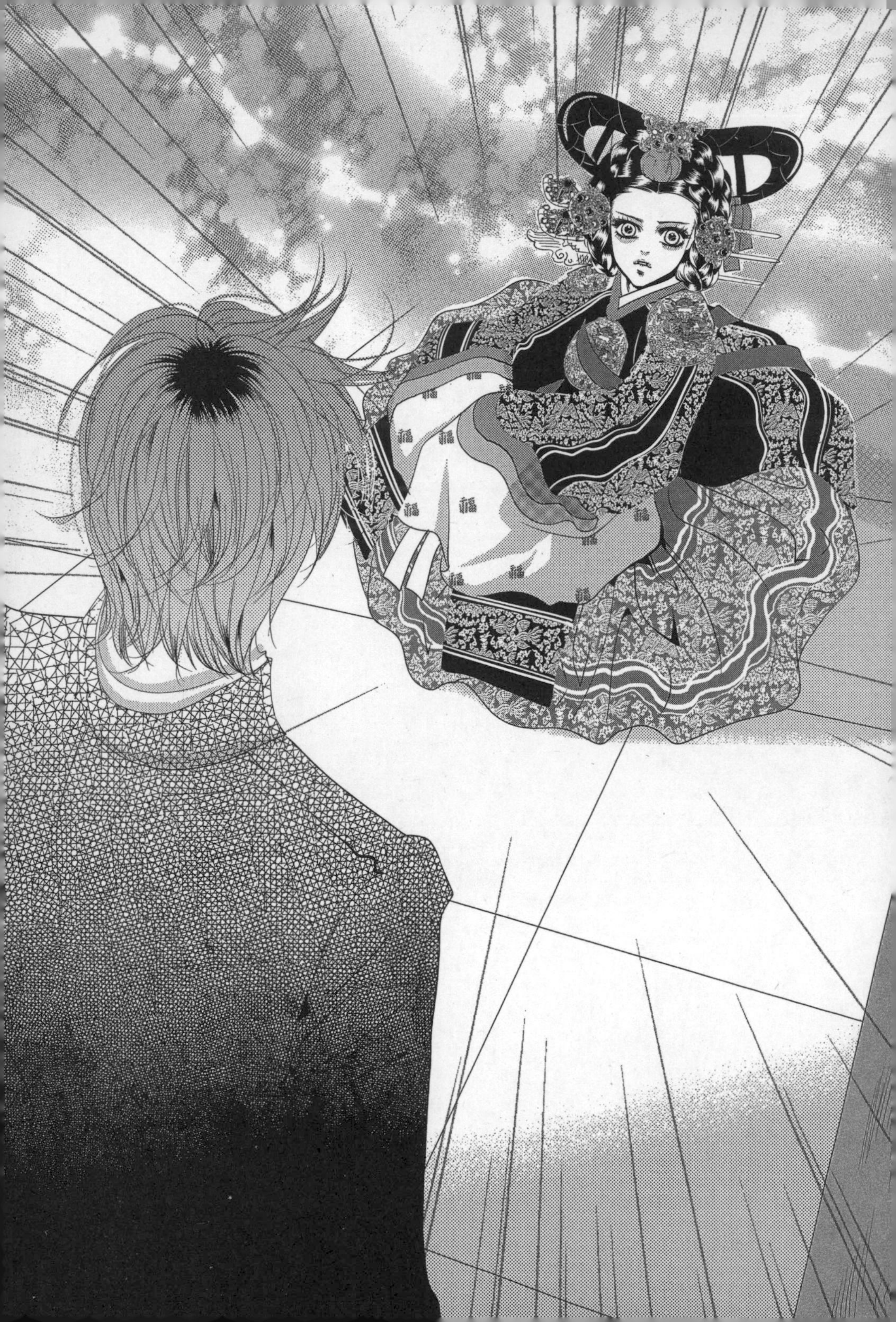

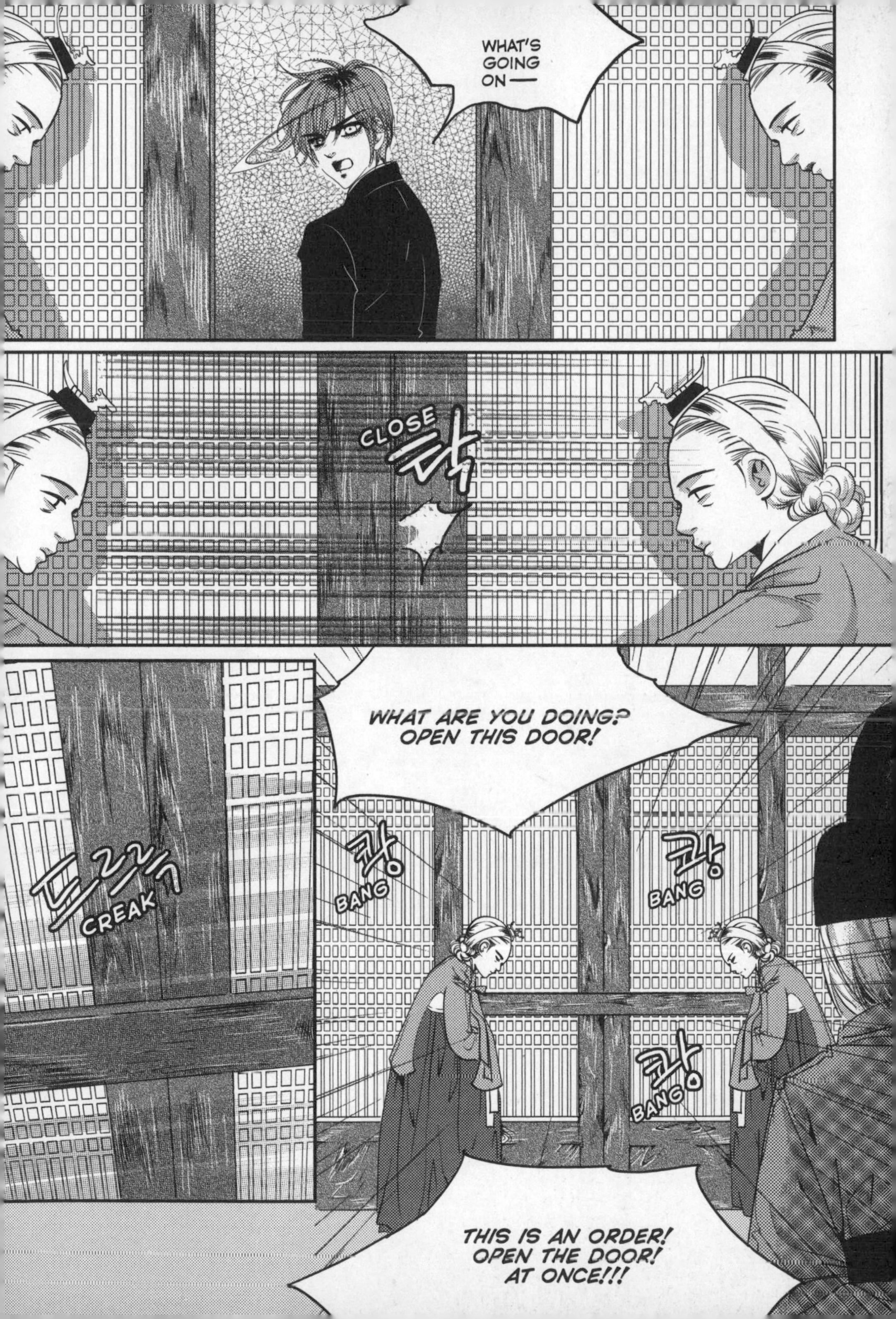
WHAT'S GOING ON—
CLOSE
탁
CREAK
WHAT ARE YOU DOING? OPEN THIS DOOR!
쾅
BANG
쾅
BANG
쾅
BANG
THIS IS AN ORDER! OPEN THE DOOR! AT ONCE!!!

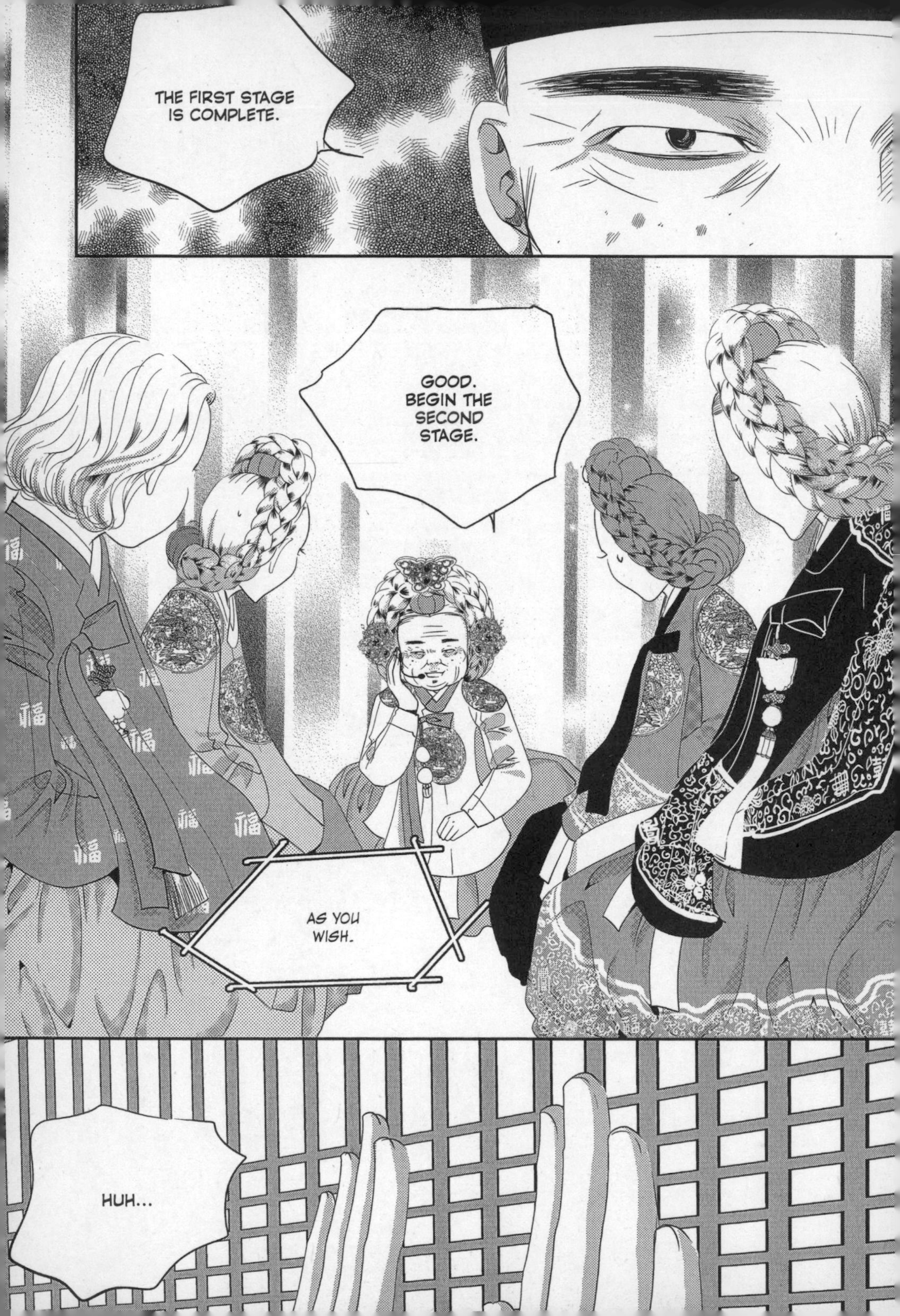
THE FIRST STAGE IS COMPLETE.
GOOD. BEGIN THE SECOND STAGE.
AS YOU WISH.
HUH...

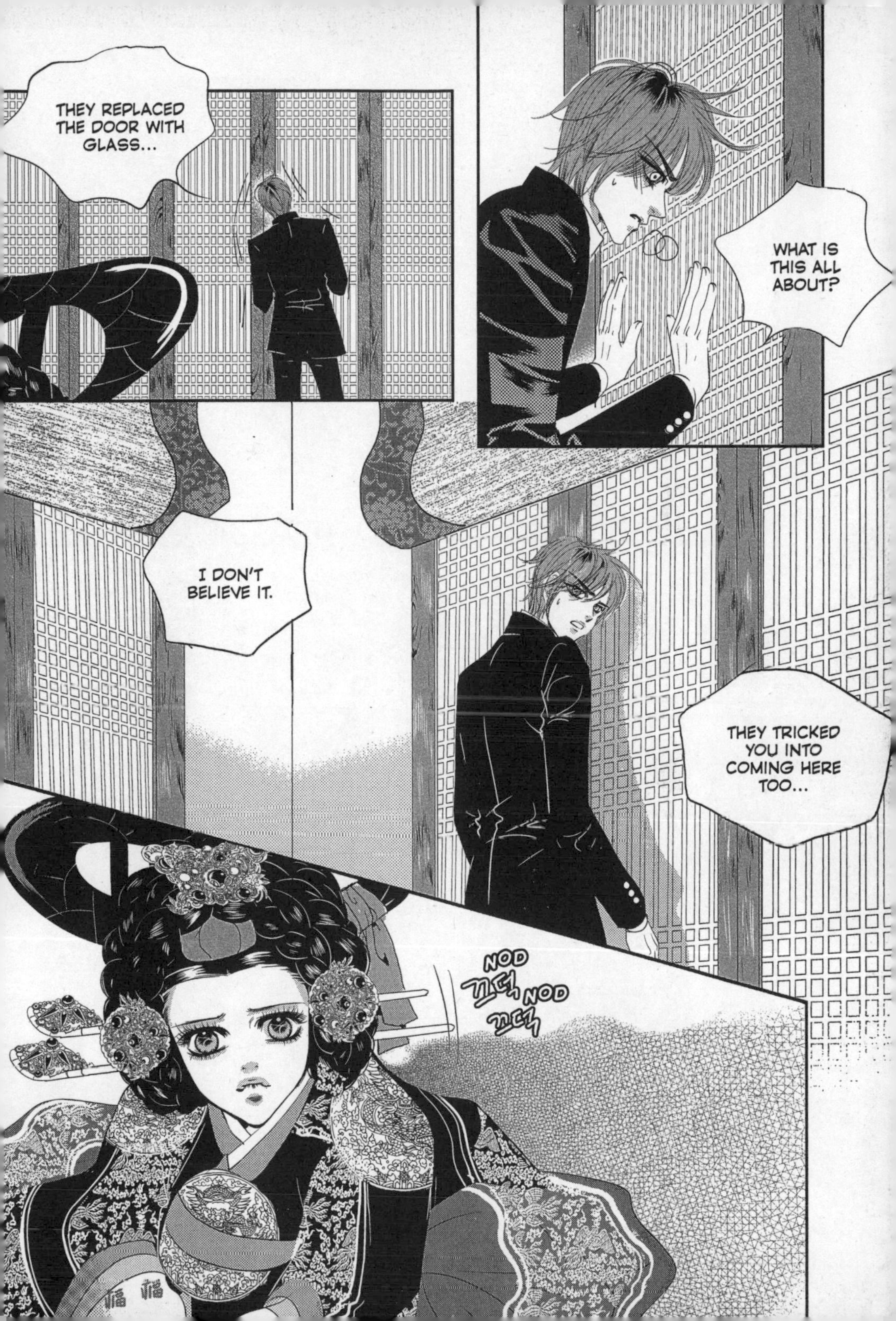
THEY REPLACED THE DOOR WITH GLASS...
WHAT IS THIS ALL ABOUT?
I DON'T BELIEVE IT.
THEY TRICKED YOU INTO COMING HERE TOO...
NOD 끄덕 NOD 끄덕

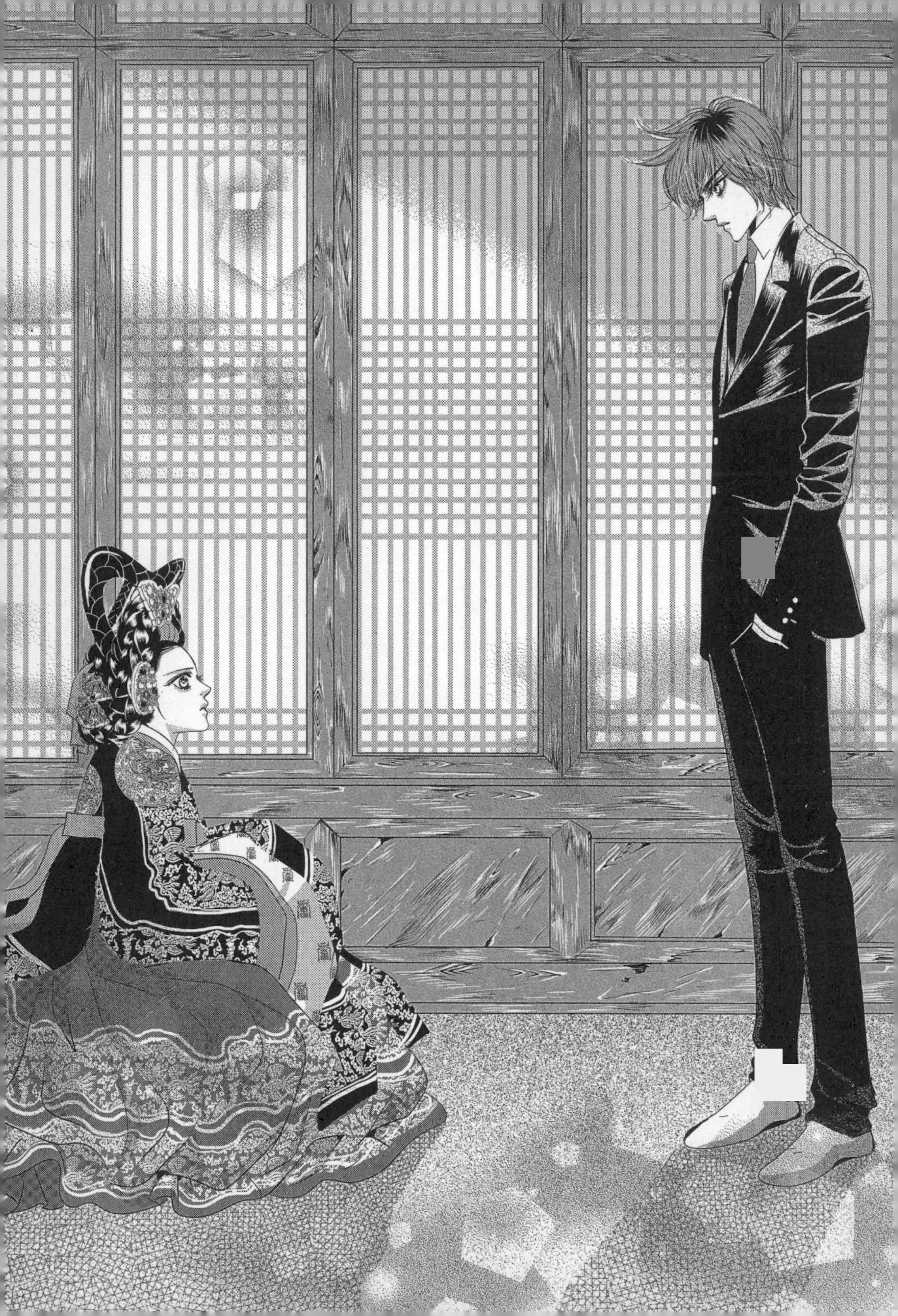

THE STORY OF SPENDING A NIGHT TOGETHER: PART 2
—WHAT HAPPENED IN THE BEDROOM—

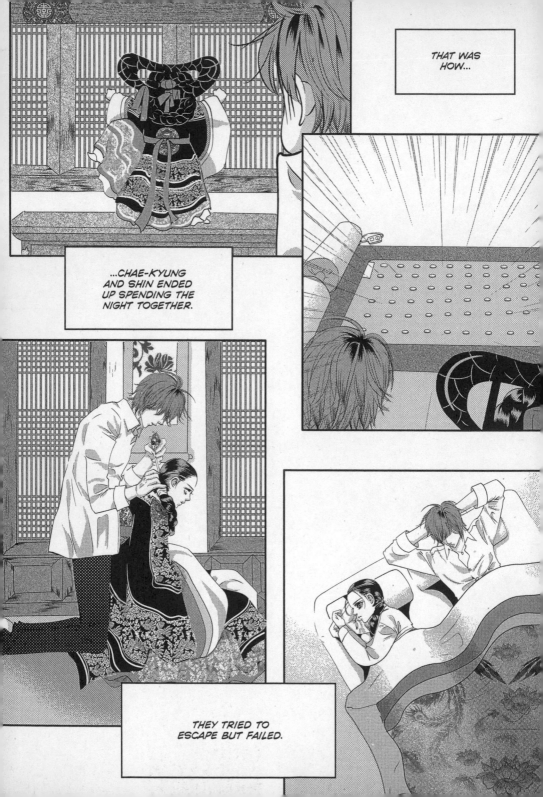

THAT WAS HOW...

...CHAE-KYUNG AND SHIN ENDED UP SPENDING THE NIGHT TOGETHER.

THEY TRIED TO ESCAPE BUT FAILED.

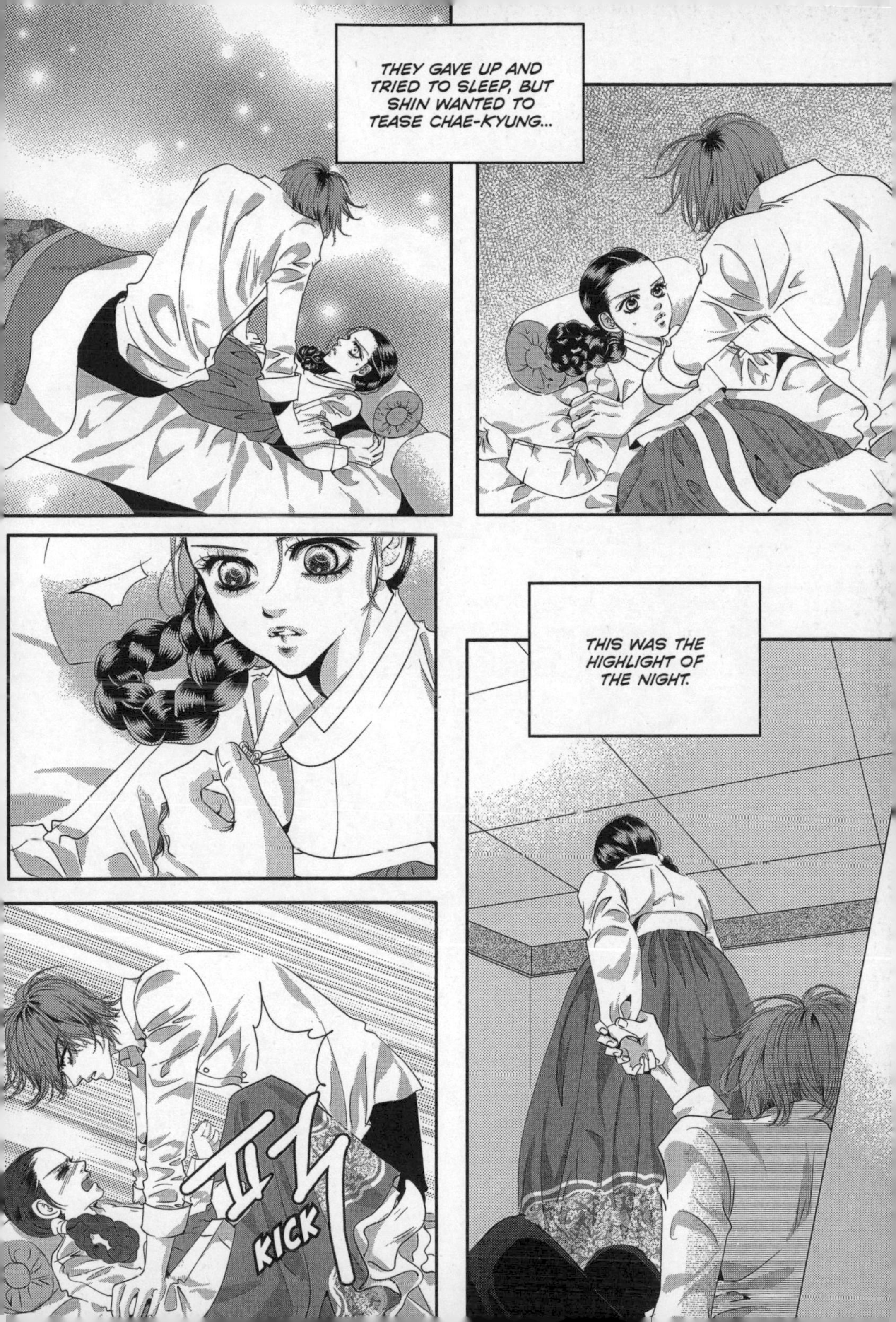
THEY GAVE UP AND TRIED TO SLEEP, BUT SHIN WANTED TO TEASE CHAE-KYUNG...
THIS WAS THE HIGHLIGHT OF THE NIGHT.
KICK

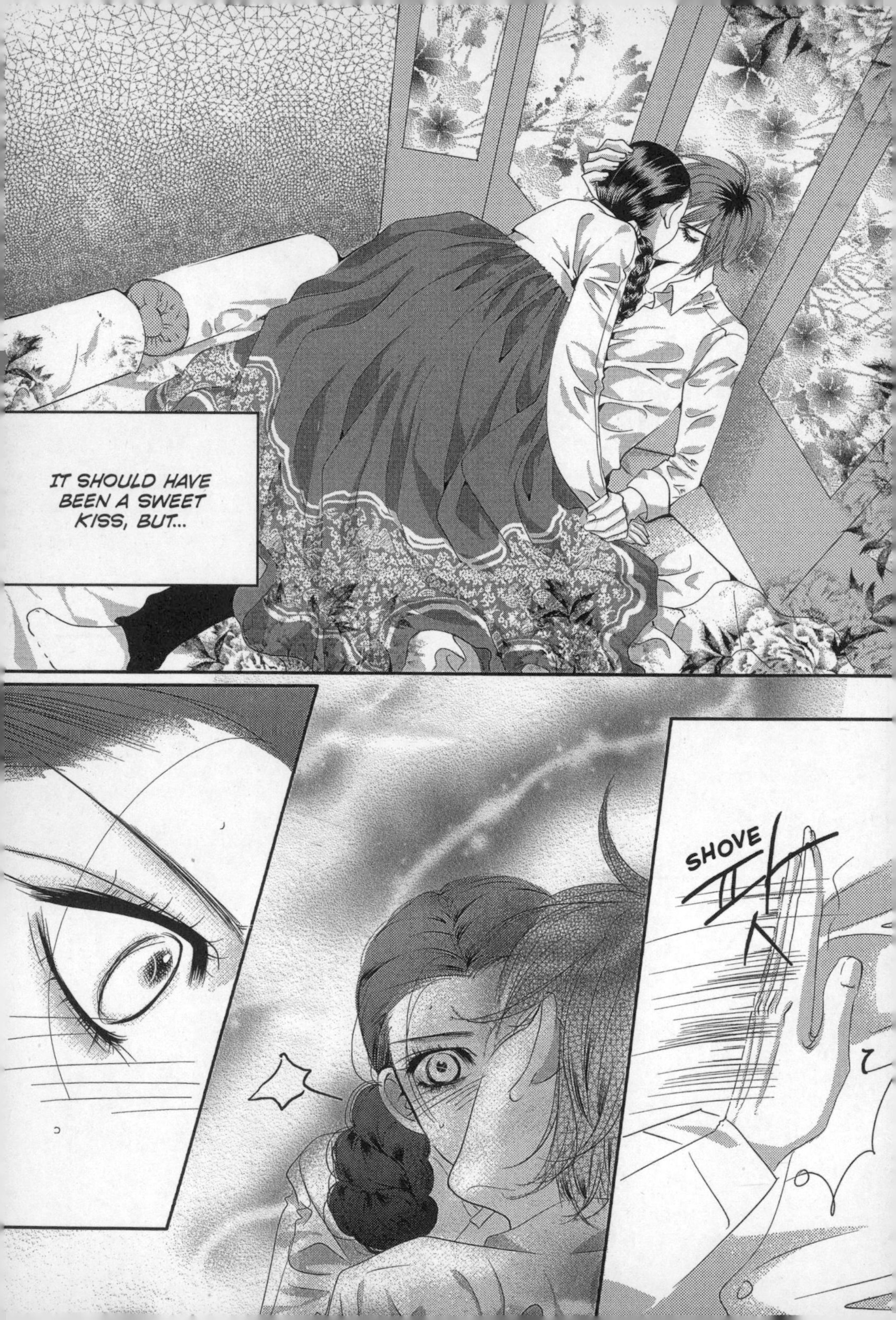
IT SHOULD HAVE BEEN A SWEET KISS, BUT...
SHOVE

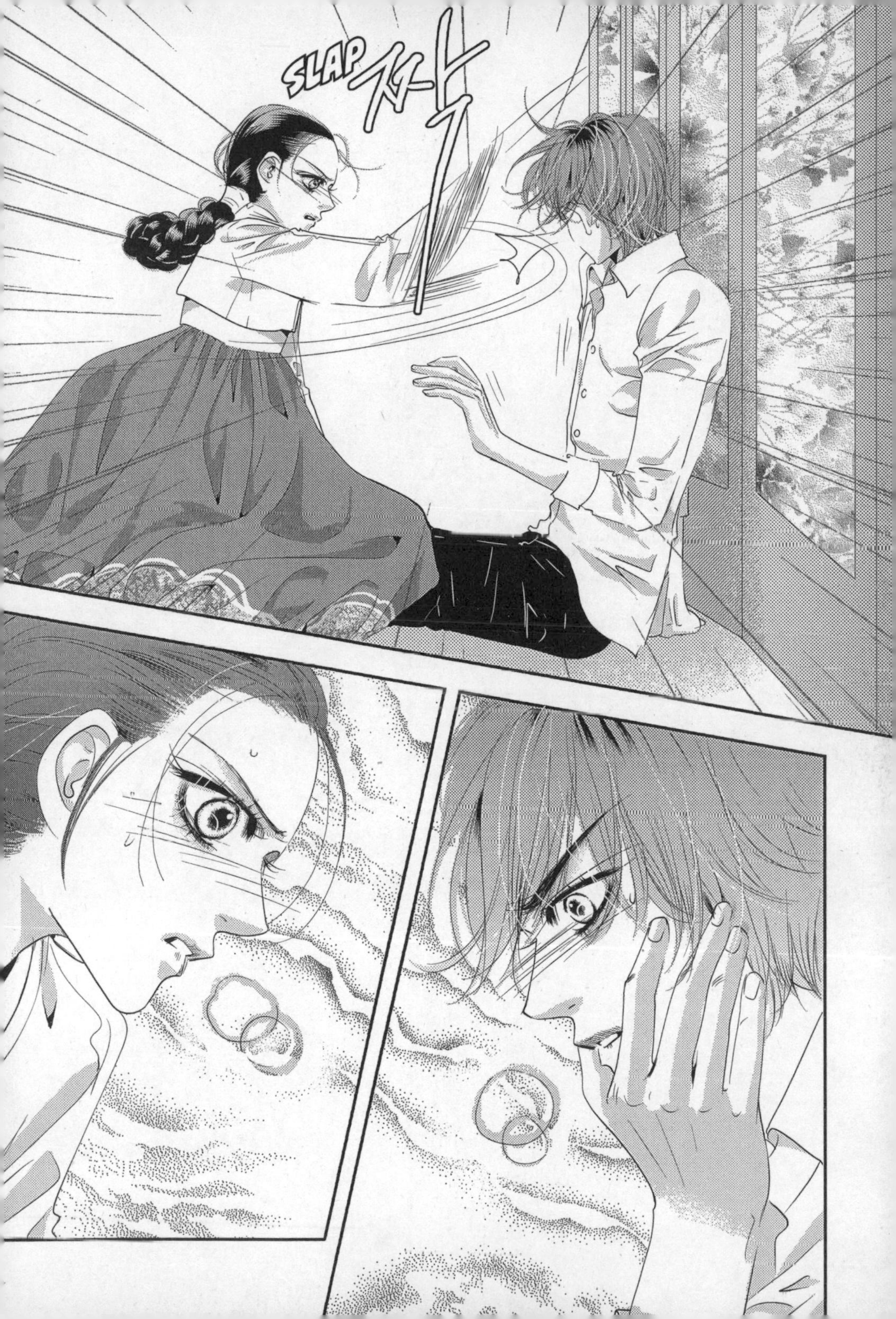
SLAP

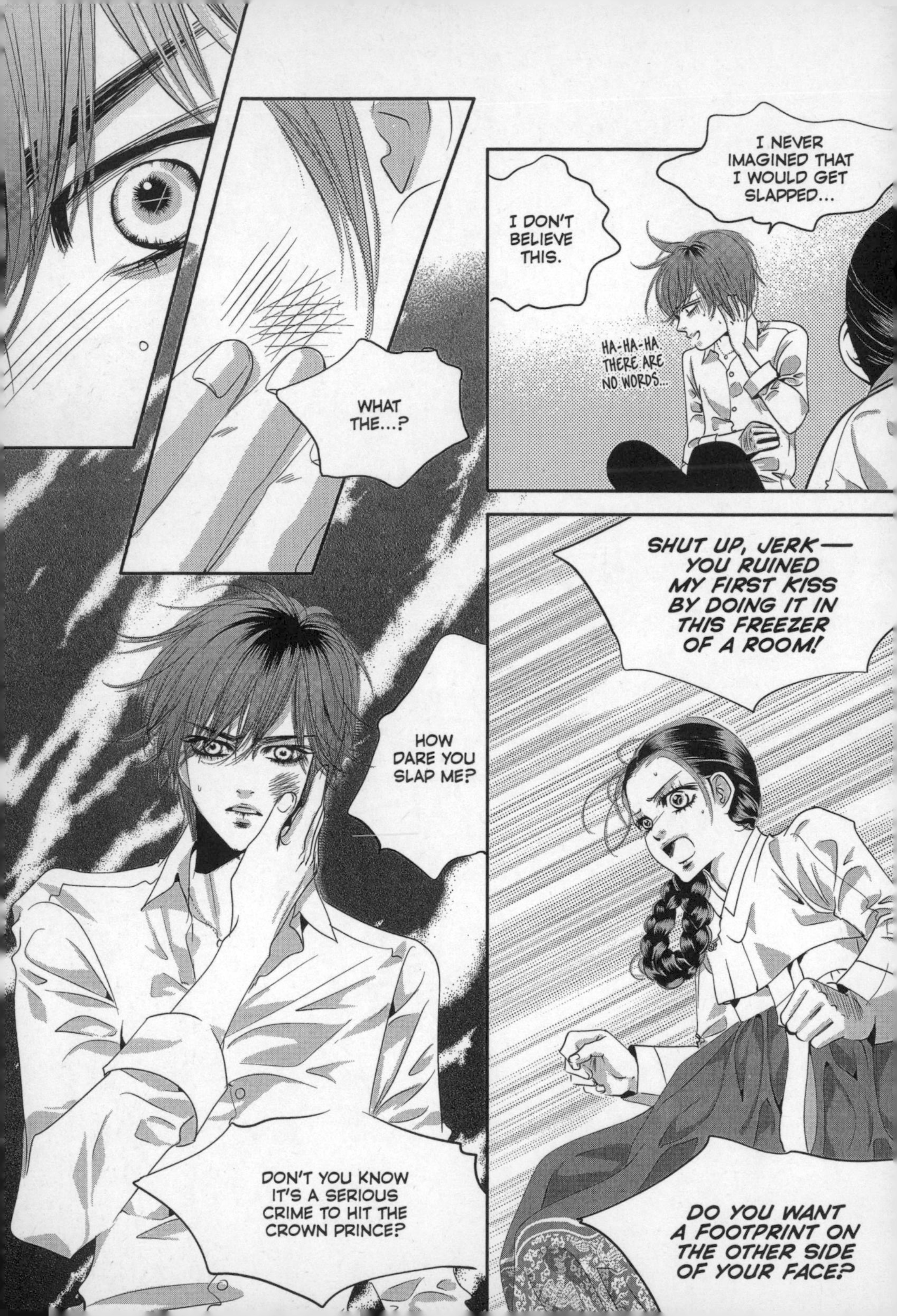

WHAT THE...?
I NEVER IMAGINED THAT I WOULD GET SLAPPED...
I DON'T BELIEVE THIS.
HA-HA-HA. THERE ARE NO WORDS...
HOW DARE YOU SLAP ME?
DON'T YOU KNOW IT'S A SERIOUS CRIME TO HIT THE CROWN PRINCE?
SHUT UP, JERK— YOU RUINED MY FIRST KISS BY DOING IT IN THIS FREEZER OF A ROOM!
DO YOU WANT A FOOTPRINT ON THE OTHER SIDE OF YOUR FACE?

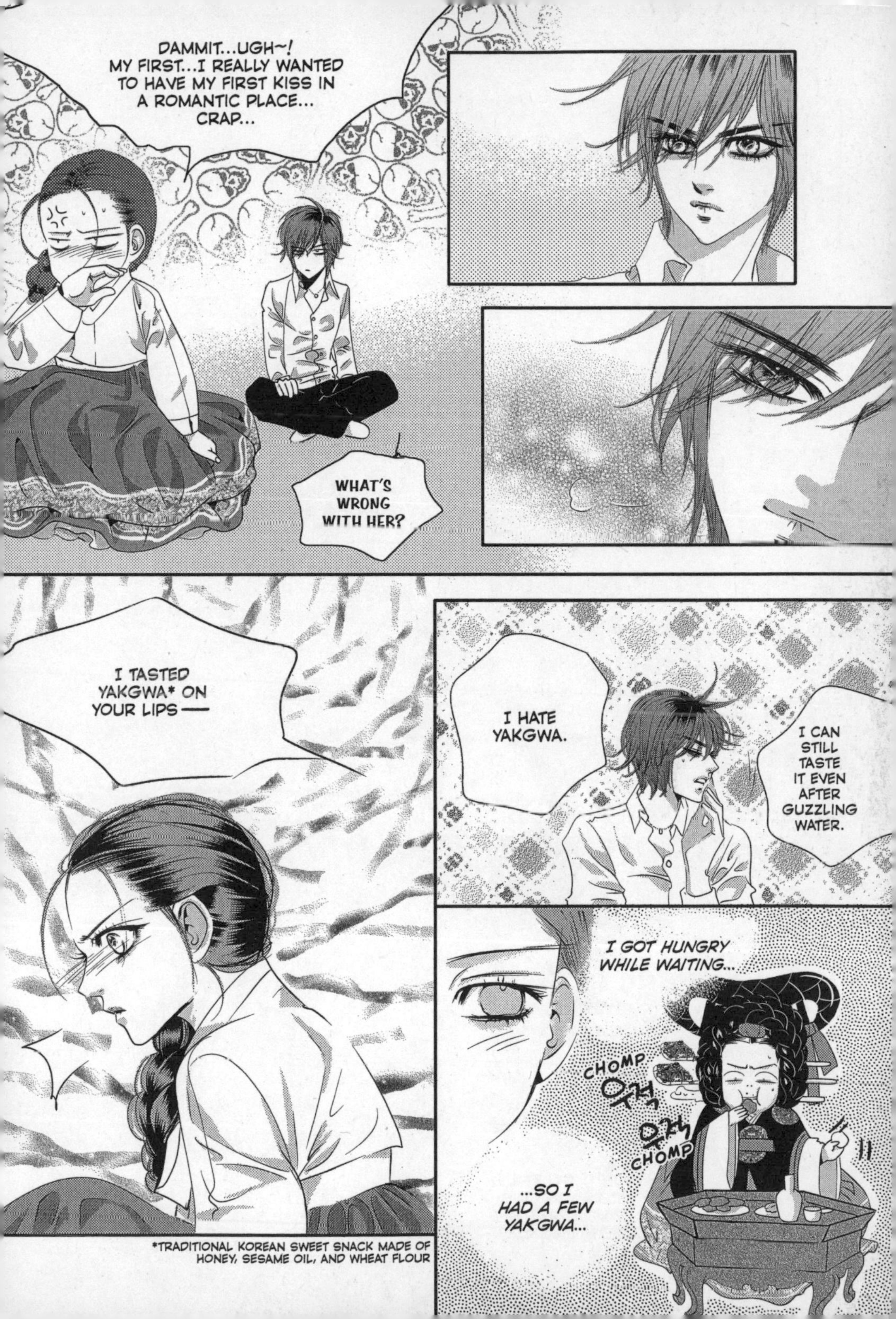
DAMMIT...UGH~! MY FIRST...I REALLY WANTED TO HAVE MY FIRST KISS IN A ROMANTIC PLACE... CRAP...
WHAT'S WRONG WITH HER?
I TASTED YAKGWA* ON YOUR LIPS—
I HATE YAKGWA.
I CAN STILL TASTE IT EVEN AFTER GUZZLING WATER.
I GOT HUNGRY WHILE WAITING...
CHOMP
우적
우적
CHOMP
...SO I HAD A FEW YAKGWA...

*TRADITIONAL KOREAN SWEET SNACK MADE OF HONEY, SESAME OIL, AND WHEAT FLOUR

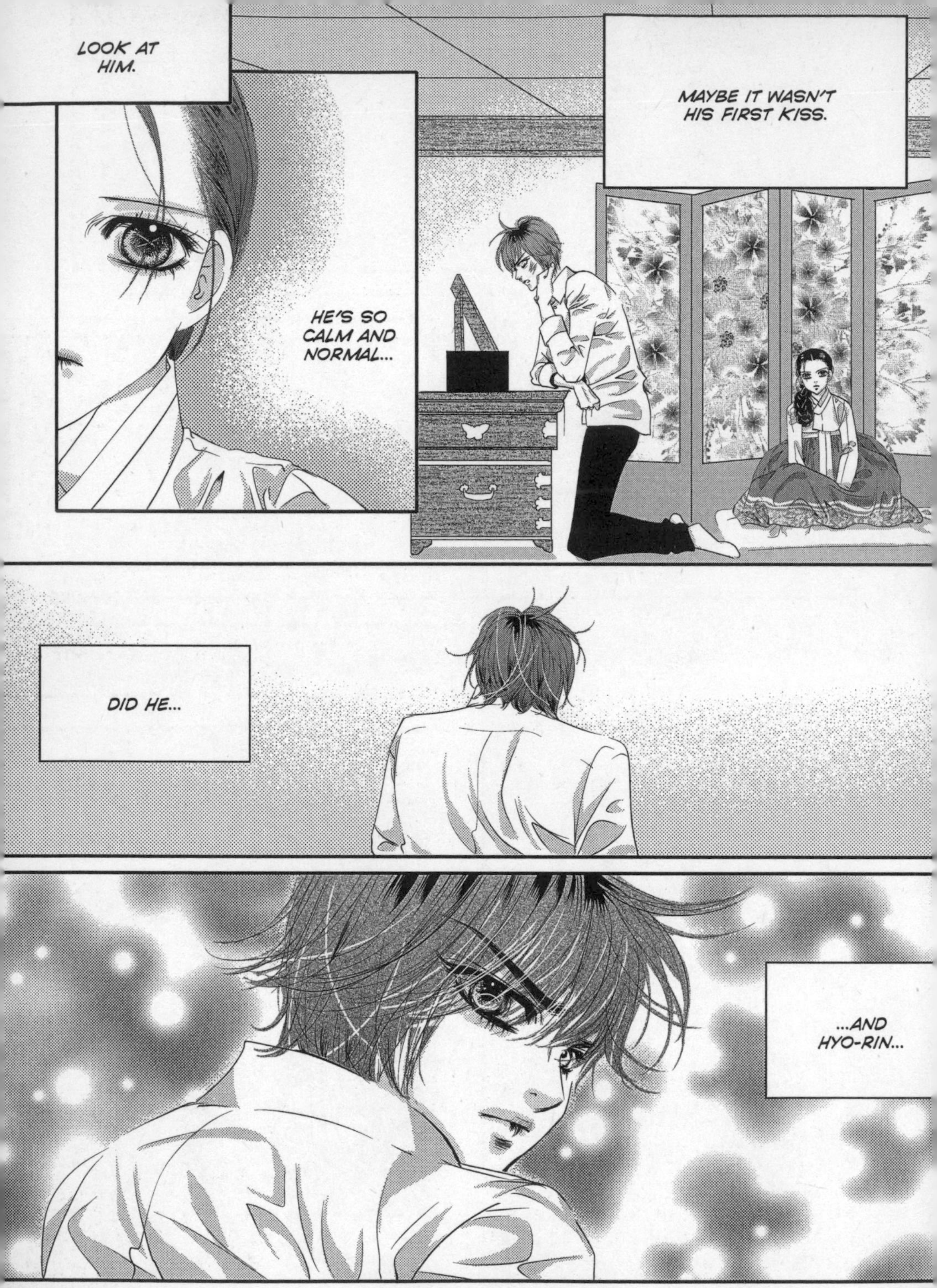
LOOK AT HIM.
MAYBE IT WASN'T HIS FIRST KISS.
HE'S SO CALM AND NORMAL...
DID HE...
...AND HYO-RIN...

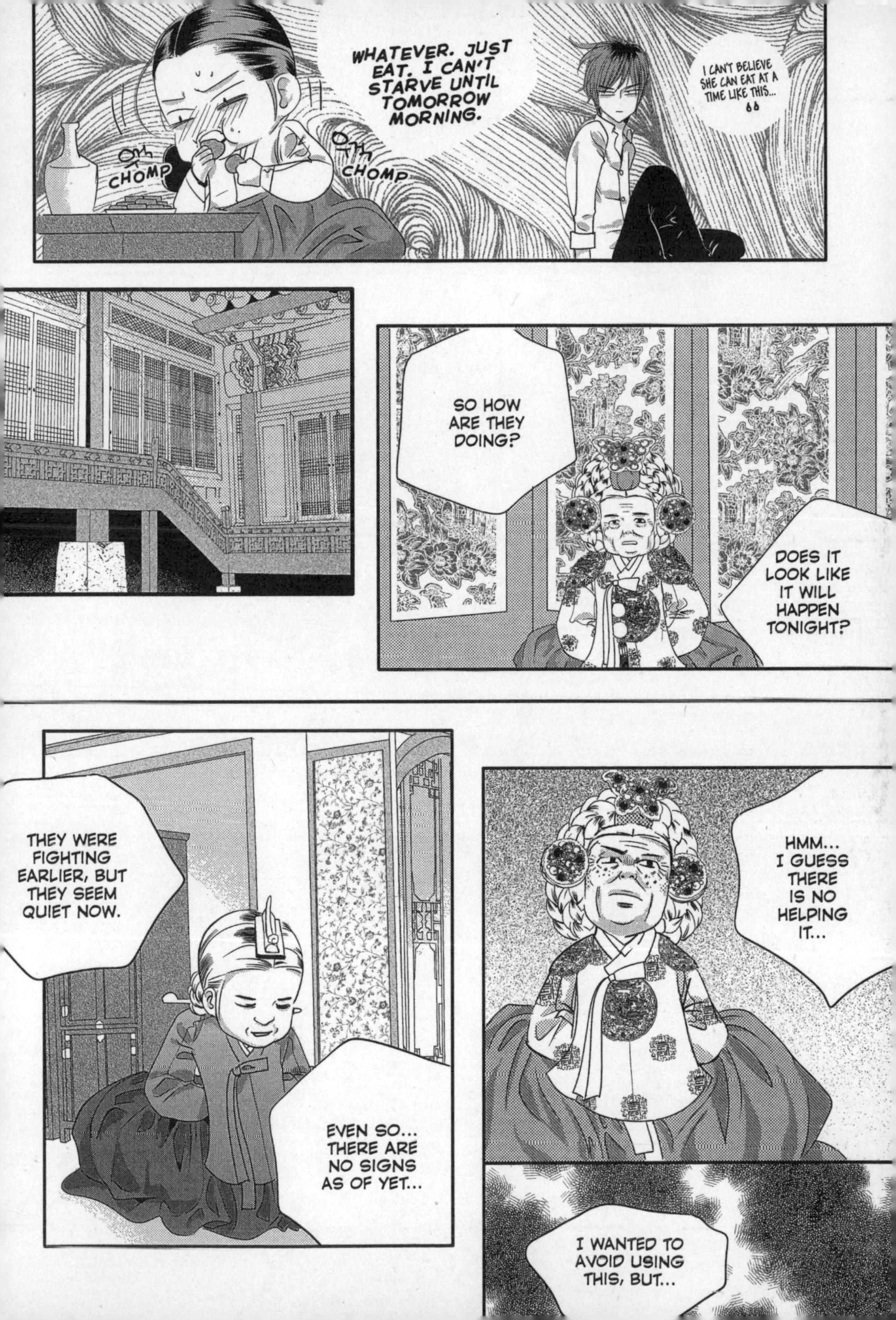
CHOMP
CHOMP
WHATEVER. JUST EAT. I CAN'T STARVE UNTIL TOMORROW MORNING.
I CAN'T BELIEVE SHE CAN EAT AT A TIME LIKE THIS...
SO HOW ARE THEY DOING?
DOES IT LOOK LIKE IT WILL HAPPEN TONIGHT?
THEY WERE FIGHTING EARLIER, BUT THEY SEEM QUIET NOW.
EVEN SO... THERE ARE NO SIGNS AS OF YET...
HMM... I GUESS THERE IS NO HELPING IT...
I WANTED TO AVOID USING THIS, BUT...

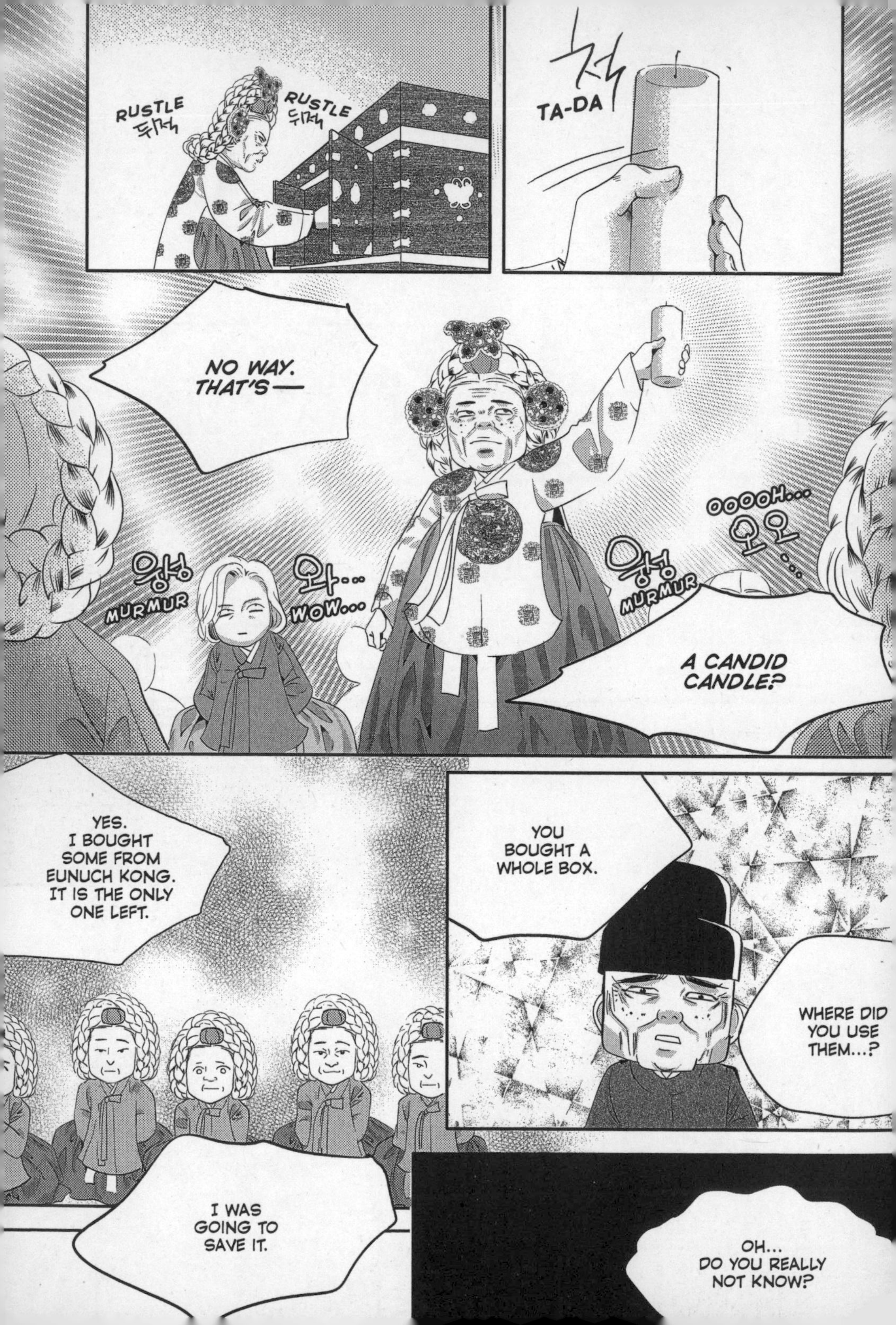
RUSTLE
뒤적
RUSTLE
뒤적
척
TA-DA
NO WAY. THAT'S—
웅성
MURMUR
와...
WOW...
웅성
MURMUR
OOOOH...
오오...
A CANDID CANDLE?
YES. I BOUGHT SOME FROM EUNUCH KONG. IT IS THE ONLY ONE LEFT.
I WAS GOING TO SAVE IT.
YOU BOUGHT A WHOLE BOX.
WHERE DID YOU USE THEM...?
OH... DO YOU REALLY NOT KNOW?

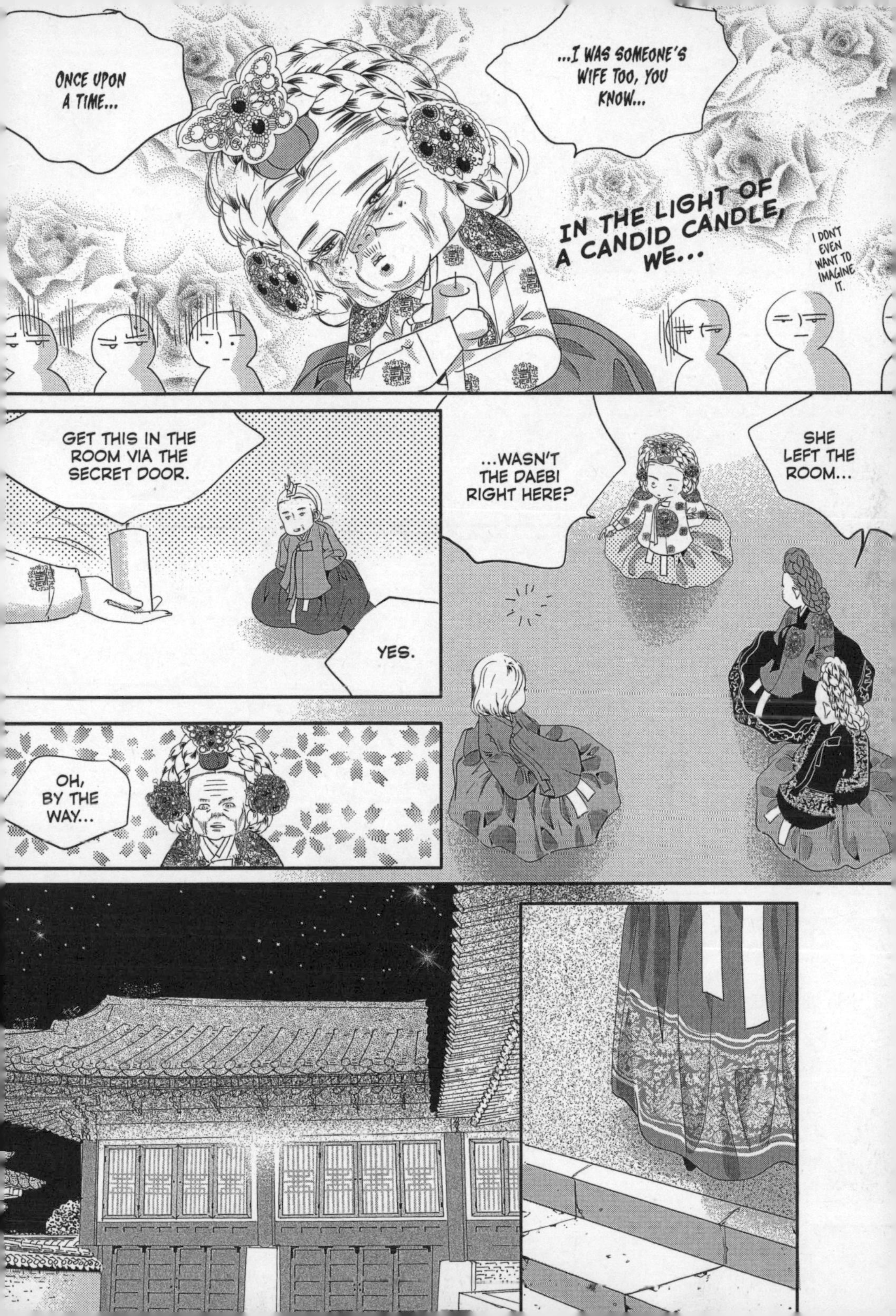
ONCE UPON A TIME...
...I WAS SOMEONE'S WIFE TOO, YOU KNOW...
IN THE LIGHT OF A CANDID CANDLE, WE...
I DON'T EVEN WANT TO IMAGINE IT.
GET THIS IN THE ROOM VIA THE SECRET DOOR.
YES.
...WASN'T THE DAEBI RIGHT HERE?
SHE LEFT THE ROOM...
OH, BY THE WAY...

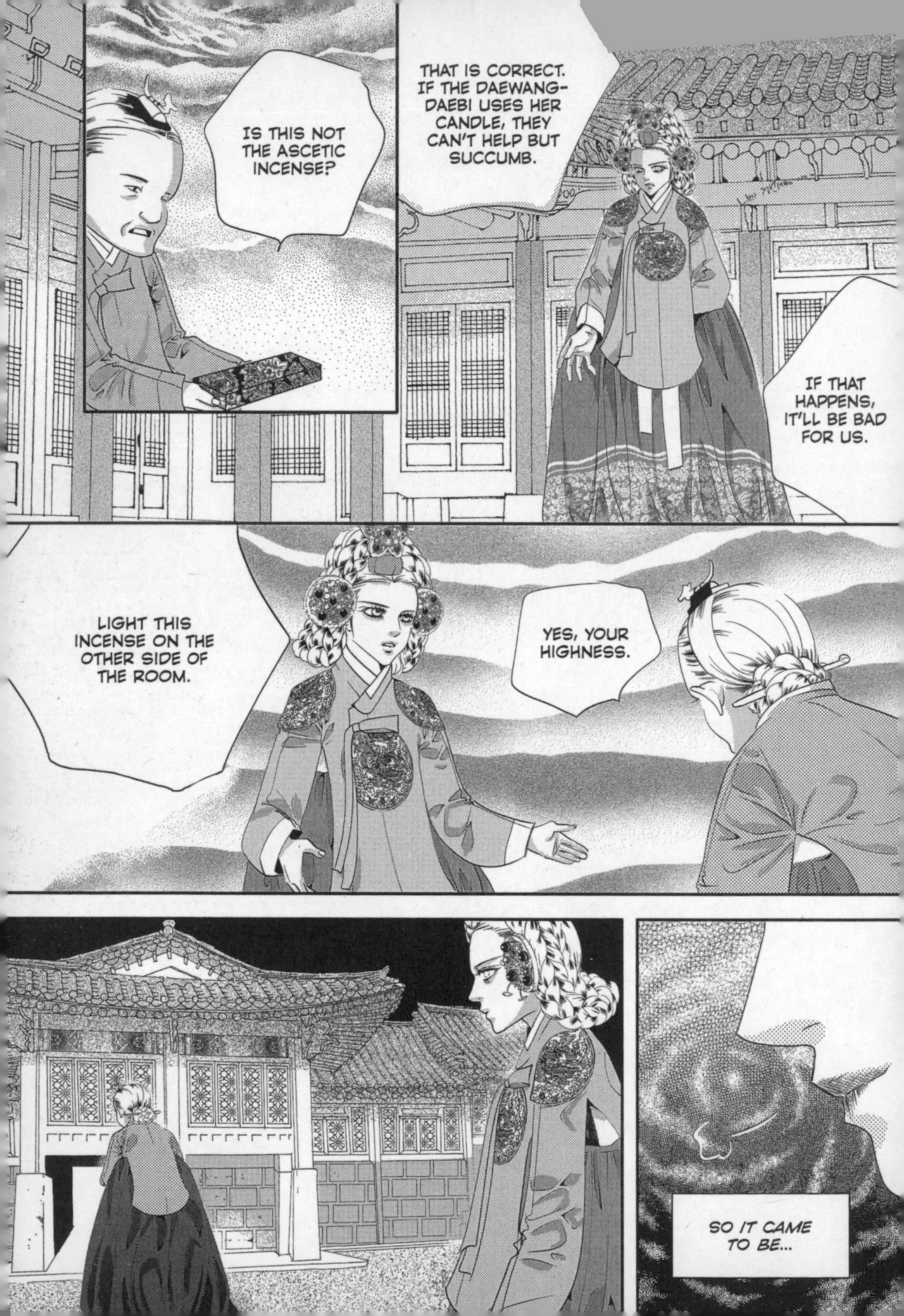

IS THIS NOT THE ASCETIC INCENSE?
THAT IS CORRECT. IF THE DAEWANG-DAEBI USES HER CANDLE, THEY CAN'T HELP BUT SUCCUMB.
IF THAT HAPPENS, IT'LL BE BAD FOR US.
LIGHT THIS INCENSE ON THE OTHER SIDE OF THE ROOM.
YES, YOUR HIGHNESS.
SO IT CAME TO BE...

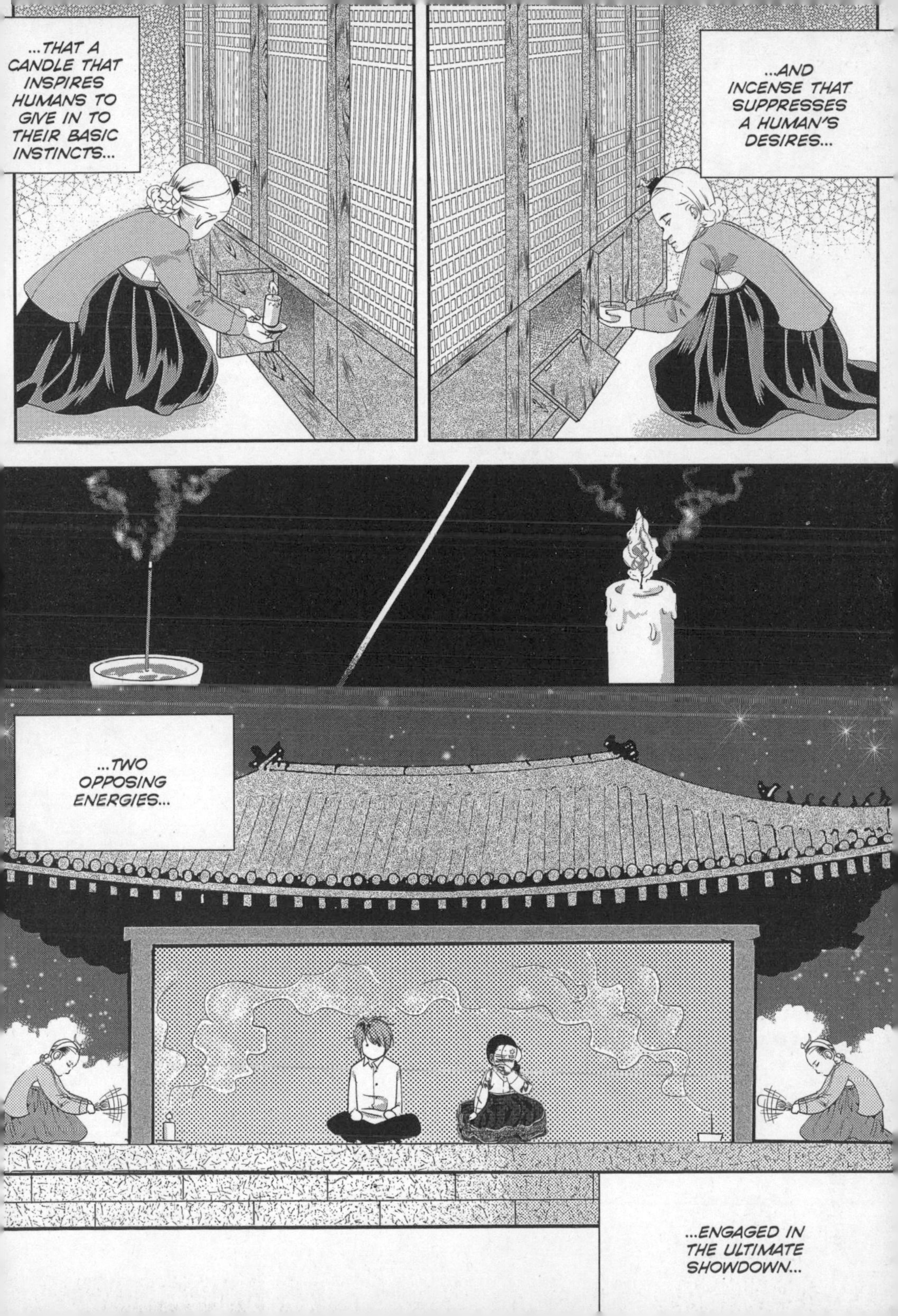
...THAT A CANDLE THAT INSPIRES HUMANS TO GIVE IN TO THEIR BASIC INSTINCTS...
...AND INCENSE THAT SUPPRESSES A HUMAN'S DESIRES...
...TWO OPPOSING ENERGIES...
...ENGAGED IN THE ULTIMATE SHOWDOWN...

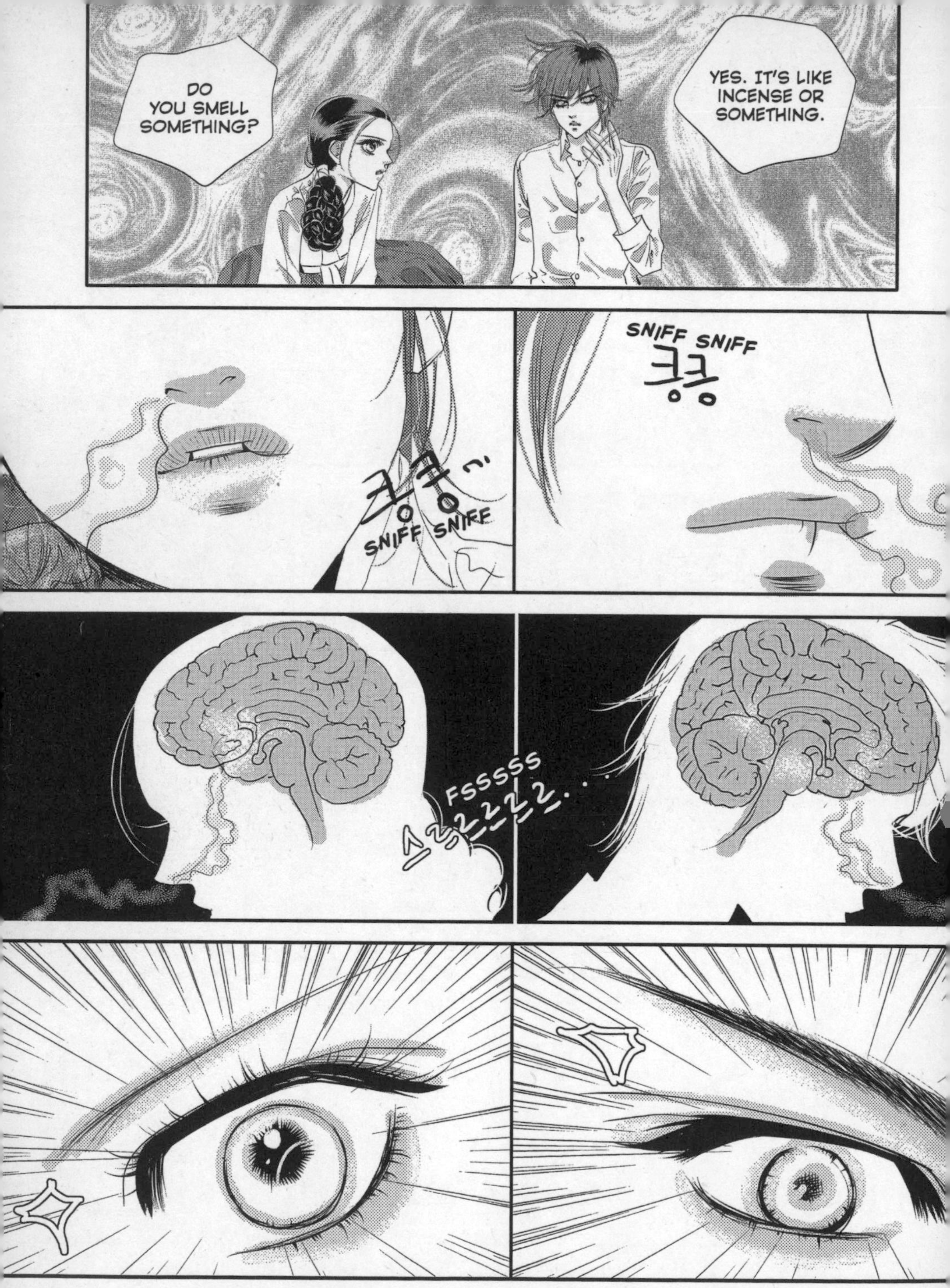
DO YOU SMELL SOMETHING?
YES. IT'S LIKE INCENSE OR SOMETHING.
킁킁
SNIFF SNIFF
SNIFF SNIFF
킁킁
FSSSSS
스으으으으...

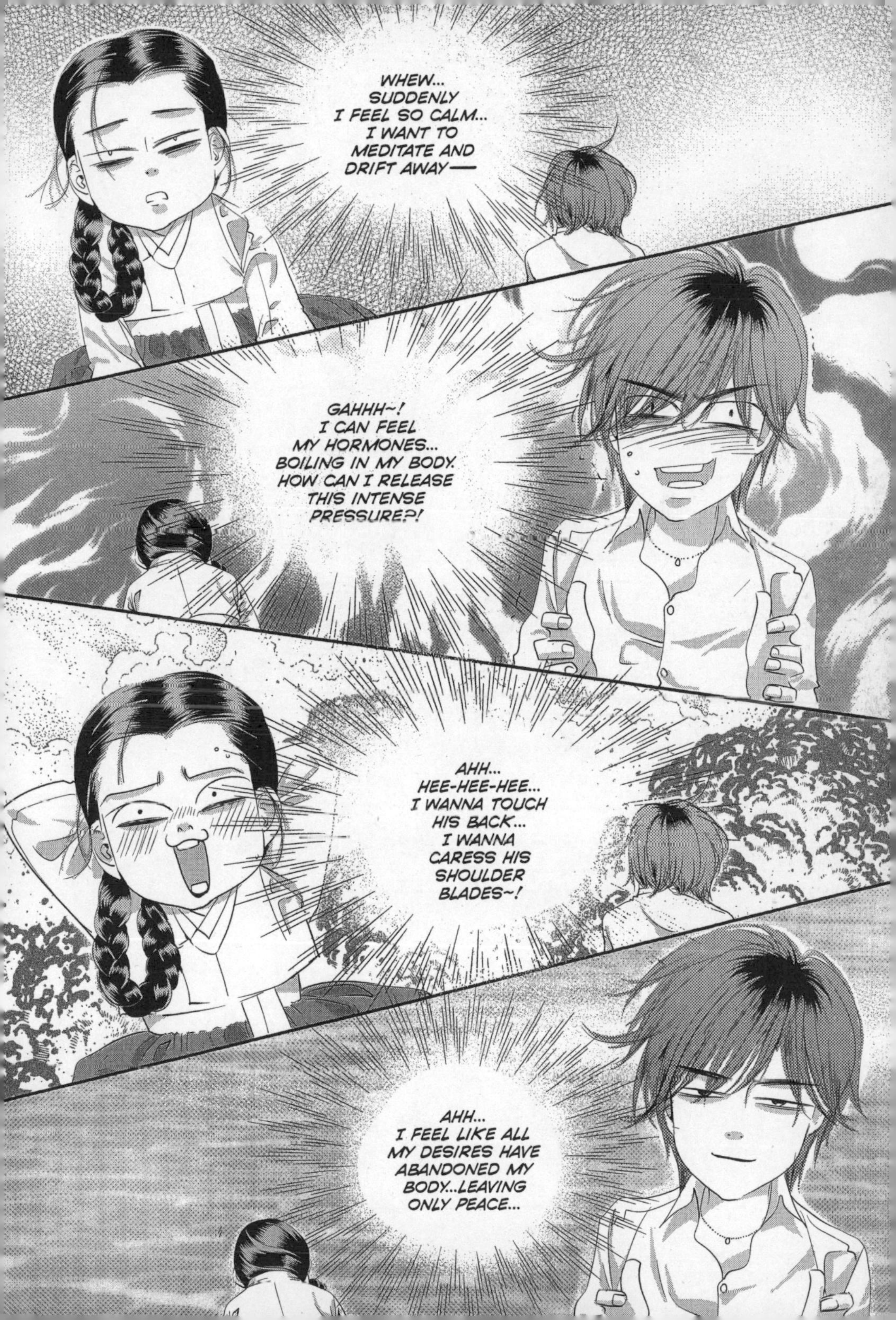
WHEW... SUDDENLY I FEEL SO CALM... I WANT TO MEDITATE AND DRIFT AWAY—
GAHHH~! I CAN FEEL MY HORMONES... BOILING IN MY BODY. HOW CAN I RELEASE THIS INTENSE PRESSURE?!
AHH... HEE-HEE-HEE... I WANNA TOUCH HIS BACK... I WANNA CARESS HIS SHOULDER BLADES~!
AHH... I FEEL LIKE ALL MY DESIRES HAVE ABANDONED MY BODY...LEAVING ONLY PEACE...

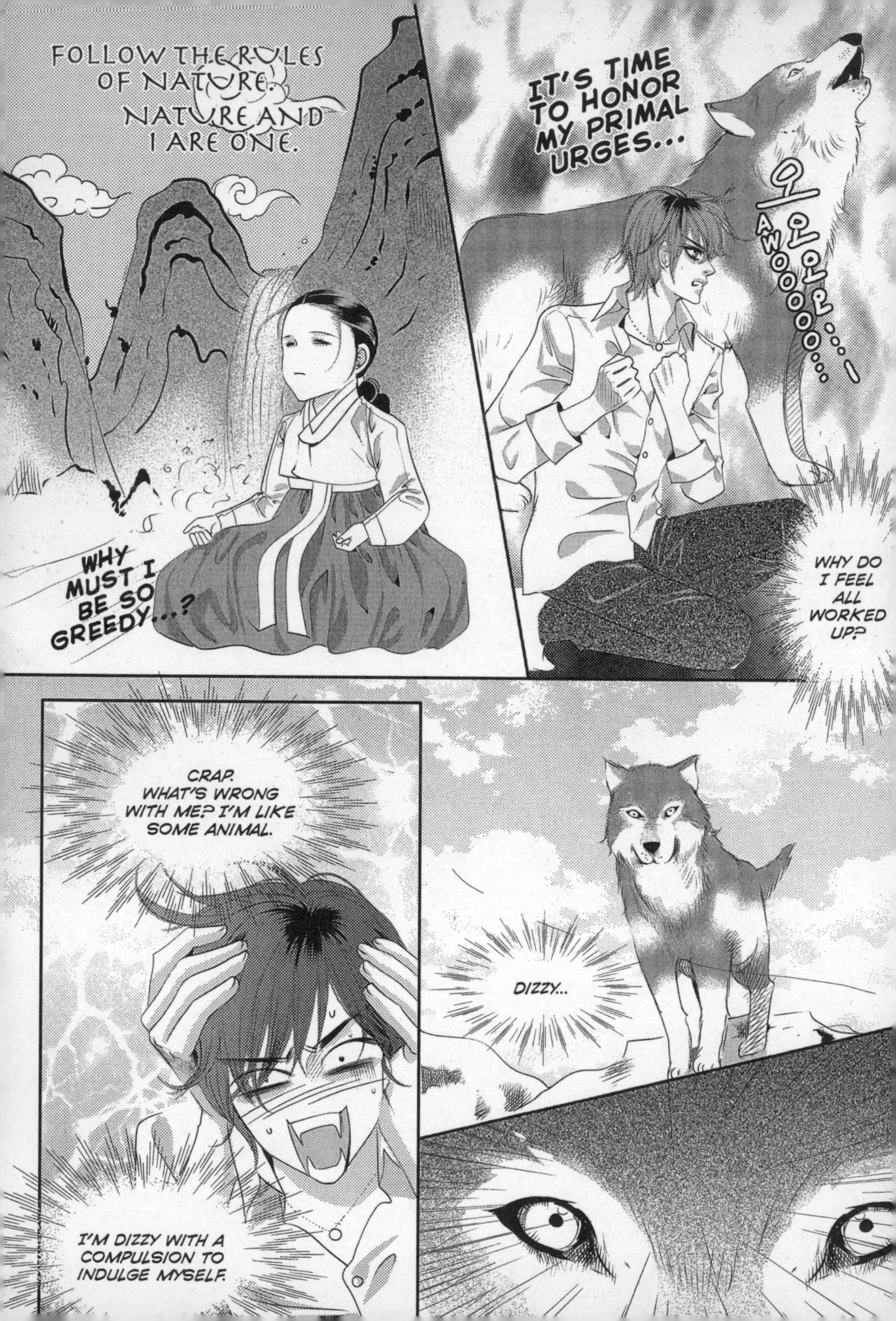
FOLLOW THE RULES OF NATURE. NATURE AND I ARE ONE.
WHY MUST I BE SO GREEDY...?
IT'S TIME TO HONOR MY PRIMAL URGES...
오—
AWOOOOOO...
WHY DO I FEEL ALL WORKED UP?
CRAP. WHAT'S WRONG WITH ME? I'M LIKE SOME ANIMAL.
I'M DIZZY WITH A COMPULSION TO INDULGE MYSELF.
DIZZY...

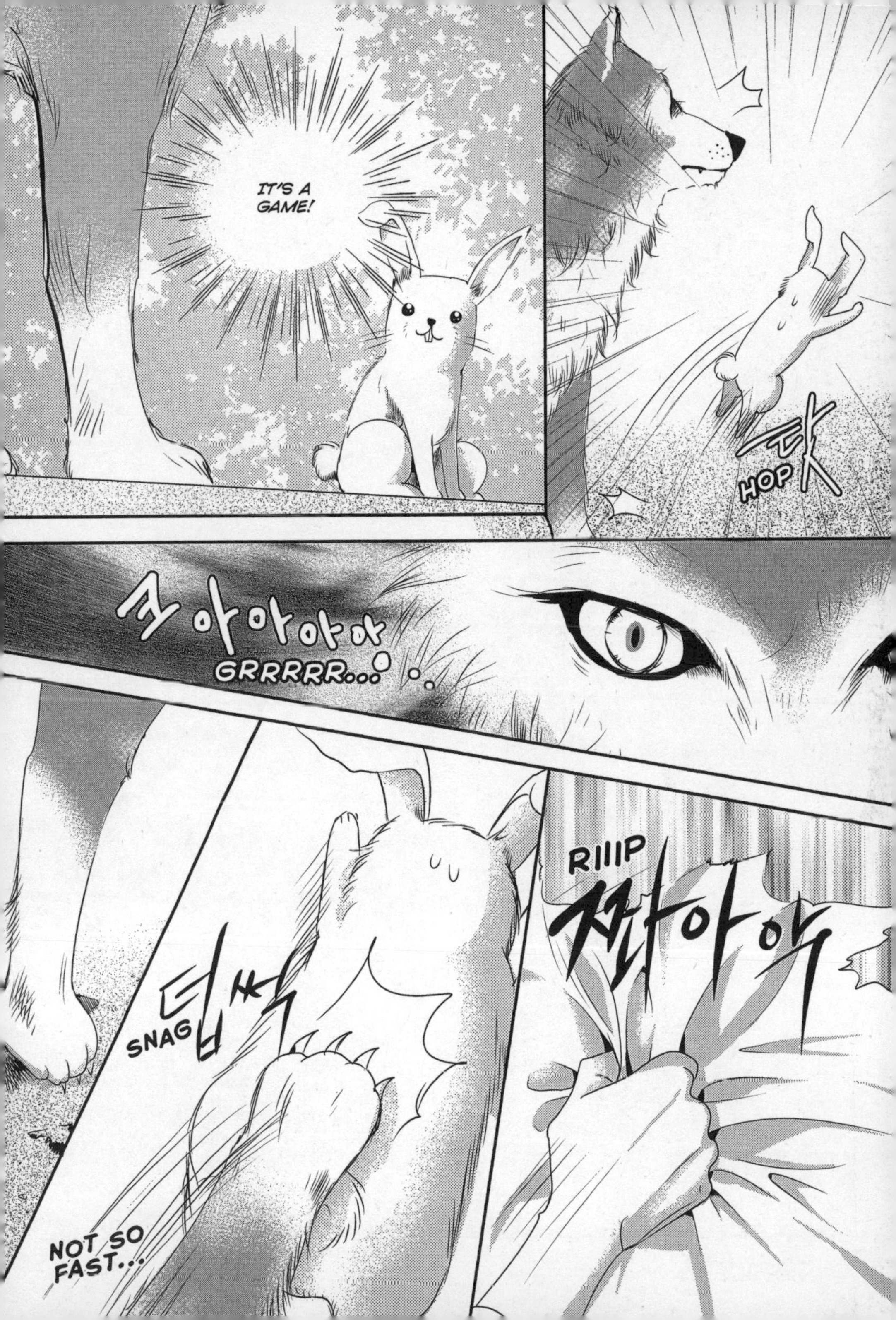
IT'S A GAME!
탓
HOP
크아아아아
GRRRRR...
덥썩
SNAG
NOT SO FAST...
RIIIP
쫘아아악

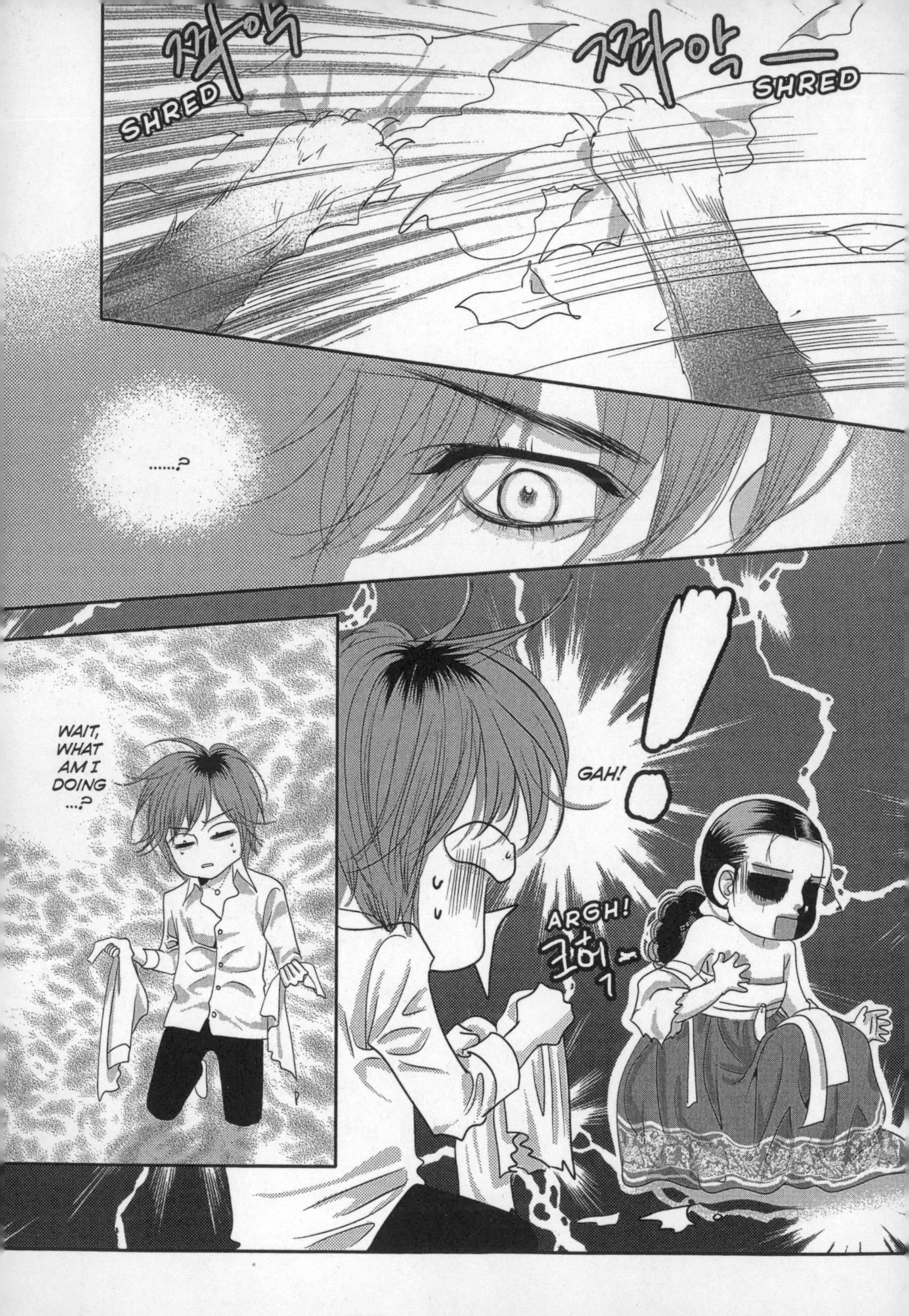
SHRED
SHRED
......?
WAIT, WHAT AM I DOING ...?
GAH!
ARGH!

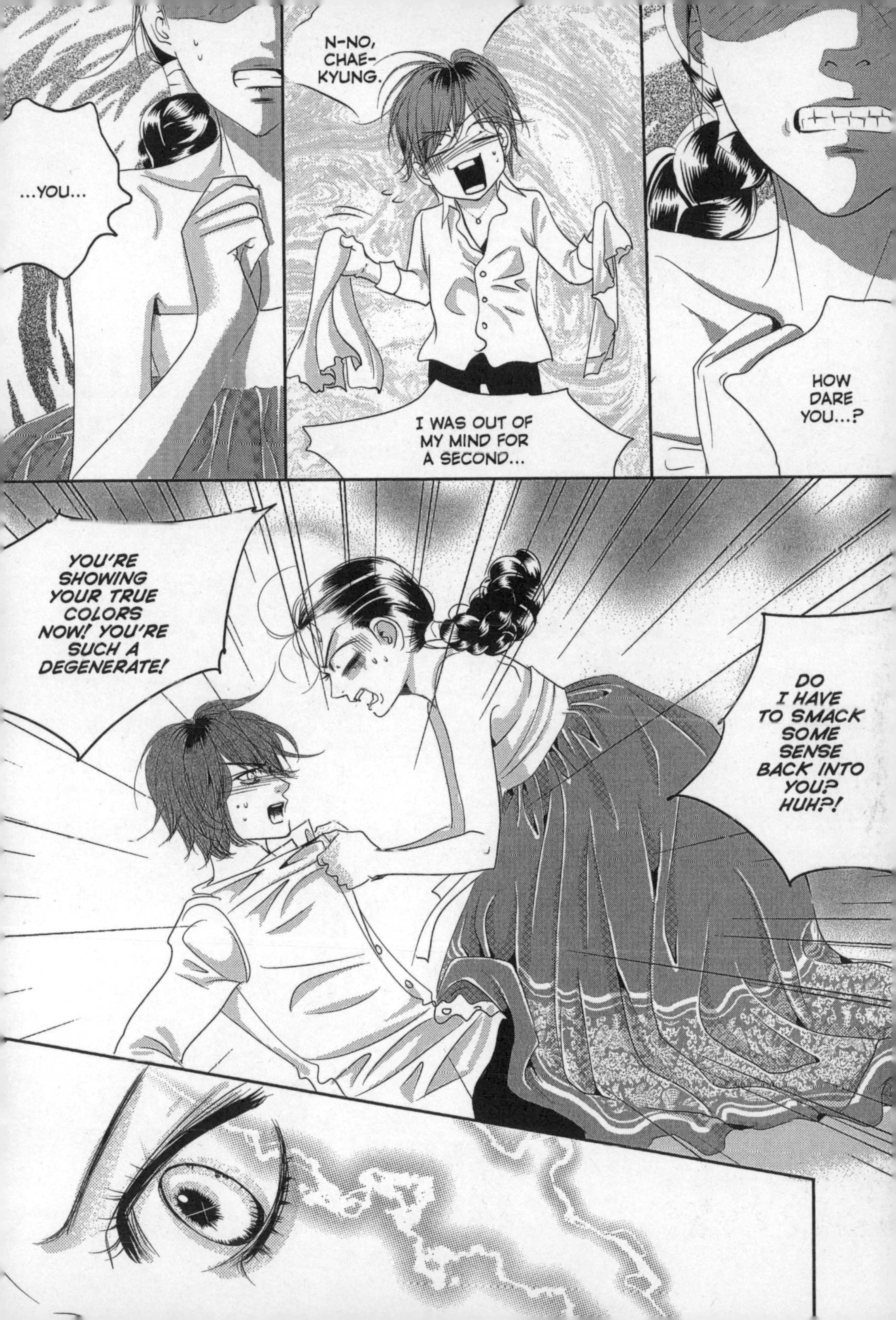
...YOU...
N-NO, CHAE-KYUNG.
I WAS OUT OF MY MIND FOR A SECOND...
HOW DARE YOU...?
YOU'RE SHOWING YOUR TRUE COLORS NOW! YOU'RE SUCH A DEGENERATE!
DO I HAVE TO SMACK SOME SENSE BACK INTO YOU? HUH?!

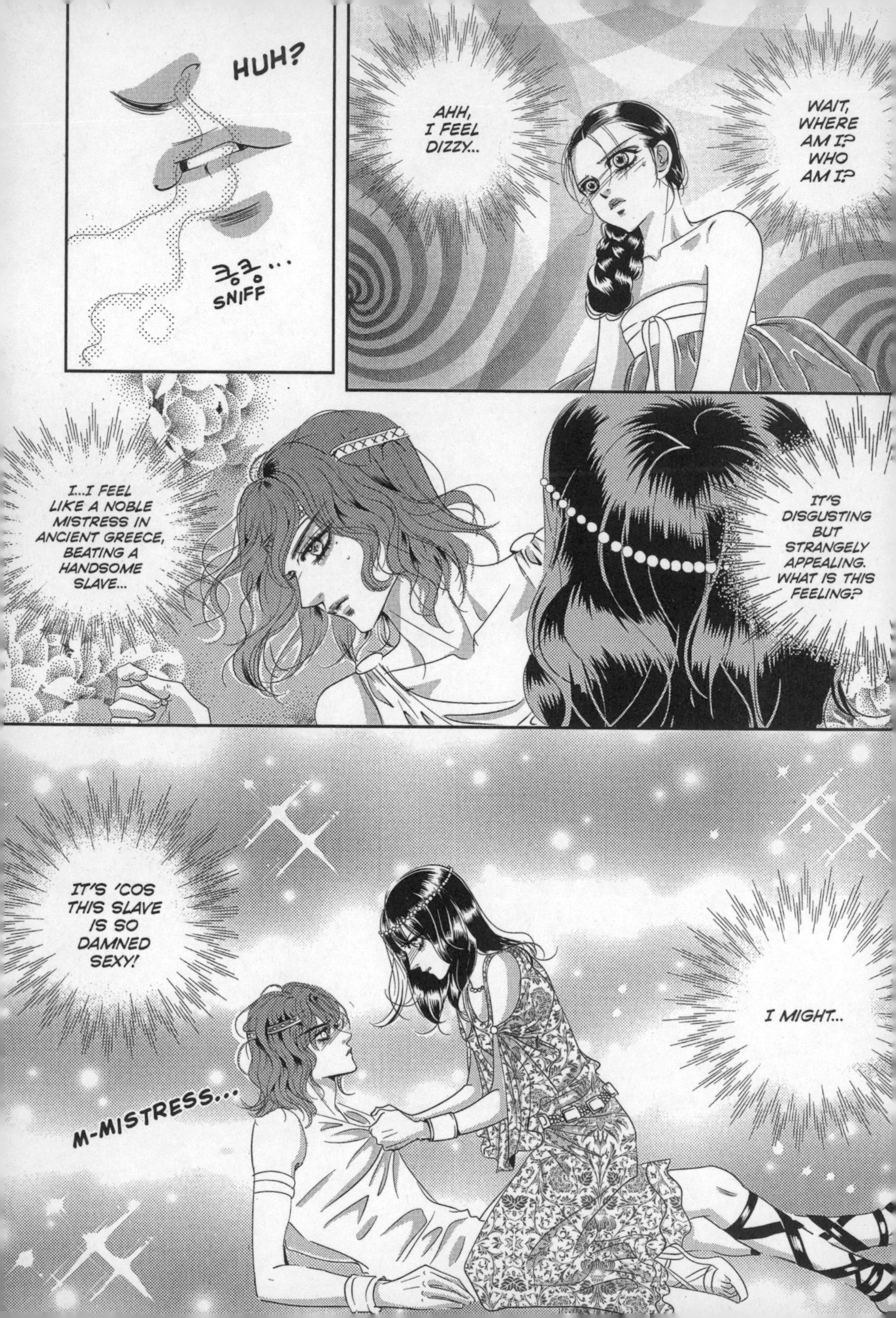
HUH?
킁킁...
SNIFF
AHH, I FEEL DIZZY...
WAIT, WHERE AM I? WHO AM I?
I...I FEEL LIKE A NOBLE MISTRESS IN ANCIENT GREECE, BEATING A HANDSOME SLAVE...
IT'S DISGUSTING BUT STRANGELY APPEALING. WHAT IS THIS FEELING?
IT'S 'COS THIS SLAVE IS SO DAMNED SEXY!
M-MISTRESS...
I MIGHT...

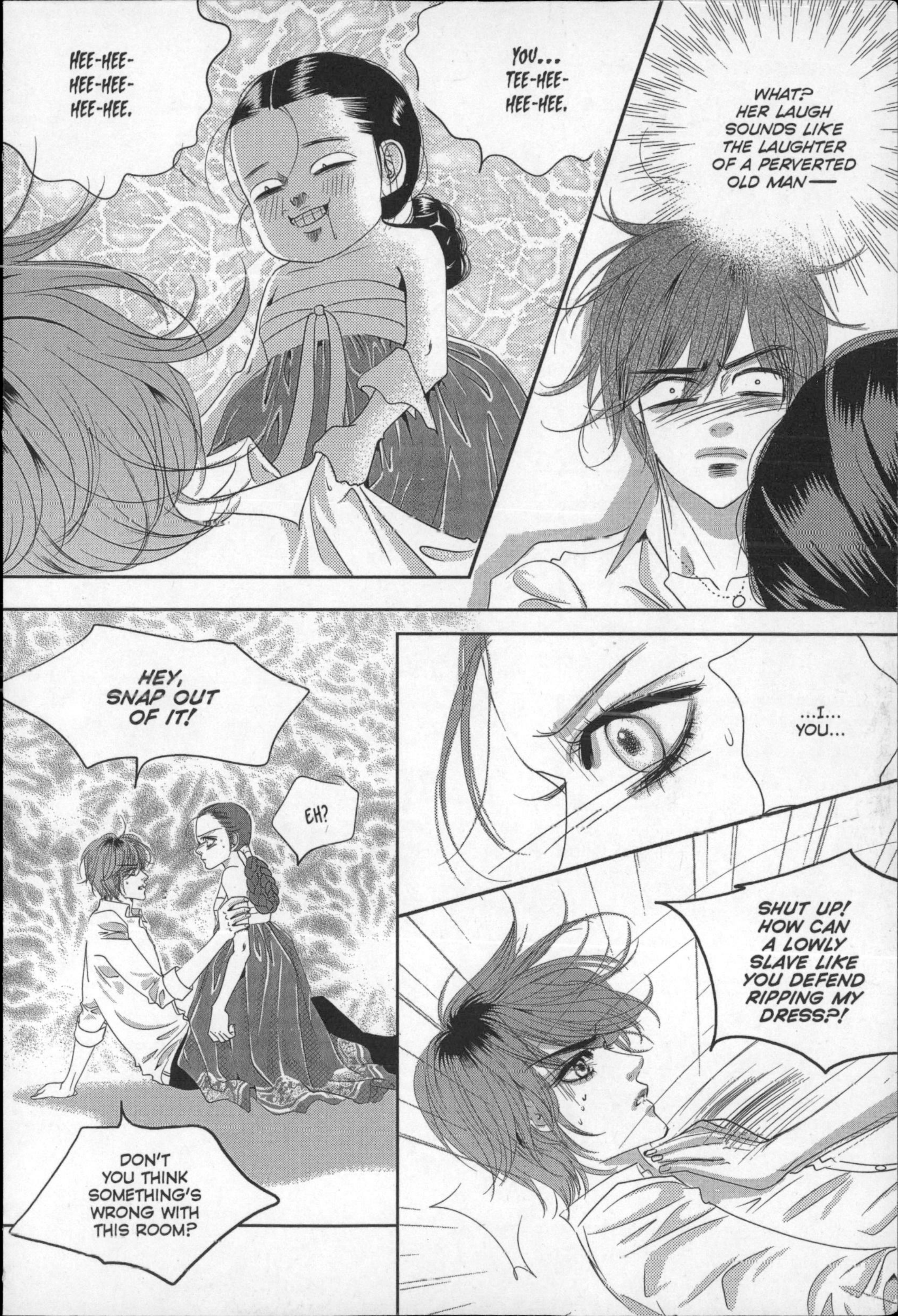
HEE-HEE-
HEE-HEE-
HEE-HEE.
YOU...
TEE-HEE-
HEE-HEE.
WHAT? HER LAUGH SOUNDS LIKE THE LAUGHTER OF A PERVERTED OLD MAN—
HEY, SNAP OUT OF IT!
EH?
DON'T YOU THINK SOMETHING'S WRONG WITH THIS ROOM?
...I... YOU...
SHUT UP! HOW CAN A LOWLY SLAVE LIKE YOU DEFEND RIPPING MY DRESS?!

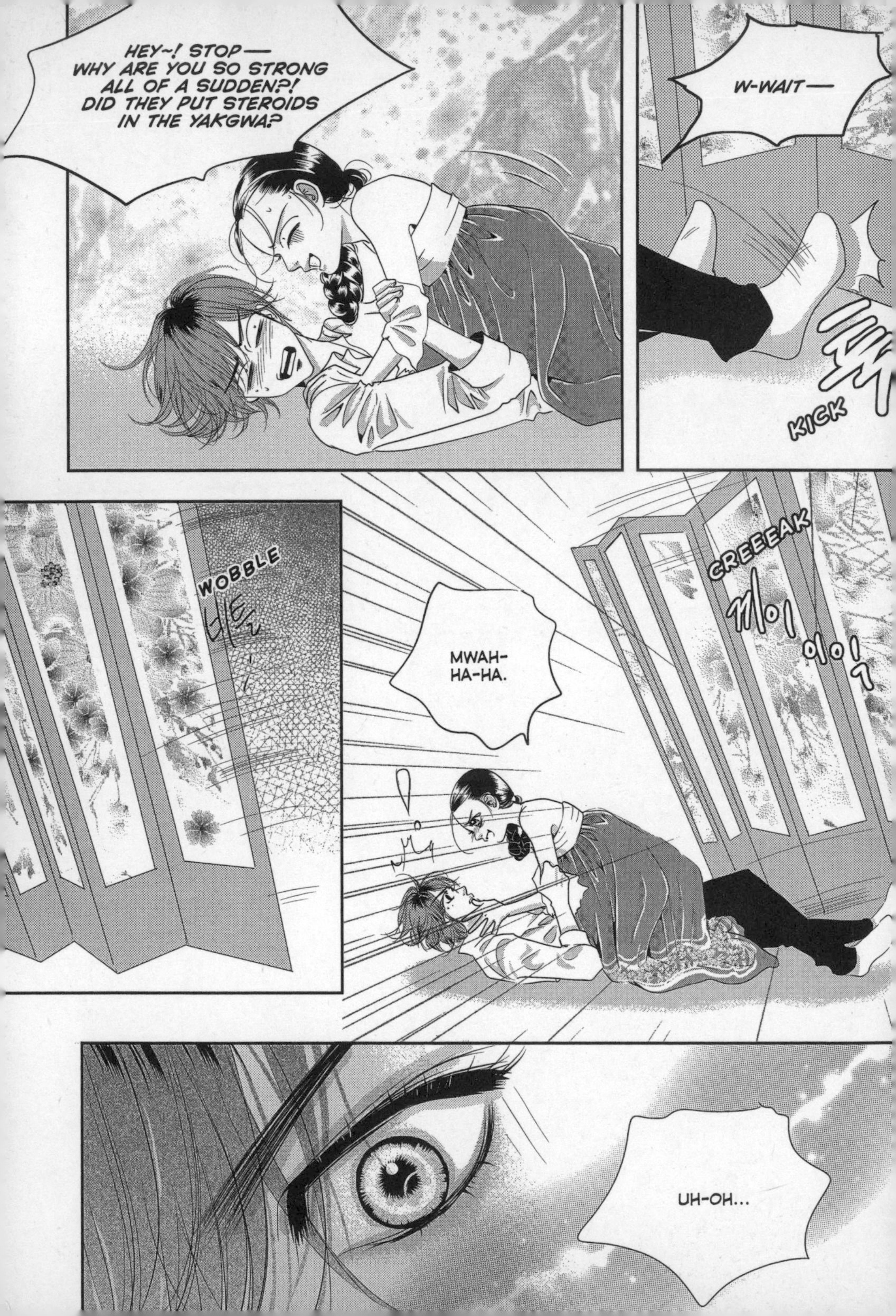
HEY~! STOP— WHY ARE YOU SO STRONG ALL OF A SUDDEN?! DID THEY PUT STEROIDS IN THE YAKGWA?
W-WAIT—
KICK
WOBBLE
MWAH-HA-HA.
CREEEAK
UH-OH...

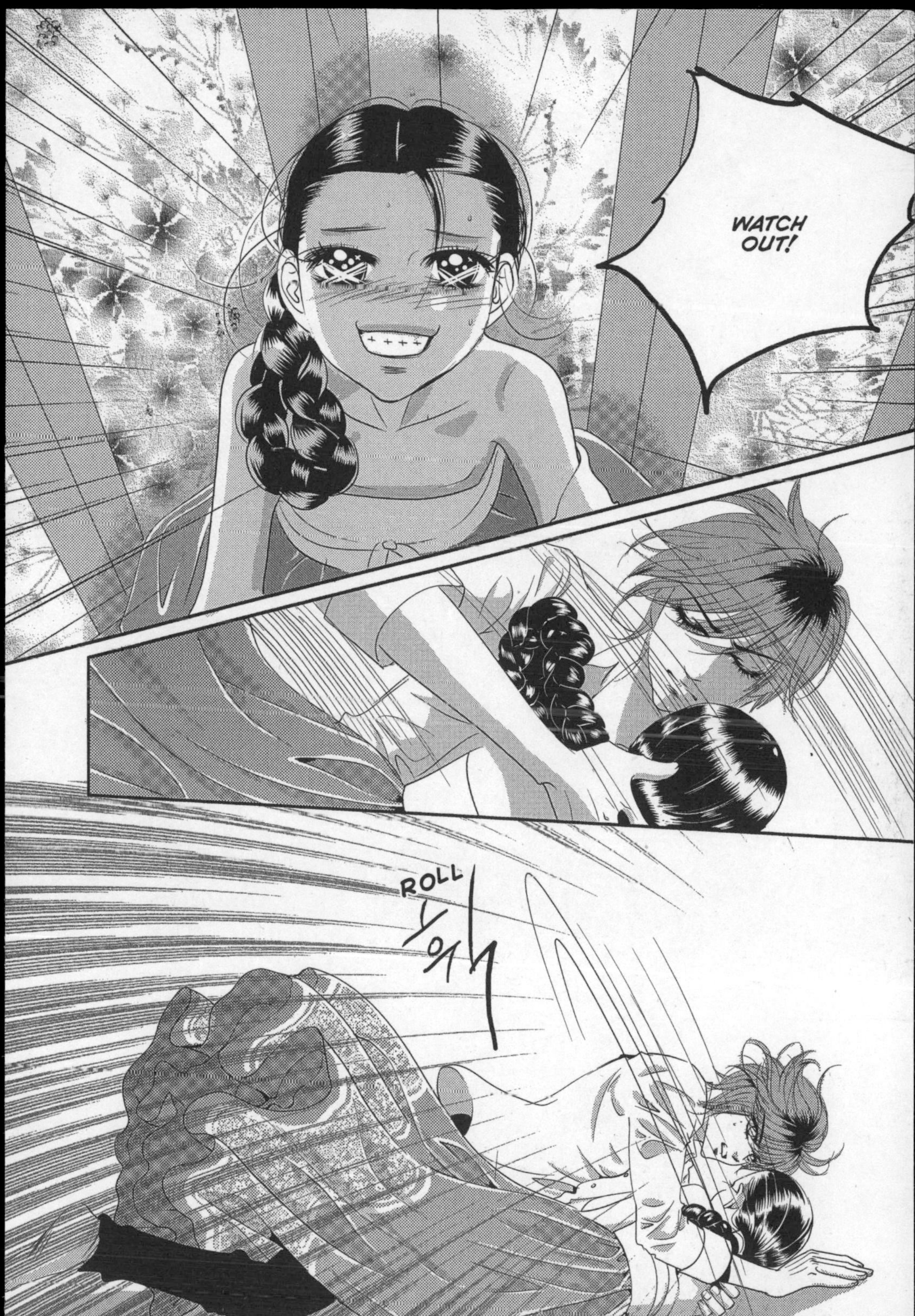
WATCH OUT!
ROLL

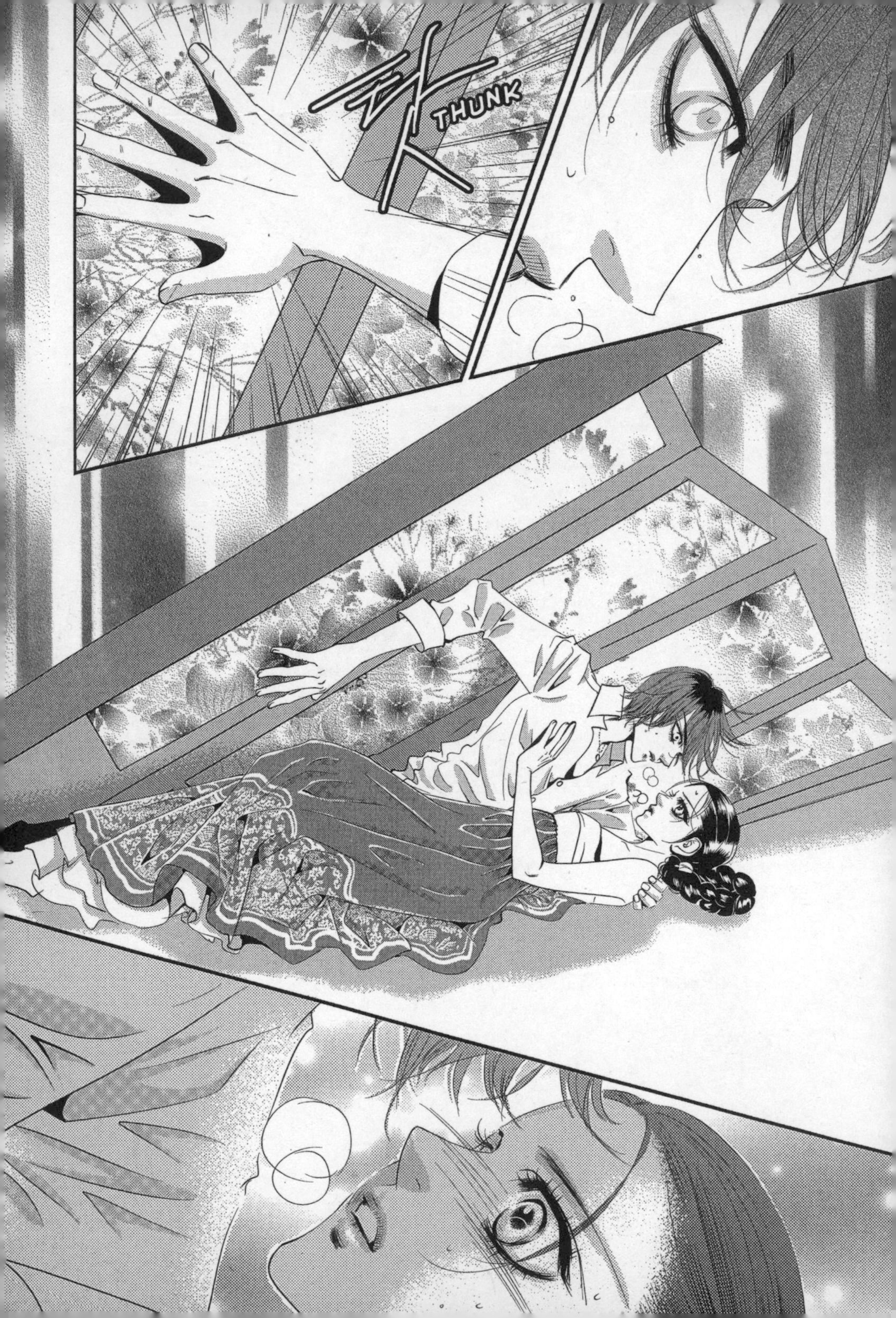
THUNK

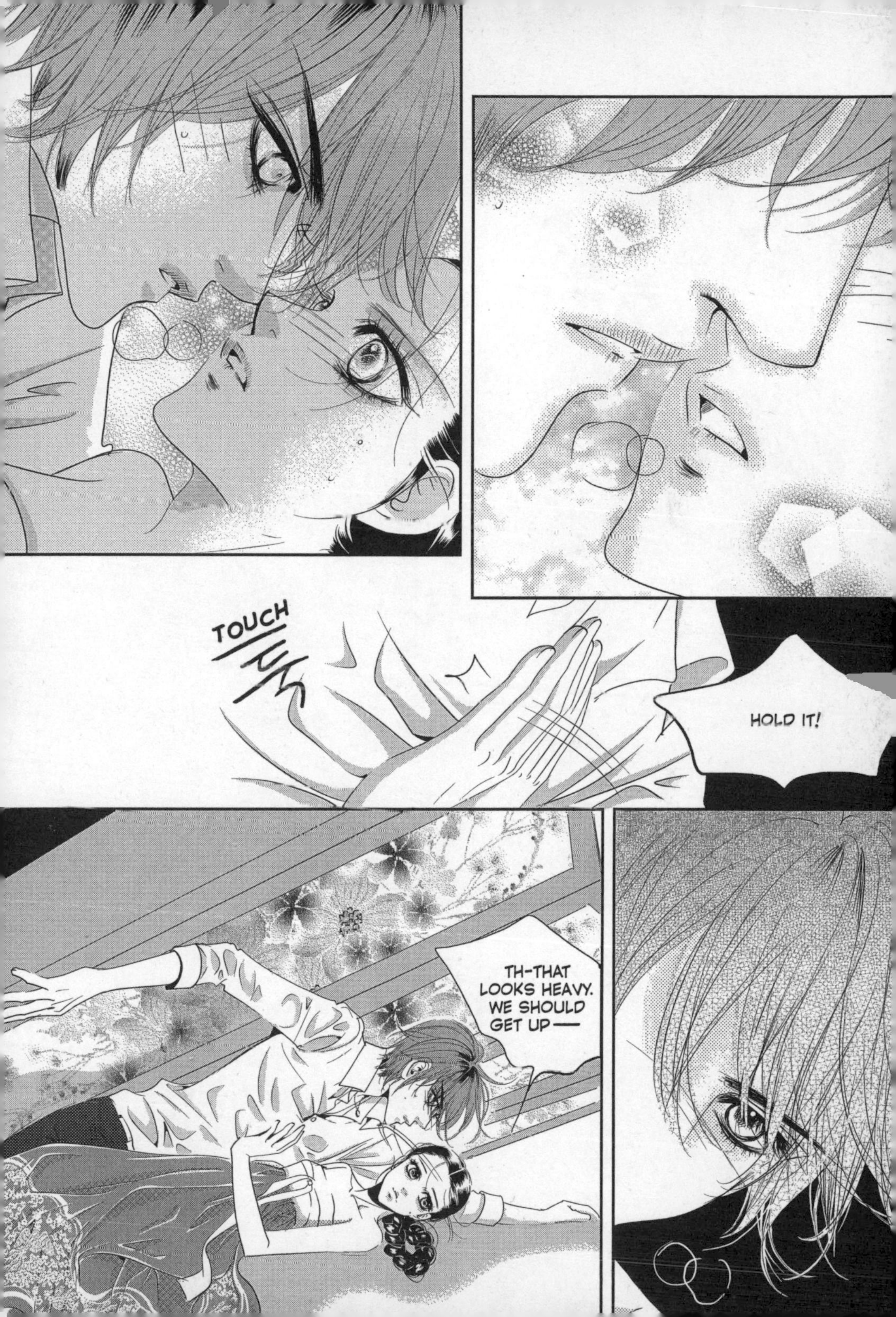
TOUCH
HOLD IT!
TH-THAT LOOKS HEAVY. WE SHOULD GET UP—

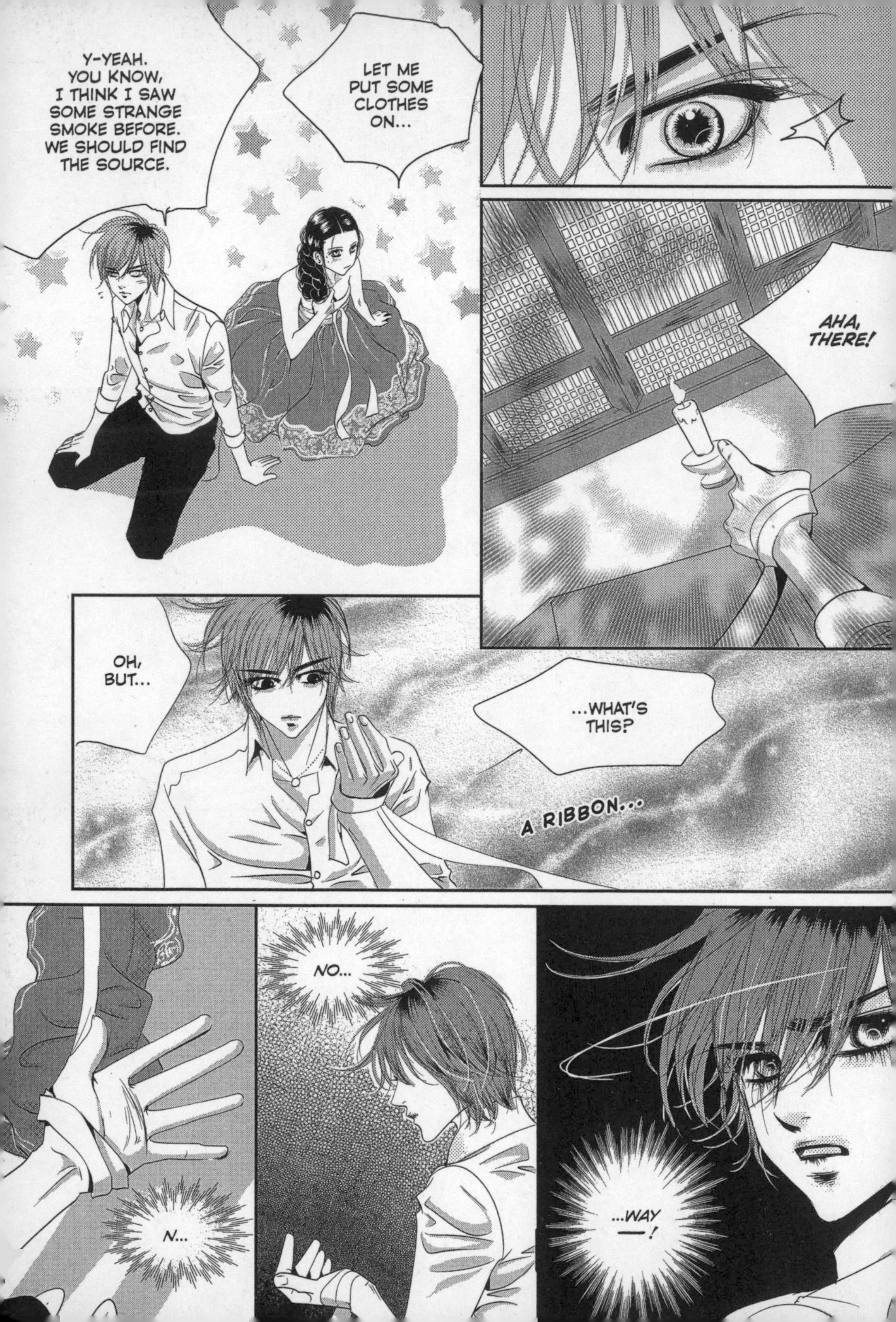
Y-YEAH.
YOU KNOW,
I THINK I SAW
SOME STRANGE
SMOKE BEFORE.
WE SHOULD FIND
THE SOURCE.
LET ME
PUT SOME
CLOTHES
ON...
AHA,
THERE!
OH,
BUT...
...WHAT'S
THIS?
A RIBBON...
N...
NO...
...WAY
—!

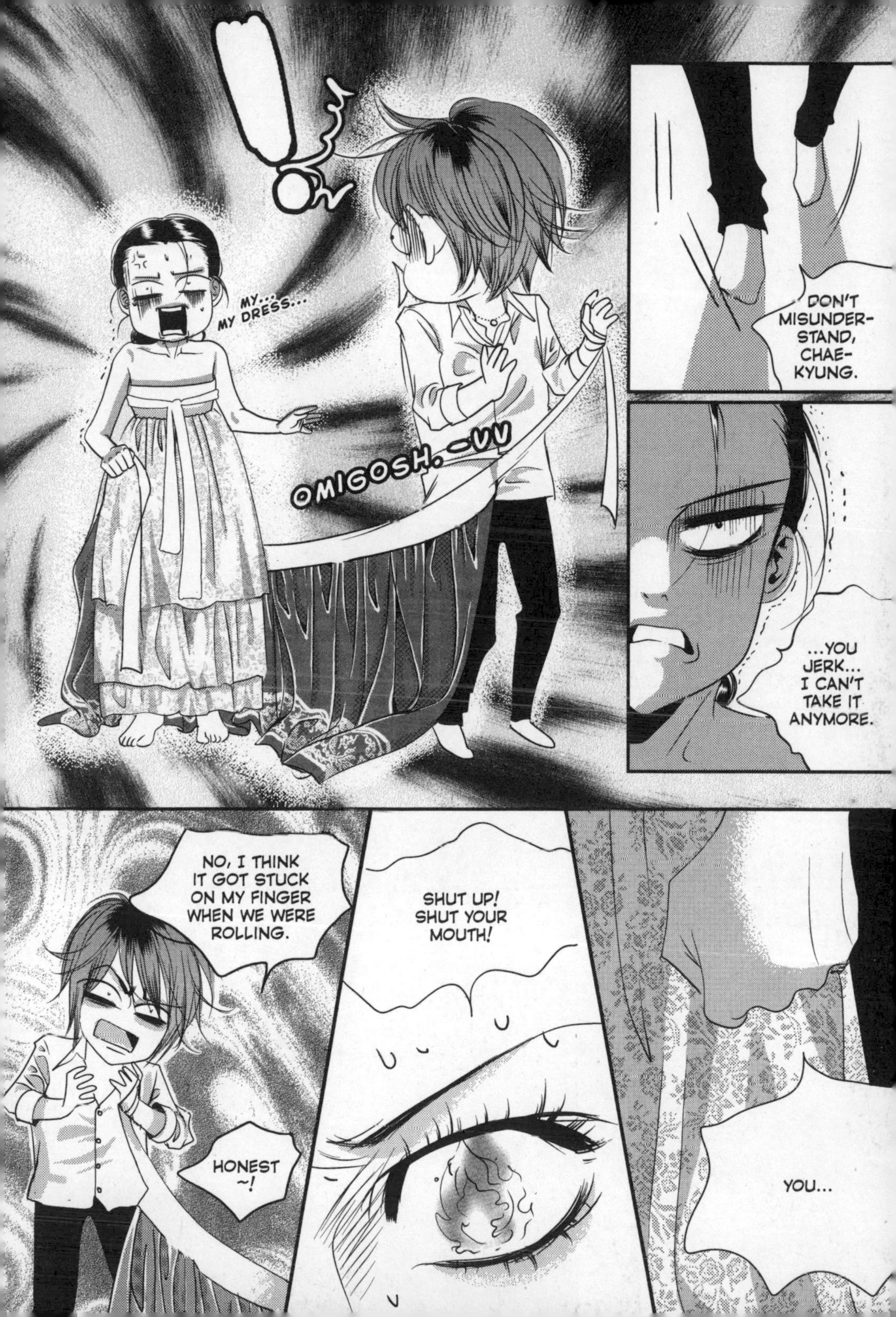
!
MY... MY DRESS...
OMIGOSH. —VV
DON'T MISUNDERSTAND, CHAE-KYUNG.
...YOU JERK... I CAN'T TAKE IT ANYMORE.
NO, I THINK IT GOT STUCK ON MY FINGER WHEN WE WERE ROLLING.
HONEST ~!
SHUT UP! SHUT YOUR MOUTH!
YOU...

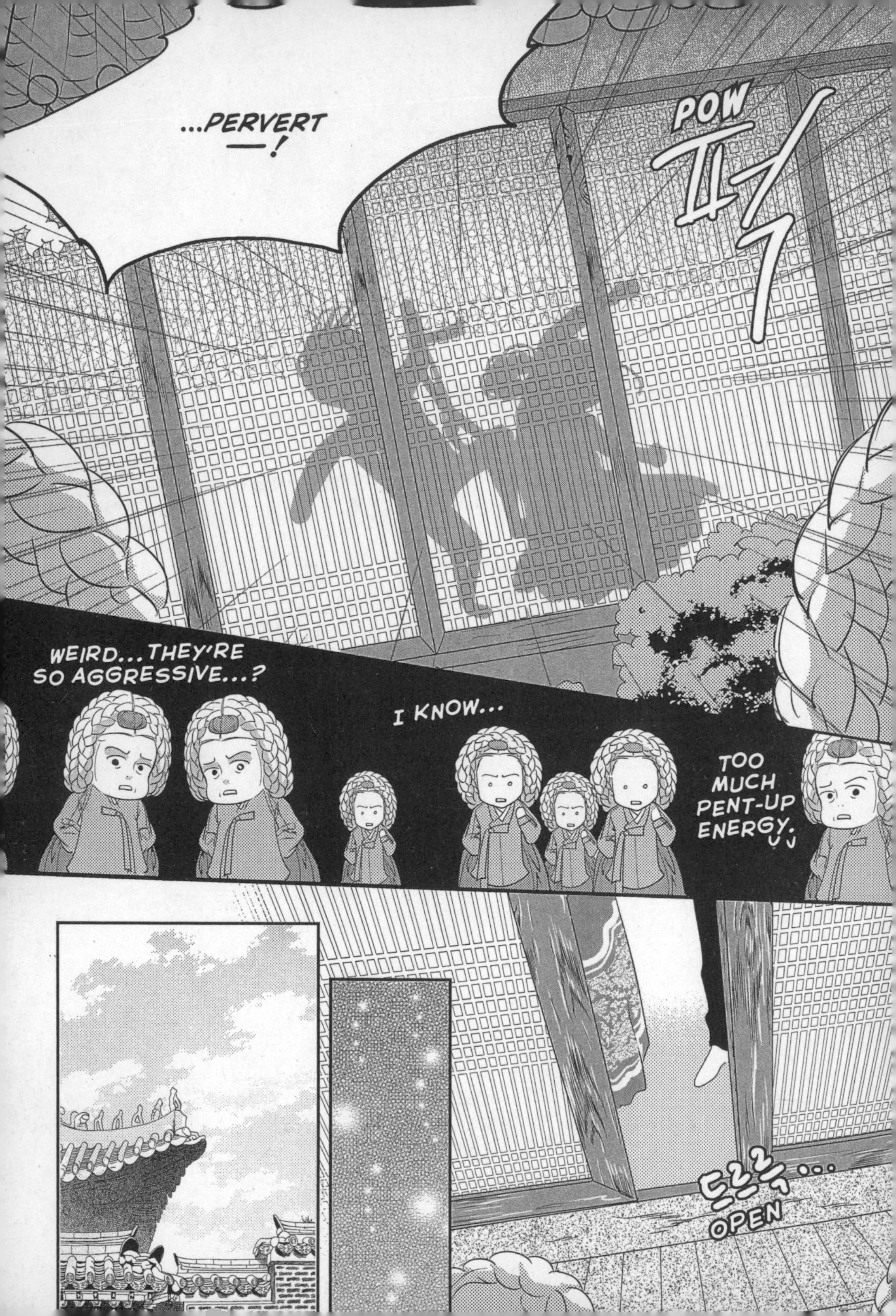
...PERVERT —!
POW
WEIRD... THEY'RE SO AGGRESSIVE...?
I KNOW...
TOO MUCH PENT-UP ENERGY.
OPEN

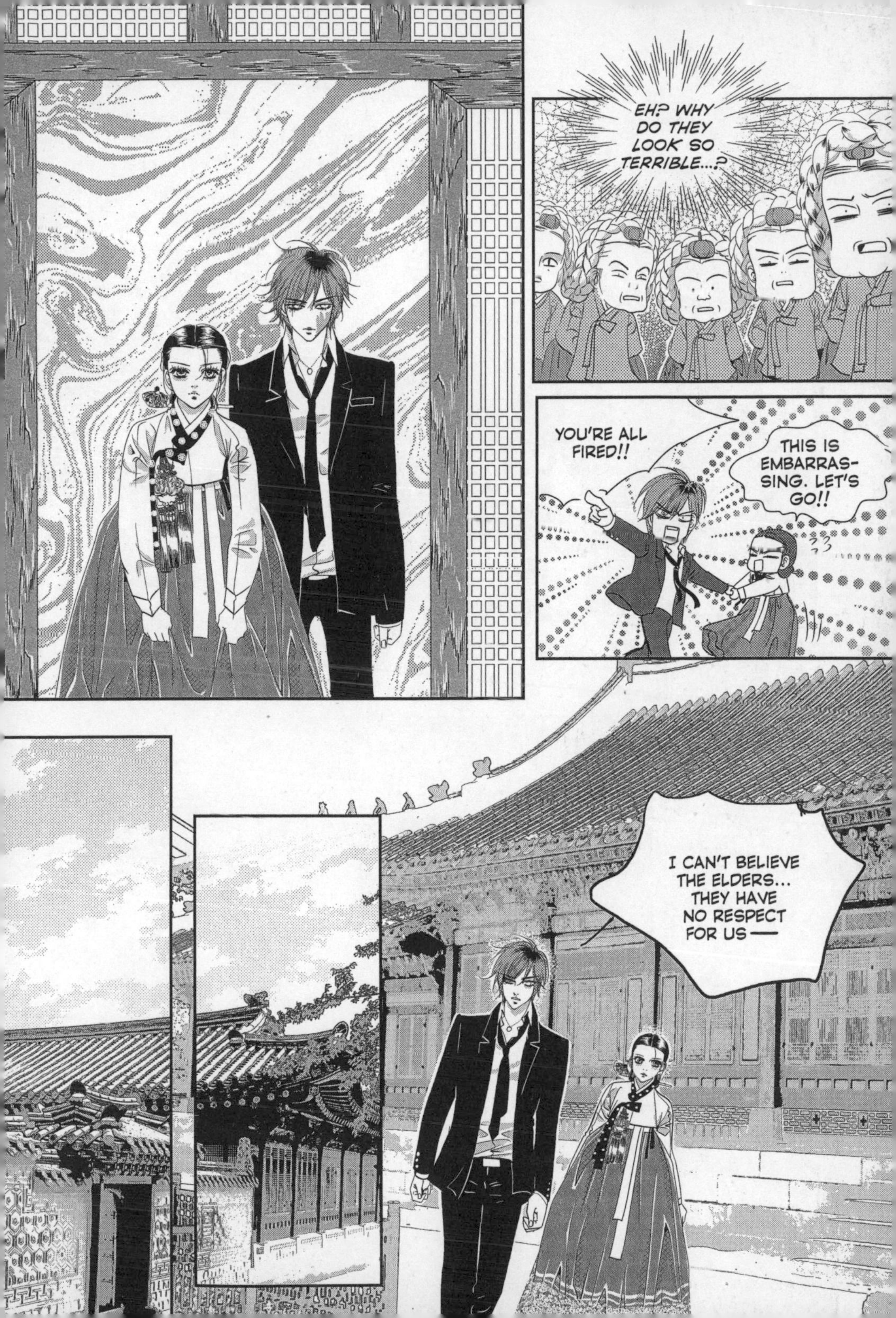
EH? WHY DO THEY LOOK SO TERRIBLE...?
YOU'RE ALL FIRED!!
THIS IS EMBARRAS-SING. LET'S GO!!
I CAN'T BELIEVE THE ELDERS... THEY HAVE NO RESPECT FOR US—

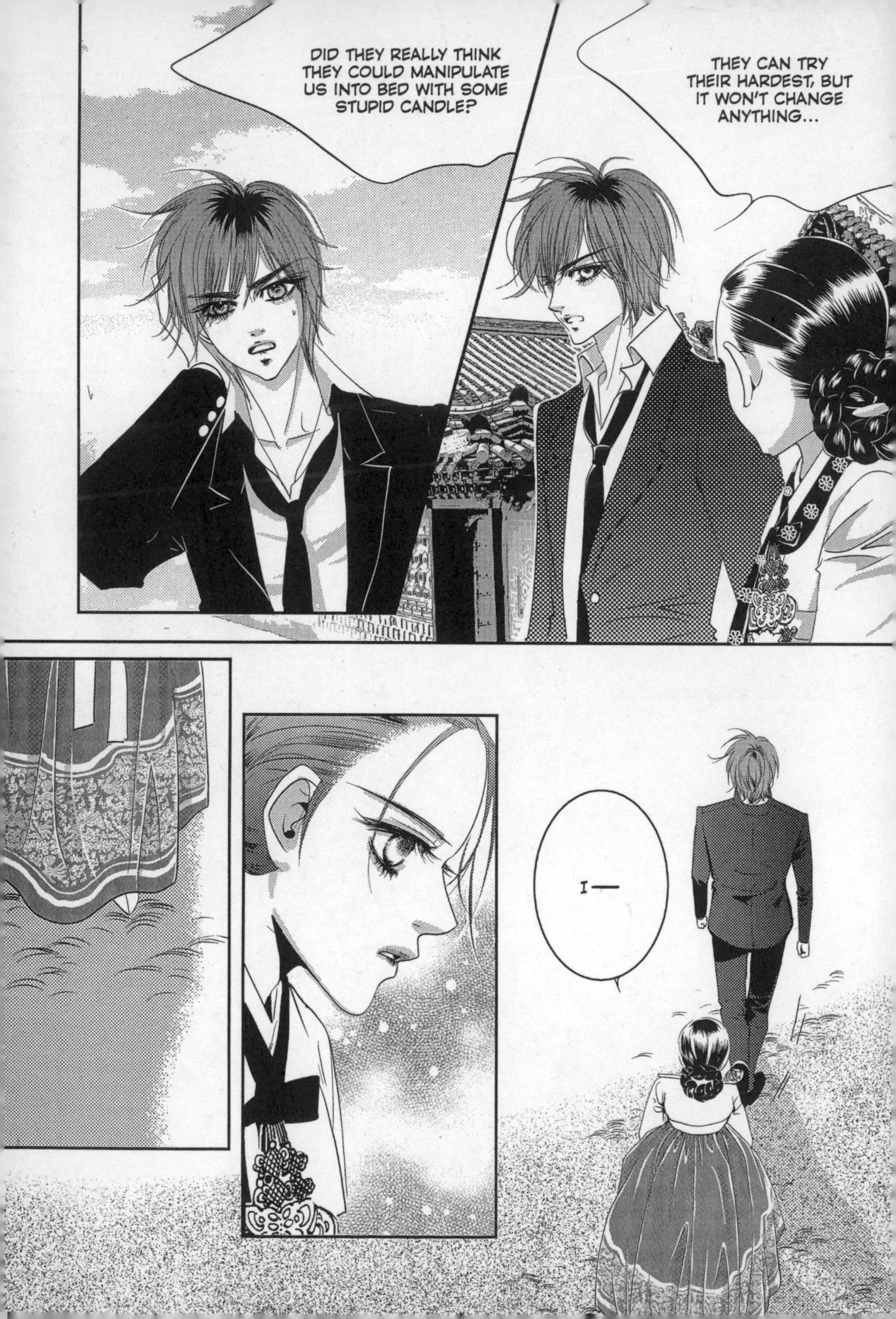
DID THEY REALLY THINK THEY COULD MANIPULATE US INTO BED WITH SOME STUPID CANDLE?
THEY CAN TRY THEIR HARDEST, BUT IT WON'T CHANGE ANYTHING...
I—

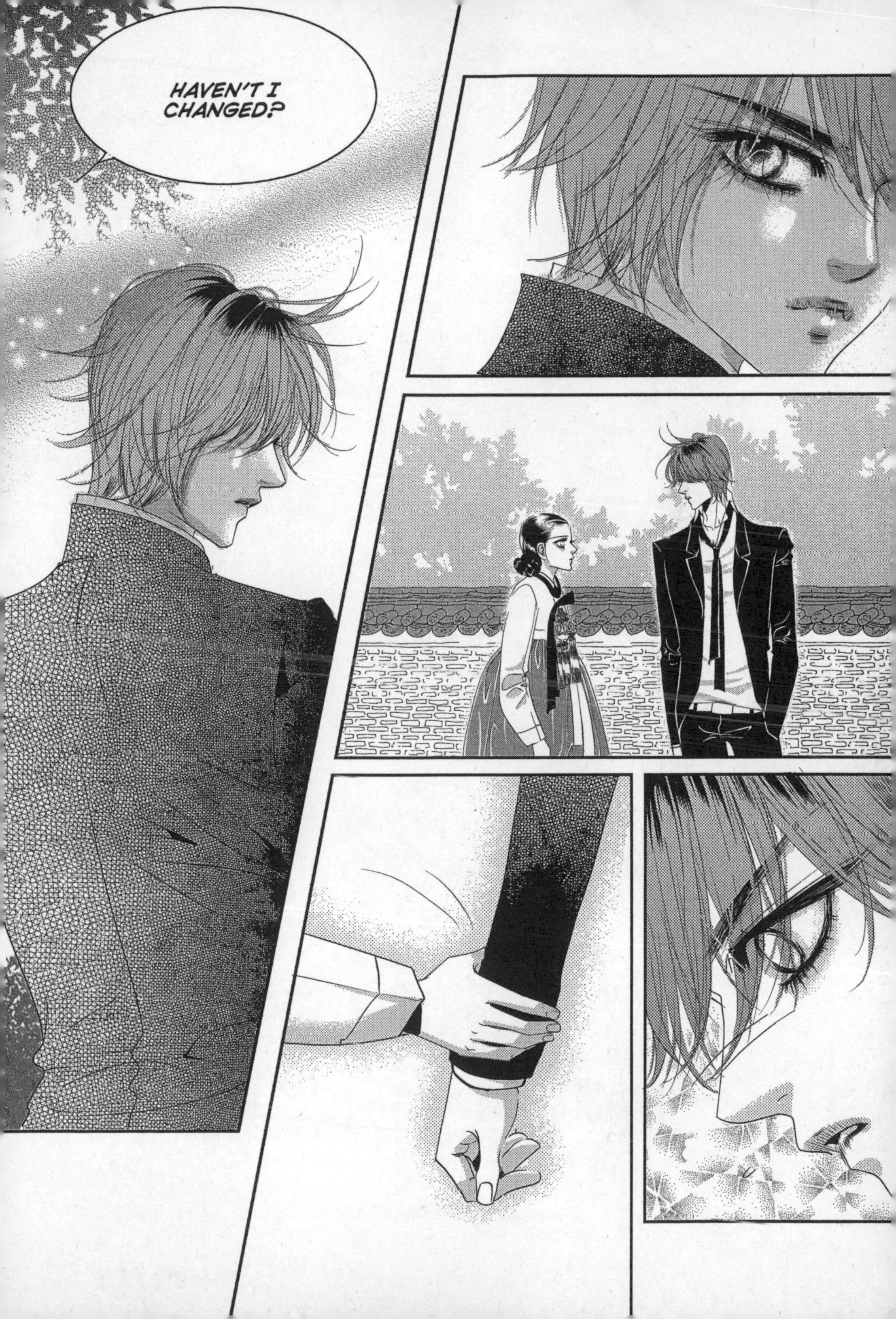
HAVEN'T I CHANGED?

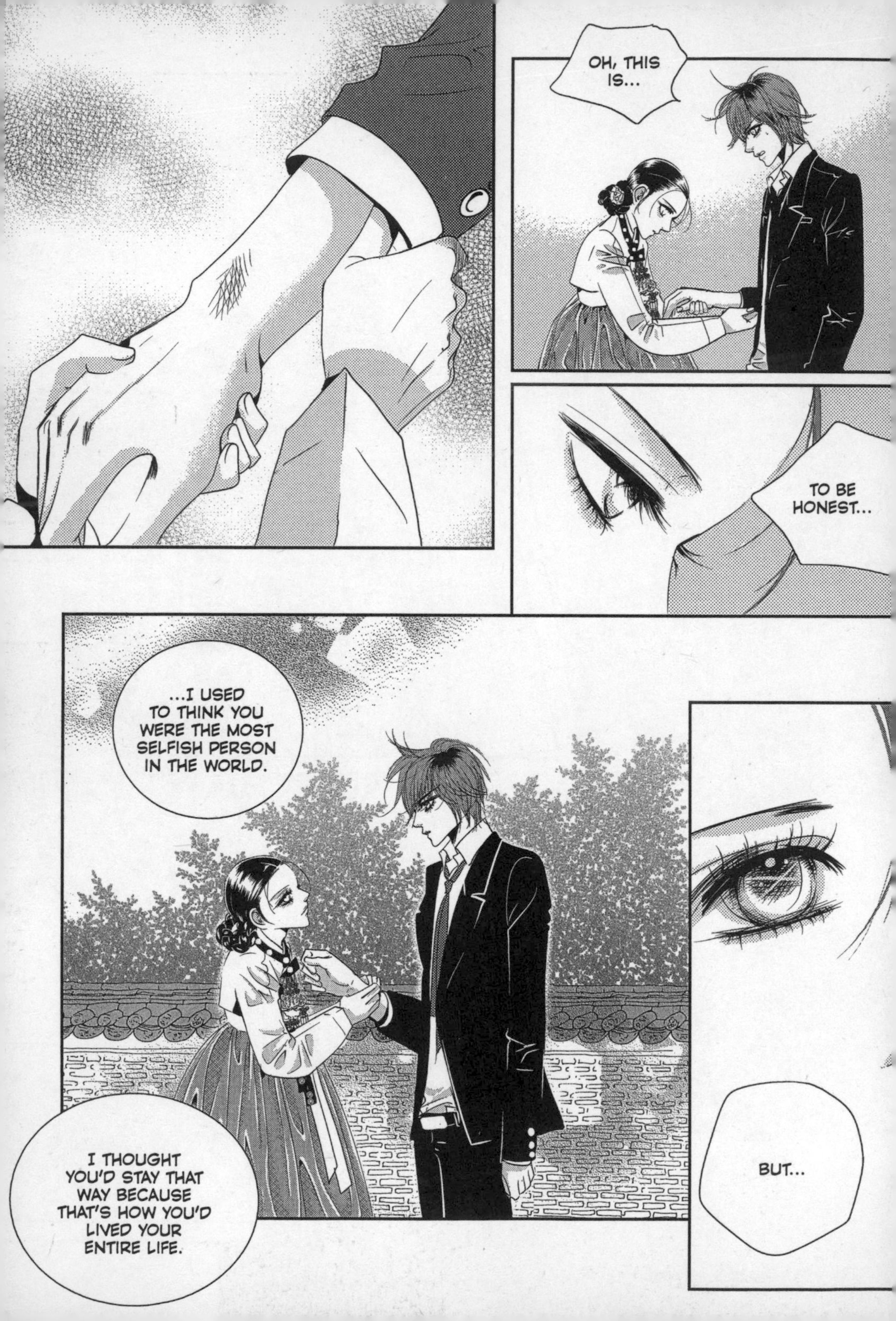
OH, THIS IS...
TO BE HONEST...
...I USED TO THINK YOU WERE THE MOST SELFISH PERSON IN THE WORLD.
I THOUGHT YOU'D STAY THAT WAY BECAUSE THAT'S HOW YOU'D LIVED YOUR ENTIRE LIFE.
BUT...

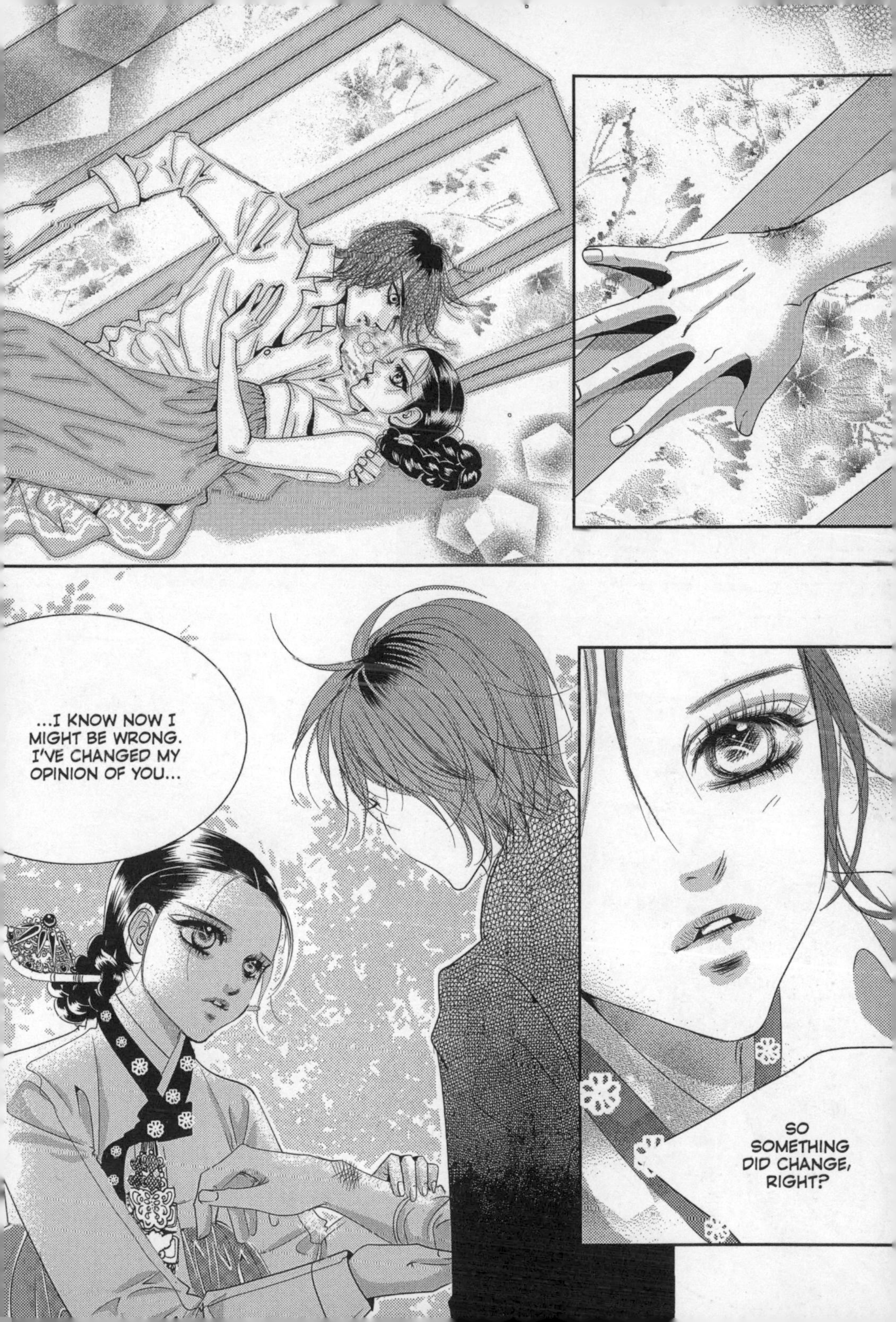
...I KNOW NOW I MIGHT BE WRONG. I'VE CHANGED MY OPINION OF YOU...
SO SOMETHING DID CHANGE, RIGHT?

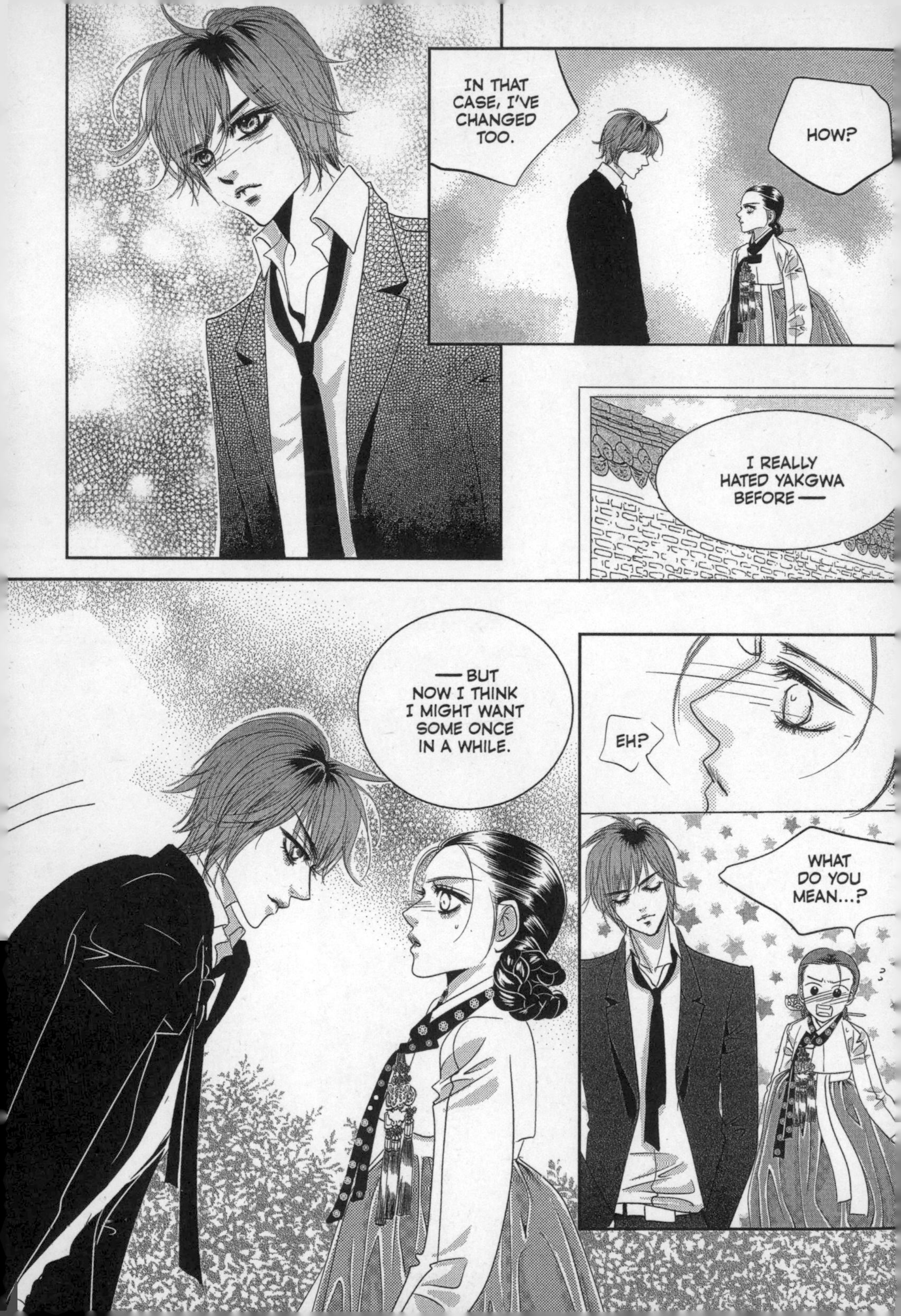
IN THAT CASE, I'VE CHANGED TOO.
HOW?
I REALLY HATED YAKGWA BEFORE —
— BUT NOW I THINK I MIGHT WANT SOME ONCE IN A WHILE.
EH?
WHAT DO YOU MEAN...?

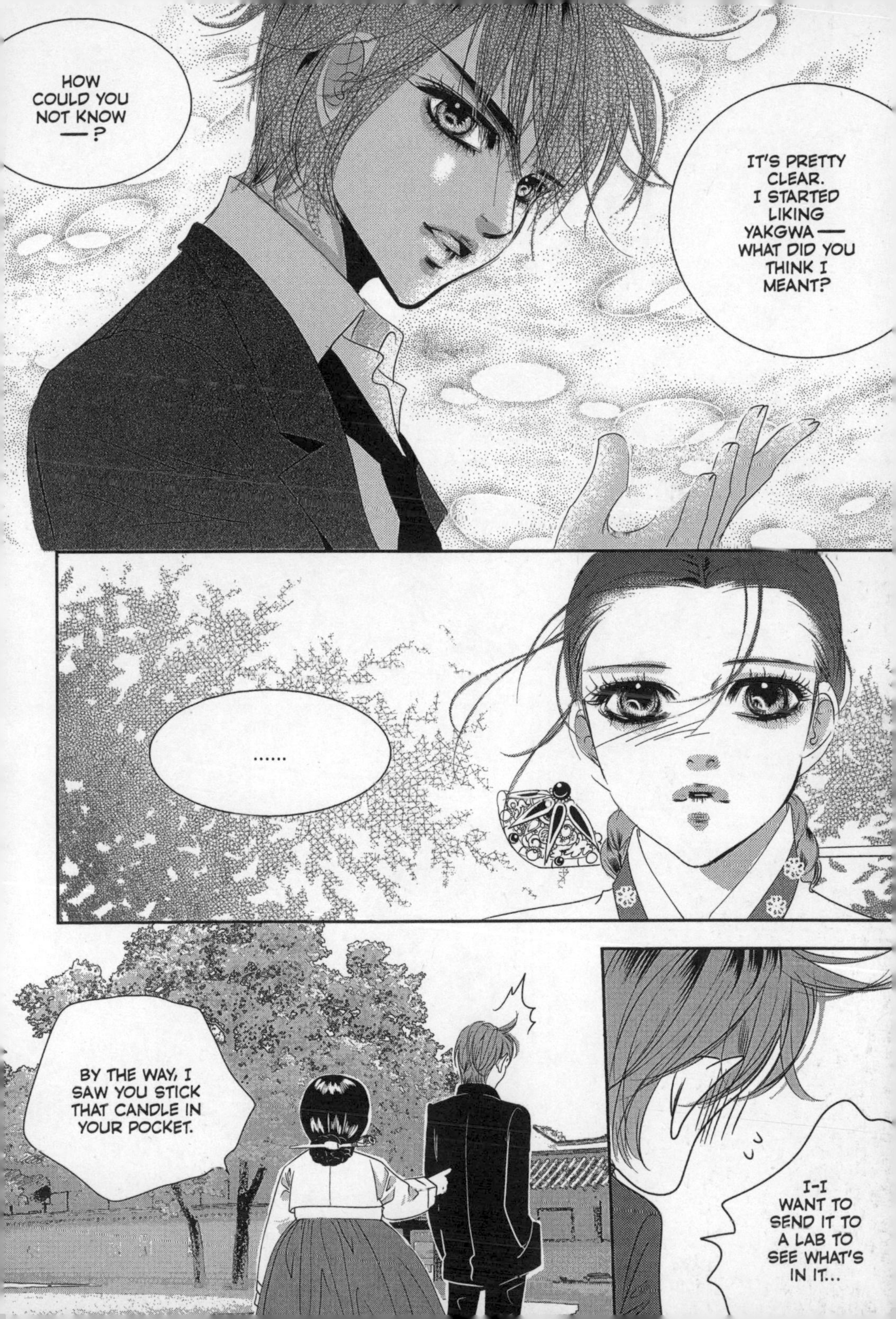
HOW COULD YOU NOT KNOW —?
IT'S PRETTY CLEAR. I STARTED LIKING YAKGWA — WHAT DID YOU THINK I MEANT?
......
BY THE WAY, I SAW YOU STICK THAT CANDLE IN YOUR POCKET.
I-I WANT TO SEND IT TO A LAB TO SEE WHAT'S IN IT...

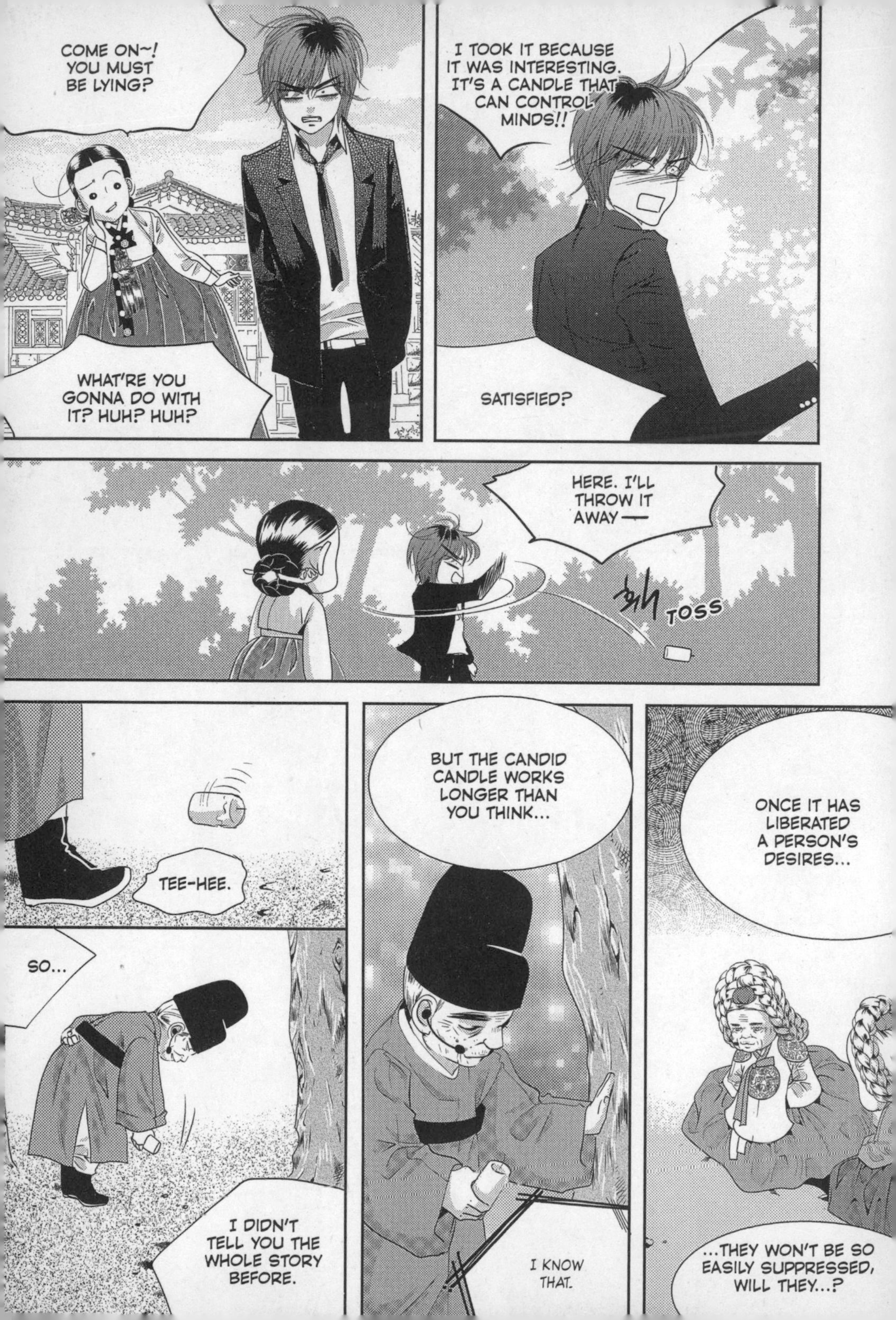
COME ON~! YOU MUST BE LYING?
WHAT'RE YOU GONNA DO WITH IT? HUH? HUH?
I TOOK IT BECAUSE IT WAS INTERESTING. IT'S A CANDLE THAT CAN CONTROL MINDS!!
SATISFIED?
HERE. I'LL THROW IT AWAY—
TOSS
TEE-HEE.
SO...
I DIDN'T TELL YOU THE WHOLE STORY BEFORE.
BUT THE CANDID CANDLE WORKS LONGER THAN YOU THINK...
I KNOW THAT.
ONCE IT HAS LIBERATED A PERSON'S DESIRES...
...THEY WON'T BE SO EASILY SUPPRESSED, WILL THEY...?

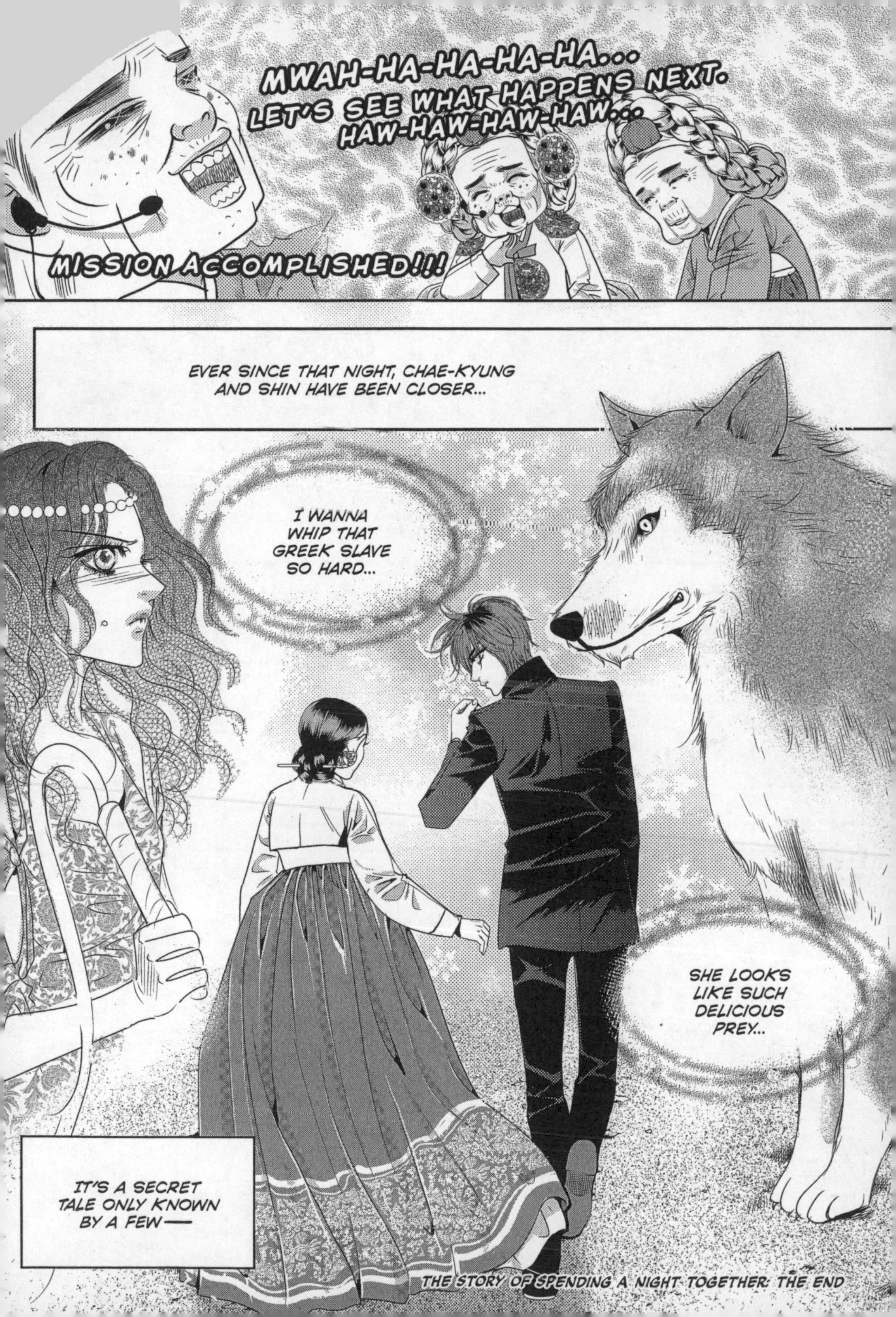
MWAH-HA-HA-HA-HA...
LET'S SEE WHAT HAPPENS NEXT.
HAW-HAW-HAW-HAW...
MISSION ACCOMPLISHED!!!
EVER SINCE THAT NIGHT, CHAE-KYUNG AND SHIN HAVE BEEN CLOSER...
I WANNA WHIP THAT GREEK SLAVE SO HARD...
SHE LOOKS LIKE SUCH DELICIOUS PREY...
IT'S A SECRET TALE ONLY KNOWN BY A FEW—
THE STORY OF SPENDING A NIGHT TOGETHER: THE END

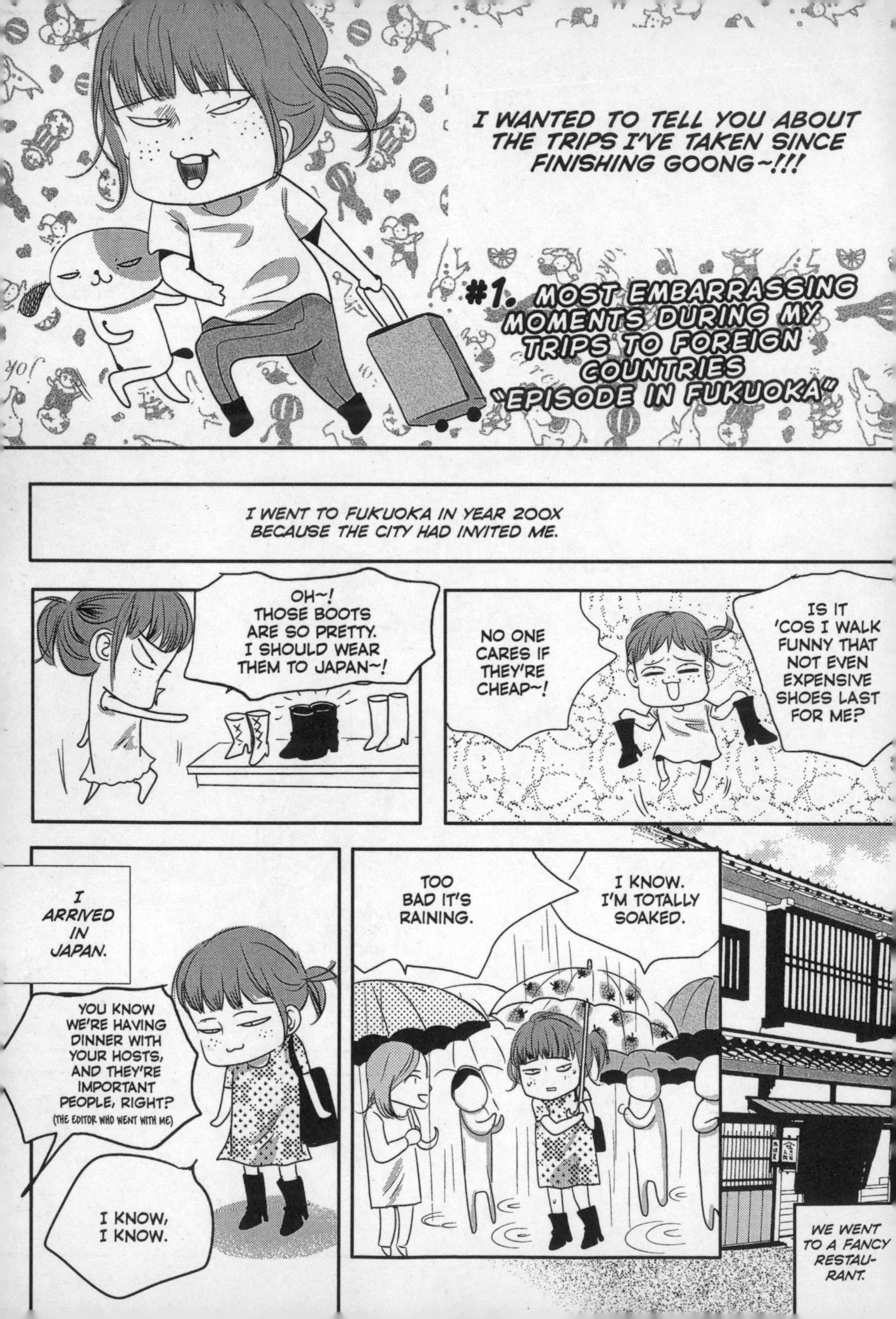
I WANTED TO TELL YOU ABOUT THE TRIPS I'VE TAKEN SINCE FINISHING GOONG~!!!
#1. MOST EMBARRASSING MOMENTS DURING MY TRIPS TO FOREIGN COUNTRIES "EPISODE IN FUKUOKA"
I WENT TO FUKUOKA IN YEAR 200X BECAUSE THE CITY HAD INVITED ME.
OH~! THOSE BOOTS ARE SO PRETTY. I SHOULD WEAR THEM TO JAPAN~!
NO ONE CARES IF THEY'RE CHEAP~!
IS IT 'COS I WALK FUNNY THAT NOT EVEN EXPENSIVE SHOES LAST FOR ME?
I ARRIVED IN JAPAN.
YOU KNOW WE'RE HAVING DINNER WITH YOUR HOSTS, AND THEY'RE IMPORTANT PEOPLE, RIGHT?
(THE EDITOR WHO WENT WITH ME)
I KNOW, I KNOW.
TOO BAD IT'S RAINING.
I KNOW. I'M TOTALLY SOAKED.
WE WENT TO A FANCY RESTAU-RANT.

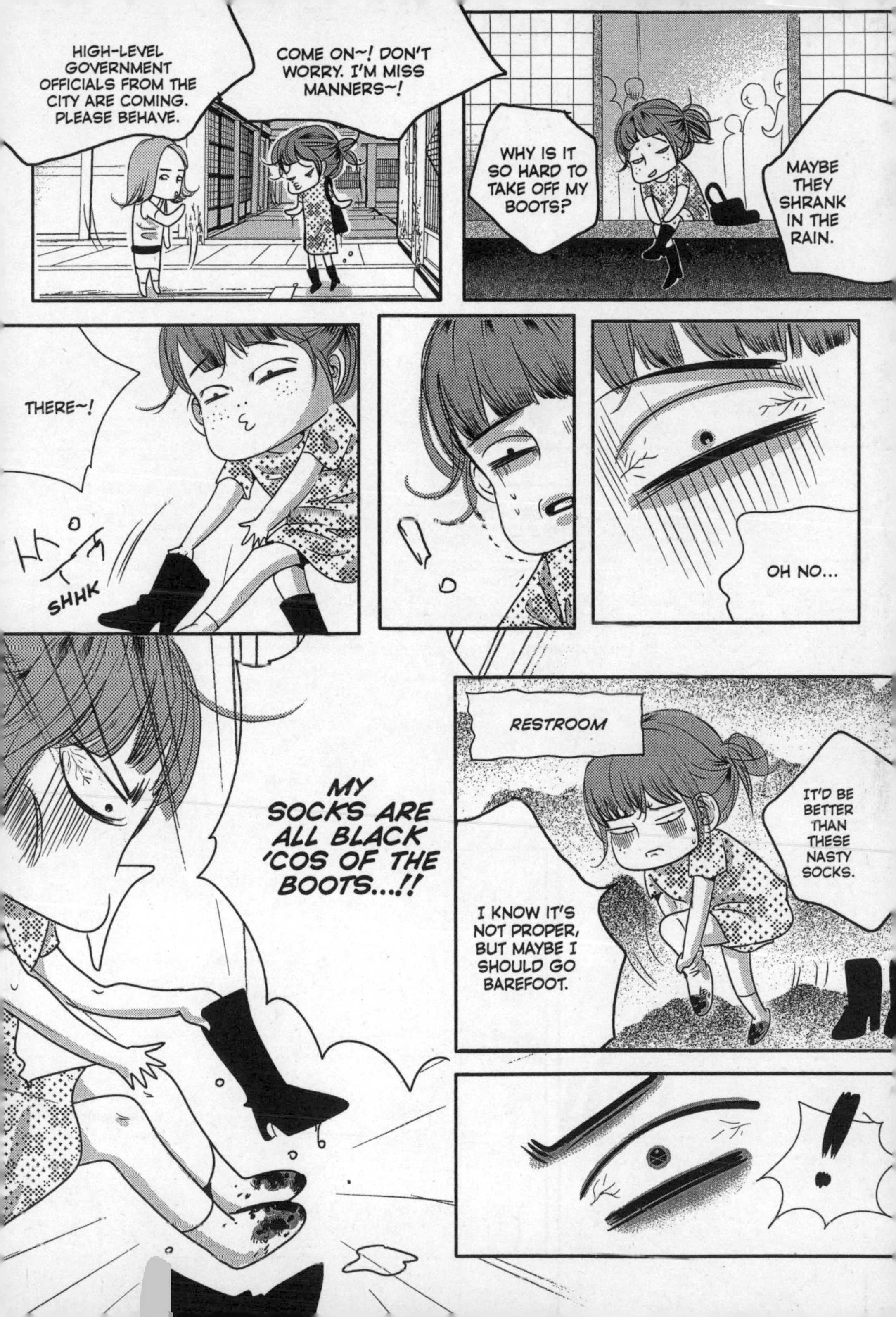
HIGH-LEVEL GOVERNMENT OFFICIALS FROM THE CITY ARE COMING. PLEASE BEHAVE.
COME ON~! DON'T WORRY. I'M MISS MANNERS~!
WHY IS IT SO HARD TO TAKE OFF MY BOOTS?
MAYBE THEY SHRANK IN THE RAIN.
THERE~!
SHHK
OH NO...
MY SOCKS ARE ALL BLACK 'COS OF THE BOOTS...!!
RESTROOM
IT'D BE BETTER THAN THESE NASTY SOCKS.
I KNOW IT'S NOT PROPER, BUT MAYBE I SHOULD GO BAREFOOT.
!

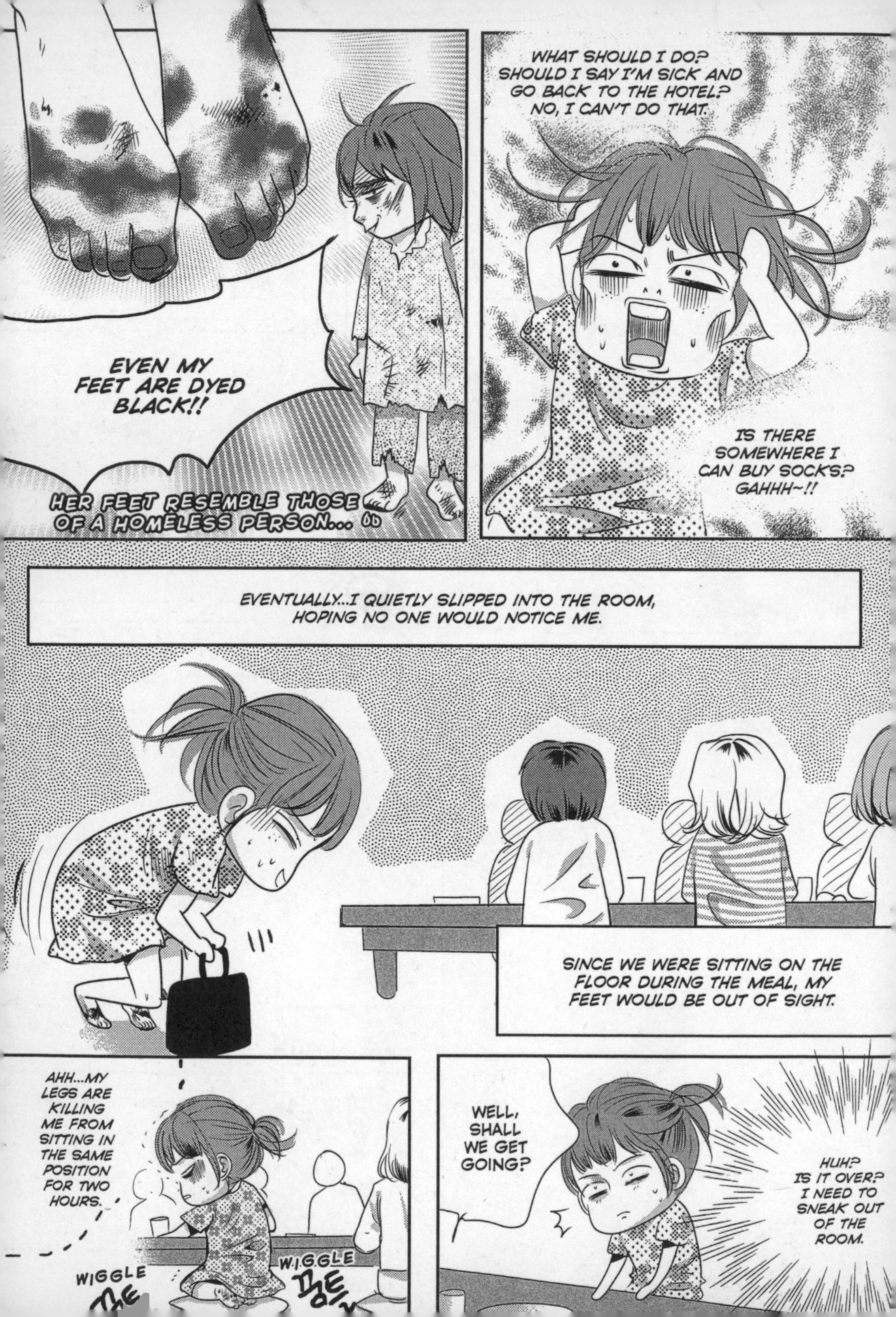
EVEN MY FEET ARE DYED BLACK!!
HER FEET RESEMBLE THOSE OF A HOMELESS PERSON...
WHAT SHOULD I DO? SHOULD I SAY I'M SICK AND GO BACK TO THE HOTEL? NO, I CAN'T DO THAT.
IS THERE SOMEWHERE I CAN BUY SOCKS? GAHHH~!!
EVENTUALLY...I QUIETLY SLIPPED INTO THE ROOM, HOPING NO ONE WOULD NOTICE ME.
SINCE WE WERE SITTING ON THE FLOOR DURING THE MEAL, MY FEET WOULD BE OUT OF SIGHT.
AHH...MY LEGS ARE KILLING ME FROM SITTING IN THE SAME POSITION FOR TWO HOURS.
WIGGLE
WIGGLE
WELL, SHALL WE GET GOING?
HUH? IS IT OVER? I NEED TO SNEAK OUT OF THE ROOM.

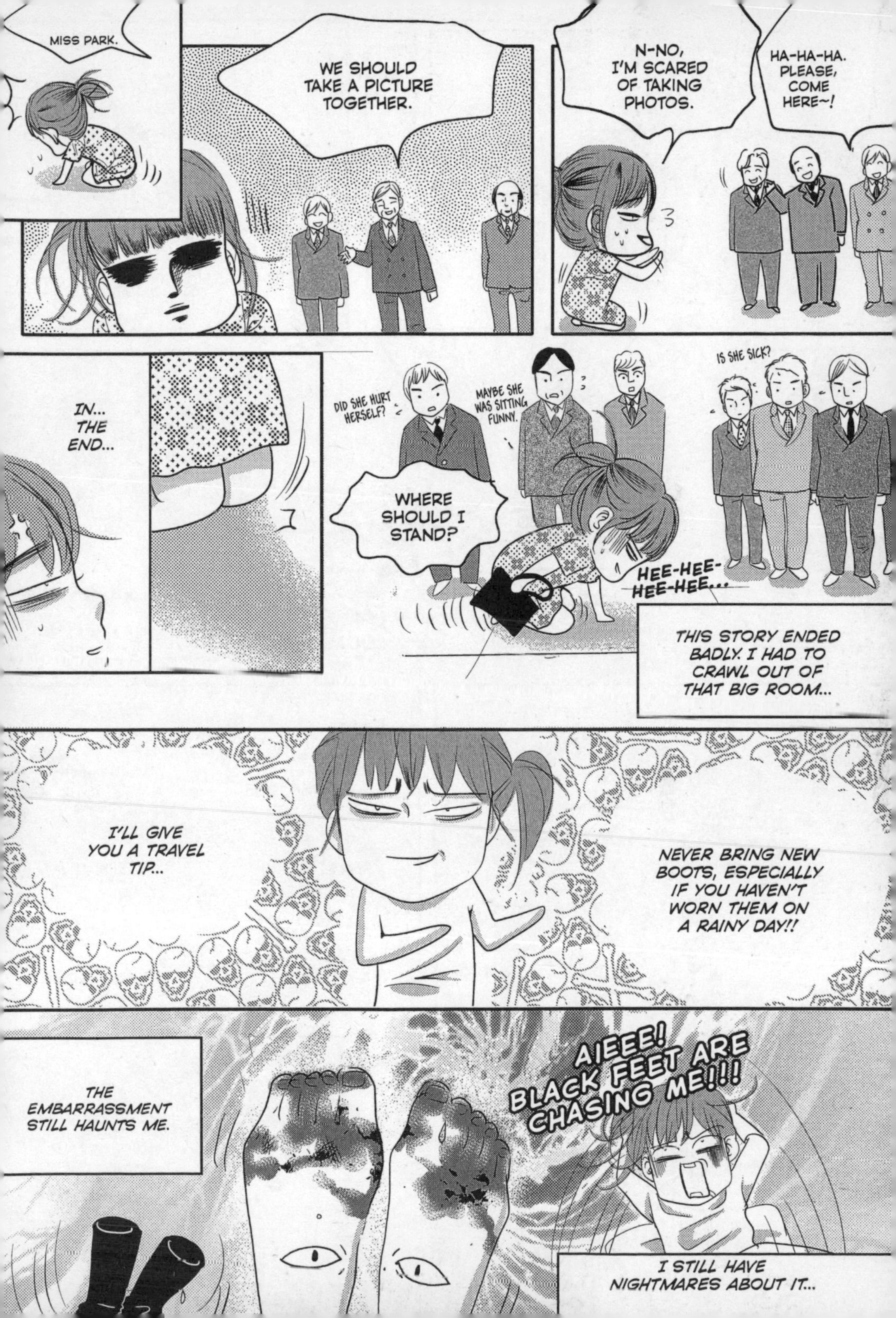
MISS PARK.
WE SHOULD TAKE A PICTURE TOGETHER.
N-NO, I'M SCARED OF TAKING PHOTOS.
HA-HA-HA. PLEASE, COME HERE~!
IN... THE END...
DID SHE HURT HERSELF?
MAYBE SHE WAS SITTING FUNNY.
IS SHE SICK?
WHERE SHOULD I STAND?
HEE-HEE-HEE-HEE...
THIS STORY ENDED BADLY. I HAD TO CRAWL OUT OF THAT BIG ROOM...
I'LL GIVE YOU A TRAVEL TIP...
NEVER BRING NEW BOOTS, ESPECIALLY IF YOU HAVEN'T WORN THEM ON A RAINY DAY!!
THE EMBARRASSMENT STILL HAUNTS ME.
AIEEE! BLACK FEET ARE CHASING ME!!!
I STILL HAVE NIGHTMARES ABOUT IT...

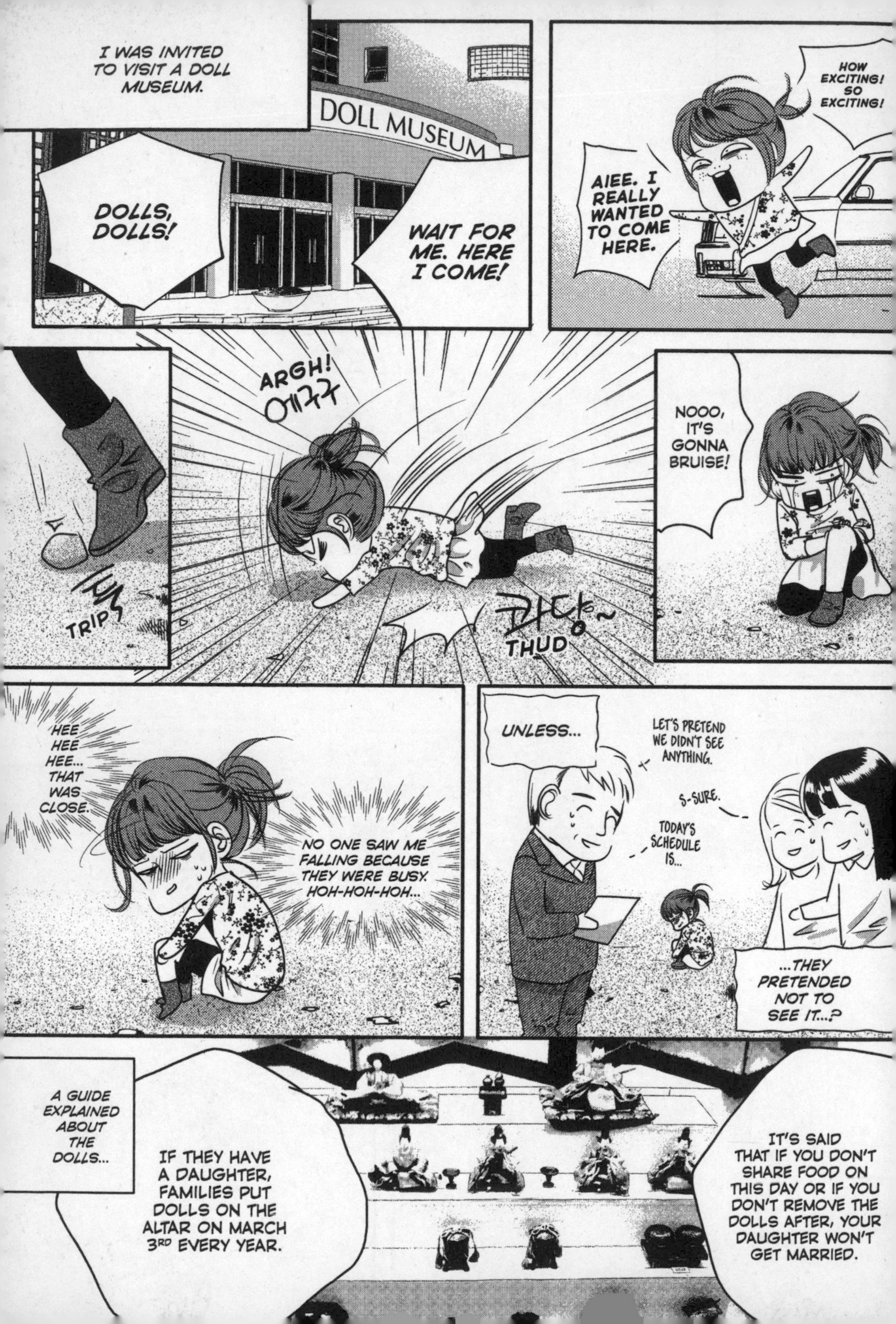
I WAS INVITED TO VISIT A DOLL MUSEUM.
DOLL MUSEUM
DOLLS, DOLLS!
WAIT FOR ME. HERE I COME!
HOW EXCITING! SO EXCITING!
AIEE. I REALLY WANTED TO COME HERE.
TRIP
ARGH! 에구구
과당~ THUD
NOOO, IT'S GONNA BRUISE!
HEE HEE HEE... THAT WAS CLOSE.
NO ONE SAW ME FALLING BECAUSE THEY WERE BUSY. HOH-HOH-HOH...
UNLESS...
LET'S PRETEND WE DIDN'T SEE ANYTHING.
S-SURE.
TODAY'S SCHEDULE IS...
...THEY PRETENDED NOT TO SEE IT...?
A GUIDE EXPLAINED ABOUT THE DOLLS...
IF THEY HAVE A DAUGHTER, FAMILIES PUT DOLLS ON THE ALTAR ON MARCH 3RD EVERY YEAR.
IT'S SAID THAT IF YOU DON'T SHARE FOOD ON THIS DAY OR IF YOU DON'T REMOVE THE DOLLS AFTER, YOUR DAUGHTER WON'T GET MARRIED.

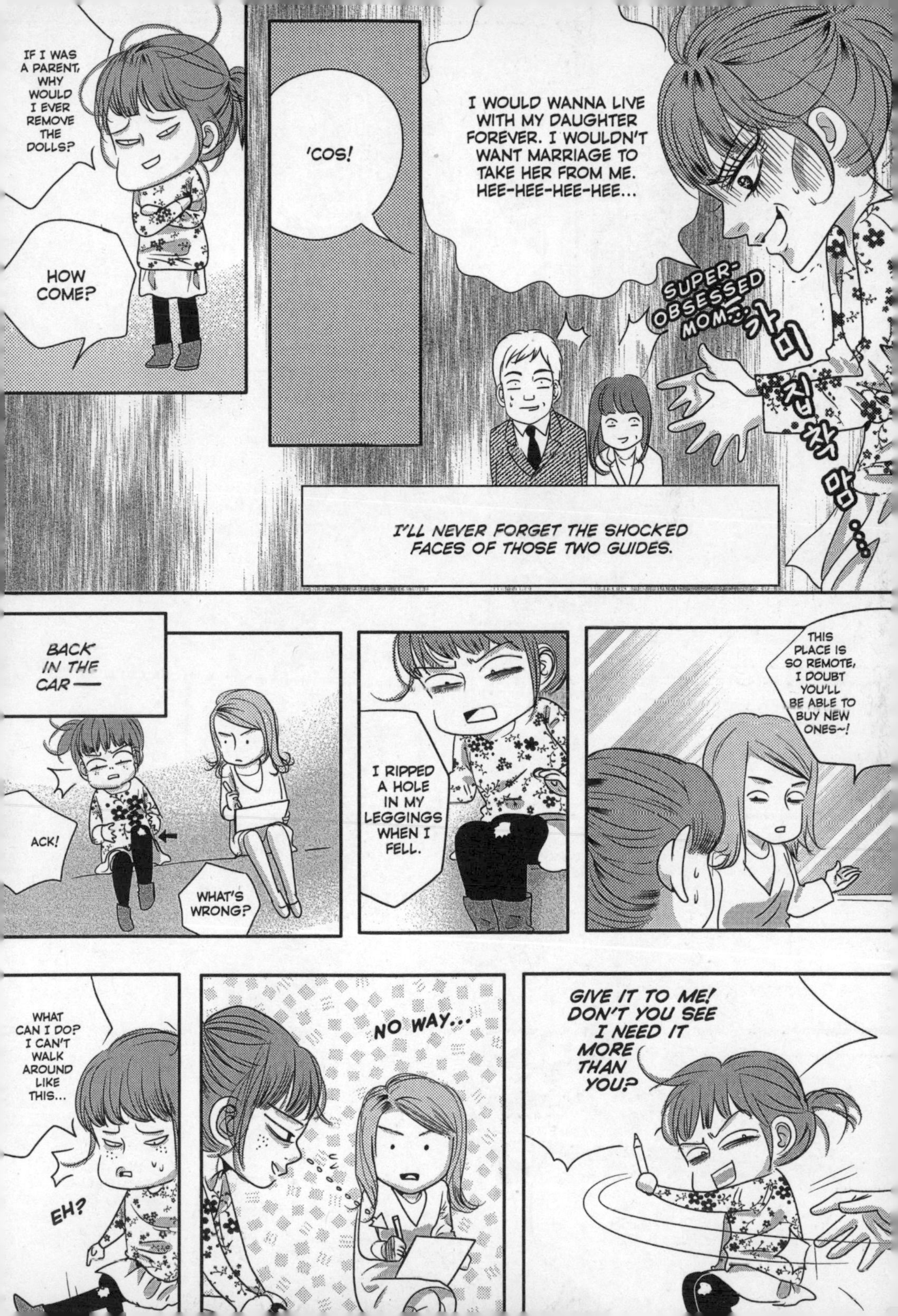
IF I WAS A PARENT, WHY WOULD I EVER REMOVE THE DOLLS?
HOW COME?
'COS!
I WOULD WANNA LIVE WITH MY DAUGHTER FOREVER. I WOULDN'T WANT MARRIAGE TO TAKE HER FROM ME. HEE-HEE-HEE-HEE...
SUPER-OBSESSED MOM
가미 집착 맘...
I'LL NEVER FORGET THE SHOCKED FACES OF THOSE TWO GUIDES.
BACK IN THE CAR—
ACK!
WHAT'S WRONG?
I RIPPED A HOLE IN MY LEGGINGS WHEN I FELL.
THIS PLACE IS SO REMOTE, I DOUBT YOU'LL BE ABLE TO BUY NEW ONES~!
WHAT CAN I DO? I CAN'T WALK AROUND LIKE THIS...
EH?
NO WAY...
GIVE IT TO ME! DON'T YOU SEE I NEED IT MORE THAN YOU?

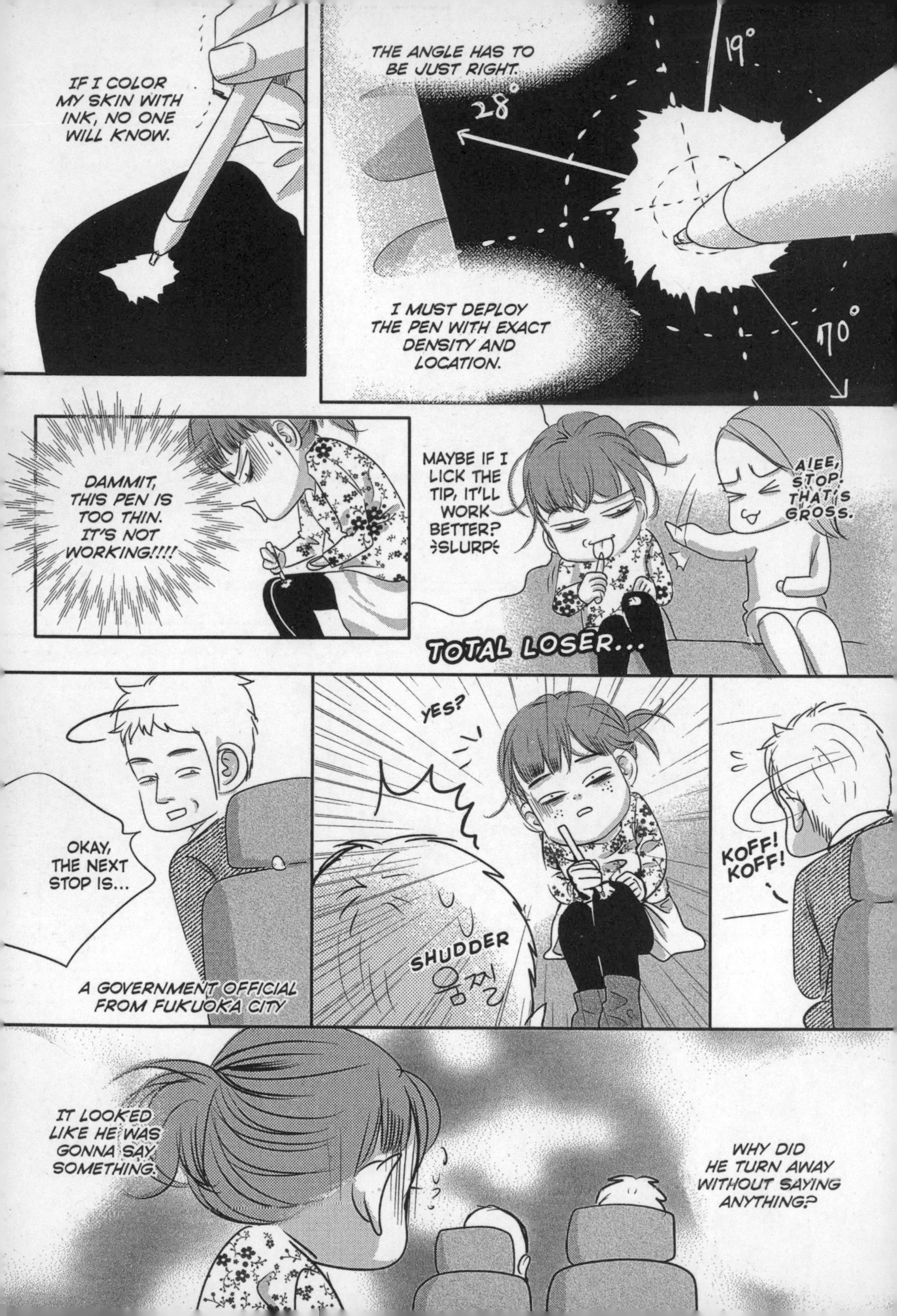
IF I COLOR MY SKIN WITH INK, NO ONE WILL KNOW.
THE ANGLE HAS TO BE JUST RIGHT.
28°
19°
I MUST DEPLOY THE PEN WITH EXACT DENSITY AND LOCATION.
70°
DAMMIT, THIS PEN IS TOO THIN. IT'S NOT WORKING!!!!
MAYBE IF I LICK THE TIP, IT'LL WORK BETTER?
SLURP
AIEE, STOP. THAT'S GROSS.
TOTAL LOSER...
OKAY, THE NEXT STOP IS...
A GOVERNMENT OFFICIAL FROM FUKUOKA CITY
YES?
SHUDDER
움찔
KOFF! KOFF!
IT LOOKED LIKE HE WAS GONNA SAY SOMETHING.
WHY DID HE TURN AWAY WITHOUT SAYING ANYTHING?

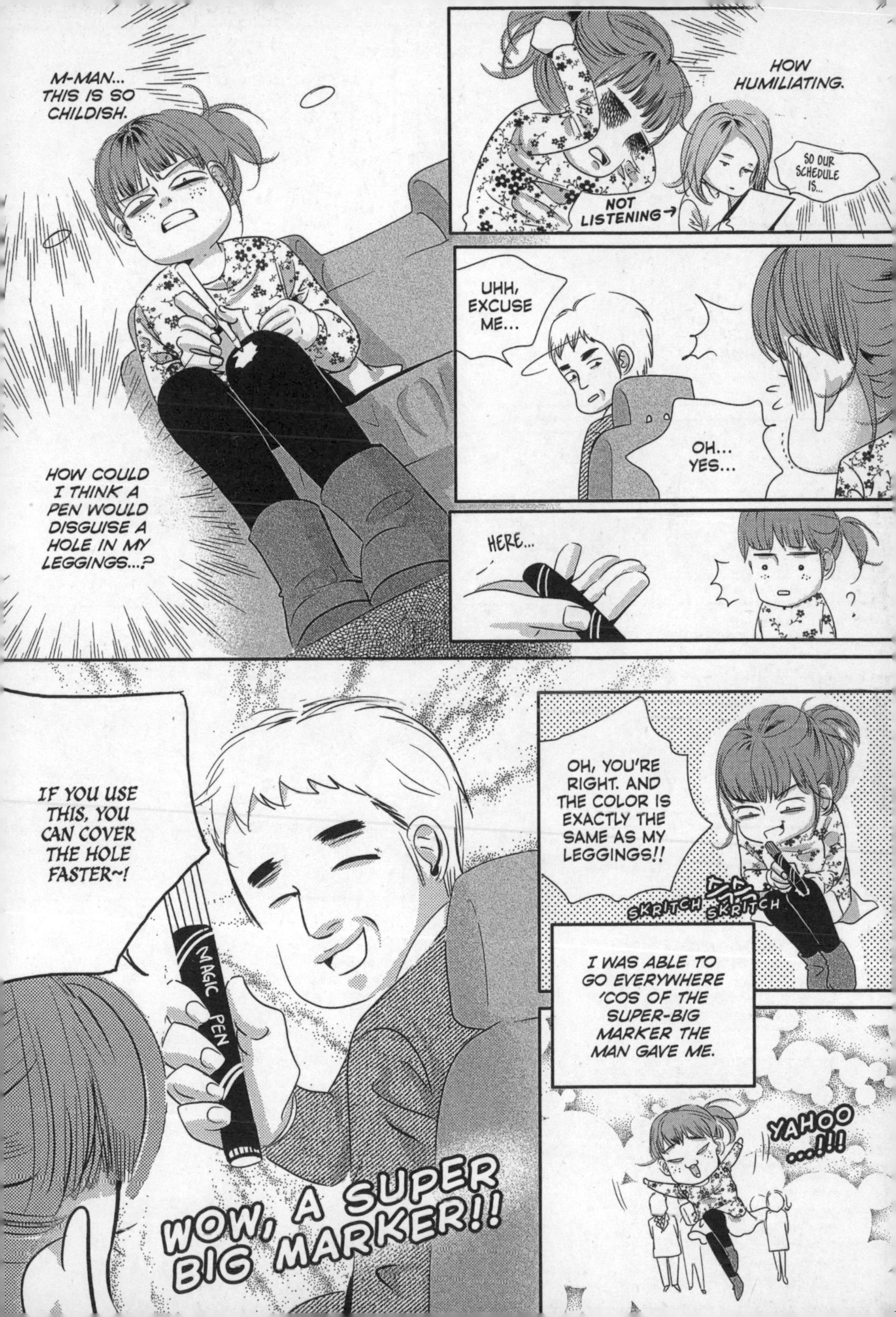
M-MAN... THIS IS SO CHILDISH.
HOW COULD I THINK A PEN WOULD DISGUISE A HOLE IN MY LEGGINGS...?
HOW HUMILIATING.
SO OUR SCHEDULE IS...
NOT LISTENING→
UHH, EXCUSE ME...
OH... YES...
HERE...
IF YOU USE THIS, YOU CAN COVER THE HOLE FASTER~!
MAGIC PEN
WOW, A SUPER BIG MARKER!!
OH, YOU'RE RIGHT. AND THE COLOR IS EXACTLY THE SAME AS MY LEGGINGS!!
SKRITCH SKRITCH
I WAS ABLE TO GO EVERYWHERE 'COS OF THE SUPER-BIG MARKER THE MAN GAVE ME.
YAHOO ...!!!

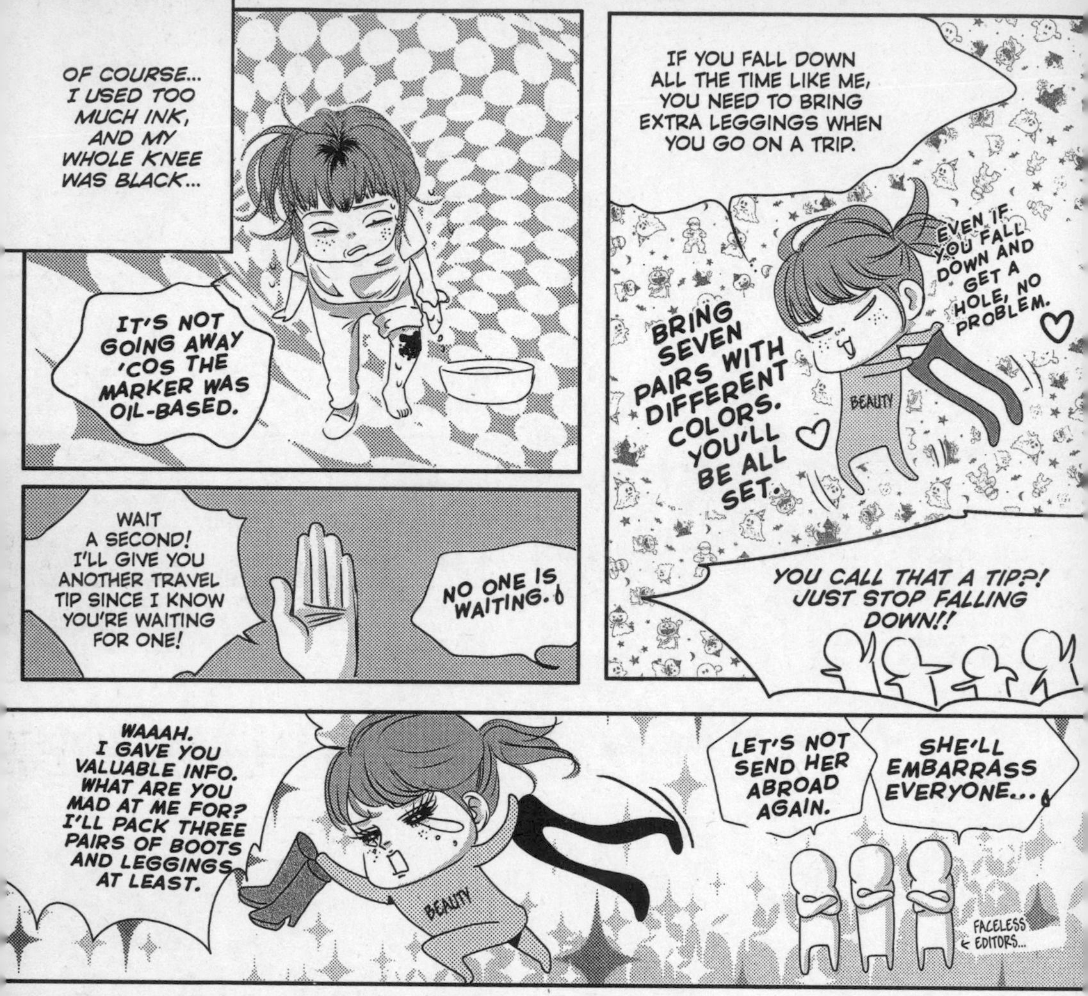
OF COURSE... I USED TOO MUCH INK, AND MY WHOLE KNEE WAS BLACK...
IT'S NOT GOING AWAY 'COS THE MARKER WAS OIL-BASED.
WAIT A SECOND! I'LL GIVE YOU ANOTHER TRAVEL TIP SINCE I KNOW YOU'RE WAITING FOR ONE!
NO ONE IS WAITING.
IF YOU FALL DOWN ALL THE TIME LIKE ME, YOU NEED TO BRING EXTRA LEGGINGS WHEN YOU GO ON A TRIP.
BRING SEVEN PAIRS WITH DIFFERENT COLORS. YOU'LL BE ALL SET.
EVEN IF YOU FALL DOWN AND GET A HOLE, NO PROBLEM.
BEAUTY
YOU CALL THAT A TIP?! JUST STOP FALLING DOWN!!
WAAAH. I GAVE YOU VALUABLE INFO. WHAT ARE YOU MAD AT ME FOR? I'LL PACK THREE PAIRS OF BOOTS AND LEGGINGS AT LEAST.
BEAUTY
LET'S NOT SEND HER ABROAD AGAIN.
SHE'LL EMBARRASS EVERYONE...
FACELESS ← EDITORS...

#2. I SAW A MONSTER IN A TAXI.

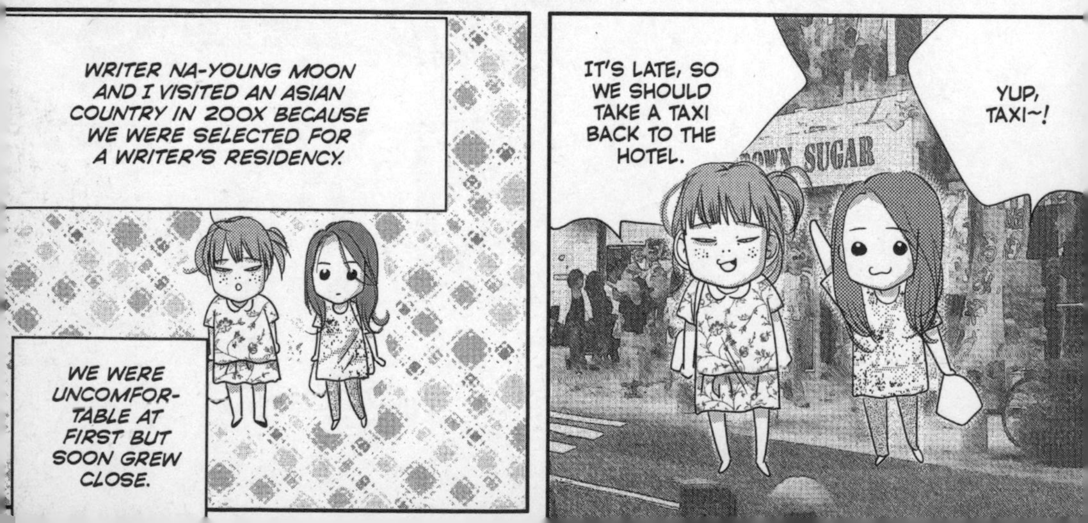
WRITER NA-YOUNG MOON AND I VISITED AN ASIAN COUNTRY IN 200X BECAUSE WE WERE SELECTED FOR A WRITER'S RESIDENCY.
WE WERE UNCOMFORTABLE AT FIRST BUT SOON GREW CLOSE.
IT'S LATE, SO WE SHOULD TAKE A TAXI BACK TO THE HOTEL.
YUP, TAXI~!
SUGAR

THE HOTEL IS CLOSE BY, SO IT WON'T COST MUCH, WILL IT?

YOU THINK? WE COULD'VE WALKED IF THE STREET WASN'T SO DANGEROUS—

HUH? WAIT A MINUTE...

WHY DOES THE METER KEEP GOING UP!?

5000

THE DRIVER KEEPS PRESSING SOMETHING!

CLICK CLICK CLICK

*ABOUT ONE DOLLAR

1,000 WON* SHOULD'VE BEEN MORE THAN ENOUGH.

1700
3000
5000
9500
11000

CONVERTED TO KOREAN WON TWO TIMES, FOUR TIMES, EIGHT TIME MORE.

TH-THIS IS CRAZY. IT SHOULD ONLY BE ABOUT 1,500 WON.

<HEY, I SEE YOU!!>

<STOP!!>

YOU'RE SO BAD. I SAW YOU. STOP, STOP!

IT'S ALREADY MORE THAN 10,000 WON!

QUIT CRANKING THE METER! STOP IT!

TOTAL KONGLISH ^^

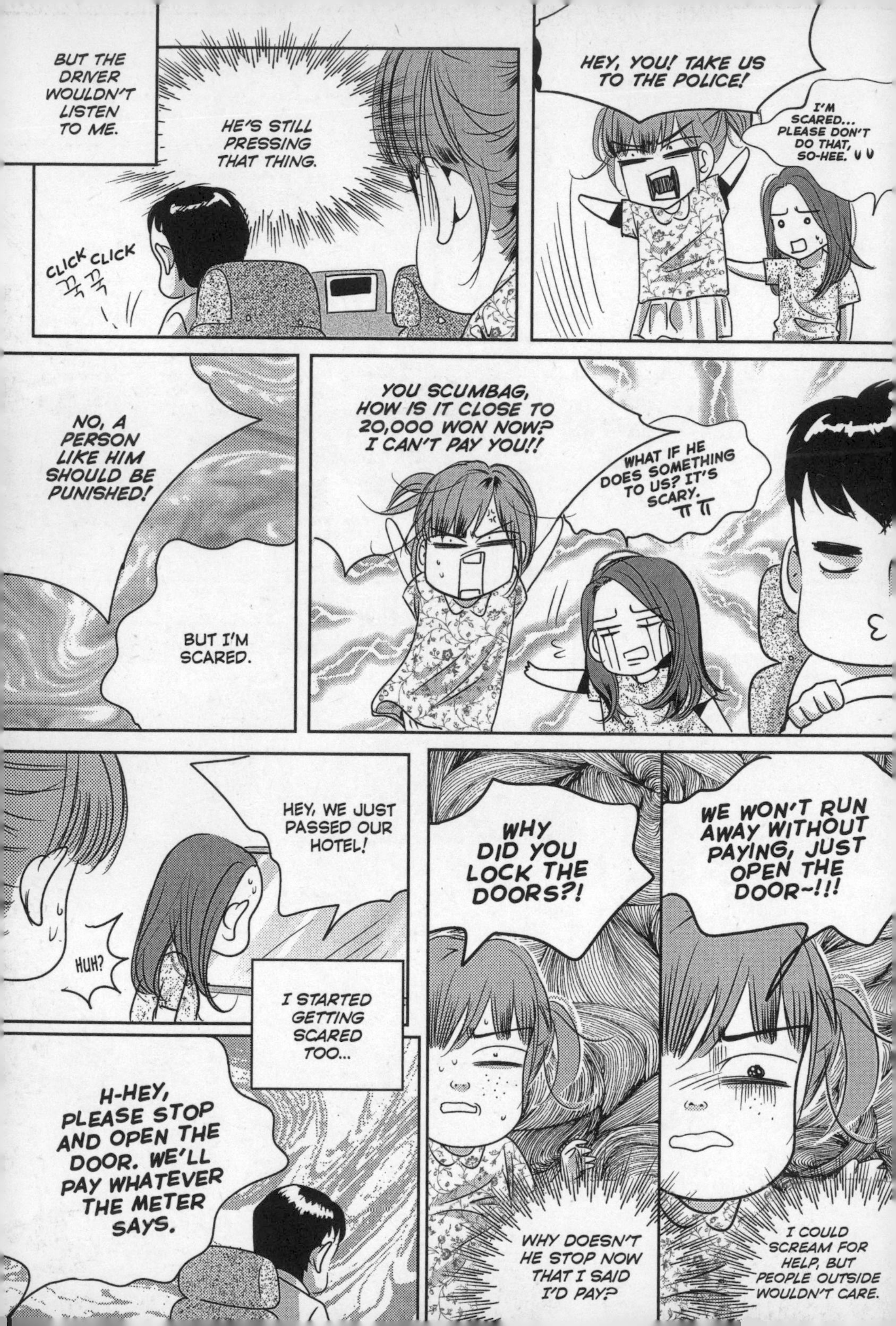
BUT THE DRIVER WOULDN'T LISTEN TO ME.
HE'S STILL PRESSING THAT THING.
CLICK CLICK
꾹꾹
HEY, YOU! TAKE US TO THE POLICE!
I'M SCARED... PLEASE DON'T DO THAT, SO-HEE.
NO, A PERSON LIKE HIM SHOULD BE PUNISHED!
BUT I'M SCARED.
YOU SCUMBAG, HOW IS IT CLOSE TO 20,000 WON NOW? I CAN'T PAY YOU!!
WHAT IF HE DOES SOMETHING TO US? IT'S SCARY. ㅠㅠ
HEY, WE JUST PASSED OUR HOTEL!
HUH?
I STARTED GETTING SCARED TOO...
H-HEY, PLEASE STOP AND OPEN THE DOOR. WE'LL PAY WHATEVER THE METER SAYS.
WHY DID YOU LOCK THE DOORS?!
WHY DOESN'T HE STOP NOW THAT I SAID I'D PAY?
WE WON'T RUN AWAY WITHOUT PAYING, JUST OPEN THE DOOR~!!!
I COULD SCREAM FOR HELP, BUT PEOPLE OUTSIDE WOULDN'T CARE.

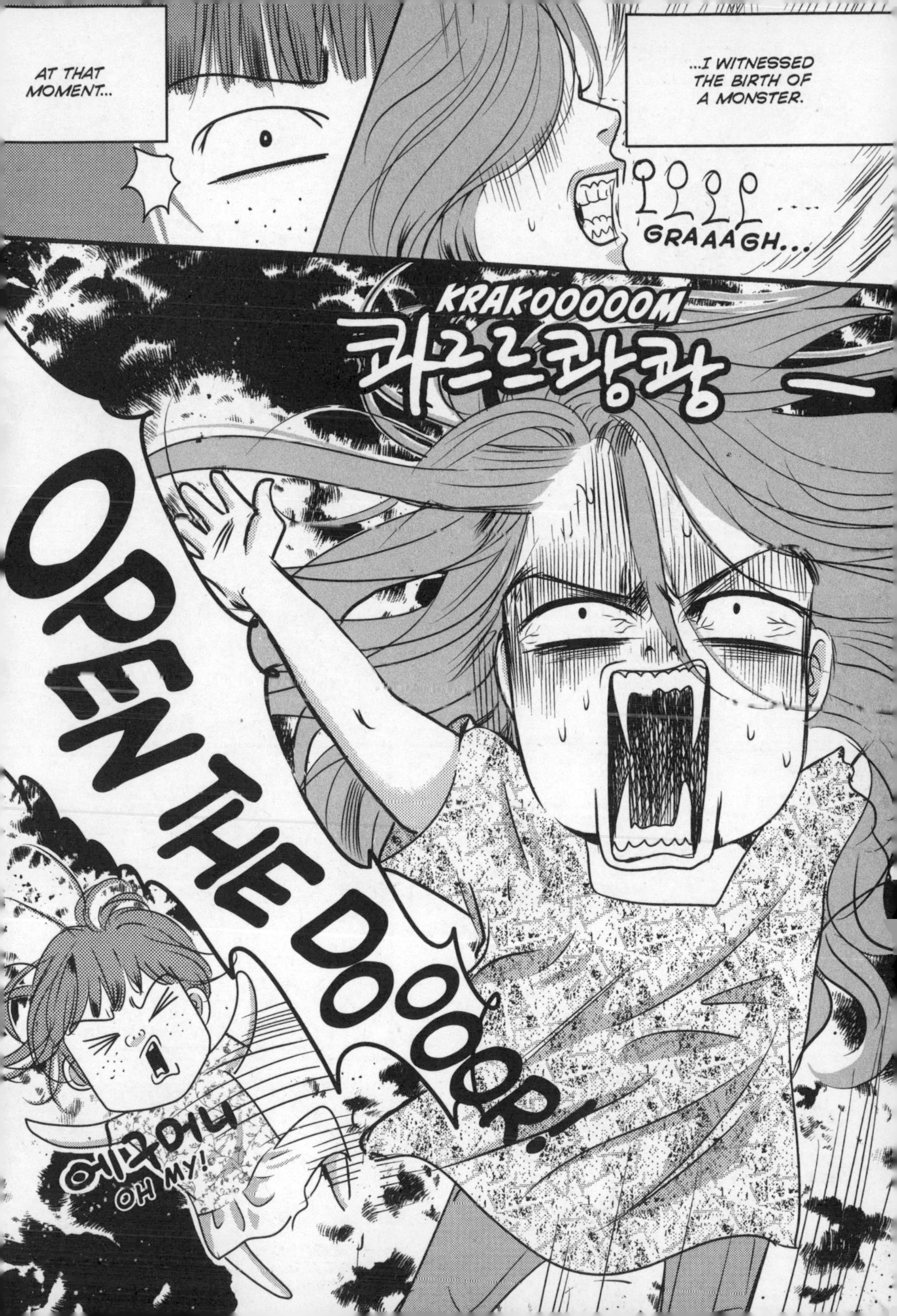
AT THAT MOMENT...
...I WITNESSED THE BIRTH OF A MONSTER.
으으으으...
GRAAAGH...
KRAKOOOOOM
콰르르쾅쾅
OPEN THE DOOOOR!
어머나
OH MY!

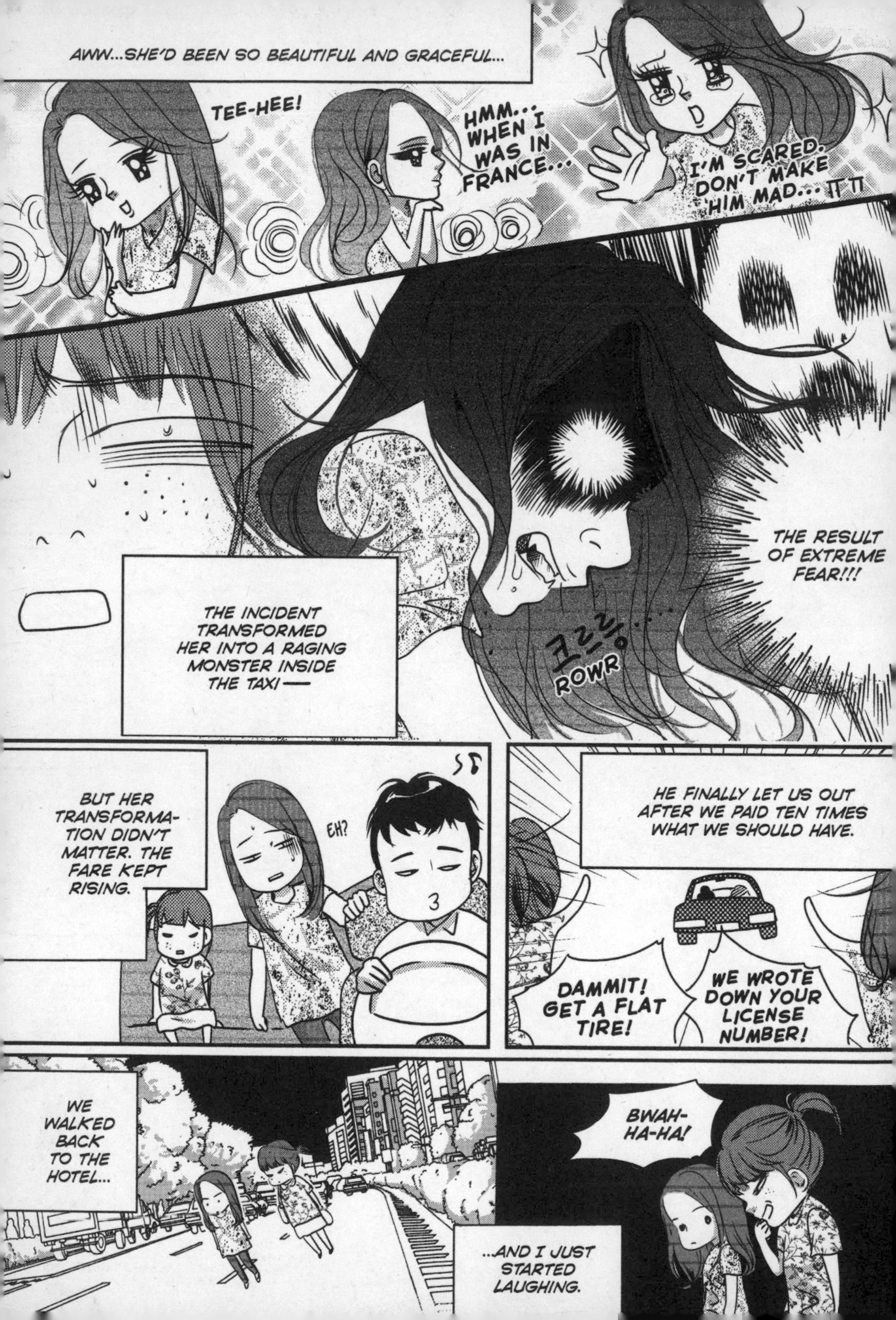
AWW...SHE'D BEEN SO BEAUTIFUL AND GRACEFUL...
TEE-HEE!
HMM... WHEN I WAS IN FRANCE...
I'M SCARED. DON'T MAKE HIM MAD... ㅠㅠ
THE INCIDENT TRANSFORMED HER INTO A RAGING MONSTER INSIDE THE TAXI—
THE RESULT OF EXTREME FEAR!!!
ROWR
BUT HER TRANSFORMATION DIDN'T MATTER. THE FARE KEPT RISING.
EH?
HE FINALLY LET US OUT AFTER WE PAID TEN TIMES WHAT WE SHOULD HAVE.
DAMMIT! GET A FLAT TIRE!
WE WROTE DOWN YOUR LICENSE NUMBER!
WE WALKED BACK TO THE HOTEL...
BWAH-HA-HA!
...AND I JUST STARTED LAUGHING.

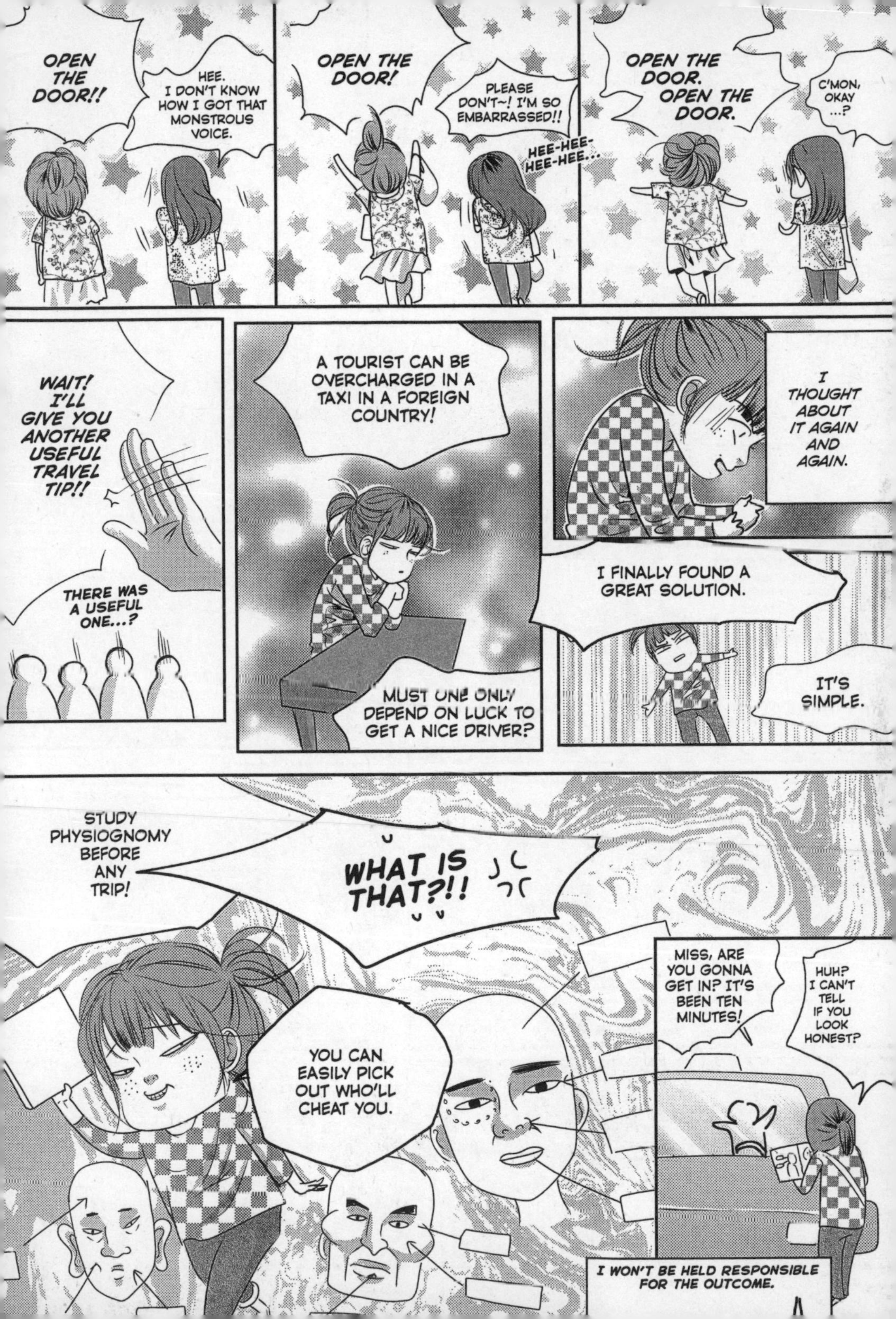
OPEN THE DOOR!!
HEE. I DON'T KNOW HOW I GOT THAT MONSTROUS VOICE.
OPEN THE DOOR!
PLEASE DON'T~! I'M SO EMBARRASSED!!
HEE-HEE-HEE-HEE...
OPEN THE DOOR. OPEN THE DOOR.
C'MON, OKAY ...?
WAIT! I'LL GIVE YOU ANOTHER USEFUL TRAVEL TIP!!
THERE WAS A USEFUL ONE...?
A TOURIST CAN BE OVERCHARGED IN A TAXI IN A FOREIGN COUNTRY!
MUST ONE ONLY DEPEND ON LUCK TO GET A NICE DRIVER?
I THOUGHT ABOUT IT AGAIN AND AGAIN.
I FINALLY FOUND A GREAT SOLUTION.
IT'S SIMPLE.
STUDY PHYSIOGNOMY BEFORE ANY TRIP!
WHAT IS THAT?!!
YOU CAN EASILY PICK OUT WHO'LL CHEAT YOU.
MISS, ARE YOU GONNA GET IN? IT'S BEEN TEN MINUTES!
HUH? I CAN'T TELL IF YOU LOOK HONEST?
I WON'T BE HELD RESPONSIBLE FOR THE OUTCOME.

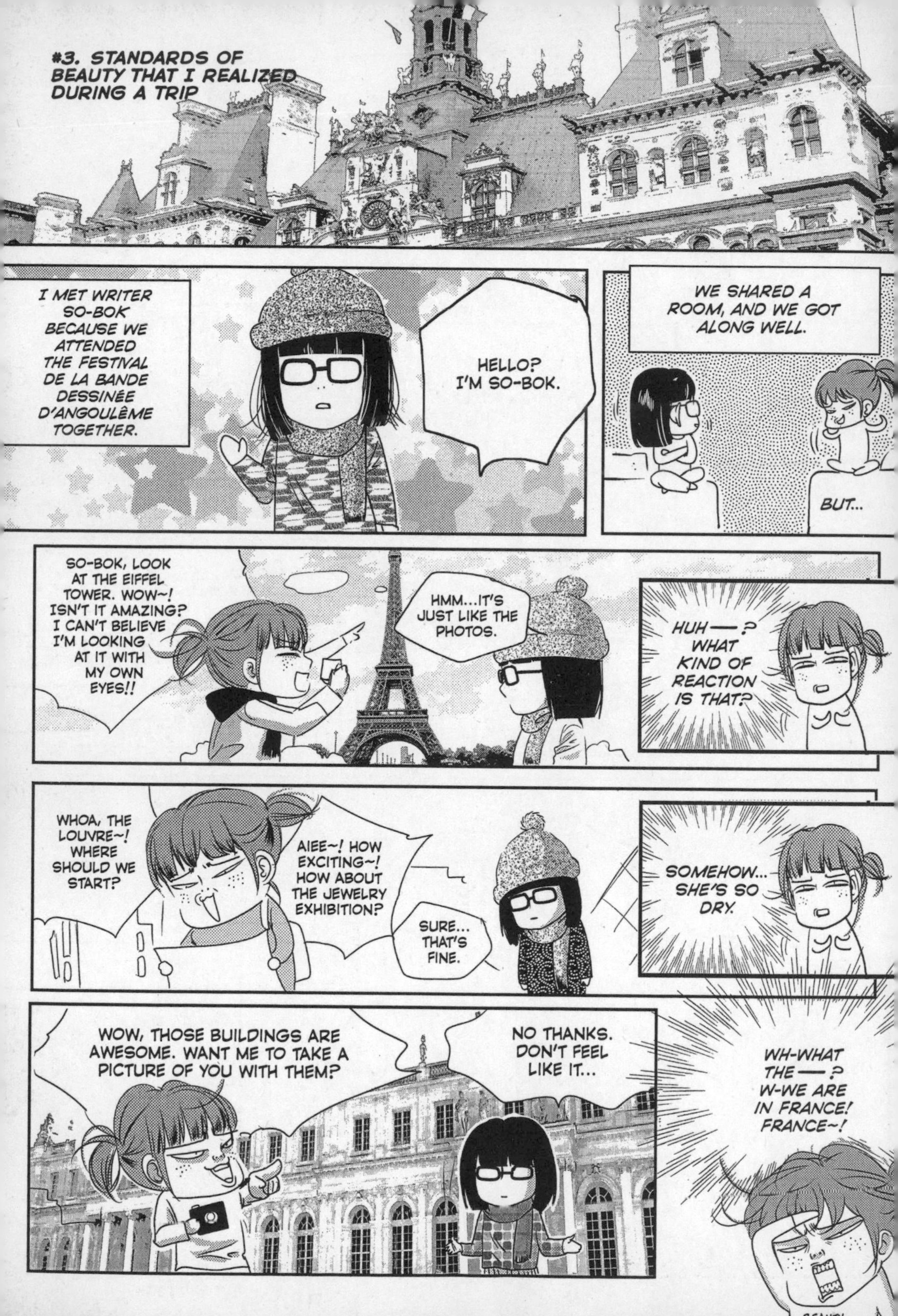
#3. STANDARDS OF BEAUTY THAT I REALIZED DURING A TRIP
I MET WRITER SO-BOK BECAUSE WE ATTENDED THE FESTIVAL DE LA BANDE DESSINÉE D'ANGOULÊME TOGETHER.
HELLO? I'M SO-BOK.
WE SHARED A ROOM, AND WE GOT ALONG WELL.
BUT...
SO-BOK, LOOK AT THE EIFFEL TOWER. WOW~! ISN'T IT AMAZING? I CAN'T BELIEVE I'M LOOKING AT IT WITH MY OWN EYES!!
HMM...IT'S JUST LIKE THE PHOTOS.
HUH—? WHAT KIND OF REACTION IS THAT?
WHOA, THE LOUVRE~! WHERE SHOULD WE START?
AIEE~! HOW EXCITING~! HOW ABOUT THE JEWELRY EXHIBITION?
SURE... THAT'S FINE.
SOMEHOW... SHE'S SO DRY.
WOW, THOSE BUILDINGS ARE AWESOME. WANT ME TO TAKE A PICTURE OF YOU WITH THEM?
NO THANKS. DON'T FEEL LIKE IT...
WH-WHAT THE—? W-WE ARE IN FRANCE! FRANCE~!

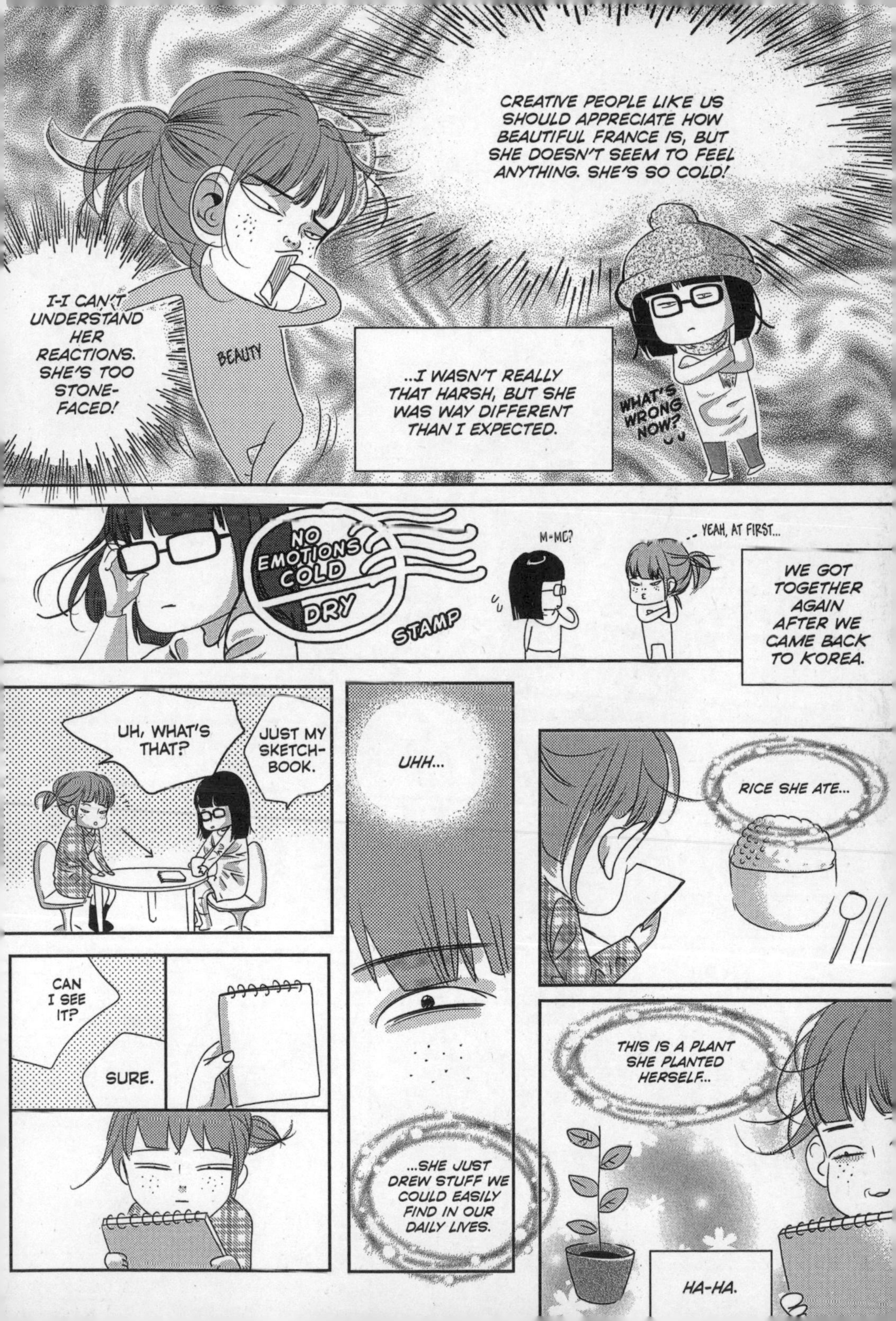
CREATIVE PEOPLE LIKE US SHOULD APPRECIATE HOW BEAUTIFUL FRANCE IS, BUT SHE DOESN'T SEEM TO FEEL ANYTHING. SHE'S SO COLD!
I-I CAN'T UNDERSTAND HER REACTIONS. SHE'S TOO STONE-FACED!
BEAUTY
...I WASN'T REALLY THAT HARSH, BUT SHE WAS WAY DIFFERENT THAN I EXPECTED.
WHAT'S WRONG NOW?
NO EMOTIONS
COLD
DRY
STAMP
M-MO?
...YEAH, AT FIRST...
WE GOT TOGETHER AGAIN AFTER WE CAME BACK TO KOREA.
UH, WHAT'S THAT?
JUST MY SKETCH-BOOK.
CAN I SEE IT?
SURE.
UHH...
...SHE JUST DREW STUFF WE COULD EASILY FIND IN OUR DAILY LIVES.
RICE SHE ATE...
THIS IS A PLANT SHE PLANTED HERSELF...
HA-HA.

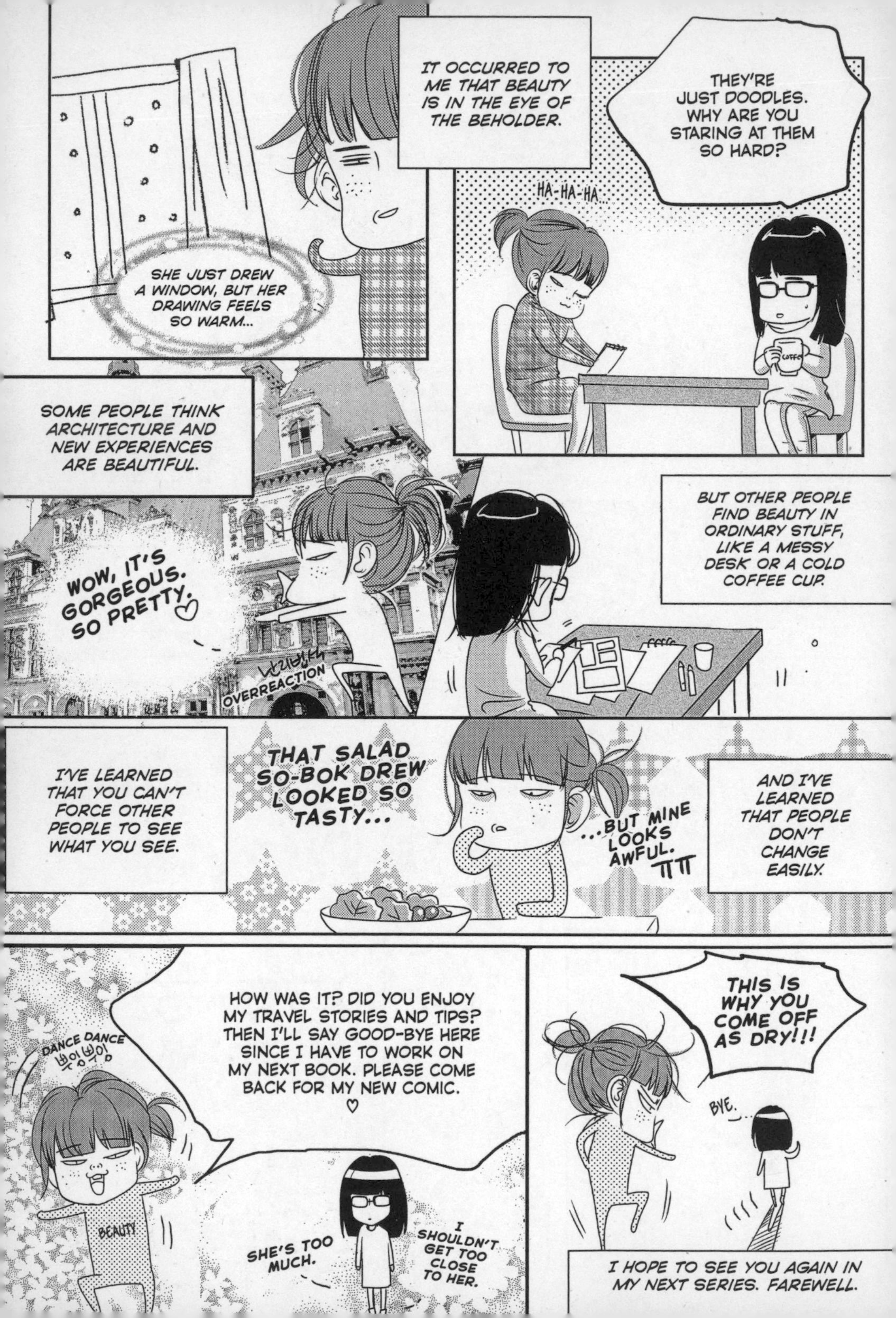
IT OCCURRED TO ME THAT BEAUTY IS IN THE EYE OF THE BEHOLDER.
SHE JUST DREW A WINDOW, BUT HER DRAWING FEELS SO WARM...
HA-HA-HA
THEY'RE JUST DOODLES. WHY ARE YOU STARING AT THEM SO HARD?
SOME PEOPLE THINK ARCHITECTURE AND NEW EXPERIENCES ARE BEAUTIFUL.
WOW, IT'S GORGEOUS. SO PRETTY. ♡
OVERREACTION
BUT OTHER PEOPLE FIND BEAUTY IN ORDINARY STUFF, LIKE A MESSY DESK OR A COLD COFFEE CUP.
I'VE LEARNED THAT YOU CAN'T FORCE OTHER PEOPLE TO SEE WHAT YOU SEE.
THAT SALAD SO-BOK DREW LOOKED SO TASTY...
...BUT MINE LOOKS AWFUL. ㅠㅠ
AND I'VE LEARNED THAT PEOPLE DON'T CHANGE EASILY.
DANCE DANCE
HOW WAS IT? DID YOU ENJOY MY TRAVEL STORIES AND TIPS? THEN I'LL SAY GOOD-BYE HERE SINCE I HAVE TO WORK ON MY NEXT BOOK. PLEASE COME BACK FOR MY NEW COMIC. ♡
BEAUTY
SHE'S TOO MUCH.
I SHOULDN'T GET TOO CLOSE TO HER.
THIS IS WHY YOU COME OFF AS DRY!!!
BYE.
I HOPE TO SEE YOU AGAIN IN MY NEXT SERIES. FAREWELL.

THE ROYAL PALACE
Goong

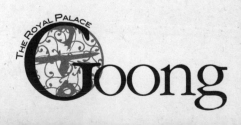

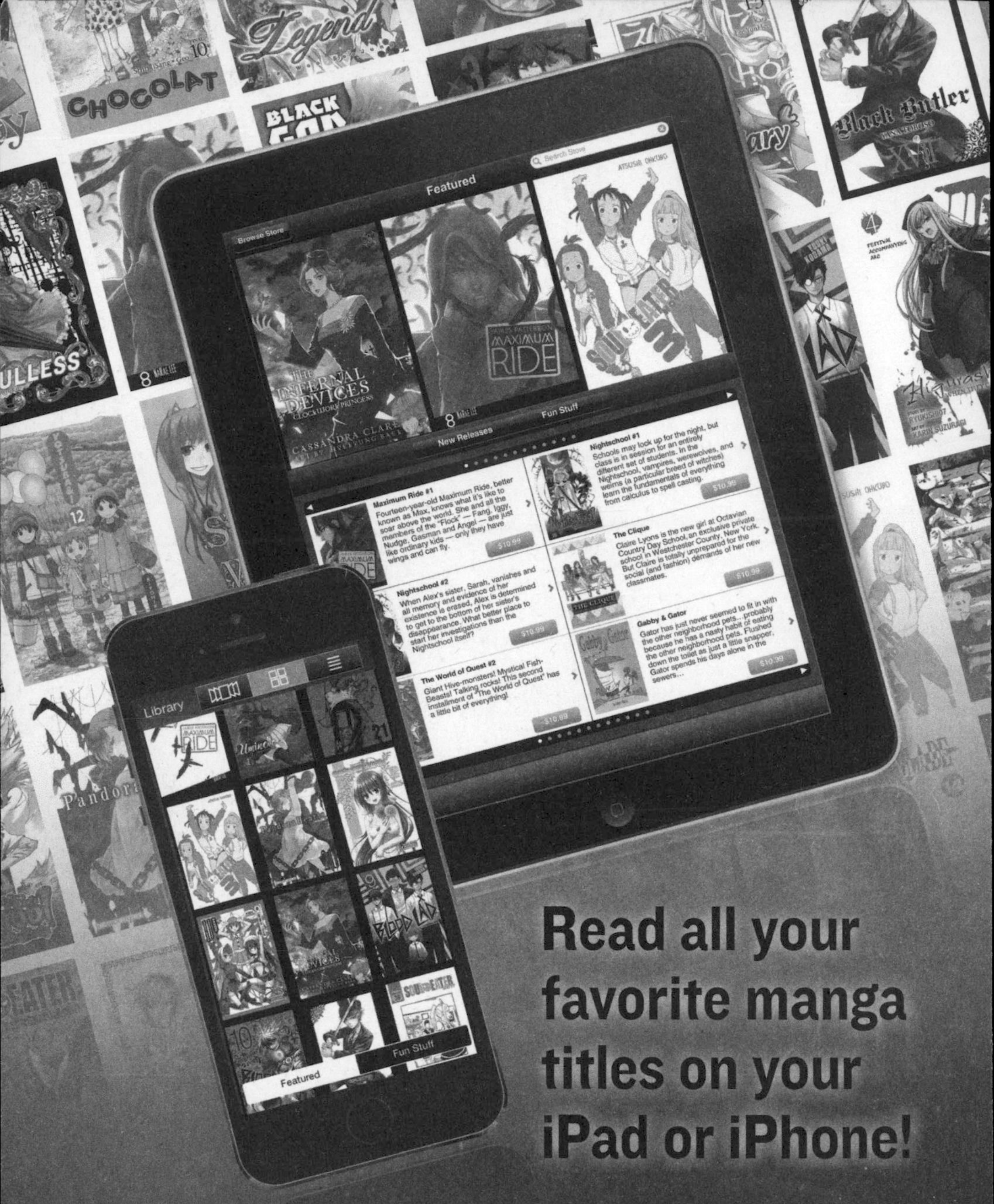
Read all your favorite manga titles on your iPad or iPhone!

Available at bookstores near you!

CHOCOLAT

1~7

Shin JiSang · Geo

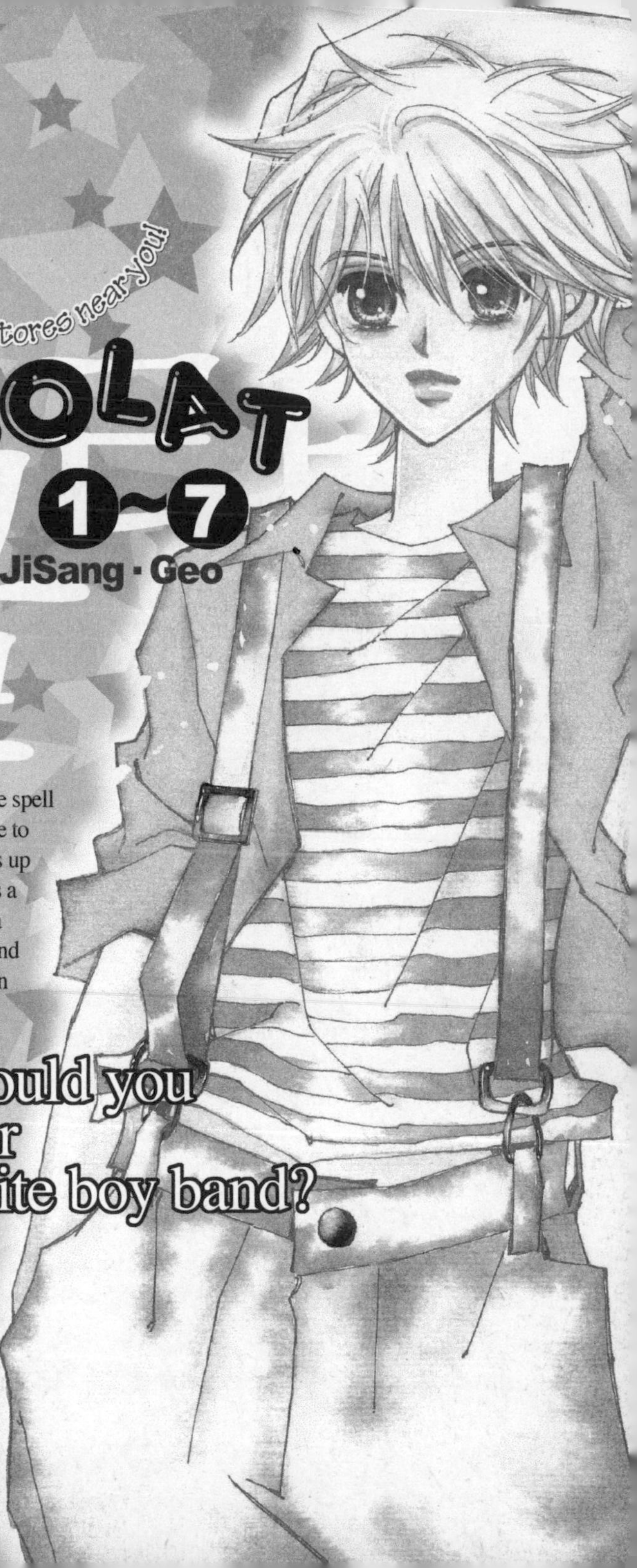

Kum-ji was a little late getting under the spell
of the chart-topping band, DDL. Unable to
join the DDL fan club, she almost gives up
on meeting her idols, until she develops a
cunning plan–to become a member of a
rival fan club for the brand-new boy band
Yo-I. This way she can act as Yo-I's fan
club member and also be near Yo-I,

How far would you
go to meet your
favorite boy band?

who always seem to be in the
same shows as DDL. Perfect
plan...except being a fanatic is a lot
more complicated than she
expects. Especially when you're
actually a fan of someone else. This
full-blown love comedy about a fan
club will make you laugh, cry, and
laugh some more.

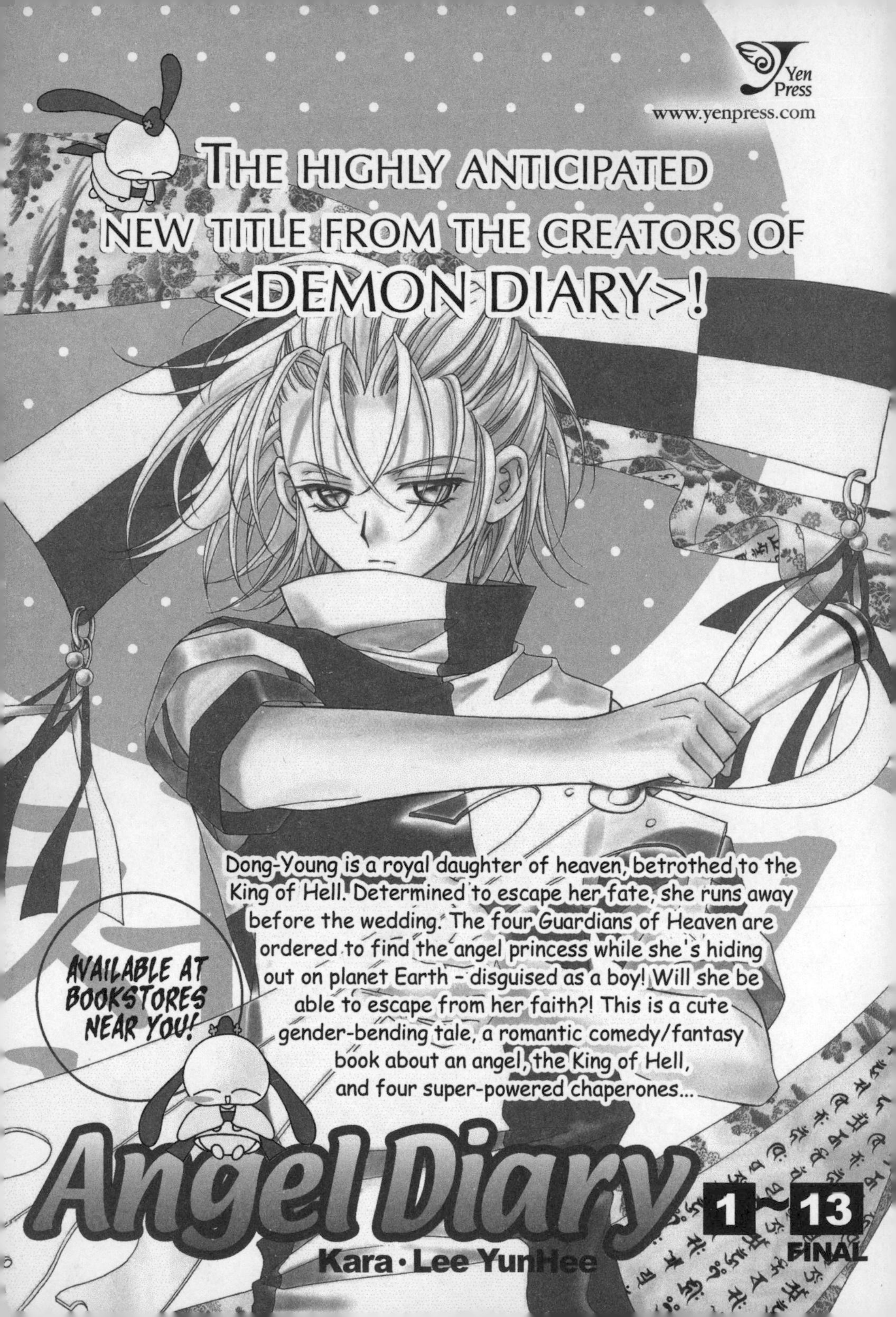
Yen Press
www.yenpress.com
THE HIGHLY ANTICIPATED
NEW TITLE FROM THE CREATORS OF
<DEMON DIARY>!
Dong-Young is a royal daughter of heaven, betrothed to the King of Hell. Determined to escape her fate, she runs away before the wedding. The four Guardians of Heaven are ordered to find the angel princess while she's hiding out on planet Earth - disguised as a boy! Will she be able to escape from her faith?! This is a cute gender-bending tale, a romantic comedy/fantasy book about an angel, the King of Hell, and four super-powered chaperones...
AVAILABLE AT BOOKSTORES NEAR YOU!
Angel Diary
1~13
FINAL
Kara · Lee YunHee

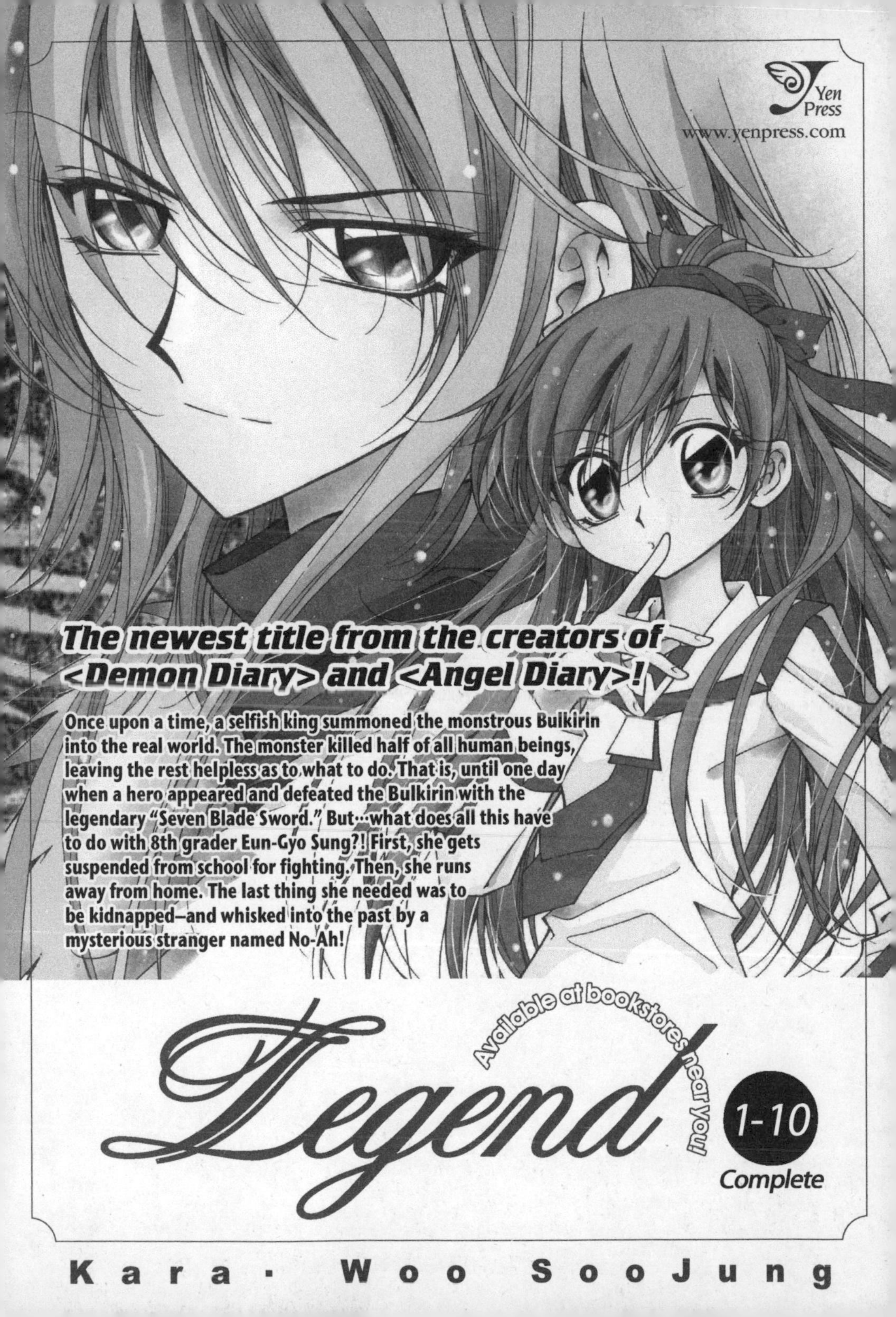
Yen Press
www.yenpress.com
The newest title from the creators of
<Demon Diary> and <Angel Diary>!
Once upon a time, a selfish king summoned the monstrous Bulkirin into the real world. The monster killed half of all human beings, leaving the rest helpless as to what to do. That is, until one day when a hero appeared and defeated the Bulkirin with the legendary "Seven Blade Sword." But…what does all this have to do with 8th grader Eun-Gyo Sung?! First, she gets suspended from school for fighting. Then, she runs away from home. The last thing she needed was to be kidnapped–and whisked into the past by a mysterious stranger named No-Ah!
Legend
Available at bookstores near you!
1-10
Complete
Kara · Woo SooJung

The Antique Gift Shop
Lee Eun

1~10 COMPLETE

CAN YOU FEEL THE SOULS OF THE ANTIQUES?
DO YOU BELIEVE?

Did you know that an antique possesses a soul of its own?
The Antique Gift Shop specializes in such items that charm and captivate the buyers they are destined to belong to. Guided by a mysterious and charismatic shopkeeper, the enchanted relics lead their new owners on a journey into an alternate cosmic universe to their true destinies.
Eerily bittersweet and dolefully melancholy, The Antique Gift Shop opens up a portal to a world where torn lovers unite, broken friendships are mended, and regrets are resolved. Can you feel the power of the antiques?

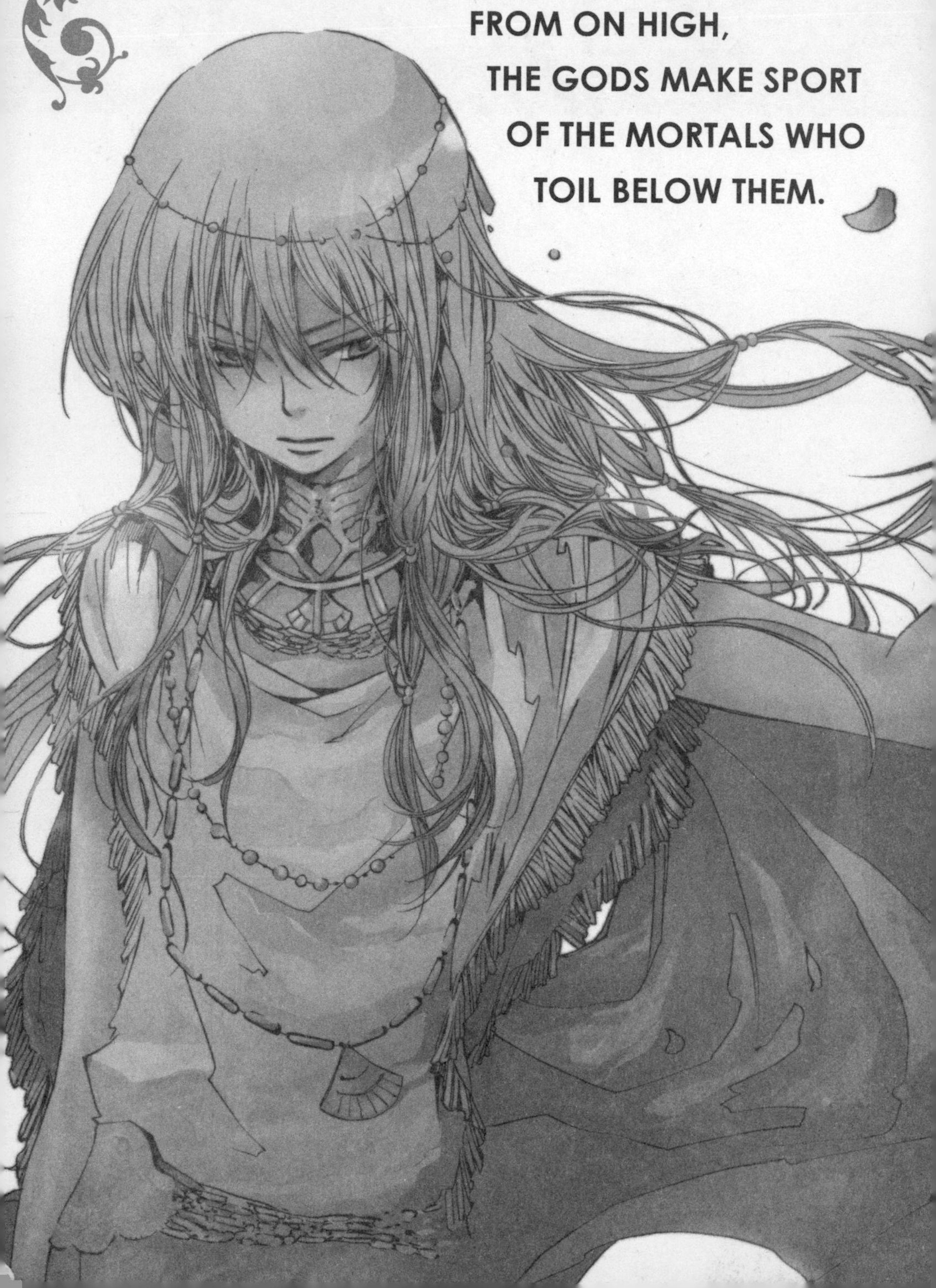
FROM ON HIGH,
THE GODS MAKE SPORT
OF THE MORTALS WHO
TOIL BELOW THEM.

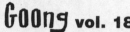

Goong vol. 18

Story and art by SoHee Park

Translation HyeYoung Im
English Adaptation Jamie S. Rich
Lettering Alexis Eckerman

Goong, Vols. 27 & 28 © 2011, 2012 SoHee Park. All rights reserved. First published in Korea in 2011, 2012 by SEOUL CULTURAL PUBLISHERS, Inc. English translation rights arranged by SEOUL CULTURAL PUBLISHERS, Inc.

English edition copyright © 2015 Hachette Book Group, Inc.

Yen Press
Hachette Book Group
1290 Avenue of the Americas
New York, NY 10104

www.HachetteBookGroup.com
www.YenPress.com

Yen Press is an imprint of Hachette Book Group, Inc.
The Yen Press name and logo are trademarks of Hachette Book Group, Inc.

The publisher is not responsible for websites (or their content) that are not owned by the publisher.

First Yen Press Edition: May 2015

ISBN: 978-0-316-32226-3

10 9 8 7 6 5 4 3 2 1

BVG

Printed in the United States of America